The Middle East in Modern World History

The Middle East in Modern World History

Ernest Tucker

United States Naval Academy

Boston Columbus Indianapolis New York San Francisco Upper Saddle River Amsterdam
Cape Town Dubai London Madrid Milan Munich Paris Montréal Toronto Delhi
Mexico City São Paulo Sydney Hong Kong Seoul Singapore Taipei Tokyo

Executive Editor: Jeff Lasser
Editorial Project Manager: Rob DeGeorge
Editorial Assistant: Julia Feltus
Senior Manufacturing and Operations Manager for Arts & Sciences: Mary Fischer
Director of Marketing: Brandy Dawson
Senior Marketing Manager: Maureen E. Prado Roberts
Marketing Coordinator: Samantha Bennett
Marketing Assistant: Diana Griffin
Senior Managing Editor: Ann Marie McCarthy
Senior Project Manager: Denise Forlow
Manager of Central Design: Jayne Conte
Operations Specialist: Laura Messerly
Manager of Central Design: Jayne Conte
Cover Designer: Bruce Kenselaar
Cover Image: Aleksandar Kamasi/Shutterstock
Full Service Project Management: Anand Natarajan/Integra
Composition: Integra
Printer/Bindery and Cover Printer: R.R. Donnelley/Harrisonburg
Text Font: Garamond 10/12

Credits and acknowledgments for material borrowed from other sources and reproduced, with permission, in this textbook appear on the appropriate page within the text.

Many of the designations by manufacturers and seller to distinguish their products are claimed as trademarks. Where those designations appear in this book, and the publisher was aware of a trademark claim, the designations have been printed in initial caps or all caps.

Library of Congress Cataloging-in-Publication Data
Tucker, Ernest
  The Middle East in modern world history/Ernest Tucker.
    p. cm.
  Includes bibliographical references and index.
  ISBN-13: 978-0-13-615152-4 (alk. paper)
  ISBN-10: 0-13-615152-3 (alk. paper)
  1. Middle East—History—19th century.   2. Middle East—History—20th century.   I. Title.
  DS62.7.T83 2013
  956—dc23

                                                              2011043722

10 9 8 7 6 5 4 3 2 1

ISBN-10:   0-13-615152-3
ISBN-13: 978-0-13-615152-4

Dedication

*I dedicate this book to my mother, Carlyn Collins,
and my father, Ernest Tucker.*

CONTENTS

PREFACE

This text provides an introduction to the modern history of the Middle East. The term "Middle East" will be used to refer to the region of the world between the Nile River in Africa and the Oxus (Amu Darya) River in Central Asia (from west to east), and between the Balkans (in southeastern Europe) and the Indian Ocean (from north to south). The book focuses on the history of this region over the past two hundred years.

This was a period in which the Middle East regained its traditional importance as a strategic conduit between East and West. It was also when the region's riches in natural resources, particularly petroleum, were discovered. Finally, the region became more and more closely linked to the world economy at this time through global trade networks that fed the Industrial Revolution. Although the Industrial Revolution had its earliest impact on Europe, it profoundly affected the rest of the world as well. This work will examine how broad global trends during this period both shaped the modern Middle East and were shaped by it.

The title of this book reflects the enormous changes in the world over the past two centuries. The phrase "Middle East" did not originate in the Middle East, but translations of it are widely used in various Middle Eastern countries today. It began as a description of how the region fits into the modern world, making it useful and appropriate for this text. "Middle East" was coined in the early 1900s to describe how this region fit into the larger strategic context of Asia.

In particular, it was used to discuss the Great Game: the nineteenth-century competition between Britain and Russia for predominance in Asia. Alfred Thayer Mahan, an American naval historian, called the area surrounding the Persian Gulf the "Middle East."[1] When his article on this subject was reprinted in the London *Times*, it was soon followed by a series of twenty essays by another analyst, Valentine Chirol, compiled into a 1903 book entitled *The Middle Eastern Question*. This publication helped popularize the term quite rapidly.[2] The earlier phrase for the region between Egypt and Central Asia had been the "Near East," which, in contemporary academic circles, has become a way to refer specifically to the pre-Islamic era of Middle Eastern civilizations.

The title of this book is designed as a reminder that events that took place in the Middle East, particularly in modern times, often were closely linked to what was happening across the globe in other regions. This work will explore those links, as well as things that set the Middle East apart, to encourage investigation of the history of this key area of the world.

---

[1]A.T. Mahan, "The Persian Gulf and International Relations," *National Review* (September 1902): 27–45.

[2]Valentine Chirol, *The Middle Eastern Question or Some Political Problems of Indian Defence* (New York: Dutton, 1903).

ACKNOWLEDGMENTS

So many people have been helpful in the writing of this text that it is difficult to mention them all. I wish to thank in particular my colleagues in the History Department at the U.S. Naval Academy for their encouragement and support, particularly Dr. Tom Sanders and Dr. Brian VanDeMark. In addition to many other professional colleagues, Dr. Camron Amin of the University of Michigan and Dr. Sholeh Quinn of the University of California offered many valuable suggestions in the preparation of this work. For their continued support of all my scholarly activities, I thank all of my friends and family, in particular my son Carl Tucker, daughter Claire Tucker, and my beloved wife Sarah Hyde.

CHRONOLOGY

Note: All dates are Common Era, except BCE= "Before the Common Era" and AH= "Hegira Year"

3500 BCE	Origins of earliest human civilizations in the Middle East.	1071	Defeat of the Byzantine Empire by Rum Seljuks at Manzikert.
c. 550–330 BCE	Achaemenid (Persian) Empire.	1095–1291	Era of the Christian Crusades in the Eastern Mediterranean.
356–323 BCE	Life of Alexander the Great.	1187	Salah al-Din (Saladin) al-Ayyubi defeated Crusader armies at Battle of Hattin.
224–651	Sassanian (Persian) Empire.		
395–1453	Byzantine (East Roman) Empire.	1243	Defeat of Rum Seljuks by Mongols at Kose Dag.
570	Birth of Muhammad.	1258	Mongol conquest of Baghdad.
610	According to Muslim belief, angel Gabriel (Arabic: "Jibril") appeared to Muhammad and began to communicate revelations.	1250–1517	Mamluk Sultanate.
		1299	Osman I became the first independent Ottoman ruler.
615	Group of Muhammad's followers took refuge in Ethiopia.	1299–1923	Era of Ottoman rule.
		1380–1405	Conquests of Tamerlane.
		1389	Battle of Kosovo.
619	Muhammad's wife Khadija and his uncle Abu Talib died.	1453	Ottoman conquest of Constantinople.
620	Muhammad experienced *Isra* and *Miraj*.	1501–1722	Safavid dynasty ruled Iran.
622	Hijra (Hegira) from Mecca to Medina.	1514	Ottomans defeated Safavids at Battle of Chaldiran.
624	Battle of Badr.	1520–1566	Reign of Ottoman Sultan Suleyman I (the Magnificent).
625	Battle of Uhud.		
628	Truce of Hudaybiya.	1529	First Ottoman siege of Vienna.
632	Death of Muhammad.	1571	Battle of Lepanto.
632–661	Rightly-Guided (Arabic: "Rashidun") Caliphs.	1683	Second Ottoman siege of Vienna.
661–750	Umayyad Caliphate.	1699	Treaty of Karlowitz.
680	Battle of Karbala.	1740	French King Louis XV recognized as protector of Ottoman Catholic subjects.
711	Beginning of Muslim conquest of Spain.		
750–1258	Abbasid Caliphate.	1745–1818	First Saudi state in Nejd (central Arabian Peninsula).
762	Founding of Baghdad.		
909–1171	Fatimid Dynasty ruled in North Africa and Egypt.	1774	Treaty of Kuchuk Kaynarja. Russian Empress Catherine the Great acknowledged as protector of Ottoman Orthodox subjects.
969	Founding of Cairo.		
970–972	Founding of al-Azhar.		

1791	Russian Jews required to live in special area called the Pale of Settlement.
1794–1925	Qajar dynasty ruled Iran.
1798	(July 2) French expeditionary force led by Napoleon Bonaparte occupied Alexandria, Egypt.
	(July 21) Mamluk commander Murad Bey defeated by French at Battle of the Pyramids.
	(July 24) Napoleon entered Cairo.
1804	Serbian nationalist uprising led by Karageorge Petrovic against Ottomans.
1805–1849	Muhammad Ali ruled Egypt.
1811–1812	Muhammad Ali crushed Mamluk political power.
1818	Ibrahim Pasha, son of Muhammad Ali, destroyed Saudi home village of Diriya in Nejd.
1821–1832	Greek War of Independence.
1822	Muhammad Ali began drafting peasants into new army.
1826	Mahmud II eliminated Ottoman Janissary corps.
1827	Modern medical school established near Cairo by French doctor Antoine-Barthélémy Clot (Clot Bey).
	European fleet sank many Ottoman ships at Navarino on October 20.
1828	Persian-Russian treaty of Turkmenchay.
1833	Convention of Kutahya.
1839	Muhammad Ali's son Ibrahim destroyed Ottoman Army at Battle of Nezib (near Urfa in modern Turkey).
1839–1876	Tanzimat era of Ottoman reform.
1839–1842	First Anglo-Afghan War.

1840	London Convention curbs power of Muhammad Ali.
1853–1856	Crimean War.
1856–1857	Anglo-Persian War.
1857–1858	Indian Mutiny.
1861	Serfs liberated in Russia.
1863	Semi-official Ottoman government bank established.
1869	Suez Canal completed.
1875	Ottoman fiscal and political crisis.
1876	(May) European bankers took control of Egyptian finances.
	(December) First Ottoman constitution proclaimed.
1877–1878	Russo-Turkish War.
1878–1880	Second Anglo-Afghan War.
1879	Persian Cossack Brigade established.
1881	(June) Muhammad Ahmad proclaims himself *mahdi* in the Sudan.
	(December) European bankers took control of Ottoman finances.
1882	British occupation of Egypt.
1890	Monopoly on producing and selling tobacco in Iran granted to an Englishman.
1892	Popular demonstrations and religious opposition forced end of foreign tobacco concession in Iran.
1897	(April–September) Greco-Turkish War (last Ottoman war victory).
	(August) World Zionist Organization founded by Theodor Herzl.
1902	Beginning of modern Saudi state.
1905	Beginning of Iranian Constitutional Revolution.
1907	Britain and Russia divided Iran into spheres of influence.

1908	(May) Oil discovered in southwestern Iran (first find in central Middle East).
	(July) Young Turk Revolution in the Ottoman Empire. Reinstatement of 1876 Ottoman Constitution.
1911–1912	Italo-Turkish War.
1912–1913	First Balkan War.
1913	(January) CUP veiled coup in the Ottoman Empire.
	(June) First Arab Congress held in Paris.
	(June–September) Second Balkan War.
1914–1918	First World War.
1914	(June 28) Assassination of Austrian heir Archduke Franz Ferdinand in Sarajevo, Bosnia-Herzegovina (outbreak of World War I).
	(August 2) Secret Ottoman-German pact.
	(October 29) Ottoman ships shelled Russian Black Sea ports, causing Russia and Britain to declare war on Ottomans.
	(October 31) Ottoman government ordered all men of military age to report for duty.
1914–1915	Battle of Sarikamish.
1915	(February) Enver Pasha issued an order to disarm Armenians in the Ottoman army.
	(April) Allied landings at Gallipoli.
	(May) Ottoman "*Tehjir Kanunu*" [Turkish: "Deportation Law"]) issued, causing deportation of hundreds of thousands of Armenians from Anatolia to Syria and their deaths.
	(July) Hussein-McMahon Correspondence began.
1916	(May) Sykes-Picot Agreement.
	(June) Beginning of Arab Revolt of 1916.
1917	Balfour Declaration issued.
1918	Ottomans signed armistice with Allies on a ship in Mudros harbor in the Aegean Sea.
1919	Treaty of Versailles signed.
1919–1923	Turkish War of Independence.
1920	(April) San Remo Agreement on Mandate System.
	(June) Beginning of armed uprising against British rule in Iraq.
	(July) French defeated Faisal, independent Hashemite ruler of Syria, at Battle of Maysalun, and established control over Syria.
	(August) Treaty of Sèvres signed, establishing British mandate of Mesopotamia (renamed "Iraq" in 1921).
1921	(April) Establishment of the Emirate of Transjordan as autonomous under British protection.
	(August) Establishment of the Hashemite Kingdom of Iraq under Faisal I.
1922	Britain decreed Egypt to be an independent country.
1923	(January) Greek-Turkish population exchange.
	(July) Treaty of Lausanne signed.
	(September) British mandate of Palestine and French mandate of Syria recognized.
	(October) Republic of Turkey established.
1925	Reza Khan became Reza Shah Pahlavi of Iran.

1927	Oil discovered in Iraq.
1929	Western Wall incident and riots in Palestine.
1932	Iraq given independence by Britain.
1936	Lebanon and Syria to be given independence by France, but treaties not ratified.
1939	British White Paper on Palestine issued.
1939–1945	Second World War.
1941	(June–July) Operation Exporter (Allied invasion of Syria and Lebanon). (August) British-Russian invasion of Iran. Deposition of Reza Shah and accession of Mohammad Reza Pahlavi to Iranian throne.
1942	First and Second Battles of El Alamein between Germany and Allied forces.
1943	Lebanon finally given independence by France.
1945	Syrian finally given independence by France. Creation of Arab League.
1946	(January–December) Kurdish Republic of Mahabad in Iranian Azerbaijan. (March) Greek civil war began. (May) Independent Hashemite Kingdom of Jordan established.
1947	(July) Strategic cooperation agreement between United States and Turkey. King David Hotel bombing in Jerusalem. (November) UN partition plan for Palestine.
1948–1949	Israeli War of Independence (First Arab-Israeli War).
1950–1953	Turkish troops served in Korea under UN command.

1951	Turkey became NATO member.
1952	Free Officers' Movement in Egypt overthrew King Farouk and proclaimed a republic.
1953	(August) Operation Ajax (Secret British-U.S. operation to overthrow Iranian Prime Minster Mosaddeq). (November) Death of Abd al-Aziz, founding ruler of modern Saudi Arabia.
1955	(February) Creation of Baghdad Pact (also known as "Central Treaty Organization" or CENTO). (September) Nasser signed major arms agreement with Czechoslovakia.
1956	(June) Gamal Abdel Nasser became president of Egypt. (July) Nasser nationalized Suez Canal. (October) Suez Crisis, resulting in Second Arab-Israeli War.
1958	Military coup in Iraq, ending Hashemite monarchy.
1958–1961	United Arab Republic, uniting Syria and Egypt.
1959	Iran-U.S. defense agreement.
1960	(May) Army staged nonviolent coup in Turkey. (August) Cyprus given independence as republic. (September) Establishment of OPEC (Organization of Petroleum Exporting Countries).
1962	Outbreak of civil war in North Yemen.
1963	White Revolution in Iran.
1964	(May) Palestinian National Charter established Palestine Liberation Organization (PLO).

(October) Status of Forces Bill gave immunity to U.S. military serving in Iran and their families.

1967 Family Protection Law reformed marriage, divorce, and family law in Iran.

Six-Day War (Third Arab-Israeli War):

(April) Major aerial battle over Golan Heights between Syria and Israel.

(May 18) Egypt asked United Nations Emergency Force (UNEF) to leave Sinai and closed straits of Tiran to Israeli traffic.

(May 30) King Hussein signed surprise mutual defense treaty with Egypt.

(June 5) Israeli jets attacked Arab airfields. By end of June 6, Israel wiped out most of the Egyptian, Jordanian, Syrian, and Iraqi air forces.

(June 7) Israeli General Dayan authorized troops to occupy Jerusalem's Old City.

(June 8) Israel secured control of Sinai Peninsula. American reconnaissance ship USS *Liberty* attacked by Israeli units.

(June 9) Syria accepted Cease-fire at 3 A.M. General Dayan ordered his troops at 7 A.M. to begin land invasion of Syria. By nightfall, Israeli forces secured Golan Heights.

(June 11) Lasting Cease-fire arranged to end fighting.

(June 27) Israel incorporated East Jerusalem and adjacent areas of the West Bank into Jerusalem's municipal boundaries.

(August) Six-Day War also forced Egypt to end its involvement in Yemen.

(August 29) Khartoum Summit.

1969 Lebanon signed Cairo Agreement permitting PLO to launch attacks from Lebanese soil.

1970 Death of Gamal Abdel Nasser. Anwar Sadat became Egypt's leader.

1971 (February) Hafez al-Assad became Syria's leader.

(August) Bahrain became independent from Britain.

(October) Celebration of 2,500 years of monarchy in Iran.

(December) United Arab Emirates formed.

1973 (October 6) Syria and Egypt launched surprise war against Israel on Jewish holy day of Yom Kippur. (Fourth Arab-Israeli War).

(October 16) Huge oil price increase.

1974 (July 15) Cyprus President Makarios deposed.

(July 20) Turkish troops landed on Cyprus to protect Turkish Cypriots.

1975 (February) Turkish Republic of Northern Cyprus established.

(December) Black Saturday in Beirut began first round of Lebanese Civil War.

1976 (June) Syria intervened in the Lebanese Civil War, keeping troops there until 2005.

(October) Cease-fire declared to be "end" of Lebanese Civil War.

1977   (March) Lebanese leader Kemal Jumblatt assassinated in attack linked to Syria.
(November) Surprise visit of Sadat to Israel began process leading to Camp David peace negotiations.

1978   (January 8) Massacre of protestors in Qom, Iran, led to cycle of demonstrations in Iran every forty days.
(March) Operation Litani resulted in Israeli occupation of southern Lebanon.
(August) CIA issued report stating that Iran was not on verge of revolution.
(September 8) Thousands of protestors demonstrated in Tehran.
(October) General strike shut down Iran's economy. Ayatollah Khomeini exiled from Iraq to France.

1979   (January 16) Mohammad Reza Shah Pahlavi left Iran.
(February 1) Ayatollah Khomeini returned to Iran.
(March) Israel-Egypt Peace Treaty signed.
(October) Shah of Iran allowed to enter United States for medical treatment.
(November 4) U.S. Embassy in Tehran seized and its diplomats taken hostage.
(November 20) Saudi dissidents seized Mecca's Grand Mosque. November 20 was also the first day of 1400 A.H.: first year of the Islamic fifteenth century.
(December 24) First Soviet troops entered Afghanistan.

1980   (September 12) Military coup in Turkey.
(September 22) Saddam Hussein invaded Iran.

1981   (January 20) U.S. hostages in Iran released.
(October 6) Egyptian President Anwar Sadat assassinated by Islamic militants.

1982   (February) Massacre of Muslim activists in Hama, Syria.
(June-August) Lebanon War conducted by Israel (Fifth Arab-Israeli War).

1983   (April) U.S. embassy in Beirut hit by suicide bomber.
(October) Suicide bombings against U.S. and French troops in Lebanon killed 241 American and 58 French soldiers.
(December) PLO moved headquarters to Tunis, Tunisia.

1984–1887   Tanker war in Persian Gulf.

1984   (February) Multinational Force left Lebanon.
(August) Beginning of Kurdish unrest in Turkey.

1985   Lebanese Hezbollah formally declared its mission.

1987   (May) Iraqi missile attack on USS *Stark*.
(July) UN Resolution 598 to end Iran-Iraq War. Cease-fire finally took effect in July 1988.
(December) First Palestinian Intifada began.

1988   (July) USS *Vincennes* shot down Iranian civilian airliner.
(November) Palestinian "Declaration of Independence" issued.

1989   (February 14) Ayatollah Khomeini issued fatwa calling for death of British author Salman Rushdie.

	(February 15) Last Soviet troops left Afghanistan.
	(June) Death of Ayatollah Khomeini, selection of Ali Khamenei as new Supreme Leader.
1990	Iraq invaded Kuwait.
1991	(January 17) Start of the military campaign in Operation Desert Storm to remove Iraq from Kuwait.
	(February 28) U.S. President Bush announced cease-fire in Operation Desert Storm, declaring Kuwait liberated.
	(March) Operation Provide Comfort established no-fly zone over northern Iraq.
1992	Operation Southern Watch established no-fly zone over southern Iraq.
1993	(April) First Hamas suicide bombing attack in West Bank.
	(September) Oslo Accords signed between Israel and the PLO.
1994	Israel-Jordan peace treaty.
1995	Israeli Prime Minister Yitzhak Rabin shot in Tel Aviv.
1998	(February) Osama Bin Laden issued fatwa against United States and allies.
	(August) Al-Qaeda bombings of U.S. embassies in Kenya and Tanzania resulted in deaths of over three hundred people.
1999	Turkey became candidate for full membership in the European Union.
2000	(May) Israeli withdrawal from southern Lebanon.
	(October) Attack on USS *Cole* in Yemen.
	(July) Camp David Summit.

	(September) Visit of Ariel Sharon to Temple Mount, beginning of al-Aqsa Intifada.
2001	(September 9) Assassination of Afghan warlord Ahmad Shah Massoud.
	(September 11) Terrorist acts carried out in New York and Washington by al-Qaeda teams.
	(October 7) Beginning of Operation Enduring Freedom (Invasion of Afghanistan by United States and allies).
2002	First UN *Arab Human Development Report* issued.
2003	Beginning of Operation Iraqi Freedom (invasion of Iraq by United States and its allies).
2004	Death of Yasser Arafat.
2005	Israel removed its troops and settlers from Gaza Strip.
2006	(January) Hamas won large plurality in first Palestinian Legislative Council elections since 1996.
	(March 2006–June 2007) Conflict between Fatah and Hamas.
	(May) First government of Iraq under new constitution took office.
	(June–July) Operation Summer Rains (Israeli incursion into Gaza).
	(July–August) War between Hezbollah and Israel.
	(November) Operation Autumn Clouds (Israeli incursion into Gaza).
2008	(February–June) Members of Hamas and other Gaza militants shot Qassam rockets into Israel.

(November) Israel placed blockade on Gaza that continued intermittently over the next three years.

(December) U.S.-Iraq Status of Forces Agreement approved.

2009 (January) Israeli army invaded Gaza Strip for three weeks.

2010 (May) Israel boarded and seized six ships of "Gaza Freedom Flotilla" coming from Turkey. Incident worsened historically good Israeli-Turkish relations.

(December) Political suicide of street vendor in Tunisia led to political upheaval, which spread to numerous other Arab countries in 2011.

2011 (February) Egyptian President Hosni Mubarak forced to leave office.

(May) United States hunted down and killed Osama Bin Laden in Abbottabad, Pakistan.

(October) Libyan leader Muammar Qaddafi killed in his hometown of Sirt, Libya.

NOTE ON TRANSLITERATION

Except for names that have standard recognized spellings in English, all Arabic, Persian, and Turkish names are transliterated generally according to the IJMES style, except that cedillas, diacritical marks, and final "h"s are omitted. Turkish "c" is transliterated as "j." The Glossary indicates common variant spellings of names.

1

The Middle East in Early Islamic History

INTRODUCTIONS

Civilization in the Middle East

To set the stage for discussion of modern developments, it is helpful to begin with an overview of the region's deeper historical contexts. The origins of civilization in the **Middle East** can be found in **Mesopotamia** and the Nile River valley in Egypt around 3500 BCE. Mesopotamia (located in modern Iraq) was the center of a series of the earliest civilizations in human history. Possibilities for irrigated cultivation near the confluence of the Tigris and Euphrates Rivers in Mesopotamia paralleled the agricultural potential of the steady flow of the Nile River in Egypt. The regular and constant water supply available in both places became the key ingredient for civilizations to flourish. From such beginnings, civilization spread along the shores of the Mediterranean and inland throughout the arable parts of the Middle East.

Sassanian Empire

By the sixth century BCE, the **Achaemenid Empire** controlled a large part of the modern Middle East, with its center in Mesopotamia and Persia. It was followed by several other empires that dominated a similar region, most recent of which before the rise of **Islam** was the **Sassanian Empire**. It arose in the second century CE and ruled over much of the eastern Middle East until defeated by the Muslim conquerors of Persia in the seventh century CE. The Sassanian state religion was **Zoroastrianism**, a dualistic monotheism with origins in the teachings of the prophet Zoroaster, who lived in Iran probably before the sixth century BCE. It focuses on the eternal struggle of good and evil, using water and fire as cleansing agents for ritual purification.

Another very important aspect of the Sassanian Empire was its use of elements of Greek and Hellenistic culture spread across Asia by Alexander the Great and his successors between the fourth and first centuries BCE. Nowhere is this seen more clearly than in the scientific and academic center of Gundeshapur. Located in modern southwestern Iran, Gundeshapur was founded by the Sassanians in the third century CE. It was described as a place where Iranian

Greek, Arab, Indian, and Roman scientists were encouraged to visit, do research, and exchange ideas. There, translations of many ancient scientific works were made into **Pahlavi**, the written form of the Persian language used by the Sassanian rulers.

Byzantine Empire

By the end of the first century BCE, Rome had taken control of all the coastal areas of the Eastern Mediterranean, including much of the western Middle East. Under Roman rule, this area became closely linked with Europe and North Africa in a single political and economic unit. Even areas not directly annexed became strongly influenced by the Roman Empire, the most powerful political and cultural entity in this region for centuries. It used two official languages, Greek and Latin, with Greek predominating in its eastern domains. When the Roman capital was transferred from Rome to **Constantinople**, founded in 330 CE on the site of the ancient city of Byzantium, the influence of Greek culture and language became gradually stronger. After the Roman Empire split into eastern and western halves late in the fourth century CE, the Eastern Roman Empire, now governed from Constantinople, developed into the Byzantine Empire. Over many decades in the sixth and seventh centuries CE, it continually fought the Sassanian Empire for control of the Middle East.

By the fourth century CE, Christianity had become the dominant religion in the Roman-ruled Middle East. From this time on, the state religion of the Byzantine Empire evolved into Orthodox Christianity. Christianity had emerged as an independent religion out of the complex milieu of first-century CE Jewish Palestine. As Roman imperial rule over Palestine was being consolidated at that time, Jews, as well as early Christians, were continually challenged by Roman authority at first because they could not recognize Roman pagan gods. By the Byzantine several hundred years later, Christianity had the *the* official imperial Roman faith. The Byzantine emperor was also head of the church, joining secular and religious authority in a relationship sometimes called "caesaropapism."

MUHAMMAD ibn ABDULLAH

The Arabian Context

On the edges of the Sassanian and **Byzantine empires**, the Arabian Peninsula was an important trade conduit for both. Merchants from its cities did business with traders from many places, exporting and importing spices as well as other valuable commodities. Cities in the peninsula were also good places to bargain for goods coming from Africa and for slaves being imported from there. One of the main trading cities in the western part of the peninsula known as the Hejaz was **Mecca**.

According to Muslim tradition, Mecca's history can be traced to **Abraham** (called in Arabic "Ibrahim"). He was believed to have built the **Kaaba** (a black stone structure surrounding a meteorite located in the center of Mecca) in ancient times helped by his eldest son Ishmael (corresponding to the Biblical Ishmael and called in Arabic "Ismail"), when the inhabitants of the place then called "Bakka" had fallen away from Abraham's belief in one god. Apart from this tradition, little is known about the Kaaba before the 400s CE.

By Muhammad's time, the Kaaba served as a place to worship deities revered by various Arab tribes. Its key god was Hubal, venerated there by the **Quraysh** tribe that had ruled Mecca for two centuries by the early 600s CE. The Quraysh made their money as merchants and traders as Mecca prospered under their rule. Arabia's stark terrain meant that life there remained a constant struggle. **Bedouin** tribes engaged in continual low-level conflicts with each other. Each year, there was a temporary truce and pilgrimage to Mecca to pay homage to tribal gods and drink from the sacred well of **Zamzam**. The pilgrimage was also an occasion for major tribal disputes to be mediated, debts to be paid, and much trade to occur.

Muhammad's Life

Muhammad was born into the Banu Hashim, an important subgroup of the Quraysh, in 570 CE. His father died before he was born, and his mother passed away when he was a young child, so he was raised in the household of his uncle Abu Talib, leader of the Banu Hashim. After he grew up, Muhammad became a merchant and at age twenty-five married Khadija, a widow fifteen years older than him. He was married to Khadija for twenty-five years and took no more wives while she was alive.

Muhammad had several daughters and sons by Khadija, but the only one recognized by all Muslims to have survived him was his daughter **Fatima**. Descendants of Muhammad through her are given the honorific titles *sharif* ("noble") or *sayyid* ("lord"). As Muhammad's only universally recognized descendants, they are respected by both **Sunni** and **Shii** Muslims, but Shii Muslims value this lineage connection more highly.

Revelation

Muhammad would retire to a cave near Mecca by himself to meditate for several weeks each year. The Muslim belief is that in the year 610 CE, during one of these sessions, the angel Gabriel (called in Arabic "Jibril") appeared and commanded Muhammad to recite the following:

> Recite, in the name of your Lord who created man from a (mere) clot of congealed blood. Recite, and your Lord is the Most Generous. He, who taught [use of] the pen, taught man what he did not know (Quran 96:1–5).

He received no more revelations for three years, but then they resumed. Quranic verses revealed to Muhammad when he was still in Mecca focused on man's responsibility to believe in one god, the resurrection of the dead, the final judgment followed by heaven and hell, and signs of God's presence in daily life.

Muhammad's wife **Khadija** was the first to recognize him as a true prophet. She was followed in this belief by his cousin **Ali** and then by Muhammad's close friend **Abu Bakr**. When Muhammad preached in public about what had been revealed to him, he was ignored or ridiculed by most of his fellow Meccans, although a few became his followers. They became known as "Muslims" or followers of "Islam." "Islam" can be defined as "submitting to God's message as communicated to Muhammad." Muhammad made some people angry when he recited verses condemning idol worship and polytheism.

His monotheistic message threatened Mecca's city fathers, in particular those from his own Quraysh tribe. They were guardians of the Kaaba, the focal point of Mecca's polytheistic worship. It functioned as the center for pilgrimages upon which much trading wealth was based. A group of the city's merchants offered to arrange a choice marriage for Muhammad, bringing him into the elite if only he would stop preaching, but he refused.

EARLY MUSLIM COMMUNITY

Muslims under Pressure

In 615 CE, some of Muhammad's followers took refuge in Ethiopia and two years later, leaders of other Quraysh clans declared a boycott against the **Banu Hashim** clan until it withdrew protection from him. Although this ended when the Banu Hashim refused to disown Muhammad, he continued to be a liability for his tribal group. Two more blows came in 619 (known later as the "Year of Sorrow"), when his wife Khadija and his uncle **Abu Talib** died, leaving him without financial or family support.

Islamic tradition records that just when his personal situation had reached this low point, Muhammad experienced in 620 the *Isra* and *Miraj*: two parts of a miraculous one-night journey. In the *Isra*, he was carried on a mystical winged horse ("Buraq") from Mec to "the farthest mosque" (Arabic: "*al-masjid al-aqsa*"), later identified by Muslims with the al-Aqsa **Mosque** in Jerusalem. In the *Miraj*, Muhammad was reported to have been taken on a tour of heaven and hell, and spoken with earlier prophets such as Abraham, Moses, and Jesus. Soon after this, a delegation from **Yathrib** (a town later called "Medina" located two hundred miles north of Mecca) came to Muhammad and asked him to mediate between opposing tribes at war there for years.

Hijra (Hegira)

Sensing a good opportunity to leave Mecca, Muhammad told his followers in 622 to go to Yathrib, which they did. When he learned of a plot against him, Muhammad slipped away with Abu Bakr and arrived in Yathrib himself in September 622. His Meccan followers who went there became known as the *muhajirun* (emigrants) or "those who made the *hijra*." The importance of the *hijra* (hegira) in Islamic history is recognized by the fact that the Muslim calendar begins with the year when Muhammad and the *muhajirun* emigrants fled from Mecca.

Among the first things Muhammad did on arrival in Yathrib (soon renamed "Madinat al-Nabi" ["City of the Prophet" or simply "Medina"]) was to create a document later known as the "**Constitution of Medina**." It specified rights and duties for all of Medina's inhabitants and relationships between different groups there, including those between Muslims, Jews, and other People of the Book. The term "**People of the Book**" refers to other monotheists such as Jews and Christians, whom Muslims accepted as legitimate believers in God. The Constitution of Medina defined the community as the *umma*, an Arabic word that came to be used to describe the community of ll Muslims in the world.

Sections of the **Quran** revealed at Medina sed on the creation of a Muslim commu- a task defining the Medinan period of

Muhammad's leadership. Muslim converts from among Medina's natives became known as *ansar* ("helpers"), because they helped Muslim emigrants from Mecca find shelter there. To transcend family loyalties and promote Muslim unity, Muhammad had his close companions among the "emigrants" and "helpers" choose spiritual brothers, with Muhammad himself choosing his son-in-law Ali as his own spiritual brother.

Meccans against Muslims

After the hegira, Mecca's leaders confiscated the properties of those "emigrants" who had fled with Muhammad to **Medina**. These emigrants, in turn, began raiding Meccan caravans: acts legitimized by Quranic revelations Muhammad continued to receive. While the attacks interfered with Mecca's trade, they provided needed wealth for the Muslims. Hostilities culminated in the March 624 **Battle of Badr:** a significant victory for Muslim forces against great odds. Muhammad and his followers saw this success as a confirmation of divine support, which strengthened the Prophet's position in Medina.

The Meccan defeat at Badr committed them to go after Muhammad to regain prestige. When the two forces met again at the mountain of Uhud in 625, the Meccans did win a modest victory but were unable to crush the Muslim forces totally. New Quranic verses revealed to Muhammad that this defeat was partly punishment for disobedience to God and partly a test of Muslim determination. Mecca's chief **Abu Sufyan** then assembled a large force to attack Medina directly and get rid of the Muslims once and for all.

Despite diplomatic efforts, Muhammad failed to prevent the formation of a tribal confederation against him. When the Meccans arrived at Medina with 10,000 men against the 3,000 Muslims there and began a siege, Muhammad tried a new tactic. Aided by a Persian convert to Islam with some engineering skills, Muslims dug a trench to supplement Medina's natural fortifications against a cavalry attack. The Meccans were stymied by this new ditch and abandoned their siege after a few days.

Muhammad received Quranic verses calling for the **hajj** pilgrimage to be made to Mecca, but Muslims had not been able to perform it due to the existing state of hostilities. In 628, Muhammad ordered preparations to be made for a pilgrimage to Mecca despite this situation, saying that God had promised him that this goal would be fulfilled. Another military confrontation almost took place, but Muhammad and the Meccans finally signed the Truce of Hudaybiya. This agreement ended hostilities between Mecca and the Muslims. Soon after this, the first pilgrimage, not a full hajj pilgrimage but the lesser version of the pilgrimage called an "*umra*," took place in 629.

Muhammad's Last Years

After this truce had lasted two years, a proxy war between the allies of the Meccans and Muslims erupted with a battle between the Banu Khuzaa, a group loyal to Muhammad, and the Banu Bakr, with close ties to Mecca. After this skirmish, Muhammad sent a message to Mecca that either Meccans should pay blood money for the dead members of the Khuzaa tribe and end their alliance with the Banu Bakr or the truce of Hudaybiya would be canceled.

The Meccans mistakenly chose to end the truce. In 630, Muhammad attacked and easily conquered Mecca. After he arrived there, he declared forgiveness for its inhabitants' transgressions against him. At that point, most Meccans became Muslims and statues of Arabian tribal gods near the Kaaba were destroyed. Muhammad's return to Mecca allowed him to complete the first full hajj pilgrimage. After performing this, he delivered his "Farewell Sermon." It proclaimed an end to existing tribal feuds upon the creation of this new Islamic *umma* (community). Muhammad died in 632 in Medina, where he was buried.

EARLY ISLAMIC EXPANSION
Building a Muslim Domain

There was considerable debate about who should succeed Muhammad as the *umma's* leader. Abu Bakr (r. 632–634 CE) was fairly quickly recognized as a consensus candidate to become the first caliph ("successor") of Muhammad. His first task was to combat a wave of false prophets and apostates who had arisen after Muhammad's demise. Once such rebellions had been quelled, Abu Bakr embarked on new campaigns of conquest to bring more lands and peoples under Islamic control. He began with Mesopotamia (modern Iraq), richest province of the Sassanian Empire, and continued on to Roman Syria, a prosperous area of the Byzantine Empire. Already an elderly man when he assumed power, Abu Bakr died within two years of taking office.

His designated successor **Umar** (r. 634–644 CE) was a talented military commander who led Muslim forces into Iran and Egypt. Since lengthy recent wars between the Byzantines and Sassanians had left both empires exhausted, Islamic armies were able to bring all of Mesopotamia, Syria, Palestine, Egypt, and the whole Persian Empire under Muslim control by 643 CE. Umar's administrative skills matched his military talents. He was renowned for a strict approach to governing, but recognized for his sense of justice and fairness. He paid with his life for Muslim success under his rule when he was assassinated by a Persian slave, but just before his death in 644, Umar appointed a committee of six Meccan "emigrants" (but no Medinan "helpers") to select the next **caliph**.

The committee's choice was **Uthman** (r. 644–656 CE): a Meccan with a reputation for being very practical. The Medinan "helpers" were displeased that the Prophet's cousin and son-in-law Ali had not been chosen instead. Uthman's first years as caliph, however, went smoothly. He continued Islamic conquests, securing North Africa from the Byzantines. His most enduring achievement was to oversee the production o a formally compiled text of the Quran. Toward the end of his reign, his government had financial troubles, setting off a revolt against him in Medina. Rebels attacked Uthman's house and killed him while he was reading the Quran.

After Uthman's demise, leaders of the *umma* selected Ali (r. 656–661 CE) to succeed him. Ali dismissed several provincial governors with close ties to Uthman, installing his own trusted aides. He also moved the Muslim capital from Medina to Kufa, a recently established Muslim garrison town in southern Iraq. These changes were not well received in Syria, then being administered by Muawiya, one of Uthman's close kinsmen. These tensions led to the first Muslim civil war, which continued through the brief caliphate of Ali.

Ali fought off numerous challenges to his rule. First, at the "Battle of the Camel," Ali's forces confronted a large army of Muslims from Medina led by two of Muhammad's companions. They were joined by Muhammad's widow Aisha, who sought to avenge Uthman's death. Soon after this, Uthman's relative Muawiya fought Ali at the Battle of Siffin. Although Siffin ended in a stalemate, Ali was killed in 661 by the distraught relative of one of his own mutinous soldiers.

Ali's eldest son (Muhammad's grandson) **Hasan** then served very briefly as caliph. Hasan ultimately agreed to retire to Medina, allowing Muawiya to replace him when he found that he could not secure power. Hostilities ended upon Muawiya's assumption of the caliphate, an event later considered the beginning of the Umayyad caliphal dynasty. The period of struggle during Ali's caliphate is often called the **first *fitna*** (disturbance), a time of conflict that ended the early unity of the Islamic *umma*. Civil conflict between Muslim factions slowed the process of expansion for a number of years, giving the Byzantine Empire time to recover.

Muslims and Those They Conquered

e important aspect of these conquests be found in the Muslim treatment of Muslims in the lands they occupied.

All who believed in one God such as Jews, Christians, and Zoroastrians were known as "People of the Book" and given *dhimmi* ("protected") status under Islamic law. Those who converted to Islam were treated exactly like other Muslims, enjoying all the same legal rights, but Islamic law prohibited forced conversions.

Those who chose not to convert were allowed to continue their religious practices as before, and their communities were permitted to retain a certain amount of legal, political, and social autonomy. Their only formal requirements were to pay the *jizya* (an annual tax) and to conduct their religious activities in an inconspicuous manner. One factor that may have aided early Muslim conquests were the doctrinal differences between Christians in different regions of the Byzantine Empire. There were almost no objections recorded by contemporary Egyptian Christian chroniclers to the rule of the early Muslim conquerors, in contrast to the numerous, angry complaints about the rule by fellow Christians who disagreed with them on theological questions.[1] This suggests that in some cases, it may have been easier for Christians to be ruled by Muslims than by fellow Christians with whom they had serious doctrinal disagreements.

THE UMAYYAD CALIPHATE

Arab Exclusivity

The first four caliphs were remembered in Islamic history as the "**Rightly-Guided**" (Arabic: *Rashidun*) caliphs, leading the *umma* when it was still relatively cohesive and united. They were followed by the **Umayyad caliphs**, who ruled the Islamic *umma* between 661 and 750 CE with their capital at Damascus. After the last Umayyad

---

[1]For discussion of this question, see Terry Wilfong, "The non-Muslim Communities: The Christian Communities," in Carl Petry, ed., *The Cambridge History of Egypt* (Cambridge: Cambridge University Press, 1998), 178.

ruler was overthrown by the Abbasids in 750, the Umayyads relocated to al-Andalus (Muslim Spain), where they eventually established the caliphate of Cordoba in 929. The Umayyad period of Islamic history saw an immense and rapid territorial expansion, which created numerous administrative and cultural challenges. The Umayyads favored the old ruling Arab elite of Mecca, in particular their own clan, over new converts to Islam, called *mawali* ("clients").

The Umayyads can be credited with promoting Arabic as the official language of the Muslim empire. The Umayyad dynasty has been depicted as transforming the caliphate from a religious institution (as it had been under the first four Muslim rulers (the "Rightly-Guided" caliphs) into a dynastic, kingly one. This perspective does not take into account how Umayyad rulers saw themselves as upholders and defenders of Islamic law, as presented by the word of God found in the Quran and **hadith** accounts (reports of Muhammad's deeds and sayings). In fact, it was during the reign of the Umayyad caliph **Umar ibn Abd al-Aziz** (r. 717–720 CE) that the first collections of hadith accounts were assembled.

Modern Arab nationalists view the Umayyad period as an early part of the Arab Golden Age that they want to emulate and revive. This is particularly true in Syria, with its capital, like that of the Umayyads, at Damascus. White, one of the four Pan-Arab colors (black, white, red, green) featured on many modern Arab flags, signifies the Umayyads.

Defining the *Umma*

Muawiya (r. 661–680 CE) was the first Umayyad ruler (although Uthman belonged to the Umayyad family and thus technically was the first Umayyad caliph). Muawiya's reign was marked by internal consolidation and external expansion. He oversaw military advances across North Africa and into Central Asia. His eastern campaigns resulted in the Islamic conquest of Kabul, capital of modern Afghanistan, as well as Bukhara and **Samarkand**, two major cities now in modern Uzbekistan. Upon his death in 680, the office of caliph passed to his son, **Yazid I**. Many prominent Muslims, including **Husayn ibn Ali** (Muhammad's grandson and Ali's younger son), opposed Yazid's automatic inheritance of the caliphate from his father. This led to a conflict later called the "Second *Fitna*."

In October 680, Husayn was heading to Kufa to assemble an army to fight Yazid. On Yazid's orders, an Umayyad force intercepted him on his way there and killed him, along with his family members and companions, at what became known as the **Battle of Karbala**. This event, which took place on the tenth of Muharram, 61 AH [Muslim year] (October 10, 680 CE) is remembered as the day of **Ashura**: one of the primary commemorations of martyrdom among Shii Muslims. **Shiis** consider Husayn to be the Third **Imam**, following his brother Hasan (the Second Imam) and his father Ali (the First Imam).

For many years, revolts organized by loyalists of Ali's descendants continued to challenge the legitimacy of the Umayyad caliphs. To bolster their Islamic credentials, the Umayyad rulers had the **Dome of the Rock** built on the Temple Mount in Jerusalem over the very stone where Muslims believe Muhammad commenced his miraculous "Night Journey" to heaven. This coincided with the location considered by many scholars to be the center of the Jewish Second Temple.

The Umayyads continued to expand Islamic control of territory. An Umayyad force commanded by Tariq ibn Ziyad made a successful landing at Gibraltar (a Romanized version of the Arabic "*Jabal al-Tariq*" ["Tariq's Mountain"]) in April 711. This incursion marked the start of the Muslim conquest of the Iberian Peninsula. Much of what was later Spain and Portugal became known in Arabic as "*al-Andalus*," portions of which would remain under Muslim rule until 1492.

EARLY ABBASID CALIPHATE

The Abbasid Revolution

Within less than one century, the Umayyads were displaced by another group with Meccan roots: the Abbasids. They descended from Muhammad's youngest uncle Abbas, but the revolution ultimately bringing them to power in 750 originated in a series of attempts to install a member of Ali's family as caliph. They began with Muhammad ibn al-Hanafiya (637–700). He was not a son of Ali by Muhammad's daughter Fatima, but by a woman of the Banu Hanifa tribe.

Husayn's martyrdom at Karbala in 680 made Muhammad ibn al-Hanafiya the ostensible head of Ali's family, since he was Ali's eldest surviving son. Based on this status, one of Muhammad ibn al-Hanafiya's loyal followers raised a rebellion to make him caliph. Although this did not succeed, a story later circulated that Muhammad ibn al-Hanafiya's son Abu Hashim had named his own distant cousin Muhammad ibn Ali to be *his* heir as he lay dying, keeping claims on the caliphate alive in this branch of Ali's family.

The son of Muhammad ibn Ali, **Abu al-Abbas Abdullah al-Saffah**, started asserting his right to become caliph in the 740s. To build his case, al-Saffah (who also happened to be descended from Muhammad's uncle Abbas) focused his activities on Khorasan. This was a region in northeastern Iran where many mawali (non-Arab Muslims) lived. These mawali resented the Umayyads, whom they perceived as prejudiced against non-Arab Muslims.

When Hisham, a successful Umayyad caliph who had stayed in power for two decades, died in 743, he was followed by a series of brief, unsuccessful rulers. Their unpopularity led the Abbasids to launch a popular uprising in Khorasan in 747 that quickly spread to Iraq. Al-Saffah, supported loyalists to Ali's family, as well as non-Arab lim mawali and other dissidents, brought rces to victory, ousting the last Umayyad Marwan II, in 750 CE.

Loyalists to Ali and his family were now being labeled "Shiis," since they belonged to his faction (in Arabic: "*shia*" means "faction"). Many of these "Shiis" had backed al-Saffah, hoping that he might be the Mahdi or at least the Mahdi's precursor. *Mahdi* is an Arabic term that means "redeemer of mankind who will come to earth just before the Day of Judgment and end injustice and tyranny." Throughout Islamic history, different groups of Muslims have turned to charismatic leaders whom they identified as the Mahdi, acting on hopes of a messiah or deliverer shared by Muslims with Christians and Jews.

Al-Saffah soon disappointed this group. Just after he took power, he not only dismissed all remaining Umayyad governors and officials but turned as well against Shiis allied with him. When al-Saffah was proclaimed caliph at Kufa's Great Mosque in 749, Shiis felt betrayed when he did not step aside and allow the Sixth Imam, **Jafar al-Sadiq** (great-grandson of Third Imam Husayn), to rule.

Although only caliph for a brief time, al-Saffah strongly promoted education and increased international trade. Some of the first paper mills outside of the Far East were built in the Central Asian city of Samarkand (in modern Uzbekistan) during his reign. These facilities were reportedly established by Chinese prisoners captured at the **Battle of Talas** (in modern Kyrgyzstan) in 751. Al-Saffah encouraged non-Muslims and non-Arabs to join his army, choosing the talented Abu Muslim (an Iranian from Balkh [in modern Afghanistan]) to lead his troops. Although al-Saffah died only four years after deposing the Umayyads, his brother and successor al-Mansur continued his polices, consolidating Abbasid rule during his more than two decades in power.

Establishing Abbasid Authority

The Abbasid dynasty governed the Islamic world for just over five centuries (750–1258 CE). Twelve years after they had taken power from the Umayyads, the Abbasids built a new

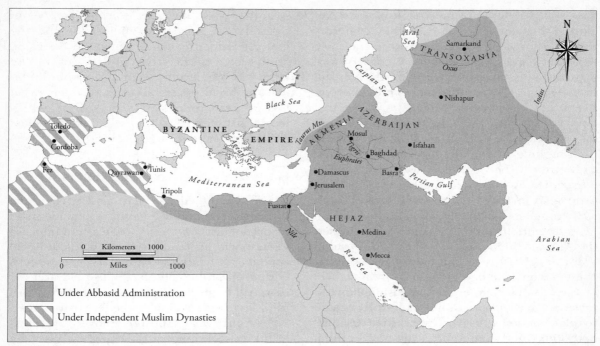

MAP 1.1   Islamic World in the Ninth Century

capital city called "**Baghdad**" about twenty miles northwest of Ctesiphon, the former Sassanian capital. Just as the Umayyads drew much from Roman and Byzantine tradition, so the Abbasids, with Baghdad so near the old Sassanian capital, borrowed and adapted much from their Persian predecessors.

The Islamic world had become so vast that even after their first few years in power, the Abbasids had still not established themselves as rulers everywhere in it. There were constant rebellions in many areas of the Middle East, particularly when new caliphs took power. Although Shiis were briefly stymied by Abbasid rejection, they soon reemerged as dangerous and dedicated foes of the dynasty. The problem of pretenders from Ali's line seeking to rule resurfaced again and again in different forms.

When Sixth Imam Jafar al-Sadiq died in 765, Shiis split into two groups. One accepted Jafar's son Ismail as the authentic Seventh Imam. They became known as Ismailis, and adopted many of the ideas and doctrines of the vanquished Hanafiya movement (see p. 8). The other group recognized Musa al-Kazim, another of Jafar al-Sadiq's sons, as *their* Imam. Musa is still recognized as the Seventh Imam by Twelvers (Shiis who believe in Twelve Imams) today.

In this uncertain situation, Abbasid rulers began to trust only members of their close family. Even Abu Muslim himself, one of the early supporters of the Abbasid revolution, fell under suspicion. Like other revolutionaries in world history, the Abbasids soon found that the radical agendas of their anti-Umayyad movement no longer remained useful as they tried to manage a large, imperial government.

Abbasids as Conservatives

Beginning under Caliph al-Mansur (r. 754–775 CE) the Abbasids began to emphasize government continuity and promoting orthodox relig above all. The official suppression of the more extremist elements of the Abbasid coalition caused a string of popular revolts in Iran. On the other hand, al-Mansur's more conservative approach reassured many people, which aided in the maturation of Abbasid institutions over the twenty-one years of his reign.

The Abbasid era also marked the real beginning of the institution of Islamic viziers: high-ranking and skilled political advisers to the ruler. The first viziers were all from a Persian family known as the Barmakids. They originated in Balkh (in modern Afghanistan) as a prominent family of landowning Buddhist priests before their conversion to Islam. Under the Abbasids, influences of the Persian tradition through advisers like these became more marked with each new ruler.

As a substitute for the diminishing importance of Arab identity, **Abbasid caliphs** began to place more stress on upholding Islamic **orthodoxy** and conformity. This conformism, as a conscious public policy, did not preclude an enormously dissolute private life for the elite behind closed doors, but what was done in private was not discussed in Abbasid circles, except as gossip. The Abbasids rebuilt Mecca and Medina, organized pilgrim caravans from Iraq, and generally reinforced orthodoxy by persecuting various heretical movements.

Harun al-Rashid's caliphate (786–809) is often perceived as the height of Abbasid power from an intellectual, cultural, and social perspective. Politically, it was also a time that saw the proliferation of independent rulers across the Muslim world. After 787, independent dynasties took power in Morocco and Tunisia, so that the Abbasid caliphs no longer retained real authority west of Egypt. By this period, Islamic domains were no longer expanding as they once had been. Harun waged a few minor campaigns against the Byzantines in Anatolia and Cyprus, but these were the last military conquests made by Muslim forces for a long time.

Soon Byzantine forces began to test Muslim defensive points in Syria and Anatolia, while invaders from the steppes of Central Asia seized Islamic territory in the Caucasus and Armenia. The fall of the Barmakid family of **viziers** from power during the latter part of Harun's reign also caused problems. Abbasid rulers began to rely somewhat less on Persian aristocrats as advisers, which meant that their court counselors now had less political and administrative expertise.

Early Challenges to Abbasid Rule

A civil war erupted upon Harun's death between his sons Amin and al-Mamun. Al-Mamun, who enjoyed much support in northeastern Iran and Central Asia, contemplated moving the caliphal capital from Baghdad to Marv (in modern Turkmenistan) to consolidate his hold over the east. Although he eventually abandoned this idea, such a plan revealed the fear that increasing autonomy and power enjoyed by rulers in the west was now also being exercised by those in the east, too. Although most Iranian and Central Asian Muslim rulers still accepted the Abbasids as their nominal overlords, this was quickly becoming only a formality.

The financial situation of the caliph's government also contributed to the central government's weakness. The expensive Abbasid court and its inflated bureaucracy recorded chronic financial deficits, made worse by the loss of revenues from increasingly autonomous provinces in addition to the exhaustion of mines and other sources of state revenue. The caliphs found a short-term fix: tax-farming by provincial governors. Governors were given virtually unlimited authority over their domains in exchange for regular monetary payments. If these governors were also army commanders, the caliphs ultimately retained little influence at all over them.

Caliph al-Mutasim (r. 833–842 CE) became one of the first Muslim rulers to import Turks from Central Asia to serve as his soldiers. Soon Turks formed the dominant group in the military. A wide gap arose between the caliph, surrounded by his elite army and government, and ordinary people. Caliph al-Mutawakkil (r. 847–861 CE) tried to reverse this trend but did not succeed. When he tried to break the Turkish troops' power and rally support among the common people against them, he was murdered by a Turkish soldier in 861.

The next four caliphs followed one after another in quick succession, but the autonomy of Turkish troops at the court was steadily increasing, and provincial governors were asserting more and more independence. There was also a massive revolt at this time among the **Zanj**: black slaves working in the salt marshes around Basra. A Zanj leader soon secured effective control over much of southern Iraq and southwestern Iran. By 877, Zanj rebels were conducting raids within a few miles of Baghdad.

After al-Muwaffaq took power in 875 (as a regent for his brother Caliph al-Mutamid), his twenty years in power did much to restore the health of Abbasid rule. By 883, he had crushed the Zanj rebellion. He was succeeded by several energetic and capable rulers, and real caliphal authority over Egypt and Iran was restored. Despite all the ups and downs, because of its relative success and endurance, the Abbasid caliphate had developed by the end of the ninth century into a cosmopolitan empire with a sophisticated mercantile and economic life.

At the same time, the rapid growth of large cities, with their concentrations of capital and labor, subjected the loose social structures of the Abbasid realm to huge stresses, causing constant widespread urban unrest. The rapid expansion of intellectual life created a lot of ferment as well. There were constant clashes between dissonant cultural traditions of different groups and their worldviews, as well as conflict between new ways of thinking about the world and more traditional views.

This all prepared the way for heretical movements to spread. Such groups, in a deeply religious society, provided the only real channels for moral or material dissent from the existing order. The endemic turmoil and unrest

of the late 800s and early 900s CE continuously tested caliphs' ability to preserve peace and order in their domains. Challenges ranged from the revolutionary militancy of the **Qarmati Shii** movement that had arisen in Bahrain, Syria, and the southern Arabian Peninsula, to the more subtle and but also more damaging critique provided by dissident urban moralists and mystics in Baghdad itself.

Threats posed by the Qarmatis receded as the movement's sympathizers blended into the emerging Shii communities of Bahrain and the **Persian Gulf** coast. At the same time, a branch of Ismaili Shiis (see p. 9) established a rival "anti-caliphate" through a dynasty—the **Fatimids**—who ruled first in Tunisia and later in Egypt from the tenth to the twelfth centuries CE.

LATER ABBASID CALIPHATE

Rise of the Buyids

In northern Iran, the **Buyids**, a military family loyal to Shiism, formed a new dynasty that was on the verge of conquering Iraq by the early tenth century. The death of Caliph al-Muqtadir (r. 908–932 CE) while fighting his own general Munis reflected the degree of confusion in established hierarchies and ranks in the Abbasid government. The next caliphs, al-Qahir and al-Radi, began to share authority with their main military commanders, now given the title "*amir al-umara*" ("commander of commanders").

This title recognized the existence of a supreme secular authority who had political and military power but was *not* the caliph. The caliph was reduced to serving as the titular head of state and religion, the embodiment of the religious unity of the *umma*.

In 945, when the Buyid commander Muizz al-Dawla took Baghdad and was recognized as the *amir al-umara*, the caliph had not only surrendered political control over the capital city to a military leader but to a *Shii* military leader as well. This unprecedented situation was overshadowed by the fact that the Abba bureaucracy had become so dysfunctional that Buyid rulers were forced to establish a new administrative system for the caliphate. The military now became the most important political group under their rule.

The caliph's responsibilities were narrowed almost totally to religious affairs. This caused a leadership vacuum, since the legitimacy of military leaders was completely based on their demonstrated military abilities. Military commanders began to carry out operations designed to showcase their warrior skills, instead of focusing primarily on the defense of the community.

Buyid politics was strongly influenced by clan and personal loyalties. Major commanders retained key officials on their payrolls, creating networks of allies and clients. At the outset of the Buyid period, the bulk of their troops consisted of compatriots from Daylam near the Caspian Sea in northern Iran. Buyid generals, like the caliphs, soon discovered that Turkish slave soldiers could be controlled more easily than their fellow Daylamis. Just like the caliphs who had first employed Turks, Buyid commanders came to depend on the goodwill of these troops.

Despite the Buyid rise to political and military dominance in the society, Abbasid caliphs still retained immense prestige across the *umma*. They continued to supervise and lead the judicial and religious bureaucracies: appointing judges and supervising the maintenance of public religious observances. This was complemented by the Buyids' ability to transcend their own Shii allegiances and govern pragmatically. Although they did offer financial assistance to Shii clerics and religious establishments in Baghdad, there is no ʾvidence that Buyid administrators ever acted ʾinst Sunnis because they were Sunnis, at ʾ in Iraq.[2] Most Turkish troops under Buyid

command were Sunnis, so any Buyid policy directed against Sunni institutions would have been highly unproductive.

The coming of Fatimid rule in Egypt in the mid-tenth century CE created further anomalies. The Shii Fatimid ruler there now styled himself a "caliph," in direct competition with the Abbasid ruler, who remained the Buyids' sovereign. In spite of religious commonality between the Fatimids and Buyids, their relations seem to have been shaped more by the political circumstances of competing empires. In the end, the Buyids enjoyed a certain independence as Shii soldiers supporting a Sunni ruler not available to them under a Shii monarch.

Pre-Islamic Nostalgia of the Buyids

Another revealing characteristic of the Buyids was their willingness to adopt pre-Islamic Iranian monarchical titles to bolster their legitimacy, given the disapproval shown in Islamic holy texts such as the Quran and hadith for pre-Islamic expressions of kingship. Several Buyid rulers issued coins referring to themselves as *shahanshah* (the pre-Islamic Sassanian "king of kings").

As anomalous as this seems, Buyid commanders even asked the Abbasid caliphs to grant them such titles officially. These honorifics could hardly be considered proper from an Islamic perspective, since to label a human being "king of kings" would be to assert that he was like God. In 1031, one Buyid commander asked to be called *"shahanshah al-azam"* ("the greatest king of kings"): an unusual mix of Persian and Arabic words. Although the caliph agreed, when his consent to this was announced at Friday prayers, a large group of people began to protest and threw bricks at the prayer leader. A committee of Islamic legal scholars investigated this matter and prohibited the use of such a title, since only God could be considered the "king of kings." All of this suggests the enormous enduring power of pre-Islamic symbols and references in the Abbasid era, not surprising

ʾe detailed discussion of the Buyids, see Joel
Humanism in the Renaissance of Islam:
al Revival during the Buyid Age (Leiden: E.J.

given Baghdad's close proximity to the ruins of past imperial centers and the Buyids' own ethnic origins near the Caspian coast.

Political Fragmentation and Economic Prosperity

The rise of the Buyids threw changes in the Abbasid military system into sharp relief. The Arab element had gradually lost its importance, and pensions formerly paid to Arabs were now discontinued except for serving soldiers. The core of the early Abbasid army had consisted of Arabs and Persians from Khorasan. In time, this gave way to the Turkish slave troops, who after the time of al-Mutasim became the main element in the army, providing support for various emirs and commanders whose power supplanted that of the caliphs.

For a long time, the political fragmentation of the Abbasid caliphate during the ninth and tenth centuries, along with the decline and eventual collapse of central authority in Baghdad, did not have measurable negative effects on economic and cultural life. A great economic revival had accompanied the Abbasids' accession to power, which was made possible by their skillful promotion of industry and trade, as well as the development of a vast commercial network within the Muslim world and beyond it. The original Arab warrior caste gave way to a ruling elite of landowners and bureaucrats, professional soldiers and literary figures, as well as merchants and men of learning. Islamic towns evolved from garrison cities into centers of commerce and cultural exchange. The Abbasid caliphate of this time became known later as the "golden age" of Islam: when a new, rich, and creative civilization arose with the confluence of many peoples and traditions.

Abbasids after the Buyids

During the three centuries between the Buyids' arrival in Baghdad and the Mongol conquest of the city, Abbasid caliphs functioned more and more as figureheads. They continued to personify the spirit of the Muslim *umma* and provided legitimation to secular rulers who held actual sovereignty in various places across the Muslim world. Except for a brief revival of their autonomy in the twelfth century, the caliphs themselves were appointed and removed by secular rulers, and only one caliph from this later period, al-Nasir, had a measurable historical impact in political terms. As secular sovereigns assumed greater and greater importance, many of them began to use the title "**sultan**" (an Arabic word meaning "ruler with temporal, secular power").

The greatest challenge to the Abbasids at this time came from the Fatimids, Shiis who ruled Egypt from the mid-tenth to the mid-twelfth centuries. They did not recognize the legitimacy of the Sunni caliphate, but installed their own caliph, whose authority was supported by an extensive network of religious propagandists and sympathizers across the Muslim world. The Fatimids attempted to divert Asian trade away from the Persian Gulf to the **Red Sea**. Despite extensive efforts, the Fatimids were never able to displace the Abbasids, except for one fleeting period.

In 1055, the Abbasid caliph had recognized a Seljuk Turkish commander, Tughril Beg, as "sultan." Three years later, he had to go to Mosul to take that city back from a Seljuk rival, his brother Ibrahim. Tughril's absence from Baghdad allowed a Fatimid missionary (al-Basasari) and his followers to capture the city briefly in 1058. After he took it, al-Basasari had the Friday sermon and prayer pronounced in the name of al-Mustansir, the Fatimid caliph, in the main mosque of Baghdad and had the caliph's throne, robes, pulpit and staff sent to the Fatimid capital in Cairo. The expelled Abbasid caliph (al-Qaim) took refuge with an emir in a different city in Iraq for a year.

After subduing his brother, Tughril Beg returned to Baghdad with a large army, causing al-Basasari to escape with his close associates. Tughril reinstated the Abbasid caliphate a year after it had been displaced in December 105... He also sent a group of soldiers in pursuit ... al-Basasari, who was soon killed. This invol...

of the name of a new monarch at the Friday noon prayer, a classic symbol in the Muslim world of a change in the political order, in this case only lasted for as long as domestic political problems preoccupied the main military commanders of the empire, now increasingly Seljuk Turks, members of a group that had recently migrated from Central Asia to Iran.

Rise of the Seljuks

In the eleventh century, different Abbasid territories quickly began to establish distinct political identities. Several large areas came to be controlled by the **Seljuks**. The Seljuk "Great Sultanate" that endured from the late eleventh through the twelfth centuries marked another step in the evolution of secular sovereignty in the Middle East, with an increasingly important role played by Turkish rulers. Turks in the Middle East after the rise of the Seljuks were no longer just slave or freed soldiers brought in from Central Asia. Now, whole confederations of nomadic, free Turks started to migrate westwards. This influx in time altered the ethnic configuration of the eastern parts of the Middle East, particularly in Iran and Anatolia.

This brought political and religious change as well. The Seljuks, as Sunni Muslims, actively tried to suppress Shii dynasties and movements. To promote Sunni belief on an intellectual level, they commissioned the construction of a large network of new religious schools (**madrassas**) to defend Sunni orthodoxy against Shii missionaries and propaganda. This campaign in turn prompted a strong reaction from extremist Shiis, particularly from one militant branch of the Ismailis in northern Iran known as the **Assassins**. As Shii radicals, they targeted high Sunni government officials for assassination, giving the name of their [...] to this activity. Their movement though, [...] resented a real challenge to Seljuk rule [Sun]ni orthodoxy, although their tactics [ide]alism inspired other revolutionaries [...] by the continued use of the term [to d]escribe a wide variety of killers.

CALIPH AL-NASIR'S ABBASID REVIVAL AND THE MONGOL INVASION

The Seljuk Great Sultanate soon broke up into numerous local principalities. The collapse of unified Seljuk power did enable Abbasid Caliph al-Nasir (r. 1180–1225 CE) to make one final attempt to restore caliphal power. By his reign, the Fatimids had collapsed, and their successors, the **Ayyubids**, were battling European Crusader forces in Egypt and Syria. The main rulers in Muslim Central Asia, the Khwarazmshahs, were first focused on wars against Turkish rivals in their region and then had to confront the Mongol onslaught. In this power vacuum, al-Nasir secured control over Baghdad by relying on popular support from urban youth organizations. When this failed, the Mongols rapidly brought the Abbasid caliphate to an end.

The Mongol conquest of Baghdad in 1258 and the end of the Abbasid caliphate have often been described as one of the major catastrophes of Islamic history. This event certainly marked the close of an important era in Islamic history. From another perspective, the Abbasid caliphate had not been a very effective ruling institution for many years. While the end of the caliphate did result in the formal fragmentation of the Muslim world, the first stages of this trend had started long before. The new reality created by the Mongol invasions left a propitious situation for energetic new military groups, particularly those made up of Turks from Central Asia, to establish themselves as rulers of the Middle East.

ABBASID "SHADOW" CALIPHS: CODA TO A "GOLDEN AGE"

Long after the fall of the Abbasids, the power of the unifying idea of a single Islamic caliphate continued to attract Muslim political thinkers and rulers seeking legitimacy. The first attempt to continue with a caliphal paradigm was made by the **Mamluks**. The Mamluks, mostly Turkish military slaves originally from Central Asia, established a realm in which military slaves ruled an Islamic empire based in Egypt for almost three centuries (1250–1517 CE). They were among the only Muslim military forces ever to defeat the Mongols. They bested them at the **Battle of Ayn Jalut** (today in northern Israel) in 1260, primarily because the main Mongol expeditionary force in the Middle East had been forced to return to Mongolia to attend the election of a new great **khan**. The Mamluks also showed considerable skill in cavalry warfare at this encounter, pitting the Mongols against adversaries who used the same military tactics as effectively as they did.

The Mamluk Sultan Baybars (r. 1260–1277 CE) rose through the ranks from being a lowly military slave to serving as an important field commander. He was credited with first defeating the European armies of the Seventh Crusade in 1254, then the Mongols at Ayn Jalut in 1260. As a military leader, Baybars identified himself very strongly as a defender of Sunni Islam, and as a man of lowly slave origin, he also sought to bolster his legitimacy however he could. To further advance his claim to be Islam's true protector, he recognized a relative of the last Abbasid ruler, now living in Cairo, as "caliph" in 1261. This man's successors, who began to be called "**shadow caliphs**" because they had no formal ruling powers, asserted their inherited authority to bestow religious legitimacy upon secular rulers from their base in Mamluk Egypt up to 1517, when the **Ottomans** conquered the Mamluk Empire and incorporated it into their own domains.

One story goes that after this, al-Mutawakkil III, the last "shadow caliph," had been captured with his family and brought to Istanbul. It was reported that when he got there, he agree to bestow the title of caliph, as well as the regalia that went along with it (Muhammad's sword and cloak), upon Ottoman Sultan **Selim I**. The Ottoman sultans began to attach more and more importance to the concept of the caliphate as they extended their empire over a similar territorial expanse as the Abbasids. The importance placed by the Ottoman sultans on connections to Muhammad can be seen even today in the display of his regalia visited daily by tourists in the old Ottoman **Topkapi Palace**.

Questions to Think About

1. What are the origins of the phrase "Middle East"?
2. How did the Byzantine and Sassanian Empires shape the Middle East on the cusp of the Islamic era?
3. What is the meaning of Muhammad's life for Muslims?
4. How did the Muslim community evolve after the hegira was made to Medina?
5. What were the most important similarities and differences between the Umayyad and Abbasid Caliphates?
6. How did the Abbasid Caliphate become fragmented? What effects did this have?
7. What were the origins of Shii Islam?

For Further Reading

Armstrong, Karen. *Muhammad: A Prophet for Our Time*. New York: HarperCollins, 2006.

Brown, Peter. *The World of Late Antiquity: AD 150–750*. New York: Harcourt Brace Jovanovich, 1971.

Daryaee, Touraj. *Sasanian Persia: The Rise and F[of an Empire*. London: I.B. Tauris & Co. Ltd., 2C

Donner, Fred McGraw. *The Early Islamic Conqu Princeton, NJ: Princeton University Press, 1[*

Donner, Fred McGraw. *Muhammad and the Believers: At the Origins of Islam*. Cambridge: Harvard University Press, 2010.

Ibn Hishām, 'Abd al-Malik, Muhammad Ibn Ishāq, and Alfred Guillaume. *The Life of Muhammad: A Translation of Ishāq's Sīrat Rasūl Allāh*. Karachi: Oxford University Press, 1997.

Kennedy, Hugh. *When Baghdad Ruled the Muslim World: The Rise and Fall of Islam's Greatest Dynasty*. Cambridge, MA: Da Capo Press, 2005.

Lassner, Jacob. *The Shaping of 'Abbasid Rule*. Princeton, NJ: Princeton University Press, 1980.

Rodinson, Maxime. *Mohammed*. New York: Pantheon Books, 1971.

Shaban, M. A. *The 'Abbasid Revolution*. Cambridge: Cambridge University Press, 1970.

Watt, W. Montgomery. *Muhammad: Prophet and Statesman*. London: Oxford University Press, 1974.

2

Islamic Civilization: The Classical Era

By Abbasid times, Islamic civilization in the Middle East had reached a prosperous and successful state. Developments in the Abbasid era were often seen by later Muslim thinkers as examples to be followed in their times, and many things that happened during this period had a lasting impact on Middle Eastern life in later centuries.

ISLAMIC BELIEFS AND PRACTICES

Islam had evolved into a thriving and prevalent religion by the Abbasid era. A review of Muslim beliefs and practices that were established by then reveals a faith in full flower. For Muslims, according to what was revealed to Muhammad, God's final prophet, Islam defines the complete and final version of an eternal, universal monotheism revealed to mankind many times and places before.

Those who received God's revelations before Muhammad included many prophets revered by Christians and Jews. Prime examples of these (all mentioned in the Quran) are Abraham, Moses, and Jesus. Muslims do accept Jesus as God's true prophet but reject the doctrine of the Trinity or any concept of Jesus as the son of God, viewing such beliefs as veiled polytheism. For Muslims, the Quran provides God's final revelation to mankind: the verbatim words of the one, unparalleled God ("Allah" in Arabic) as communicated to Muhammad. They consider Muhammad to be the greatest example of a human being, although not divine in any way. Reports (hadiths) of Muhammad's teachings and behavior (in Arabic called the *sunna*) are followed and revered as holy scripture. The word *Islam* in Arabic means "submission (to the will of God and God's message)." *Muslim*, the word for a believer in the Islamic faith, is the Arabic active participle of the same verb for which "Islam" is the verbal noun. Muslim religious practices begin with the **Five Pillars of Islam**: the most basic required acts of worship. Islamic Holy Law (Arabic: "**Sharia**"), based on the Quran and hadith reports (compiled during the Umayyad and Abbasid eras into collections), offers guidance on all aspects of life and culture.

FIVE PILLARS OF ISLAM

The basis for all Islamic belief is the idea of *tawhid* (Arabic: "God's unity and oneness"). In the first of the Five Pillars of Islam, *tawhid* is expressed by reciting the *shahada* (the testament of faith): "There is no god but God, Muhammad is the Prophet of God." God transcends all human understanding. God is mentioned, above all, in the Quran as "compassionate" (Arabic: *al-rahman*) and "merciful" (Arabic: *al-rahim*). Muslims believe that their lives' main purpose is to worship God. The most important step in becoming a Muslim is to pronounce the *shahada* with sincerity.

The first of the five pillars requires affirmation of belief, while the other four prescribe practices. One is that a short ritual prayer (Arabic: *salat*) must be performed five times daily in the direction of the Kaaba in Mecca. The function of prayer is to focus believers' minds on God. Although prayers may be performed alone, performing them in a group is recommended to enhance the spirit of the *umma* (community of Muslims) worshiping together. To facilitate this gathering, calls to prayer are issued from mosques shortly before each prayer time. An *imam* (an Arabic word with the basic meaning of "prayer leader") stands in front of those assembled in a mosque (from Arabic "*masjid*" meaning "place of prostration [in prayer]") to guide them through the sequences of recitation and prostration that ritual prayer requires. All these prayers are recited in Arabic by the assembled believers in unison.

Another pillar is the requirement for Muslims to give alms to the poor (Arabic: *zakat*). They are required to donate some part of their accumulated wealth, but are encouraged in Islamic holy texts to give away, of their own free will, as much as they are able. In traditional Islamic society, *zakat* was given to the government for it to distribute, but great emphasis was placed by legal scholars on the idea that this did not constitute a tax merely because it was collected and distributed by government officials. Instead, it was described as a way to enhance social solidarity by taking wealth from those who had lots of it and giving it to those who needed it most.

During the month of **Ramadan**, Muslims must not eat or drink between dawn and dusk. This pillar of ritual fasting (Arabic: *sawm*) is also designed to bring the believer's spirit nearer to God. It is to remind the faithful of the fragility of their existence and how much they owe their good fortune to God. During Ramadan, it is customary to read a section of the Quran each night and to have an *iftar* (Arabic: "breaking of the fast") with invited guests just after dusk. Fasting is not obligatory for believers for whom it would constitute an undue burden (such as pregnant women or sick people). There is flexibility in performing the fast, according to individual situations. Muslims should make up fast days missed during Ramadan, but this should be done as soon after the missed day as possible.

HAJJ PILGRIMAGE

One of the most meaningful of all the pillars is the requirement to go on a pilgrimage (during the Islamic month of Dhu'l-Hajj) to Mecca on the *hajj* once in a lifetime (if it can be afforded and one is physically able to do it). Carrying this out requires entering into the state of "*ihram*": an Arabic term to describe both the spiritual cleanliness, purity, and ease of a pilgrim during the pilgrimage as well as the simple garment that is worn. Men are asked to dress in just two seamless white sheets, while women wear simple, modest clothing. Before entering this ritual state, pilgrims bathe, ritually cleanse themselves, trim their nails and hair, and verbally pronounce their intention to perform the hajj.

Over several days, they perform a series of rituals to celebrate key Islamic religious themes. These include feeling what it will be like to be in heaven moving around God's throne by circling the Kaaba counterclockwise seven times. Pilgrims also pay homage to the power of God's forgiveness by visiting Mount Arafat. According to Islamic belief, this is where Adam and Eve were reunited and forgiven by God for their sins after wandering the earth for many years after their expulsion from the Garden of Eden. Hajj participants experience the joy of Abraham (Arabic: "Ibrahim") when God permitted him to sacrifice a ram instead of his son (identified by most Muslim scholars as Ishmael [Arabic: "Ismail"]) to show his devotion. They remember this by sacrificing a sheep or goat whose meat is given away as alms to the needy. Although visiting Medina is not a formal part of the hajj ritual, most people include this in their journey in order to visit Muhammad's tomb and the first Islamic mosques there.

The rituals of the hajj are designed to remind Muslims why Mecca and the Kaaba are so important. Mecca is regarded by Muslims as the site of the first place on earth established to worship God, as well as the location of many important events in the life of Abraham (Ibrahim), his son Ishmael (Ismail), and his wife Hagar (Arabic: "Hajar"). Muslims, Christians, and Jews all define principal aspects of their religions through special connection to Abraham. Christians and Jews perceive this link to be made for them through Abraham's son by Sarah, Isaac (Arabic: "Ishaq"), while Muslims perceive their connection to be made through Ishmael (Abraham's other son, by Hagar).

The annual hajj pilgrimage has also had a political dimension for centuries. Official sponsorship of pilgrimage caravans became an important mark of prestige for Muslim rulers beginning in the Abbasid era. In modern times, the Ottomans, the Hashemite rulers of the Hejaz, and the monarchs of **Saudi Arabia** have all been recognized throughout the Muslim world when they served as "custodians/servitors of the two holy places [Mecca and Medina]" by being the recognized political rulers of the two cities.

Taken together, the five pillars constitute the foundations of Islam. It is a religion that attaches importance both to **orthopraxy** (the importance of following correct ritual practices) and orthodoxy (the importance of having correct beliefs about God and his message). The three monotheisms (Christianity, Judaism, and Islam) all have elements of orthodoxy and orthopraxy but emphasize different aspects of each.

JIHAD: AN ISLAMIC DUTY

The term *jihad*, which means "to strive or struggle" (to fulfill God's wishes), has been considered by some Muslim thinkers as a "sixth pillar" of the Islamic faith. One definition of the word, sometimes described as the "lesser" jihad, has been associated with waging war to defend (or in some cases expand) territories ruled by Muslims. Another definition, labeled the "greater" jihad by some thinkers, describes an individual's struggle to improve him or herself religiously and morally. According to Islamic law, the "lesser" jihad is the only legal way to wage war. Since it is seen as a collective duty whose performance and supervision are really the responsibility of the sovereign alone, it only becomes a religious duty for the rest of the people if the legitimate ruler declares a "just war" according to Islamic legal requirements.

ISLAMIC HOLY SCRIPTURES

Also in common with other Abrahamic monotheisms, Islam attaches primary importance to its holy scriptures: the Quran and collections of hadith reports. The Quran is the final book revealed by God to his last prophet, Muhammad. The Muslims accept the validity of previously revealed scriptures, such as the Torah (Arabic: "*Tawrat*") and the Gospels (Arabic: "*Injil*") but believe that through human error, their texts became altered and distorted.

Muslim belief holds that the text of the Quran was written down while Muhammad was still alive, but was compiled in the time of the first caliph Abu Bakr and its text verified during the time of the third caliph Uthman. It is divided into 114 chapters (*suras*) arranged in descending order of length (except for the first sura). The suras revealed at Mecca focus on questions of salvation and anticipation of Judgment Day and the end of world, while those revealed after the hegira to Medina pertain more to the rules and order of the *umma* (the Muslim community then developing there).

For Muslims, the only religiously valid text of the Quran is its original Arabic version, because of the belief that it cannot be accurately translated. For this reason, all translations of it, even those done by Muslims, are considered only interpretations or commentaries on its meaning. The Umayyad and Abbasid periods saw the development of *tafsir*, the science of interpreting the Quran and commenting on its meanings.

Hadith collections provide the comprehensive written record of what Muhammad said and did during his life. They both augment the Quran and help in its interpretation. Although Muslims do not consider Muhammad to be divine in any way, his life is regarded as exemplary for all human beings, with his actions and words forming the sunna (broadly defined as the "proper life path" from which the adjective "Sunni" is also derived). Two of the most important Islamic scholars of the Abbasid period, Muhammad al-Bukhari (from Central Asia) and Muslim ibn al-Hajjaj (from Iran), produced hadith collections in the ninth century that have remained fundamental Islamic reference works ever since.

SHARIA: ISLAMIC HOLY LAW

The Abbasid caliphate saw the elaboration of a structure to interpret and administer Islamic Holy Law (Arabic: "*Sharia*"). Since Sharia covers all aspects of life, from government administration to foreign relations to business practices, family life, and daily routines, it became the basis for legal and judicial systems in the premodern Middle East. Its prescriptions and prohibitions are often defined in broad or ambiguous terms, so that the interpretation of its rules became a very important activity for Muslim scholars as the Islamic empire grew.

This gave rise to the *ilm al-fiqh* (Arabic: "science of jurisprudence"): a discipline focused on how to apply religious legal rules in practice. According to rules codified during the Abbasid era, Islamic law was (and still is) based on interpretations by skilled jurists relying on (in descending order of importance) the Quran, the sunna (as found in hadith collections), consensus of Muslim legal scholars on a given issue (Arabic: *ijma*), and finally, use of reasoning by analogy (Arabic: *qiyas*) or logical inference (Arabic: *ijtihad*) to formulate legal opinions. Islamic jurisprudence groups all human behavior into five categories. All actions are classified as obligatory, recommended, neutral, discouraged, or forbidden.

Given the context of the caliphate as a combined religious and political system, Sharia law did not sharply differentiate between the religious and political spheres. Islamic legal scholars were thus considered both jurists and theologians, which gave them considerable power and significance in traditional Islamic societies. Beginning as early as the Abbasid period, Muslim rulers supplemented religious courts with a parallel system of administrative law (Arabic: "*mazalim*") courts over which they had sole control.

Although these courts did not function under the detailed rules of Islamic jurisprudence, they were considered legitimate by Islamic legal scholars. They were seen as providing a way for "public interest" (Arabic: "*maslaha*") to be invoked according to the rulers' discretion in prohibiting or permitting things. This parallel legal system later became a way for Islamic political reformers and modernists in the nineteenth century to establish legitimacy for attempts to integrate and harmonize modern Western law and Sharia law.

Schools of Islamic Legal Interpretation

Islam is a faith in which daily religious practice is fundamentally important. Since the discernment of what is forbidden, what is encouraged, and what is permitted—the essence of Islamic jurisprudence—provides such key guidance in the Muslim world, it is differences in jurisprudence that define the real differences between Muslim groups. This is often confusing for non-Muslims, since Muslims agree on so many things.

All Muslims, for instance, accept the five basic pillars of Muslim belief and regard the same Arabic text of the Quran as God's message to Muhammad. However, because Sunni and Shii scholars rely on different hadith collections, this is where divergences begin. Although a majority of hadith reports in Sunni and Shii collections are identical, enough are different to create challenges of interpretation for Islamic scholars. In addition, even in interpreting identical hadith reports, different schools of thought have emerged within the Sunni community itself, without even taking into account the significantly different approaches of Shii scholars.

By the end of the ninth century CE, four major Sunni schools of legal interpretation (*madhhabs*) had become established, named for the legal scholars who founded them: the Hanafi, Shafii, Maliki, and Hanbali schools of jurisprudence. All relied primarily on the Quran, Sunni hadith collections, scholarly consensus (*ijma*), and analogical reasoning (*qiyas*) to form legal opinions, but differed in how they applied these in given situations. Each school was recognized by most Sunni rulers as a legitimate source of Islamic law, but different rulers favored schools whose interpretations best suited them. Sunni Muslim rulers after the era of the caliphs often tended to favor the Hanafi school, because it offered the most flexibility for rulers in approaches and methods.

Important Differences between Sunni and Shii Islam

Shii scholars also began with the Quran, but followed a different path beyond it in legal reasoning. They used different hadith collections from the Sunnis and were more cautious about using consensus and analogy as bases for legal argument, since they were perceived as too easily straying from divine intention. Although they lacked political power, Shii Imams were active during the Abbasid period, creating distinctive Shii approaches to Islamic jurisprudence at the same time that Sunni scholars were developing the four legal schools of Sunni Islam. These two groups of Muslim scholars did exchange ideas quite a bit during this time. For example, the Sixth Shii Imam Jafar al-Sadiq was so highly regarded as a legal scholar by Sunni clerics that **Abu Hanifa**, founder of the Hanafi school, became one of his main students.

Because of their belief in the special status of the Imams (the Shii title for all of Muhammad's direct descendants through Fatima and Ali), Shii scholars accepted these Imams' actions and words as extensions of Muhammad's own sunna, and thus gave them equal theological weight. In place of consensus and analogy, Shii scholars championed the use of techniques of pure logic (Arabic: *mantiq*) to verify how compatible their rulings were with the Quran as well as this Shii version of the sunna, which included the wisdom of the Twelve Imams.

Shiis recognize the Imams as infallible conduits of the esoteric truth of God's message sent through Muhammad. This sets Shiism starkly apart from Sunni Islam, with its fervent insistence on Muhammad as the "seal of the prophets"—the end of prophetic wisdom. Not all Shii groups, however, recognize the same line of Imams. The best-known Shii group, the Twelver Shiis, recognize twelve lineal descendants of Muhammad as their Imams. The last and twelfth one, **Muhammad al-Mahdi**, was believed to have gone into hiding in the 870s CE and expected to return just before the Day of Resurrection. Another major Shii group, the Ismailis, concur with Twelver Shiis up through the Sixth Imam, Jafar al-Sadiq, but recognize a different son of his (Ismail instead of Musa al-Kazim) as the Seventh Imam, following a totally different line of succession after him as well.

For Twelver Shiis, the fact that the **Twelfth Imam** went into mystical hiding in the ninth century has created some complexities for how Islamic religious law should be applied. For example, some Twelver Shii scholars have argued that jihad involving offensive warfare can only be lawfully declared by the current divinely sanctioned religious leader or a deputy appointed by him for this task. Since the recognized religious leader remains the Twelfth Imam, the ability to proclaim a jihad has been theoretically in suspension since he went into hiding (although this has not prevented later governments led by Twelver Shiis from initiating military action).

Shii "Fundamentals of Faith" and "Practices of Faith"

Although Twelver Shiis agree with all the principles presented in the Five Pillars of Sunni Islam, their own "Fundamentals of Faith" (*Usul al-Din*) and "Practices of Faith" (*Furu al-Din*) add more elements to reflect particular Shii doctrines and practices. The Shii "Fundamentals of Faith" are (1) the doctrine of the oneness of God (contained in the "Testament of Faith" pillar), (2) God's justice (not presented by Sunni scholars as a fundamental of faith, but accepted by them), (3) prophethood of all legitimate prophets (implicit in the Sunni "Testament of Faith" pillar), (4) legitimate leadership of the current Imam (not accepted by Sunni Muslims), (5) belief in the Day of Resurrection (accepted by Sunni Muslims).

Shii "Practices of Faith" are (1) prayer (as for Sunni Muslims, but often fewer times per day), (2) fasting during Ramadan (as for Sunnis), (3) pilgrimage to Mecca (as for Sunnis), (4) giving charity to the poor (as for Sunnis), (5) giving *khums* (20 percent of yearly profits, of which the first half must be given to the current Imam or, during his current absence, to a respected Shii scholar) and the second half to needy descendants of Prophet Muhammad (known as *sayyids*), (6) jihad (but only if declared by the current Imam [now in hiding] or his designated representative.

Two other basic practices are also important to the Sunnis, but not as pillars: "commanding the just" and "forbidding the evil." Except in issues linked to specific doctrinal differences, most of the basic principles of Shiism closely parallel those of Sunni Islam. The difficulty is that as with disagreements between believers in any given religion, the smallest divergences have the potential to cause great strife in a specific political or social context.

Law in Traditional Middle Eastern Islamic Societies

Sunni and Shii jurisprudence are very similar in many aspects of property and business law. While Islamic law recognizes private property, it regards all property as owned ultimately by God, with an obligation to be shared with those in need. If the proceeds of any property were formally dedicated to charity, the title to this property was then declared to be transferred to God, and its proceeds were then given to particular beneficiaries as a *waqf* (Arabic for "charitable foundation"). The institution of *waqfs*, which greatly expanded under the Abbasids, permitted the continued support of numerous public institutions, such as hospitals, schools, marketplaces, and mosques, some of which in the Middle East today are still supported by *waqfs* begun centuries ago.

This egalitarian approach also shapes Islamic business and contract law, designed to prevent unequal exchange and unfair advantage being taken in commerce. This is the reason that Islamic law forbids what is called in Arabic "*riba*": defined as charging any interest on loans, as well as conducting any other transaction in which risks are taken that are not proportional to the potential return for those involved.

MUSLIM WOMEN

Women and Islamic Law

Although women are regarded in the egalitarian spirit of Islamic theology as equal to men as human beings in the eyes of God, in the context of traditional Muslim life, they were considered to be different from men because of their places and roles in society. One example of this can be found in the rules of inheritance under Islamic law, in which a woman's portion is generally half of what a man gets in the same circumstances. One explanation for this is that property will tend to flow away from a family when female inheritors take their shares with them to the families into which they marry.

Another aspect of difference between men and women in the traditional Muslim social context was the consent given to polygamy. According to traditional Islamic law, a Muslim man was permitted up to four wives. However, this appears to have been implicitly discouraged in the Quran. It stated in one passage that a man was required to treat all of his wives equally, but it was mentioned in another verse that this could never be achieved. All of the wives by law were permitted to have separate living quarters and to receive equal attention, financial support, and inheritance. Muslim rulers often married women from among conquered opponents in order to create ties of kinship with new subjects. Under Islamic law, though, marriage was formally recognized as a legal contract, which required a woman's formal consent to be valid. Married women also retained control over their own wealth, which gave them a measure of autonomy in medieval Middle Eastern patriarchies.

Although the Quran itself imposed similar rules on men and women to dress modestly, men are only required to be covered from knee to waist, while women must cover all of their bodies except the hands and face. However, since the rationale deduced for these rules is to avoid having men and women view or be viewed by each other as sexual objects, the actual implementation of these rules has continued to be a matter of legal interpretation for centuries and has differed greatly in different times and places.

Women in Traditional Middle Eastern Muslim Societies

In traditional Islamic societies, relations between men and women were shaped more by a concept of complementarity than equality. Women were primarily enjoined to nurture and promote the family, while the husband was to support his family financially and defend its honor. Despite such formal differences in roles, women still had major importance in many aspects of medieval Middle Eastern society. One way was through the support many prominent women gave to founding major Islamic educational institutions, often by helping to create *waqfs* to support them. The foundation of the University of al-Karaouine, in Fez, Morocco, one of the oldest universities still functioning in the world today, was sponsored by the daughter of a prominent merchant of that city, Fatima al-Fihri, in 859 CE.

Through the Abbasid era, there were countless examples of prominent women patrons who helped establish such *waqfs* to fund all types of social institutions. Some women even became scholars and academics, and it has been estimated that as many as 15 percent of medieval hadith scholars were women. Women were involved in a diverse range of economic activities in Abbasid times. They often served as both nurses and physicians in medieval Muslim hospitals, given the need to keep genders apart in the intimate settings of medical treatment. With the diversity in interpretation of Islamic law and rules in different traditional Muslim societies, the roles and positions of women radically differed from one place and era to the next.

SUFISM

Sufism and Orthodox Islam

From the earliest period of Islamic history, there were many Muslims who wanted to go beyond the mere observance of the rules of holy law. Some people sought a more mystical path to God to transcend the experience of religion in the material world. There was also an increasing concern among others that the phenomenal and rapid success of Islamic expansion and the wealth of the caliphate had created an atmosphere of too much luxury and indulgence, from which a truly pious person could only save himself by withdrawing.

The earliest ascetics reportedly wore rough wool cloaks ("suf" in Arabic) to protest this ostentatious wealth, hence their name: "sufis." They sought to deepen their relationship with God by reciting the *dhikr:* ritual chanting of the names of God and short Quranic verses, pronounced repeatedly to induce a hypnotic state. Other ways of seeking unity with God were playing music and listening to recitations of vivid poetry, in particular love poetry. In these poems, the "beloved" was God, with amorous activities, sometimes described in vivid detail, considered as descriptions of relations with God. Hearing such poetry was designed to put the devotees into a mystical ecstatic state, often enhanced by rhythmic dancing.

The Sufi devotee abandoned the world as far as he could in order to dedicate himself to God. He battled his own base instincts and lusts that kept him from truly renouncing the world and exclusively surrendering to the divine. His goal was annihilation (Arabic: *fana*) of self, which could only occur when he was totally absorbed into God and ceased autonomous existence. Only by making the conscious journey toward this goal, down a long road (Arabic: *tariqa*) of devotion and self-denial, could he achieve satisfaction. This Arabic word for "road" (*tariqa*) was also used later to refer to Sufi orders: organized groups making this journey together.

Although Sufis, like more orthodox Muslims, relied on the Quran and sunna, their approach to discovering truth in these texts was entirely different. Instead of seeking these texts' apparent or perceptible (Arabic: *zahir*) meanings, their goal was to uncover their esoteric and hidden (Arabic: *batin*) truths. Sufi mystics believed that their pursuit of knowledge of the inner self and its esoteric reality was superior to any focus on the apparent and perceptible. While they acknowledged that the conventional scholarly approach was an important part of enhancing understanding of some aspects of theology, they did not accept that it could discern ultimate truth.

By the tenth century, Baghdad evolved into a center of intellectual mysticism, replacing Basra, one of the first Sufi towns. A number of Sufi masters appeared in the eastern part of the caliphate, particularly in cities near the Oxus River in Central Asia (in modern Afghanistan and Uzbekistan). This period of intellectual development culminated in the career of **Muhammad al-Ghazali** (1058–1111 CE).

Originally from northeast Iran, al-Ghazali became a major professor at the al-Nizamiya university in 1091 CE. Al-Nizamiya was one of the first Muslim universities founded in Baghdad. This institution had been established in 1065 by Nizam al-Mulk, a celebrated Iranian scholar at that time serving as vizier for the Seljuk Sultan Alp Arslan. Al-Ghazali's lectures there attracted hundreds of students, and his reputation spread across the Islamic world. Within a few years, he suffered a spiritual crisis, resigned from his academic position, and wandered around the Middle East for a number of years as a mendicant holy man. Eventually, he resumed his academic career, producing numerous works on philosophy and theology. His master work *Revival of the Religious Sciences* (*Ihya Ulum al-Din*) offers a creative synthesis of an orthodox approach to studying the apparent and perceptible meanings of texts with a mystical attempt to probe their more esoteric dimensions.

Sufism and Poetry

Over the next few centuries, Sufi scholars began to write in Persian, with poetry and **Sufism** increasingly linked in Persian literary masterpieces. Some of the most famous Sufi poems were penned by Attar (1145–1221 CE). His most famous work *Conference of the Birds* chronicles a mystical quest by the birds of the world to find their king, a mythic flying creature known in Persian as the "Simurgh." Their quest takes them through seven valleys that present many trials and challenges. Only thirty of the birds finally reach Simurgh's dwelling place, but what they finally discover is that they themselves are *simurgh*. While *simurgh* was the name of a legendary mythical bird, the word also just means "thirty birds" in the Persian language.

Another major Sufi poet was **Jalal al-Din** Rumi (1207–1273 CE) who remains a major poetic figure across the world today. Born in Balkh (in modern-day Afghanistan), Rumi spent many years in Konya (in modern Turkey) and traveled widely through the medieval Islamic world. His most famous poem, the *Masnavi-ye Manavi (Spiritual Couplets)*, is sometimes described as the "Quran of Sufism." It offers voluminous explanations about how to reach the Sufi goal of perfect union with God by pursuing truth through mystical contemplation.

A near contemporary of Rumi, Ibn al-Arabi (1165–1240 CE), was born in Muslim Spain, but later spent much time in Syria and Anatolia. His concept of "the unity of being" (*wahdat al-wujud*) describes God not only as the main agent of creation but as the one thing that exists all alone and whose existence encompasses all other existences. In al-Arabi's view, all things that exist borrow their existence ultimately from God, who remains the perfect, transcendent essence of existence and being itself.

Beginning in later Abbasid times and extending beyond the end of the caliphate, Sufi mystical activity came to be organized into orders (*tariqas*) in which disciples (*murids*) followed the teachings of a particular master (sheikh or *murshid*). These orders came to have more fixed rules of membership as well as leadership hierarchies, and greatly expanded in Ottoman times.

CULTURE AND SCIENCE IN THE ISLAMIC "GOLDEN AGE"

The development of civilizations globally has always been closely tied to the prosperity and flourishing of cities and trade, and the Islamic Golden Age was no exception. This term refers to the period of time roughly corresponding with the Abbasid caliphate (750–1258 CE), and describes an era when the Islamic world became one of the principal world centers of innovation and growth in a wide variety of disciplines and activities. Because of their unique location at the crossroads of Eurasia, scholars in the medieval Islamic world mastered earlier traditions, preserved them, blended their legacies, and made contributions of their own. The Middle East became the main intermediary in trade and intellectual exchange between East and West, given that Islamic rule extended from Spain to India. In addition, the relative tolerance with which medieval Islamic rulers treated their non-Muslim subjects, particularly Christians and Jews as "People of the Book," allowed the skills and energies of followers of many different faiths to contribute to this success.

Abbasid caliphs relied on experts in many fields. Caliph al-Mansur appointed a vizier (Khalid ibn Barmak) who used two Persian astrologers to lay out the plan for Baghdad before it was built. Al-Mansur wanted to enhance Baghdad's reputation, so he invited numerous scholars from neighboring cities to live there. As they moved there in significant numbers, they began to form a scholarly class, some of whom eventually rose to high positions in the Abbasid administration.

Abbasids and the "House of Wisdom"

In 765, al-Mansur fell seriously ill and was advised to summon the renowned physician Jirjis for treatment. At that time, Jirjis presided over the medical teaching academy and hospital of Gundeshapur (see pp. 1–2).

After Jirjis had treated al-Mansur successfully, he was asked to remain in Baghdad for a few years. This created a continuing link between the Abbasid caliph's court in Baghdad and Gundeshapur. The connection grew over the next few decades, until Caliph al-Mamun established the Bayt al-Hikma ("House of Wisdom") in Baghdad itself. This House of Wisdom was modeled after the Academy of Gundeshapur and staffed by its graduates. Although its exact period of operation has not been verified, it seems to have flourished for many years after that. The House of Wisdom was not provided with the same level of support by all later caliphs, but it reportedly survived right up to the thirteenth-century Mongol invasion of Iraq.

The interchange of knowledge embodied by the House of Wisdom did have tangible products. It seems fairly certain that much medical information later passed on to Europe came first from texts written in Syriac and Greek that were translated into Arabic there or in institutions like it. Much mathematical and astronomical information conveyed by works produced in Baghdad seems to have been based more directly on translations of Indian sources, as seen for example in the texts of the main Middle Eastern mathematicians of this era such as al-Khwarizmi.

"Translation Movement" in Abbasid Baghdad

Abu Muhammad ibn al-Muqaffa (flourished in the mid-eighth century CE) typified the translators of the era. He was an Iranian who had been an employee of an uncle of the first two Abbasid caliphs. His scholarly efforts focused on the translation of many important works from the Pahlavi Persian language, such as the stories of *Kalila wa Dimna*. *Kalila wa Dimna*, which became a classic work of Arabic literature, was itself translated and adapted from the Pahlavi Persian version of a classic set of Sanskrit animal fables from India: the *Panchatantra*. Another translation he produced was an Arabic version of the Persian *Khudainama,* a biographical history of the Persian kings. Although this Arabic work has been lost, it formed the basis for the Islamic-era Persian poet Ferdawsi to create the *Shahname* (*"Book of Kings"*) in modern Persian. Ibn al-Muqaffa is also responsible for producing some of the first "mirrors for princes" in Arabic. Based on Persian models, these were manuals of good government, etiquette, and the duties of civil servants. They became an important genre in Middle Eastern literature several centuries later.

The "translation movement" focused not only on rendering new versions of classic works on good government and administration, but on producing scientific texts. One of the most prolific scientific translators was Hunayn ibn Ishaq (809–873 CE), a Nestorian Christian Arab from southern Iraq. Hunayn translated many classic works of philosophy and other disciplines into Arabic, but he is best remembered for his versions of the classic medical texts of Galen: the second-century CE Roman physician who has been credited with creating the very discipline of medicine and whose investigations were later continued in Alexandria. The result of Hunayn's efforts was to make the complete curriculum of the ancient medical school at Alexandria available for contemporary Middle Eastern students.

Abbasid Scientists

Muhammad ibn Musa al-Khwarizmi (780–850) was born in Central Asia (with his name indicating a connection to al-Khwarizm, located in modern Uzbekistan). Al-Khwarizmi became one of the main scholars to work at the **House of Wisdom**, and studied a wide variety of topics there. Among his best-known contributions was his technique for solving linear and quadratic equations. He presented this in his *Compendium on the Calculation of Completing [Equations] and Balancing [Them]*: a work composed during the first half of the ninth century. This book presented such a concise way to solve these equations that it led to an entirely new branch of mathematics being called "algebra," of which this work remains a foundational text. "Algebra" is the medieval Latin version of the Arabic word *al-jabr* (meaning "completion" or "reuniting," and used to describe the setting of a broken bone).

Another important work of his was *On Calculation with Hindu Numerals*. Written about the same time as his algebra manual, it set forth the main basis for all subsequent development of mathematics in the Middle East and Europe: describing a positional, decimal system of numbers that featured a way to represent zero or a null value. The work was translated sometime in the twelfth century CE into Latin under the title *Algoritmi de Numero Indorum*: immortalizing al-Khwarizmi's own geographical surname as the Western mathematical term *algorithm*.

His contributions were not confined to mathematics. Al-Khwarizmi corrected the geographical information presented by Ptolemy in the second century CE to locate places in Africa and the Middle East more accurately. He also assisted in projects to calculate the Earth's circumference and to draw a world map for Caliph al-Mamun. Other works of his described mechanical devices such as the sundial and astrolabe, as well as presenting astronomical tables based on Indian models that helped launch the modern study of astronomy.

Scientific activity in this period did not remain confined to Baghdad and the inner circle around the caliphs' courts. A somewhat later key figure was **Husayn ibn Sina** (980–1037 CE). Known in the West as "Avicenna," he was originally from a town near Bukhara (also in modern Uzbekistan). By his time (as noted), the Abbasid caliph had become more of a figurehead presiding over a dynamic group of regional military leaders who controlled

various regions. Ibn Sina thus moved around Central Asia and Iran a few times in search of new patrons for his work. Early in his career, he developed a reputation for being a good physician. While he served as a doctor to numerous rulers, he worked on many treatises, the most voluminous of which, the multivolume *Qanun fi al-Tibb* (*Canon of Medicine*), remained a medical reference book in the Middle East and Europe until the eighteenth century.

It became renowned for its numerous pioneering discussions on a diverse range of medical topics. The *Canon* was among the first diagnostic manuals to present ways of dealing with infectious diseases, techniques of experimentation in medicine, and hygienic medical practices. Ibn Sina was credited with being among the first authors to describe the anatomy of the human eye correctly, along with discussing its ailments such as cataracts. Although European physicians initially rejected the work's claim that tuberculosis was contagious, scientific research later confirmed that this was true.

His work is also one of the first to document the benefits of regular exercise instead of relying on drugs to preserve health. "Once we direct the attention toward regulating exercise as to amount and time, we shall find there is no need for such medicines as are ordinarily required for remedying diseases...."[1] Although Avicenna was best known for his medical works, he produced treatises on a broad range of other topics, including an analysis and commentary on the works of Aristotle.

Although the philosopher **Abu al-Walid Muhammad ibn Rushd** (1126–1198 CE; known in the West as "Averroes") was not part of the initial wave of Abbasid-era scientific activity, he built his work on what had been accomplished before him in Abbasid times. Ibn Rushd, a native of Cordoba, is considered one of the most significant intellectual figures

---

[1]Avicenna, *The Canon of Medicine (al-Qanun fi al-Tibb)*, vol. 1, trans. Laleh Bakhtiar, Oskar Cameron Gruner, and Mazhar H. Shah (Chicago: Kazi, 1999), 377.

of Muslim Spain. He conducted an intellectual conversation, as had Muslim thinkers before him, with the great scientific and philosophical masters of the pre-Islamic past. This can be seen in his commentary on Plato's *Republic*. In it, he argued that Plato's ideal state of "philosopher-kings" closely corresponded to the ideal form of the Islamic caliphate.

His main philosophical work, *The Incoherence of the Incoherence* (*Tahafut al-Tahafut*), was a defense of Aristotle's philosophical methods against the criticism presented by al-Ghazali in his work *The Incoherence of the Philosophers* (*Tahafut al-Falasifa*). Al-Ghazali, the great religious thinker who had reconciled mystical and more orthodox approaches to theology in other writings, argued in this work that Aristotle's methods, particularly as explained in Ibn Sina's commentaries, contradicted each other and insulted Islamic teaching. Ibn Rushd argued that since Ibn Sina had not presented Aristotle's philosophical methods correctly, al-Ghazali's arguments based on them were also mistaken. Ibn Rushd, who had received extensive training as an Islamic scholar and had served as a judge in Muslim Spain, perceived no conflict between religion and philosophy, arguing that they provided different ways to reach the same ultimate truth.

Ibn Rushd did not have as large a following in the Muslim world as in Europe, perhaps partly because he worked in Spain and North Africa, somewhat at a remove from the main currents of intellectual discourse in central Muslim lands. In contrast, as "Averroes," he had a notable impact in medieval Europe. There, literary tribute was paid to him by Dante in the *Divine Comedy*, putting Ibn Rushd in "Limbo": his netherworld for all respected non-Christians.

Broad Impact of Medieval Islamic Civilization

The intellectual contributions of such thinkers did not merely have impact on the scholarly elite of the Middle East. Their influence and achievements made the Muslim world into a real center of global civilization during this period.

So many aspects of contemporary life were either created or significantly refined during this era of Middle Eastern history. These included material advances such as the widespread use of paper, the use of bank checks, and the introduction of much higher qualities of glass, chemicals, and pharmaceuticals, as well as the formation of new social institutions such as public libraries, hospitals, observatories, and universities. The relative economic power of the Middle East in Eurasia at this time is reflected by the large number of Abbasid coins found in buried coin caches recently unearthed all over Europe.

This can also be seen in such anomalies as a rare gold coin minted in England sometime after 774 CE. It was an exact copy of an Abbasid dinar with that date, but with the king's name "Offa" added on one side in Roman letters. Like their Roman forerunners, but unlike European medieval counterparts, Muslim cities had advanced water supply systems with public baths, drinking fountains, and widespread public toilet and bathing facilities.

The region's thriving literary culture had a lasting impact as well, with the most famous work being *The Book of One Thousand and One Nights* (*The Arabian Nights*): a collection of traditional Middle Eastern folktales. One Middle Eastern story of this period, *Hayy ibn Yaqdhan*, the morality tale of a child growing up on a desert island in seclusion, has been identified as an inspiration for the eighteenth-century English novel *Robinson Crusoe*. Dante's *Divine Comedy*, considered one of the great European medieval epics, may have borrowed aspects of its style and many of its episodes from a genre of Arabic works chronicling Muhammad's "Night Journey" to heaven (the *Miraj*).

MEDIEVAL ISLAMIC CIVILIZATION AND NON-MUSLIM MIDDLE EASTERNERS

Some of the most important participants in all aspects of this "golden age" were Middle Eastern Christians and Jews. Their status in the medieval Islamic caliphate as "people of the book" was quite different from that of Muslims, since they were regarded as inferior to them. These "People of the Book" (also known as "*dhimmi*" or "*ahl al-dhimma*": "people under [Muslim] protection") had to live with numerous restrictions designed to reduce their visibility as non-Muslims and paid a monetary tribute each year (*jizya*) to their Muslim rulers to symbolize their subservience (as well as provide a source of government revenue). The level of tolerance they experienced varied enormously according to where and when they were living. For periods of time during the Muslim "Golden Age," *dhimmis* were able to live relatively successful lives. At other points, they were severely persecuted and had huge restrictions placed on them.

Although it remains difficult to generalize about the overall status of "people of the book" during the medieval "golden age" of the Middle East, there are some groups on whom considerable research has been possible, such as the medieval Egyptian Jewish merchants documented in the "Geniza fragments." The details of the lives of members of Cairo's medieval Jewish community were recorded by chance in documents on fragments of paper. These fragments had to be kept (and put in the "Geniza" ["storeroom"] of the old synagogue in Cairo) because they contained sacred epithets such as the Hebrew word for "God."

By chance, this offers a huge storehouse of information on medieval social history. According to information from these sources, several Jewish merchants were able to prosper through long-distance trade in this era. In the 1120s, one young Jewish man from Cairo, Abraham Ben Yiju, went to India to make money in trade there. Documents concerning his life show that he achieved considerable financial success by sending iron and spices from India to his Jewish trading partners in Aden (in modern Yemen), while bringing arsenic, paper, and other items to India.[2] Other documents in this collection describe Ben Yiju's later problems in keeping his particular business going, but overall, the collection offers a picture of a vibrant Jewish commercial network across Eurasia at this time.

END OF THE MUSLIM MEDIEVAL PERIOD

The conventional view has been that the end of the Islamic "golden age" coincided with the Mongol invasions of the thirteenth century CE. These invasions did cause much destruction and ended the caliphate as it had existed for centuries. They have long been viewed as a turning point from which the Middle East never really recovered its central economic, political, military, and social role in Eurasia.

Alternatively, it has been also argued that the success of the Ottoman Empire, which revived the region's prosperity and endured for another few centuries, reduced the importance of any perceived "end" to such a "golden age." In any event, the situation after the end of the caliphate did result in the political fragmentation of the Muslim world, which had preserved at least a pretense of Islamic unity (with a few significant exceptions) up to that time. Since then, the Islamic "Golden Age" has, for some in the region (particularly beginning in the nineteenth century), taken on the aura of an idealized time whose conditions ought to be restored. The next chapter will examine the rise of the Ottoman Empire and the emergence of its Safavid rival in Iran, both of which were in some ways continuing, in other ways reviving, and in still other ways, vastly different from the Middle East of the "Golden Age."

---

[2]S.D. Goitein, *A Mediterranean Society,* vol. 5, *The Individual* (Berkeley: University of California Press, 1988), 229–230.

Questions To Think About

1. What are the most important beliefs and practices for Muslims? Why are they important?
2. What is the meaning of the hajj for Muslims?
3. What are the most important holy scriptures for Muslims?
4. How does Holy Law form an integral part of the Muslim faith?
5. What are the most important similarities and differences between Sunni and Shii Islam?
6. How has Islamic law defined the role of women? How did this shape the roles of women in traditional Islamic society?
7. What is the relationship of Sufism to orthodox Islam?
8. Why did scientific activities flourish during the Abbasid Caliphate?
9. What were the greatest contributions made to scientific research during the Abbasid Caliphate?
10. What was the status of non-Muslims living under Abbasid rule?

For Further Reading

Ahmed, Leila. *Women and Gender in Islam: Historical Roots of a Modern Debate*. New Haven: Yale University Press, 1993.

Badeau, John Stothoff, and John R. Hayes. *The Genius of Arab Civilization: Source of Renaissance*. Cambridge: MIT Press, 1983.

Bulliet, Richard W. *The Case for Islamo-Christian Civilization*. New York: Columbia University Press, 2004.

Esposito, John L. *Islam: The Straight Path*. New York: Oxford University Press, 2005.

Hill, Donald Routledge, and David A. King. *Studies in Medieval Islamic Technology: From Philo to Al-Jazari, from Alexandria to Diyar Bakr*. Aldershot, UK: Ashgate, 1998.

Holt, P. M., Ann K. S. Lambton, and Bernard Lewis. *The Cambridge History of Islam*. Cambridge: Cambridge University Press, 1970.

Lapidus, Ira M. *Muslim Cities in the Later Middle Ages*. Cambridge: Harvard University Press, 1967.

Lassner, Jacob, and Michael David Bonner. *Islam in the Middle Ages: The Origins and Shaping of Classical Islamic Civilization*. Santa Barbara, CA: Praeger, 2010.

Lindsay, James E. *Daily Life in the Medieval Islamic World*. Westport, CT: Greenwood Press, 2005.

Meri, Josef W., and Jere L. Bacharach. *Medieval Islamic Civilization: An Encyclopedia*. New York: Routledge, 2006.

Momen, Moojan. *An Introduction to Shi`i Islam: The History and Doctrines of Twelver Shi`ism*. New Haven: Yale University Press, 1985.

Morgan, Michael Hamilton. *Lost History: The Enduring Legacy of Muslim Scientists, Thinkers, and Artists*. Washington, DC: National Geographic, 2007.

Rahman, Fazlur. *Islam*. Chicago: University of Chicago Press, 1979.

Rippin, Andrew. *Muslims: Their Religious Beliefs and Practices*. London: Routledge, 2005.

3

Ottoman and Safavid Empires

THE MONGOL ERA

Conquest and World Empire

The end of the caliphate and the rise of a Mongol world empire in the thirteenth century had a huge impact on the Middle East. This broke central Eurasia up into an entirely new set of political units based on the Mongol tradition of dividing tribal lands among several sons. Known as an "appanage" system, it was quite different from primogeniture, which made the eldest son inheritor of all lands.

Before the rise of **Temujin** (later given the title "Genghis Khan"), Mongol and Turkic tribes engaged in continuous battles for primacy on the steppes of Central Asia. Lasting predominance usually eluded any one group, because no enduring political confederations could ever be formed. Temujin, a leader who emerged in the late twelfth century, did succeed in uniting a band of Mongol and Turkic tribesmen under him. He was reputed to have treated his defeated enemies either very kindly or very severely, and became known for dividing the spoils of conquest among all warriors allied to him equally. In 1206, Temujin was recognized as ruler of the whole *ulus* (Mongol for "nation") at a general council of leaders. He assumed the title "Chingis Khan" ("Genghis Khan"; meaning "oceanic" or "universal" ruler): an event later seen as the beginning of the Mongol Empire.

Genghis Khan rewarded his loyal followers with important positions in his army, giving high positions to previously low-ranking warriors. Relying on the remarkable cavalry and archery skills of his forces, as well as their prodigious endurance, the united army of Genghis was able to expand quickly east and west. Although Genghis assigned different sons to administer different parts of his empire, it remained an important principle that as a whole, all conquered territories belonged collectively to the whole family.

By the time Genghis Khan died in 1227, the Mongol Empire ruled lands from the Pacific Ocean to the Caspian Sea—an extraordinarily rapid conquest of such a vast territory given the resources available. Expansion did not stop, but continued under his successors Ogedei, Guyuk, and Mongke. After Mongke's death in 1258, the empire effectively split into different parts, with the Middle Eastern section being run by the Ilkhan dynasty, whose founder was Mongke's brother Hulegu Khan.

After Hulegu had crushed the Abbasid Caliphate, his forces moved on to Syria, which they quickly conquered, and then onto Palestine. They were finally stopped there at Ayn Jalut in 1260 by the Mamluks, military slaves who had recently taken power in Egypt. Part of the problem was that Hulegu himself was unable to command this force in person, since he had gotten news of Mongke's death and had to return to Mongolia with much of his main force to participate in a general family council to select a new leader. As a result, this battle marked the western limit of Mongol expansion in the Middle East. When Kubilai Khan was selected as the next universal Mongol leader, there was dispute over the succession. This soon caused the breakup of the world empire into separate realms in China, Central Asia, the Middle East, and Russia.

The Mongols developed a reputation as ruthless warriors, and the initial impact of their conquests was utter devastation. Mongol invaders destroyed many of the major cities of medieval Islamic society, killed significant percentages of its inhabitants, and laid waste to its infrastructure in ways that would require centuries of recovery.

On the other hand, certain aspects of life slowly got better after the initial calamity of the Mongols' arrival. For example, international communications ultimately experienced considerable improvement under Mongol rule, with trade and cultural exchanges finally flourishing again between Asia and Europe. Evidence of this can be found in the way Chinese royal textile patterns influenced Armenian decorations, and Middle Eastern miniatures began to reflect a Chinese aesthetic.

Many different varieties of trees and vegetables were exchanged between China and Iran, with technological innovations also making their way on Mongol trade routes to the Middle East and Europe. But renewed trade connections also facilitated the spread of the Black Death from southern China to a variety of other places now all controlled by the Mongols. By the mid-fourteenth century, spread of the plague devastated the new trade networks and created political chaos for several decades.

Ilkhan Dynasty and Timur (Tamerlane)

Ghazan (r. 1295–1304), Mongol Ilkhan ruler of the eastern part of the Middle East, persisted in his predecessors' conflict with the Mamluks and even defeated a Mamluk army, temporarily reoccupying Syria in 1299. However, raids on his eastern frontier launched by Mongol rivals from Central Asia kept his attention there and prevented him from taking over more of the Middle East.

Ghazan converted to Islam by 1295, which raised some issues, particularly with regard to what law should apply under his rule. Genghis Khan proclaimed a new law code for the empire (called "*Yasa*" in Mongolian) that incorporated existing nomadic customary laws and allowed religious freedom based on the loose Mongol tradition of worshiping the sky god. Even as a Muslim, Ghazan still respected Mongol tribal religion. The *Yasa* law code remained in place as tribal medicine men were allowed to function in the Ilkhan empire and remained politically influential for a number of years. However, ancient Mongol shamanistic traditions went into decline by the 1320s, with Ilkhan rulers espousing an increasingly purified form of Islam.

Mongol opponents began to cast their battles in a more religious light as well. **Ibn Taymiya** (1263–1328), a scholar of the fairly strict Hanbali school of Islamic jurisprudence, penned one of the strongest contemporary Muslim statements against the Mongols in a fatwa he issued in support of the Mamluks in one of their campaigns. In it, he labeled jihad against the Mongols not merely just, but obligatory. His justification for this was that since they continued to follow their "*Yasa*" law code even after claiming to have converted to Islam, this proved that they were living in *jahiliya* (a traditional Islamic term describing the pre-Islamic state of ignorance before Muhammad and the revelation of the Quran).[1] This innovative use of *jahiliya* to refer to something other than pre-Islamic beliefs was later adopted by militant radical Islamist thinkers in the twentieth century such as **Sayyid Qutb** (see Chapter 16).

The Mongols weathered such criticisms. By 1323, the Ilkhan ruler Abu Said Khan (r. 1316–1335) signed a lasting peace treaty with the Mamluks, but continually faced more and more severe internal challenges to his authority. Upon his death in 1335, Ilkhan domains in Persia and Iraq collapsed into political anarchy. Within a year, the dynasty's territory had been divided between various warlords.

Out of this upheaval emerged Timur (Tamerlane) (1336 –1405): a conqueror who secured control of much of Central Asia, the eastern part of the Middle East, Anatolia, and the northern part of the Indian subcontinent between 1370 and 1405. Timur, from Shahr-i Sabz (in modern Uzbekistan), and his descendants ruled over parts of this vast area for many years. His descendant Babur created the Mughal Dynasty in the early 1500s. The Mughals eventually conquered most of northern India, surviving until 1857 as titular rulers there (although by then long under de facto British control).

Timur was of Turco-Mongol origin. His career embodied the paradoxical relationship between steppe nomadic culture and Islamic norms of political legitimacy and government. On the one hand, he presented one of his main goals as the restoration of a unified Mongol world empire, celebrating tribal traditions that honored Mongol warrior prowess. On the other hand, the empire Timur sought to "rebuild"

was also described as an Islamic domain. His most significant fighting, which he carried out as a "*ghazi*" (Arabic: "warrior for Islam"), took place against other steppe nomadic monarchs also identifying themselves as Muslim *ghazis*, such as the khans of the Golden Horde and Ottoman sultans. **Timur** was a great patron of urban mosques and buildings, but also presented himself as a simple tribal warrior.

While the Mongols rapidly conquered large parts of Eurasia, the quick collapse of their empire and its constituent Middle Eastern part (the realm of the Ilkhan dynasty) introduced a trend of fragmentation that would continue in the Middle East between 1350 and 1500. Timur created an impressive empire very rapidly, but only pieces of it survived longer than a century.

IBN KHALDUN

A versatile North African scholar, **Ibn Khaldun** (1332–1406), made one of the first attempts to analyze the dynamic of these nomadic conquests in the *Muqaddima* (Arabic: "Introduction"): first volume of his general history of the world. In it, he presents a theory of social conflict. Nomadic conquerors are at first usually very successful in a military sense against sedentary opponents, because they have a strong sense of *asabiya* (Arabic: "group feeling") created and reinforced by their difficult nomadic lives. Once they conquer a sedentary society, however, they lose this advantage as they become seduced by attractions of sedentary life, losing their martial spirit and prowess.

Ibn Khaldun traces this process of change through several generations of sedentarization. He was among the first sociologists to explore the dichotomies of sedentary versus nomadic life, as well as the concept of evolution through "generations," by exploring how martial skills dissipated when desert and steppe warriors conquered and tried to govern cities.

His theory concludes with the idea that when conquerors become completely

---

[1]See Carole Hillenbrand, *The Crusades: Islamic Perspectives* (New York: Routledge, 2000), 242–243.

sedentarized, they are then easily vanquished by leaner, hungrier nomads with greater levels of group feeling, and the cycle starts over. Ibn Khaldun has been regarded as one of the first scholars to explore change over time in societies as political and social organizations evolve. His theories on nomadic-sedentary relationships shed particular light on the social dynamics of this period of Middle Eastern history.

The two most important Middle Eastern dynasties to emerge from the tumult following the Mongol invasion both had nomadic roots: the Ottomans (r. 1352–1923) and **Safavids** (r. 1501–1722). The Ottomans, staunch defenders of Sunni Islam, created one of longest-lasting Islamic empires ever. The Safavids established one of the first governments to adopt Twelver Shiism as its official religion. A brief look at how these empires started and became established will introduce the main subject of this work: the modern history of the Middle East in the world as it developed during the nineteenth, twentieth, and twenty-first centuries.

OTTOMANS

Origins

The Ottomans originated as vassals of the Turkish Seljuk Sultans of Rum. The **Rum Seljuks** ruled over a fairly substantial empire in Anatolia and the Middle East between the late eleventh to the early fourteenth centuries, since in medieval Middle Eastern geography "Rum" was another name for Anatolia. These "Rum Seljuks" had split off from the Great Seljuks, earlier established as "sultans" under the Abbasid caliphate.

By the thirteenth century, Anatolia had become a frontier zone between the Byzantines and the Rum Seljuks. These regional powers had both been weakened in recent major defeats: the Byzantines by the Rum Seljuks in 1073 at Manzikert, and the Rum Seljuks by the Mongols in 1243 at Kose Dag. This emboldened minor rulers in the area to establish more autonomy. In this border area, the Ottomans emerged not far from the Byzantine capital of Constantinople as one of several small Turkish principalities in Western Anatolia.

In 1299, their leader Osman (Turkish version of Arabic "Uthman") proclaimed himself "sultan": an event later considered the founding of the Ottoman dynasty. During his reign, Osman captured towns and fortresses belonging to the Byzantines, as well as seizing lands from rival neighboring Turkish warlords. Soon after Osman's son Orhan (r. 1324–1362) took over from his father in the mid-1320s, the Ottomans captured the city of Bursa. This became their new capital from which they extended control in various directions. Orhan also married the daughter of a prominent Byzantine nobleman, John VI Kantakouzenos, which created an important family tie.

Kantakouzenos relied on Ottoman help to prevail in the 1341–1346 civil war between him and supporters of the young Byzantine Emperor John V Palaeologus. Based on good relations with John VI, Orhan was able to occupy the castle of **Tzympe** (Turkish: "Jinbi") on the European side of the Dardanelles. This castle became an important base, from which Ottoman forces extended their control over the fortress of Gallipoli and much of the Gallipoli peninsula.

This in turn provided the Ottomans a strategic foothold in Europe, where they pursued numerous military projects. This was something that none of the Ottomans' Turkish rivals in western Anatolia could do, because the Ottomans alone had a presence on the European side of the Dardanelles. The Ottomans quickly resettled Turkish troops from Anatolia on the Gallipoli peninsula, launching a series of quick campaigns to occupy Thrace. After taking Thrace, the Ottomans controlled principal overland routes between Constantinople and the Balkans.

Orhan's son Murad I soon took Adrianople (now known by its Turkish name "Edirne" as a major city in modern Turkey) and was poised to advance farther into Europe. Ottoman successes in Thrace made the rulers of Bulgaria, Serbia, and the Byzantine Empire very anxious, since none were ready to confront this threat. For a while, Balkan rulers received a respite when Sultan Murad was called away to deal with rival Turkish rulers in Anatolia and intrigue at the Byzantine court.

Murad I's problems in Anatolia emboldened Serbian and Bulgarian rulers who had earlier been his vassals to sever their ties with him. In the end, this proved a tragic mistake. After consolidating his position in Anatolia, Sultan Murad assembled the largest Ottoman force ever gathered in the Balkans to secure control there. At the battle of Kosovo Polje (the "Field of Blackbirds") on June 28, 1389, Murad I confronted the Christian lords who had defied him, achieving a swift and substantial victory. This was important for continued Ottoman expansion into the Balkans, since the Christian rulers brought all their reserve troops to the battle and had nothing left after that.

Within three years, Serbian regional lords had all been compelled to become Ottoman vassals again. Serbia would remain under Ottoman control for the next four hundred years, and the battlefield at Kosovo has remained a place of bitter memories for Serbs ever since then.

Beyazid I

When Murad I was killed at Kosovo by a Serb assassin just after this battle, his son and successor, Beyazid I, lost no time in avenging him and renewing the Ottoman drive for further advances in the Balkans. Beyazid forced yet more local princes in Albania to become his vassals and began settling more Turkish nomads from Anatolia in Macedonia. The situation continued to be unsettled in various parts of the region through the 1390s, but the Ottomans achieved victory in most military encounters there.

After Beyazid started a blockade of Constantinople in 1394, the king of Hungary assembled a coalition two years later to start a crusade against the Ottomans. This force

collapsed in spectacular failure at the 1396 Battle of Nicopolis (in modern Bulgaria): a disaster causing the end of Bulgaria's existence as an independent country for several centuries. After this victory, Beyazid returned to consolidating Ottoman control over Albania and staging intermittent raids into Hungary, Wallachia (in modern Rumania), and Bosnia.

Meanwhile, an Ottoman blockade of Constantinople persisted through 1402. Byzantine Emperor Manuel II, once an Ottoman vassal, traveled to Europe to solicit help, but monarchs there only sent token forces. True relief for the Byzantines, which allow their evaporating empire a few more fleeting decades of existence, occurred when Beyazid rushed to Anatolia to do battle with Timur (Tamerlane).

At Ankara, the Ottomans' Anatolian Turkish forces and Balkan vassal troops came against Timur's veteran Central Asian forces and were annihilated. Timur took Beyazid prisoner, and he died in captivity. This sparked an Ottoman civil war that continued over the next decade, which took some pressure off the Balkans. The next two Ottoman rulers (Mehmed I [Turkish version of the name "Muhammad"] and Murad II) both merely had to focus on restoring Ottoman power to what it had been. By the end of Murad II's reign, he was able to sign peace treaties formally restoring Ottoman control over substantial areas of the Balkans.

Mehmed the Conqueror

Murad II's young son **Mehmed II** ("the Conqueror") had briefly been sultan between 1444 and 1446, but came to the Ottoman throne on a more permanent basis following Murad's death in 1451. Within a few months, he scored several diplomatic and military victories in preparation for what would become his main priority: conquest of Constantinople.

By the 1450s, he had many reasons to pursue this goal. The city provided a natural link between East and West in both land and sea trade. Conquest of it would immortalize him. Mehmed prepared his assault in a very deliberate fashion. He organized a naval force to cut the city off from outside help, assembled a large amount of artillery to bombard it, and sealed off the Bosphorus north of the city by constructing a huge fortress on the European shore. Mehmed concluded an agreement with the Venetians to keep them from helping the Byzantines, while the rest of Western Europe focused on its own internal struggles (the French and English, for example, were exhausted at the end of their "Hundred Years' War").

In the fall of 1451, the Byzantines requested that the Ottomans double the stipend they were paying to an Ottoman pretender being held by the Byzantines as a hostage. They announced that if the Ottomans refused, they would release this man to create a succession crisis. Mehmed used this threat as a pretext to void all treaties with the Byzantines, placing Constantinople under siege in April 1453.

Because he had made careful preparations and blocked outside help, the city's defenses were substantially weakened. Ottoman artillery first knocked substantial holes in its huge land walls. After two months, Turkish attackers stormed through these holes and quickly took control in a predawn assault on May 29, 1453. After over a millennium as capital of the Christian Roman Empire, Constantinople suddenly became the new center of an Islamic Ottoman Empire (although it did not acquire "Istanbul," the name Turks had given it for a long time informally, as an official title until several hundred years later).

Following its capture, Mehmed started to build the Topkapi Palace (near the site of one of the old Byzantine palaces) in 1462 and moved the Ottoman seat of government there. Mehmed added to his titles the phrase "Kaysar-i Rum" ("Roman Caesar")—styling himself the worthy successor of the Byzantines he had just overthrown. Thereafter, one of the Ottoman goals for conquest in Europe remained the "*Kizil Elma*" ["Red Apple"]: an Ottoman nickname for Rome. The Hagia Sophia, main cathedral of the Byzantine Empire, became a mosque, as numerous other religious buildings were also reconfigured for Ottoman use.

Nevertheless, as an Islamic ruler, Mehmed carefully respected the rights of the city's non-Muslim inhabitants in order to preserve its commercial continuity and stability. Even by this time, the city had still not recovered from the destruction caused by European knights in the Fourth Crusade of 1204. Mehmed soon launched a huge redevelopment program to revive it economically. After some time, it grew into a prosperous multicultural and multiethnic metropolis for the Ottoman Empire.

Mehmed, now entitled "the Conqueror," turned to consolidate Ottoman control in the Balkans for once and for all. Over the following decade, he pursued a series of military offensives to secure strong defensive lines along the Danube against Hungary and along the Adriatic coast against Venice. He brought Greece and Serbia firmly under Ottoman control, and had secured Albania and Wallachia, as well as Bosnia-Herzegovina, by his death in 1481. South of the Danube, only the city of Belgrade, still held by the Hungarians, remained outside of Ottoman control.

OTTOMAN EXPANSION

Selim I

Sultan Mehmed's conquest and remaking of Constantinople into an Islamic capital decisively established the Ottoman Empire as the dominant military force in the Balkans and the eastern Mediterranean. This enabled it to commence a period of even greater expansion by now extending its control across the central lands of the Middle East, including Mecca and Medina, as well as pushing all the way to the gates of Vienna in Europe. The increasing power of the Ottoman navy and the particular advantages that land units such as the Janissaries possessed were important factors in this success.

The mercantile prowess displayed in Abbasid times by long-distance merchants between Asia and Europe again reemerged, with centers of Middle Eastern trade now shifting to important Ottoman cities such as Bursa, Izmir, and Istanbul. Ottoman success in controlling trade routes more effectively than previous Middle Eastern rulers may have offered an extra incentive for European powers to find alternate routes to the treasures of East Asia. Paradoxically, Ottoman achievements may have been a real impetus for Ferdinand and Isabella to fund the voyages of discovery led by Columbus.

The next great sultan after Mehmed II, Selim I (r. 1512–1520; whose nickname was "Yavuz" ["Grim"]), defeated the Safavids and the Mamluks, bringing all of Anatolia, Syria, and Egypt under Ottoman control. He became the first Ottoman ruler to claim the title "custodian/servitor of the two holy places" in recognition of his conquest of Mecca and Medina.

Upon becoming sultan, Selim perceived the Qezelbash as one of the most important threats to Ottoman control of Anatolia. "Qezelbash" was the name given to Shii sympathizers among the Turcoman tribes in eastern Anatolia, deriving from the Turkish phrase for "red head" that referred to their distinctive red headgear. In recent years, more and more Qezelbash had become attracted to the Safavid cause, since the Safavids had been sending missionaries to spread Shii religious propaganda among them.

The Safavids, who spoke Turkish and were from Ardabil near the Caspian coast in Azerbaijan (in modern Iran), began as a Sufi order in the thirteenth century. By the early sixteenth century, they had emerged as a messianic Shii movement led by their charismatic adolescent leader, Esmail. He took the title "Shah Esmail I" in 1501 when Safavid armies captured the city of Tabriz.

This victory gave the Safavids enormous momentum, and their movement soon began to threaten Ottoman domains. Selim carried out a purge of suspected Qezelbash loyalists, rounding up thousands of Turcoman who were imprisoned or killed. When **Esmail** became convinced that he had divine support and could attract the military backing of **Qezelbash** Turcoman and other forces in Anatolia, he marched to confront Selim's army at the **Battle of Chaldiran** in August 1514. At first, the Iranian heavy cavalry overwhelmed the Ottoman light infantry. However, repeated salvos from the Ottomans' fortified artillery wagons, combined with precision small-arms fire, soon defeated the main Safavid cavalry force. This turned the tide for the Ottomans.

Shah Esmail was wounded by a bullet and nearly captured. Although he physically survived, the battle called his legitimacy into question, since his followers had believed before this confrontation that Esmail's special connections with the Twelve Imams would protect him. At a more mundane level, Chaldiran revealed the power of the Janissaries' skilled use of firearms: weapons not regularly used by Iranian armies until much later.

After this victory, Sultan Selim I was able to secure control over all the main cities in eastern Anatolia and some in Azerbaijan, proclaiming Ottoman rule for some years even over the city of Tabriz, which until then had served as the Safavid capital. This was facilitated when Sunni Kurdish rulers in the area, whose ancestral territories had been taken away by Shii Qezelbash followers of the Safavids, now pledged loyalty to the Ottomans. Through the agency of Idris Bidlisi, who had been an advisor to the Turcoman rulers of eastern Anatolia and was also closely linked with these Kurdish rulers, Selim appeased the Kurds by officially recognizing their hereditary rights.

The Ottomans also placed an embargo on all silk traffic between Persia, the Ottoman lands, and Europe that was kept in place for several years after Chaldiran. Silk had become a critically important trade good for the rulers of Iran to earn foreign currency, so this dealt a further blow to them.

The Safavid shah was not the only Ottoman rival in the east—another was the

Mamluk sultan. Sensing a threat from the Ottomans with Selim I's forceful approach, the Mamluks tried not to confront the Ottomans directly, but made alliances with Turcoman rulers who controlled northern Syria to go after the Ottomans just as they were confronting the Safavids. Selim had enlisted his own Turcoman allies and after defeating the Safavids, decided to incorporate these Turcoman lands into Ottoman territory. As they had done with Kurdish rulers, the Ottomans were careful to recognize existing rulers and land rights among the Turcoman military elite, which greatly eased the integration of these lands into the Ottoman system.

Although conflict with the Safavids could be legitimized since they were Shiis, it was more difficult for the Ottomans to justify war on religious grounds with the Mamluks, with their reputation as staunch defenders of Sunni Islam. Powerful economic forces ultimately drove the Ottomans to wage war on them. The cities of Syria then under Mamluk rule, particularly Aleppo, had become very closely linked commercially with Bursa and Izmir. Mamluk naval forces had also fallen short in the Red Sea and Indian Ocean, where they were never really able to protect Middle Eastern merchants trading with India against the Portuguese. Although the Portuguese had arrived in the region only a few years before (around 1502), they had already established a formidable naval presence in the Indian Ocean, the Red Sea, and the Persian Gulf.

When Portugal began to make threatening noises about trying to capture Mecca and Medina, and destroyed the Mamluk navy (such as it was) in 1509 in a battle on the Red Sea, the Mamluk sultan implored the Ottomans to send him naval commanders and shipbuilding materials. They sent expert advisers and lumber, but Ottoman leaders took this as a sign. It might be time to replace the Mamluks, particularly if they were not capable of defending the holiest sites of Islam against Christian attack. Soon, Mamluk governors of Aleppo and Damascus had established secret relations with the Ottomans and were won over to their side, along with many other Mamluk officials, through promises of future employment.

Mamluk Sultan Kansuh al-Ghawri feared an Ottoman naval attack, particularly when he found out in 1515 that Ottoman naval construction had suddenly increased substantially. Various accusations flew back and forth between the Mamluks and the Ottomans about how the other side was violating Islamic law and principles, but the immediate cause of the war was the Mamluk demand for the Ottomans to withdraw from Turcoman territory in northern Syria and eastern Anatolia, which both sides now claimed. The Mamluk army reluctantly confronted the Ottoman army at Marj Dabiq (a few miles north of Aleppo) in August 1516.

As at Chaldiran, the Ottoman technique of using armored artillery wagons chained together, along with their skilled use of muskets, was a key factor in their success. The Mamluks, like the Safavids, relied heavily on the skill of cavalry troops that could not stand up to well-trained artillery units. The Mamluk Sultan was killed in the battle, and the Ottomans were able to secure control over Syria within a few weeks.

Selim decided to advance on Egypt without pausing. When he faced the logistical challenge of how to provide adequate water to his troops as they crossed the Sinai desert, a camel force with thousands of water bags was prepared. To confront the Ottoman army by using its own tactics against it, the new Mamluk Sultan Tuman Bay constructed a strong fortified line of artillery and ditches at a site on the approach to Cairo. When battle was joined there in January 1517, the main Ottoman force attacked in front, but another force went around the Mamluks and attacked from the rear. Although the Mamluks fared better at first here than they had at Marj Dabiq, the Ottomans still prevailed in the end, again because of their more agile use of firearms. Once the Ottomans took Cairo, they had won the war.

Upon news of the fall of the central Mamluk sultanate, other Arab lands quickly switched allegiance. Selim's appointment of Khair Bey, a former high Mamluk official, as Ottoman governor of Egypt, was an important step in reconciling Mamluk officials to the new administration. In the fall of 1517, Selim reportedly sent numerous residents of Cairo to Istanbul by ship, including the last Abbasid shadow caliph al-Mutawakkil III.

After defeating the Mamluks, Selim began to consider himself as their legitimate successor, and took on their title of *khadim al-haramayn al-sharifayn* (custodian/servitor of the two holy places). It was alleged in later sources that al-Mutawakkil III had officially transferred his status as caliph to Selim at that time, although no contemporary source has ever been located to confirm this report. In any event, neither the Mamluk nor the Ottoman sultan had any formal right to replace al-Mutawakkil as caliph according to Islamic law, because they could not claim ancestry from the Quraysh tribe of Muhammad.

Nevertheless, having defeated the Mamluks, Selim did assert his status as spiritual guardian of the entire Islamic world, evidenced by his fight against heretics and his increased responsibility now to protect Muslim pilgrimage routes. With the new Portuguese threat to capture Mecca and Medina, the need to protect Islamic holy sites seemed more urgent. Presenting themselves as the "foremost of *ghazi* warriors" Selim I and the son who succeeded him, **Suleyman I**, claimed to be the protectors of all Muslims.

Ottoman success against the Mamluks and Safavids at this time was helped by the fact that European nations had shifted focus to building overseas empires, particularly in the New World, and fighting wars against their European rivals. War within Europe was also fueled by the onset of the Protestant Reformation, significantly increasing internal military and political conflicts there for a long time.

While consolidating rule over his new acquisitions in the east, Selim took care to preserve the status quo in relations with European powers. After he conquered the Mamluks, for example, he confirmed the robust status of Venice's trade relationships with Egypt, but instructed that the tribute of 8000 gold ducats paid annually by Venice to the Mamluks for control of Cyprus would now go directly to him.

Suleyman the Magnificent

The next sultan, Selim's son Suleyman (ruled 1520–1566) has long been considered one of the greatest Ottoman rulers. In domestic affairs, he was credited for making beneficial changes in how justice was administered and law used in the Ottoman system, with the result that his nickname in the Middle East was "Suleyman the Lawgiver." His legal regulations (*"kanuns"*) provided administrative guidance for the empire for centuries. The art, literature, and architecture produced under Suleyman's patronage are still considered masterpieces.

His wife, "**Haseki Hurrem Sultan**" (originally a slave concubine known in Europe as "Roxelana," probably of Ukrainian origin), made such a partnership with Suleyman that he had five children by her, freed her, and officially married her. Hurrem Sultan was famous in her own right as Suleyman's adviser, as well as in her capacity as the founder of numerous charitable institutions across the empire. One of the most significant was the Haseki Sultan Hospital, established in 1551 and still an important teaching hospital in Istanbul today.

Suleyman as Leader

Unlike his father, Suleyman had no brothers, and so faced no succession struggles when he took the throne in 1520. Beginning in 1521, he conducted a series of imperial campaigns that he personally led in Europe and Asia. In August 1521, Suleyman first took Belgrade, whose great fortress had long eluded Ottoman control. A few months later he began the successful conquest of Rhodes. It had become an outpost of piracy in the Mediterranean against the Ottomans, controlled by the Knights of St. John of Jerusalem. Although it took over a year to secure this island, Suleyman received good publicity from how he had conducted his campaign there, allowing the Knights to leave Rhodes as freemen once they had surrendered.

His next target was Hungary. As in recent battles in the Middle East, Ottoman artillery easily vanquished obsolete Hungarian cavalry troop units using the same artillery tactics that Hungarians in the previous century had used against them. This offensive culminated in the summer of 1526 with the Battle of Mohacs: another substantial Ottoman victory. Despite this success, Suleyman was not able to secure control over all of Hungary. All of a sudden, he had to rush back to Istanbul to deal with a new Turcoman insurgency that had erupted in Anatolia. Because these revolts required two years to suppress, the political situation in Hungary continued to evolve.

It is true that the Ottomans had only occupied the Hungarian capital of Buda for ten days in 1526, but after their campaign there, they had secured recognition of their control over southern Hungary. By 1528, the problem was that two candidates (elected by different assemblies of notables) now battled to be recognized as the legitimate ruler of Transylvania. This led to another Ottoman campaign in Hungary, after which Suleyman confirmed his vassal as Hungary's king and reoccupied Buda with no problem. He then decided to attack Vienna, but did not arrive until September 27, 1529. His first famous siege there, which only lasted for twenty days, ended after four attempts to enter the city failed before the arrival of winter.

Suleyman arranged a truce with the Habsburgs in July 1533, just in time to reengage militarily against the Safavids on his eastern front. The Ottomans and Safavids had maintained a relative truce since the 1514 Battle of Chaldiran, but tensions persisted in their relationship due to the Safavids' religious influence over Turcoman rebels who continued to cause instability in Anatolia. The proximate cause of the new round of hostilities was the defection of a Kurdish emir in eastern Anatolia, Sheref Bey of Bitlis, to the Safavids. This triggered an Ottoman campaign against Iran, led by Grand Vizier Ibrahim Pasha.

Ibrahim's other agenda was to try to place Sam Mirza, a brother of the reigning Safavid monarch Shah Tahmasb I, on the Iranian throne as a ruler friendlier to the Ottomans. When he reached Tabriz in the summer of 1534, he found that Safavid forces had evacuated it. From there, he headed southwest and took Baghdad, also without opposition. After securing the areas of Erzurum and Van in eastern Anatolia, Ibrahim concluded what became called the "Campaign of the Two Iraqs [Arab Iraq and Persian Iraq]" by the beginning of 1536 and established the future boundary between the two empires.

Two months after the campaign ended, Ibrahim Pasha was strangled on the orders of the Sultan. Suleyman apparently feared that he was growing too powerful. After the loss of Ibrahim, Suleyman achieved no more spectacular victories, although he conducted many more campaigns. Over the next few years, Ottoman-Habsburg rivalry reached its height. The recent struggle in Hungary made up only one area of this conflict. Both the Habsburg and Ottoman rulers saw themselves as rightful masters of the world and refused to acknowledge each other's legitimacy. With the passage of time, Ottoman fleet operations played an increasingly important role in Suleyman's plans against the Habsburgs.

Habsburg naval forces had recently acquired an expert new commander, the Genoese mariner Andrea Doria. Suleyman found his own naval leader in the person of Barbaros Hayrettin Pasha, a Turkish privateer originally from the Aegean island of Lesbos ("*Midilli*" in Turkish) who was made *kapudan pasha* (admiral of the Ottoman fleet) in 1533. Suleyman also adopted clever diplomatic strategies to check his Habsburg rivals.

He concluded an unprecedented alliance with a Christian European power: the French monarch Francis I. Francis had approached the

Ottomans after being defeated and held captive by Habsburg Emperor Charles V following the Battle of Pavia in 1525. By the 1530s, the Ottoman and French rulers had developed quite a rapport. At that time, in addition to offering French citizens special commercial and judicial privileges as part of a diplomatic alliance, Suleyman tried to create an ambitious joint operational plan for the French and the Ottomans to cooperate in several attacks. This did not succeed because of logistical problems and errors, but the close relations with France that he had established at that time set the stage for cooperation with it over the next two centuries.

In the end, difficulties of logistical support often placed severe limits on Ottoman naval operations. The Ottoman fleet experienced a few successes, with victories at Preveza (off the coast of modern Greece) in 1538, the 1551 capture of Tripoli (in modern Libya), and the conquest of the Tunisian island of Jerba from Spain in 1560. Ottoman ships dislodged Genoa from its last holding in the Aegean, the island of Chios (in Turkish "Sakiz"), in 1566.

The Ottoman navy had much less success in more remote operations that took place in the Red Sea, Persian Gulf, and Indian Ocean. It had deployed ships in these bodies of water after defeating the Mamluks, in order to counter the Portuguese. In 1538, the Ottoman governor of Egypt set out to attack the Portuguese colony at Diu (on the Gujarat coast of India) in command of seventy-two ships. He initially met with success when he took Aden back from the Portuguese. From there, he sent this force, the largest Ottoman fleet ever deployed in the Indian Ocean, to lay siege to Diu starting in November in cooperation with the forces of the local Indian ruler of Gujarat. The Portuguese meanwhile had sent a relief fleet, and the ruler of Gujarat was not cooperating as much as the Ottomans had hoped, so the Ottoman fleet was compelled to lift the siege within a fairly short time.

On the way back to Egypt, the Ottoman commander did reorganize the province of Yemen to enhance Ottoman control there. There were a few more naval encounters between the Ottoman and Portuguese fleets in the Indian Ocean, but no Ottoman victories. Ottoman naval presence in that region was able to stop the attempt by the Portuguese to block trade in the Red Sea and the Persian Gulf, but never was able to remove the Portuguese presence from the Sea of Oman and the coasts of India: a presence that in retrospect only marked the tentative beginning of the massive European naval and maritime expansion into the seas around the Middle East that followed in the late seventeenth and early eighteenth centuries.

Ottoman military focus had always remained on land operations, following the early example set by Suleyman. Despite the ups and downs of many campaigns, he remained an army commander to the end. Although not physically very well, he died leading a 1566 expedition through Hungary against the Habsburgs. The day after he succumbed, Ottoman troops conquered a fortress they had kept under siege for weeks. Suleyman was buried next to Haseki Hurrem Sultan in the mosque complex built in his name by the master Ottoman architect Mimar Sinan.

OTTOMAN IMPERIAL INSTITUTIONS

The Ottoman Empire developed a general structure by the time of Sultan Suleyman I that persisted long after his demise, so it is worth briefly exploring.[2] The Ottomans never possessed a true aristocracy. Instead, they relied on a meritocracy of soldiers (many of whom were technically the sultan's slaves) as well as bureaucrats and clerics who had risen through the system. All members of this meritocracy belonged to the *askeri* ("ruling") class (defined in general as "those who receive tax revenues"),

---

[2]It must be noted that what follows is a description of the ideal of the system, not its actual functioning. As in all governments, there is significant difference between the actual and the ideal.

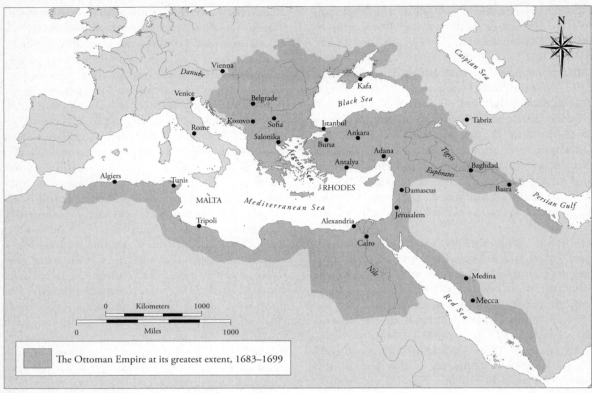

MAP 3.1   Ottoman Empire in the Seventeenth Century

in contrast to the *reaya* class of those who grew food and produced goods ("those who pay taxes"). The Ottoman *askeri* ("ruling") class resembled classical Islamic ruling institutions whose origins can be found in the Seljuk period. At their top was the sultan: keeper of the **"well-protected domains"** charged with ensuring justice, defending the realm, and securing prosperity.

Harem

The sultan kept a large retinue of family and servants in his harem: the inner, guarded sanctuary of the palace where the sultan's wives, concubines, and their children lived. The accepted leader of the harem was usually the mother of the reigning sultan (*valide sultan*).

As dominant voice there, she held sway over one of the most important power centers of the Ottoman court. Particularly during the seventeenth century, *valide sultans* got involved in state politics on a regular basis. During one period, these women effectively controlled daily activities in the empire during what was called the "Sultanate of Women." Below her was a complex hierarchy of other women, with current sultan's wives ranking just below the *valide sultan*. Wives outranked the sultan's concubines, who in turn had a higher station than female retainers and servants.

There was a parallel hierarchy for men in the **harem**. All men living there not directly related to the sultan were eunuch slaves, captured in war or recruited from within the empire. The chief black eunuch (usually from the Sudan) commanded the entire eunuch corps. Because of position and access, chief black eunuchs came to enjoy the sultan's confidence on important political issues.

The chief black eunuch's main deputy was the chief white eunuch. He supervised other white eunuchs who controlled message traffic between the sultan and the rest of the world. The chief white eunuch also ran the palace school and at first was the only person in the sultan's retinue allowed to speak privately with him.

Divan and *Askeri*

The sultan was advised by the imperial **divan**: a cabinet of royal advisers. It included the grand vizier (chief military officer and administrator of the empire), head scribe, chief accountant, and chief judges for Rumelia (Ottoman Europe) and Anatolia, as well as other high officials. Below this but still part of the *askeri* class, the government was divided into "men of the sword" (the military), "men of the pen" (bureaucrats), and "men of *ilm* ["religious knowledge"]" (meaning religious officials and judges in the court system). These three parts of government functioned quite separately and had separate career paths. The military carried out state administration and government at the provincial and local levels, while the other two bureaucracies (religious and bureaucratic) had their representatives at every level of government: national, provincial, and local. Military officials answered to their military superiors, bureaucrats to their bosses, and religious officials to their senior religious leaders. All three groups formed separate chains of power and authority ultimately leading to the sultan.

The empire was divided into small territories known as *kazas* ("judgeships"): each under the jurisdiction of a *kadi* ("judge"). These judges had all received Islamic education and embodied the sultan's judicial authority by trying cases according to Islamic law as interpreted by the Hanafi school of Muslim legal thought (see p. 21). Military officials ("beys") held civil authority in the *kazas*. A military official could only punish a criminal on the verdict of a *kadi,* while *kadis* were not allowed to carry out punishments on their own.

Devshirme

One of the main ways to populate the meritocracy of the military part of the *askeri* class was through the *devshirme* system. The *devshirme* system annually conscripted several thousand boys between eight and twenty years old. They were taken as a tax from non-Muslim (usually Christian) peasant communities, mostly in the Balkans. The system was denounced, particularly by Balkan intellectuals, as a form of child stealing, but there was actually some incentive for peasant families to allow their children to be taken away. If a *devshirme* conscript one day became a high official or military commander; this might prove very lucrative and beneficial for his relatives.

Each boy conscripted into the *devshirme* system became a *kapikulu* "servant of the [imperial] Porte [a euphemism at this time for the sultan]." A *kapikulu* was neither free nor an ordinary slave. He was subject to strict discipline, but received a salary and was provided a pension on retirement. Men conscripted through the *devshirme* system created a distinctive social group that rapidly became a major component of the Ottoman ruling class.

Many trained to join the **Janissary** corps, and the most capable and qualified were invited to enroll in the palace (*enderun)* school. For graduates of this elite training academy, there were excellent career opportunities. Sokollu Mehmed Pasha (1506–1579) was this sort of *devshirme* conscript. Born in Bosnia, he began his service as a Janissary, and under three sultans rose to become grand vizier, effectively become the real ruler of the Ottoman Empire for more than fourteen years.

JANISSARIES The Janissaries (Turkish: *Yenicheri* ["new soldier"]) were infantry troops that formed an elite Ottoman military force. The force was first created in the late fourteenth century using male children levied through the *devshirme* system from conquered countries and ultimately abolished by Sultan Mahmud II in 1826. The Janissary corps had distinctive uniforms, was paid regular salaries, and marched to distinctive martial music played by the *mehter* military band.

They have been compared to the Praetorian Guard of Rome and had some important parallels with the Mamluks who had been ruling in Egypt, but had no real equivalent in contemporary European armies. Their units were close-knit communities, effectively functioning as a soldier's family. Janissaries lived in barracks and did duty as policemen and firefighters during peacetime.

Originally, they were a well-equipped elite force, provided with support units to clear travel paths, set up tents, and cook for them. Janissaries were given substantial privileges and benefits to reward their staunch loyalty and preparedness in combat. These troops received military instruction in the ascetic environment of *ajemi oglan* ("cadet") schools. Since they technically were the property of the sultan, these cadets were taught to regard him as their father, and the Janissary corps as their family.

While Janissaries were expected to convert to Islam, they were also initiated as disciples of the Bektashi Sufi order, a very popular Sufi group in the Ottoman Balkans. A distinctive quality of the Bektashi order was that it welcomed a wide spectrum of religious beliefs and practices not always acceptable to more orthodox Muslims, and thus may have been more welcoming for those recruited from non-Muslim backgrounds. Bektashi leaders served as mentors to the Janissary corps from the time it was first organized.

By the early sixteenth century, the Janissaries had developed a reputation for skill in the use of gunpowder weapons, particularly muskets and primitive forms of grenades. Within just a century, though, they were becoming anachronisms. Military technology and tactics were changing swiftly as a result of the Military Revolution that began in Europe around 1450 and rapidly spread to the Middle East. During the last century of their existence, the Janissaries became more of a social class of businessmen and craftsmen than an organized military force, since their original discipline and monastic living rules had been relaxed, and they were not really useful in battle anymore.

PALACE SCHOOLS   Not all the boys conscripted in the *devshirme* system became Janissaries. The main tool for creating the elite members of the meritocracy was the palace school system. Palace schools comprised not a single track, but two. First, selective madrassa schools (Turkish: *medreseler*) educated promising pupils not recruited through the *devshirme* system to become scholars and state officials. There was also the *enderun* palace school. This was a boarding school located in the Ottoman royal palace complex whose students were drawn from the most promising boys among those taken in the *devshirme* levy. The palace schools were fairly successful in turning out qualified graduates, and produced many statesmen. This system functioned to create government servants who ideally would devote themselves permanently to public service.

Land Tenure

The Ottoman Empire was divided into provinces, and each province's governor was also an important military commander. The organization of each province was broken down along the lines of successively smaller military units, since many military officers derived their salaries from revenues collected on land grants known as "*timars*."

In the Ottoman Empire, much land was originally part of the *timar* system. The *timar* system distributed the projected revenue of newly conquered and previously acquired territory in the form of temporary land grants to the *sipahis* (cavalrymen) and some other members of the *askeri* ruling class. These landholders were given the revenues from this land as compensation for their military service, for which they received no other pay. Timars could be of different sizes, but originally had an average annual value of less than twenty thousand *akches* (*akche*: Ottoman silver coin). This system of land tenure was most common in Ottoman lands between the fourteenth century and seventeenth centuries.

Like other military land tenure systems, the *timar* system was created by financial, political, and expansionist pressures. It was designed to meet the Ottoman government's need to pay its troops, to increase the number of cavalry soldiers, and to help gradually bring conquered regions under more direct Ottoman control. The Ottoman Empire allowed *timar* holders, usually *sipahis* (cavalry officers), to have control over all arable lands, wastelands, fruit trees, forests, and waters within a *timar*'s territory. These *timar* holders employed agents to collect revenues and keep watch over how the land was cultivated. A *timar* holder was rewarded if he settled vacant land, but penalized and punished if he caused already cultivated land to be abandoned. *Timar* holders and their agents had police authority to pursue and arrest criminals within their territories. However they did not exercise any judicial powers, which were all reserved for the local judge (*kadi*) as part of the clerical religious/judicial bureaucracy.

The main responsibilities of a *timar* holder were to protect peasants and persons in his territory and to join the Ottoman army when needed on military campaigns. The *timar* holder did not *own* the land—it all belonged to the Ottoman sultan. *Timars* were at first not considered to be heritable, and holding a *timar* was contingent on active military service. In some parts of the empire, a regular rotation system of *timars* was enforced so that *timar* holders were dismissed from a particular *timar* after serving for a limited period of time there.

By 1600, the *timar* system of land tenure had started to unravel substantially, but as late as the 1520s, *timar* holders still remained one of the large and important components in the Ottoman army. *Timar*-holding *sipahis* had to pay their own expenses, including provisioning during campaigns, and secure their own equipment, as well as providing auxiliaries and grooms. With the onset of firearms, cavalry units, which had once formed the backbone of the Ottoman army, were becoming obsolete. Long and costly wars during the seventeenth century against the Habsburgs and Iranians now required the formation of modern standing armies paid in cash. Many *timars* thus became tax farms to provide the central government with more cash revenue.

Reaya and *Millets*

Townspeople, villagers, and farmers formed a lower class called the *reaya*. This class had nothing to do with what religion one belonged to, but included anyone not part of the *askeri* class. In accordance with Muslim principles on how "people of the book" were to be treated, major non-Muslim religious groups under Ottoman rule were allowed to establish their own self-governing communities. Each was called a "*millet*" (Turkish for "nation"). Under the sultan's protection, *millets* were allowed to live according to their own religious laws, traditions, and language. Each *millet* was led by a religious leader, who had secular/judicial as well religious authority over his community. This often provided religious leaders more authority and power than they had enjoyed in pre-Ottoman times, sometimes significantly shifting the internal balance of power in these *millet* communities. Paradoxically, non-Muslim *millet* leaders sometimes became staunch defenders of the Ottoman status quo, because they owed their own status in their communities to the millet system.

OTTOMANS AFTER SULEYMAN

In addition to the encroachment of the Portuguese on Indian Ocean trade routes, the expansion of Muscovite Russia southwards under Ivan IV "The Terrible" (r. 1533–1584) intruded into areas controlled by the Tatar Khans, longtime Ottoman vassals, and disrupted pilgrimage and trade routes coming from these areas.

Sokullu Mehmed Pasha, one of the most thoughtful grand viziers of this era, tried to build a canal between the Don and Volga rivers in 1569 to counter this trend and facilitate long-distance trade and communications. However, this proved too ambitious a project, given the logistical and financial obstacles. The Ottomans fell back to relying on their vassals, the Crimean Khans to secure this frontier, which worked well enough for another century.

New challenges to the Ottomans in the Mediterranean emerged at this time, too. The Spanish assembled another Catholic coalition to confront the Ottomans at sea and succeeded in gaining an important victory over the Ottoman fleet at the **Battle of Lepanto** (off the coast of modern Greece) in 1571. Although this removed the aura of invincibility that had settled on the Ottomans after recent conflicts, Lepanto had more immediate symbolic than military significance, because the Ottomans were able to assemble an entirely new fleet within a few months of this defeat.

Based on this quick Ottoman recovery, Venice was persuaded to conclude another peace treaty with the Ottomans in 1573, and the Ottomans consolidated their hold over newly-acquired portions of North Africa. Following Lepanto, the Ottoman-Habsburg land frontier was unsettled by a "Long War" between 1593 and 1606. Then, as a result of the 1606 Peace of Zsitvatorok, Ottoman-Habsburg relations settled back into a relatively quiescent stalemate, broken only by a series of minor skirmishes over the next few decades.

During this period of relative military quiet, the Ottoman army still continued to fall behind in technology as the "Military Revolution" remade European tactics and weaponry. The Ottomans lacked the financial power to keep up with this, unlike European powers who could now pay for their innovations with greater wealth derived from overseas

colonies. The opening of the New World drastically affected the Ottoman economy because of the rapid devaluation of silver, one of the key metals of the Ottoman treasury, due to massive new influxes. Previous Ottoman military innovations, such as the Janissaries, no longer were relevant on a battlefield in which sharpshooters were paid in cash. The economic upheaval also spread to the agricultural system, when unpaid soldiers turned to brigandage in the Jelali revolts between 1595 and 1610. This created anarchy across the empire when the Ottomans could least afford it.

At this same time, the influence of the *valide sultans* (sultans' mothers) became dominant in the so-called Sultanate of Women. Although these women served very capably to keep the Empire running, their sons were not very competent rulers, which weakened it in the long run. A large part of the problem for sultans was that by this time in Ottoman history, princes were being confined to the harem section of the Ottoman royal palace until they reached maturity in an arrangement known as the "*kafes*" ["cage"] system. Although this avoided any bloody succession struggles breaking out upon a monarch's death, it created many princes with few "real-world" leadership skills.

In addition to the powerful sultans' mothers, much power and authority during this period devolved to the grand viziers, some of whom were very skilled and others not. During the **Koprulu Era** (1656–1703) for example, the empire was essentially run by a series of very able grand viziers from the Koprulu family, who achieved substantial renewed Ottoman military success on various frontiers. Unfortunately for the Ottomans, this period of renewed success also saw calamities, for example when Grand Vizier Kara Mustafa Pasha tried to take Vienna a second time and failed decisively in May 1683.

The coalition that had held Vienna against this second Ottoman siege then launched a "War of the Holy League." It lasted for almost two decades, ending with the 1699 Treaty of

Karlowitz: an agreement that formalized the Ottoman Empire's first permanent loss of substantial European territory. After this, the Ottomans gradually shifted to a more and more defensive strategy, which totally changed their relationships with European powers that were now beginning to have a real global presence.

SAFAVIDS: OTTOMAN COUNTERPARTS

In Iran, the reign of the Safavids bore striking resemblances to the Ottomans, but differed from them essentially as well. Although they only lasted from 1501 to 1722 CE, they created the most significant Iranian empire since before the Islamic conquest of Iran in the seventh century CE. It was also the first Islamic government to establish Twelver Shiism as its official religion.

The Safavids originated as a Sufi brotherhood of Turcomans based in Azerbaijan, but their evolution was marked by two great transformations. The Safavids began as a Sufi order, but evolved into a messianic movement promoting a heterodox version of Shiism. Finally, this charismatic movement developed into a large Islamic empire supporting orthodox Twelver Shiism as its established faith.

There is much uncertainty about the original ethnic identity of the Safavids. There has been speculation that they may have been of Kurdish origin, but the original followers of the Sufi brotherhood they led were mostly Turcomans: Turkish-speaking nomads living in eastern Anatolia and western Iran who had migrated there around the time of the Seljuks. The Safavid order was founded by Safi al-Din (1252–1334 CE), who soon gained numerous followers in Azerbaijan. Over the next two centuries, it gradually gained more supporters as its leadership passed through a chain of Sufi masters, each of whom was a son of the previous master.

When Sheikh Jonayd, one of this chain, became the leader in 1447, he recast the movement to acquire more political power. To achieve this, he began to cultivate relationships with other Turcoman rulers in that area (as well as challenging any military rivals). The Safavid order was soon transformed into a political movement now championing Shiism.

Its followers were Turcoman tribesmen who adopted a distinctive red headgear. They were called "Qezelbash" (Turkish for "red head") and were now staunch defenders of Ali, the Twelve Imams, and Twelver Shiism in general. Leadership of the Safavid order finally passed to Esmail in 1494.

At that time, he was a seven-year-old child who was in hiding to avoid being captured or killed by Turcoman rivals, since they had killed his father and grandfather when they had been the group's leaders. His Qezelbash followers, who saw themselves as spiritual warriors, began a campaign to take power, resulting in Esmail's capture of Tabriz and his proclamation as "shah" in 1501 at the age of fourteen.

Even at a young age, Esmail had a reputation for being brave and charismatic, and was virtually worshiped by his Qezelbash soldiers. He was a skilled poet who composed verse suggesting that he himself was a descendant of Ali. This caused widespread speculation about his possible connections with (or identity as) the Twelfth Imam: the great hope of Shii believers for justice to be restored to the world. The Safavids rapidly secured control over Azerbaijan and established authority over much of the rest of modern Iran within a decade after taking power. This immediately put them into conflict with the Ottomans as they moved into the border lands of eastern Anatolia. For the Ottomans, the major threat the Safavids represented was that they had created a fifth column among **Turcomans** there, ostensibly under Ottoman authority. The result was the decisive 1514 Battle of Chaldiran, which decisively checked the Safavids' messianic momentum.

This defeat had an important psychological impact as well. It destroyed Qezelbash devotees' belief in Esmail's invincibility, diminishing their perceptions of his charisma. Turcoman tribal rivalries subsumed in the fervor of the early

Safavid movement gradually reappeared. After Esmail died young in 1524, ten years of civil war between different tribes followed. Esmail's son, who took the throne when he was ten years old as "Shah Tahmasb I," finally stabilized the situation and asserted control by the mid-1530s upon reaching adulthood.

Tahmasb I's reign of fifty-two years was the longest in Safavid history. During this period, the Uzbeks, Turkic rulers in Central Asia, attacked Iran's eastern province of Khorasan numerous times, while the Ottomans (led by Sultan Suleyman) invaded Iran from the west several times as well. Although Iran permanently lost some territory in the west in Iraq, and the Safavids had to move their capital to Qazvin, the dynasty's control over the central regions of modern Iran was not challenged.

Tahmasb's death in 1576 threw Iran into another decade of upheaval and struggle between rival factions for power. Foreign powers capitalized on this unsettled state, and both the Ottomans and Uzbeks took border territories that they had long coveted. Finally, Shah Abbas I (r. 1587–1629) came to power after a palace coup that unseated his father Shah Mohammad Khodabande (r. 1578–1587) who had functioned more as a figurehead than as an actual monarch, since he was almost blind.

Shah Abbas I

Abbas learned about leadership the hard way, by surviving continuous court intrigue and political maneuvering. Upon taking the throne, he decided that Iran's military weakness against the Ottomans and Uzbeks had resulted in a continual series of defeats. His first step was to arrange a peace agreement in 1590 with the Ottomans to quiet his western frontier. Then he set about reorganizing his armed forces. To carry this out, he enlisted the help of two English brothers who had traveled to Iran, Robert and Anthony Sherley. The reorganization of the Iranian military by Abbas was designed to create a force that resembled that of the Ottomans with their artillery corps and Janissary units. **Abbas I's** version of the Janissaries was to be a group of paid, well-disciplined military slaves called the "ghulams," a unit composed of boys taken (in an Iranian version of the Ottoman *devshirme* levy) from Christian populations in Georgia and Armenia.

He also moved the Safavid capital to Isfahan, to locate it in a more central part of Iran. Across the river from the new city of Isfahan, Abbas I created a suburb called "New Julfa," to house merchants and craftsmen brought in from Armenia. The international trade conducted by them for the shah made a lot of money for him, particularly through the silk trade. Abbas built Isfahan into a show-place, spending liberally to create an urban center that became one of the masterpieces of the classical Persian architectural aesthetic. Isfahan became both a thriving commercial and intellectual center, with a population estimated to be around 400,000 by the end of Abbas's reign.

Abbas led his improved military forces to victory over the **Uzbeks**, recapturing Herat and Mashhad from them by 1598. He was also successful against the Ottomans, recapturing Baghdad, eastern Iraq and parts of the Caucasus by 1622. Finally, he was able to dislodge the Portuguese from the Persian Gulf, first from Bahrain in 1602 and then from Hormuz in 1622 (with the assistance of the British). Income from Iran's expanded commercial ties to the British and Dutch East India Companies augmented the Safavid royal treasury. This allowed Abbas I to strengthen his new standing army and reduced the ability of Qezelbash tribal forces to challenge his central authority.

Later Safavids

The death of Shah Abbas I in 1629 created a great problem for the Safavids, because he had left no qualified heir to succeed him and lead the empire. The power of Qezelbash forces

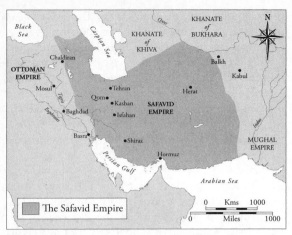

MAP 3.2   Safavid Empire in the Seventeenth Century

had also waned. This left real power in the empire more and more in the hands of merchants, many of whom were ethnic Armenians, Georgians and Indians. Many Safavid rulers after this time also became more interested in the frivolities of court life than in ruling the empire. The realm suffered accordingly.

The international situation was also changing to cause more problems for Iran. In addition to the Ottomans and Uzbeks, Iran now had to contend with the rise of Russia as it gradually extended its domains farther south. Iran dealt with unrest on its Afghan border: an area always in dispute between it and the Mughal rulers of India. In economic terms, East-West trade routes gradually shifted away from Iran toward India, causing a loss of commerce and trade, and further diminishing Iran's financial health.

The fatal blow to Safavid authority was struck by Afghan rebels. As staunch Sunnis, the Afghans rose up against the Shii Safavids (who had recently brought Afghanistan under Iranian control). In particular, they opposed the harsh policies of the Safavid governor of Afghanistan, Gurgin Khan (a *ghulam* originally from Georgia). When the Afghans vanquished the Safavid detachment in Kandahar, they were emboldened to invade Iran proper led by the Afghan Ghilzai leader Mahmud. Within a short time, the Afghans took Isfahan and overthrew the Safavids entirely, with Mahmud acknowledged as Iran's new monarch in October, 1722.

Within a few years, Nader Quli Khan was able to check the Afghans. Nader was a Turcoman military leader who had risen to lead a branch of the Afshar Turcoman tribe in Khorasan under the Safavids. After he defeated Afghan forces in 1729 at the Battle of Mehmandust, they fled back to Afghanistan. Nader pursued them there on his way to India, which he conquered in 1739 after having himself crowned in 1736 as "Nader Shah": Iran's new monarch.

Nader kept Safavid rulers as figureheads until he took the throne himself. Members of the Safavid family were also used later in the eighteenth century as figureheads by other Iranian rulers such as Karim Khan Zand (r. 1750–1779). The effective end of real Safavid authority though, had been the Afghan invasion of Iran in 1722.

Shiism and the Safavids

Perhaps the most enduring contribution of the Safavids was to make Iran the first Twelver Shii empire in Middle Eastern and Islamic history. At the time that the Safavids took power in the first decade of the 1500s, Shah Esmail I promoted an extremist version of Shii belief. Esmail's successors, though, gradually brought in more mainstream Shii leaders from Iraq and Lebanon to create a powerful and more conventional Shii clerical establishment by the end of the Safavid era. One sign that Shiism as practiced in Safavid Iran became more orthodox over time was the gradual prohibition by the Safavid shahs of most Sufi groups, despite the Sufi origins of the dynasty.

At first, followers of the Safavid movement in its messianic phase believed its rulers to be legitimate because the first, Esmail, was thought either to be descended from the Seventh Imam or to be the harbinger of (or even *be*) the returning Twelfth Imam.

Once Safavid rule had lost its charismatic, radical element, a more mundane theory of its legitimacy emerged. High-ranking Safavid clerics explained that although Safavid rule could not be considered actually legitimate in an absolute sense (since it was not directly under the Hidden (Twelfth) Imam), it remained the best form of government during the period of waiting for the Hidden (Twelfth) Imam's return.

One of the key factors in the clerical establishment's increased financial autonomy in Iran was the right to collect the *khums* tax independent of the secular rulers (an important basic privilege allowed the clergy in Shii law [see p. 22]). This income stream caused its independent power to increase substantially.

Among Shii clergy under Safavid rule, there was a revival of philosophical study. This was based in part on the fact that Shii jurisprudence emphasized the importance of rational thinking and logic in formulating legal opinions. Figures such as **Mulla Sadra** (c. 1572–1640) and Mir Damad (d. 1631) built on the philosophical insights of thinkers like Averroes of the medieval Islamic "Golden Age" and added new scholarly contributions of their own.

Usulis and *Akhbaris*

There was also disagreement within the clergy about how much pure logic should be employed in legal opinions. The proponents of the Akhbari movement, which arose in the early seventeenth century, declared that only the Quran, authorized Shii hadith collections (including collections of legal opinions issued by the Twelve Imams), and scholarly consensus were valid sources upon which to base legal opinions (*fatwas*). They rejected the use of pure reason as a basis for such opinions. The supporters of the Usuli movement disagreed entirely, arguing that pure reason was the best basis for legal opinion, if it were used carefully by eminent recognized scholars.

The Usuli approach came to dominate Twelver Shii thinking about how to approach religious law. One result was the increased importance among Shii legal scholars of the concept of *ijtihad* (the Muslim legal term for "independent legal reasoning") and the increased status of Shii *mujtahids* (scholars capable of employing *ijtihad*) in Iran during the eighteenth and early nineteenth centuries. According to the Usulis, all Shii Muslims were either *mujtahids* or *muqallids* (those who should follow [*taqlid*] the rulings of a *mujtahid*).

Later regarded as one of the greatest *mujtahids*, Mohammad Baqer Majlesi (1616–1699) was a scholar prominent toward the end of the Safavid era whose main goal was to purge Sufi and extraneous philosophical influences from Twelver Shii thought. He promoted specifically Shii ritual practices such as visiting tombs of the Twelve Imams and stressed the importance of the Imams as man's true links to God. His collections of wisdom and legal interpretations remain very important texts for faithful Twelver Shiis around the world today.

EUROPE IN THE EIGHTEENTH-CENTURY MIDDLE EAST

Quite apart from the important theological developments occurring in Safavid domains in the seventeenth and eighteenth centuries, political changes beginning to take place globally with the rise of European power also had an obvious impact on the Middle East. The **Treaty of Karlowitz** for example, concluded between Austria and the Ottoman Empire in 1699 at a town in the Vojvodina region of present-day Serbia, was the enduring result of the failure of the Ottomans' last campaign to conquer Vienna, since it marked the first substantial and permanent loss of territory for the Ottomans in Europe.

Karlowitz has often been presented as the beginning of the end of Ottoman predominance in southeastern Europe and portrayed by generations of historians as the start of the Ottoman Empire's inevitable decline toward its final collapse two centuries later—the period when it became labeled "the sick man of Europe."

Recent scholarship has successfully challenged such categorical negative statements about the final centuries of Ottoman rule. Studies have made clear that the empire remained quite viably independent and relatively autonomous from the mid-fifteenth through the mid-eighteenth century.[3] The Ottoman economy remained self-sufficient in the production of both necessary consumer goods and military supplies, while its international trade was primarily in luxury goods. Ottoman sultans enjoyed relatively stable reigns during this era, despite the ebb and flow of international and domestic politics as well as the sweep of global economic change. Nevertheless, it is true that by the turn of the nineteenth century, Ottoman economic, political, and social systems were being affected by the world in ways that would in the end produce profound changes.

Following the fall of the Safavid dynasty in 1722 to Afghan invaders, Iran experienced far more internal upheaval in the eighteenth century than the Ottomans. As defenders and promoters of Twelver Shiism, the Safavids had established stable rule over Iran during the two centuries prior to this invasion, but their sudden collapse ushered in a chaotic transition period that saw Iran broken up for a few years into different realms. Like the Ottomans, the Iranians had enjoyed considerable independence in their premodern domestic economic, political, and social systems, but for Iran, the process of becoming more tied to the world economy took place during a period of political turmoil. One result was that demand for their most profitable export, silk, shifted to more reliable alternative sources such as India. Iran's political uncertainty produced a succession of rulers, none of whom could

secure lasting legitimacy until Fath Ali Shah Qajar established his authority in the early nineteenth century.

By 1800, all of the Middle East started to feel the effects of the economic revolution sweeping the world since European voyages of discovery three centuries earlier. During this time, the rise of global commerce had a growing impact on more and more sectors of Middle Eastern domestic economies. This was intensified by the fact that European capitalists enjoyed real advantages with their trading companies in emerging world markets over their non-Western counterparts.

Still made up in the eighteenth century of societies whose wealth flowed mostly from agriculture, the Middle East had to contend with the swift expansion of European economic power, but it had to use tools developed for an earlier, calmer era of international trade. Wealth in the region was still primarily transferred in kind, not cash. In addition, except for a few merchant family networks, there were no unified military/economic Middle Eastern business enterprises like the emerging British and Dutch trading companies. Long-distance commerce in the region was often dominated by religious minorities, thus less regulated and integrated with the society's ruling elite than in Europe.

The Ottomans also began to confront real political change in the 1770s as the empire was drawn into the rapidly evolving global system created by expanding European powers. Although the Ottomans and Russians fought many battles over preceding centuries, the **Treaty of Kuchuk Kaynarja** ending the Russo-Turkish War of 1768–1774 introduced important changes in their relationship. Henceforth, Crimea would be part of the Russian Empire, but with the Ottoman sultan now recognized only as the spiritual head of Muslims there. In turn, the Russian Emperor was acknowledged as the protector of all Orthodox Christian subjects of the Ottoman Sultan. In addition, the Black Sea would be opened to Russian military and commercial ships.

---

[3]See, for example, Suraiya Faroqhi and Donald Quataert, *An Economic and Social History of the Ottoman Empire* (Cambridge: Cambridge University Press, 1997).

These treaty provisions required the Ottomans to rethink boundaries between the Ottoman and non-Ottoman worlds. At a material level, the Crimea had for centuries provided important food supplies, raw materials, and military manpower to the Ottomans that were easily accessible via the Black Sea. Now, this body of water now would no longer be reserved for exclusive Ottoman use. In political terms, the Ottomans had derived considerable symbolic legitimacy from their status as overlords of the Crimean Khans, who claimed direct descent from Genghis Khan and the Mongols, but this was now finished.

It was not only these Ottoman losses, but the European acquisition of status that changed the situation. As early as 1740, the Ottoman sultan had officially confirmed the French king as the official protector of all Ottoman Catholics in a move designed to bolster Ottoman-French ties. The sultan's similar acknowledgment of the Russian emperor's status as protector of Ottoman Orthodox subjects in the 1774 treaty was even more significant, due to the large Orthodox populations in strategic Ottoman areas near the Russian borderlands, as well as the historical connections between Russia and the Byzantine Empire.

Russian monarchs had long seen themselves as successors to the Byzantine emperors, sometimes referring to Moscow as the "Third Rome" after Constantinople/Istanbul and Rome itself. The conquest of the Crimea became viewed by some Russian intellectuals as the true beginning of Russia's move southward: the first key step in a long process of bringing back to the fold communities of Orthodox Christians now under Ottoman rule. A few hoped that this process would culminate in the restoration of Constantinople (which had been renamed "Istanbul" by the Ottomans) as a true Christian capital city—a desire that heightened Ottoman distrust. To mark progress toward that goal, the Russians held a large celebration in the Crimea in 1787 on the twenty-fifth anniversary of the reign of Tsarina Catherine the Great (1762–1796) just as the region became fully incorporated in the Russian Empire.

Another big change in European-Ottoman relations occurred when the Ottomans opened permanent diplomatic missions in the capitals of Europe. This created a new group of Ottoman officials with much more exposure to European daily life as well as to European languages than ever before. They were positioned to connect with Western culture in far more profound ways than the previous main contact group between the Ottomans and the West: the *terjumans* (dragomans), a group composed mostly of Greeks native to the city of Istanbul who had served the Ottomans for centuries as official court translators.

Questions To Think About

1. What were the negative and positive effects of the Mongol conquest of the Middle East?
2. Who was Ibn Taymiya and what was his later impact?
3. How did Timur (Tamerlane) draw on Mongol and Islamic traditions?
4. What were Ibn Khaldun's theories of social change?
5. How were Ottoman conquests in the Balkans an essential phase of the Ottomans' consolidation of imperial power?
6. What was the impact of the Ottoman conquest of Constantinople?
7. How did Selim I extend Ottoman control over the central Middle East? What were the differing consequences of his victories over the Safavids and the Mamluks?
8. How and why can the era of Suleyman II be considered a successful time for the Ottoman Empire?
9. How did the classical Ottoman system of government and social organization function?

10. What happened to the Ottoman system of government and administration after the reign of Suleyman I?
11. How did the Safavids establish Twelver Shiism as the dominant religion in Iran?

12. What impact did Europe start to have on the Middle East in the eighteenth century?

For Further Reading

Dale, Stephen Frederic. *The Muslim Empires of the Ottomans, Safavids, and Mughals*. Cambridge: Cambridge University Press, 2010.

Faroqhi, Suraiya. *The Ottoman Empire and the World Around It*. London: I.B. Tauris, 2004.

Finkel, Caroline. *Osman's Dream: The Story of the Ottoman Empire, 1300–1923*. New York: Basic Books, 2006.

Fromherz, Allen James. *Ibn Khaldun: Life and Times*. Edinburgh: Edinburgh University Press, 2010.

Ibn Taymiyah, Ahmad ibn `Abd al-Halim, and Yahya Michot. *Muslims under non-Muslim rule: Ibn Taymiyya on fleeing from sin; kinds of emigration; the status of Mardin; domain of peace/war, domain composite; the conditions for challenging power*. Oxford: Interface Publications, 2006.

İnalcık, Halil. *The Ottoman Empire: The Classical Age, 1300–1600*. New York: Praeger Publishers, 1973.

İnalcık, Halil, and Donald Quataert. *An Economic and Social History of the Ottoman Empire, 1300–1914*. Cambridge: Cambridge University Press, 1994.

Itzkowitz, Norman. *Ottoman Empire and Islamic Tradition*. Chicago: University of Chicago Press, 1980.

Manz, Beatrice Forbes. *The Rise and Rule of Tamerlane*. Cambridge: Cambridge University Press, 1989.

Morgan, David. *The Mongols*. Malden, MA: Blackwell Publishing, 2007.

Soucek, Svatopluk. *A History of Inner Asia*. Cambridge: Cambridge University Press, 2000.

Streusand, Douglas. *Islamic Gunpowder Empires: Ottomans, Safavids, and Mughals*. Boulder, CO: Westview, 2010.

4

The Middle East and Early Modern Europe

SELIM III AND THE FIRST PHASE OF REFORM

Various economic and political developments that began in the early eighteenth century marked Europe's emergence as a global force. Within a few decades, this trend became so strong that it caused an Ottoman reaction. Economies and societies of the Middle East became gradually reshaped not only by profound changes in the rest of the world, but by local rulers' attempts to manage their impact. Nowhere was this more evident than in reforms caused by growing concern about how the Ottoman military was beginning to fall behind its European opponents.

The 1699 Treaty of Karlowitz marked the first enduring Ottoman surrender of territory to the Habsburgs. It may be viewed, in retrospect, as the beginning of the end of Ottoman control over the Balkans. Nevertheless, it did not have as immediate an impact as later losses of land would. The Ottomans were able to retake some of what the Habsburgs had occupied in the next round of conflict three decades later, even if only for a limited time. In contrast, the 1774 end of Ottoman rule over Crimea was perceived as a real disaster by contemporary Ottoman political analysts. They began to wonder whether fundamental changes in their empire's institutions might be required for it to survive and prosper.

Loss of the Crimea marked a new turning point for the Ottomans. This region was regarded as one of the empire's true heartlands, and for centuries Crimean cavalry units had been essential in Ottoman campaigns in Europe and the Middle East. Moreover, the steppe lineage of the Crimean khans represented a direct link for the Ottomans to Genghis Khan. The termination of the Crimean khans' status as key Ottoman vassals thus weakened a centuries-old system of loyalties and legitimacy. The war that preceded the loss of the Crimea also confronted Ottoman commanders and observers with the inadequacy of their forces against the Russian army. The Russian military, like its European counterparts, was being reshaped by the transformation of tactics and weapons then underway in Europe.

Ottoman observers reacted to this setback in different ways than they had before. Commentators in the 1600s had diagnosed the causes of the empire's defeats at that time as transient. They judged that the realm's basic structure remained sound, but merely needed to be reinvigorated. Ottoman writers of the late eighteenth century, in contrast, blamed defeat in the Crimea directly on superior European military techniques and weapons, arguing that Ottoman armies should undergo basic structural reforms to forestall any further setbacks.

Calls for change were held in check by Ottoman conservatism. Despite mounting evidence of military problems in the military, Ottomans generally still perceived their sultan as the true guardian of the empire's "well-protected domains": the pinnacle of a political system that was regarded, in its ideal form, as a model of Islamic governance. Critics thus had to present calls for reform not as plans to change the larger Ottoman system in any substantive way, but rather as slight correctives to insure that this "well-protected" realm remained impervious to foreign incursions.

Diverse remedies were proposed for its perceived military weakness. Conservatives saw a need to return to successful practices of the past. Reformers sought either to blend old and new military methods or in some cases, to transform the Ottoman military completely into a force that emulated its European opponents. At first, Ottoman rulers chose to focus on military reforms that would minimally affect other aspects of government and society.

However, the impact of such changes went far beyond correcting the problems that the reforms were supposed to address. European societies had already begun to feel the effects of similar military changes. The new types of weapons, warfare, and troops that started to appear there in the sixteenth century had a huge impact on political, economic, and social trends over the next two centuries. This process, later labeled "the Military Revolution," involved the creation of mass armies and the adoption of modern military techniques. It had enormous secondary effects on the creation of modern nation-states and on the emergence of modern concepts of nationalism and national identity, because this revolution changed so profoundly how military force was used in societies. This transformation of Europe's armies took place in parallel with a "Commercial Revolution" that rapidly expanded Europe's economies as they began to interact more closely with other parts of the globe.

To defend their domains against this growing European power, Middle Eastern rulers decided to implement significant military reforms themselves, beginning in the late eighteenth century. Compared to what was happening in Europe, of course, the impact of such reforms was small in scale, but they nevertheless had enormous importance. Since the Middle East was still dominated by military elites at that time, military reform there proved a real harbinger of change in many other aspects of life as well.

Among the first Ottoman witnesses of the effects of Europe's Military Revolution were two emissaries in Europe: Ahmed Resmi Effendi (1700–1783) and Ebubekir Ratib Effendi (1750–1799). Resmi Effendi met the renowned Prussian military reformer Frederick the Great (1712–1786). He was so impressed by Frederick's military reforms that he wrote up a short report for an Ottoman military commander who had just suffered a terrible defeat at the outset of the 1768–1774 Russo-Turkish War: an especially propitious moment for a military leader to be receptive to lessons from outsiders.

Ratib Effendi also traveled across Europe. He authored a treatise in the late 1770s, arguing that if ancient Ottoman military rules were restored, while at the same time a "new order" (called "*nizam-i jedid*" in Ottoman Turkish) that included European military techniques and doctrines was implemented, the Empire's ability to defend itself and protect its domains would be restored. Ratib later became a close associate of Sultan **Selim III** (r. 1789–1807): the Ottoman ruler credited with introducing the first comprehensive program of modernizing military reform.

Selim and his court started paying serious attention to reform proposals following the disastrous outcome of the next Ottoman-European war (1787–1792). This conflict had been started by Selim's uncle Abdulhamid I (r. 1774–1789), who had apparently felt pressure to initiate this war, the fifth against the Russians and the third against the Austrians, as a hasty attempt to recapture long-lost territory.

This war had also been fueled by growing Ottoman popular resentment of European rulers, who touted recent territorial gains to bolster their prestige. There was apparently a strong reaction in Istanbul against Catherine the Great's 1787 ceremonial tour of the Crimea. Accompanied by a grand entourage that included the Austrian Emperor Joseph II (traveling incognito in the guise of a lesser nobleman), Catherine visited there to celebrate Russia's triumphs in the south and to foreshadow future victories over the Ottomans.

When hostilities commenced in August 1787, the Ottomans quickly suffered a string of military setbacks after a few initial victories. The worst occurred with the Russian destruction of the Ottoman fleet on the Black Sea at Ochakov (Ozu) in December 1788, followed by the Austrian recapture of the strategic fortress of Belgrade in the fall of 1789. Sultan Abdulhamid I became stricken and died in April 1789, apparently unable to accept the debacle at Ozu. He was succeeded by his nephew, who ruled as Sultan Selim III. The treaty finally ending this war was signed at Jassy, Moldavia, in January 1792. It was the first major agreement signed by Selim III and surrendered still more territory to Russia (although it restored Belgrade to Ottoman control).

Selim's experience before he took the throne was considerably different from many of his immediate predecessors. To avoid succession struggles, it had been customary among the Ottomans since the early seventeenth century to confine princes for virtually their whole lives to seclusion in special apartments at the Topkapi Palace. Selim's father, Sultan Mustafa III (r. 1757–1774), treated him differently, allowing him to observe battles in the field as they took place.

Selim thus became an eyewitness to one of the earliest Ottoman uses of modern artillery. These weapons were fired by a unit under the command of a French military advisor, Baron de Tott, against the Russians in a battle near the Danube during the Russo-Turkish War of 1768–1774. In addition, Mustafa assigned intellectuals (including Ratib Effendi) to Selim's entourage to school him in emerging new military techniques and theories.

Implementing Reforms

Despite growing acceptance at the highest levels of the need for military reforms, implementing them would prove neither easy nor smooth. Ottoman military evolution was severely constrained by key parts of the traditional army, in particular the Janissary corps. The Janissaries had been a mainstay of the Ottoman army with their once-revolutionary infantry organization and training. By the late eighteenth century, however, their focus had shifted from military to commercial activities, so they were no longer effective contributors to imperial efforts to hold back the European tide. Through vast networks of investment and patronage built up over centuries, they had amassed substantial economic power as a group, particularly in the main imperial cities such as Istanbul.

Mindful of the Janissaries' entrenched power, Selim bypassed them to create totally new military units that employed European concepts and equipment. He had these forces train in remote locations away from public scrutiny. Like any new units based on unfamiliar models, these detachments were not easy to create and maintain. They existed in constant tension with traditional military organizations, sometimes resulting in severe clashes between the two groups of soldiers.

In 1792, Sultan Selim hired a staff of renegade German, Russian, and French officers to train a group of peasant soldiers (belonging to the Ottoman subject class known as *reaya)* in new European military techniques, using muskets provided by the British embassy. To avoid attracting attention, they conducted this training away from the center of Istanbul in a location far from the Janissary barracks. After much discussion, a decision was also taken to create a new treasury for this force.

Fiscal Change and Military Reform

The potential for military reform in the Middle East was always directly linked to the ability to pay for such innovations. To avoid placing additional financial burdens on the imperial treasury and to allay suspicion among the traditional armed forces that their positions were being usurped, a large portion of revenues generated through the tax-farming (*iltizam*) system were allocated to support these new troops.

Tax-farming had been expanded in the Ottoman Empire in the mid-seventeenth century as a way to generate more cash for the central government. Previously, revenues had been paid in kind by peasants to a *timar* (land grant) holder, generally a cavalry officer who owed the sultan military service instead of revenue. This system eventually became strained in two ways. The value of the Ottoman treasury became drastically reduced with the sudden influx of New World silver in the late sixteenth and early seventeenth centuries. Also, new techniques of warfare introduced during the European Military Revolution focused more on guns than horses. Infantry soldiers, usually paid in cash, became more important than cavalry troops funded by income from land. The vastly increased need for cash was partially met by the introduction of tax-farming, which brought in considerably more revenue.

These more robust revenue streams funded new military forces called "*nizam-i jedid*" ("new organization") units. Although they were implemented at first for only a few years, the changes in Ottoman military

strategy, organization, and tactics initiated by the "*nizam-i jedid*" experiment had far-reaching effects not merely on the Ottoman military, but on the society as a whole.

This new system challenged long-standing barriers between classes. Ottoman society traditionally had been broken down into ruling elites (*askeri*) and ruled subjects (*reaya*). The term *askeri*, with its root meaning of "military" or "ruling class," referred to the social class that received salaries from tax revenue through land grants such as the *timars*, while *reaya* traditionally included non-military subjects of the Sultan who did not *collect*, but *paid* taxes. Military members of the *askeri* class were allotted *timars*, land grants whose revenue funded their participation in sultans' military campaigns. In earlier Ottoman times, *timars* would be reassigned every few years to different officers to restrict the power of *timar* holders over particular areas.

However, maintenance of this system required constant vigilance on the part of the central government. By the eighteenth century, *timars* had largely given way to networks of hereditary fiefdoms in various regions. Provincial lands were virtually transformed into the property of prominent families whose allegiance to the sultan now had to compete with their own provincial networks of loyalty. In addition, as a measure of bureaucratic expediency and to ease tax collection, many areas were parceled out to tax-farmers, whose obligation to the central authority was no longer military service but consisted only of the remittance of tax revenues.

In addition to all the fiscal changes taking place with the decline of the *timar* system, this new military organization represented something radically different socially as well. Instead of being made up of members of the elite military *askeri* class, the *nizam-i jedid* units were composed almost entirely of ordinary Muslim urban and rural peasants. This was in striking contrast to units such as the Janissaries.

The radical modifications introduced by *nizam-i jedid* units to the military's composition directly paralleled vast changes in military organization then taking place in various European states. The European Military Revolution created a rising demand for salaried artillery and musket forces, forcing central governments to collect more cash and to modernize tax structures. The Ottoman shift to tax farming to pay for the *nizam-i jedid* forces show how Ottoman military budgets, too, increasingly depended on cash, not agricultural wealth.

Nizam-i jedid units grew swiftly, increasing from 500 recruits in 1796 to 24,000 officers and men just 10 years later in 1806. These troops were successful whenever they were sent into military action, although they never comprised more than about 10 percent of total Ottoman forces. As their reputation spread, traditional forces began to view them with suspicion and refused to serve alongside them. Despite this skepticism, these units achieved striking success against the French army led by Napoleon besieging Acre in 1799 in order to take Palestine—a force they helped push back to Egypt.

FRANCE AND EGYPT

Egypt was one of the first places in the Middle East to see the impact of changes taking place in Europe at this time. This happened due to Egypt's importance on the trade route to Asia, as well as its close connections with France. France had remained one of the main mercantile powers in the Mediterranean for centuries, and its economic ties to Egypt through the cotton and linen trade only increased during the eighteenth century with the beginning of modern industrial fabric production in Europe. This also meant that when changes happened in France, their impact was bound to be felt in Egypt.

Egypt's place in the eighteenth-century international system was also in transition. Although still an integral part of the Ottoman Empire, by this time Egypt was beginning to assert a measure of autonomy from central Ottoman authority. This became particularly evident when Ali Bey, a Mamluk originally from the Caucasus, held power there between 1760 and 1773. He brought in European military advisors and experimented with using European military techniques in his armed forces, although was toppled from power in the end by the severe internal rivalries that defined late eighteenth-century Egyptian politics.

The various phases of the French Revolution that ensued after 1789 thus had a substantial impact on all the Middle East, but particularly on Egypt. After successfully campaigning in Italy in 1797, Napoleon returned to France, where he was then asked by the Directory government to create a plan to invade England. After some deliberation, he concluded that it would be more prudent and feasible to strike against British India, instead of the British Isles themselves. Moreover, the first place to secure on the way there, in his view, was Egypt: key to controlling Asian trade routes.

The Directory accepted his proposal. It also decided that the creation of a canal at Suez as well as bringing the values of the Enlightenment to the Egyptian people would be worthwhile side projects. The government authorized an Egyptian expedition to include soldiers and scientists. Many politicians also perceived Napoleon as a potentially serious threat to their power. Having him travel to Egypt to spread the spirit of the Enlightenment and the French Revolution while challenging Britain's rising global influence would also have the additional benefit of keeping him occupied in foreign military campaigns.

Napoleon in Egypt

A French force occupied Alexandria on July 2, 1798. Murad Bey, the Mamluk leader and governor of Egypt, fought and lost to the French at the Battle of the Pyramids on July 21, and Napoleon entered Cairo on July 24. This expedition became the most visible Western military activity in a central Middle Eastern country since the **Crusades**.

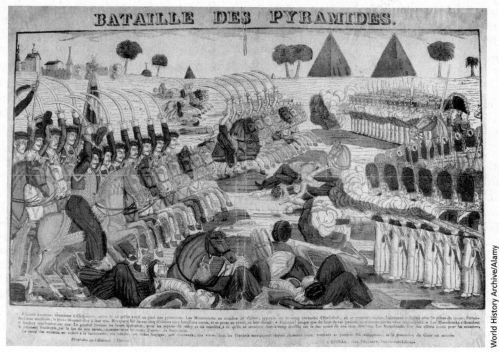

Battle of the Pyramids (July 21, 1798)

Upon his arrival in Alexandria, Napoleon issued a proclamation to the Egyptians declaring that he would liberate them from the oppression of the Mamluks and British and that he respected "God, His Prophet [Muhammad], and the Quran more than the Mamluks." It declared him to be a friend of the Egyptian people and Muslims in general. While this document might be read as part of a cynical *realpolitik* strategy to curry favor among the locals and discredit their overlords, it was indeed couched in the idealistic rhetorical style of declarations issued in the first few years after the French Revolution.

The Egyptian perspective on this was another matter. The concept of a French Christian ruler defending Muslims against other Europeans did not ring true to contemporary Egyptian commentators such as al-Jabarti, and the population as a whole remained unmoved by appeals to support French activities there. Although the French occupiers did not let this stop them, the Egyptian people were a hard sell.

Napoleon arranged for a hot air balloon to fly over Cairo to dazzle the Egyptian public with French technological prowess, but al-Jabarti dismissed this innovation as nothing more momentous than "the kites carpenters make at the time of festivals." His attitude reveals a deep skepticism among Middle Easterners at that time about the benefits of European innovation. Such a view was based on received stereotypes of European inferiority, formed centuries earlier in the era of the Crusades when Europe did lag far behind the Middle East culturally and technologically.

Such stereotypes were now to be challenged, as the power of the modern French army was on display in Napoleon's advance down the Nile toward Cairo. French troops' use of innovative formations, such as stationing squares of riflemen around groups of artillery and cavalry units, has been given credit for his decisive victory there and left a strong impression on local commanders and observers.

However, the triumph of this force was tempered by the destruction of almost the entire French fleet by ships of the Royal Navy under the command of British admiral Lord Nelson in the harbor of Abukir on August 1. Nelson's destruction of these French vessels severely compromised Napoleon's occupation of Egypt, since this defeat severely curtailed logistical support available to French troops on the ground.

Despite this setback, Napoleon did not give up on the agendas of promoting the Enlightenment and revolutionary values. He had brought with him a team of scholars who by late August established the *Institut d'Égypte* in Cairo. This organization was the first official European group charged with collecting historical, cultural, and natural information about Egypt. Although it functioned only during the three years of the French occupation, it collected an immense amount of information and important artifacts, including the Rosetta Stone, whose inscriptions finally provided the vehicle for the eventual deciphering of ancient Egyptian hieroglyphs. This material was published in nine volumes over the next three decades in a series that laid the foundations for modern Egyptology. These findings also sparked a popular European fascination for the ancient Middle East that would promote the development of modern archaeology in the region.

After securing Egypt, Napoleon turned to Palestine, which he invaded by land from the Sinai Peninsula, having lost so much of his fleet. As noted, contingents of Ottoman *nizam-i jedid* troops helped defend Acre (modern Akko, Israel) as it lay under a French siege in the spring of 1799. These forces also played a role in blockading the French at Rosetta near Alexandria in the following year. It is ironic that one of the first serious opponents to do battle with this new military force was the invading French army, itself emerging as a newly reorganized force after the tumultuous early years of the French Revolution.

Napoleon's Impact

Although brief, the three-year occupation of Egypt by the French (1798–1801) had a lingering impact on the Middle East throughout the nineteenth century. This episode shaped the reigns of **Muhammad Ali Pasha** (r. 1805–1849) and his descendants, who governed Egypt for the next 150 years. Egypt's experience, in turn, had a profound effect on developments in the central Ottoman Empire under Sultan Mahmud II (r. 1808–1839) and his successors.

Napoleon himself was in Egypt for only about sixteen months, but his time there had a lasting effect on him as well. It helped him plan how he would reconfigure the Republic upon his return to France into a Consulate and later into an Empire. In doing this, Napoleon blended traditional with novel symbols and ceremonies to garner popular support, drawing on his experience of blending old and new in innovative ways for a similar purpose in Egypt.

The Napoleonic invasion of Egypt severely disrupted Ottoman-French relations for a few years, but it had a more profound effect on how and by whom Egypt was ruled. Powerful Mamluks such as Ali and Ibrahim Bey who had dominated Egyptian politics in the final decades of the eighteenth century were pushed aside by the French. After the French departed, Muhammad Ali rose to prominence.

From an Albanian family in Macedonia, he came to Egypt as deputy commander of a regiment of Ottoman volunteers to fight the French. By 1805, he had built a network of supporters in Egypt so powerful that the Ottoman sultan was compelled to recognize him as governor. Muhammad Ali consolidated his power over the next few years in a deliberate series of attacks on powerful rivals. He was such a skilled politician that within the first few years of his reign, he had established his independence from the central Ottoman government, ruling Egypt until 1849 with virtual autonomy. In addition, continuing French influence on Muhammad Ali's government and his policies in turn strongly affected measures carried out by the central Ottoman government, so the French occupation of Egypt had importance beyond its short duration.

After 1802, Ottoman-French friendship was revived with all of the long-standing French privileges known as "**capitulations**" restored. "Capitulations" were provisions in agreements going back to 1536 that gave French imports preferential tax treatment in Ottoman markets and recognized the French king as the protector of Ottoman Catholic subjects. Such preferential treatment was later to be granted also to other European states as they competed for status and influence in the Middle East.

MODERNIZATION UNDER MAHMUD II

After this Ottoman-French rapprochement, Sultan Selim III was persuaded by 1806 to launch another war against Russia in parallel with the French advance eastward under the command of Emperor Napoleon I. As in previous such encounters, the Ottomans achieved a few minor victories at first, but suffered a series of defeats over the next six years, culminating this time in the loss of Bessarabia (modern Moldova).

These military failures now brought on a May 1807 coup against Selim, after which the Janissaries and their allies imprisoned him and tried to eliminate all traces of his reform program by abolishing the *nizam-i jedid* units. Efforts to rescue him were organized by one of his main reformist associates, Bayraktar Mustafa Pasha, but before Mustafa Pasha's army could reach Istanbul, Selim was put to death. The Janissaries and their conservative allies installed a compliant Mustafa IV, Selim's nephew, on the throne. To legitimize their move, the chief Ottoman religious official known as the **Shaykh al-Islam** issued a fatwa (religious opinion) condemning Selim's innovations as anti-Islamic. In a countercoup the next spring, Mustafa IV's younger brother became Sultan Mahmud II. Bayraktar Mustafa

Pasha, as a provincial notable, was now able to enlist the support of other provincial leaders to reinstate Selim's reforms and have Mahmud sign a "Document of Agreement" in October 1808 confirming that he would support this effort. Although the document was vague, it gave implicit approval for Selim's programs to be continued under other names.

Just one month later, Bayraktar Mustafa and his associates died under suspicious circumstances when a gunpowder depot in which they had taken refuge blew up. Following this, Mahmud II was forced to disband the revived new army units and again put a brake on reforms. He had to bide his time, nurturing modernizing programs more covertly over the next eighteen years.

During this interlude, he shifted focus to supporting elements of the traditional Ottoman army that had already been somewhat modernized, such as the artillery corps, which he refashioned as an effective counterweight to the Janissaries. Although the organized suppression of Selim's reform programs continued for some time after traditional forces had reestablished primacy, veterans from Selim's new military units were able to lie low and serve in provincial units until the tide finally shifted back in their favor.

With such tensions, Mahmud began his reign with a gradualist strategy toward reform. One key area of change became the Ottoman navy, with a new set of regulations written in 1810 to enforce stricter discipline on ships. An attempt was also made to make the navy a more Muslim force and more homogenous. Mahmud exerted influence over the Janissaries indirectly, appointing supporters to important leadership positions in their ranks and eliminating opponents of reform among them on an individual basis. In the first years of his reign, Mahmud's status was quite tentative, although he remained the Ottoman prince in most direct line of succession. Reformist and conservative factions continually vied for influence, but reformers gained the upper hand in the 1820s when they could blame the Janissaries for Ottoman losses in the Greek War of Independence.

CHALLENGES TO EMPIRE

Nationalism in Serbia and Greece

With the upheavals of the Napoleonic Era, it was not surprising that the Ottomans suddenly faced real challenges to their rule from among their Balkan Christian *reaya* subjects: first in Serbia with the 1805 Karageorge Petrovic uprising and then in Greece during the 1821–1829 War of Independence.

Witnessing how easily the Austrians were able to defeat the Ottomans in the early 1790s, Serbian leaders began to contemplate their own uprising against their Turkish overlords. Selim III had issued decrees in the 1790s to propitiate the Serbs, granting them more rights, establishing the right for local Serbian rulers (*"knezes"*) to collect taxes, and guaranteeing freedom of trade and religion in Serbia. He also ordered the Janissaries out of Belgrade, since they had developed a bad reputation for treating ordinary peasants harshly there.

These measures did not have the desired effect, since Serbs perceived attempts to modernize the Ottoman administration as signs of weakness. These new policies were in any case rather short-lived, since by 1799, the Janissaries had been permitted to come back and reestablish themselves in Serbia, ruling in virtual autonomy from the central Ottoman government.

Upon their return, they radically increased taxation, seized land, and required peasants to perform even more forced labor. The Serbs rose against them in February 1804, choosing Karageorge Petrovic as their leader. Over the next three years, they successfully battled the Ottomans and took control of Belgrade. Although the Serbs then established a constitutional democracy, Karageorge, an autocrat, refused to cede power to it. The Ottomans reoccupied Serbia in 1813 after they had concluded their most recent war with Russia. Only

a few years later, another Serbian leader, Milos Obrenovic, compelled the Ottomans to recognize him as prince of Serbia, establishing it thereafter as an independent nation.

Ottoman Greeks, like their Serbian counterparts, had been inspired by the revolutionary fervor of the French and formed a secret group called the "Society of Friends" in the Black Sea port of Odessa, now part of the Russian Empire, in 1814. Russia supported this group as a way to put pressure on the Ottomans, and it drew members from Greek communities in many parts of the Ottoman Empire. In 1821, just as the Ottomans were preoccupied with a new war against Iran, the society joined forces with the *klephts* (armed Greek highwaymen) and launched a revolt.

This grew into the Greek War of Independence (1821–1829), resulting in the establishment of the modern nation of Greece. This war saw European powers and prominent intellectuals intervene in defense of the Greeks, motivated by the spirit of Philhellenism. This nineteenth-century movement supported Greek independence fighters as the modern embodiments of ancient Greek virtue. It inspired European intellectuals such as Lord Byron to give their lives fighting alongside these revolutionaries. To counter this, the Ottomans received help from Muhammad Ali, the Ottoman soldier who ruled Egypt after 1805. By the 1820s, he had achieved such success in implementing reforms in Egypt that he inspired the Ottomans to follow suit and begin their own new era of modernization.

Egypt and Muhammad Ali

Indeed, the second phase of Ottoman reforms that began in the 1820s was directly inspired by the activities of Muhammad Ali, who had transformed Egypt since he had taken power there two decades earlier. He benefited from the power vacuum that existed when he became governor, since Egypt's existing ruling establishment had been pushed aside by the French intervention. Muhammad Ali had no real allies

Muhammad Ali (1769–1849)

World History Archive/Alamy

century. It called on Muslims to return to the ways in which Islam had been practiced in the Prophet Muhammad's time. Wahhabis believed that most contemporary Muslims, particularly Sufis, were not true believers at all. Despite their defeats by Muhammad Ali and Ibrahim, the **Saudis** survived into modern times to create the Kingdom of Saudi Arabia in 1932 under **Abd al-Aziz ibn Saud**.

In the process of securing power, Muhammad Ali experimented with various kinds of military units modeled on French units, the Mamluks, and Ottoman Janissaries. By the 1820s, he had created his own new military force, called the *Nizamiya*. It was certainly inspired by the Ottoman *nizam-i jedid* experiment, but was even more closely patterned on British and French forces. He instituted the first system of mass conscription in the Middle East, modeled on the French *levée en masse* first organized during the French Revolution.

In the spring of 1822, Muhammad Ali sent teams to various Egyptian provinces to draft peasants into his new army. He created new artillery and logistics units, while also modernizing the Egyptian navy along the lines initiated by the Ottomans decades earlier. Not content merely to update his force structure, he foresaw the need to secure and even manufacture modern military equipment and began to assemble munitions and war materiel in the 1810s.

A key question for him, as it had been for the Ottomans, was how to finance such plans. He was much more ambitious in securing sources of funds than Selim III had been, establishing state enterprises to produce cash crops of cotton, sugar, rice, and indigo on a scale hitherto unknown in Egypt. To make this work, he imposed an autocratic agricultural system that was centrally planned and directed in order to replace the tax farming system entirely. In addition, beginning in 1816, he established textile mills to produce finished cotton and silk products. By 1830, he had brought in a steam engine from Europe to power a clothing factory with 150 looms.

among the Mamluks, but relied on Bosnians and Albanians personally loyal to him to build his own power base in Egypt.

Muhammad Ali clearly derived many ideas from the French. Numerous French advisors stayed on during his reign, but he blended his own ideas with concepts brought in from a wide variety of sources. His first striking political act was to kill his most powerful Mamluk rivals after inviting them to a reception at the Cairo Citadel on March 1, 1811: an action emulated years later in Istanbul by Mahmud II when he crushed the Janissaries. Muhammad Ali then established credibility as a loyal Ottoman vassal by campaigning against the Saudis to dislodge them from Mecca and Medina, sending his son Ibrahim to destroy the Saudis' home village of Diriya in central Arabia near Riyadh in 1818.

The Saudis were a tribal nomadic group based in the central Nejd region of Arabia. They were Wahhabis, followers of Muhammad ibn Abd al-Wahhab (1703–1792), an Iraqi cleric who began a conservative revival movement in central Arabia in the mid-eighteenth

Muhammad Ali also improved living conditions for peasants whom he brought into this system, creating new clinics and public health facilities. In 1827, one of the first modern medical schools in the region was established at Abu Zabal near Cairo by Antoine-Barthélémy Clot (Clot Bey), a French doctor. This evolved into the modern medical faculty of Qasr al-Ayni: an institution still in operation today.

By the 1830s, Muhammad Ali had secured his status as Egypt's ruler and governed a domain, now including Sudan, that controlled a considerable portion of the Nile. He pressed on despite such setbacks as the 1827 naval disaster of Navarino off the western coast of Greece, in which a flotilla of European warships sank a large part of the main Ottoman fleet, including many of Muhammad Ali's best ships. Undaunted, Muhammad Ali expanded his shipyards at Alexandria and Bulaq (near Cairo) and soon rebuilt his fleet.

Eventually his growing stature threatened his Ottoman overlords. When Muhammad Ali demanded that Sultan Mahmud II give him control of Syria and Mahmud refused, the ruler of Egypt started a war that nearly resulted in the overthrow of the Sultan. Muhammad Ali did succeed in expanding his power according to the terms of the treaty that ended the conflict: the 1833 Convention of Kutahya. In it, Muhammad Ali's son Ibrahim was made governor of Syria and other territories were transferred to his control.

Muhammad Ali's rising stature now began to have repercussions beyond the Middle East. The fact that the Russians brokered the Convention of Kutahya bothered the French and British a great deal. Beginning in the late eighteenth century, they had grown more and more wary of Russia's attempts to expand its influence farther south.

British and French mistrust of Russian intentions produced the "Eastern Question": the perennial worry about Russia's rise and the Ottoman Empire's decline in Europe and Asia. In any event, the Kutahya document was short-lived in its effect. By 1838, Muhammad Ali was planning another military move against the Ottomans. Now his goal was to establish control over more territory to have access to enough iron, coal, and timber to develop industries he had begun to create.

With the Eastern Question on their minds, European powers were jolted into action after Muhammad Ali's son Ibrahim destroyed the Ottoman army at the Battle of Nezib (near Urfa in modern Turkey) on June 24, 1839. France and Britain feared that Muhammad Ali might supplant the Ottomans entirely, continue on a path of unchecked expansion, and establish a level of autonomy for himself that might threaten the regional balance of power. When the Ottoman Sultan Mahmud II died immediately after this battle took place and was succeeded by his sixteen-year-old son who took the throne as Abdulmejid I, new concerns arose about the staying power of the Ottomans.

The Europeans first tried to appease Muhammad Ali. In July 1840, Britain, Austria, Russia, and Prussia issued the London Convention. It promised that if Muhammad Ali withdrew his troops from the Syrian hinterland and the coastal regions of **Mount Lebanon**, while also reducing the size of his army, he and his descendants could continue to rule Egypt and he could retain control of the province of Acre (in modern-day Israel) during his lifetime. When he refused such terms, the Europeans shifted to military pressure. British and Austrian ships were sent to blockade the Egyptian coastline, while other European forces were dispatched to force Muhammad Ali out of Acre. After this show of force, Muhammad Ali agreed to accept the terms of the Convention and to reduce his military forces. No foreign diplomatic document had ever granted such terms to an Ottoman viceroy and his descendants, a sign of how much direct European intervention in Ottoman politics had increased since Napoleon's time. This document became an important guarantee, since Muhammad Ali's family continued to rule Egypt until King

Farouk, last of the line, was removed from power in 1952.

Mahmud II: Impact of Muhammad Ali

Muhammad Ali's activities as ruler of Egypt made a profound impact on Mahmud II from the very beginning of his reign. This began when he ousted the Wahhabis from Mecca and Medina, rendering important assistance to the new Ottoman sultan in the latter's capacity as protector of the Islamic Holy Places. Mahmud then called on Muhammad Ali's new troops to battle Greek nationalists in the Greek War of Independence where they performed effectively in combat, aside from the naval debacle of Navarino.

Mahmud borrowed many ideas from Muhammad Ali while implementing his own reforms, but he did not copy his Egyptian vassal blindly. As Muhammad Ali had eliminated the Mamluks in 1811 all at once, Mahmud did away with the Janissaries in one decisive attack in 1826 on their main barracks. The end of the Janissary corps marked the final establishment of a modern Ottoman army, again given the name "*nizam-i jedid*" ("New Order"). To give

these forces a new look, Mahmud gradually introduced new military clothing styles, based on European uniforms, but with a distinctive Ottoman fez as the prescribed headgear.

To get beyond the Navarino naval catastrophe, Mahmud II also bought the first steamships for his navy. In 1829, he had the Imperial Naval Shipyard on the Golden Horn in Istanbul build the *Mahmudiye*, for many years the largest warship in the world. It stayed in service forty-five years, playing a key part in the Siege of Sevastopol during the Crimean War (1853–1856).

Mahmud's reforms were not limited to the military. Through various legal measures, he reduced the power of local emirs and pashas, establishing the sultan as the final recourse of judicial appeal for all levels of the society. Unlike his predecessors, Mahmud II began regularly to attend meetings of the *Divan-i Humayun* (Imperial Council) in person, instead of observing them from behind a screen above the meeting chamber. Following in the footsteps of Muhammad Ali, Mahmud II placed the revenues of *waqf* (religious endowment) lands more closely under state administration

The Battle of Navarino (October 20, 1827)

Ute Franz/Art Resource, Inc.

and control. As described before, *waqfs* were religious endowments of land whose income was used to pay for charities such as hospitals, mosques, schools, and soup kitchens. They had traditionally been kept beyond the control of the central government, making them good vehicles for families to shelter funds by endowing *waqfs* and establishing themselves as the trustees By putting *waqfs* more directly under government control, both Mahmud and Muhammad Ali estranged the religious authorities, but the quickly rising need for more revenue overshadowed any concerns about violating Islamic norms.

Mahmud attempted to regularize the taxation system by abolishing *avariz* (Arabic: *awarid*) taxes in an 1834 edict. *Avariz* taxes were extraordinary requests of money or labor that, in the traditional Ottoman system, could be demanded at will from subjects. Now, no revenues were to be collected, except for funds taken at two regular half-yearly periods. He ended the traditional *timar* system entirely, since *timars* by his time had become more sinecures than sources of revenue for active soldiers. He also suppressed, at some cost, the power of the *derebeys* ("mountain valley chiefs") who now held power as hereditary petty princes in almost every corner of the empire.

This era witnessed the gradual pacification of provincial tribes, beginning in Anatolia and later spreading to the Arab provinces of the empire. Tribes were sedentarized and brought into the settled economy in various ways that integrated the empire even more closely into the global economy. With the expansion of the Russian Empire toward the Black Sea, entire Muslim groups such as the **Circassians** sought refuge with the Ottomans, who resettled them in various marginal and frontier areas such as the north Arabian Peninsula.

Many modernization initiatives became opportunities for reasserting central state power, but with updated methods. With the goal of bringing a diverse set of lands, peoples, and resources more under central control, Mahmud presented an early version of the centralizing strategies adopted by later modernizing regimes in the Middle East. Such modernizing agendas also paralleled the goals of Western powers in the region during the nineteenth century. Europeans were in favor of a more centralized Ottoman administration that could work more efficiently with them.

Early Nineteenth-Century World Economy and the Ottomans

All such developments took place at a time of immense changes in global trade, which eventually precipitated a major restructuring of the Ottoman economy. Foremost was a substantial increase in the production of raw materials in the Ottoman Empire for export. Through the first half of the nineteenth century, agricultural products comprised about 90 percent of total Ottoman foreign exports. With about four-fifths of the entire population of the empire living on the land and employed in agricultural production, the rise of cash crops had a gradual but substantial effect on society over the nineteenth century.

Before this time, the Ottoman economy had been constrained by policies designed to promote state monopolies on certain goods and the retention of raw materials for domestic markets. In this new era, Ottoman agricultural exports steadily rose as a percentage of total agricultural production, so that the impact of changes caused by shifts in the international market was gradually felt more strongly. Although the rising ease of access to cash crop imports such as coffee, cotton, and tobacco from the New World by the beginning of the nineteenth century had somewhat diminished the Ottomans' status as an essential supplier of such products to Europe, this did not change the main trend of the Ottoman economy to focus gradually more and more on the export of raw materials *to* and the import of finished goods *from* the West. This was especially true of the period between 1826 and 1860, when Ottoman markets became more open to free trade.

Many of the military and political reforms already discussed also had important economic impacts. Foremost among these was the dissolution of the Janissaries. By the early nineteenth century, the Janissaries had evolved into an economic class tightly integrated into the traditional Ottoman guild structure, so their destruction opened previously closed traditional markets and cleared the way for economic liberalization to expand its reach.

Political treaties had unforeseen economic effects as well. A good example is the **Anglo-Turkish** (Balta Limani) Convention of 1838, which the Ottomans signed in order to gain British support for their campaigns against Muhammad Ali. One of its long-term effects was to unleash British merchants to pursue free trade in Ottoman lands, because it lowered the tax rates so much for British imports there. Egypt was also required to accept the same free-trade provisions of this agreement (favoring British exports) when it agreed to the 1840 London Convention described above.

These agreements shifted the relative importance of Ottoman trading partners as well. Until 1789, the French had dominated much European trade with the Ottomans. Over the following twenty years of upheaval, the British managed to supplant them. Thereafter, even after it had restored normal trade relations with the Ottomans, France lagged behind Britain as a trading partner with the Ottomans. The gradual incorporation of the Ottoman economy into a global system of trade based on economic liberalism, which began during the first half of the nineteenth century, would become an increasingly important factor in the empire's economy by the second half of the century: a trend that the existing political, economic, and military systems of the Ottoman Empire were not well-equipped to manage, even though significant reforms were being undertaken.

IRAN

The Early Modern Era

All the social, political, and economic trends occurring in the Ottoman Empire were also present in Iran, but in a very different context. Iran, after experiencing considerable turmoil through the eighteenth century following the invasion of Afghan forces and the fall of the Safavid dynasty in 1722, had regained its equilibrium under the Qajar dynasty. That dynasty's founder, Aqa Mohammad Khan (r. as Qajar shah 1794–1797), had a reputation as a fierce warrior. He secured control of most of the old Safavid domains, but it was only during the reign of his nephew, Fath Ali Shah (r. 1797–1834), that stability returned to many aspects of Iranian life. This consolidation was aided by a revival of symbols with cultural authenticity and a depth of tradition from the pre-Islamic era.

Fath Ali Shah celebrated the heritage of pre-Islamic Iran, promoting artifacts that linked him to that time such as the "*Taj-e Kayani*" ("Kayanid Crown"). This was a crown first worn by his uncle to commemorate the Kayanids, traditionally celebrated as Iran's first ruling dynasty. Fath Ali Shah also commissioned the poet Saba to produce a *Shahanshahname* ("Book of the King of Kings") modeled on the *Shahname* ("Book of Kings"): Ferdawsi's eleventh-century masterwork of Persian epic poetry.

The force of the French Revolution and the subsequent upheavals of Napoleonic times were felt in Iran but from a distance. France was always less important politically there than Britain or Russia: both already vying for primacy at the outset of the "Great Game." Iranians were certainly aware of Ottoman reform initiatives epitomized by the *nizam-i jedid*, but were far more focused at the beginning of the nineteenth century on restoring traditional sources of military and political power that had eroded since the fall of the Safavids. Militarily and socially, this focus on restoration persisted through the 1820s and 1830s, when the swift spread of globalization and European influence forced Iran to confront global trends more directly.

Iran had its most serious political and military confrontations during this time with Russia, against whom it fought two wars (1805–1813) and (1826–1828). Both ended in Russian victory, allowing the Russians to consolidate their control over the Caucasus. The Treaties of Gulistan (1813) and Turkmenchay (1828) both recognized northern Iran as a Russian "zone of influence" where Russia would henceforth be free to play a major part in Iran's internal affairs. The British, in turn, began to establish a greater presence in the Persian Gulf, as they secured the approaches to their main Asian colony in India. It was the continued presence of officials, soldiers, and merchants from these two Great Powers to enforce their respective zones of influence that made their impact seem more direct than in the Ottoman Empire—an involvement that decisively shaped the course of events in Iran throughout Qajar times.

Early Military Reforms

Just as it had for the Ottomans, military defeat became a catalyst for Iranian rulers to think about change and reform, but from a different point of departure. The strength of the Iranian army still remained its tribal cavalry. Originally, both the Ottoman and Iranian forces had evolved from a Turco-Mongol steppe military tradition that emphasized the use of mounted archers. The Ottomans had undergone a far more comprehensive military evolution, including development of a cadre of slave-soldier Janissaries and artillery troops. The Safavids tried to imitate this with their own *ghulam* units established under Shah Abbas I in the early seventeenth century, but the development of such forces placed heavier financial demands on the central government than it could support. Because these financial needs required more centralization of power

and authority than the Safavids were able to sustain, they saw far less evolution beyond traditional military systems than occurred under the Ottomans.

In fact, tribal cavalry remained the paramount military force in Iran through the relatively peaceful seventeenth century, as well as the chaotic eighteenth century. Qajar rulers had only just begun to recover from this time of chaos as they confronted the renewed Russian push against them after the Napoleonic era in the two wars mentioned above. At first, they reacted to the Russian advance by having a traditional call for jihad against infidel invaders issued, but swiftly shifted after the debacle of the 1826–1828 war to seeking real military and political change to secure the very survival of Qajar rule in the face of advancing Western power. Suddenly such reforms began to seem essential.

Mirza Abu al-Qasem Farahani (1779–1835) exemplified this change in perspective. As the principal adviser to Abbas Mirza, Qajar heir apparent and viceroy who ruled Azerbaijan, Farahani arranged for the publication in 1818 of a collection of fatwas on jihad (here with the meaning "holy war"). In its introduction, he discussed the need to take up arms against the Russians in terms that echoed traditional exhortations. In contrast, the poetry that he composed *after* the defeats of the conflict of 1826–1828 conveyed skepticism about the usefulness of a religious approach to confronting foreign invaders, now arguing that careful containment of Russia's advances and diplomacy with them might produce a better result.

Given their greater remove from European trends, Iranian attempts to create new units modeled on the Ottoman *nizam-i jedid* troops had a less substantial impact there than among the Ottomans. Experiments in new Iranian military units began as early as 1807 in Azerbaijan under the tutelage of French instructors brought in by Abbas Mirza. These French advisers were expelled two years later upon the conclusion of a friendship treaty between Iran and Britain and were replaced by a British military mission. Unfortunately, the first European-trained Iranian troops suffered a severe defeat fighting against the Russians, so these British advisers were also sent away by 1815, their advice not deemed very useful.

Two main problems dogged attempts at military and other types of reform in Iran over decades. The first was a severe lack of continuity in foreign advisers, with a parade of officers from different countries being brought in as the Qajars changed alliances. The other was the issue of how to pay for military forces at all, given the formidable financial problems of the Iranian central government.

Abbas Mirza tried to address this issue by creating a conscription program called the *buniche* system, which required each landowner to provide a certain number of peasants for the army. This system bore some resemblance to the way in which Muhammad Ali had brought peasants into his army, and it also apparently took inspiration from the Russian system of peasant levies developed by Peter the Great to man his military units. Whatever its origins, the troops produced by this system were no more successful in the second Russo-Persian War of 1826–1828 than they had been in the first, suffering multiple defeats.

Despite this, Abbas Mirza brought in another British military mission in 1833. This group's impact was limited by the deaths, within a short time, of both Abbas and Fath Ali Shah. This left the British to navigate the complexities of the ensuing succession struggle. But if this were not a big enough problem, the new ruler, Abbas Mirza's son Mohammad Shah, decided to show his military prowess by invading Afghanistan in 1837—an act that caused the British to sever all relations with Iran. Now the British delegation was replaced with another French team. It was largely composed of retired sergeants who spent most of their time trying to secure payment for their services.

The late eighteenth and early nineteenth centuries marked the first era of reform in the Middle East. There was change in areas of greatest perceived need, principally the military. Because reform efforts at this time were partial and transient, their impact and success were limited. They can be seen as harbingers of larger and more substantial changes about to happen. Broader change would have to wait for the era of **Naser al-Din Shah** in Iran and the **Tanzimat** period of Ottoman history. The continuing challenge for all processes of reform in the nineteenth century was the ongoing shortage of funds to pay for them. Such financial weakness, in stark contrast to the growing material prosperity of Europe as it took center stage in the increasingly globalized world economy, would decisively shape the Middle East's relations with the rest of the world in this next era.

Questions to Think About

1. Why did modernizing reforms start with the military in Middle Eastern societies?
2. What was new about the Treaty of Kuchuk Kaynarja?
3. What were Russian agendas in the Middle East in the eighteenth and nineteenth centuries?
4. Why did the Janissaries oppose reform in the Ottoman Empire?
5. What was tax farming? Why did it become so popular in the nineteenth-century Ottoman Empire?

6. What was the impact of Napoleon's occupation of Egypt?
7. How did Muhammad Ali change Egypt?
8. Who were the Wahhabis? Why were they considered a threat to the Ottoman Empire?
9. What role did the Ottoman Empire come to play in the nineteenth-century global economy?
10. How and why did modernizing reforms have a very different impact in Iran from the Ottoman Empire?

For Further Reading

Cole, Juan. *Napoleon's Egypt: Invading the Middle East* (New York: Macmillan, 2008).

Pamuk, Şevket. *The Ottoman Empire and European Capitalism, 1820–1913: Trade, Investment and Production* (Cambridge: Cambridge University Press, 2010).

Sayyid-Marsot, Afaf Lutfi. *Egypt in the Reign of Muhammad Ali* (Cambridge: Cambridge University Press, 1984).

Shaw, Stanford. *Between Old and New: The Ottoman Empire under Sultan Selim III, 1789–1807* (Cambridge: Harvard University Press, 1971).

Zürcher, Erik Jan. *Turkey: A Modern History* (London: I.B.Tauris, 2004).

5

From "New Order" to "Re-Ordering": The Tanzimat

BEGINNINGS OF THE TANZIMAT

The Tanzimat Decree

The transformations of the Ottoman Empire that began under Sultan Mahmud II continued after 1839 under his sons Abdulmejid (r. 1839–1861) and Abdulaziz (r. 1861–1876). The period 1839–1876 in Ottoman history is often called the "Tanzimat" (Turkish/Arabic: "Reordering" or "Reorganization") Era, recalling the "Tanzimat" decree issued just months after Abdulmejid took the throne. This document, also known as the "**Noble Rescript of the Rose Chamber**" ("*Gulhane Firmani*)" after the park next to the Topkapi Palace where it was proclaimed, reinterpreted the basis of the sultan's sovereignty and legitimacy while redefining Ottoman subjects as "citizens" of the empire with specific rights. It set the stage for reforms already decreed to develop into formal rules and institutions.

Its language borrowed heavily from the European Enlightenment in its call for the protection of the "life, honor, and fortune" of Ottoman subjects, as well as its charge to create systems of taxation and military service that applied equally to all persons, regardless of religion or ethnic identity. It decreed that written law codes should be drawn up to regulate this, to be created by assemblies of notables and government officials. These notables and officials were to receive adequate salaries and be restrained by effective laws to curtail the effects of favoritism and bribery. The Gulhane Decree proclaimed that it sought "to reinvigorate pure religion [*mujerret din*], government [*devlet*], and the nation [*millet*]" through "a thorough alteration [*tagyir*] and renewal [*tejdit*] of ancient customs [*usul-u antika*]."[1]

---

[1]Suna Kili, A. Şeref Gözübüyük (eds.), *Türk anayasa metinleri: Senedi Ittifaktan gününmüze* (Istanbul: Türkiye İş Bankası Kültür Yayınları, 1985), 13.

It offered the most concrete expression of a new reformist vision of Ottoman government. This vision was actively promoted at this time by a group of young officials led by Mustafa Reshid Pasha, but the document's appearance at a moment of political crisis sheds light on the complexities of reform politics. The army of Muhammad Ali, the semi-independent ruler of Egypt who had carved his own empire out of Ottoman territory, had just defeated Ottoman forces rather decisively in June 1839 at the Battle of Nezib in southeastern Anatolia. Koca Husrev Mehmed Pasha, then grand vizier, was in favor of transferring authority over the provinces of Syria and Adana to Muhammad Ali as a way of acknowledging the Egyptian ruler's greater status. To complicate matters, Sultan Mahmud II died on July 1, replaced by his sixteen-year-old son who took the regnal name "Abdulmejid I."

Mustafa Reshid Pasha

This change of rulers exposed a rift that had developed between bureaucratic modernizers led by Mustafa Reshid Pasha and the military elite put in place by the first wave of reforms beginning in the 1810s, a faction now led by Husrev Pasha. Both Reshid and Husrev had been longstanding supporters of reform, particularly within the military, but with differing views of how this ought to happen. Husrev forged close ties with Russia in the mid-1830s, when he hired Russian advisers to help create new "Victorious Armies of Muhammad" units as part of the military reforms taking place.

Mustafa Reshid Pasha and his circle, in contrast, had long been skeptical of Russian motives in the Ottoman Empire. Their suspicions had risen especially following the secret 1833 Ottoman-Russian agreement, which required the Ottomans to close the Dardanelles to all non-Russian ships in wartime. Reshid Pasha served for many years as an Ottoman diplomat in Paris and London and became identified with the British. He was a close

friend of Lord Palmerston, then serving as British foreign minister.

Since Reshid had played a key role in securing British support for Ottoman efforts to contain Muhammad Ali throughout the 1830s, the Sultan allowed him to have the Gulhane Decree issued, perhaps partly to make clear to Britain and France just how serious the Ottomans were about implementing reforms. It would be misleading, however, to portray its issuance as merely an attempt to appease the British and French. Reshid had already established himself as a supporter of political reform, having taken several initiatives as foreign minister in 1837 and 1838. These included having Sultan Mahmud issue decrees banning bribery and the arbitrary confiscation of property, as well as establishing advisory councils to promote economic, administrative, and financial innovation.

Reshid always took care to respect traditional Ottoman religious and social norms in formulating policy. His father had been the administrator of Sultan Beyazid's *waqf*: an important position in the religious establishment. Reshid's own career path steered him toward the nonreligious clerical bureaucracy. What he encountered in this service determined his later commitment to reform. He served as a staff aide to his uncle during the Greek War of Independence in the 1820s and witnessed the logistical and technical problems experienced by the Ottoman army on the battlefield there.

His experiences as an official and diplomat combined with his religious education to shape him as a reformer whose goal was to blend innovation with Islamic and Ottoman tradition. Reshid Pasha's approach epitomized Tanzimat-period attempts at change. Tanzimat methods contrasted with what had happened during the reigns of Selim and Mahmud, which had been defined more by adopting foreign models wholesale without trying to harmonize them with existing cultural norms.

Balancing tradition and innovation was a difficult task, as shown by the text of the Gulhane Decree itself. Its attempt to create a system of legal equality for citizens had no real precedent in Ottoman or Islamic tradition. Ottoman religious minorities, known as *millets*, lived as tolerated groups and enjoyed formal privileges under Muslim law. However, they were never considered legally equal in status to Muslims. This document came much closer to treating them as equals, particularly in the realm of taxes and military service, for which they had previously been subject to different rules.

Implementing the Tanzimat

The Gulhane Decree was only one document, subject to cancellation or modification by the sultan. It was also just one part of a larger process. Actual implementation of reforms based on this decree took a long time, was slow to achieve, and met with only partial success. Nevertheless, the reform process had commenced long before this document was ever issued. The stage had been set in the 1820s for sweeping changes in the Ottoman government by the destruction of the Janissaries and the centralization of the administration of charitable religious endowments (*waqfs*). In the 1830s, Reshid himself, while serving in various parts of the Ottoman government, helped create new administrative structures to facilitate reform.

Building on these earlier accomplishments, Reshid and his two main protégés, Mehmed Emin Ali Pasha and Kechejizade Mehmed Fuad Pasha, retained the support of Sultan Abdulmejid I and his brother and successor Abdulaziz I through almost four decades. Throughout the seventeenth and eighteenth centuries, Ottoman politics had been shaped by the ebb and flow of power between the grand vizier (the Ottoman chief minister whose office was often called "the Sublime Porte" or simply the "Porte") and the sultan. With this new cohort of reformers and bureaucrats, the dynamic center of Ottoman politics shifted decisively toward ministers of the Porte and away from the sultan for many years.

The Gulhane document did prove to be milestone in the process of change that ushered in a myriad of new institutions: development of a new secular school system, completion of the reorganization of the Ottoman military that had started much earlier, and creation of a centralized postal system. This happened simultaneously along with numerous innovations that reshaped the role of the central state in the economy and transformed the tax-farming system into a land regime based more and more on private ownership of property.

In this era of upheaval, the outcome of projects to redefine the Ottoman Empire as a modern nation-state also became more and more problematical. Changes introduced to modernize it also contributed to its weakening and destabilization. For good and bad, economic and social changes begun during the Ottoman Tanzimat period had such sweeping effects that they continued to shape Middle Eastern societies long after the fall of the Ottoman Empire.

Tanzimat reforms also happened in the context of major developments reshaping the mid-nineteenth century world, such as the spread of the Industrial Revolution and the rapid expansion of communications and transportation systems. This era saw the emergence of new European nation-states such as Germany and Italy that soon played pivotal roles in international politics. Finally, disputes over the Eastern Question continued. This now began to include the problem of who would have most influence over Ottoman territories establishing their independence. Differences over this issue precipitated a series of military conflicts, most serious of which was the Crimean War (1853–1856). These wars drew the Ottomans into ever closer connections with European states, thrusting the Ottoman world ever more directly into processes of social, economic, and political change then sweeping the globe.

Staffing the Tanzimat Reform Process

The Ottoman reform process also gained momentum after 1839 as change in the rest of the world had a growing local impact. For years, Sultan Mahmud had played different reform groups against one another by continually alternating major appointments between them. His young and inexperienced son Abdulmejid was not able to manage these bureaucrats as easily.

For the first few years after taking power, he retained Rauf Pasha, considered fairly neutral in factional politics, as grand vizier (1840–1846), replacing him only for one year (1841–1842) by a follower of Husrev. Rauf concentrated on foreign affairs. His tenure centered on stabilizing relations with Muhammad Ali, who finally had to comply with the 1840 London Convention that forced him to acknowledge Ottoman sovereignty but allowed him to retain control of Egypt. Rauf was also in office for the signing of the 1841 London Straits Convention that opened the Bosphorus and Dardanelles to non-Russian warships. European powers felt satisfied that these documents secured the Ottomans' international situation and restored the status quo in the region.

This appearance of restored stability in foreign affairs, though, contrasted with changes in domestic policy that began to unfold rapidly over the next few years. In 1840 and 1841, Reshid played a major part in extending army reforms to the provincial level and in instituting a new commercial code based on French models. Both actions raised the hackles of provincial religious leaders, who denounced his actions as anti-Islamic.

To appease them, Abdulmejid had Reshid removed as foreign minister and appointed as ambassador to Paris between 1841 and 1846. He concurrently served as governor of Edirne province beginning in 1843. Edirne was a place where modernizing reforms were actually being implemented, so Reshid was able to supervise the process there more closely. After 1846, he and his protégés Ali and Fuad Pasha began serving as grand viziers for large parts of the next two decades, creating some continuity in policy despite the sultans' continued efforts to balance the strength of different factions.

Ahmed Jevdet Pasha: Education and the Tanzimat

In the end, implementation of reform beyond a superficial level would require the development of new cohorts of officials well-schooled in modern techniques and ideas. The first substantial group of modernizing Ottoman officials had been largely made up of former students in the **Translation Bureau** (*terjume odasi*), created in 1821 by Mahmud II to educate Muslims (not just Christians and Jews serving as dragomans [translator/interpreters]) on how to translate important books and documents from foreign languages into Ottoman Turkish. Such translations directly exposed a much more substantial group than ever before to innovative foreign concepts. By the 1840s, modern specialized schools had also already been established for many years in fields such as medicine and military science, although they were primarily technical training institutions designed for students at a relatively advanced level of preparation.

The lack of secondary schools made bridging the gap between traditional primary education and advanced higher education quite difficult. One of the most important developments of the Tanzimat period was a huge expansion in the number of secondary institutions to fill the niche between elementary *mektebs*, still under the firm control of the clerics (ulema), and highly specialized technical academies designed for a fairly small number of advanced pupils. These new intermediate institutions, called "**Rushdiye**" ("adolescence") schools, gave several generations of students a broad exposure to modern arts and sciences in a system that survived even after the Ottoman Empire's collapse.

The Rushdiye schools were inspired by new educational concepts around the world, in particular the Lancasterian monitor school that became popular in England and the United States in the 1810s and 1820s. The Lancasterian system tried to promote mass education beyond simple religious instruction. Later criticized as too rigid and mechanical, it relied on using more successful students to mentor less successful peers to allow more pupils to be in one class with a single teacher. The system drew praise for its much lower cost and became a model for public school expansion in Europe and North America.

The Lancasterian system came to the attention of the Ottomans as a direct consequence of the influx of foreign missionaries, particularly Protestant Christians. William Goodell, one of the first American Protestant missionaries to become established in Istanbul, opened a Lancasterian school there for Greek and Armenian boys on his arrival in 1831. One year later, he added a branch for Greek and Armenian girls. These schools produced a strong negative reaction among local Greek and Armenian Orthodox priests and bishops, who saw these schools and the activities of their Protestant teachers as direct threats to their own authority and power.

Nevertheless, these educational experiments soon attracted the attention of prominent Muslim military officers, who visited them and within a short time set up their own pilot schools of this type for the Muslim community. Such innovation now alarmed Muslim clerics, who began to assert more stringent control over Muslim primary education through the Shaykh al-Islam (still the highest-ranking official in the traditional religious/judicial bureaucracy).

Despite such resistance, the reform-minded "Council of Public Works" (*Mejlis-i Umur-u Nafia*) had approved in 1838 the establishment of a group of Rushdiye schools. What really got these new institutions to flourish was the creation of a teachers' training academy for them in 1846. In 1850, this academy was placed under the direction of **Ahmed Jevdet Pasha** (1822–1895), later one of the main architects of Ottoman judicial reform.

With his background reminiscent of Reshid Pasha's, Jevdet first trained in a religious primary school and joined the *ilmiye* (religious/judicial/educational) section of the Ottoman bureaucracy. By coincidence, one of his first assignments was to be sent in 1846 as a religious tutor for Mustafa Reshid's family, which landed him in the midst of Tanzimat activities and completely reshaped his career path. Holding a series of important official positions beginning in the 1840s and continuing through the 1890s, Jevdet played important roles in a wide range of Tanzimat-era modernization projects. It was once rumored that Jevdet might be a candidate for the office of Shaykh al-Islam but was opposed by more conservative clerics. He made his most enduring contribution at the end of the Tanzimat period as compiler of the *Mejelle*, the first codified Ottoman legal code. It was formally based on Sharia law, but employed the style, vocabulary, and form of modern European legal systems.

THE CRIMEAN WAR

Implications for the Tanzimat

The Tanzimat did not take place in a vacuum. The encounter between Ottoman and foreign concepts that shaped its reform processes happened simultaneously with ongoing international political developments. Trends elsewhere had a growing impact on the Ottomans, particularly what was going on in Russia. Its renewed push southward, as well as the steady Austrian advance into the Balkans, again threatened the Ottomans' concept of empire, continuing to nibble away at what they had conquered centuries earlier.

For a few years around 1800, Russia and Austria became distracted from their long-term policies of southward expansion by the revolutionary fervor that swept Europe after the rise of Napoleon. Soon, their southerly focus returned as conflict within Europe subsided following the Congress of Vienna in

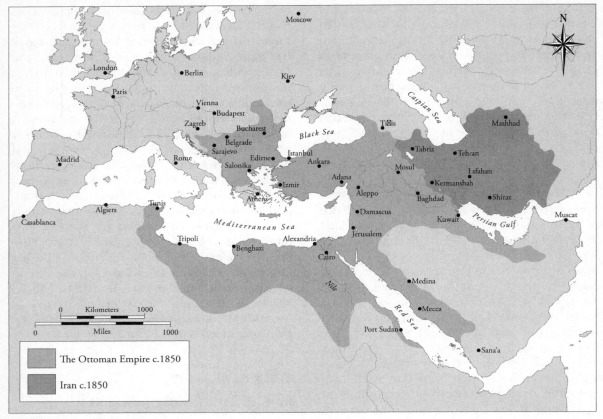

MAP 5.1   Middle East in 1850

1815. Britain and France became increasingly concerned about renewed Russian plans for expansion. Tsar Nicholas I (r. 1825–1855), a staunch nationalist, revived imperialist dreams of Peter and Catherine the Great. He again pushed for Russia's continuous expansion southward, ever with an eye on reclaiming the lost Byzantine capital of Constantinople: wellspring of Orthodox Christianity. Russia flexed its muscles in the 1820s in support of the Greek rebels and again in the 1830s during the conflicts between the Ottomans and Muhammad Ali. Populist excitement across Europe was reignited in 1848, later dubbed the "Year of Revolution."

All these trends helped set the stage for the next world conflict with a significant impact on the Ottomans: the Crimean War. A spirit of revolutionary sentiment once again erupted in France, but led now to the enthronement of Louis-Napoleon Bonaparte (Napoleon I's nephew) as Emperor Napoleon III. The Crimean War arose from his seemingly trivial challenge to Russia that France, instead of Russia, was entitled to symbolic control over certain holy sites in Palestine, which included possession of the keys to the door of the Church of the Nativity in Bethlehem. When Napoleon forced the Ottomans to acknowledge France's authority in these places, Russia demanded that its longstanding rights over Orthodox Christians and *their* holy places in the Ottoman Empire be affirmed and additional privileges be granted them.

But the Ottomans refused this request, prompting the Russians to march into

Moldavia and Wallachia in July 1853. These Balkan areas were still under nominal Ottoman sovereignty, but Russia had been granted increasing amounts of actual authority over them since the 1820s. Known as the "Danubian Principalities," they took advantage of being controlled neither fully by the Ottomans nor the Russians, and asserted increasing local autonomy. After 1848, their fragile political system was thrown into turmoil by nationalist uprisings in Moldavia, giving the Russians a pretext to invade. This in turn led Britain and France to join the Ottomans in a war against Russia in February 1854 after the Russians had destroyed an Ottoman fleet at anchor.

Although Russia soon withdrew its troops from Moldavia and Wallachia, Britain and France decided to use the war as a chance to settle the Eastern Question. They made four demands on Russia for a peace treaty. Russia would have to (1) end its protectorate over the Danubian Principalities, (2) give up the right to intervene in Ottoman affairs as the recognized protector of Orthodox Christians there, (3) agree to revise the Straits Convention of 1841 to reduce its naval control over the Black Sea, and (4) guarantee freedom of navigation along the Danube.

Russian refusal of these demands really started the Crimean War. After a few inconclusive battles in the fall of 1854, the war became defined by the long siege of Sevastopol between October 1854 and September 1855. It produced neither a substantial change in control of territory nor caused the fall of a government, so had little impact as a conventional war. Instead, the Crimean conflict was noteworthy as one of the first "modern" conflicts because of how it juxtaposed traditional and modern military tactics, strategy, and technology in ways that changed how wars would be planned and fought around the world. It was among the first wars to be covered by mass-circulation newspapers and of which photographs were taken.

The Crimean conflict was one of the first media wars in the modern sense. The British public became enthralled by frontline dispatches from William Howard Russell in the London *Times*. In one, Russell depicted a "Charge of the Light Brigade" at the Battle of Balaclava in a vivid and grim report published in his newspaper only three weeks after the event, prompting Alfred Tennyson's poem of that name that appeared one month later in a rival London newspaper. The British government became concerned about negative effects on morale when versions of Tennyson's poem started to circulate among troops in the field. Roger Fenton was allowed to take a series of photographs and William Simpson to draw a series of illustrations designed to portray events in a more positive light. But Fenton's photographs depicted war with a brutal immediacy never before possible, to be replicated a few years later by Matthew Brady's daguerreotypes of the American Civil War.

Vivid newspaper accounts from the Crimea moved **Florence Nightingale** to set up one of the world's first modern military hospitals. Housed in the Selimiye barracks of the Ottoman army in Uskudar, across the Bosphorus from Istanbul, the equipment and methods she used there became models for modern army medical care. This took place in an Ottoman military building named for Sultan Selim III, built in 1800 as part of the *nizam-i jedid* military modernization initiative. Another important artifact of early Ottoman naval modernization, the European-style tall ship *Mahmudiye* constructed by Mahmud II in 1829, played an important role in the siege of Sevastopol during the war. The *Mahmudiye* was for many years the largest warship in the world and continued in Ottoman service until 1875. The Crimean War also saw the first serious military use of railroads and telegraphs as well as prototypes of rifles that fired the Minié ball: a new type of bullet with radically improved accuracy and deadliness.

The war was not just a showcase for medical and technological innovations: It also exposed how traditional military practices, such as the sale of officer commissions by the

Florence Nightingale's military hospital in Istanbul (Crimean War)

British army and the Russian use of serfs as troops, greatly hampered military effectiveness. Karl Marx described the Crimean War as a conflict that passed "supreme judgment upon social organizations that have outlived their vitality": a prelude in his view of the coming global revolution of the working class.[2] The immediate impact of the war on the Ottomans was more local and specific than it was on Europe. When the conflict was over, the Ottomans suddenly owed large sums to British and French lenders: a very challenging situation for an empire with limited experience in the contemporary European financial system.

Costs of the War

The modern European financial system had an increasingly greater impact on the Ottomans as they became integrated into the world economy in the nineteenth century. With the expenses

generated by the modernization processes of the Tanzimat era, the Ottoman economy was becoming gradually more cash-based and integrated into global financial networks. This was demonstrated by the first issuance of Ottoman paper money in 1840 and the establishment of an Ottoman central bank in the early 1850s.

The Crimean War produced an immediate and sudden need for large amounts of cash to pay for materiel and military supplies. In 1854 and 1855, the Ottomans took out two loans at relatively low rates of interest from European financiers to help finance their military debt. British and French bankers offered these loans on very attractive terms, but also set up a control commission to oversee how their proceeds were being spent—beginning a process that ultimately led to European bankers taking control of the Ottoman treasury.

As quasi-official instruments of finance, these first two loans had the solid backing of the British and French governments, which shielded them somewhat from the turns and twists of the financial markets. However, when the Ottomans were not able to secure

---

[2]Karl Marx, *The Eastern Question* (New York: Burt Franklin, 1968), 576.

replacement loans in the open market for them, a fiscal crisis ensued when the original loans came due for payment in 1860. The situation only stabilized in 1863 when the private Ottoman Bank was reestablished as a semi-official Ottoman Imperial Bank upon the accession of the next sultan, Abdulmejid's brother Abdulaziz.

The War and Ottoman Society

The financial impact of the war was not the only thing that drew the Ottomans closer to their European allies. British and French politicians, reacting to negative publicity in the European press about battlefield losses in this war, developed the sense that their alliance with the Ottoman Empire against Russia had to be justified more convincingly to their constituents, given the long history of Ottoman conflicts with the West and that Western newspapers were starting to label the Ottoman Empire the "sick man of Europe." The Ottomans themselves took on the task of demonstrating why they deserved to be regarded as part of the European "Concert of Nations." Upon being awarded the French Legion of Honor in 1854, Abdulmejid proclaimed, "I firmly hope that … my Empire will prove to the entire universe that it is worthy of a prominent place in the concert of civilized nations."[3]

This sultan issued a proclamation in February 1856 extending and elaborating on the promises of the 1839 Gulhane proclamation. In this document, later called the "Imperial Rescript" or "Reform Decree," all Ottoman subjects were promised equal treatment in taxation, education, military service, justice, and an equal opportunity to serve as government officials. The Imperial Rescript was swiftly given international approval when it was cited in article nine of the 1856 Treaty of Paris ending the Crimean

War. The impact of the war, from a diplomatic perspective, was to emphasize how much Ottoman reforms were inspired by European models and how the Ottoman Empire was becoming more and more an integral part of the European diplomatic system.

One of the striking changes in domestic policy introduced in this **Imperial Rescript** was how it redefined how revenues would be collected. It got rid of the poll ("*jizye*"/"*jizya*") tax: the traditional fee paid by non-Muslims in all Muslim societies. All citizens were now subject to the same taxes and rules. This meant that, by implication, all Ottoman subjects were now subject to military conscription.

Although the law did not explicitly refer to military service obligations for non-Muslims, it created a new system in which non-Muslim men were allowed to pay *bedel-i askeri* ("military substitute tax") in place of military service. In practice, this generated more revenue while implementing the ideal of equality before the law: a good outcome for those running the government. Tax collection was also modernized and streamlined with a new imperial inspection system.

The Ottoman *millet* system had developed historically into a way for separate but not necessarily equal rights and privileges to be guaranteed for members of religious communities on a group-by-group basis. Millet communities were now given a much more formal legal status and structure in Tanzimat decrees than ever before, as well as granted the promise of equal treatment with Muslims. This applied in particular to Greeks and Armenians, whose *millet* communities became redefined as constitutional components of the Ottoman government, complete with their own legal codes and legislative bodies.

In 1860, the Greek *millet* received its own set of regulations and was asked to form a new governing council composed of clerics and lay leaders with the Ecumenical Patriarch as its head. The Armenians received a "Book of Regulations for the Armenian *Millet*" in 1863, which served as a sort of constitution for their

---

[3]"Remise du grand cordon de la Légion d'honneur par l'ambassadeur de France a Constantinople," *L'Illustration*, no. 673 (1856): 35–36.

community. Both groups were tasked with policing themselves and administering justice as a way to preserve their communal identities within a modern constitutional framework.

Such reform programs were opposed both by *millet* leaders, who saw their power threatened, as well as by mid-level Muslim government officials and military officers, who felt that too many privileges were being given to non-Muslim groups in the Empire without Muslims receiving much in return. Some began to see the changes initiated by the Imperial Rescript as a way to undermine the Ottoman system and impose undesired European values and practices.

At the same time, there was resentment among some Muslims about Ottoman subjects of other religions being granted equal status. This was exacerbated by the continuation and expansion of the *berat* system. The *berat* ("certificate") system allowed foreign nations to bestow privileges on certain non-Muslim Ottoman subjects in exchange for payment. It had been around for centuries, but more and more countries were now being permitted to use it, such as the British, who became formally recognized as the protecting power for Ottoman Jews and certain Ottoman Protestant Christians in the 1850s.

The Imperial Rescript was only the beginning of how Ottoman law would evolve during this period. Other statutes passed soon afterwards had similar far-reaching effects. One was the penal code of 1857 that introduced law codes resembling European legal systems. This effectively set up a criminal justice system that endured through the rest of the Empire's history, but it displaced religious judges from their roles as direct administrators of the criminal justice system, reversing centuries of Ottoman legal tradition.

Even more radical legal changes were to be found in the 1858 and 1867 **Land Laws**, with their attempts to establish a more coherent system for distinguishing between state and private lands. As with other Tanzimat innovations, these were presented as reassertions of traditional Ottoman land ownership categories in order to curb the power of provincial landlords. The actual result of these laws was to increase local notables' power, since more and more land came to be registered in the names of local lords by peasants, always leery of central government oversight. These changes also greatly accelerated the sedentarization of tribes in Iraq, for example. Vast stretches of tribal lands there came to be registered in the names of a few tribal leaders, with ordinary tribesmen reduced to landless sharecroppers.

The 1850s also witnessed the influx of large numbers of Muslim refugees from territories recently acquired by Russia, particularly from the Crimea and the Caucasus. The 1857 Refugee Law, issued to manage this influx, gave refugees amnesty from taxes and military service for six to twelve years and made provisions for settling them. It placed them in areas where their assimilation into the local culture proved difficult, which created new ethnic tensions in many areas.

The swift pace of Tanzimat reforms resulted in a backlash from various constituencies threatened by rapid change. The Kuleli incident of 1859 was typical of such reactions. It was an abortive coup attempt at one of the new modern military schools along the Bosphorus, whose goal was to depose Sultan Abdulmejid in the vain hope that a new ruler might simply retract all the reform decrees that had been issued.

LARGER IMPACT OF THE TANZIMAT

Reform and the Ottoman Provinces

Reaction against the reform policies of the 1850s was not confined to the Ottoman capital. There were a series of disturbances across the Empire that signaled discontent in many places. One was Lebanon.

By the mid-nineteenth century, it had become an increasingly important center of the economy of Eastern Mediterranean. For about a century and a half, the area had been ruled by members of the Shihab clan, the leading family among Maronite Christians there. Leaders of the Druze, a sect with roots in Shiism that had many followers in the Mount Lebanon region, were challenging the Shihabs for power by the early nineteenth century. In 1840, the major Shihab ruler Bashir II (in power since 1788) chose to support Muhammad Ali when his forces occupied Syria and was deposed by the Ottoman government for his disloyalty. The Ottomans installed another Shihab as "Bashir III," but he only lasted a few months. Then, a Druze massacre of Maronites at Dair al-Qamar in 1841 plunged Lebanon into civil conflict.

The Ottomans tried to resolve the situation by dividing Mount Lebanon into Druze and Maronite sections, creating an uneasy peace that lasted for a few years. The reform process inaugurated by the 1856 Imperial Rescript upset this fragile situation, because it precipitated a revolt by the Maronite peasants against their Christian feudal overlords. These peasants now wanted to see the implementation of any new reform measures that could lighten their tax burdens and make the system of military service obligations fairer.

This struggle between different social classes of Maronite Christians unpredictably boiled over into a full-scale civil war between the Maronites and the Druze, but with the Druze leaders now supported by Ottoman forces. Foreign powers now got involved as well, and Napoleon III sent 7,000 French troops to defend the Maronites in an enclave that they created.

Peace prevailed again in Ottoman Lebanon after 1861, now based on a power-sharing arrangement recognizing the rights of each religious community. Based on its claim to defend its Maronite religious brethren, France asserted its presence in Lebanon as never before. All subsequent Ottoman governors of this region were Europeans subject to British and French approval.

The climate of reform created by the Tanzimat emboldened groups in other parts of the empire as well. In 1858, 8,000 inhabitants of the island of Crete joined together to form an assembly. It threatened to revolt if the promises of the Tanzimat reform decrees were not implemented on the island, particularly with regard to building new local schools and roads. The Ottoman government appointed a succession of new governors there over the next few years, but did not address these grievances.

Finally in 1866, a group of Greek Cretans submitted a petition to the sultan demanding the cancellation of new taxes introduced under the reform laws. The Ottoman authorities decided to manage this problem by putting Crete under the authority of Egypt, whose government offered it better roads and schools. The Cretans rejected this change and at a "General Assembly of the Cretans," proclaimed the end of Ottoman rule over the island and announced its union with Greece. These rebels brought in volunteers from Greece to create a formidable fighting force.

After several years of fighting between the rebels and the Ottomans, the sultan had his grand vizier at that time (the reformer Ali Pasha) issue an "Organic Law" in September 1868 for the island. This featured an intricate power-sharing arrangement between Christians and Muslims modeled on the Lebanese agreement between **Druze** and **Maronites**. Within a few months, Crete was once again peaceful, a situation that endured for another ten years. Nevertheless, the island then embarked on a gradual path toward union with Greece, which occurred just before World War I.

The Ottomans succeeded in implementing just enough modernizing reforms in various problem areas such as Crete and Lebanon to reduce the growing pressure on them to relinquish control over lands they had ruled for centuries. In both areas, outside powers became more involved in internal affairs than ever before.

This greater foreign involvement was accompanied by much closer European scrutiny of what was happening in the Middle East after the mid-nineteenth century. European public opinion, as expressed in the mass media and by politicians, was shaped by

Europe's rapidly increasing economic superiority over the Ottomans. Based on perceptions of this changing relationship, Europeans felt increasingly emboldened to attack Ottoman practices, principles, and policies that they did not like. Because the Ottomans were trying to win acceptance as legitimate members of the Concert of Europe, they could not just ignore these concerns.

Slavery and the Tanzimat

A good example of how European public opinion affected policies toward the Ottomans can be seen in attitudes toward slavery in the Ottoman Empire. The question of slavery had become of the most emotionally charged issues in the Western world at that time. By the 1850s, abolitionism around the world had become a major crusade for western antislavery activists, who put significant pressure on their governments to fight slavery through direct and indirect means. The Ottoman Empire ruled over a series of well-established trade networks that supplied slaves for domestic and manual labor, principally from Africa and Central Asia. The Ottomans perceived no particular moral or religious sanction to abolish this practice, which was not formally prohibited by Sharia law. They did not feel much pressure to get rid of it, except in the case of slaves from Circassia, viewed as Muslims unlawfully in bondage.

European abolitionists focused on freeing enslaved Africans and on pressuring the Ottomans to prohibit the African slave trade. This prompted a strong negative reaction in Jedda, capital of the Ottoman province of the Hejaz and one of the traditional centers for buying and selling African slaves. Local merchants there supported their imam when he criticized European attempts to outlaw slavetrading practices permitted in Islamic law. Because of extreme local displeasure with foreign antislavery activities there, the French and British consuls along with some other foreigners were murdered. In spite of such local tensions, Ottoman authorities took a series of measures designed to diminish the slave trade gradually.

They encouraged the freeing of slaves and promoted the issuance of manumission documents (*mukatabat*), using the rationale that although Islamic law does not prohibit slavery, it describes man's natural state as free. By referring to an implicit Islamic critique that opposed keeping fellow humans in bondage, the Ottomans handled the slavery issue much as they managed other dilemmas in this early era of modernization. They appealed to traditional norms to legitimize new and unfamiliar ideas. The challenge, as always, was how to harmonize traditional values as much as possible with modern trends by introducing the latter in a careful, balanced way appropriate to each particular situation.

International Relations in the Tanzimat Era

To bolster these attempts to harmonize the traditional with the modern, the Ottomans actively sought ties to emerging international organizations, because foreign recognition of their efforts could help blunt domestic opposition to change. Still, they had to be sensitive about how to manage conflicts that emerged. For example, they were among the first signatories of the original Geneva Convention of 1864: the treaty that established the framework and organization of the International Red Cross and Red Crescent societies. However, the Ottomans eventually had to implore the Swiss to allow them to use a red crescent instead of a red cross on the flag flown by medical personnel in battle, since the cross evoked so many negative images from previous Muslim-Christian conflicts such as the Crusades.

The Ottomans also recognized that they were part of an emerging new global transportation system created by steamships and railroads, linking the world economically and socially with a speed never seen before. The travel networks created by these new vehicles permitted a vast increase in the number of

Muslims able to perform the hajj, with many implications for the Ottoman government.

Among these was the need to prevent the spread of infectious diseases among pilgrims. Disease prevention, in turn, was getting easier due to Pasteur's breakthroughs in understanding the transmission of illness. To strengthen ties to the European medical community, the Ottomans chose to host the third International Sanitary Conference in Istanbul in February 1866 to discuss in particular the problem of cholera epidemics, one of which had just broken out.

The increased ease of international travel also allowed for the only trip ever made by a reigning Ottoman ruler to Europe to take place: the visit of Sultan Abdulaziz to France and Britain in 1867. This voyage marked a high point of Ottoman participation in the Concert of Europe, when Abdulaziz was cordially welcomed by Emperor Napoleon III as a fellow European monarch. This hospitality was reciprocated with the visit of Napoleon's wife, Empress Eugenie, to Istanbul in the fall of 1869 on her way to the opening of the Suez Canal in Egypt.

The Ottoman section of the 1867 Paris International Exhibition, which Abdulaziz toured during his visit there, displayed a new Ottoman style blending traditional Islamic and western motifs. It was based in part on the European rediscovery of the medieval Spanish Islamic style of the Alhambra. This fashion had been in the European public eye since the Alhambra Court exhibit at London's 1851 Great Exhibition: the first of the large nineteenth-century world's fairs. The Alhambra "Moorish" style of this exhibit directly inspired the architectural designs of the Balian family, designers of many major public buildings being built in Istanbul at that time.

These expanded cultural connections between Europe and the Ottomans also promoted "Orientalist" views of the Middle East far more widely, with the circulation of many Western popular accounts about the region and its major figures. Mark Twain thus described a ceremonial procession that he witnessed which featured Napoleon III and Abdulaziz during the 1867 Paris visit. "Napoleon III, the representative of the highest modern civilization, progress and refinement; Abdul Aziz, the representative of a people by nature and training filthy, brutish, ignorant, unprogressive, superstitious – and a government whose Three Graces are Tyranny, Rapacity, Blood. Here in brilliant Paris, under this majestic Arch of Triumph, the first century greets the nineteenth!"[4] Although Twain often relied on such overstatement for artistic effect, his view of an abiding contrast between East and West was widely shared in the West, as the rapid progress of the Industrial Revolution heightened popular perceptions of a vast dichotomy between the two regions. The Middle East became constructed in popular western media more and more as the "orient" of seductive human vice, luxury, mystery, and secrecy.[5]

Missionaries and the Tanzimat

Other new Western accounts of the Middle East by observers with more measured perspectives on cultural differences, began to be produced. Many were written by Protestant missionaries who had set out across the world from Britain and the United States during the Second Great Awakening (1790–1850) on evangelical missions. Many of them traveled in particular to the Ottoman Empire: the location of so many places mentioned in the Bible. The Ottomans were challenged by this new influx of foreigners, but found ways to use them to their advantage. Missionaries were strictly forbidden from proselytizing Muslims, but the Ottomans used them to keep native Christian leaders in check, allowing Western missionaries to try to convert native Christians and Jews to their faiths.

---

[4]Mark Twain, *Innocents Abroad* (Hartford: American Publishing Company, 1869), 126–127.
[5]For the definitive study of this trend, see Edward Said, *Orientalism* (New York: Vintage Books, 1978).

Among the greatest imports brought by the missionaries were modern methods of education, particular in science and medicine. In the more tolerant atmosphere of the Ottoman Empire in the 1860s after two decades of Tanzimat reforms, American Protestants were permitted to open two important schools of higher learning that had lasting impacts on education in the Middle East: **Robert College** (now Bosphorus University), founded in Istanbul in 1863, and the **Syrian Protestant College** (now the American University of Beirut), founded in Beirut in 1866. Both institutions had a significant impact on the Middle East because of the numbers of their graduates who joined the social and political elites of countries across the region. By the end of the Tanzimat period, mission schools at all levels had been established and were thriving across the Ottoman Empire, catering primarily to Christian Ottoman subjects, but not exclusively.

Missionaries played an important role in forming impressions among the western public of how the Ottomans were treating native Christians. To a certain degree, missionary literature cultivated a negative view of life among local Christians to promote fundraising at home, and this intensified negative stereotypes about Middle Easterners in general. Through the 1870s, more romantic impressions of life in the region also spread: visions of a distant magical place filled with genies and magic carpets. This was epitomized in 1870 when the "Ancient Arabic Order of the Nobles of the Mystic Shrine" (known today as the "Shriners") was founded in New York City as a Masonic charitable organization whose rituals and regalia were based on Middle Eastern motifs and designs.

End of the Tanzimat

Education had been important in launching and sustaining the Tanzimat reforms through these years, given the number of reformers who had been educated in new types of schools. Although Mustafa Reshid Pasha was himself a product of the traditional Ottoman scribal bureaucracy, his two main protégés who each served many years as grand vizier, Ali and Fuad Pasha, both graduated from modernizing schools established during the reign of Mahmud II. When Fuad passed away in 1869, followed by Ali two years later, Sultan Abdulaziz took the opportunity to reclaim some of the power that had flowed to these architects of Tanzimat reform. The Sultan, although a supporter of the Tanzimat, wanted to exert more personal control over the pace of events, so he picked Mahmud Nedim Pasha, also originally Mustafa Reshid's protégé but later out of favor with him, to serve as grand vizier upon Ali's death in 1871.

Figures like Nedim represented the decline of the Tanzimat spirit, because although the reform programs kept going, they were not pursued as before. He was said to have remarked that "happiness and peace in the affairs of state derive from loyalty."[6] Espousing such a sentiment, he was not going to be vigorously promoting any aspects of the Tanzimat that challenged the sultan. The last true reformer of the Tanzimat period, Ahmed Shefik Midhat Pasha, succeeded Nedim briefly as grand vizier, but then was dismissed as being too sympathetic to the reformist group.

Midhat, like Ali and Fuad, had risen through the Ottoman bureaucracy under the tutelage of Mustafa Reshid Pasha, but possessed significantly more experience in the day-to-day running of government in the Ottoman provinces than them. By the late 1860s, he had risen to a very high position in the central government, but was always seen as a bit too sure of himself by many senior officials. His personality conflicts with Ali drove him into exile as governor of Baghdad between 1869 and 1872, but he used this experience to regain the sultan's favor.

Although Midhat impressed Abdulaziz at first, he was ousted after only three months as

---

[6]Mahmud Nedim Pasha, in Ş. Hanioğlu, *A Brief History of the Late Ottoman Empire* (Princeton: Princeton University Press, 2008), 109.

grand vizier in 1872, replaced by a swift succession of lesser bureaucrats over the next four
years. This created somewhat of a power vacuum that allowed Sultan Abdulaziz to bolster
his position of authority from the new Yildiz
Chalet, a palace sequestered in a forest on the
hills overlooking the Bosphorus. Midhat then
spent a considerable period of time outside of
government, becoming more and more closely
associated with a political reform organization
known as the "Young Ottomans."

The "Young Ottomans" had originally
been created in 1865 as a secret society
supported by Ottoman political exiles in
Europe, but emerged in the open by the early
1870s after the death of Ali Pasha and the
loosening of the political climate. Opposed
to the methods of what they viewed as the
"modernizing absolutism" of the first Tanzimat
reformers Reshid, Fuad, and Ali, the Young
Ottomans called for the establishment of a true
constitutional government to promote reform,
but based on a more careful and creative
understanding of Islamic law viewed in light
of Enlightenment theories of democracy and
constitutionalism such as those presented by
Montesquieu and Rousseau.

Having pushed the reformers and their
ilk out of power, Sultan Abdulaziz suddenly
found himself under huge political pressure
as the Empire was overtaken by a fiscal
and political crisis in 1875. Ottoman lands,
particularly those in Anatolia, had been hit
by a drought in 1873, forcing the Ottomans
to declare bankruptcy in October 1875. This
crisis precipitated two major rebellions of
Orthodox Christians in the Balkans: first in the
summer of 1875 in Herzegovina and then in
April 1876 in Bulgaria. The Ottomans were not
very successful in quieting down the situation
in Herzegovina, but they effectively quelled the
Bulgarian uprising with irregular troops, many
of whom were drawn from refugees recently
escaped from areas in the Caucasus and Crimea
now occupied by Russians.

These troops were soon accused by the
European press of perpetrating monstrous
atrocities. This quickly became a huge political
issue in Britain, with opposition leader William
Gladstone severely chastising the government
of Benjamin Disraeli then in power for
defending Turkish actions in this conflict. The
crisis also rekindled the spirit of **Pan-Slavism**:
an ideology that promoted the union of Slavic
peoples and their liberation from Ottoman rule.

On May 30, 1876, Midhat, in collaboration with the current grand vizier and minister of war, took the opportunity presented by
these crises to depose Abdulaziz in a coup that
brought Abdulaziz's nephew to the throne as
Sultan Murad V. With Pan-Slavic sentiments
rising in the Balkans, Serbia and Montenegro
took this change of government as their chance
to declare war on the Ottomans, their nominal
rulers, on June 30.

Meanwhile, the coup plotters' plan was
to have Murad V issue a formal constitution for the Empire that would legitimize the
whole reform process in a more formal and
legal manner. Unfortunately, he turned out
to be mentally unstable and was deposed by
a fatwa of the Shaykh al-Islam on August 31.
He was replaced by his brother, who became
Sultan **Abdulhamid II**. The **Young Ottomans**
were hopeful that Abdulhamid would support
their plan, and he did in fact proclaim the first
Ottoman constitution on December 23, 1876,
selecting Midhat to be his grand vizier.

This declaration did not occur on that
date by chance. December 23 was the day
after the end of a European peace conference
that had been meeting for the previous two
weeks in Istanbul, to which the Ottomans
paradoxically had not been invited. The
peace conference resolved that three Ottoman
provinces, Eastern and Western Bulgaria, as
well as Bosnia-Herzegovina, would stay under
Ottoman authority, but henceforth be governed
by Christian officials appointed by the sultan,
subject to the approval of the European Great
Powers. Midhat protested that under the new
constitution that had just been proclaimed, all
Ottoman citizens were granted totally equal
rights. He argued that this removed any need

for such novel governing arrangements in the Balkans and thus rejected these European peace terms.

At that point, the Russians, asserting solidarity with the Balkan Slavs, declared war on the Ottomans. The Russo-Turkish War that followed was marked by two prolonged struggles: the siege of Plevna in Rumania (July–December 1877) and a very bloody confrontation in eastern Anatolia that finally resulted in the Russian takeover there in February 1878. Based on momentum generated by hard-fought victories on several battlefronts, the Russians forced the Ottomans to sign the Treaty of San Stefano (now a suburb of Istanbul known as "Yeshilkoy") in March 1878. This document granted independence to Romania, Serbia, and Montenegro, leaving Bulgaria as an autonomous component of the Ottoman Empire.

Other European powers totally rejected this new settlement and convened the Congress of Berlin that summer to create a substitute for it. This meeting produced yet another treaty restoring to the Ottomans much of what they had ceded to the Russians in the Yeshilkoy/San Stefano agreement.

The 1877–1878 Russo-Turkish War produced yet another group of Muslim refugees fleeing from the Balkans into central Ottoman territory, but nowhere more so than from Bulgaria, where thousands of Muslim peasants were displaced. A final important result of the war was that since he feared the complete disintegration of his empire, Abdulhamid suspended the Ottoman parliament's activities, although without formally dissolving it. This state of affairs lasted for thirty-two years until July 1908.

Sultan Abdulhamid II ruled during this interval as an absolute monarch, but the spirit of democratization popularized by the Young Ottomans persisted through various clandestine organizations, as did a rising consciousness of "Turkish" (in contrast to a more general "Ottoman") identity. One of the earliest and most influential proponents of Turkish nationalism was one of the founders of the Young Ottoman group, **Namik Kemal** (1840–1888), whose *Vatan yahut Silistre* (*Fatherland or Silistria*) was a dramatization of the siege of Silistria that caused the Crimean War to break out in 1854.

EGYPT DURING THE TANZIMAT ERA

Egypt had experienced a remarkable period of prosperity under Muhammad Ali, who was ably assisted by his adopted son, Ibrahim Pasha, in the 1820s and 1830s. By 1848, though, both son and father were so ailing that Ibrahim actually died before Muhammad Ali, after insisting that the Ottoman ruler Abdulmejid appoint him as regent. The successor to both, Muhammad Ali's grandson Abbas I, was murdered less than six years into his reign. He was in turn succeeded by his uncle Said, who ruled for only nine years (1854–1863). Said spoke French very well and favored France in international relations, granting the concession to build the Suez Canal to a French businessman, Ferdinand de Lesseps, over British objections. He even sent a group of Sudanese troops to help French forces defending Emperor Maximilian in Mexico in the 1860s.

Neither Abbas nor Said had as much of an impact on Egypt as Ismail, Ibrahim Pasha's son, who ruled from 1863 until he was removed by the British and French in 1879. Far more than his immediate predecessors, Ismail followed the path traced by Muhammad Ali and Ibrahim Pasha in devoting energies to the modernization of Egypt. In 1878, he remarked, "My country is no longer in Africa. We are now a part of Europe." His education in Paris no doubt increased his affinity for the task of making Egypt more European. He paralleled the Tanzimat reformers in Istanbul by reviving the industrial expansion programs of his grandfather, building railroads, combating the slave trade, and creating Egypt's first legislative "assembly of delegates" in 1866 composed of village headmen and urban notables. He pushed for the completion of the Suez Canal, which was finished by 1869.

Suez Canal (around 1894)

To confirm the European cultural focus of his regime, he commissioned Giuseppe Verdi to write the opera *Aida*. Set in pharaonic Egypt, it had its premiere in Cairo in December 1871, its debut delayed by the outbreak of the Franco-Prussian War. Also like his forebears, he engaged in expensive foreign military adventures, sending troops to Sudan and Ethiopia on unsuccessful empire-building campaigns.

In another parallel to what was happening to the central Ottoman government, Ismail's modernization plans and military activities plunged Egypt into serious debt by the 1870s. This culminated with Egypt selling its interest in the Suez Canal to Britain in 1875, and European bankers taking control of Egyptian finances in 1876. Ismail was reduced to the status of a constitutional monarch with a British finance minister and a French minister of public works—a situation that would ultimately unleash considerable public anger at him. This change also marked the end of the impact of the Ottoman Tanzimat period in Egypt, such as it was, since with this

far greater European involvement in the day-to-day running of the government, there was much less room for any initiative on the part of the local rulers than there had been before the late 1870s.

NASER AL-DIN SHAH: BEGINNING IRAN'S MODERN ERA

Iran, while more removed than the Ottoman Empire from the vast social and economic changes sweeping over nineteenth-century Europe, remained close to the center of the Great Game, the continuing struggle between Britain and Russia for supremacy in Asia during the century preceding World War I. As a result of the **Treaty of Turkmenchay**, Russia had secured a very influential role in internal Iranian politics by the middle of the nineteenth century, particular in the northern areas of Iran near the Caspian Sea. The British began to establish their permanent presence in the Persian Gulf and to wield influence in southern Iran as early as the eighteenth century. Britain had signed formal treaties of alliance with various emirates there by the 1820s (along the shoreline known as the "Trucial Coast" because of these agreements, known as "truces"). The British "**Persian Gulf Residency**" was created in 1822. It had its headquarters in Bushehr, Iran, operating under the aegis and control of the British East India Company in Mumbai.

Prompted by these European diplomatic and military activities in and near Iran, Abbas Mirza, the country's heir-apparent and governor of Azerbaijan through the 1820s, experimented with modernizing his armed forces, creating army units loosely modeled on the Ottoman *nizam-i jedid* corps. His untimely death in 1834 ended this first period of reform in Iran. The next important period of change began in 1848, when Naser al-Din, Abbas Mirza's grandson, took the throne. Continuing for forty-eight years, the era of Naser al-Din can be usefully divided into what happened before and after 1873, the year of his first journey to Europe. This trip accelerated connections between Iran and the west in many dimensions.

At first, Naser al-Din Shah tried to be both modernizer as well as traditional Iranian monarch and conqueror—an ambitious goal for any ruler. His first guide in implementing reform was his mentor Mirza Taqi Khan Farahani (known in Iranian history as "Amir Kabir"). He appointed Amir Kabir as grand vizier and had him embark on a comprehensive reform program reminiscent of the Ottoman Tanzimat in its scope and intention. To solidify connections with Amir Kabir, Naser al-Din arranged for him to marry his sister. Amir Kabir, of peasant origin, had achieved his status because his father had served as Fath Ali Shah's cook. He was ruthless in cutting government expenses and reforming the bureaucracy in many areas.

Amir Kabir succeeded in getting large numbers of Iranians vaccinated for the first time against smallpox and founded the Dar al-Fonun in 1848, Iran's first European-style university that evolved into the modern University of Tehran. He sponsored the publication of one of the first newspapers in Iran: an official gazette

that began circulation in 1851. Plans were made under his direction for the establishment of a variety of industrial factories in Iran and for the creation of a modern navy.

Implementation of such projects depended upon securing a more stable official budget and trimming spending deficits. He saw a way to accomplish this by curtailing the large annual salaries paid to members of the Qajar royal family. When news of this plan reached the shah's mother and her retinue, she became very angry and began to scheme against him. Since he was of humble social origin, Amir Kabir had no powerful kinsmen to shield him from such attacks. Allegations circulating against him finally convinced Naser al-Din Shah to dismiss Amir Kabir and exile him to Kashan, where he was put to death by an assassin authorized by the monarch in 1852. Despite Amir Kabir's relatively brief time in power, the reform measures that he was able to carry out laid the groundwork for a process of modernization that continued after his death.

Iran experienced two other episodes in the 1850s that set the stage for what transpired later in Naser al-Din Shah's reign: the emergence of Bahaullah (1817–1892) as the prophet of a new religion, the Bahai faith, and the 1856–1857 Anglo-Persian War, which further defined the terms of the Great Game.

Bahaullah was the disciple of a charismatic seer named Sayyid Mirza Ali Muhammad (1819–1850). Mirza Ali Muhammad, who became known by his followers as the "Bab" ("gate" or "door"), declared that he was the Islamic mahdi (messiah) and the harbinger of a new revelation. He quickly attracted numerous followers, but was savagely attacked by the Islamic clergy as a heretic for claiming to be a prophet after Muhammad, considered by Muslims to be the last and final prophet. The Bab and his followers were hunted down, and he was put to death in 1850.

In his writings, the Bab spoke of a "Promised One" who would come after him as another messenger. Bahaullah's followers believe his designation as the Bab's "Promised

One" to have taken place during his imprisonment as a follower of the Bab in 1852 in a Tehran prison known as the "Black Pit" ("*Siyah Chal*"). Bahaullah waited until 1863, after he had gone into exile from Iran in Ottoman Iraq, to openly declare himself a prophet. He ended up in Acre (Akka; now in modern Israel but then located in Ottoman Palestine), where he lived under house arrest and became recognized by a growing group of international followers as the founder of the Bahai faith. Despite the fact that Bahaullah never returned to Iran, his religion developed numerous adherents there. They played important roles in subsequent Iranian history, despite official condemnation and persecution from the clergy and government.

Naser al-Din Shah also chose in 1856 to invade Afghanistan in order to "reincorporate" Herat into Iranian domains. Herat had not really been controlled by Iran since late Safavid times, but its "recapture" had been contemplated in 1838 and again in 1852 as an assertion of the Qajars' ability to exercise authority over areas once controlled by Iran. Both times, British diplomacy forced Iran to back down before actual conflict ensued. The main British goal, as part of the emerging Great Game, continued to be the maintenance of Afghanistan as a unified, neutral buffer state between British domains in India and the expanding Russian empire, just then consolidating its control over recent acquisitions in Central Asia and Transoxiana.

Although precipitated by the Iranian seizure of Herat, the Anglo-Persian War of 1856–1857 was fought almost completely along the Persian Gulf coast. The British had no desire at all to go into Afghan territory in the wake of their disastrous defeat there in the First Afghan War (1839–1842), but were confident of the Royal Navy's ability to sort out problems with Iran on its own terms. Indeed, the British Navy swiftly occupied Bushehr, which it then easily held despite some tactical setbacks.

Faced with this show of force, the Iranians quickly withdrew from Herat and signed a treaty with the British that permitted Britain yet more commercial concessions in Iran, relinquished any Iranian claims over Herat, and promised Iranian help in suppressing the slave trade in the Persian Gulf. This was a comprehensive victory for Britain, since all of its provisions promoted specific, if disparate goals of British foreign policy in the region at the time.

In the end, the social tensions arising from Bahaullah's messianic vision and his movement had been exported and defused (to some degree) upon his departure from Iran while the danger posed by Iran's invasion of Afghanistan to the strategic balance of the Great Game in its invasion of Afghanistan had also been averted. Nevertheless, Naser al-Din severely weakened Iran by pursuing policies at cross-purposes with one another. He intermittently followed the ambitious path of a traditional Persian warrior-conqueror monarch while at the same time, promotied modernization programs in a very lackadaisical, half-hearted way. For Naser al-Din to have had any chance at success, Iran would have needed far more wealth than it actually had. Iran's economic dependency on the West steadily increased as it sought ways to finance its activities. This in turn produced greater western influence on all aspects of this society, as it did also in other places across the Middle East at this time.

Questions To Think About

1. What was the Gulhane Proclamation?
2. What was the Tanzimat?
3. Who was Mustafa Reshid Pasha, and what was his real impact in the Ottoman Empire?
4. Why were European powers afraid of Muhammad Ali, and what did they do to limit his power?
5. Why did power at the top of the Ottoman government shift away from the sultan

and toward the grand vizier during the Tanzimat?

6. What was the Eastern Question? Why did it worry European powers so much?

7. What was the Great Game? What was Iran's importance in the Great Game?

8. How did the Ottoman educational system change during the Tanzimat period?

9. What were Ahmed Jevdet's contributions to the Tanzimat?

10. How did the Tanzimat reforms affect non-Muslims in the Ottoman Empire?

11. What was the real importance of the Crimean War in world history?

12. How and why did the Ottoman Empire try to become more "European" during the Tanzimat period?

13. What was the Ottoman attitude toward slavery?

14. What was the impact of Christian missionaries in the Ottoman Empire?

15. How was the experience of the Tanzimat different in Egypt from how it affected the central Ottoman Empire?

16. What made being Iran's monarch particularly difficult for Naser al-Din Shah?

17. What was the context of Bahaullah's movement in Iran, and why was it so threatening to Iran's rulers?

For Further Reading

Ali Haydar Mithat. *The Life of Midhat Pasha*. New York: Arno Press, 1973.

Amanat, Abbas. *Resurrection and Renewal: The Making of the Babi Movement in Iran, 1844–1850*. Ithaca, NY: Cornell University Press, 1989.

Badem, Candan. *The Ottoman Crimean War, 1853–1856*. Boston: Brill, 2010.

Davison, Roderic H. *Reform in the Ottoman Empire, 1856–1876*. New York: Gordian Press, 1973.

Findley, Carter V. *Bureaucratic Reform in the Ottoman Empire: The Sublime Porte, 1789–1922*. Princeton, NJ: Princeton University Press, 1980.

Findley, Carter V. *Turkey, Islam, Nationalism, and Modernity: A History, 1789–2007*. New Haven: Yale University Press, 2010.

Green, Dominic. *Three Empires on the Nile: The Victorian Jihad, 1869–1899*. New York: Free Press, 2007.

Kasaba, Reşat. *The Ottoman Empire and the World Economy: The Nineteenth Century*. Albany: State University of New York Press, 1988.

Makdisi, Ussama Samir. *Artillery of Heaven: American Missionaries and the Failed Conversion of the Middle East*. Ithaca, NY: Cornell University Press, 2008.

Makdisi, Ussama Samir. *The Culture of Sectarianism: Community, History, and Violence in Nineteenth-Century Ottoman Lebanon*. Berkeley: University of California Press, 2000.

Maoz, Moshe. *Ottoman Reform in Syria and Palestine, 1840–1861; The Impact of the Tanzimat on Politics and Society*. Oxford: Clarendon Press, 1968.

Mardin, Şerif. *The Genesis of Young Ottoman Thought; A Study in the Modernization of Turkish Political Ideas*. Princeton, NJ: Princeton University Press, 1962.

Pamuk, Şevket. *The Ottoman Empire and European Capitalism, 1820–1913: Trade, Investment, and Production*. Cambridge: Cambridge University Press, 1987.

Sayyid-Marsot, Afaf Lutfi. *Egypt in the Reign of Muhammad Ali* (Cambridge: Cambridge University Press, 1984).

Toledano, Ehud R. *Slavery and Abolition in the Ottoman Middle East*. Seattle: University of Washington Press, 1998.

Ufford, Letitia Wheeler. *The Pasha: How Mehemet Ali Defied the West, 1839–1841*. Jefferson, NC: McFarland & Co, 2007.

Zürcher, Erik Jan. *Turkey: A Modern History* (London: I.B.Tauris, 2004).

6

Indirect European Influence in the Middle East

BRITISH IN EGYPT

The opening of the Suez Canal in 1869 suddenly transformed international commerce, with Europe now linked to Indian Ocean and East Asian trade routes more directly than ever before. Because of the Canal's importance, Britain gradually assumed a more direct role in promoting Egypt's stability, since it was a conduit on the way to India. Egypt's dilemma was that British policy there was shaped less by what might have been best for the country, but more by what was required to develop and maintain the *Pax Britannica*: the late nineteenth-century period of peace when Britain controlled the world's maritime trade routes and enjoyed unchallenged naval supremacy. Through the early 1880s, France had been Britain's partner in securing Egypt. With their own imperialist projects in Southeast Asia and Africa, the French gradually acceded to British primacy along the Nile—a situation that would prevail through the middle of the twentieth century.

Although Britain developed into Egypt's main protective power only a few months after intervening in its affairs in 1882, its authority there was left ambiguous. Britain strongly preferred to maintain at least the façade of Ottoman control. Thus, it managed Egypt as a "**Veiled Protectorate**" in which its officials would wield real power in government and administration, but only behind the scenes in consultation with Egyptians remaining formally in charge.

Britain promoted a diverse set of political and economic goals in Egypt at this time. It wanted above all, to keep Egypt politically quiet as well as economically and socially stable, while simultaneously encouraging aspects of modernization. Although the British did want Egypt to become modernized, its main role from the British perspective in the world economy, in addition to serving as a conduit for international commerce, was to produce raw materials as well as consume imported finished goods. Such economic goals were at cross-purposes with the self-sufficiency programs initiated by Muhammad Ali and his successors, designed to move Egypt beyond its longtime status as a supplier of raw materials and promote its manufacturing capabilities.

The result of British supervision of Egyptian affairs over several decades beginning in 1882 was the selective expansion and updating of Egypt's transportation, communication, and public health systems, but without any focus on aspects of development that would have permitted Egypt to attain greater economic independence. This is particularly noticeable in the way that education was systematically neglected by the British, hindering the development of a literate and knowledgeable group of Egyptians to run the country.

Even more serious than the gradual reversion of the Egyptian economy to a role as a provider of raw materials was its debt crisis of the 1870s. This was brought on by several factors. The value of Egyptian cotton, the export seen as the main revenue base for the modernization projects of Muhammad Ali's grandson Ismail, had become artificially inflated during the American Civil War. When cotton prices collapsed after 1865, the costs of his plans and military activities suddenly had to be met by European loans at exorbitant rates of interest. In addition, he had agreed to very unfavorable terms with the Suez Canal Company, allowing it a free ninety-nine year lease on the Canal territory and use of large amounts of wealthy agricultural land next to the Canal. Egypt's insolvency crisis culminated with it selling its own shares in the Company to Britain in 1875 and a committee of European bankers taking control of Egyptian finances in 1876.

Ismail was reduced to the status of a limited monarch with foreign officials supervising his government in the "Dual Control" system. When foreigners took on such important roles in the Egyptian government, this sparked great public anger and prompted an uprising that forced Ismail to remove them. The British and French would not tolerate this interference in their plans, so they replaced Ismail with his son Tawfiq in June 1879.

However, this did nothing to quell Egypt's continued political instability. A faction of the army led by Colonel **Ahmad Urabi** kept up pressure to prevent European control of the government through 1881. Colonel Urabi was one of the highest-ranking officers in the Egyptian army of "*fellah*" (indigenous Egyptian peasant) origin, in contrast to the "Turco-Circassian" Mamluk military elite who had run the country for centuries. To take charge of the situation, the British military intervened, beginning with a naval bombardment of Alexandria in July 1882.

This started a war in which Urabi had three religious leaders from the religious university **al-Azhar** issue a fatwa declaring Tawfiq a traitor, implicitly deposing him as the country's legitimate ruler. For two months, Egypt was split between two governments, one in Alexandria, controlled by Tawfiq and his British supporters, and the other in Cairo, ruled by Urabi and his army cohort. This lasted until Urabi's decisive defeat at Tal al-Kabir by British forces on September 11.

There was some sentiment initially in favor of Urabi's cause among parts of Gladstone's Liberal party government then in power in Britain, but in the end, the imperial agenda to promote stabilization at all costs won out. Urabi's revolt has been characterized as the first broad uprising of Egyptians against foreign domination, but it may have been mostly the product of popular anger over burdensome taxation and poor government. After the Urabi uprising had been suppressed and its leaders sent into exile, Evelyn Baring (Lord Cromer), a British financial official who had served both in Cairo and in India, was installed in Egypt as Britain's consul-general in September 1883. He now functioned as the country's effective ruler over the next few years.

Lord Cromer

At first, Cromer's intervention in Egyptian governmental affairs was perceived as a temporary expedient, designed only to ensure the implementation of measures needed to stabilize Egypt's economy. Over the course of time, Cromer came to believe that because of Egyptian administrative incompetence, a long period of British supervision would be essential to implement any sort of lasting reforms, with particular attention paid to guarding the security of the Suez Canal zone. The British government, although led by several prime ministers with differing political agendas, continued to agree with him. His tenure in this role thus persisted for thirty-four years through 1907.

Cromer's new system was designed to obscure the degree to which Britain had actual control over Egyptian affairs. Tawfiq, although relatively subservient to the British, sanctioned this state of affairs as the surest guarantee of his continued tenure on the throne. With the advent of this new system, the Egyptian army was gradually weakened, forcing the nation to rely more and more on British troop garrisons there for security and defense.

During Cromer's years as consul-general, the Egyptian nationalist movement was suppressed and forced into exile, showing few signs of life until the very end of his tenure. Cromer felt that "'subject races' were totally incapable of self-government, that they did not really need or want self-government, and that what they really needed was a 'full belly' policy which fed the population, kept it quiescent and allowed the elite to make money and so cooperate with the occupying power."[1] Although, at least rhetorically, the goal of British intervention had initially been to restore the existing status quo, the longevity of the Veiled Protectorate created a new status quo that assumed British dominance and Egyptian subservience: a paradigm that endured through fall of King Farouk, the last ruler of Muhammad Ali's dynasty, in 1952.

---

[1]Lord Cromer, quoted in Afaf Lutfi al-Sayyid Marsot, *A Short History of Modern Egypt* (Cambridge: Cambridge University Press, 1985), 75–76.

Events in the Sudan

Britain's perceptions of its proper role in Egypt were shaped by what was going on at this time in the Sudan. Ismail sought to emulate his grandfather Muhammad Ali, who had invaded the Sudan in 1820, as well as to rival European powers scrambling to claim territory all over Africa, particularly near the source of the Nile.

For Ismail, activities in the Sudan shifted focus away from the problems of governing Egypt. He took steps to tighten control over isolated parts of the Sudan, suppressed the slave trade there, and tried to modernize Sudan's army and society in ways that paralleled the modernization that had taken place in Egypt over the previous decades. He extended his authority farther south than his predecessors had done, establishing an "Equatoria" province (Arabic: "*al-Istiwaiya*") in southern Sudan in 1869 governed by Sir Samuel Baker, a renowned Victorian explorer, big-game hunter, and confirmed abolitionist.

Baker was succeeded by Charles "Chinese" Gordon, a British officer who had acquired fame in China. After clashing with the Egyptian governor of northern Sudan, Gordon succeeded in getting himself appointed as Ismail's governor for the whole country. In this position, he faced the opposition of slave traders in the north, who resisted the Egyptian government's attempts to suppress their activities, and tried with limited success to broker peace with Ethiopia. Gordon resigned his position at the beginning of 1880, but was recalled to the Sudan in 1883 by the British. As part of stabilizing the situation in Egypt, they were trying to arrange an orderly withdrawal of Egyptians and foreigners from the Sudan following the unrest produced by the rise of Muhammad Ahmad.

Muhammad Ahmad was a charismatic Muslim leader who proclaimed himself the Mahdi (Islamic messiah) in 1881, leading an army of devotees calling themselves the "*ansar*" ("helpers"; alluding to Muhammad's helpers from Medina). This popular uprising was touched off in part by the stresses caused by Ismail's modernization efforts. There was a great deal of resentment among the Sudanese people that they had to provide housing for Egyptian troops and that they were being forced to work on public projects. They also did not support Ismail's appointment of non-Muslims such as Baker and Gordon to be their governors as well as being angry about his categorical suppression of the slave trade— formerly an integral part of the Sudanese economy.

By the fall of 1883, the Mahdist forces had consolidated their control over large parts of Sudan, and defeated a large Anglo-Egyptian force at al-Ubayd under the command of Colonel William Hicks. The Anglo-Egyptian forces that remained in Sudan after this defeat were now led by Gordon. They retreated to Khartoum, from where they were ordered to conduct an orderly withdrawal from the country.

After a series of tactical miscalculations, Gordon became trapped in Khartoum for a siege of nine months. In order to gain popular support, Gordon remitted taxes, made slavery legal again, and sought the help of his old adversary Zubayr Pasha, a former Sudanese slave trader, against the Mahdi's forces. None of these measures prevented Gordon from being massacred along with his troops there. While this disaster ended British and Egyptian involvement in the Sudan for another thirteen years, the problems there also became an important factor keeping the British Veiled Protectorate in place in Egypt, due to a continuing fear that the revolutionary spirit of the Mahdi and his followers might spread there as well.

Abbas Pasha and the Veiled Protectorate: 1892–1907

By the 1892 installation of Abbas II as Egypt's ruler upon the death of his father Tawfiq, Cromer's policies had stabilized the financial and security situation there. Abbas, who had studied at a military academy in Austria, saw

the British as standing in the way of his rightful assertion of power and prestige as monarch. At first, he challenged British officers who commanded Egyptian units, but Cromer forced him to retract such criticisms and gradually made him into a ruler who did not directly defy the British.

The situation in the Sudan also calmed down in the first part of his reign. Both France and Belgium had previously asserted claims over parts of southern Sudan but had given these up by the mid-1890s. A joint Anglo-Egyptian force reestablished control over the country following its triumph at the Battle of Omdurman in 1898, imposing a shared Anglo-Egyptian sovereignty there that lasted until 1956.

Despite collaborating with the British on many important issues, Abbas maintained some rapport with various anti-British elements in Egyptian politics: in the first part of his reign, with pan-Islamic activists such as Sheikh Ali Yusuf; and after 1900, more with Egyptian nationalist leaders such as Mustafa Kamil.[2] Two episodes in particular catalyzed the anti-British feeling of nationalist and Islamic Egyptians: the Taba and Dinshaway incidents of 1906. When Lord Cromer sent Anglo-Egyptian troops to assert Egyptian control over the town of Taba on the Gulf of Aqaba, they were thrown out by the Ottoman garrison there. Mustafa Kamil's newspaper used this incident to rally support for the Ottoman Sultan Abd al-Hamid II as Taba's legitimate ruler and as an Islamic sovereign not under the control of any foreign power.

At Dinshaway, a village in lower Egypt, a group of British soldiers had gone pigeon-hunting, apparently without receiving official permission from the village elder. Just as one of the British officers started to shoot, a fire broke out in a nearby grain pile. This prompted its owner to grab the officer's gun, which fired, wounding five villagers. At this

---

[2]"Pan-Islamism" as a movement had arisen from the thought of Jamal al-Din al-Afghani, who is discussed in Chapter 7.

point, the leader of the British group ordered his men to give up their guns and walk back to their vehicles. When an angry crowd of villagers surrounded and went after them, one British officer was killed. In a special tribunal created by Cromer for such cases, four villagers were sentenced to be hanged, eight flogged, and two sentenced to life in prison. These verdicts unleashed a firestorm of criticism both in Egypt and England, with George Bernard Shaw including an indictment of this case in a preface to a play he had just written about Ireland: *John Bull's Other Island.*

The negative impact of the Dinshaway incident forced Lord Cromer to resign as consul-general, but his successors, Sir Eldon Gorst and Field Marshall Herbert Kitchener, adhered to similar policies. The end of Cromer's career in Egypt coincided with the return of the Liberal Party to power in the British parliament, which may have reshaped official British attitudes toward Egypt and boosted support for its right to be autonomous. In December 1914 after the entry of the Ottoman Empire into World War I on the German side, Britain declared a formal protectorate over Egypt, formally severing its links to the Ottomans. This marked the end of Egypt's ruler (referred to since Ismail's time as the "**Khedive**") as a deputy of the Ottoman Sultan. Abbas II was deposed as the last Khedive with his uncle Husayn Kamil proclaimed as "Sultan of Egypt and the Sudan." World War I would have an important impact on Egypt, as it would on the rest of the Middle East.

IRAN CONTINUES TO MODERNIZE UNDER NASER AL-DIN SHAH

The reign of Naser al-Din Shah after his 1873 trip to Europe witnessed an increase in connections between Iran and the West in many areas. This visit had a large impact on him, since he could see firsthand what Europe had achieved after several decades of the Industrial Revolution. He captured this in a diary that he wrote on this voyage. This text was translated into English and published in Britain within one year of its production, as well as published in Persian and widely circulated in Iran at that same time. Naser al-Din Shah seemed struck by the sheer size of the crowds he encountered, becoming the central participant in well-planned modern mass events the likes of which he had never experienced at home.

He was most captivated by the Crystal Palace, the original exhibition hall for the 1851 Great Exhibition. This was the first of the World's Fairs that became so popular in the last half of the nineteenth century. The Qajar capital of Tehran began to incorporate certain influences from this trip as it started to feature broader avenues and more open palace architecture. The city began developing on a considerably expanded scale from its older, more defensive structure and layout. The *Takiye-ye Dowlat*, a new amphitheater for the performance of *taziyes* (Shii ritual plays depicting the martyrdom of Imam Husayn), was designed to make this important religious occasion into a public event resembling European "urban ceremonies" glimpsed by Naser al-Din on his trip.

The trip had been very costly, so new ways needed to be discovered to pay for it. The Shah tried to grant concessionary privileges on a number of fiscal items to the British Baron Julius de Reuter in 1873, but had been forced to cancel this under Russian pressure. In March 1890, a key concession—the monopoly on producing and selling tobacco—was granted to another Englishman, Major Gerald Talbot. This surrender of control over a commodity so basic to ordinary Iranians united the ulema and merchants in a tobacco protest and boycott. This dissent was given religious sanction by a fatwa in December 1891 issued by Mirza Mohammad Hasan Shirazi prohibiting smoking of any type until the tobacco concession was canceled. When the shah was forced to end the concession in January 1892, this demonstrated that coordination between the religious classes and the merchants in confronting the monarch could be successful. This clerical-merchant alliance has often been described as a precursor to similar coalitions leading to the **Iranian Constitutional Revolution** of 1905.

Naser al-Din Shah achieved some progress in modernization and reform, but could not go very far beyond the traditional paradigm of an absolute Iranian monarch. Iran paid a substantial price for this, suffering considerable economic, social, and political stagnation over the nearly five decades of his reign. The repressive atmosphere of the country ultimately resulted in Naser al-Din's assassination in 1896 by a frustrated nationalist/Islamic activist named Mirza Reza Kermani, just two years before he would have celebrated his royal jubilee. Kermani was a follower of **Jamal al-Din al-Afghani**, a peripatetic Islamic modernist. Under the second half of Naser al-Din's rule, Iranians became frustrated at their declining prosperity, reflected in the number of government services that had been sold off to the highest foreign bidders for the government to amass as much cash as it could. As bad as things got though, there were still reformers and dreamers such as Jamal al-Din al-Afghani thinking about how to create a better society.

ZIONISM IN NINETEENTH-CENTURY EUROPE

As modernization proceeded in Egypt and Iran, the nineteenth century saw the awakening of nationalist aspirations among many other ethnic groups across Europe and the Middle East, including Jews. For Jewish groups, the idea of returning to the ancestral homeland of Israel had remained a central theme of Jewish life for centuries: the constant desire to return to the Holy Land from various exiles and diasporas as first recorded in the Bible.

Despite ups and downs, there had been a continuous Jewish presence in Palestine since Roman times. Various movements, some with messianic leaders, had arisen through the centuries in Europe and the Middle East with the goal of leading Jews back to Israel.

In 1648, **Sabbatai Zevi** led a group of Jews traveling toward Israel through the Ottoman Empire. There, they ended up converting en masse to Islam and establishing a special community centered in the Aegean Ottoman city of Salonika (later Thessaloniki, Greece), where they became known as *donmes* (Turkish for "converts").

In addition to being augmented by the followers of messianic movements, the Jewish population of Palestine slowly grew as immigrants gradually moved there during the period of Ottoman rule that began in the sixteenth century. As rulers, the Ottomans remained relatively tolerant of Christians' and Jews' comings and goings in the Holy Land. The city of Safed became an important Jewish population center during this period, as well as Jerusalem, Hebron, and Tiberias.

European Jews and Modern Nationalism

The European Enlightenment of the eighteenth century led to a European Jewish enlightenment movement known in Hebrew as the "**Haskalah**". By the mid-nineteenth century, European Jews enjoyed a legal status in many countries more or less equal to their Christian compatriots. This new cohort of nonreligious Jews became strongly influenced by prevailing trends of rationalism, romanticism, and nationalism. The rise of modern nationalism and the creation of new nations in Europe at the same time also promoted increased levels of anti-Jewish prejudice.

What had previously been unorganized religious persecution now evolved into racial anti-semitism. Antisemites now defined Jews in pseudo-scientific terms as members of an alien religious, national, and racial group in Europe and actively sought to bar them from acquiring equal rights and citizenship. This new anti-semitism became most widespread in the Russian Empire as the century progressed.

Jews had long faced pogroms and persecution in Tsarist Russia, but ironically, pressures on them increased after the liberation of the serfs in 1861. This reform created new social groups who now saw Jews more directly as economic competitors. At the same time, official restrictions had increased for Jews in Russia beginning in 1791, when they were officially required to live only in an area known as the "Pale of Settlement" in the western part of the Empire. The Russian government imposed severe quotas on the number of Jews able to attend schools and universities or even live in cities.

Beginning in 1827, Jewish males became subject to military conscription at age twelve, which could mean twenty-five years of required service in the Russian army. Such measures, intended to destroy Jewish identity, in fact radicalized a large sector of Russian Jews and familiarized them with nationalism and socialism with greater exposure to the outside world through military service. With such pressures increasing, several million Jews left Russia between 1880 and 1928. Many immigrated to the United States and other countries in North and South America, but a few headed for Palestine. At the same time, the intellectual foundations of **Zionism** were being developed by Jewish thinkers in Western Europe. Authors such as Moses Hess argued for the creation of a modern Jewish homeland in Palestine as the best way to solve the problem of Jews never being able to assimilate fully into European society (commonly called the "Jewish question").

British and American Zionists

The idea of restoring a Jewish presence in the Holy Land also had great resonance in Britain and America at the time of the Second Great Awakening: the revival of Protestant Christianity that occurred throughout the English-speaking world during the first half of the nineteenth century. Britain established a consulate in Jerusalem in 1838, and the next year, the Presbyterian Church of Scotland sent observers to document the condition of Jews there as a way to highlight the benefits of improving and promoting a Jewish presence in Palestine.

Evangelically oriented Americans shared such sentiments. In 1842, the Mormon prophet Joseph Smith sent a representative to dedicate Palestine for the return of the Jews, and an American Protestant theologian, William Eugene Blackstone, submitted a petition in 1891 to U.S. President Benjamin Harrison calling for a Jewish return to Palestine. This gradually developed into a movement called "Restorationism." It argued for the return of the Jews to Palestine either on religious grounds, as a necessary preliminary step for Christ's Second Coming, or on the secular grounds of creating a refuge for the Jews from persecution everywhere else, particularly in Russia.

First Aliyah

Such sentiments also moved prominent Jews in Europe and the United States to donate money to help their brethren in the Ottoman Empire and to build communities in Palestine to which European Jews could move. The eminent British Jewish philanthropist Sir Moses Montefiore visited Palestine numerous times and fostered development of the Jewish community there. He helped construct the settlement of *Mishkenot Sha'ananim* ("Tranquil Dwellings" in Hebrew): the first Jewish neighborhood in Jerusalem to be built outside the ancient city walls there in 1860. In the same year, a group of French Jews founded the *Alliance Israelite Universelle* (Universal Jewish Alliance) to help defend Jewish rights and establish modern Jewish educational facilities throughout the world.

In the late 1870s, European Jewish philanthropists such as Montefiore and his family, as well as the Rothschilds, also began to sponsor agricultural settlements for Russian Jews in Palestine. The immigration of Jews in this period is known as the "First Aliyah." In Hebrew, *aliyah* means "ascent" or "going up." Jews who physically moved to the Holy Land were thus metaphorically "ascending" to a better life there, so the term *aliyah* encapsulated the basic goal of modern Zionism. Petah Tikva was the first such Zionist agricultural settlement, created in 1879. Rishon LeZion (Hebrew for: "First in Zion") was founded just south and inland from the Ottoman port of Jaffa in 1882 by a small group mostly of Ukrainian Jews know as the "Lovers of Zion," whose plan was to establish a group of Jewish agricultural settlements in Palestine.

These first outposts did not have a large immediate impact on the native Arab population. Land for them had been legally purchased according to the new Ottoman land laws, and only a few hundred people would come at any one time to any given area. Many of these early settlements did not prosper like later ones. Their members often realized that they felt more comfortable in urban settings, and about half ended up moving to towns.

Despite these issues, such communities planted the seeds for a larger Zionist and Jewish presence not merely in the cities, but in rural parts of Palestine. Their focus on the land was shared by the Zionist movement that rose to prominence in the 1890s under the aegis of **Theodor Herzl** and the World Zionist Organization.

Questions To Think About

1. How and why did the status of the British change in Egypt in the last half of the nineteenth century?
2. How did events in the Sudan affect Egypt and its politics?
3. What was the meaning of the Taba and Dinshaway incidents in Egyptian politics?
4. How was the second half of Naser al-Din Shah's reign in Iran different from the first?
5. Why did Zionism originate in nineteenth-century Europe?
6. What was the First Aliyah and what was its impact in Palestine?

For Further Reading

Amanat, Abbas. *Pivot of the Universe: Nasir Al-Din Shah Qajar and the Iranian Monarchy, 1831–1896.* Berkeley: University of California Press, 1997.

Chenevix Trench, Charles. *The Road to Khartoum: A Life of General Charles Gordon.* New York: Norton, 1979.

Churchill, Winston, and F. Rhodes. *The River War: An Historical Account of the Reconquest of the Soudan.* London: Longmans,Green and Co., 1899.

Green, Dominic. *Three Empires on the Nile: The Victorian Jihad, 1869–1899.* New York: Free Press, 2007.

Laqueur, Walter. *A History of Zionism.* London: Weidenfeld and Nicolson, 1972.

Mansfield, Peter. *The British in Egypt.* New York: Holt, Rinehart and Winston, 1972.

Mitchell, Timothy. *Colonising Egypt.* Cambridge: Cambridge University Press, 1988.

Tignor, Robert L. *Modernization and British Colonial Rule in Egypt, 1882–1914.* Princeton, NJ: Princeton University Press, 1966.

Vital, David. *The Origins of Zionism.* Oxford: Clarendon Press, 1975.

7

Responses to Increased European Presence

ALTERNATIVE REACTIONS TO CHANGE

Abdulhamid II Rediscovers Muslim Symbols

With the Balkans finally quiet after the end of the Russo-Turkish War of 1877–1878, Abdulhamid turned his attention to consolidating political control and bolstering the empire's financial and strategic situation. Like Egypt, the central Ottoman government had spent beyond its means to modernize during the Tanzimat. By 1881, an Ottoman Public Debt Administration was created to administer the finances of the empire on behalf of a group of European bankers. Unlike in Egypt, European intervention in the affairs of the central Ottoman Empire never went beyond the financial sector, so that Abdulhamid was able to function as an absolute ruler for most of the three decades that he remained in power.

He tried to rule with an "enlightened absolutism." Abdulhamid promoted Islamic values and governed with an iron fist, while simultaneously encouraging economic and technological development. It is revealing that he never abolished the 1876 constitution and the parliament it created. He claimed that he had merely suspended it until such time when the empire had attained sufficient stability for democratic government to function smoothly. All critics who decried such hypocrisy were ruthlessly suppressed, but Abdulhamid did manage to extend the life of the Ottoman Empire for several decades. This was at a time when observers had for years been predicting its imminent natural demise as the "sick man of Europe," already described by the Russian Tsar Nicholas I in the 1850s.

Abdulhamid relied on Islamic sources of legitimacy more directly than his immediate predecessors by asserting more forcefully a claim to be recognized as caliph. The Ottomans had referred to their sultan as caliph more and more since the 1774 Treaty of Kuchuk Kaynarja allowed the Ottoman ruler to retain religious authority as caliph over Crimean Muslims now ruled politically by Russia. By the late nineteenth century, the title "caliph" had a greater international impact. In india,

The Print Collector/Alamy

Sultan Abdulhamid II (1842–1918)

Muslim intellectuals had taken up the cause of pan-Islamic unity, arguing that Abdulhamid II could legitimately assert authority over the larger world Muslim community if he were recognized by all as caliph: a position he was glad to promote from afar.

At the same time, Abdulhamid sought to strengthen his European alliances, forging closer ties with the new unified Germany (since 1871) of Kaiser Wilhelm II. The Ottomans admired Germany for how it combined techno-logical and scientific achievement with a robust tradition of strong monarchical power. There had been extensive cooperation between the Ottoman and German (previously Prussian) militaries since the early Tanzimat era, with Prussian Field Marshall Helmuth von Moltke serving early in his career as a military adviser to the Ottoman army during the late 1830s. By the 1890s, Germany was also helping the Ottomans build their infrastructure through such projects as the Anatolian, Baghdad, and Hejaz Railways. In Ottoman eyes, Germany's new status as a major European power usefully balanced Britain, France, and Russia, with their longstanding imperialist agendas.

Hamidiyan Modernization: The Case of the Red Crescent Society

If the Tanzimat can been characterized as the "opening" of Ottoman society, particularly to the concepts of political liberalism, the reign of Abdulhamid II (known as the "Hamidiyan" era) can be contrasted to this as a more conservative era, in which the empire became less open to innovation while the sultan focused more on its defense and preservation. However, it can be viewed as a time when he allowed modernization programs begun in the Tanzimat era to continue, but to be presented with more deference shown to traditional values. One example **is the Ottoman Red Crescent Society**. This organization, a component of the original Geneva Convention (which the Ottomans joined in 1868), embodied the spirit of civic voluntarism and international linkage that arose during the Tanzimat period, yet its activities did not cease during the reign of Abdulhamid II.

Under him, the Ottoman Red Crescent Society became part of a policy to maintain the sultan's image as guardian of the Islamic *umma* and Muslim tradition on one hand, while presenting him as a progressive and modern European monarch on the other. Modernization could continue, but through the more gradual evolution of "tacit knowl-edge" that lay behind the workings of modern society and government: a "tacit knowledge" that remained hidden behind a façade but was still evident in Red Crescent activities.

This can be seen with the adoption of The Red Crescent symbol in November 1876. The Swiss administrators of the Red Cross Movement first balked at this, arguing that the original Red Cross was nothing but the Swiss flag in reverse with no ostensible reli-gious meaning. The Ottoman government was requesting permission to use the Red Crescent, because the Red Cross had offended its Muslim soldiers on the battlefield and pre-vented the Ottomans from exercising their Geneva Convention rights. Such an appeal to Swiss practicality prompted the International

Red Cross to approve this change for the duration of armed conflict only. Many more years of discussion ensued, after which use of the Red Crescent symbol was finally made permanent. This provided a lasting way to honor both Islamic values as well as the concept of a community of nations embodied in the Red Cross Movement.

After the end of the First Constitutional Period in 1878 and Abdulhamid's seizure of absolute power, Tanzimat institutions such as the Red Crescent Society became perceived as potential political threats, yet the Society continued to function and expand its mission. Throughout this period, the Ottomans were mindful of the swiftly rising status of the international Red Cross movement as well as increasingly negative reports in the Western press about Ottomans' treatment of their Christian subjects. Such coverage led the American Red Cross to dispatch a relief mission to the Armenians in 1896 to Anatolia led by its founder, Clara Barton. The Ottoman government at first impeded this mission's activities, but Abdulhamid in the end bestowed a medal on Barton never before awarded to a woman. This can be explained as a mere diplomatic gesture, but it did signal Ottoman acknowledgment of the international cachet of this world organization. Abdulhamid accepted, even if only tacitly, that humanitarian service was something to be rewarded in a "modern" context.

As a result of this evolution, the Ottomans soon found themselves receiving and supporting international humanitarian assistance in ways that before would have been unimaginable. The sultan accepted the donation of a Russian field hospital during the brief 1897 Greco-Turkish war. The Ottoman Red Crescent itself then donated medical supplies to both sides in the 1905 Russo-Japanese War.

As in all areas of Ottoman life at this time, though, the problem of finances still loomed large over the affairs of the Ottoman Red Crescent Society. Soon after approving the Society's request for funds to donate medical supplies to both sides in the Russo-Japanese War, the sultan sent a letter to the grand vizier inquiring about how much money the Red Crescent Society then controlled, and officials immediately tried to lay hands on this sum. Dellasuda Faik Pasha, a prominent military medical commander and a member of the Society's board of directors, stopped them from requisitioning all of the group's funds, but it was not easy to defend its operating budget from the grasp of a needy Imperial treasury.

Nationalisms: "Young Ottomans," "Young Turks," and Others

During the Tanzimat period, a clear interest arose in cultivating an "Ottoman" sense of identity, reflected by the adoption of an Ottoman national flag and national anthem in the 1840s. As revealed in the writings of one of its most prominent members, the playwright and poet Namik Kemal (1840–1888), the "Young Ottoman" group had tried to forge a new identity based on a shared sense of "Ottoman" values.

This began with a "modern" reading of traditional Islamic principles in an Ottoman context. The nation was to be identified with the *umma*, or Islamic community, in a manner closely modeled on Enlightenment concepts of the nation. The sultan (now increasingly also called the "caliph") became defined as the defender of the *umma*'s rights and as the ruler implicitly chosen by its members, defense of whose individual freedoms (for which Kemal used the Turkish/Arabic word "*hurriyet*") constituted the ultimate basis of political sovereignty.

Kemal consciously adopted the Turkish/Arabic term "*vatan*" to translate the French *patrie* ("fatherland" or homeland"). This blurred the distinction between the words *vatan* and *umma*, which otherwise represented quite distinct concepts of "nation" versus "religious community." As a reaction to this, Kemal's intellectual heirs such as **Ziya Gokalp** eventually adopted a far more specific definition of *vatan* as "homeland or nation of a particular ethnic group," in place of the earlier, looser definition just as "nation."

In the late Tanzimat era, intellectual leaders in the Young Ottoman movement moved to various European cities to escape severe constraints imposed on all political activities within the Ottoman Empire itself. Except for the brief period of openness between December 1876 and February 1878 after the proclamation of the first Ottoman constitution, Abdulhamid would not abide experiments in free expression, quashing all open political discussion and forcing dissident groups underground or into exile.

To defend his regime, Abdulhamid created a secret police rivaling the Okhrana: the legendary intelligence apparatus of the Russian tsar. He also adopted another tactic from the Russians by organizing Kurdish horsemen into special units known as "Hamidiye" regiments modeled on the Cossacks. They were assigned to enforce the sultan's writ over the many ethnic groups of the Empire, which included Armenians. This resulted a series of very bloody attacks by **Hamidiye units** against Armenians in 1895–1896: the very situation that had prompted Clara Barton's visit.

Despite this tightening of political controls, not all dissent could be suppressed. The growing worldliness and sophistication of students at the modern schools established during the Tanzimat period and before meant that covert political discussion groups began to form to debate how modernization should continue in the Empire. In 1889, a small group of students at the Ottoman Imperial Military Medical School (one Albanians, two Kurds, and an Azeri) formed a secret society known first as the Committee of Ottoman Union.

This was the forerunner of the Committee of Union and Progress: the most important component of the movement known in Europe as the "Young Turks." The Young Turks included proponents of many different sorts of governments and ideologies. What generally united them though, was some shared vision of the importance of popular sovereignty: a real challenge, however defined, to longstanding concepts of the monarchical legitimacy of the Ottoman dynasty.

Support for "popular sovereignty" became a common thread in many nationalist movements that emerged in the Ottoman Empire during the late nineteenth century, but with vastly different definitions of what this phrase meant. For example, two Armenian nationalist revolutionary movements active in the Ottoman Empire after the 1880s, the *Hinchak* ("Bell") and *Dashnaktsutiun* ("Federation") groups, both championed popular sovereignty and self-determination, but in the context of creating a nation for the Armenian people with less attention given to the status of other ethnic groups in the Ottoman Empire.

On other hand, the multiethnic nationalism that had been part of "Ottomanism" in the Tanzimat period and beyond still remained an ideal to inspire many **Young Turks**. This concept ultimately proved a useful way to unite disparate nationalist groups in support of the 1908 revolution that launched the Second Constitutional period. In the end, such an inclusive concept was pushed aside by more nationalist and exclusive views of ethnic identity. The evolutionary process of all these political philosophies was continually stymied by the severe repression of political discussion and activity that continued during most of Abdulhamid's time in power.

Religious Revival Movements: Return to the Original *Umma*

Parallel to the emergence of nationalist and religious ideologies in the mainstream of Ottoman politics, the nineteenth century also witnessed the rise of popular Islamic religious revival movements on the margins of the Ottoman Empire. Such movements developed either as rejections of Ottoman Islam as a corruption of "pure" Islam, or appeared as resistance movements in areas newly conquered by expanding European empires. Despite their diversity in location and activities, a common goal of these movements was to revive and restore rules of the *umma* in Medina as led by Muhammad: the ideal of Islamic government and society. "Rejectionist" revivalism was epitomized by the Wahhabis in Arabia and the followers of the Mahdi in the Sudan, while Abd al-Qadir in Algeria and Imam Shamil in the Caucasus are among the best examples of "resistance" revivalist leaders of this era.

As noted, the Wahhabi movement had arisen among the Saudi tribal confederation in the mid-eighteenth century as it fell under the influence of a Muslim cleric originally from the town of Uyayna in the Nejd region of the central Arabian Peninsula, Muhammad ibn Abd al-Wahhab (1703–1792). After he studied Islamic law in Basra, he performed the hajj pilgrimage. When he returned home to the Nejd, he became famous for preaching forcefully against *bida* (Arabic: "innovation") and *shirk* (Arabic: "polytheism") in Islamic practice. In one sermon against *bida*, he called for an adulteress to be stoned as a way to adhere more precisely to original principles of Islamic justice revealed to Muhammad. His admonition to destroy a venerated saint's tomb became part of a campaign against paying homage to any person or thing beyond God's revealed word and the words and deeds of Muhammad in his capacity as God's final messenger. When Muhammad ibn Abd al-Wahhab's uncompromising approach to Islamic law prompted the rulers of Uyayna to throw him out, he found refuge with the Saudis in Diriya.

Like most tribes in the Nejd, the economic basis of the Saudis' lives had been long-distance transit trade across the Arabian Peninsula, as well as income generated by raiding other tribes and settlements in the region. Soon after Muhammad ibn Abd al-Wahhab took refuge with them in the 1740s, they pledged to follow his interpretation of Islam. This was an important step to take, because when the Saudis as a group made this commitment, their rigorous approach to Muslim belief and practice became the foundation for a very powerful tribal coalition that ultimately resulted in the creation of modern Saudi Arabia as a nation in the early twentieth century.

Wahhabi doctrine gave purpose to their activity, because it justified raids on non-Saudi Muslims as actions against people who could be considered heretics or apostates due to failure to adhere to Islamic law as strictly defined. It also championed a puritan ethos for their life in central Arabia not far removed from the traditions of the original Islamic forebears in Mecca and Medina. The first two organized Saudi states (1744–1818 and 1824–1891) were essentially tribal confederations that extended control over a large part of the Nejd region and sections of the Persian Gulf coast. All of these areas were relatively marginal to the Ottomans and to European powers moving into the region, except when the Saudis captured Mecca and Medina in 1802: an unacceptable territorial loss for the Ottomans.

At this point, the Ottoman sultan sought the help of Egyptian ruler Muhammad Ali to recover the Holy Cities. An Egyptian force led by his son Ibrahim Pasha destroyed the Saudi army in 1818, razing their hometown of Diriya completely and forcing their leaders into exile. Despite this huge setback, another branch of the Saudi family managed to reestablish a Saudi state centered in Riyadh by 1824. It endured until 1891, maintaining a Wahhabi ideology, although controlling a smaller territory than before. The Saudis remained an aggravation as desert raiders, but since the main trade routes of this era were either maritime or through areas more stably under Ottoman control, they did not present a major threat to international trade or the circulation of pilgrims after Mecca and Medina had been retaken from them.

Another instance of "rejectionist" revivalism occurred in the Sudan. There, Muhammad Ahmad proclaimed himself the Mahdi (the "promised Muslim messiah") in 1881 and created a state based on novel readings of Islamic holy texts that also included instructions communicated by God to Muhammad Ahmad in nightly visions. The recitation of the Islamic testament of faith ("*shahada*") was modified to include the phrase "and Muhammad Ahmad is the Mahdi of God and representative of His Prophet." Within the five pillars, "service in holy war" replaced the hajj pilgrimage as a duty incumbent on the faithful and *zakat* (almsgiving) became equated with tax paid to the Mahdi's state. Such an innovative vision of an Islamic state and its law was immediately denounced by Muslim clerics outside of this state as *bida* (innovation), thus supremely antithetical to the Wahhabi Islamic doctrine described above. Nevertheless, the Mahdi's proclamation of the Ottoman Turks as "infidels" to be resisted echoed the Wahhabi view of them.

The other broad category of Islamic revivalism in the nineteenth century was a "resistance" revivalism promoted by Muslim leaders resisting European colonial expansion, typified by the struggles of Abd al-Qadir (ruled 1830–1847 in Algeria) and Imam Shamil (ruled 1830–1859 in the Caucasus). In both cases, these resistance movements were led by charismatic warriors affiliated with the international **Naqshbandi** Sufi brotherhood, who imposed strict codes of morality and behavior on their followers based on a return to the "original" rules of the Islamic *umma*. Once these "resistance" leaders had been defeated and co-opted by their European adversaries, their movements disbanded fairly quickly. They became remembered during later struggles, such as the Algerian War of Independence of the 1950s and the Russian-Chechen War of the 1990s, not so much as religious leaders, but as early defenders of local sovereignty against European imperialism.

THINKING ABOUT CHANGE IN NEW WAYS

Jamal al-Din "al-Afghani": Peripatetic Muslim Philosopher

While the impact of the West was felt in different ways at the popular level, it prompted members of the educated elite in the Middle East and the greater Islamic world to probe the root causes of the diminished standing of Islam in modern times. They sought answers to contemporary Muslim problems through a "modern" application of Islamic precepts and principles. Foremost among them was Jamal al-Din "al-Afghani" (1838–1897). He was apparently born and spent his childhood in Afghanistan (although he may have been originally of Iranian origin), but subsequently spent time in India, Egypt, Istanbul, and various cities in Europe.

He began his career as a court tutor in Afghanistan after undergoing a classical education in Islamic legal studies, rhetoric, and logic. He departed after ten years when a new ruler took power. His travels eventually brought him to Cairo and then Istanbul, where he was invited to give a series of lectures at various mosques and universities. His approach to Islamic studies was deemed too modernist and avant-garde by some conservative Ottoman clerics, who criticized him so strongly that he left Istanbul and went back to Cairo after only a few months in March 1871.

There, Khedive Ismail granted him a stipend. Al-Afghani became a resident public intellectual whose discourses, lectures, and discussions on many issues and subjects attracted a large following of young Egyptians. Some later rose to prominence, including Saad Zaghloul and **Muhammad Abduh**. Al-Afghani in particular cultivated relationships with young journalists and writers who went on to found numerous journals and newspapers.

When Ismail was replaced by his son Tawfiq in 1879 at the behest of the British and the French, al-Afghani was expelled from Egypt. He had attracted the hostility of conservative Egyptian clerics and was not trusted by the British, so he ended up going back to India. There, while living and giving lectures in Hyderabad, he composed his longest work: *Refutation of the Materialists*.

This included a kind of modern Muslim version of Plato's *Republic* that envisioned a society founded on basic Islamic values, such as maintaining a sense of shame, being trustworthy, and telling the truth, while promoting the development of human intelligence, strengthening pride, and promoting global justice. Al-Afghani argued that loss of belief in God and religion had doomed certain states in history, implying that this might be happening in Europe now through the influence of materialism on culture.

By 1883, he had moved to London, where he met Wilfrid Scawen Blunt (1840–1922), a famous British anti-imperialist poet and great champion of Egyptian nationalism. That same year, he went on to Paris. There, he published a refutation of the French orientalist Ernest Renan, since Renan had argued in a recent article that Islam was essentially unscientific and even antiscientific. Al-Afghani conceded that although the current state of Islamic discourse could support the idea that Islam was against science, he made the case that such an antiscientific stance went against centuries of Islamic thought that revered science and its methods.

Soon Muhammad Abduh joined al-Afghani in Paris, where together they published a newspaper, *al-Urwa al-Wuthqa* (*The Firm Bond*), between March and October 1884. Although banned and suppressed by British authorities in India and Egypt, it was distributed free of charge and did have some international impact. It attacked British activities in the Muslim world and called on Muslims to confront this challenge by rediscovering the strengths of their religion. In addition, the journal called on Muslims to embrace modern science and technology, which, it argued, had been wrongly cast aside. The articles in this journal provided among the earliest expressions of Pan-Islamic thought: the idea that Muslims worldwide should be more united.

In 1885, Abduh and al-Afghani parted ways, with Abduh focusing on more pragmatic activities to reform Muslim education while al-Afghani continued to pursue dreams of Islamic unity and traveled around Europe for a few more years. The Iranian ruler Naser al-Din Shah apparently heard about him at this time and invited him to Iran. He stayed there only briefly, since his increasing popularity and influence soon made the shah jealous. From Iran, he went to Russia for three years, where he lobbied Tsar Alexander III on behalf of Russian Muslims.

Al-Afghani was traveling to the 1889 Paris World's Fair, when he ran into Naser al-Din Shah again in Munich. The shah persuaded him to come back to Iran, but al-Afghani again so aroused Naser al-Din's jealousy after another short stay there that he was forced to take refuge in a holy shrine near Tehran. After he had stayed a few months there, the Shah threw him out of the country, and al-Afghani became his implacable opponent.

Al-Afghani's letter denouncing the Iranian Tobacco Concession and the Shah's corruption prompted a Shii cleric in Ottoman Iraq to issue a fatwa forbidding Muslims to smoke tobacco until the Iranian government canceled the concession. This declaration became part of what led to the 1891–1892 Tobacco Rebellion. Al-Afghani spent the next year back in London, publishing a litany of articles and giving lectures that denounced Qajar rule. He addressed his discussions in particular to Iranian clerics, who responded by supporting the popular reform movement that ultimately led to the 1905 Iranian Constitutional Revolution.

In a final curious episode, al-Afghani spent the last few years of his life as an invited guest of Abdulhamid II. Abdulhamid by this time had become a strong supporter of Pan-Islamism, and he perceived that al-Afghani might be most useful to him if he were kept close at hand. The sultan held regular audiences with al-Afghani, who was provided with a house in Istanbul near the royal residence at the Yildiz chalet overlooking the Bosphorus. As on earlier occasions, the rivalry and jealousy of Ottoman clerics finally caught up with him, and they spread intrigues about him in order to weaken his relationship with the sultan. When al-Afghani died from cancer in early 1897, one year after Naser al-Din Shah had been assassinated by one of al-Afghani's loyal followers, it was rumored that certain Ottoman clerics had arranged for his doctors to provide him with inadequate treatment.

Jamal al-Din al-Afghani wrote only a few lengthy pieces, since most of his writings were articles and pamphlets providing quick commentaries on current events. His work blended conventional Muslim religious condemnation of unbelief with sharp criticisms of the impact of modern Western imperialism and praise for parts of modern Western science. He packaged his discourses as appeals to Muslim unity, but also as calls on Muslims to adopt aspects of Western science and its institutions that might strengthen their faith.

His eclectic approach was shaped by the twists and turns of his career. In addition to providing a modern Muslim recasting of Plato's *Republic*, his 1881 *Refutation of the Materialists* included one of the earliest Islamic critiques of Darwin's *On the Origin of Species*. Its somewhat confused account of Darwin's theories suggests that al-Afghani might not have read Darwin's work very carefully before commenting on it. He accepted natural selection as valid, claiming it to have been been long understood by Muslim scholars, but disputed Darwin's account of evolution from apes to men. For al-Afghani, Darwin failed to explain the origin of the human soul: God's sacred gift to mankind from a Muslim perspective.

In political discussions, al-Afghani did not always insist on promoting constitutional government, but harped on the need to overthrow Muslim rulers who had been too lax or subservient to foreigners. He had been greatly disappointed by the failure of the 1857–1858 Indian Mutiny to end British rule of India. In examining this failure, he concluded that European imperialism, having conquered India, now threatened the Middle East. In al-Afghani's view, this Western onslaught could only be prevented if Middle Easterners immediately adopted modern Western technology. At the same time, he called for relying on Islam as an effective vehicle for mass mobilization against Western imperialism.

Although al-Afghani called for Muslim unity, he did not believe that all Muslims necessarily had to be united under one ruler. Instead, cooperation among Muslim nations would prove the best way to thwart Western encroachment. In al-Afghani's view, Islam and Sharia law were compatible with scientific rationality, permitting modern Western techniques and methods to be harmonized easily with a traditional Islamic social morality.

Muhammad Abduh

The philosophy of al-Afghani had a profound effect on Muhammad Abduh (1849–1905), an Egyptian who became one of the great champions of Muslim educational reform in the early modern era. Abduh was a very bright student from a peasant family who managed to end up studying at al-Azhar. He met al-Afghani just after he arrived in Cairo. They quickly established close ties. Abduh spent several years exploring different genres of classical and modern Islamic scholarly texts under al-Afghani's guidance. Inspired by him, Abduh branched out to use texts not conventionally taught in Islamic schools when he became an instructor himself, such as the Arabic translation of a modern French history and the *Muqaddima* of Ibn Khaldun.

When Khedive Ismail was deposed as Egypt's ruler and al-Afghani kicked out of the country, Abduh had to spend a year back in his home village, but was soon appointed as chief editor of an important government newspaper under the new khedive, Tawfiq. While serving in this post, he advocated for the modernization of school curricula and instruction in Egypt. In 1882, he was sent into exile for supporting the Urabi revolt and eventually linked up again with al-Afghani in Paris. Between 1885 and 1888, Abduh lived in Beirut, teaching and writing extensively on classical Islamic literature, as well as translating some of al-Afghani's works, mostly written in Persian, into Arabic. Abduh was also active as a journalist and helped establish a society to promote friendship between Muslims, Christians, and Jews.

He finally was allowed to return to Egypt, but not permitted at first to teach. Abduh was finally appointed chief mufti (religious scholar) in 1899, in which capacity he served until his death in 1905. He spent this time engaged in numerous projects and served on numerous commissions dedicated to educational reform. Abduh was always a much stronger advocate of representative government than his mentor al-Afghani. His views became widely circulated in the Muslim world through his monthly journal *al-Manar* (*The Lighthouse*), a publication edited by his student Rashid Rida. In some respects, Abduh's actual works, being more substantial than al-Afghani's, had more lasting influence across the Muslim world, but the vigorous approach to reform and modernization of both scholars continues to influence Muslim intellectuals today.

BUILDING NEW ALLEGIANCES

"Arab Awakening" and the Arab Press

Print culture had gradually expanded since the widespread introduction of presses and newspapers in the Middle East in the 1820s and 1830s. Around forty new journals and fifteen newspapers were established in Beirut alone between 1870 and 1900. The rapid growth of journalism, coupled with rising literacy rates promoted by modernizing educational systems, spawned an intellectual renaissance in the Arab world later called "*al-Nahda*" (the Awakening), whose beginnings trace back to the late eighteenth century. This movement, regarded as the genesis of Arab nationalism and the later ideology of Pan-Arabism, championed the union of all Arabic-speaking peoples into one nation. It thus helped define the first version of what became one of the main Middle Eastern political ideologies through much of the twentieth century.

One of its earliest proponents, Abd al-Rahman al-Kawakibi (1849–1902) received

a conventional Ottoman education, being born into and brought up in a family of notables in Aleppo. He worked there in local administration through the 1890s, but clashed with the local governor over censorship issues as Sultan Abdulhamid II tightened restrictions on free speech. When he had his property confiscated as punishment for opposing the government, he was forced to move to Cairo in 1898.

Al-Kawakibi had first gotten into trouble with the Ottoman censors in the 1870s by helping publish several journals and newspapers that criticized government activities. His two books, which he waited to publish until after he had been exiled to Egypt, drew extensively on arguments presented in Western works but situated them in a Middle Eastern context. One was *Umm al-Qura*, first published as a book but then made popular as a series of articles in Muhammad Abduh's *al-Manar*. Its arguments built on Wilfred Blunt's *The Future of Islam* (1882) by arguing that the Muslim caliph ought to be a member of the Quraysh family, with the general capital of the Muslim world relocated to Mecca.

Al-Kawakibi's view was that this Arab caliph would possess political authority only over the Hejaz, but enjoy wider spiritual authority as a prominent Muslim Arab religious and cultural figure. This presented a clear challenge to the conventional wisdom at this time that the Ottoman sultan was the legitimate caliph. Al-Kawakibi's other extended work was an adaptation of an denunciation of tyrants from the Napoleonic era, Vittorio Alfieri's *Della Tirannide*, called in Arabic *Tabai al-Istibdad* (*The Nature of Tyranny*). Coincidentally, a Turkish version of this work was published in Istanbul around the same time by Ottoman reformer Abdullah Jevdet Pasha.

Al-Kawakibi was not the only opponent of authoritarian rule or proponent of Arab autonomy at this time. One of the very first secret societies to espouse the cause of Arab political separation from the Ottomans was formed in 1875 by students at the Syrian Protestant College (SPC): an American

Protestant missionary school founded in 1866 and renamed the American University of Beirut (AUB) in 1920. American Protestant missionary schools played an increasingly important role in the dissemination of ideas among Arab intellectuals in Syria and Lebanon by the end of the nineteenth century. Americans had established more than thirty schools there by mid-century, partly due to this area's rapidly increasing political autonomy from the Empire's central administration.

AUB became one of the main incubators of the **Arab Awakening**, because of how it provided a congenial place for Middle Eastern students to explore ways of thinking about politics and other things far removed from their own world. Many of the college's early instructors had an overt Christian proselytizing agenda, and its enrollment had been restricted at first to Christian Ottoman students. Within a relatively short period of time, the tenor of its courses became more secular as it focused on creating an intellectual atmosphere to promote contemporary Western culture and methods of learning. Along with other European-sponsored universities in Beirut, its impact extended far beyond its own student body and campus as it began to attract a diverse cohort of students from a wide variety of countries.

Edward Said, in his groundbreaking 1978 study *Orientalism,* examines how missionaries and other Westerners intimately involved in the Middle East constructed an Oriental "other" based more on romantic concepts of the Middle East than on the realities of the region itself. This "other" then could be classified as inferior, dominated, and controlled in ways that hopelessly distorted Western perceptions of the Middle East. Said's argument provides a powerful analytical tool for thinking about how Western perceptions of the Middle East have shaped Western behavior toward it, but its analysis reveals only parts of the picture.

An example of the complexity of comparing different perceptions can be seen by contrasting local and foreign views of the impact of this school. One contemporary account, for instance, by an American missionary teacher at the Syrian Protestant College (SPC) in the early twentieth century described a track meet that he had witnessed there. For him, the success of this American-style event powerfully demonstrated the power of competitive sports to erase consciousness of ethnicity, class, and religious distinctions: providing a classic expression of the progressive spirit guiding American educational theory at that time.

From a local perspective, in contrast, one of the most enduring associations of Middle Easterners with the American University of Beirut was its renowned medical school and hospital. The SPC's School of Medicine was established in 1867 and merged in 1887 with the Prussian Hospital for Clinical Teaching to provide inpatient care. In 1902, the College established a 200-bed hospital with pioneering wards for gynecology, obstetrics, and children's diseases. This led to the AUB Medical Center becoming one of the best respected medical institutions in the Middle East today, where it is still considered a major health care "safety net" for Lebanon and the region.

Butrus al-Bustani: Creating "Modern" Arabic

One striking aspect of these new schools from the local perspective was that all this modern knowledge was no longer filtered through the centuries of commentaries and interpretations, as in the style of the classical Islamic madrasa system. Through printed materials, individuals suddenly came face-to-face with a flood of new ideas and styles of learning. For Arabic, the development of a modern press and the establishment of these new schools helped create a modernized version of the written language, now called "Modern Standard Arabic," still used today all over the Arab world.

One of the greatest contributors to this language modernization was Butrus al-Bustani (1819–1883), a Lebanese Christian peasant long associated with the American missionaries in Beirut who went on to found his own "National School" in 1863. It adopted pedagogical techniques used by the missionaries in their schools. Al-Bustani produced the first modern translation of the Bible into Arabic as well as the first modern Arabic dictionary and encyclopedia.

In 1860, he published *Nafir Suriya* (*An Appeal to Syria*), in he which he called for national solidarity to transcend religious identities. He argued that the conflicts that enmeshed his homeland were caused either by Europeans or power-hungry local rulers. His call for his compatriots to embrace a common "Syrian" identity, paralleling the Young Ottomans' appeal to "Ottomanism," marked another tentative attempt to build group loyalty beyond dynastic and religious allegiances. The first decade of the twentieth century would mark the culmination of attempts to define various national and political identities in the Middle East through constitutional revolutions in Iran and the Ottoman Empire whose impacts endure to the present.

Theodor Herzl: Creating "Modern" Zionism

Within the Ottoman province of Syria, the late nineteenth century also saw the number of Zionist settlers in Ottoman Palestine gradually increase until by 1909, the first Zionist city, **Tel Aviv**, was founded there. Tel Aviv was named after the capital city in Theodor Herzl's *Old-New Land* (1897), a speculative novel about a future Jewish state in Palestine. Herzl's other work, the *Jewish State* (1896), had even more impact. It presented a plan for a Jewish state that caught the imagination of Jews worldwide and catapulted Herzl to the leadership of the Zionist movement when it became formally established at the first World Zionist Congress in Basel, Switzerland, in 1897.

As a well-assimilated Austrian Jewish journalist, Herzl had been profoundly shocked while covering the Dreyfus Affair when he lived in Paris. This was an 1894 espionage case in which a French Jewish army officer, Alfred Dreyfus, was wrongly convicted of spying in a trial that revealed far greater anti-semitic feelings in France than assimilated Jews had realized were there. The depth of anti-semitism in France, the first country in Europe to grant Jews equal legal rights, led many to question future Jewish prospects in *any* Christian European society. This caused many to agree with the case that Herzl soon presented for the creation of a Jewish state, as a way to enable Jews to join the family of nations and escape anti-semitism for once and for all.

The first congress of the World Zionist Organization agreed that the basic goal of Zionism was to establish a home for the Jewish people in Palestine "secured under public law." To achieve this, the congress envisioned settling Jewish farmers, artisans, and manufacturers in Palestine, strengthening general consciousness of Jewish identity in Jewish communities around the globe, and securing the consent of foreign governments, if necessary, to establish a Jewish national home in Palestine. At the time, this was generally understood to mean getting legal permission from the Ottomans for Jewish immigration to the Holy Land, with the word "home" substituted for "state" and "public law" used for "international law" to avoid alarming the Ottoman ruler.

The Organization's first goal was to get the Ottoman sultan to allow Jewish settlement in Palestine by keeping up a constant small-scale Jewish immigration there. This was to be combined with setting up the **Jewish National Fund** (a charity to buy land for Jewish settlement) and the Anglo-Palestine Bank (a bank created to provide loans for Jewish businesses and farmers) in Ottoman Palestine. Although Britain offered land in 1903 for a Jewish state in East Africa, where it then controlled large territories as colonies, Zionist leaders quickly rejected this offer, since most people they hoped to persuade to immigrate to Palestine would reject it.

When the Zionist movement decided that it would also promote a Jewish cultural renaissance in Palestine by rethinking how timeless religious truths might be made more relevant to the modern world, this created a rift with Orthodox Jews that was hard to heal. At this time, many leaders of the liberal Reform Jewish movement in Europe opposed Zionism, because they saw it as inconsistent with the need for Jews to function as citizens in secular states where they were to be considered equal to everyone else.

Competing Future Visions: Zionism and the Bund

The most serious opponent of the Zionist movement in Europe became the General Jewish Labor Union, commonly known as the "Bund." Formed in Vilnius (now the capital of Lithuania, but then in the Russian Empire) in 1897, it called for Jewish autonomy within Eastern Europe, promoted Yiddish as the official Jewish language, and espoused socialism as its economic system. As socialists, some members of the Bund saw Zionism as a form of bourgeois nationalism. The Bund's influence among many Zionists, though, led to the development of Socialist Zionism: a kind of meeting of the two ideologies, which competed with the Bund for Jewish support in Europe. **Socialist Zionists** played key roles in the Second Aliyah, the wave of Jewish immigration mostly from the Russian Empire between 1904 and 1914.

Questions to Think About

1. How did Abdulhamid II try to strengthen his power and authority as Ottoman Sultan?
2. How did the Ottoman Red Crescent Society exemplify what happened to Ottoman organizations under Abdulhamid that were founded in the Tanzimat period?
3. How did Namik Kemal and the Young Ottomans try to promote an Ottoman national identity?
4. What united the Young Turks politically?
5. What were the tensions in the late nineteenth-century Ottoman Empire between religious identity and national identity?
6. What types of popular religious revival movements existed in the Middle East in the eighteenth and nineteenth centuries, and what goals did they have in common?
7. How did Jamal al-Din al-Afghani attempt to reconcile Islam and modern science?
8. What was the "Arab Awakening"
9. Who was Theodor Herzl, and why did he become one of the founders of the Zionist movement?

For Further Reading

Adams, Charles C. *Islam and Modernism in Egypt.* New York: Routledge, 2000.

Amanat, Abbas. *Pivot of the Universe: Nasir Al-Din Shah Qajar and the Iranian Monarchy, 1831–1896.* Berkeley: University of California Press, 1997.

Antonius, George. *The Arab Awakening; The Story of the Arab National Movement.* New York: Capricorn Books, 1965.

Davison, Roderic H. *Reform in the Ottoman Empire, 1856–1876.* New York: Gordian Press, 1973.

DeLong-Bas, Natana J. *Wahhabi Islam: From Revival and Reform to Global Jihad.* Oxford: Oxford University Press, 2004.

Deringil, Selim. *The Well-Protected Domains: Ideology and the Legitimation of Power in the Ottoman Empire, 1876–1909.* London: I.B. Tauris, 1999.

Herzl, Theodor, and Lotta Levensohn. *Old New Land.* Princeton, NJ: M. Wiener, 1997.

Herzl, Theodor. *The Jewish State* (complete text online at: http://www.jewishvirtuallibrary.org/jsource/Zionism/herzl2.html).

Holt, P. M. *The Mahdist State in the Sudan, 1881–1898: A Study of Its Origins, Development and Overthrow*. Oxford: Clarendon Press, 1963.

Hourani, Albert. *Arabic Thought in the Liberal Age, 1798–1939*. Cambridge: Cambridge University Press, 1983.

Keddie, Nikki R. *Sayyid Jamal ad-Din "Al-Afghani": A Political Biography*. Berkeley: University of California Press, 1972.

Laqueur, Walter. *A History of Zionism*. London: Weidenfeld and Nicolson, 1972.

Mansfield, Peter. *The British in Egypt*. New York: Holt, Rinehart and Winston, 1972.

Mardin, Şerif. *The Genesis of Young Ottoman Thought: A Study in the Modernization of Turkish Political Ideas*. Princeton, NJ: Princeton University Press, 1962.

Pawel, Ernst. *The Labyrinth of Exile: A Life of Theodor Herzl*. New York: Farrar, Straus & Giroux, 1989.

Tignor, Robert L. *Modernization and British Colonial Rule in Egypt, 1882–1914*. Princeton, NJ: Princeton University Press, 1966.

Winder, R. Bayly. *Saudi Arabia in the Nineteenth Century*. London: Macmillan, 1966.

8

Experiments in Popular Sovereignty

MOZAFFAR AL-DIN SHAH: TENSIONS IN LATE QAJAR IRAN

It is ironic that Iran, although affected later than other areas of the Middle East by European involvement and lagging behind the Ottomans in the modernization process, was the first government in the Middle East actually to experience a constitutional revolution. This was made possible in part by the relatively loose structure of the Iranian government at this time. The ability of the Qajars to exercise real authority over most of their vast domains remained strikingly weak through the early twentieth century, compared, for example, with the power enjoyed by the Ottomans over their territories. Iran's central government could not secure any firm and lasting control of the nation's military or police forces until the very end of the nineteenth century, which meant that the Qajars continued to rely on vassals and clients to maintain order in particular regions, as had been the case for centuries. Experiments in military modernization had been underway in Iran since the early eighteenth century. It was only with the establishment of the Persian Cossack Brigade in 1879, though, that the central government could enjoy a modicum of military power. Finally, it was no longer dependent on armed forces essentially made up of a set of vassal armies led by powerful regional governors.

Even the Cossack Brigade itself was commanded exclusively by foreigners: Russian officers on loan to the Qajars, until nearly the end of the dynasty's tenure. From this perspective, it was yet another example of foreign encroachment on basic governmental functions in Iran. This trend accelerated with the selling of more and more government concessions to foreigners, allowing them to profit through controlling specific official functions or monopolizing the sale of various goods. The most egregious example of this, the tobacco monopoly granted to a Belgian company in 1891, caused a protest that united the clergy with urban merchants. The success of the initial resistance created the basis for a continuing alliance between religious officials and merchants in opposition to the monarch. This tie gained strength after Naser al-Din Shah was replaced by his son Mozaffar al-Din Shah (1853–1907).

Mozaffar al-Din Shah had served as crown prince since 1861, when he was made governor of Azerbaijan: the traditional assignment for training Qajar crown princes. Instead of using this position to learn about statecraft, Mozaffar al-Din focused on enjoying himself. His father also kept him at arm's length, so he was not really prepared to take the throne when the time came. Mozaffar al-Din became Iran's ruler when its financial situation was already very tenuous, prompting him to grant even more foreign concessions to raise funds. The one with the most lasting impact was the **D'Arcy agreement** of May 1901. Upon payment of £20,000, an English/Australian mineral prospector named William Knox D'Arcy received a sixty-year concession to export all of Iran's oil, except for what was extracted in its five northern provinces. The agreement stipulated that the Iranian government would receive only 16 percent of his company's annual profits: a proportion later seen as scandalously small. Although the impact of this action would not even begin to be felt until after May 1908, when D'Arcy actually found oil just as he was on the verge of giving up his prospecting, it became viewed in retrospect by later generations of Iranians as yet another Qajar surrender of key sovereign rights for no clear gain.

The appointment of some Belgians to administer customs and collect customs duties had a more immediate impact. This resulted in merchants perceiving that they now had to pay much more tax, which they blamed on the shah. Mozaffar al-Din also took out several loans, notably from Russia, for which the Russians received a number of additional concessions as well as reduced tax rates on their merchants and the goods they imported. Finally, he used these newly acquired funds to finance three expensive trips to Europe between 1900 and 1905 in imitation of his father—a gesture that became the last straw for the merchants.

Through this period, economic conditions steadily grew worse, so secret clandestine leaflets known as *shabnames* ("night letters") denouncing the government began to be circulated. The British also paid various clerics to oppose the monarch's programs when they perceived him to be growing too close to the Russians. Iranians opposed to the shah soon began to see the situation created by the Russo-Japanese war of 1904–1905 as an appropriate time to act against him. In their view, the Russians had become too embroiled in other issues to worry much about Iran, particularly after news came of the outbreak of the 1905 Russian Revolution in January and the Japanese naval victory over the Russians at the Battle of Tsushima Straits in May.

In December 1905, when the unpopular governor of Tehran tried to punish merchants by having them beaten for raising sugar prices, a group of protestors including merchants and clerics took refuge (*bast*) in the main Tehran mosque. They were thrown out on the authority of a progovernment imam, but a much larger group then moved to take refuge at a nearby shrine in defiance of the government's authority. They insisted that the government adhere more closely to the sharia and that it establish an *adalatkhane* (house of justice), with both demands open to a wide variety of interpretations. Although the shah agreed to these demands in order to disperse this group, he did not actually take any action.

When it became clear that he was not going to act on his word, a much larger group of merchants and clergy took refuge on the expansive grounds of the British embassy in late July 1906. They now formally requested the establishment of a representative assembly (*majlis*) and wanted Ayn al-Dawla, the shah's conservative prime minister, dismissed. When he agreed to this, elections were quickly held for this assembly, which opened for business in October 1906. It quickly enacted a series of modernizing reforms including provisions to promote freedom of the press, all of which quickly angered many of the clerics who had originally supported this new institution. One of Mozaffar al-Din's last acts was to sign the first Fundamental Law: an Iranian constitution.

Based largely on a Belgian model, this document was augmented by a Supplementary Fundamental Law issued a few months later.

Struggle over Iran's Constitution

Bigger problems ensued when Mozaffar al-Din was succeeded by his son Mohammad Ali Shah in January 1907. Although the new monarch at first gave the appearance of supporting the new constitution and its legislative body, Mohammad Ali Shah was in fact opposed to the ways in which this new set of laws and assembly limited his powers, and so began to wage indirect war against this new system. In the midst of this tension, Britain and Russia signed an agreement in August 1907 to formally divide Iran into spheres of influence, with Russian authority recognized over the north and Britain accepted as predominant in the south. Assisted by the Cossack Brigade, Mohammad Ali finally shut down the parliament and went after its leaders in June 1908. The parliamentary forces, now known as Constitutionalists, were forced to flee to Azerbaijan and Gilan. Eventually they fought their way back to Tehran, where they were joined from the south by cavalry troops from the Bakhtiyari tribe. They succeeded in ousting Mohammad Ali Shah and placing his eleven-year old son Ahmad on the throne in July 1909. By this time, many conservative clerics had broken with the Constitutionalists and supported the return of a more traditional type of government.

Over the next three years, the Iranian parliament resumed its attempt to construct a stable constitutional democracy and address the country's massive financial problems, despite being more and more constrained by Britain and Russia. In order to procure the advice of someone knowledgeable about Western banking, but without any taint of association to the imperialist Great Powers, the Iranians chose an American expert, Morgan Shuster, to advise them about what they should do.

Arriving in May 1911, Shuster proposed that a special tax-collecting gendarme force be set up and led by an officer from the British Indian army, Major Claude Stokes. The Russians immediately protested this use of a British officer as a violation of the balance of power specified in the 1907 Anglo-Russian agreement and got the British to agree. When the Iranian parliament rejected this complaint as an infringement on its sovereignty, the Russians sent troops marching in the direction of Tehran. This forced the dissolution of the second parliament and got Shuster expelled from Iran by January 1912.

This first brief period of constitutional government in Iran was effectively ended. A new parliament was not elected and seated until 1914. By this time, the government had come under the close supervision and scrutiny of the British and Russians following the outbreak of World War I. What did endure from the first constitutional period was the text of the Fundamental Laws, as well as a series of governmental and financial reforms that regularized tax collection and standardized land tenure practices more than ever before. The legacy of all these laws and rules was very important in the formulation of subsequent Iranian constitutions, in particular the constitution of the Islamic Republic of Iran in 1979.

Oil and Its Impact

Another lasting legacy of this period was the way that the entire context of foreign, particularly British, interests in Iranian affairs changed forever upon the discovery of oil in southwestern Iran in May 1908—the first find of this sort in the central Middle East. This came at a very propitious time for the British, just then on the verge of converting their navy from coal to oil power. Upon news of the discovery, the Burmah Oil Company, which had stepped in to fund D'Arcy's explorations after he ran short of **cash, created the Anglo-Persian Oil** Company (APOC) as its subsidiary. Iranian production of oil products in bulk eventually started in 1913 at a refinery built on the Persian Gulf in Abadan, which for its first five decades of operation was the largest oil refinery in the world. In that same year, Winston Churchill, then serving as First Lord of the Admiralty, acquired a controlling interest in this company for the British government. He arranged to provide it with £2,000,000 in capital to ensure a stable oil supply for the Royal Navy: a step that linked Britain more closely to Iran's political fortunes than ever before. This would only become clear in the aftermath of World War I, then just on the verge of breaking out due to numerous tensions on the frontiers of the Ottoman Empire, particularly in the Balkans.

YOUNG TURK REVOLUTION OF 1908

Over many centuries, the rulers of Iran had never been able to control their subjects as well the Ottoman sultans, but Ottoman society was also exposed to European ideologies and ideas much more directly and continuously than Iranians ever were. By the early twentieth century, Abdulhamid II had built a formidable security apparatus and imposed censorship that effectively squelched dissent at home. Meanwhile, substantial communities of Ottoman political exiles had arisen in places like Paris, plotting in various ways to overturn the status quo. At the same time that the power of the Ottoman central authority grew with the rapid expansion of communications and transportation, the reach of dissident groups was also increased through the newspapers, pamphlets, and leaflets in continual covert circulation.

Nowhere was this felt more strongly than in the Balkans, scene of many Ottoman experiments in modernization. This was also the part of the Ottoman Empire in closest proximity to the large-scale social upheavals that accompanied the recent rise of nationalism across Europe. Throughout this region, both the Ottoman opposition and government forces tried to co-opt one another.

One of the most successful examples of this underground struggle for influence occurred when Abdulhamid's agents persuaded several important Young Turk leaders in exile abroad to come back to the empire to help implement reforms in the wake of the unexpected Ottoman victory over Greece in 1897. This transpired at exactly the same time when many Young Turk activists already serving in government positions were being put on trial and sent into internal exile for their political activism. The net impact of this confused web of loyalties and hostilities was to destabilize the opposition. It was already a fragile mosaic of activists with differing agendas and goals, but it became even more fragmented between those who chose to collaborate with the Hamidiyan regime and those who refused.

Opponents of the regime had difficulty achieving any coordination at all between their activities: a major reason for convening the Congress of Ottoman Liberals in Paris in 1902. It soon became clear at this meeting, attended by representatives from a diverse spectrum of ethnic, religious, and political dissident groups, that there was an irreconcilable difference between those supporting the use of violence and those against it. The activists attending this gathering, moreover, were mainly philosophers and intellectuals who delighted in debating what to do for several more years without producing any real plan of action.

Meanwhile, a group of young Ottoman army officers stationed in Macedonia, who commanded units that had been greatly weakened by the irregularities and lapses of the military pay system, became galvanized by the fear that Abdulhamid would soon relinquish this province to non-Ottoman control. In 1906, they organized an Ottoman Freedom Society in the provincial capital of Salonica. Its founder was Mehmet Talat (1874–1921), a postal clerk sent there from Edirne in internal exile for political activism. His organization recruited numerous followers in both the Second and Third Ottoman armies based in the region, and eventually made contact with the more established dissident exile groups in Paris.

In October 1907, various Ottoman opposition groups came together under the name first used in the mid-1890s: the **Committee of Union and Progress** (CUP).

SECOND OTTOMAN CONSTITUTIONAL PERIOD

This newly assembled organization grew so quickly in Macedonia that it set off a rebellion in the Ottoman garrisons there. When troops sent in from Anatolia refused to quell this insurrection because of CUP activists within their own ranks, the sultan quickly determined that this foreshadowed the possibility of a far more general upheaval. On July 24, 1908, Abdulhamid announced that the original 1876 constitution, in abeyance for thirty years, would now be restored. He justified this action by explaining that he had kept this document on hold until the people were "ready" for its implementation. News of this decision, which was somewhat slow to spread due to the massive censorship apparatus, soon produced huge spontaneous celebrations in all the major cities of the empire among a wide variety of ethnic and religious groups.

This unleashed a series of workers' strikes, prompted by the revolutionary mood and a tough economic situation. All such outbursts were quickly suppressed, since the CUP leaders who stood at the forefront of this revolution had paradoxically risen up to promote order and stability, not necessarily to defend popular democracy and enfranchisement. They did not really support the rights of common workers to govern themselves freely, but favored the guidance of the professional and business classes in coordination with the military to maintain social harmony and save the empire from disintegration.

Because they had come together as members of a clandestine group, the CUP leaders, mostly consisting of junior military officers as well as intellectuals just returned from exile, did not put themselves in positions of overt power, but acted behind the scenes. They were promoting seemingly contradictory political agendas. While they continued to support the restoration of the constitutional government and the multifaceted democracy that this entailed, they also sought to keep popular fervor for democratic change from getting out of control by suppressing mass demonstrations.

RISE OF THE COMMITTEE OF UNION AND PROGRESS (CUP)

Evolution of the CUP

This diverse set of goals partially grew out of the CUP leadership's attempts to blend various philosophies and ways of thinking then popular in certain European circles. The young officers, for example, who were a key part of the CUP's core leadership cadre, were mostly graduates of the Ottoman Imperial Military School. There the ideas of the German military theorist Colmar von der Goltz and the French psychologist Gustave Le Bon had been popular. From von der Goltz (who himself spent many years on the faculty of the Ottoman Imperial Military School), they took the lesson that the health of societies depended on having militaries organized for extended conflict using well-trained mass armies. This was a type of struggle that he labeled *Volkskrieg* or "People's War": oddly anticipating how World War I battles would actually be fought in Western Europe. From Le Bon, they derived the idea of the power of mass psychology and the need to inculcate a population collectively in a doctrine or belief system for it to become mobilized toward a goal. These young officers had studied how the Japanese, during the period of the Meiji Restoration (1868–1912), developed a modernized constitutional government by blending traditional practices and institutions with modern techniques of organization and government. The power of this approach was confirmed in their mind by the recent success (1905) of the Japanese in defeating the Russians in a modern, technological war: a milestone for a non-European power in the early twentieth century.

CUP behind the Scenes (1909–1913)

At first, there were no drastic changes in the leadership of the government, as the CUP acted discretely to place its high-ranking sympathizers such as Huseyin Hilmi Pasha in formal positions of authority and to prop up support for Sultan Abdulhamid as the newly reconstructed champion of constitutionalism. New elections brought politicians from a broad spectrum of political parties into the parliament. The reopening of parliament, although celebrated as the true measure of the revolution's success, exposed abiding tensions and disagreements within the Young Turk movement as well as providing a forum for conservatives opposed to it.

These negative feelings built up over several months and exploded in the countercoup of April 1909. This was carried out by conservative military officers and soldiers in alliance with religious students. They claimed to be seeking restoration of the Sharia to the preeminent role that they perceived it to have played *before* modernizing government reforms. It was not clear what exactly they meant by this, but it soon emerged that their real goal was to remove the CUP from power and depose all government officials affiliated with it.

One faction of the original Young Turk opposition movement, the Liberal Union Party headed by Prince Sabahettin (and now at odds with the CUP although it had participated in the 1908 revolution) tried to take the control of this uprising away from the conservatives and promote its own agendas. Meanwhile, the main CUP leaders had retreated to Salonica, where they organized an "Action Army" that mobilized to retake Istanbul, squelch the countercoup, and depose Sultan Abdulhamid II by the end of the month. The conservative countercoup revealed many divisions among the army troops, particularly between the *mektepli* officers (those trained in modern military schools) and the *alayli* officers (those who had risen through the ranks). Its main lasting effect, however, was to demonstrate to the CUP inner circle that it would have to rely primarily on its loyalists in the army to counter challenges from opposing political groups.

To reestablish control, the CUP replaced Abdulhamid on the throne with his brother Mehmed Reshad (who essentially functioned thereafter as a puppet ruler crowned as "Sultan Mehmed V"). It resumed the implementation of its vision of modernization and constitutional reform, but in a more regimented and disciplined way. As noted, in the old Ottoman system power had oscillated between the sultan's court and government bureaucrats, but now, because of internal struggles and external threats, power was shifting to the military to a degree not seen since the early nineteenth century.

The reinstatement of the 1876 constitution had unleashed enormous pent-up waves of political energy, shown by the active debates in parliament and the vibrant energy of the newly uncensored press during this period. This forced the CUP to act somewhat stealthily, as it tried to promote its agendas of maintaining stability while simultaneously honoring an ideological commitment to representative democracy. In contrast to its forceful reaction to the countercoup, most of the CUP central committee's activities between 1909 and 1913 continued to be carried out behind the scenes, as the CUP evolved into a political movement with both overt and covert dimensions. This level of continued secrecy in many of its activities, combined with its continued open support for parliamentary debate and freedom of speech, meant that although its parliamentary enemies continued to oppose its programs and initiatives, they were not able to diminish its influence and standing very much.

To ensure that it did not lose control, the CUP resorted to a variety of measures to preserve its standing, such as enacting a series of laws designed to curtail political freedoms without entirely abolishing them. These measures were often issued as "temporary laws" confirmed by imperial decree while the parliament was not in session to skirt the legislative process. The CUP also paid careful attention to the press, creating a sophisticated propaganda system to counter its critics in newspapers and journals.

As part of its official message, it attached much more importance than ever before to promoting the concept of national sovereignty (even coining a new term for it in Ottoman Turkish: *hakimiyet-i milliye*). This idea had emerged as early as the beginning of the Tanzimat period, but the CUP used it more skillfully than it ever had been before. When the CUP finally carried out its own coup in January 1913, the grand vizier whom it was then deposing wrote a letter explaining that he was stepping down at the demand of the armed forces. Enver Bey, the CUP's coup leader, had him change this sentence to state that his action was taken "at the demand of the *people* and the armed forces": a subtle but very meaningful change in emphasis.

War over Libya (1911–1912)

External pressures also helped to deflect domestic opposition to the CUP's strong-arm tactics. In October 1911, Italy invaded Libya, ostensibly to defend its interests there, but it really just wanted to grab territory to parallel France's recent acquisition of neighboring Tunisia. The Ottoman government, although trying very hard to avoid another entanglement in defending the empire's frontiers, was forced into a war there that presented enormous logistical obstacles.

From October 1911 through the summer of 1912, the Ottomans, despite their formidable military disadvantages, were able to fight to a stalemate against the Italians, who made pioneering use of airplanes and armored cars in combat. In the end, the Italians used their clear naval superiority to attack and seize

Ottoman islands in the Aegean and to assault the Dardanelles, forcing the Ottomans to sign a treaty formally recognizing that Libya now fell under Italian sovereignty. Although the Ottomans lost this war, it became a rallying point for numerous patriotic young officers who volunteered to serve in it. They had arranged for their own transportation there via circuitous routes and organized local Bedouin tribesmen into an irregular but effective resistance force. Such volunteers included Enver Bey, the CUP leader who spearheaded the 1908 revolution and the later 1913 coup, as well as **Mustafa Kemal** (later Ataturk), then a captain in the Ottoman army.

In the middle of this war, when the CUP perceived that it had begun to lose parliamentary by-elections, it arranged for an "election with a stick" to make sure that it retained certain seats by fixing ballots and employing a variety of other questionable electoral techniques. An even more dangerous challenge to it ensued when a group of anti-CUP army officers formed a group whose main agenda was to separate politics entirely from army activities. In the summer of 1912, this new group went on the offensive against the CUP, but their initiative was quickly overshadowed by what was happening in the Balkans.

First Balkan War (1912–1913)

As a direct consequence of the Young Turk Revolution, Austria-Hungary formally annexed Bosnia-Herzegovina, and Crete proclaimed its union with Greece in October 1908. Since that time, Balkan nations had been pursuing agendas of territorial expansion as conditions permitted. By 1912, they sensed another opportunity to move against the Ottomans, now weakened by the conflict with Italy. The Ottoman situation in Europe had also deteriorated because of what had been happening in Albania. Since 1910, a nationalist revolt had smoldered there: a situation that perplexed the government in Istanbul because the CUP had so many sympathizers among the Albanians. However, many Albanians resented new laws introduced after 1908 that curbed their autonomy and raised their taxes.

The Ottoman government sent Sultan Mehmet V on a goodwill trip to Kosovo in June 1911, delivering a promise of greater respect for Albanian autonomy. This placated some people in the north of the country, but not in the south, where a rebel army was formed to demand a united Albania governed by Albanians only. By September 1912, the Ottoman government and Albanian rebels had worked out an agreement that gave Albania greatly expanded self-rule, but this ultimately gave the Ottomans only a brief respite.

Perceiving the success of all these strategic challenges as propitious for their plans, Serbia, Greece, Montenegro, and Bulgaria put aside their differences and joined forces long enough to create a "Balkan League" and declare war against the Ottomans in October 1912, just as they signed a final peace treaty with Italy ending the Libyan war. This new conflict took Ottoman commanders by surprise, resulting in the loss of most of the remaining Ottoman territory in Europe (including major cities such as Salonica) within only a few weeks. This rapid pace of events prompted the European powers to convene a rushed peace conference in London.

However, the proposed settlement would have required the Ottomans to surrender the historic town of Edirne to the Bulgarians. This shocked the CUP into taking full control. It staged a coup on January 23, 1913, when CUP leader Enver led a volunteer force into the main building of the Sublime Porte, forcing anti-CUP Grand Vizier Kamil Pasha to resign at gunpoint. The CUP still did not in fact seize overt power, appointing the nonpolitical but CUP-friendly Mahmud Shevket Pasha to be the new grand vizier and naming only three CUP members to his new cabinet. Despite taking control, the CUP leadership still lost Edirne to the Bulgarians before the war ended in May 1913.

CUP after the 1913 Coup

The Second Balkan War broke out just a month after the end of the First Balkan War, and in this second round of conflict, the Ottomans retook Edirne. When serving military commanders refused to take the initiative in this offensive, more junior officers associated with the CUP such as Enver took charge on the battlefield. The forces that reconquered Edirne were associates of Enver Pasha known as *fedais* ("volunteers"): from the Arabic word commonly used in the Middle East to refer to irregular forces in battle, in this case from various political and ethnic groups struggling to define their positions in the empire. After Edirne had been secured, yet another group of volunteers allied with the CUP undertook to organize guerrilla resistance among Turkish Muslims in Western Thrace to put pressure on the Bulgarians before another peace treaty was signed in September 1913.

In the wake of the internal and external upheavals of 1913, the CUP central committee gradually dropped any pretense of tolerance for its political opponents in the parliament, particularly after a sympathizer of one of the opposition parties assassinated Mehmed Shevket Pasha, the long-time CUP ally then serving as grand vizier, in June 1913. Within a short time, although not every member of the assembly was formally affiliated with the CUP, the body became a virtual rubber stamp for its policies. The CUP was always led by a central committee, but three of its members, Enver, Talat, and **Jemal Pasha**, began to take on such great power and authority in leading the Ottoman Empire from that time until the end of World War I that they became known as the "CUP Triumvirate" of leadership.

RISE OF "TURKISH" CONSCIOUSNESS

It was also around 1912 that the allegiances of the Young Turks emerged more explicitly as "Turkish" rather than "Ottoman." Turkish ethnic consciousness had its roots in nineteenth-century works like A.L. David's grammar of the Turkish language (1832): the book that launched the search for common Turkic ethnic bonds.[1] This investigation was carried out by scholars like Armin Vámbéry (1832–1913), a Hungarian orientalist who traveled across Central Asia in search of common Turkic cultural characteristics. In 1865, he mused about a Turkic "empire extending from the shore of the Adriatic far into China."

One of the Young Ottoman group Ali Suavi focused on the common ethnic origins of Turkic peoples when he wrote about the Central Asians of Khiva, whom he called "Turkish Muslims who were of our religion and our tribe and our family."[2] In the nineteenth century, Turkish ethnic and cultural connections of Ottomans with others were never as strongly promoted as strongly as Islamic ties between Ottoman subjects, and the focus was on inculcating a concept of "Ottomanism" and loyalty to the dynasty above all.

Consciousness of a common Turkic identity was probably most strongly promoted in the expanding Russian Empire by intellectuals like the Tatar writer Ismail Bey Gaspirali (1851–1914). He was searching for something to counter Russian and Slavic nationalism as it served to legitimate Russian imperialism. Gaspirali was the founder of *Terjuman (Translator)* (published 1883–1918): a newspaper written in a simplified "common" Turkish, featuring articles calling for Turkic unity around the world. Even with the stringent press censorship under Abdulhamid, this newspaper circulated in Ottoman circles, and Gaspirali stayed in touch with Istanbul and Cairo. He managed to avoid angering either the Russian government or the traditional Central Asian Islamic establishment, so his newspaper helped foster nationalist consciousness among different Turkic groups through several decades.

Another man who discussed the importance of Turkish and Turkic identity was Yusuf Akchura (1876–1935). Akchura, a man of Tatar origin who had grown up in Istanbul but had spent time in both the Russian and Ottoman empires, was related through marriage to the family of Gaspirali. In 1904, he published *Uch Tarz-i Siyaset (Three Types of Policies)*, in which he identified Ottomanism, Islamic allegiance, and Turkish ethnic identity as three potentially unifying political doctrines. He noted that the Ottomans had promoted the first two, but he now called for a reappraisal of whether or not to focus on the third as something stronger. Akchura became an important contributor to new societies designed to promote Turkish literature and culture organized after 1908. The most influential was the **Turkish Hearth (*Turk Ojagi*) association**, first assembled by a group of students in Istanbul at the Imperial Military Medical School in the summer of 1911 and then formed into a more national organization in March 1912 under the aegis of the CUP. The Hearth Association provided a way for the modernizing and nationalist ideas of the CUP to be disseminated.

Another important philosopher who became active in the Hearth Association was Ziya Gokalp (1876–1924). Less interested than Akchura in reaching out to Turkic communities beyond Ottoman domains, Gokalp is regarded as one of the founders of modern Turkish nationalism. He envisioned a synthetic balance of Turkism, adherence to Islam, and modernism in which each of these components complemented the other in a holistic way.

Gokalp's work was instrumental in the development of the modern concept of Turkish national identity. He believed that a modern state required a uniform culture, religion, and national identity to flourish. His work distinguished *Avrupalilik* ("Europeanism"; "acting as Europeans") from *Modernlik* ("Modernity; acting in a modern fashion"), describing

---

[1]The adjective "Turkic" refers to all peoples across Asia and Europe identified as "Turks" and the languages they speak, while "Turkish" refers specifically to Turks from the former Ottoman Empire or Iran and the languages that they speak.
[2]Ali Suavi in Şerif Mardin, *The Genesis of Young Ottoman Thought* (Syracuse, NY: Syracuse University Press, 2000), 371.

the latter as the preferable course. Japan was presented as a model for how to do this properly, since it was apparently able to modernize without sacrificing its fundamental cultural identity. Based on his understanding of the French sociologist Emile Durkheim, Gokalp perceived the promotion of "culture" (which he described as altruistic, public-spirited, and reinforcing of social solidarity) as a way to correct the problems presented by "civilization" (which he viewed as embodying utilitarianism, selfishness, and individualism). For Gokalp, nationalism offered a very effective way to create "social solidarity": the essential pre-requisite for "cultural unity." All of this seemed more and more elusive in the multiethnic contexts of Ottomanism and Ottoman identity, but easier to promote with a Turkish identity: a lesson not lost on the empire's leaders as the Ottomans headed into World War I.

EVENTS OF 1908: DIFFERENT IMPACTS ON DIFFERENT GROUPS

The promising rhetoric of the early Second Constitutional Period and the first elections in the fall of 1908 raised the hopes of politicians in various ethnic groups about the possibilities of change in the empire at last: a change that would allow these groups to declare their agendas and goals openly. **The Armenian Revolutionary Federation**, a group founded in Tsarist Georgia in 1890 and commonly called the Dashnak Party, as well as its slightly older Armenian revolutionary cousin, the Hinchak (Bell) Society, had fought against Abdulhamid II for better treatment of Ottoman Armenians since their founding. They based their campaigns specifically on the need to defend rights granted to *all* Ottoman subjects in the 1876 Constitution.

As noted, the sultan organized Hamidiye cavalry units to quell this dissent. Part of the difficulty with them was that such units were manned mainly by Kurds, who, as nomadic tribesmen, had been shut out of the economic gains afforded to sedentary peasants, such as

the Armenians, as a result of the Tanzimat. When the government then gave these troops license to terrorize Armenians in eastern Anatolia, particularly during the disturbances of the 1890s, they became all too willing to enrich themselves at villagers' expense, given the bleak poverty and despair that they otherwise faced in this era of modernization.

With both groups in the exiled opposition in 1902, the Dashnaks had joined forces with the Young Turks then to attend the Congress of Ottoman Liberals in Paris. Although the Young Turks at that meeting disagreed with the Armenians about the efficacy of seeking foreign help, the Dashnak Party supported the Young Turk coalition in the activities that led to the reinstatement of the Ottoman constitution in July 1908.

The success achieved in 1908 produced a wave of optimism among various Armenian communities about their community's future prospects within an Ottoman framework. At that time, one group of Armenians even formed a new group called the Armenian Constitutional **Democrat Party** in Alexandria, Egypt. It opened a branch in Istanbul to make clear that its main agenda was to act within the framework of the restored Ottoman Constitution to promote Armenian rights. In the first elections under the new regime, twelve Armenians were elected to the Ottoman parliament.

Among them were two members of the Dashnak Party from Erzurum. One, Karekin Bastirmadjiyan, had participated in an assault on the Ottoman Bank in 1896 carried out by Dashnak revolutionaries. By the fall of 1908, he had agreed to join in supporting the Young Turk's own revolutionary experiment. The newly chosen Armenian Orthodox Patriarch at that time, Madteos Izmirlian remarked to a British diplomat "that the changed conditions in Turkey implied that Armenians has ceased to exist as a separate national entity and were merged in the Ottoman whole...." It was his opinion that the future for the Armenians "lay in working in loyal union with the Turks on the line of prudence and moderation and eschewing all extremist ideas in the way of autonomy...."[3]

Because of the pressures that the Young Turk Revolution had unleashed, this honeymoon ended fairly soon. Just after the April 1909 countercoup, for instance, there was a coordinated attack on Armenians in the city of Adana by Muslim conservatives angry about how the new constitution gave Christians equal status with Muslims. Another factor that produced huge strain on relations between the Ottoman government and its Armenian subjects was the flood of new refugees pouring into Anatolia from territories lost by the Ottomans in Europe during the Balkan Wars. These vast new groups of people placed an enormous burden on a government that was already virtually bankrupt and having a difficult time just keeping itself together even *without* a large new contingent of people to settle. To ease stress on its overtaxed systems, the Ottoman government in fact tried to resettle these immigrants in rural areas, where they clashed with the existing residents, who were often Armenians.

From another perspective, not all of the new laws and programs brought in by the Young Turks were welcomed by all Armenians. With their declaration of universal equality, the new laws envisaged the final end of the *millet* system that had defined Ottoman state relations with minorities for centuries. Suddenly, minority groups were now to be subject to military conscription and could presumably expect to have their taxes rise to reflect their newly equal status as well. In addition, members of the Armenian elite particularly in Istanbul who had long been empowered by the *millet* system saw their importance as community leaders diminish as the Young Turks promoted social equality. This was a political change supported by the Dashnak Party, which had its supporters among the more rural constituency of eastern Anatolia. Finally, because of the systemic

inefficiencies of late Ottoman government and administration, the actual implementation of reforms varied enormously from place to place. The potential transformations in social organization that went along with the new laws quickly raised tensions between groups, particularly under the stress of the nearly continuous wars in which the Ottoman Empire became involved starting in 1911.

Arabs in the Ottoman Empire faced a differed set of problems from the Armenians, but shared with them the stresses of sudden political change. They too welcomed the possibilities of political liberalization, but when the scions of great Arab notable families suddenly found themselves dismissed from government in the fall of 1908 and replaced by Turks (since the CUP had become a more heavily Turkish organization after that time), this created resentment and fear. Arab intellectuals began slowly to shift to a more consciously Arab orientation, but still taking great pains at first to stay with the fabric of Ottoman political allegiance.

A vanguard of Arab nationalist thinkers had begun to formulate a concept of Arab independence from the Ottomans in 1905, when Najib Azuri (1873–1916), a Lebanese Christian who had served as an Ottoman bureaucrat in Jerusalem, published (in French) *The Awakening of the Arab Nation* (*Le Reveil de la Nation Arabe*): one of the first clear calls for an independent Arab state not under Ottoman authority at all. Given its date, his work was fueled by the strong sentiments that had arisen against Sultan Abdulhamid II, whose ouster in 1909 gave hope even to Arabs displaced by the turmoil of the previous revolutionary year.

It is striking that as late as January 1913, a large number, perhaps even a majority of Arab politicians remained broadly loyal to the Ottoman cause. At that time, some of the Syrian notables disenfranchised by the events of 1908 and disillusioned by the CUP's rigged elections in 1912 formed an Ottoman Party of Administrative Decentralization in Cairo. It was modeled on the Liberal Union Party led

---

[3]British Foreign Office Documents. Fitzmaurice to Lowther, 54D, Nov. 30, 1908, FO 195/2281.

by Prince Sabahettin and focused in similar ways on highlighting particular aspects of the Young Turk plan that could accommodate greater Arab demands for autonomy within existing power structures. Just after that, however, in June 1913 the first "Arab Congress" was held in Paris. It assembled representatives of several different groups, including delegates from the newly created Decentralization Party as well as Midhat Shukri, secretary-general of the CUP, who had been sent there by the CUP central committee in Istanbul. The result was that the CUP, at least on the surface, agreed to certain demands for greater Arab autonomy and appointed Arab leaders to important posts.

In the end, the government that seized power in Istanbul following the coup in January 1913 did not follow through on these promises. It did allow an Arab, Said Halim Pasha, the Egyptian grandson of Muhammad Ali, to continue as Ottoman grand vizier between 1913 and 1916 even though he had serious disagreements with the CUP leadership on a number of matters. Despite such gestures, secret Arab societies issued manifestos after this congress that began to call in definite terms for liberating the Arabs from Ottoman control, charging that the CUP had been treating them "like a herd of livestock" to be exploited.

Even after the Constitutional Revolution, all roads in the Ottoman world led one way or another through Istanbul, and this produced interesting encounters between contemporary intellectuals. One took place between Sati al-Husri and Ziya Gokalp. From a Syrian Arab family but born in Yemen, al-Husri had been educated and risen in the Ottoman bureaucracy as an educational reformer. After 1908, he was first assigned to Macedonia, where he came into close contact with the CUP, and later to Istanbul, where he served as director of the Teachers' Training College through 1912.

In the more open atmosphere of this period, al-Husri began to give speeches and publish articles while working in this job. In them, he advocated a liberal "Ottomanism," favoring the decentralization and autonomy supported by the Liberal Union Party and by most of the Syrian elite. In his written responses to al-Husri, Gokalp sharpened and articulated his concept of the need to inculcate popular support for "Turkism" as the salvation for the empire's problems. Despite the actual changes enacted into law after the Constitutional Revolution, most such discussion of the issues facing the empire after 1913 was academic, since the CUP had by then assumed total control of government policy and administration. The consequences that flowed from discussion of these issues did begin to have real impact on the lives of ordinary people during World War I and afterwards, when figures like Sati al-Husri, having left Ottomanism behind, would emerge as one of the staunchest proponents of Arab nationalism and Pan-Arabism.

WOMEN GET INVOLVED IN POLITICS

The expansion of political discourse resulting from this wave of constitutionalism also marked the first real entry of women into the public arena in both the Ottoman Empire and Iran. The story of Halide Edip Adivar (1884–1964) provides one of the best early examples of this. Educated in a girls' school in Istanbul founded by American Protestant missionaries, she became associated with the post-1908 modernization process underway in the Empire by advocating women's rights in lectures and articles that she produced while working at an Istanbul teachers' college.

Her life before 1908 had been the fairly sheltered existence of an upper-class Ottoman bureaucrat's daughter and wife, but was transformed by the turmoil set in motion by the Young Turk uprising. Her father had been one of Sultan Abdulhamid's scribes, but upon the sultan's ouster following the 1909 counter-coup, Adivar and her two young sons had to flee to Cairo.

Soon after her return to Istanbul, her husband announced that he was going to marry a second wife, upon which she divorced him and set out on her own path.

As a budding journalist and novelist, she became good friends with philosophers such as Ziya Gokalp, who visited her house regularly for several years. In 1912, Adivar published a utopian novel *New Turan* (*Yeni Turan*) about an imagined future Turkish model society. In her autobiography, she recounted that she had been "largely affected by the apostolic sincerity and austerity[E1]" of Gokalp in composing this work. It was around this time as well that Adivar became associated with the Turkish Hearth association and, over the next few years, continued to provide a strong woman's voice in discussions about how a new society should emerge in the years following the Ottoman Constitutional Revolution.

A parallel major female leader in the Arab world can be found in Huda Sharawi (1879–1947). She began to advocate for women's rights in her youth, when she went to a store in Alexandria to buy her own clothes instead of having them brought to her home. In 1909, Sharawi became one of the main organizers of the *Mabarrat Muhammad Ali* (Charitable Organization of Muhammad Ali): one of the first social service organizations in the Middle East for women to be run by *women*. This activity set the stage for the increased involvement of Arab women in political and social life after World War I: the period that became the modern watershed for this region in so many different ways.

Iran, like its Middle East neighbors, witnessed an evolution in the status of women in the years following its 1906 Constitutional Revolution. Within a short period of time after this event, various women's societies and a women's newspaper were organized, creating a public space for women that led them to participate in social and political life as never before there. Naser al-Din Shah's daughter Taj al-Saltane (1884–1936), who became active in the Society for Women's Freedom, published accounts in her 1914 autobiography (*Crowning Anguish*) of many traditional practices that had oppressed women in Iran and called for

women's unveiling to promote social equality and freedom. Another Iranian female writer, Esmat Tehrani (1869–1911) with the pen name "Tayere," argued in a 1909 series of essays that the education and empowerment of women would enormously enrich and strengthen society. Her discussion recalled the arguments presented by European women's rights crusaders during the era of the French Revolution such as Mary Wollstonecraft.

The entry of women into the public sphere, in all these countries, in ways not been seen before, was a common aspect of the period of constitutional revolutions and experimentation. As in other areas, the possibilities of change and reform raised many more questions than could be solved easily or swiftly. Substantive changes in women's status often did not occur until much later, when material and economic circumstances had changed significantly in this region.

CHANGES IN THE ZIONIST MOVEMENT AND THE SECOND ALIYAH

After the turn of the twentieth century, the small Zionist community in Ottoman Palestine began to expand more quickly. The widespread pogroms that accompanied the 1905 Russian Revolution had been fueled by Pan-Slavic nationalist and anti-semitic groups called the Black Hundreds. In addition, the threat of military conscription for the Russo-Japanese war led many young Russian Jewish men to leave for Palestine.

This new wave of immigrants, known later as the "Second Aliyah," really began to construct a vision of Zionism that transcended its European nationalist roots. The town of Tel Aviv, established in 1909 just north of Jaffa on the Mediterranean coast, was the location of the Herzliya Hebrew High School: the first modern school whose language of instruction was Hebrew. In Jerusalem, foundations were laid for a Jewish university (the

Hebrew University) which would also teach only in Hebrew. In Haifa, the cornerstone was laid for a Jewish technical school, called the "Technion." Supported by the Zionist financial institutions already mentioned, Jewish immigrants and organizations continued to make large land purchases all during this period, buying up malarial swamps in particular (of which there were many near the Mediterranean coast) and draining them to produce highly fertile land.

EMERGENCE OF SOCIALIST ZIONISM

As noted, the chief ideological rival to Zionism among young Jews in Eastern Europe was the socialist movement. Many Jews supported the Bund, which was an important factor in the emergence of a new Zionist group that quickly began to dominate politics in the Jewish community in Palestine: the **socialist Zionists**. They argued that centuries of Jewish oppression in anti-semitic societies had made Jews meek and vulnerable, simply creating more anti-semitism. According to this view, Jews now had to redeem themselves as farmers, workers, and soldiers in their own country to escape a "diaspora mentality." The Socialist Zionists also generally rejected any strong affiliation with Jewish religious tradition and practices as being part of this archaic way of thinking. This group, known as "Zionist pioneers," established rural communal collective farms in Palestine beginning in 1909 called "kibbutzim" and rejected Yiddish as a language of exile, embracing Hebrew as their common tongue.

Some of them maintained that since the Jews lacked a "normal" class structure, different social classes that constituted a nation would have to be created artificially. This gave them further impetus to become Jewish peasants and a proletariat, focusing on settling the land and working on it. According to one of the most prominent Zionists of this new wave (although not a socialist himself) Aaron David Gordon (1856–1922), "One thing is certain, and that is that the land will belong more to the side that is more capable of suffering for it and working it."[4] This group also focused on developing agriculture and water resources to be able to sustain large numbers of Jewish immigrants and became a dominant force in Ottoman Palestine just before the outbreak of World War I.

However, the rise of this socialist group deepened the schism between Zionism and some groups of Orthodox Jews, since the latter continued to believe that any nationalist planning for a homeland ahead of the Messiah was blasphemous and sacrilegious. Meanwhile, strong Socialist Zionist groups in Eastern Europe formed youth movements that operated training programs in Europe to prepare young Jews for migration to Palestine. As a result, many Socialist Zionist immigrants around the time of World War I arrived in Palestine already speaking Hebrew and prepared for life there.

Before World War I, all Jews in Palestine had to operate under the aegis of Ottoman rule, and the hope among many was that the experiments in constitutionalism that had begun with the Young Turk Revolution of 1908 could be very advantageous to the Zionist project as it matured. As for others in the region, the whole political and social situation would change with the onset of the war, which would reshape the situation of Ottoman Palestine swiftly and tumultuously.

REFORM EXPERIMENTS: A SUMMARY

In both the Ottoman Empire and Iran, the first decade of the twentieth century saw experiments take place in the creation or restoration of constitutional rule. They were soon curtailed by governments that did not really see the need to democratize or

---

[4]A.D. Gordon, in Zeev Sternhell, *The Founding Myths of Israel* (Princeton: Princeton University Press, 1999), 68.

reflect true popular sentiment, although they retained a democratic façade. Instead, they either were heavily influenced by domestic authoritarian groups, such as the CUP in the Ottoman Empire, or were decisively shaped by the interventions of outside powers, as in the case with Russia and England in Iran. In spite of this, neither state foresaw going back to the more traditional forms of absolutism embodied by Naser al-Din Shah or Sultan Abdulhamid II. In both Iran and the Ottoman Empire, the amount of actual potential reform at this time was limited by many factors, not least of which was the financial strain caused by such change.

More serious problems, though, were about to explode for the region, and the world, when the house of cards upon which the system of alliances and power balances that had arisen to define international relations was overturned following the assassination in Bosnia of the Austrian crown prince, Franz Ferdinand, by a Serbian nationalist agitator, Gavrilo Princip, in June 1914: an act of violence that arose from the same visceral nationalist impulses that fueled the First and Second Balkan Wars.

Questions to Think About

1. Why did a constitutional revolution happen in the Middle East first in Iran, and how did Iran's experience with a constitution compare with the Ottoman Empire's?
2. What was the impact of the discovery of oil in Iran?
3. How did the Russo-Japanese war and the Russian Revolution of 1905 affect the Middle East, particularly Iran?
4. Who was Morgan Shuster, and what was his importance?
5. What caused the Young Turk Revolution of 1908?
6. What were the origins of the CUP, and how did its goals evolve?
7. What were the impacts of the Libyan War as well as the First and Second Balkan Wars on the Ottoman government?
8. What led to the rise of "Turkish" consciousness in the Ottoman Empire, and what were its effects?
9. Who was Ziya Gokalp, and why was he important in the creation of the modern Turkish national identity?
10. What was the impact of the 1908 Young Turk Revolution on Armenians and Arabs in the Ottoman Empire?
11. Who was Halide Edip Adivar and why is she important in the history of modern Turkey?
12. What was Socialist Zionism, and how did it affect the Zionist movement's plans for a Jewish homeland in Palestine?

For Further Reading

Adıvar, Halide Edib. *Memoirs of Halidé Edib*. New York: Century Co., 1926.

Adıvar, Halide Edib. *The Turkish Ordeal: Being the Further Memoirs of Halidé Edib*. New York: Century Co., 1928.

Afary, Janet. *The Iranian Constitutional Revolution, 1906–1911: Grassroots Democracy, Social Democracy & the Origins of Feminism*. New York: Columbia University Press, 1996.

Ahmad, Feroz. *The Young Turks: The Committee of Union and Progress in Turkish Politics, 1908–1914*. Oxford: Clarendon Press, 1969.

Akmeşe, Handan Nezir. *The Birth of Modern Turkey: The Ottoman Military and the March to World War I*. London: I.B. Tauris, 2005.

Browne, Edward Granville. *The Persian Revolution of 1905–1909*. London: Frank Cass, 1966.

Hourani, Albert. *Arabic Thought in the Liberal Age, 1798–1939*. Cambridge: Cambridge University Press, 1983.

Hovannisian, Richard G. *The Armenian People from Ancient to Modern Times*. New York: St. Martin's Press, 1997.

Laqueur, Walter. *A History of Zionism*. London: Weidenfeld and Nicolson, 1972.

Longhurst, Henry. *Adventures in Oil: the story of British Petroleum*. London: Sidgwick and Jackson, 1959.

Shuster, W. Morgan. *The Strangling of Persia*. New York: The Century Co, 1912.

Somakian, Manoug Joseph. *Empires in Conflict: Armenia and the Great Powers, 1895–1920*. London: Tauris Academic Studies, 1995.

Tibi, Bassam, Marion Farouk-Sluglett, and Peter Sluglett. *Arab Nationalism: A Critical Enquiry*. New York: St. Martin's Press, 1990.

Vital, David. *Zionism: The Crucial Phase*. Oxford: Clarendon Press, 1987.

Zürcher, Erik Jan. *The Young Turk Legacy and Nation Building: From the Ottoman Empire to Atatürk's Turkey*. London: I. B. Tauris, 2010.

9

World War I: The Last Ottoman War

From an Austrian perspective, World War I might have been seen at first as a "Third Balkan War" designed to secure Bosnia-Herzegovina. Austria-Hungary had taken this territory from the Ottomans in 1878, but only formally annexed it in 1908 just after the Young Turk Revolution. Serbia also saw Bosnia-Herzegovina as a part of its rightful domain, given the substantial Serbian Orthodox population there. In contrast to Serbia and Austria-Hungary, the Ottomans no longer paid much attention to Bosnia, although a large percentage of Bosnia's population remained Muslim. Instead, the Ottomans worried much more about retaining control of *any* territory on European soil at all in the wake of recent disastrous conflicts that had ended their rule over all but a part of Eastern Thrace.

The end of an Ottoman presence in the Balkans after the First and Second Balkan Wars (1912–1913) had caused all the European powers to reassess the strategic balance of the Eastern Mediterranean region. The French and British now perceived the Ottomans to be so weak that they began to focus more on the challenges of a rising Russia and the newly independent Balkan nations, secretly planning how to manage the possible breakup of the remaining Ottoman Empire. Germany began to fear that British and French plans for the future of the Middle East might exclude it and was alarmed by the friendly relations that Britain and France had developed with Russia in recent years.

Germany had been building stronger economic ties to the Ottoman Empire for some time as well. It had been constructing a railway link between Berlin and Baghdad since the early 1900s and had helped create a number of other Ottoman railway lines, including the Hejaz train that ran from Damascus to Medina via Amman. By 1914, the line to Baghdad had reached Eastern Anatolia, well on its way to entering northern Iraq and thus connecting ultimately to the Persian Gulf. When complete, it offered Germany a connection with East Asian trade not dependent on transit through the Suez Canal, by then long under British control.

Germany had already decided that with tensions rising rapidly in the world, it would be prudent to send skilled advisers to the Ottomans who could

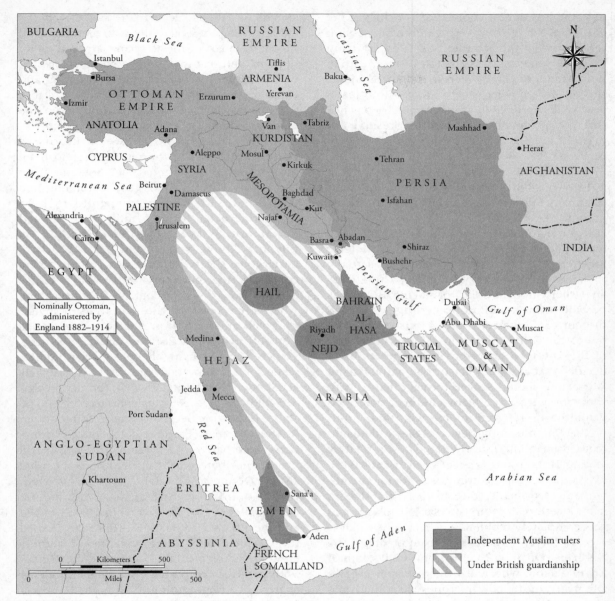

MAP 9.1   Ottoman Empire and Persia in 1914

strengthen their military capabilities in order to help them defend what remained of their empire. In October 1913, Lieutenant General Otto Liman von Sanders was appointed to command the First Ottoman Army Corps, assisted by a delegation of German officers.

Use of foreign military commanders was a longstanding Ottoman tradition. Liman von Sanders's compatriot Count Colmar von der Goltz had served as inspector general of the entire Ottoman army at the same time that British Admiral Sir Arthur Limpus (1863–1931) held the position of commander-in-chief of the Ottoman Navy. However, a quick succession of events in the summer of 1914, starting with the June 28 assassination of the Austrian heir Archduke Franz Ferdinand in Sarajevo, Bosnia-Herzegovina, swept away within just a few weeks a fragile diplomatic/military balance that the Ottomans had tried to preserve for decades in their relations with various foreign powers.

Upon the general outbreak in August 1914 of hostilities between the Central Powers (Germany and Austria-Hungary) and the Triple Entente (France, Britain, and Russia), neither side envisioned the Ottoman Empire as a major part of the conflict. However, its strategic location suggested that it could not actually remain neutral for very long. Departing from an earlier Ottoman policy of staying as aloof as possible from intra-European struggles (which the current Sultan Mehmet V wished to continue), the CUP leaders who had seized control of the Ottoman government in January 1913 decided that after the catastrophe of the Balkan Wars, they should seek a formal alliance with some foreign power. Many Ottoman statesmen would have preferred joining with the nations of the Entente, only because they calculated that Ottoman interests would be best served by joining Britain and France. Even before these two countries rejected proposals for an alliance with the Ottomans, CUP leader **Talat Pasha** made overtures to Russian Tsar Nicholas II, but was completely rebuffed.

In the end, the Ottomans approached the Germans. On July 22, 1914, the CUP's **Ismail Enver Pasha**, who had recently taken over as Ottoman minister of war, proposed a formal military alliance with Germany, which its ambassador in Istanbul, Hans von Wangenheim, promptly refused after consulting with Liman von Sanders. These two determined that the Ottoman army was too weak, its government too poor, and its leadership too uncertain. Nevertheless, based on the final decision of the central German government as well as Enver Pasha's continued lobbying, a secret Ottoman-German pact was signed on August 2, 1914. It stated that the Ottoman Empire would ally with Germany and Austria-Hungary if the Russians attacked either of them, and that the German advisory mission was to play an important role in planning and executing Ottoman military operations: a clause that would have a substantial impact on the Ottoman conduct of the war.

The competition between European powers to influence the Ottomans had been intensifying for a long time. Several years before the current crisis, the Ottomans had contracted with British companies to have two modern battleships built, to be named the *Sultan Osman I* and the *Reshadiye*. By July 1914, these vessels had been launched, undergone sea trials, and were ready to be commissioned into the Ottoman Navy. Crews had already arrived in England to collect them when First Lord of the Admiralty Winston Churchill announced on August 3 that due to the outbreak of hostilities between Britain, France, and Germany, these vessels would be taken for incorporation into the Royal Navy as HMS *Agincourt* and HMS *Erin*: an action that was allowed by their sales contracts.

This seizure became immensely unpopular in the Ottoman Empire, since public donations there had partially funded the ships, and major contributors to them had been awarded "Navy Donation" medals. Just as Ottoman public opinion turned against Britain, the Germans sent two key warships, the *Goeben* and the *Breslau,* to Istanbul. There they joined the Ottoman fleet along with their complete crews, now renamed the *Yavuz* and the *Midilli*. With pro-German popular sentiment suddenly soaring, German Admiral Wilhelm Souchon (1864–1946) replaced Admiral Limpus as commander-in-chief of the Ottoman Navy.

The first hostile acts taken by a military unit under an Ottoman flag were in fact under the command of Souchon, who led a naval squadron that shelled the Russian Black Sea ports of Sevastopol and Odessa and destroyed the Russian minesweeper *Prut* on October 29. This put the Ottoman government in a somewhat difficult situation. Although they had not formally authorized Souchon to carry out this operation, they could not now back away from what it had unleashed. In fact, it caused the Russians to declare war on the Ottomans, followed by Britain a few days later. By November 12, 1914, the Ottoman government officially declared war on the Triple Entente.

Although hesitant at first, once the Ottomans had officially declared war, the CUP threw its full support behind mobilization efforts, now seeing this as a chance to right old wrongs and regain lost standing. The Ottoman government ordered all Ottoman men of military age to report for duty on October 31, creating large processing delays as well as compromising the fall harvest in many areas that depended on manual farm labor.

The government also took the unusual step of having the Ottoman Shaykh al-Islam issue a fatwa to legitimize the war as a jihad that all Muslims around the world were invited to join. This was intended primarily as a unifying device for Muslims across the Ottoman Empire and proclaimed in mosques across the Middle East: a gesture more reminiscent of the Pan-Islamist vision of Abd al-Hamid's time than the modernizing programs of the CUP. The fatwa was also directed at Muslims in places ruled by the Entente powers such as India, Africa, and Central Asia, calling them to join the Ottoman cause and oppose their colonial masters on religious grounds.

An archaeologist who worked for the German Foreign Office, Baron Max von Oppenheim, had written a secret study several years earlier explaining how such an appeal might undermine British, French, and Russian authority in these areas. With the coming of the war, von Oppenheim now served as head of a German "Intelligence Office for the East." This office publicized the fatwa, reminding Muslims of the Ottoman sultan's status as caliph in an attempt to stir up anticolonial sentiments through propaganda in a variety of languages.

FIRST OTTOMAN BATTLE PLAN: RETAKE EASTERN ANATOLIA

The CUP leadership focused more on immediate action. The first opportunity for this came when a Russian army attacked in Eastern Anatolia just after the initial declarations of war. This first attack was thwarted fairly easily by the Ottoman Third Army, then under the command of the veteran General Hasan Izzet Pasha. To build on this success, Hasan Izzet Pasha argued for a defensive strategy based on holding the fortress at Erzurum, but Enver Pasha disagreed. Buoyed by the positive momentum of this initial victory and the possibility of reclaiming territory lost in 1878, Enver devised a comprehensive strategy for a bigger campaign in Eastern Anatolia.

Much of Enver's plan was based on his training in Prussian and Napoleonic techniques of combat at the Ottoman Imperial Military Academy. It depended on Ottoman forces being mobile and able to arrive at specific objective points at exact times—impossible goals to achieve given the arduous battlefield terrain and logistical difficulties in the area. Due to his dissent, Hasan Izzet Pasha was asked to resign as the Third Army commander, and Enver himself travelled to the front in mid-December to take personal charge of the situation.

During the ensuing Battle of Sarikamish, the Russians retained a key logistical advantage because they kept control of the railway line that connected Kars and the Caucasus region. In addition, despite the large number of regular troops being called away to help fight the Germans, the Russians were able to secure the cooperation of local irregular forces, particularly Armenian volunteers called *fedais* (the same term employed for Ottoman volunteers in the Second Balkan War). For the first few days of this clash, despite enduring severe cold and serious losses, Ottoman forces retained the offensive, and Enver's plan appeared to be working. However, by the time that the first Ottoman troops actually reached the Russian front lines at Sarikamish on December 29, only a few hundred were still in good enough physical condition to attack the city, and they were easily repelled by its defenders.

This marked the beginning of Ottoman defeat in this encounter. The next few days saw a series of retreats and losses due to enemy fire, cold, and illness. Enver's complex theoretical plan of operation could not be translated into reality. The disaster that ensued became one of the worst Ottoman defeats of the entire war, occurring only two months after fighting began.

The involvement of Armenian volunteers on the Russian side was an important factor at Sarikamish. Some Armenians had volunteered to help the Russians upon the outbreak of hostilities, because they decided that there was no further possibility for fulfilling Armenian political aspirations in an Ottoman Empire that was now at war and under attack. The head of the Armenian Orthodox Church (in Russian Armenia) blessed this effort, and Tsar Nicholas II even made a trip to the Caucasian front to thank these troops in person.

The exact number of Russian versus Ottoman Armenians serving with the Russian troops there remains hard to determine. Since the 1878 war, the border in Eastern Anatolia between regions controlled by Russia and the Ottomans had been quite porous. The defeat at the Battle of Sarikamish definitely marked a turning point in CUP attitudes about Ottoman Armenians because of the perception that Armenian forces had played a key role in securing Russian victory there.

At the last congress of the Ottoman Armenian Revolutionary Federation Dashnak Party, held just before the war in Erzurum at the end of July and beginning of August 1914, the party's leaders had still reaffirmed the organization's loyalty to the Ottoman Empire. However, the delegates to this meeting rejected an offer presented to them by a high-ranking CUP delegation. This group communicated to them that if they were willing and able to incite subversion among Russian Armenians in the coming conflict, the Ottoman Empire would be well-disposed to agree to an autonomous Armenian government under its aegis, including all of Russian Armenia as well as parts of the Ottoman provinces of Erzurum, Van, and Bitlis. The rejection of this offer has been characterized as the beginning of an unbridgeable gap between the Ottoman Armenians and their government. In any event, the Ottoman-Armenian divide deepened rapidly as the war progressed.

OTTOMAN ATTACK ON THE SUEZ CANAL

Eastern Anatolia was not the only battle-front where the CUP saw a chance to regain lost territory. In February 1915, the Ottoman Fourth Army led by Jemal Pasha (with the assistance of his German advisor General Friedrich Freiherr Kress von Kressenstein) attacked the Suez Canal. Because of logistical difficulties there and their inadequate equipment, they were easily turned back by British, Egyptian, and Australia and New Zealand Army Corps (ANZAC) troops after only one day of fighting. At the outbreak of hostilities, Britain had declared Egypt to be totally independent of the Ottomans and a British protectorate. This major rebuff of the Ottoman effort to reclaim it was another serious setback for CUP war plans.

ARMENIAN CRISIS AND THE GALLIPOLI CAMPAIGN

In the wake of these early military disasters, the Ottoman leadership had a crisis of confidence and took drastic measures to shore up what was perceived to be a quickly deteriorating situation. The greatest victims of this reaction were to be the Ottoman Armenians, who as recently as 1908 had been on a path to becoming full partners in the Ottoman system. Only a few months into the war, they were now suddenly seen by the CUP leadership as some of the greatest potential enemies of the empire. They were treated accordingly.

Enver Pasha issued an order on February 25, 1915, that all Armenians serving in the **Ottoman Army** should be disarmed and transferred to labor battalions. These units had been formed at the beginning of the war in order to disarm Armenians (serving as regular members of the Ottoman army in significant numbers since 1908) and have them serve instead in military support functions. While some were employed for legitimate labor activities, many of these groups, particularly by the early months of 1915, became the pretext for simply getting rid of Armenian men, and they were placed under the control of irregular Ottoman military units. The situation came to blows in the city of Van in April 1915, when the Ottoman governor there, Enver Pasha's brother-in-law Jevdet, tried to assemble Armenian men to be conscripted into labor battalions. This quickly degenerated into an outright war between Armenians and Ottomans in the city that broke out on April 20.

A few days later, an order was issued to round up Armenian intellectuals in Istanbul at almost precisely the same time that the Allies were making their first major landings on the Gallipoli Peninsula just west of the Dardanelles Straits. Using a force that included a substantial number of ANZAC troops, this landing was the second phase of a military campaign whose main goal was to seize the Dardanelles. The plan was to block sea-lanes to Istanbul and the Black Sea, which would effectively cut the main supply artery of the Ottoman Empire and force the Ottomans out of the war.

The initial landing operation, successful at first, quickly degenerated into a stalemate that lasted over nine months. The Gallipoli campaign was marked by a series of grinding clashes that eventually claimed more than 131,000 lives on both sides. This had significant political repercussions in Britain when it was revealed that military planning and coordination between naval and land forces for

ANZAC soldiers landing at Gallipoli (1915)

Science and Society/SuperStock

the campaign had been inadequate and rushed. Gallipoli became remembered in Australia and New Zealand as the first great conflict experienced by these young nations, whose losses are still commemorated every year there on ANZAC Day (April 25). Lieutenant Colonel Mustafa Kemal (later Ataturk) also achieved fame there. He served as the commander of one of the main Ottoman units that successfully resisted the invading force, the 19th Division, which overcame tremendous odds to stop the ANZAC troops in August 1915 during the Battle of Chunuk Bair (*Jonk Bayiri*).

Although the Ottomans were relieved to have thwarted Allied plans to seize the Dardanelles and Gallipoli for the time being, their problems in Eastern Anatolia continued to grow. The initial Armenian resisters to the Ottomans at Van in April were aided by a Russian force sent there under the command of General Yudenich, the victorious general of Sarikamish. His troops occupied Van in late May 1915, as Armenian irregular forces tried to establish control over the surrounding countryside.

This situation did not last long, because Ottoman forces retook Van in early August. Thousands of refugees who had joined the Russians there fled eastwards. The Ottomans again had to pull back and evacuate the city at the end of September 1915, prompting some who had fled to return. Russian and Ottoman forces fought back and forth over different parts of Eastern Anatolia for much of the next two years, with neither side establishing stable control over the whole region for a prolonged period of time.

As Eastern Anatolia devolved into a zone of continuous conflict, the CUP government decided to take further action against Ottoman Armenians. On May 29, 1915, the Ottoman government issued a "Temporary Law concerning measures to be taken by the army with respect to those who are resisting government activities in wartime" (a decree later known as the *Tehjir Kanunu* ["Deportation Law"]). This law ordered that whole villages and districts where people (either individually or as a group) had violated rules put in place by the military or had conducted acts of espionage or treason be sent away and settled in other locations.

The deportations resulting from this order consisted of hundreds of thousands of Ottoman Armenians being expelled from all over Anatolia to Syria (principally to the town of Dayr al-Zawr on the Euphrates and to Damascus and Aleppo) as well as huge numbers fleeing into Russia and other countries over the next few years: a process that claimed untold lives. The final result was the end of the Armenian community in Anatolia. This historical trauma, at the heart of the modern Armenian experience, has remained the focal point of controversy and enmity between Armenians and Turks ever since.

Most Armenians, along with most foreign scholars and many foreign governments, remember this event as the "Armenian genocide," perceiving it as the deliberate destruction by Ottoman rulers of the Ottoman Empire's Armenian population at the time of World War I and during its aftermath.

Most Turks, along with some foreign scholars and foreign governments, deny this charge, challenging the veracity of sources used to prove it and pointing out the extreme suffering also endured by Muslim Ottomans and others during World War I. In addition, they put these events in the context of the horrible treatment suffered by Muslims fleeing from the Russian Empire and the Balkans to Anatolia around the turn of twentieth century. This continuing unresolved dispute reveals the intensity of emotions about national consciousness and nationalisms that boiled over in the cauldron of World War I. In this way, the conflict marked the final cataclysm of the Ottoman Empire, in whose former territories more than thirty modern nations have been established.

PROBLEMS IN OTTOMAN SYRIA

The war also unleashed the nationalism of the Ottoman Empire's Arab provinces, particularly with the increasingly "Turkish" emphasis of the CUP government in the years just before the war. Although most Arabs began the war as loyal Ottomans, new ways of thinking about an "Arab" nation and people beckoned some of them. The desire to identify oneself as an "Arab" only grew stronger after the initial setbacks of the war revealed substantial Ottoman military and political weaknesses. Another source of friction for Ottoman Arabs was how the CUP had begun to replace members of the traditional ruling elite with its own functionaries in provincial posts after the Young Turk Revolution. This created serious discontent, particularly in Syria.

After the war started, the situation became even more challenging when Jemal Pasha, another member of the CUP's inner circle, took over as governor of Syria, operating under a May 1915 decree that gave him extraordinary powers. After the failure of the first Suez offensive a few months earlier, he took a harsh approach to governing this land. His harshness pushed a number of Arab intellectuals into the enemy camp, but he kept Ottoman Syria (a territory comprising modern Syria, Jordan, Israel, Lebanon, as well as parts of Turkey and Iraq) more or less pacified, with rising Arab nationalist sentiments suppressed.

SHARIF HUSSEIN: PLANS FOR REVOLT

At the outset of the war, the British searched for ways to harness these growing anti-Ottoman feelings. They found a successful strategy by courting **Sharif Hussein ibn Ali**, former Ottoman governor of the Hejaz and leader of the Hashemites: clan of the rulers of Mecca and Medina related to Muhammad. After 1908, Hussein, like many of his Arab counterparts, found himself at odds with the CUP and feared that they would try to replace him. His second son, **Abdullah ibn Hussein**, had been elected to the Ottoman parliament in 1908. Early in 1914, Abdullah started a dialogue with the British High Commissioner in Cairo, Sir Herbert Kitchener. He wanted to see if the British would support Sharif Hussein and his family if the CUP

moved against them." Kitchener made no firm commitments at that time. After the Ottomans entered the war on the German side in the fall, Kitchener, in his new capacity as British secretary of state for war, communicated that the British would now favor an independent Arab state led by Hussein if he allied with them.

When the Ottomans secured a fatwa from their Shaykh al-Islam legitimizing their declaration of war in November 1914 as a *jihad*, the Sultan made a direct appeal to Sharif Hussein, in his capacity as hereditary ruler of Mecca and Medina, to support the Ottoman war effort and contribute troops to it. Soon after this, representatives of two Arab nationalist secret societies based in Syria, "al-Fata" and "al-Ahd," visited Hussein in Mecca in January 1915. Their mission was to persuade him to lead a revolt against the Ottomans. At about the same time, Hussein's eldest son Ali learned of an Ottoman plot to depose Hussein as Sharif of the Hejaz in favor of Ali Haydar, head of a rival branch of the Hashemite family.

Hussein ordered his third son Faisal to confront the Ottoman government in Istanbul with evidence of this plot. On the way there, he stopped in Damascus to discuss the possibilities of a revolt with leaders of Arab secret societies. Faisal left skeptical about the strength of this movement and did not believe that a revolt could succeed without outside assistance. In Istanbul, when the Ottoman government conveyed to him that it was extremely urgent that his father join in their declaration of *jihad*, Faisal interpreted this as a sign that they were about to move against his family.

On his return trip, Faisal visited Damascus again, where he formally accepted the invitation for his branch of the **Hashemites** to cooperate with Arab nationalist societies against the Ottomans. They gave him a document that became known as the "Damascus Protocol." This was a plan for the Arabs to commence a revolt against Ottoman rule in alliance with Great Britain, in return for British recognition of Arab independence in an area bounded by the 37th parallel of latitude (now near the southern border of modern Turkey) in the northeast, the Iranian border and the Persian Gulf in the east, the Mediterranean in the northwest, and in the south by the Arabian Sea.

In discussions Hussein had with his sons Faisal, Ali, and Abdullah in the Hejaz in June 1915, Faisal argued for caution, Ali was against rebellion, while Abdullah wanted action. In the end, Hussein chose June 1916 as the tentative date to commence an armed revolt against the Ottomans. Based on this plan, he opened negotiations with the new British High Commissioner in Egypt, Sir Henry McMahon, exchanging a series of letters between July 1915 and January 1916 later known as the "Hussein-McMahon Correspondence." The most important letter was one sent from McMahon to Hussein in October 1915. In essence, it affirmed that the British government would officially recognize an independent Arab state led by Sharif Hussein with the frontiers specified in the Damascus Protocol, but with two key provisions. First, this territory would not extend to parts of Syria that were west of Damascus, Homs, Hama, and Aleppo, nor would it include the Ottoman districts of Mersin or Alexandretta. Second, it would include all areas within the proposed boundaries in which Great Britain was "free to act without detriment to interests of her ally France." These particular territorial provisions were to cause big problems after the war, but the exchange of letters allowed the Arab Revolt to begin as planned by the summer of 1916.

At this point in the war, Allied morale sank with news of the carnage of the battle of Verdun and the setbacks at Gallipoli, and the latest information from Iraq was not encouraging either. There, after a successful landing in which the British captured Basra and the southern part of the country, several thousand British and Indian troops became trapped in Kut al-Amara, a town 200 miles north of Basra on the Tigris where they endured a siege of 147 days. About half of the 13,000 British and Indian soldiers who

surrendered there to the Ottomans in April 1916 died from disease or starvation while imprisoned.

THE ARAB REVOLT

On the other side of the region, things were looking up for the Allies when the Arab Revolt commenced with an attack by several thousand Arab horsemen on the Hejaz port of Jedda on June 10, 1916. They were assisted by British warships and seaplanes and secured the city within one week. Aided by the Royal Navy, this Arab army was then able to occupy many cities along the Red Sea, capturing several thousand Ottoman prisoners by September.

In October, the British government in Egypt sent out a young officer to work with them who had done graduate study on Crusader castles and ancient Middle Eastern archeology as well as traveled in the region before the war: Captain T. E. Lawrence. His most important operational contribution to the revolt was to convince Faisal and Abdullah, then leading tribal forces on behalf of their father Sharif Hussein, to pursue their campaigns in close coordination with the British. He persuaded them to bypass a large Ottoman garrison in Medina and to attack the Hejaz railway instead on many occasions. This effectively tied up a lot of Ottoman troops, who were obliged to protect the railway and constantly repair damage to it.

In January 1917, Faisal advanced on the west Arabian city of Wajh from the south with a force consisting of thousands of camel riders and foot soldiers, in coordination with a small party of Arabs and British troops attacking from the north. This joint operation caught the Ottoman garrison there by surprise and forced them to surrender within two days. The Ottomans were increasingly pushed into a defensive position of holding onto a few bases and railway stations, while the Arab army kept attracting more volunteers based on its successes.

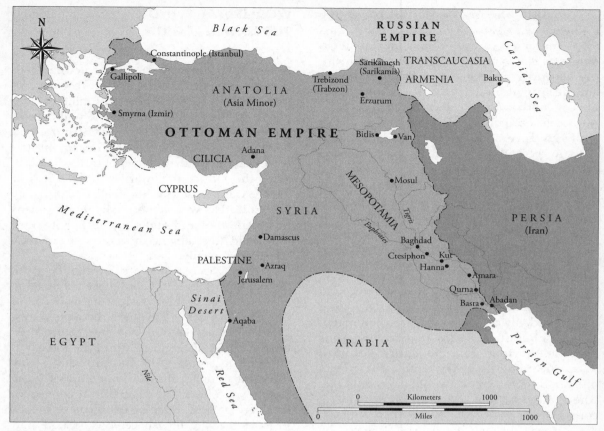

MAP 9.2 World War I in the Middle East

Capitalizing on the growing reputation of this Arab force, Lawrence was able in the summer of 1917 to recruit a new group of Arab irregulars led by a shaykh of the Syrian Huwaytat tribe, Auda Abu Tayi, who had formerly been an Ottoman vassal. This new contingent mounted a successful assault from the desert to capture the port city of Aqaba on July 6. This was a significant victory, since Aqaba was the only Red Sea port still under Ottoman control that could threaten the right flank of the British Egyptian Expeditionary Force, then just preparing to advance into Palestine. After Aqaba fell, Lawrence rode 150 miles to Suez to arrange for the Royal Navy to bring food and supplies to the 2,500 Arabs and 700 Ottoman prisoners in the city.

The success of all these Arab military operations gave much-needed momentum to Allied efforts on the Mediterranean coast. For some time, the Egyptian Expeditionary Force had not been faring so well. After a second Ottoman assault on the Suez Canal failed in the summer of 1916, the British mounted two successive attacks on Gaza in March and April of 1917 that were repulsed. With the Ottomans now weighed down by the Arab army coming up from the Hejaz, the new British commander General Edmund Allenby successfully broke through the main Gaza-Beersheba Ottoman defensive line in southern Palestine in November, which led swiftly to the capture of Jerusalem just before Christmas, 1917.

In 1918, the Arab cavalry kept gaining followers who sensed victory at hand. This force continued to use its now-familiar techniques as it advanced: harassing Ottoman supply networks, attacking their small garrisons, and destroying railroad lines. Its operations were immortalized by Lowell Thomas, a young American journalist who spent several weeks with Lawrence and the Arab army in March 1918. At the end of the war, Thomas produced one of the first multimedia shows about this offensive, which he presented on a world tour that made Lawrence a legendary figure and shaped popular images of the Middle East in the early 1920s.

The whole campaign culminated in the Battle of Megiddo in late September 1918, which quickly turned into an Ottoman rout. As the Ottoman Seventh Army fled down a road going east from Nablus into the Jordan Valley, it was suddenly attacked by a large contingent of RAF aircraft. A series of bombing runs essentially wiped out the entire Ottoman force, including its heavy equipment, within one hour. T.E. Lawrence would later write that "the R.A.F. lost four killed. The Turks lost a corps."[1]

In part through the damage inflicted by Arab irregular troops on Ottoman logistics and supplies and also through the tactical air superiority now established by the British, General Allenby's final offensive led swiftly to the fall of Damascus on October 1: an event that signaled the end of the war in the Arab provinces for the Ottomans. When Allied forces marched into Damascus, they found the Arab Revolt flag already raised there by nationalist sympathizers. This was also very near the final end of the war as a whole for the Ottomans, who signed an armistice with the Allies on October 30 on a ship anchored in the harbor of Mudros, just off the Greek island of Lemnos, located in the Aegean Sea south of the Dardanelles.

---

[1] T.E. Lawrence, *Revolt in the Desert* (Garden City, NY: Garden City Publishing Company, 1927), 295.

WORLD WAR I AND THE JEWISH LEGION

The progress of the war marked the shift of Zionist allegiances from careful neutrality to becoming aligned with Britain as that nation's fortunes rose with its successful military campaigns in the Middle East. At the outbreak of the conflict, the World Zionist Organization's headquarters were situated in Berlin, but the organization tried to stay politically neutral. After the Ottoman Empire entered the war on the German side in the fall of 1914, many Zionist leaders were deported by the Ottomans from Palestine and ended up in Egypt, since they held Russian passports and were thus considered enemy aliens.

Two Zionist leaders originally from Russia, Ze'ev Jabotinsky and Josef Trumpeldor, created a unit in the British army made up of Zionist deportees in Egypt that became known as the "Jewish Legion." As the "Zion Mule Corps" it first distinguished itself in combat at Gallipoli in spring 1915 and provided a way to recruit Zionist Russian immigrants for the British war effort. Although British commanders were at first wary of using these troops in Palestine, the Jewish Legion did take part in the 1917–1918 British campaign there, for which Jabotinsky was awarded a medal.

In Britain, a new government came to power after the Shell Crisis of 1915, in which it was revealed that the previous government had not produced enough artillery shells to supply the war effort. In this new administration, David Lloyd-George became the minister responsible for armaments. Before the war, he had been a Christian supporter of the Zionist movement and had represented them in legal dealings with the British government. One of the Zionist leaders in Britain at that time was the chemist Chaim Weizmann. By coincidence, Weizmann had just developed a method for the mass production of acetone that allowed Britain to meet its armament production needs. According to Lloyd-George, Weizmann told him that he wanted no payment for this, only for Zionist rights in Palestine to be officially recognized by the British government. The result was that when Lloyd-George became prime minister in 1916, he helped arrange for his foreign secretary, Arthur Balfour, to issue a declaration in November 1917 supporting a Jewish "national home" in Palestine, the consequences of which would only become clear after the end of the war.

FINAL OTTOMAN DRIVE TO THE EAST

Meanwhile, the Arab army assembled by Faisal, Sharif Hussein's third son, together with the Egyptian Expeditionary Force commanded by General Allenby, now given the title Viscount Allenby for his triumph at Megiddo, had terminated Ottoman control over Syria, and hostilities in the western part of the Ottoman Empire had drawn to a close. However, Ottoman forces remained engaged in one area in the fall of 1918: the Caucasus region. Russia's war efforts there suddenly collapsed when the November 1917 Bolshevik Revolution plunged the whole Russian Empire into civil war.

This caused the withdrawal of Tsarist Russian forces from Eastern Anatolia, which in turn brought further suffering for refugees, particularly Armenians fleeing the Ottoman advance as the Russians withdrew. Russian commanders in the area and Vehip Pasha, chief of the Ottoman Third Army, signed an armistice at Erzinjan, the point marking the farthest western Russian advance, in December 1917. Ordinary Russian soldiers started to leave the Caucasus battlefront attempting to return home, but their exodus created a huge power vacuum in that region, which others quickly attempted to fill.

ENVER PASHA AND THE "ARMY OF ISLAM"

Shortly after signing an armistice with the Russians at Erzinjan, the CUP managed to establish friendly relations at first with the Bolsheviks who had just taken power. The Ottoman-Russian friendship treaty signed on January 1, 1918, was one of the first international agreements concluded by the Bolshevik government. This was soon followed by the March 1918 Treaty of Brest-Litovsk (between the Central Powers [Germany, Austria-Hungary, and the Ottoman Empire] and Russia), which completely took Russia out of the war.

This treaty and the vagaries of the war had changed the geopolitical situation to a great degree for the Central Powers. The old concept of a strategic link from Berlin to Baghdad had gone by the wayside when the British finally captured Baghdad in February 1917. However, the upheaval in the Russian Empire that had erupted at about the same time caused some to envision a different connection to the East: one that linked Berlin with Baku (in Russian Azerbaijan) and Bukhara (in Russian Turkestan) instead.

In any event, these diplomatic agreements did not halt the movement of armies on the ground in this region. Between March and May, 1918, the Ottoman Third Army led by Vehib Pasha reoccupied Kars, Batum, Ardahan, and other areas beyond even the 1878 boundaries, taking advantage of the prevailing chaos of war to seize new territory. The Germans, in turn, established a new military mission and presence in Georgia. When the Ottomans signed "friendship" treaties in June with the new independent governments of Armenia, Azerbaijan, and Georgia, Georgia and Armenia had to agree to reductions in their territories and to permit the Ottomans free passage to Azerbaijan. Some dissatisfied Armenian guerrilla leaders such as Andranik Ozanian continued resistance for several months, but this had become the one battlefront where the Ottomans suddenly enjoyed renewed power and influence.

All this activity translated for some members of the Ottoman CUP leadership into an opportunity to act on old Pan-Turkic dreams to use the Caucasus as a stepping stone for expansion toward the East. Just after the Erzinjan Armistice, Ottoman minister of war Enver Pasha ordered the creation of a new military force to be called the "Army of Islam" as a vehicle for this plan. It would have no German advisers, but be manned by volunteers and not officially attached to the Ottoman Army, to avoid any charges that the Ottomans were violating the Brest-Litovsk agreement. Its ostensible mission would be to link Turkic populations in the southern and eastern Caucasus, particularly in Azerbaijan, with the Ottomans: the first step in a larger project to connect all the Turkic peoples of the collapsing Russian Empire with their Ottoman cousins.

Enver Pasha's other obvious agenda was to put the Caucasus region under Turkish suzerainty in order to give the Central Powers control over the Baku oil fields. Finally, a presence on the Caspian coast might really open the way to further expansion in Central Asia and possibly even British India. To promote all this, the CUP created a special Caucasian Department under the direction of Hasan Rusheni, who was sent on a secret mission in March 1918 to Baku to prepare the way for more Ottoman engagement there.

The Army of Islam was assembled in Azerbaijan under the command of Enver's half-brother Nuri Pasha by the late spring of 1918 out of a combination of units from the Ottoman Fifth Army, as well as Azeri and other irregular forces from the Caucasus. Its creation occurred around the time Azerbaijan declared its independence, since it was asserted that Nuri had been ordered to commence military operations there to free Azerbaijan from Bolshevik rule as requested by its new "independent Islamic government." The Army of Islam and the Azerbaijani national government were both situated in Ganja, because the capital city of Baku had fallen under the control of a Bolshevik-led organization, the Baku Commune, in April.

Nuri's main civilian advisor was Ahmet Agaoglu. Agaoglu ("Aghayev") was a prominent Azerbaijani supporter of "**Pan-Turkism**" who had spent considerable time in Istanbul and became a close associate of Yusuf Akchura and other activists there. They tried to steer the Azerbaijani government's policies

away from the socialist and communist programs being militantly promoted by the Baku Commune toward the Ottomanist/Pan-Islamic/Pan-Turkic constitutionalist agendas of the CUP. This abstract appeal to Pan-Turkic unity only went so far. Even Azeris allied with Nuri soon began to resent his interference as a foreigner.

The other problem was that by the summer of 1918, the Ottomans began to diverge quite substantially from the Germans in their plans for the Caucasus. With the Brest-Litovsk Treaty, Germany accepted the Communist takeover of the Russian Empire and sought to do business with the Bolsheviks now ruling it, particularly in the area of exporting oil from Azerbaijan. Germany became concerned that the Ottomans might disrupt this supply (even if just because of the logistical difficulties created) if they defeated the Baku Commune, now closely allied to the Bolsheviks ruling in St. Petersburg.

As the Ottoman forces and the Army of Islam gained ground in their push toward Baku, the Bolshevik leader of the Baku Commune, Stepan Shahumian, requested Red Army reinforcements from Moscow and food from the North Caucasus. These did not arrive, being diverted to Tsaristyn, where Stalin was at that very moment waging a pivotal battle of the Russian Civil War; after his victory the city was later renamed Stalingrad. Just as the Army of Islam was on the verge of capturing Baku on July 26, the Baku Commune Soviet (the ruling council) dissolved in disagreement. A majority of its members voted to invite a British force to come there and keep the Ottoman-led army away. When Bolshevik members resigned in protest, remaining council members formed a new anti-Soviet Central Caspian Dictatorship.

Several non-Bolshevik members of the Baku Soviet who formed this new government had been in communication with a British commander in Iran: General Lionel Dunsterville. He commanded a small elite group of less than one thousand British, Australian, and New Zealand officers and NCOs formed in

Baghdad in January 1918, which became known as the Dunsterforce. Its mission was to keep Germany and the Ottoman Empire out of Iran and the Caucasus region. When he received Baku's request for help, he proceeded there with his troops. The Dunsterforce landed in Baku on August 16, just in time to prepare for battle with the Army of Islam on August 26.

At this time, Germany made an offer to the Soviet government that it would quell the Army of Islam in exchange for guaranteed access to Azerbaijani oil. They signed a codicil to the Brest-Litovsk Treaty on August 27 with the Russian government to formalize this arrangement. However, when the Germans requested their Ottoman allies to halt the assault of the Army of Islam on Baku, Enver Pasha ignored them. Between August 26 and September 1, Ottoman forces established positions, which they consolidated over the next two weeks, and were reinforced by another Ottoman division. The early part of September saw the lessening of German opposition, now that Ottoman forces faced British troops instead of Bolshevik forces.

The Baku Army, now commanded by the officers of the Dunsterforce and fighting against the Army of Islam, was a mixed group of soldiers. Many of its troops were Armenian veterans of years of combat against the Ottomans, who treated the Muslim inhabitants of Baku with some cruelty and massacred a number of civilians there. In the end, much of this Baku Army had to flee by ship across the Caspian together with the British to Iran on the night of September 14, but not before Muslim residents of Baku exacted harsh revenge for what had been done to them.

All this activity became a footnote to history when the Ottomans surrendered with the Armistice of Mudros on October 30. Soon after that, a new British commander, General William Thomson, landed in Baku with 2,000 Indian Army troops, ordered all Ottoman troops to leave immediately, refused to recognize the Azerbaijani government, and put the country under direct British military rule.

He also ended the long-running insurgency of Armenian guerrilla forces in the Karabakh region, and placed this mountainous area under the control of the Azerbaijanis: an action that fueled the ethnic tensions culminating in the Nagorno-Karabakh War (1988–1994) between Armenia and Azerbaijan.

IRAN IN WORLD WAR I

British troops in Azerbaijan had traveled across the Caspian Sea from Iran, where World War I also had a substantial impact. Already in 1907, Iran had been divided into Russian and British spheres of influence. Despite the fact that the newly enthroned Ahmad Shah Qajar issued a decree proclaiming Iran's neutrality on November 1, 1914, the war was bound to affect the country significantly. The two countries who kept troops there (Britain and Russia) were military allies against Iran's western neighbor: the Ottoman Empire.

At the beginning of the war, various powerful factions in Iran favored the Germans because they were neither British nor Russian. Since the Germans had not been engaged in the imperial game as long as their British and Russian adversaries, however, they were at a disadvantage logistically and diplomatically. This was demonstrated by what happened to the German secret agent Wilhelm Wassmuss. He achieved striking success in 1915 by infiltrating the British zone of influence in southern Iran and stirring up feelings against them among the tribal populations there. He even established loose political control and influence over some areas. Yet the British, with their large presence in nearby India, were able to create a new military unit called the South Persia Rifles to stabilize the situation there within a couple of years.

A bigger problem was the fact that German strategic goals in Iran, although they overlapped with Ottoman aims, were not identical to them. The Germans saw Iran as a staging ground for taking on the British in India. Some members of the Ottoman CUP leadership perceived it, particularly its

Azerbaijan province, as a stepping stone for ambitions to create Pan-Turkic ties.

Neither the Russians nor the British were going to allow any rivals in their spheres of influence, but not all Iranians would simply acquiesce to the status quo of British-Russian dominance. In November 1915, the Russians got wind of a plan for Iran to declare war on the Allies and receive German help, and their soldiers marched on Tehran. Most political leaders who opposed the British and Russians from among the parliamentary deputies, newspaper editors, and members of the gendarmerie fled from Tehran to Qom. The shah was persuaded by the British and the Russians not to join them, but because there was no longer a quorum in the parliament, it was closed temporarily and a new pro-British prime minister was appointed as its caretaker.

In Qom, the dissident group, now known as the Emigrants (*muhajirun*), began to form a "Provisional Government," which, with German help, asserted its official status in March 1916. By this time, the group had arrived at Qasr-i Shirin, staying just ahead of Russian forces pursuing it. There, it received official greetings and recognition from the Ottoman and German governments as the legitimate authority in Iran. One month later, just as the group was about to be captured by the Russians, it fled to Iraq, where it remained until returning to Kermanshah, Iran, after the Ottoman army conquered that city. For the next seven months, this Iranian "Provisional Government" ruled areas of Iran under Ottoman military control: Kermanshah, Hamadan, Kordestan, Lorestan, and Persian Iraq. It even managed to put in a telegraph line and build a road, although it was plagued from the start by ruinous financial problems. The group wrote to the shah to express its allegiance and loyalty, inviting him to join them. He replied that he would ally with the Central Powers when the Ottoman Empire won the war, as he had communicated to the German Kaiser in an official letter. Ultimately, as Ottoman fortunes began to wane in Iraq, support for this government

diminished, and it ceased operations within a few months after it started.

The central government in Tehran lost control of many other parts of the country during the war. Tabriz, the capital of Azerbaijan and a key city in the Russian sphere of influence, saw occupiers come and go, dealing at various times with the Ottomans, Russians, and British. The Ottoman entry into Azerbaijan made northern Iran in general a contested territory. The CUP circulated propaganda in favor of reuniting Russian and Iranian Azerbaijan, a proposal that was designed to appeal to Azeris as well as those who supported closer links to the Ottomans. Taking advantage of Russian weakness at various times, the Ottomans occupied Tabriz briefly in early 1915 and again in the summer of 1918, holding onto it from then until the Mudros Armistice.

In the south near the border with Ottoman Iraq, **Khuzestan** remained firmly under the control of Sheikh Kazal, a tribal leader under British protection, although he nominally recognized the shah as his sovereign. Farther east, the port of Bushehr (Bushire) came under the direct occupation of the British in 1915, given its strategic importance for the Persian Gulf. In Gilan on the south Caspian coast, Mirza Kuchek Khan led the Jangali (Forest) revolutionary movement throughout the war, whose main goal was to restore and revive the ideals of the 1905–1906 Iranian Constitution. In June 1918, he and his comrades were defeated at a major battle at Manjil by an army consisting of the Dunsterforce led by General Dunsterville (then on its way to Baku) and an isolated detachment of White Russians led by Colonel Lazar Bicherakov. In spite of this setback and the fact that he was not really a Bolshevik (although he had once been a Bolshevik ally), Mirza Kuchek Khan survived until 1920 to found the Socialist Republic of Gilan with Soviet help, although he was killed the next year by Reza Khan (who took the throne as Reza Shah only four years later).

The end of World War I, conventionally marked by the armistices signed at Mudros (October 30) and in the forest of Compiègne

(November 11), did not in fact signify an end to war in the Middle East. The real clashes in the region that would define its modern boundaries were just starting or about to begin. Many of them were caused by dreams, promises, and expectations that arose as World War I was unfolding. It is ironic to note just how this "war to end all wars" led to what David Fromkin aptly calls the "peace to end all peace" after the war.

Questions to Think About

1. Why could World War I have been perceived at first as a "Third Balkan War"?
2. Why did the Ottoman Empire end up as an ally of Germany and Austria-Hungary in World War I?
3. Why did the Ottomans start the war in Eastern Anatolia, and what was the impact of their loss at the Battle of Sarikamish?
4. What caused the Armenian crisis in World War I, and what became its impact?
5. How did the Arab Revolt break out?
6. What role did the Arab Revolt play in the Allied war effort during World War I?
7. What was the Hussein-McMahon Correspondence and why was it important?
8. What role did the Jewish Legion play in World War I?
9. Who was Chaim Weizmann, and why was he friends with David Lloyd-George?
10. What was the Balfour Declaration?
11. What was Enver Pasha trying to do with the Army of Islam in the Caucasus?
12. What was the military mission of the Dunsterforce?
13. Who was Wilhelm Wassmuss, and what were his goals in Iran?

For Further Reading

Atabaki, Touraj. *Iran and the First World War: Battleground of the Great Powers*. London: I.B. Tauris, 2006.

Balakian, Grigoris, trans. Peter Balakian, and Aris G. Sevag. *Armenian Golgotha*. New York: Alfred A. Knopf, 2009.

Dadrian, Vahakn N. *Warrant for Genocide: Key Elements of Turko-Armenian Conflict*. New Brunswick, NJ: Transaction Publishers, 1999.

Erickson, Edward J. *Ordered to Die: A History of the Ottoman Army in the First World War*. Westport, CT: Greenwood Press, 2001.

Ford, Roger. *Eden to Armageddon: World War I in the Middle East*. New York: Pegasus Books, 2010.

Hourani, Albert. *Arabic Thought in the Liberal Age, 1798–1939*. Cambridge: Cambridge University Press, 1983.

Hovannisian, Richard G. *The Armenian People from Ancient to Modern Times*. New York: St. Martin's Press, 1997.

Korda, Michael. *Hero: The Life and Legend of Lawrence of Arabia*. New York: Harper, 2010.

Laqueur, Walter. *A History of Zionism*. London: Weidenfeld and Nicolson, 1972.

Lawrence, T. E. *Seven Pillars of Wisdom: A Triumph*. Garden City, NY: Doubleday, Doran & Co, 1938.

Lewy, Guenter. *The Armenian Massacres in Ottoman Turkey: A Disputed Genocide*. Salt Lake City: University of Utah Press, 2005.

McCarthy, Justin. *The Ottoman Peoples and the End of Empire*. London: Arnold, 2001.

McMeekin, Sean. *The Berlin-Baghdad Express: The Ottoman Empire and Germany's Bid for World Power*. Cambridge: Belknap Press of Harvard University Press, 2010.

Moorehead, Alan. *Gallipoli*. New York: Harper, 1956.

Reynolds, Michael A. *Shattering Empires: The Clash and Collapse of the Ottoman and Russian Empires, 1908-1918*. Cambridge: Cambridge University Press, 2011.

Teitelbaum, Joshua. *The Rise and Fall of the Hashimite Kingdom of Arabia*. New York: New York University Press, 2001.

Turfan, M. Naim. *Rise of the Young Turks: Politics, the Military and Ottoman Collapse*. London: I.B. Tauris, 2000.

10

Redefining the Middle East

WORLD WAR I AGREEMENTS

When the Ottomans signed the Mudros Armistice with Britain and France, it ended the formal state of war but did not bring peace to the Middle East. As in Europe, the cease-fire brought a turbulent period of territorial shifts sometimes resulting in the transfer of whole populations and areas. With the final collapse of empires, nationalist ideologies that excluded all who were not from a certain group grew much stronger. At the same time, ambiguous wartime promises made by the victors created much confusion and misunderstanding in postwar negotiations over how to define the region anew.

The prewar concept that Britain and France supported the Ottomans to maintain stability in the region was swept away when the Ottoman Empire entered World War I on the German side. Now, ideas about how to reshape and possibly dismantle it guided British and French policy in the Middle East. Different visions of how to do this clashed and often were overtaken rapidly by events as the war dragged on and intensified. In addition, the Allies made agreements and declarations as the war took place primarily to achieve victory, with little worry about whether their terms might later contradict each other.

As noted, British High Commissioner in Cairo, Sir Henry McMahon, had agreed in October 1915 in a letter to Sharif Hussein to "recognize and uphold the independence of the Arabs" in territories to be ruled by Hussein. This provided a clear declaration of support for Arab independence, which launched the **Arab Revolt** in the spring of 1916. British promises to Hussein became constrained by other commitments made soon after that.

Within two months, the British concluded a secret understanding with the French in January 1916 about the disposition of Ottoman territories after the war known as the **Sykes-Picot Agreement**. In it, Britain formally expressed its consent to French predominance in the coastal regions of Ottoman Syria, with an acknowledgment of French claims in Palestine. The Sykes-Picot accord called for direct British and French control over certain areas (modern Lebanon and southeastern Anatolia for the French and southern Iraq for the British) and more

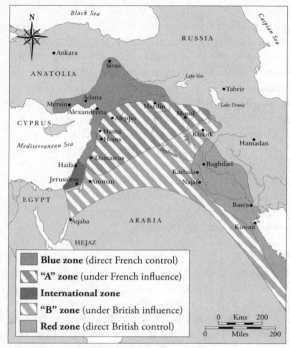

MAP 10.1 Sykes-Picot Agreement Proposed Map (1916)

Map legend:

Blue zone (direct French control)

"A" zone (under French influence)

International zone

"B" zone (under British influence)

Red zone (direct British control)

the British officials in Cairo in continuous contact with Hussein, which created uncertainties among the Arabs at a critical point in the war.

A bigger concern was raised by the **Balfour Declaration**. This document was delivered in early November 1917 by Arthur Balfour, then British foreign secretary, to the head of the British Zionist Federation, Lord Rothschild. It formally declared for the first time the British government's official support for the establishment in Palestine of "a national home for the Jewish people... it being clearly understood that nothing shall be done which may prejudice the... rights of existing non-Jewish communities [there]...."[1] The phrase "national home" took the place of any more explicit call for a "nation" or "state," showing sensitivity to the diplomatic complexities of the situation.

The issuance of the Balfour Declaration has been explained in several ways. Following the February Revolution in Russia in early 1917, the British became terribly worried about losing that nation as its ally in the war. Some officials argued that just such an expression of support for a Jewish presence in Palestine might prove useful in garnering support among the worldwide Jewish community: a group seen as having influence among revolutionaries who had just taken power in Russia. By the fall of 1917, the October Revolution was now unfolding, bringing a government to Russia whose clear intention was to leave the war entirely, rendering such diplomatic gestures moot. From another point of view, the establishment of a sympathetic Jewish presence near the Suez Canal was also seen as potentially useful for Britain's greater strategic interests.

In any event, more diplomatic damage control became necessary. In January 1918, David Hogarth, one of the directors of the British Arab Bureau in Cairo, called on Sharif Hussein in Jedda to present him a letter from Sir Mark Sykes later called the Hogarth Message. It explained that the Balfour

indirect influence over others (inland Syria and northern Iraq for the French and Jordan along with northern Arabia for the British), together with joint British/French control of Palestine.

Controversy over these arrangements erupted when the full text (shared confidentially with the Russians) was released by the Bolsheviks after they took power in November 1917 and made all the tsar's secret archives public. Some interpreted the Sykes-Picot accord as conflicting with the Hussein-McMahon Correspondence, while others (including Sir Mark Sykes, one of its authors) argued that the two agreements were actually quite compatible. In fact, Sykes and Picot had traveled together to Jedda in May 1917 to reassure Sharif Hussein of the Allies' continued support for the establishment of an independent Arab state in Syria. What soon became clear was that the British foreign office saw the situation in the Middle East quite differently from

---

[1]http://wwi.lib.byu.edu/index.php/The_Balfour_Declaration (accessed August 27, 2010).

Declaration did not conflict with the terms of the Hussein-McMahon Correspondence and that Britain still fully supported an independent Arab state under Hussein's suzerainty as promised. Arab opposition to the Sykes-Picot and Balfour documents spread rapidly. This was encouraged by the Ottomans, who portrayed these documents as clear evidence of Allied plans to colonize the Middle East. They launched a propaganda offensive in late 1917, appealing to Pan-Islamic sentiments of the Arabs in order to thwart Allied plans and blunt the momentum of the Arab Revolt. However, the success of the Arab army and Allenby's Egyptian Expeditionary Force against the Ottomans through the fall of 1918 diminished the appeal of such information campaigns, as well as putting discussions of postwar promises on hold for a while.

The positive momentum generated by the string of military victories lasted only until the end of hostilities. One week after Mudros, France and Britain agreed to encourage "the establishment of indigenous Governments and administrations in Syria and Mesopotamia [Ottoman Iraq]."[2] Tactically, this declaration was designed to assuage Sharif Hussein's son Faisal and his Arab Revolt army, whose forces had only a few days earlier marched into Damascus as triumphant liberators. In practical terms, the situation was quickly transformed by the end of the war, as all sides negotiated for promises made to be fulfilled and to arrange for the victors to provide them with additional concessions.

THE PARIS PEACE CONFERENCE

In January 1919, just two months after the cessation of hostilities, the Allies convened a comprehensive conference in Paris designed to set terms for peace with the defeated Central Powers (Germany, Austria-Hungary, and the Ottoman Empire) and divide up their empires. Ethnic groups from around the world,

particularly from the Middle East, saw this as a golden opportunity to right old wrongs. Because the situation on the ground changed so drastically as a result of the fighting, promises made early in the war would have to be revisited and perhaps renegotiated. It took a long time for leaders and ordinary citizens of countries to accept the fact that the war had been as bloody, lengthy, and costly as it turned out to be. The unprecedented number of civilian and military deaths, in which whole age groups in many European nations were decimated, caused an upsurge in pacifism and antiwar feelings, as well as creating a desire for vengeance and retribution.

The war came to be described as the "Great War," partly in an attempt to honor sacrifices made. The entry of the United States in the spring of 1917 also changed how it was viewed. Many in the Middle East were encouraged by Woodrow Wilson's **Fourteen Points** speech of January 1918. This address cast the conflict in a moral light, envisioning a postwar peace in this same vein. In particular, Middle Easterners focused on its twelfth point. This called for the Turkish portion of the Ottoman Empire to be "assured a secure sovereignty," but specified that other groups under Ottoman rule should be offered an "absolutely unmolested opportunity of autonomous development."[3] This was welcomed by many nationalist groups as a way to legitimize their plans for independence.

Based on such hopes, numerous delegations from across the region tried to attend the Paris Conference to stake claims of nationhood, with varying degrees of success. As the war was about to end in late 1918, a group of Egyptian nationalists formed a group called the **Wafd** (Delegation) led by Saad Zaghloul, a veteran Egyptian politician and disciple of Ahmad Urabi (leader of the 1882 anti-British revolt). Their main agenda was to attend the negotiations to make a case for Egypt's total independence and to call for an end to British

---

[2]*The Fortnightly Review* 107 (January–June 1920): 255.

[3]*The Independent* 101 (March 13, 1920), 403.

authority there. When they explained their plan at large public rallies across Egypt, this unleashed enormous popular support for them.

To dampen such enthusiasm, Britain detained the group's leaders in Malta for several weeks. Ultimately they had to be let go because their detention caused great unrest back in Egypt. As a conciliatory gesture, the new British High Commissioner in Cairo, General Allenby, allowed the Wafd to present its case at the Paris Peace Conference on April 11. Wafd leaders were disappointed to find little interest there in what they had to say. Even the U.S. delegation, upon whose support they had been counting, favored continuation of a British protectorate in Egypt.

The British alternately negotiated with and imprisoned Egyptian independence activists over the next three years, but finally relented in 1922. On February 28 of that year, they unilaterally decreed Egypt to be an independent country, except for four "reserved points" that kept Britain involved in its affairs over the next three decades. The British (along with the French) were to retain control of the Suez Canal and the country's communications system, they were to administer Sudan jointly with the Egyptians, they would defend foreign interests and the rights of religious minorities in Egypt, and they were to remain as guardians of Egypt's foreign defense.

Other delegations at the Paris conference were sent by Kurds, Greeks, and Armenians, with spokesmen for the Hashemite rulers from Arabia and the Zionist movement also present there. Most received favorable receptions at the conference, and some were given promises of autonomy and independence. In fact, the system of mandates under the League of Nations, part of the June 1919 Treaty of Versailles that established the League, foresaw the independence of Syria, Iraq, and Palestine from the Ottoman Empire. These areas were described in the treaty as territories "where their existence as independent nations can be…recognised subject to…administrative…assistance

by a Mandatory until…they are able to stand alone."[4]

The ideal of the **mandate** system as envisioned in the Treaty of Versailles was quite different from the reality of how the mandatory powers established control in the region. Many specific questions remained unresolved, such as what nation would be the mandatory power for which exact areas of the Middle East and what new states' precise borders would be. While the conference was session, events on the ground in the Middle East were reshaping how peace agreements would actually be implemented. One good example was what happened in Syria.

SYRIA UNDER THE FRENCH

In October 1918, the Arab Revolt army led by Hashemite Prince Faisal had established the first "Arab" government in Damascus. It created local governments under its control in various regions across the Ottoman province of Syria (comprising the modern nations of Syria, Lebanon, Jordan, and Israel). Soon after that, the French landed on the Syrian coast and dismissed local Arab governments there, asserting their right to control the region based on the Sykes-Picot Agreement. The British, given their support for the Balfour Declaration, had also placed Palestine off-limits for the forces of the Arab Revolt. At the same time, British troops remained in Damascus and central Syria for several more months through late 1919 to support their Hashemite ally Faisal and forestall the French from occupying these inland areas.

Meanwhile, Faisal had been at the Paris conference pleading his case and making agreements to secure his political future. In late January 1919, he even concluded an agreement with Dr. Chaim Weizmann, head of the British Zionist Organization, in which Faisal accepted an official Zionist role in a future Palestinian state. Faisal made his support for Zionism

---

[4]Charles Howard-Ellis, *The Origin, Structure and Working of the League of Nations* (Boston: Houghton Mifflin Company, 1929), 493.

contingent upon whether he and his Arab Revolt followers actually received what the British promised during the war: creation of an independent Arab state under the Hashemites to include most of the Arabian Peninsula and Ottoman Syria. When he determined that this promise had not been met, he disavowed the agreement with Weizmann.

While in Paris, Faisal arranged to have an independent commission (in the end comprised solely of Americans) travel to Syria, where it would learn the wishes of the country's inhabitants directly. This was the King-Crane Commission, named after the two Americans who ran it. The King-Crane Commission determined, through extensive interviews and polling, that most Syrians opposed having any mandate at all, rejected the Balfour Declaration, and thought that if there had to be a mandate, it ought to be run by Americans. The French and British disregarded this commission entirely and suppressed its findings for several years. British prime minister David Lloyd-George was famously reported to have remarked to French president Georges Clemenceau during one April session of the Paris conference that "the friendship of France is worth ten Syrias."[5]

During the summer of 1919, as the British prepared to leave Damascus, they tried to broker an agreement between Faisal and the French. Sensing that his time was running out, Faisal, still in Paris, began to give implicit support to Syrian nationalists who, emboldened by the King-Crane Commission, were now pushing for total independence. Although Faisal did not at first openly side with these activists, he made it known that his prestige among them as leader of the Arab Revolt would enable him to silence them on behalf of the eventual mandatory power in Syria—more and more likely to be France.

In September 1919, the British and French concluded an agreement based on the Sykes-Picot accord that essentially divided Ottoman Syria between them. Accordingly, Britain withdrew its troops from Damascus and surrounding areas. Faisal immediately protested against this at the peace conference. In the end, after protracted negotiations between him and the French, as well as the fact that the British severely curtailed his monthly financial subsidy, Faisal signed a curious treaty with the Clemenceau government of France. It acknowledged French control over Syria and accepted that Lebanon would be administered by it separately, but also recognized Faisal as Syria's legitimate monarch.

However, a new French government that chose to assert more direct control over France's overseas mandates came to power in early 1920. This set off an armed showdown between the French and Faisal in March 1920 that dragged on for several months. France's campaign to increase control over Syria was bolstered at the San Remo Conference in April 1920, which awarded this territory to the French as a "Class A" League of Nations mandate. French forces defeated the now hostile Arab nationalist army at the **Battle of Maysalun** (just west of Damascus) in July 1920, prompting Faisal to take refuge in Britain and allowing France to enjoy sole political control of its new Syrian holdings.

ANATOLIA BETWEEN GREEKS AND TURKS

A parallel set of chaotic developments occurred to the north in Anatolia during this same period. The catalyst for the events that would shape the future of Anatolia was the landing of Greek troops in Izmir (Smyrna) on May 15, 1919: an action sanctioned and even encouraged by Allied leaders such as David Lloyd-George. This encouragement was the result of the very favorable view taken at the Peace Conference of the Greeks and their energetic leader Eleftherios Venizelos, combined with the desire to curtail any Italian

---

[5]British prime minister David Lloyd George to French president Georges Clemenceau, April 25, 1919, in Arthur S. Link, ed., *The Papers of Woodrow Wilson*, vol. 58 (Princeton: Princeton University Press, 1988), p. 134.

plans to establish a presence in Anatolia. Although the Allies and Italy had signed an agreement during the war that foresaw giving Italy control over Izmir (Smyrna) in a postwar settlement, both Lloyd-George and Woodrow Wilson had come to believe that it made more sense to support Greek control there, due to the large Greek population of that part of Anatolia.

The unintended consequence of allowing this landing was to awaken fears among the Turks that the Greeks would try to establish a permanent foothold politically in Western Anatolia and to displace the Turks there as rulers. Venizelos had been a strong advocate for many years of the *Megali Idea* (Great Idea): the concept of a Greater Greece that included Thrace, possibly Istanbul (to be rechristened Constantinople), as well as large parts of Anatolia. He had also been spreading stories of Turkish atrocities against the Greek populations in Western Anatolia at the Paris conference, in order to build a case for the legitimacy of transferring these areas permanently to Greek control in any final Allied-Ottoman peace settlement.

THE TURKISH WAR OF INDEPENDENCE

By the winter of 1920, Greek forces had advanced to strategic positions deep in Western Anatolia just beyond the Menderes (Meander) River. Over this same period, the Ottoman government had become divided, with a rump administration in Istanbul and a Grand National Assembly of deputies from around Anatolia assembling in Ankara and declaring a Turkish Republic in January 1920.

The charismatic leader who had changed the whole situation there was Ottoman general Mustafa Kemal (1881–1938). He was one of the few Ottoman commanders not to have suffered a huge defeat during World War I and had achieved considerable fame for his determined stand at Gallipoli in 1915. A few months after the Mudros Armistice, the Ottoman government in Istanbul sent him to Anatolia as an

Mustafa Kemal Ataturk (March 1923)

inspector general to supervise the demobilization of Ottoman forces there.

Instead of carrying out this mission, he had a different plan. When he arrived in Samsun (on the Black Sea coast of central Anatolia) on May 19, 1919, just days after the Greek occupation of Izmir, he met with army commanders and governors in the region and proceeded to Amasya. There, he issued a declaration in late June calling for a national congress to be convened.

Upon receiving news of this initiative, the Ottoman government in Istanbul dismissed him from his post, at which time he himself resigned from the Ottoman army. At the congress, which was ultimately held in Erzurum in July, Mustafa Kemal was elected president. A decision was taken to form an alternate national government, since the Ottoman rulers had failed to preserve the empire's independence. Another congress was convened at Sivas in September, where nationalist societies from around the country joined together as the Society for the Defense of Rights in Anatolia and Thrace. After this meeting, Mustafa Kemal informed military commanders, provincial governors, and the sultan that a Council of Representatives would henceforth represent the Turkish nation, providing a clear statement of how the movement he was assembling overtly identified itself as a Turkish nationalist project.

This development caused the Ottoman government of Prime Minister Damad Ferid Pasha to fall. Mustafa Kemal promised to cooperate with the new Istanbul government led by Ali Riza Pasha, but only if it accepted decisions taken at the Erzurum and Sivas congresses. Kemal, in his capacity as chairman of the new Council of Representatives and Hulusi Salih Pasha, the Ottoman naval minister representing the Istanbul government, signed an Amasya Protocol in late October 1919. It stated that free elections would be held soon to choose representatives for a new national council. In addition, all groups would accept the resolutions and decisions made at the Sivas Congress, and the new National Assembly would be convened somewhere other than Istanbul for security reasons. Despite this document, elections were still held to choose members of the last Ottoman parliament, which met for one final session in Istanbul.

Ironically, Mustafa Kemal was elected to represent Erzurum in this body, but could not actually attend its meetings. Istanbul had been under de facto Allied military occupation since late 1918, and the Ottoman authorities there had an outstanding warrant for his arrest as a traitor. Within two months, Mustafa Kemal moved his base of operations to Ankara to coordinate the activities of his growing movement. When the final session of the Ottoman parliament convened in Istanbul on January 12, 1920, a majority of its members expressed support for the nationalist program of the Society for the Defence of Rights—now codified in the document called the National Pact (*Misak-i Milli*). In agreement with decisions taken at the Sivas Congress, the National Pact stated again

that the final status of all territories in and around Anatolia should be decided by popular referendum, and that territories not occupied by the Allies with a Muslim Turkish majority population should immediately be recognized as parts of the Turkish homeland.

The parliament's open acceptance of Mustafa Kemal's nationalist program deeply angered the British occupying force in Istanbul. Britain had viewed the parliamentary elections as a way to shore up support for the faltering Ottoman government there, in preparation for the upcoming final peace treaty between the Allies and Ottomans then being drawn up in Paris at the peace conference still in session. The British forced Ali Riza to resign as prime minister on March 3, 1920, replacing him with the more compliant Salih Pasha. Within two weeks, Britain had formally declared Istanbul to be under military occupation and imposed martial law, deporting 150 Ottoman officials to Malta as subversives. This upheaval in the Ottoman government prompted the Greek forces to launch a major offensive to move further into Anatolia. On March 19, Mustafa Kemal issued a declaration that he and his followers would work toward the establishment of a new Turkish state with its new capital at Ankara. Meanwhile back in Istanbul, Damad Ferid Pasha became prime minister yet again and assembled an army to combat Kemal's troops.

A new parliament, the **Turkish Grand National Assembly**, convened in Ankara on April 23, 1920. It elected Mustafa Kemal as its chairman, and declared that national executive and legislative power was now vested in it. The Ottoman government under Damad Ferid continued to struggle against the Ankara movement as illegitimate. The Ottoman First Martial Law Court issued a decision in May revoking Mustafa Kemal's military titles and sentencing him to death for treason. Despite the open rift between the Ottoman and nationalist governments, the nationalist forces focused on establishing control of central Anatolia and preparing to eject foreign occupying forces from Southern Anatolia. When representatives of the now vestigial Ottoman government finally signed the **Treaty of Sèvres**—the document officially ending the state of war between the Allies and the Ottoman Empire—on August 10, 1920, it was a dead letter.

No Ottoman parliament then sitting in Istanbul would have been able to ratify it, since most of the deputies of the previous parliamentary session had fled to Ankara. The Sèvres Treaty terms were quite harsh on the Ottomans, with much of Anatolia being divided up into zones of influence and control among the Greeks, Italians, and French. Only a remnant of north-central Anatolia and Istanbul were to remain totally under Ottoman control. Eastern Anatolia was to be divided between the new nations of Armenia and Kurdistan,

with Armenia being granted a lion's share of territory there due to the intercession of U.S. president Woodrow Wilson. The treaty also acknowledged the new arrangements being made for the Arab provinces of the Ottoman Empire by the Allies, as well as accepting the terms of the Balfour Declaration.

The reaction of the Turkish Grand National Assembly to this was to prepare to attack all foreign armies then occupying parts of Anatolia on various battlefronts. The first Turkish nationalist offensive against Greek forces, who had gradually been advancing inland from Izmir during the spring and summer of 1920, took place on the Aegean coast in October. An intense battle there pushed the Turkish army back into the hills. Mustafa Kemal

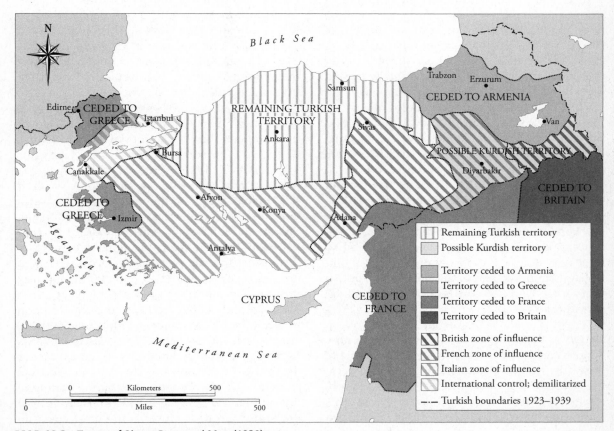

MAP 10.2 Treaty of Sèvres Proposed Map (1920)

regrouped his Western Anatolian forces and prepared to strike back. In the east, an attempt to secure the large Armenian state across much of northeastern Anatolia envisioned in the Sèvres Treaty was thwarted by Turkish troops led by General Kazim Karabekir. He succeeded in pushing the Armenian forces back into the territory that became the first modern Republic of Armenia.

In fact, the first peace treaty signed by the government of the Turkish Grand National Assembly was the Treaty of Alexandropol (Gumru), concluded with the new Democratic Republic of Armenia on December 3, 1920. This agreement resulted in a territory for Armenia about half the size of what had been allocated in the Sèvres accord, but peace with Armenia also gave Mustafa Kemal's army the chance to prepare for an impending Greek offensive in the west.

When Greek forces did advance from Bursa and Ushak to Eskishehir and Afyon, they were halted by Turkish armies under the command of Ismet Pasha, Kemal's trusted deputy, at the First Battle of Inonu on January 10, 1921. Based on the momentum of victory, a new Turkish constitution was proclaimed on January 20. After this first big Turkish success, Britain, France, and Italy convened a conference in London in February and March 1921 to try to salvage the Sèvres Treaty, but the representative there of the Ankara government refused to accept their terms. When the London negotiations collapsed, the Greek army launched another attack, which led to their next defeat at the Second Battle of Inonu in late March. At this same time, other Turkish units forced French forces in Cilicia (Kilikya) to withdraw.

The Greek army began its final offensive in Anatolia in July 1921 with a force now augmented by new troops. As this formidable army approached Eskishehir and Sakarya, the Turkish nationalist war effort suddenly appeared on the verge of collapse. Facing this crisis, Mustafa Kemal took direct command of the army. The Battle of Sakarya, which commenced on August 23, was at first marked by steady Greek advances. After capturing a key mountain, the Greek commander Anastasios Papoulas apparently panicked and ordered a tactical retreat. This one decision reversed the momentum of the advance just enough to lead to his eventual defeat. Turkish triumph at the **Battle of Sakarya**, fought on a front extending over a large territory of Western Anatolia between August and September 1921, ended the final Greek offensive in Anatolia.

After this Turkish victory, the conflict settled into a cease-fire until August 1922. A final big Turkish offensive that began that month ended the war on September 18, 1922, when the last Greek troops left Anatolia. The Mudanya Armistice, signed on October 11, 1922, led to a new peace conference at Lausanne, Switzerland. Soon after the armistice, **Sultan Mehmed VI** was deposed as the last Ottoman sultan (although he was allowed to retain his title of caliph for a few months). He left Istanbul soon after that, and peace negotiations opened in Lausanne between the Allies, the Turks, and the Greeks.

The first result of this conference occurred in January 1923, when the Turkish and Greek governments agreed to a population exchange. Orthodox Christian subjects of the Ottomans (who identified themselves as ethnically Greek but did not necessarily speak Greek as their main language of communication) were transferred to Greece at the same time as Muslim inhabitants of certain parts of Greece (except Western Thrace) were brought in to occupy dwellings that these Greeks had just left. In the end, approximately 1,500,000 Greeks left former Ottoman territories (primarily from western and central Anatolia and the Trabzon region), to be exchanged with about 500,000 Muslims from Greece. There had been mass deportations of populations in many places in the world before, but this was an unusual example of a population exchange arranged by mutual agreement. It did not include two important groups: Muslims under Greek rule in Western Thrace (about 80,000 in 1922) and

Greeks in Istanbul and the Aegean Islands assigned to Turkey (about 270,000 at that time).

In July 1923, the comprehensive Lausanne Treaty was signed, which recognized the modern Republic of Turkey with more or less the same borders that it has enjoyed ever since. Clauses of this treaty dealt with two issues that had long created problems between the Ottomans and European powers: All capitulation treaties (see p. 61) then in force were declared null and void, and the Dardanelles and Bosphorus straits were opened to unrestricted international military and civilian traffic, subject only to oversight by an International Straits Commission to be formed by the League of Nations. The last Allied troops left Istanbul in September, and the Republic of Turkey was formally established on October 29, 1923.

FRENCH MANDATES: ORIGINS OF MODERN SYRIA AND LEBANON

The conclusion of the Turkish War of Independence allowed the international focus to shift to the Arab Middle East, where Britain and France now finalized how the region would be configured. Conflicting promises made to different groups during the war continued to complicate the situation, as seen in Syria. From the League of Nations perspective, France had been awarded Syria as a Class A mandate, with the implicit expectation that this would be a pathway to its gradual independence.

Although they may have paid lip service to such a sentiment, the French did not share it. Despite success as one of the victors, France after World War I experienced a period of post-traumatic reevaluation as it sorted out the loss of so many people and the wrecking of important parts of its economy. One reaction to such a pyrrhic victory was to reassert older imperial plans. These included creating a viable French presence to dominate the eastern Mediterranean, corresponding to how France had established itself in the western Mediterranean in Morocco, Algeria, and Tunisia.

Syria was the obvious place to carry out such a project, which meant that the French quickly became serious about retaining authority over it, beyond any envisioned independence in a "mandate system." French defeat of Arab nationalist forces at Maysalun in July 1920 had given them military control of the country, but just barely.

To secure their presence more firmly, they adopted a strategy of divide and rule, splitting Syria up into six distinct "states" within the first two years of their rule. These were divided according to ethnic and geographical divisions, but with significant alterations made in the old Ottoman provincial boundaries. The result of these changes was to create lasting instability due to territorial fragmentation. The first such state to be created in 1920 was **Great Lebanon** (*Grand Liban*), soon followed by the states of Damascus and Aleppo in 1920, then Jabal Druze, the Alawite state, and Alexandretta in 1921.

The French took various other measures to secure long-term control over the country. In 1920, they established a military academy to train officers for a "Syrian Legion." This created a native armed force that had several thousand members by the 1930s, but with particular

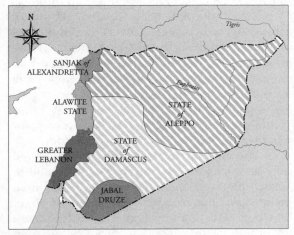

MAP 10.3 Syria and Lebanon (1920s)

characteristics. The officer corps trained at this military academy was composed largely of minorities, because the Sunni Arab elite that had dominated Syrian politics did not regard military careers very highly. The resulting predominance in the Syrian military officer corps of minorities had a decisive effect on Syrian politics after World War II.

In Lebanon, Maronite Christians, long allied with the French, derived greatest political benefit from the creation of this Great Lebanon while Muslims there were the most disenfranchised. They protested by boycotting Lebanon's first census in 1922 and refusing to accept identity cards identifying them as Lebanese. Despite this tension, the Maronites, as a numerical majority in this state at this time, were able to have it declared the Republic of Lebanon in September 1926.

The next two "states" to be created, the states of Damascus and Aleppo, corresponded roughly to regions of Ottoman Syria not placed by the French under the control of ethnic minorities. Two more, the Jabal Druze and Alawite territories, were configured to give minorities their own special territories, for whose security they would be forced to rely on the French. In July 1922, Damascus, Aleppo, and the Alawite state were brought together in a loose Syrian federation, but the Alawite state broke away in 1924, leaving the two remaining states to form a state of Syria, so that Syria's political fragmentation remained until 1936. The status of the district of Alexandretta, with its multiethnic Ottoman mozaic, remained in limbo after the French-Turkish peace agreement of 1921 until 1939, when it finally became a Turkish province. The next few years saw a constant struggle between the local populations in all parts of Syria, most of whom supported the nation's political unification, and the French, who tried to keep it fragmented. Because of this basic disagreement on political goals, problems continued for the French throughout their administration there.

BRITISH MANDATES: ORIGINS OF MODERN JORDAN AND IRAQ

In some ways, Jordan (at first called Transjordan to specify that its territorial center was *east* of the Jordan River) was among the easiest parts of former Ottoman Syria to stabilize after the war, at least in a military sense. Its situation on the peripheries of great population centers and trade routes in the region meant that it was somewhat sparsely populated, but the story even of *its* creation was complex. In the late summer of 1920, after the French defeated Faisal at Maysalun, the area of Ottoman Syria directly east of the Jordan River remained without any real government. To fill this vacuum, the British dispatched Captain Alec Kirkbride (1897–1978), an officer from General Allenby's staff, to this area. He brought it under control until Faisal's elder brother Abdullah arrived there in November 1920.

Abdullah had been decisively defeated by the advancing forces of Abd al-Aziz ibn Saud (see Chapter 11) at Turaba (on the eastern Hejaz border) in May 1919, which led him to seek ways to restore prestige. Since Faisal had been chosen as king of Syria in March 1920 by a general congress, a group of Iraqis put forward Abdullah's name as a potential king of Iraq. Such talk died down after Faisal was soon ejected from Syria by the French and began himself to be considered for the Iraqi throne.

After the defeat at Turaba, Abdullah arranged a truce with Abd al-Aziz ibn Saud and proceeded northward to Amman. There, a group of Arab nationalists had invited him to lead a movement to oust the French from Syria and restore it to Arab control. He arrived in November 1920 in Maan (about 130 miles south of Amman) via the Hejaz railway for what was described as an inspection tour.

The British themselves had established only a very tentative presence at that time in Maan. They were there to explore the potential inclusion of the area beyond the Jordan River that included this city (called "Transjordan") into the Palestine mandate recently awarded

Bettmann/CORBIS

The Hashemites in Iraq (November 1923)

to Britain. British military commanders in Palestine had sent a very limited staff out there due to financial and military constraints, but they were keen to leave the final status of this region open to negotiation. By the beginning of 1921, the British were becoming anxious to resolve the question of who would be administering exactly which regions in the Middle East.

At the March 1921 Cairo Conference, it was agreed that Faisal would rule Iraq while Abdullah would be recognized as Transjordan's monarch. Although Abdullah agreed to this arrangement only for an initial six-month period, the emirate of Transjordan (as a part of the Palestine mandate) was then created in July 1921, with Abdullah as its emir. In August 1922, the British declared that the Balfour Declaration *only* applied to territories of the Palestine mandate *west* of the Jordan River.

Functionally at this time and officially later, Transjordan became a separate political entity with Abdullah recognized as its head.

Because Abdullah was from the Hejaz, which although Arab, was not an area closely linked to the tribes that dominated Transjordan, he had to build a case to rule there virtually from scratch. The British had drawn the eastern and southern borders of Transjordan in part to facilitate the construction of an oil pipeline through it from the new British mandate of Iraq to Haifa, one of the main ports of Palestine along the Mediterranean.

The borders of Transjordan were once labeled "Winston's hiccup" to suggest that they were drawn rather randomly by Winston Churchill (then the British colonial secretary) after a liquid lunch in Cairo during the March 1921 conference that set up the boundaries of the British mandates. In reality, it appears

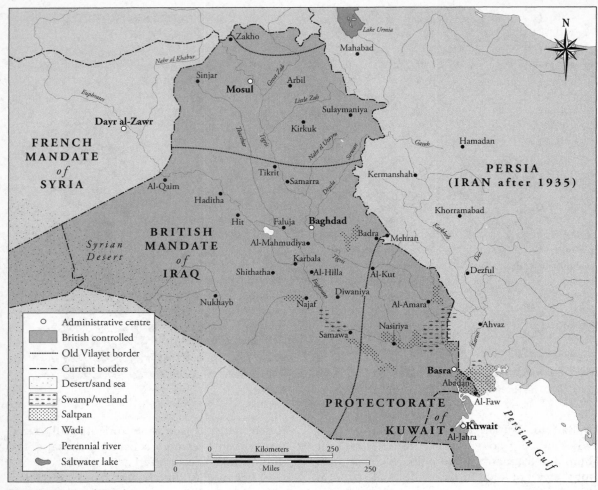

MAP 10.4 Iraq (1920s)

that frontiers were established primarily with concern for how they might divide or unite certain desert tribes, as well as to create an unbroken British air corridor between the Mediterranean and the Indian Ocean. In any event, Britain recognized Transjordan as an independent state in May 1923: a status in which it has continued ever since, still ruled by descendants of Abdullah (who took a new title upon the creation of his independent kingdom in 1946 as King Abdullah I).

The stabilization of Iraq was considerably more complicated, since it brought together

the three Ottoman provinces of Basra, Baghdad, and Mosul. All of them had been quite separate from one another over many centuries, with a diverse array of different ethnic and religious groups. Just after the end of hostilities in late 1918, secret anti-British resistance societies were organized to challenge the presence of British and British Indian troops in this area.

The formal declaration in April 1920 of the Iraq mandate at the San Remo Conference (at first called the British Mandate of Mesopotamia) unleashed various uprisings and insurgencies created by different Sunni and Shii groups. Muslim religious leaders sanctioned these rebels' actions, approving local resistance to attempts by the British, as non-Muslims, to rule Muslims. The disparate sentiments of different groups came together by the summer of 1920 to launch the Great Iraqi Rebellion: an unprecedented union of Iraqis normally at odds with one another but now united against the British.

At some cost, British occupation forces were able to stabilize affairs, but it was decided at the 1921 Cairo Conference to try a new strategy. British administrators now chose to place Faisal, newly ex-ruler of Arab Syria, on the throne of a united Iraq and to arrange for a manufactured referendum of Iraqis to "confirm" his right to rule over them. This created a potentially valuable ally for the UK in a strategic part of the Arab world. Iraq, a place with great geographical importance where oil would soon be discovered, was now ruled by a sovereign totally dependent on the British for support and legitimacy.

One important issue for this new Iraq was that the mandate government had no share in the **Turkish Petroleum Company** (renamed the Iraq Petroleum Company or IPC in 1929). This was a company begun in Ottoman times that became the major oil producer in Iraq when oil was discovered there in October 1927. The Iraqi government had been promised the right to acquire a 20 percent share of this company at the San Remo Conference (which it was not able to do), but received quite small revenues from oil production for many years due to a variety of complex factors.

Another big problem for the new mandate was the status of Kurds in northern Mesopotamia and Eastern Anatolia. Just after the Armistice of Mudros, Kurdish leaders met in Sulaymaniya with Colonel Arnold Wilson, acting British governor of Mesopotamia, in December 1918 to request support for a united and independent Kurdistan under British protection. In the subsequent Treaty of Sèvres, the Kurds were in fact promised a separate state in Eastern Anatolia and northern Mesopotamia to

include the city of Mosul. When this promise was not kept after the collapse of the Sèvres agreement, Kurdish leader Mahmoud Barzanji led two revolts against the British in the early 1920s. To defeat him, they resorted to aerial bombardments: an extreme measure taken partially because of the lack of British army troops on the ground there.

The British feared that if they allowed an independent Kurdish area to be established, this would tempt the two Arab areas of Baghdad and Basra to stage another revolt against British rule as they had done in 1920. By 1922, Britain had made peace with Sheikh Mahmoud, hoping to establish him as a buffer against the Turks, who continued to press their claims on Mosul and Kirkuk. Instead of becoming a cooperative ally, Sheikh Mahmoud soon changed course again and declared a Kurdish state with himself as its monarch, although he later accepted limited autonomy within the new state of Iraq. At this same time, the army of the Turkish Republic had been fighting numerous battles with Kurdish forces just north of the Iraqi border in Eastern Anatolia. Turkey did not accept the incorporation of the Mosul province into Iraq until June 1926, but then only after being granted a 10 percent royalty payment on oil exports from Mosul province for twenty-five years. This settled the border down for a period of time, but various Kurdish rebellions have continued to break out on both sides of it ever since.

PALESTINE: COMPLEX MANDATE

Despite earlier ambiguous statements about postwar Palestine, made just after Mudros but before the Paris Peace Conference, the British and French agreed in early December 1918 that Britain would take primary responsibility for its administration, given that it was the main focus of the Balfour Declaration. The World Zionist Organization now became very concerned about implementing the pledge to support a "Jewish national home" in Palestine. To make sure that this was being carried out, Chaim

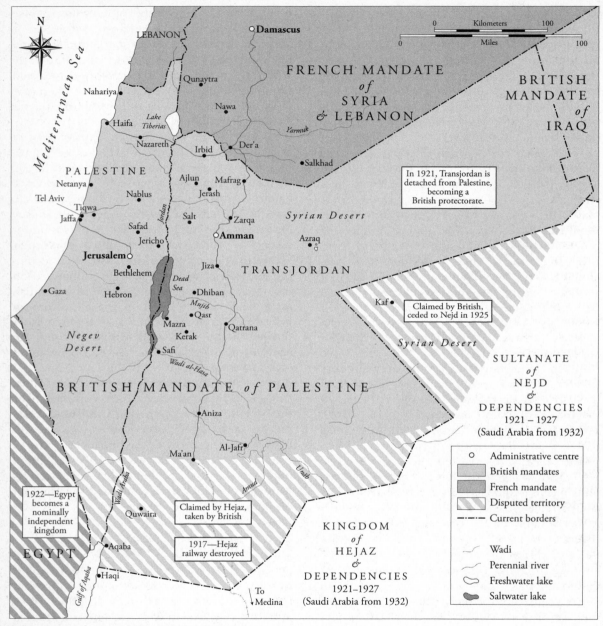

MAP 10.5 Palestine and Transjordan (1920s)

Weizmann, the organization's president, traveled to the Middle East in the summer of 1918.

Weizmann made a tentative agreement while there with Faisal, which Faisal soon canceled when the British did not meet his conditions for ratifying it. Memories of this earliest tentative Arab-Zionist agreement have lingered, but events on the ground rapidly overtook such ephemeral diplomatic gestures.

Palestine itself was directly administered by the British army from the end of hostilities until July 1920. At that time, the British appointed a civilian, Sir Herbert Samuel, to be its first High Commissioner and prepare for the finalization of the mandate structure in Palestine. Immediately after the end of the war, another wave of Jewish immigrants began to pour into Palestine (known as the Third Aliyah). This new wave was generated in part by unsettled conditions in the former Russian Empire, where the February and October revolutions had triggered yet new rounds of pogroms. Immigration to Palestine also became an escape from the perils of sorting out national identities and situations in the territories of the former Habsburg Empire in the Balkans, in which many Jews suddenly found themselves threatened and attacked.

Although the leaders of Zionist organizations were always pleased to see new immigrants, they were not prepared for this sudden influx. Soon, though, with British support and approval, they began to build a system of community organizations to accommodate these recent arrivals. In 1919, a centralized Jewish school system (in which the language of instruction was Hebrew) was organized in Palestine. One year later, an Assembly of Representatives was set up as the elected parliament of the **Yishuv** (the name given to the whole Jewish Zionist community in Palestine). Executive administration of this group was assigned to a new Jewish National Council. The **Histadrut** was created as a labor federation that offered social services, job protection, and health benefits for the Zionist *olim* ("emigrants" or "those going up to the Holy Land").

Among Arab Palestinians, the situation was different, since they were a population trying to regroup and figure out how to fit into this new Palestine after being part of the larger Ottoman Empire. In engaging the Palestinian Arabs, British administrators chose a cautious path through making ties to their existing elites. They empowered local officials in ways that had not been done before, but did not really promote or create space for Arab popular sentiments to be expressed. For example, the Ottoman-era Mufti of Jerusalem was retitled Grand Mufti of Palestine, giving the holder of that office considerably more power than any local religious official had held in Ottoman times.

The British established a Supreme Muslim Council to administer *waqfs* (religious endowments) and appoint religious judges and local muftis: functions always performed under Ottoman rule by officials in Istanbul. Hajj Amin al-Husayni, member of a prominent Palestinian family, was appointed as Palestine's first Grand Mufti, although he was young and had received the least support from Jerusalem's Islamic leaders. The British also appointed one of his greatest rivals, Raghib Bey al-Nashashibi, as mayor of Jerusalem in 1920 to replace Hajj Amin al-Husayni's uncle Musa Kazim al-Husayni. British policy fueled rivalry between the al-Nashashibi and al-Husayni families, which gradually increased over the next two decades and helped keep Palestinian Arabs divided.

Musa Kazim openly broke with the British when he exhorted crowds to sacrifice themselves for the cause of Arab Palestine during the Nabi Musa riots of April 1920. These riots happened just a few days after Faisal and his Arab nationalist followers had commenced fighting the French for control of Syria.

They were also sparked by a growing realization among the Arabs of how rapidly the Zionist movement had gained power and presence in Palestine with the coming of the British. This unrest became a way for Palestinian Arabs to stand in solidarity with their Syrian compatriots, who had just begun battling the French. One of the main instigators of the Nabi Musa uprising was Arif al-Arif. Arif was the editor of the nationalist newspaper *Southern Syria* (*Suriya al-Janubiya*) then being published in Jerusalem, which advocated the union of all of Ottoman Syria under Faisal as its monarch.

The Nabi Musa upheaval was not the only episode that challenged intercommunal relations in the first few years after the war.

They were also affected by the Jaffa riots of May 1921. These began as a May Day uprising by Communists against the British, but developed into a set of attacks by local Arabs on Zionist immigrants in Jaffa and the new city of Tel Aviv. The problems caused by these uprisings prompted the British to limit legal Jewish immigration to Palestine.

Ending all Jewish immigration became one of the main ongoing demands by Palestinian Arab community leaders of the British, who also remained under constant pressure from Zionist leaders to let more Jews come in. Another result of these first riots was that Zionist leaders who felt that the British failed to protect them from Arab violence began to set up clandestine self-defense militia units known collectively as the *Haganah* (Hebrew for "the Defense"). Finally, what transpired in these early disturbances rapidly caused Palestinian Arab leaders to view themselves less as "southern Syrians" and more uniquely as "Palestinians." The first four years of the British administration of Palestine after World War I thus set the stage for what was to come in the 1920s and 1930s.

IRAN AFTER WORLD WAR I

The situation in Iran after the war was affected quite seriously by the Russian Revolution. The rise of Soviet power in the years after 1918 at first encouraged the ongoing Jangali guerrilla movement in Gilan, fighting against the central Iranian government since the beginning of the war. Mirza Kuchek Khan, its leader, allied himself with the Bolsheviks after they had secured power on the Caspian and declared a Soviet Republic of Gilan in May 1920. Because he was actually moderately conservative and Islamic in perspective, Kuchek Khan soon came into ideological conflict with his communist allies. When they demanded that he carry out an immediate redistribution of feudal lands in Gilan, Mirza Kuchek left the capital city of Rasht and headed into the forest, leaving the Gilan Republic to be taken over by Iranian communists more closely linked to

Moscow. By 1921, Russians decided to reassert their influence over the central Iranian government and abandoned any assistance to the Gilani rebels. Soon thereafter, Reza Khan, commander of the Persian Cossack Brigade, secured central government control in the region. This was an important step in his rise to power that resulted in him taking the throne as Reza Shah in 1925.

Reza Khan had been assisted and promoted by the British after World War I, who tried (but failed) in 1919 to establish a protectorate over Iran that would have excluded Russia. When the Jangalis marched on Tehran in 1920, Reza Khan joined with Ziya al-Din Tabatabai to stage a coup in February 1921. The Qajar Ahmad Shah was kept on as monarch, but real power now went to Tabatabai as prime minister and Reza Khan, war minister as well as commander of the Iranian army. The Soviets signed a treaty with this new Iranian government in 1921 that allowed Soviet Russia to invade Iran if it believed that events there threatened its national security. In 1925, Reza forced the last Qajar Shah to leave Iran and was crowned as **Reza Shah Pahlavi**. He borrowed the pre-Islamic term "Pahlavi" as the name for his dynasty, to portray his reign as the revival of an ancient Iranian tradition. Soon, he changed the preferred name for his country from "Persia" to "Iran"—also harking back to older usage.

Some scholars describe World War I as really extending for the Ottomans from 1911, when Italy invaded Libya, until 1923, when the last sultan was deposed and the Turkish Republic established. While this concept of a longer World War I clearly applies to the central Ottoman domains, it also seems just as valid for Iran and other areas of the Middle East, which were experiencing upheaval and warfare long before 1914 and well after 1918. In fact, stability only began to return to the region as a whole by the late 1920s and early 1930s. New paradigms of society and politics were created in the region in the wake of the recent destruction and upheaval that it had suffered.

Questions to Think About

1. Did the Sykes-Picot Agreement contradict the Hussein-McMahon Correspondence?
2. How was the Balfour Declaration received in the Middle East when it was issued, and how did the British and Ottomans try to influence perceptions of it?
3. How did Wilson's "Fourteen Points" speech affect the approach of Middle Easterners to the Paris Peace Conference?
4. What was the purpose of the mandate system? Did it fulfill its goals?
5. How did the Syria mandate work under the French? How did the British help solve Syria's problems?
6. What started the Turkish War of Independence?
7. What are the origins of the Turkish Republic, and what was its relationship to the Turkish War of Independence?
8. What were the terms of the Treaty of Sèvres, and why was it never implemented?
9. Why was there a population exchange between Turkey and Greece, and what were its effects?
10. What was the Treaty of Lausanne?
11. How did the French try to govern Syria?
12. How was Transjordan created by the British, and how were its borders determined?
13. What did the British do to keep Iraq unified as a country?
14. What was the status of Kurds in the Iraq mandate, and how did the British manage them?
15. What shaped Palestine as the British took control of it?
16. What shaped the Jewish and Arab communities in Palestine in the early years of the British mandate?
17. How did "Reza Khan" become "Reza Shah" after World War I in Iran?

For Further Reading

Clark, Bruce. *Twice a Stranger: The Mass Expulsions That Forged Modern Greece and Turkey*. Cambridge: Harvard University Press, 2006.

Fromkin, David. *A Peace to End All Peace: The Fall of the Ottoman Empire and the Creation of the Modern Middle East*. New York: H. Holt, 2001.

Ghani, Sirus. *Iran and the Rise of Reza Shah: From Qajar Collapse to Pahlavi Rule*. London: I.B. Tauris Publishers, 2000.

Keddie, Nikki R. *Qajar Iran and the Rise of Reza Khan, 1796–1925*. Costa Mesa, CA: Mazda Publishers, 1999.

Khoury, Philip S. *Syria and the French Mandate: The Politics of Arab Nationalism, 1920–1945*. Princeton, NJ: Princeton University Press, 1987.

Lewis, Geoffrey. *Balfour and Weizmann: The Zionist, the Zealot and the Emergence of Israel*. London: Continuum, 2009.

MacMillan, Margaret. *Paris 1919: Six Months That Changed the World*. New York: Random House, 2002.

Mango, Andrew. *Atatürk*. Woodstock, NY: Overlook Press, 2000.

McDowall, David. *A Modern History of the Kurds*. London: I.B. Tauris, 1996.

Rogan, Eugene L. *Frontiers of the State in the Late Ottoman Empire: Transjordan, 1850–1921*. Cambridge: Cambridge University Press, 1999.

Schneer, Jonathan. *The Balfour Declaration: The Origins of the Arab-Israeli Conflict*. New York: Random House, 2010.

Sluglett, Peter. *Britain in Iraq: Contriving King and Country, 1914–1932*. New York: Columbia University Press, 2007.

Smith, Charles D. *Palestine and the Arab-Israeli Conflict*. Boston: Bedford/St. Martin's, 2004.

Tripp, Charles. *A History of Iraq*. Cambridge: New York: Cambridge University Press, 2007.

Wasserstein, Bernard. *The British in Palestine: The Mandatory Government and Arab-Jewish Conflict, 1917–1929*. Oxford: B. Blackwell, 1991.

Wilson, Mary C. *King Abdullah, Britain, and the Making of Jordan*. Cambridge: Cambridge University Press, 1990.

11

Birth of New Nations

World War I was as decisive a watershed for the Middle East as for any part of the world. The amount of civilian and military fatalities in the Ottoman Empire as a result of the war (approximately 14 percent of the total prewar population there) was rivaled only by the approximate total deaths in the entire Soviet Union of the same percentage of its population as a result of World War II: a staggering amount in both cases. As much as military defeat, the loss of populations created a totally new context in which new nations arose from the remains of vanquished empires that had been in place for centuries. This helped accelerate a process of change that has continued to the present, as new nations have continued to define their new identities, boundaries, and systems of social organization. This chapter will focus on three new nations: Turkey, Iran, and Saudi Arabia. All were created by governments newly established in all or part of the territories that they were governing by the end of the 1920s.

THE BIRTH OF MODERN TURKEY

Reform Programs of Mustafa Kemal

As observed, the First World War really came to a close in the Middle East not in 1918, but in 1923, when the **Treaty of Lausanne** established the Republic of Turkey in the Anatolian territories of the former Ottoman Empire. This treaty ended the prolonged struggle (1919–1923) for control over Anatolia between Greece and the Turkish nationalist movement under the charismatic leadership of Mustafa Kemal. Originally an associate of the leaders of the Committee for Union and Progress (CUP/Young Turks), Kemal had fallen out with them during the war, but adopted many of their positions as he formed his own political program.

An avid student of European political and military theory, Kemal began to construct a brand-new country over the next decade, which emerged as a phoenix from the ashes of the vanquished Ottoman Empire. In building this new state, he and his associates used an eclectic mix of programs and techniques to create a society that was secular, modern, and progressive. As conceived in the Turkish Constitution of 1921, sovereignty in the Turkish Republic was held by the Turkish Grand National Assembly, the parliament first convened in April 1920 during the war with Greece, as the expression of the will of the Turkish people. The new system departed sharply from Ottoman precedent in numerous ways in its exclusive reliance on popular sovereignty, secularization, and Turkish nationalism as sources of legitimacy. Ottoman experiments in constitutionalism had paved the way for this development, but the cataclysm of the war allowed for a much more comprehensive vision of modern government to be introduced.

The leadership of Kemal, a workaholic who slept only a few hours each night, put the new country on a fast course toward modernization. His leadership style was soon criticized as quite harsh and authoritarian: a paradox for someone dedicated to promoting democracy.

Defenders of Kemal pointed out that the thorough nature of changes he envisioned required a strong hand to carry out, which was seen in all aspects of his reforms. As he carried out his plans, he relied on six principles of "**Kemalism**": republicanism, populism, secularism, revolutionism, nationalism, and statism. All were adapted to the specific cultural context of post-Ottoman Turkey, making discussion of them a good way to explore how this new society was taking shape.

Republicanism had its origins in late Ottoman attempts to create a constitutional representative democracy. Despite the fact that power in this system flowed from the elected legislature, which in turn elected a president, this still included some separation of powers between judicial, legislative, and executive parts of this government to create checks and balances. *Populism* refers to the absolute sovereignty of all individual citizens as a whole, not any elite group. This is somewhat paradoxical in that Mustafa Kemal and his close associates who made the revolution could be seen as a closed elite group.

Secularism referred to the government's neutrality in religious affairs and its attempt to separate religion and politics, but in practice referred to the secularization of the entire religious component of the former Ottoman government. This included secularizing the educational and judicial systems, closing down meetinghouses of Sufi religious organizations, as well as establishing total government control over religious charitable foundations and the agricultural properties that supported them. State control over Islamic practice was eventually coordinated under a Religious Affairs Directorate designed to "conduct affairs related to the principles of Islamic belief, worship, and ethics, to enlighten the public on the topic of religion, and to administer sacred places of worship."[1] The new government asserted the equality of religions and the rights of all Turkish citizens to worship privately under the protection of the Republic. The state saw itself as protecting freedom of worship while standing aloof from all religious influence and combating political Islam, which it saw as a threat to the independence of the state.

Revolutionism meant that changes taking place needed to be swift and sometimes drastic in form, to maintain the energy of the reform campaign and to make the changes that they were instituting irreversible. *Nationalism* was not construed as referring to a Turkish ethnicity, but to the community of all who lived within the borders established at the end of the Turkish War of Independence. The Turkish people were defined as those who "protect and promote the national, moral, human, spiritual and cultural values of the Turkish Nation": a definition purposely devoid of much ethnic or racial specificity.[2] In contrast to earlier pan-Turkic movements that envisioned the linkage of Turkic-speaking communities and ethnic groups across Asia, Kemal's vision was of a nation happily living within the borders envisioned by the 1920 Turkish National Pact. Given his attempt to cultivate good relations with the new Soviet Union, Kemal had given

---

[1]See http://www.diyanet.gov.tr/english/tanitim.asp?id=13 (accessed November 9, 2011).

[2]http://www.meb.gov.tr/Stats/apk2001ing/Section_1/1Generalprincipals.htm (accessed August 27, 2010).

up on Pan-Turkish attempts to connect with Turkic brethren who now made up some of the USSR's constituent republics, just as Lenin and his Communist associates had abandoned Russian pan-Slavic visions fueling moves against the Ottomans.

Finally, Kemal's program had an economic dimension, expressed in its principle of "statism." This referred generally to the concept that the government would control and manage sectors of the nation's economy in which private enterprise either could not or would not be involved. The plan was for the national government to play an important role in promoting industry and manufacturing, while leaving space for private companies to develop at the same time.

With these principles defining his eventual goals, Kemal set about changing social practices through a series of tangible and fairly drastic steps. The closing of religious schools and the adoption of Swiss law codes were among the measures that had most impact on society. For advice on how to supplant the religious school system, he even invited the famed American educational reformer John Dewey to visit Turkey in the summer of 1924 and consult with him. In 1925, he banned the wearing of brimless hats, and in 1928 he changed the Turkish alphabet from Arabic to Roman script. Between 1926 and 1934, he ended the veiling of women, gave them the right to vote, and saw women elected to the parliament for the first time as representatives. Even in terms of his own identity, he arranged for passage of law in 1934 requiring all Turkish citizens to adopt surnames. The name Ataturk (Father of Turks) was given to him by the Grand National Assembly in recognition of what he had done for the nation.

In the economic arena, he promoted government involvement in key economic sectors to build self-sufficiency, create new economic systems, and restore infrastructure lost in recent conflicts. The revolutionary energy of his state-capitalist projects was reminiscent of large-scale industrial programs

being carried out elsewhere, for example, in the Soviet Union, but unlike them, these programs did not include rejection of private capitalist activity or complete adoption of socialism. Instead, his measures were envisioned as an intermediate step on the way toward growing economic privatization that was designed to create a strong basis for further economic development.

To ensure the spread of modernization programs at all levels of society, a network of People's Houses was created in towns across the country. Their purpose was to provide educational and entertainment programs for the general public that would attract them and reinforce Kemalist principles. They were augmented in the 1930s in small villages by People's Rooms, so that by 1950, 500 People's Houses and over 4,000 People's Rooms had been established. The net result of this campaign was to popularize Ataturk's reform plans, promote cultural activities such as plays designed to reinforce the values of the new Republic, and to raise literacy rates.

Reactions to Change: Progressive Republican Party and Sheikh Said

After the establishment of the Turkish Republic in the fall of 1923, some sectors of society resisted the cascade of reforms, but for differing reasons. By the fall of 1924, the first official opposition political group emerged as the Progressive Republican Party. Its members had all been part of the inner circle of leaders in the Turkish Independence Movement and had played major roles in the Turkish War of Independence, and so were strong supporters of the general scope of Kemal's reform programs. However, many of them, including General Kazim Karabekir, opposed the timing and methods of implementation that Kemal was using.

In particular, Karabekir became very concerned about how quickly Kemal had moved to get rid of the caliphate in March 1924: the last symbolic vestige of Ottoman rule. Although not himself a supporter of the Ottomans, Karabekir saw this as unnecessarily antagonistic for leaders who retained reverence for this symbol, and in general, saw Kemal's antireligious policies as overly strident and inflexible. The demise of the caliphate has been identified as one factor in the outbreak of one of the most important uprisings against the new regime: the Sheikh Said rebellion of 1925.

This uprising against the central government was carried out largely by Kurds of the Zaza tribe under the aegis of Sheikh Said Piran. Sheikh Said was a Naqshbandi Sufi leader from just north of the eastern Anatolian city of Diyarbekir. Historians have tried to characterize his uprising as either primarily religious or nationalist in motivation, but it appears in fact to have been a combination of both, uniting Kurds alienated by Kemal's secularizing reforms with those displaced by the collapse of existing Ottoman power structures and political networks. While Sheikh Said provided spiritual and intellectual guidance for this event, its military component was bolstered by the Azadi (Freedom) movement. This was a group founded in Erzurum in 1923 by former Kurdish members of the Ottoman Hamidiye cavalry units.

The precursor to this uprising occurred in late 1924, when it became clear that Kemal was backing away from earlier suggestions he made about supporting Kurdish autonomy and promoting Kurdish language and culture within the new Republic of Turkey. One of the last blows for Kurdish leaders had been Kemal's abolition of the caliphate, which further angered many religious Kurds. In September, five hundred Turkish army troops, who were secret Azadi sympathizers, mutinied at a garrison in Bayt al-Shabab near Hakkari, just west of the Iraqi border.

Because these rebels were unable to attract any tribal supporters, they fled over the nearby border into Iraq. Over the next few months, Sheikh Said, in alliance with the Azadi group, attempted to start a mass uprising in the region north of Diyarbakir, proclaiming his intention to restore the caliphate and declare

an independent Kurdish state. His rebellion climaxed and then quickly fizzled in March 1925 because of a lack of support from any significant group beyond his core following. This period of crisis did force the final settlement of the current border between Iraq and Turkey in 1926, following negotiations that definitively assigned the province of Mosul and its potentially great oil resources to Iraq.

The Sheikh Said upheaval produced a severe reaction from the Turkish Republican government, which set up two Independence Tribunals and a Law for the Restoration of Order. These emergency measures put much of the country under martial law for a significant period of time and set a precedent for harsh reactions to any internal threats, perceived or real, to the nation's stability, particular those arising in its eastern provinces. This crisis also put an end to the Progressive Republican Party. Some of its members were accused of having aided the Sheikh Said rebellion and were put to death or sentenced to several years under house arrest or in exile. One of this party's founders was Dr. Adnan Adivar, husband of Halide Edip Adivar and a prominent physician who had been a director of the **Turkish Red Crescent Society** as well as a member of Kemal's cabinet for periods of time between 1920 and 1923 as minister of health and minister of internal affairs. From 1925 until after Ataturk's death in 1938, he remained in exile in Europe with his wife as a result of this crackdown, which enabled Halide to write from a critical distance about developments in the reform programs being undertaken back home.

This political challenge mounted by members of the inner circle of leaders of the Turkish Republic, as well as continued unrest in eastern Anatolia, set the stage for the gradual tightening of central political control in Ankara, creating a situation that would not be relaxed until after World War II. Although there were a couple of other brief experiments made with opposition parties in the Turkish parliament during the 1930s, one-party rule became the norm through Ataturk's life and beyond.

At the same time, one of the main focuses of the reform program continued to be the promotion of education and the raising of political consciousness for ordinary citizens, a process in which Ataturk himself became personally involved. He even helped to create a basic textbook for this: *Civic Knowledge for the Citizen*. It is ironic that even though Ataturk took strong measures against those whom he saw as threatening or opposing his vision of the Turkish Republic, he stated that its government "should enforce all the requirements of democracy as the time comes."[3] With an eclectic approach, Ataturk promoted scientific and cultural research on a variety of topics, sponsoring a translation of the Quran into Turkish and commissioning the first opera in Turkish. Ataturk so ardently wanted to strengthen the credentials of his new country that he espoused pseudoscientific concepts such as the **Sun Language theory**, which held that all human languages were descended from an original Central Asian language similar to Turkish. He promoted numerous neologisms as "rediscoveries" of words in "real Turkish" (*"oz Turkche"*) for things, even when they were largely invented.

In contrast to the flights of creativity he showed when delving into questions of Turkish national identity and language, Ataturk took a very measured and deliberate approach in his conduct of foreign relations: trying to promote "peace at home, peace in the world." This involved methodically building cordial relationships with all of Turkey's neighbors. Except for a period of minor conflict with Syria in the late 1930s over the province of Hatay/Alexandretta, Turkey developed good ties with its neighboring states. It even managed to reassert Turkish control over the straits of the Bosphorus and Dardanelles under the 1936 Montreux Convention: a document that has defined the status of these waterways ever since.

By the time of his premature demise in November 1938, Ataturk had built an entirely new modern country in Turkey that endured after him. After he survived an assassination attempt in 1926, Kemal asserted, "My humble body will surely turn to dust one day, but the Turkish republic will live on forever."[4] His remarkably comprehensive and swiftly-enacted reform programs in many areas has indeed shaped the subsequent development and evolution of this country that straddles Europe and Asia in the shadows of its ancient imperial forebears ever since then.

REZA SHAH'S NEW IRAN

One of Ataturk's most ardent admirers was Reza Shah Pahlavi, who served as Iran's monarch between 1925 and 1941. When Reza

Reza Shah Pahlavi and his son Mohammad Reza (1920s)

ullstein bild/The Granger Collection, NYC

---

[3]Afet İnan, *Atatürk Hakkında Hatıralar ve Belgeler* (Ankara: Türkiye İş Bankası Yayınları, 1968), 260.

[4]Andrew Mango, *Atatürk* (Woodstock, NY: The Overlook Press, 2000), 446–47.

Shah visited Turkey in 1934, he was enthralled to view the achievements of Ataturk's modernization programs firsthand, redoubling his own reform efforts upon his return home. Reza saw his mission as bringing Iran into the modern world, much as he perceived Ataturk had done for Turkey.

Reza's more limited success in achieving this was caused by the very different geopolitical situation from Turkey in which Iran found itself in the 1920s. Unlike the Ottoman Empire, Iran ended World War I in control of more or less the same territories with which it had begun the conflict. What had changed was Russia's status as one of the two principal foreign powers with spheres of influence over it, as a result of the Bolshevik Revolution. As noted, northern Iran and the Caucasus region became the scene after World War I of several military struggles. In the end, relative calm and stability had been restored to Iran under Reza Shah Pahlavi, a former Iranian Cossack commander crowned to replace the last Qajar monarch on December 15, 1925.

Like Ataturk, he launched Iran on a rapid and comprehensive modernization scheme in all areas of society and government. Unlike Ataturk, his authoritarian approach was not tempered by the concept that undemocratic methods were being used to build what would evolve into a democratic society. He came to power in a 1921 coup designed to restore stability to Iran. Although lacking in government functionality and stability, Iran was nowhere near the state of total social collapse that prevailed in former Ottoman lands. Through a series of decisive moves, Reza was able to bring the country to a more steady state within two years and to force the last Qajar shah into exile by October 1923.

His intention at that point was to emulate Turkey and proclaim a republic, but such a change was bitterly opposed by two powerful constituencies who, in relative terms, were far more powerful in Iran than their counterparts in the former Ottoman Empire: Shii clerics and

traditional landlords. As a result of this resistance, Reza recast his plan as a bid to become Iran's monarch, promising that he would not undertake any radical land reforms and not do anything to undermine the clerics' status as guardians of Islamic law. This shift now angered supporters of constitutional government and democracy in Iran. Maintaining as their goal the restoration of the 1906 constitution (which had envisioned Iran's development into a full parliamentary democracy), they opposed Reza's consolidation of power, but were unable to stand up against his increasing control of the military and government bureaucracy.

Just after he took the throne, Reza unveiled his plan to force change on the country. One of his first steps was to impose conscription. This created a viable military force controlled by the central government, giving the monarch powers of coercion that he had never exercised before in Iran. Reza used these powers to weaken tribal leaders, disarming tribal soldiers and forcing tribes to settle down in ways that gradually increased central control of provincial life in ways never before seen there.

Another lever of power for him was use of patronage, a traditional Iran way of exercising authority, but now centralized as never before. More than previous monarchs, Reza secured personal control over many huge estates and commercial enterprises, all of whose managers and supervisors were directly bound to him. He also expanded the central government bureaucracy, creating three new ministries and fifteen provinces, where there had been only eight in Qajar times. As for the parliament, he transformed it into a powerless body filled with his supporters, and selectively did away with officials whom he perceived to be acquiring too much power.

As in Turkey, Reza tried to secularize the judicial system by creating a system of civil courts. Instead of abolishing the religious authorities powers directly, however, he took a series of measures designed to supplant the primacy of the religious legal system and sharia law gradually. Through the 1930s, he terminated various judicial privileges that the clergy had enjoyed, generally removing them from significant judicial power by 1939. He also attempted to go around the religious educational system by establishing a large number of new secular elementary and secondary schools. However, he did not abolish religious schools, but in fact permitted them to expand, so that they had considerably higher enrollments by the end of his reign than at the beginning.

In terms of personal rights, he did away with the legal distinction between Muslims and non-Muslims, but did not alter the Islamic legal status of women, except for raising the legal age of marriage and requiring the civil registration of all marriages. In 1929, men were ordered to wear a new headgear known as the "Pahlavi cap" resembling a French kepi in 1929, but in 1935, were forced to put on fedoras, called "international hats."

Reza Shah took a much bigger step by unveiling women in January 1936 as part of a comprehensive national women's reform program. Although unveiling was only sporadically enforced through the rest of his reign, it remained an important part of official propaganda and was only formally rescinded in 1943 through an act of parliament. In contrast to this change, he continued to allow men to practice polygamy and take temporary wives, both longstanding traditional Shii practices.

Many of Reza Shah's judicial reforms were carried out and guided by secular experts with foreign training, such Ali Akbar Davar (1888–1937). Davar, a legal scholar educated in Europe, held numerous important government posts in the late 1920s and early 1930s, in which he was responsible for numerous reforms. For example, he was able in March 1926 to dismantle the existing Iranian judicial system, appointing hundreds of new judges and consulting with French legal advisers to restructure how court proceedings were carried out. His many other reform projects included creating modern law codes to protect personal rights and status, as well as founding the first state insurance company in Iran. Tragically, Davar committed suicide under mysterious circumstances in 1937—perhaps the victim of political intrigues caused by pressure from foreign political and economic interests.

Reza Shah not only focused on restructuring Iran's government, he also began a program of reorienting Iran culturally more toward its pre-Islamic past by changing its traditional name, "Persia," to "Iran" in 1935 and adopting a dynastic name, "Pahlavi," that harked back to the name of the medieval Persian written language. To inculcate this new ideology, he created a scouting movement for boys and girls that would celebrate nationalist traditions as much as Iran's Islamic heritage. Iran was given a new solar calendar that began on **Nawruz**: the Persian New Year's Day that happens on the spring equinox in March. Like Ataturk, he authorized linguistic purges that stripped the Iranian language of foreign words, replacing them with Persian terms and promoting the use of Persian names.

Despite this agenda of change, he did not try to suppress religion totally in favor of secularism, in contrast to Ataturk. In fact, Reza Shah's main agenda seemed to be to try to exercise more direct control over religious teaching and practice, as a way to use religion to strengthen national unity and cohesion as well as to modernize it. He himself made several religious pilgrimages, and invited prominent Shii clerics from Iraq to transfer their activities from Najaf to Iranian religious centers such as Qom.

Mirza Rezaqoli Shariat-Sanglaji, a popular religious figure and preacher allied with Reza Shah, called for a "reformation" in order for Shii Islam to embrace modernity wholeheartedly. In responding to the controversy over banning the veiling of women, Shariat-Sanglaji called for Shii authorities to use the tool of *ijtihad* (independent judicial reasoning) to bring Islam into harmony with the modern world.

In the economic sector, Reza Shah boosted tax collection and announced in 1928 that taxes collected on foreign imported goods would be raised, with capitulations and tax exemptions granted by the Qajars now abolished. He sponsored several government projects designed to stimulate the economy, most notable of which was the **Trans-Iranian Railway** that linked the Caspian Sea to the Persian Gulf through Tehran. This was built entirely without foreign financial assistance. Although it was a significant accomplishment, creating an enterprise that employed the largest workforce in the country outside of the oil industry, its high cost was a burden on the nation's infrastructure; taking the place of many more miles of surface roads that might have served transport needs better. In addition, Reza had its tracks stop just short of the two bodies of water it was connecting as a defensive measure: a step that reduced its usability considerably.

The Iranian government at this time participated in building urban infrastructure by giving loans for industrial development, and helping to construct various mills and refineries. The top-down approach to stimulating the economy in the cities also meant that most projects were centrally administered. This led to less stringent oversight of worker's conditions, as well as increased inefficiencies and corruption associated with large government-run enterprises.

At the same time that he was building the Iranian economy, Reza took great care to prevent the growth of a workers' movement in Iran. Attempts to organize workers into unions had begun in the 1920s at the new factories and industrial enterprises that he had created, such as the Vatan textile mill in Isfahan. By the late 1920s, the Iranian Central Council of Federated Trade Unions claimed several thousand members in different industries. To suppress a series of growing May Day demonstrations, Reza had his parliament enact an anticollectivist law in 1931 to restrict the activities of communists and socialists in organizing workers. This reduced the visibility of the workers' movement in Iran until the accession of Reza's son, Muhammad Reza, to the throne in 1941. Reza was unable

to dismantle workers' groups entirely, since the rapid industrialization of Iran that continued through the 1930s transformed many more peasants into industrial laborers.

The focus of Reza Shah's program of economic change stayed in the urban sector, since he ultimately chose to promote agricultural policies in rural areas that directly benefited large landowners at the expense of peasants. This was significantly different from the more populist approach taken in Turkey, reflecting how the existing power structures of great landlords in Iran had been far less disturbed than in Turkey by World War I. As late as 1934, 95–98 percent of the rural peasant population of the country possessed no land, while a small group of large landlords owned about half of the nation's agriculturally productive property. The lack of change in the agricultural sector was a great barrier to the creation of an expanding national market for industrial goods, which in turn hindered development of urban production facilities.

In many respects, the impact of Reza Shah's modernization programs on Iran was less comprehensive than what Ataturk was able to accomplish in Turkey. The scale of activity was so much vaster in Iran, with a land area more than double that of modern Turkey. The differences also had to do with the different goals of the two leaders. In the end, Ataturk sought to raise Turkey from the impoverished, weak state to which it had sunk by the fall of the Ottoman Empire, but also to replace an autocratic monarchy with a process of evolving toward a popular democracy. Reza Shah also sought to raise Iran from the weak, dependent state into which it had fallen by the late Qajar period. He always had to remain cognizant, however, that unlike in the Turkish case, World War I had not displaced the existing holders of religious and economic power in Iran to the extent that he could forge a totally new system to replace them.

The context of change in the two societies was also quite different. Beginning with the Gulhane Decree of 1839, the Ottomans had experimented with modernization in various aspects of society and government in the decades preceding Ataturk's revolutions, many of which were the culminations of ongoing processes of change. In the Iranian case, the experience of modernization in late Qajar times was far more limited and intermittent than it had been for the Ottomans; this was reflected in the way Reza Shah was able to operate and in the successes and failures he experienced in trying to change the country.

Another key difference lay in the how foreign entanglements continued to plague Iran more severely than Turkey after World War I. Despite enduring some levels of privation and hardship, the Turks were able to establish a degree of financial autonomy for their economy after the Treaty of Lausanne, which had not been possible for the Ottomans during the last century of their time in power. Iran, if only because of the Anglo-Iranian Oil Company (AIOC, previously the Anglo-Persian Oil Company), which was the largest industrial concern and had the largest number of employees of any industrial company in the nation, continued to be more tied to foreign interests. Reza Shah was able, after strenuous negotiations in 1933, to increase Iran's share of oil profits very modestly from 16 percent to 20 percent of the AIOC's total yearly earnings, but the price of this was that the concession date was extended another 32 years to 1993. As control over Iran's oil became a more and more important political issue through the 1930s and 1940s, this became a rallying point for sentiments against Pahlavi rule.

More serious even than foreign financial connections were the political perturbations caused by Iran's increasingly close ties with Germany in the late 1930s. Much like the Ottomans before him, Reza Shah saw Germany as a rising international power with a track record that seemed less encumbered by complex imperialist agendas than the British or Russians. In addition, the cultural identification of German's new Nazi rulers with their "Aryan" origins fitted well with Reza's new focus on Iran's pre-Islamic "Aryan" past. The Germans sent large numbers of businessmen and agents to Iran in the 1930s, so that during the first two years of World War II (1939–1941), Germany became Iran's large foreign trade partner (representing nearly 50 percent of its total foreign trade).

After the tumultuous events of the first two years of the war, such expanding commercial and cultural connections between Germany and Iran quickly became intolerable for Britain and the Soviet Union. They chose to remove Reza Shah from power in September 1941 and to place his twenty-one-year old son Muhammad Reza Pahlavi on the Iranian throne, with many consequences over many years. In the end, although Reza Shah achieved some success in his modernization campaigns, reestablishing Iran's prosperity and stability after its economic decline and political upheaval in late Qajar times, he was swept away by forces beyond his control—a legacy that haunted his young son during his first years on the throne.

ABD AL-AZIZ AND MODERN SAUDI ARABIA

Quite a different independent power emerged following the First World War in the central Arabian Peninsula. There, the Saudi family, gradually rebuilding its power base after a series of defeats through the late nineteenth century, began to flourish under the visionary leadership of Abd al-Aziz ibn Saud (r. 1902–1952): the man credited with creating the modern kingdom of Saudi Arabia.

Abd al-Aziz was born in 1876 into a line of Saudi emirs who had ruled the Najd in two successive Saudi states beginning in the mid-eighteenth century. As noted, their control over central Arabia was broken for a few years in the early nineteenth century after their decisive defeat at the hands of Muhammad Ali's son Ibrahim at Diriya in 1818. Abd al-Aziz himself had been forced into exile in Kuwait in 1891 when the **Al Rashid**, a rival Nejd clan, seized Riyadh and the core of Saudi territory there. In January 1902, on a night raid, Abd al-Aziz and twenty companions took Riyadh back. This surprising victory brought him many followers in the Nejd region, and he proceeded to take back almost all of his family's old territories in the area over the next two years. When the Ottoman army heard about this, they mounted an expedition against him, but soon abandoned their offensive due to logistical problems with fighting in the desert so far from their bases.

By 1912, he had consolidated control in the Nejd and decided to create a force called the *Ikhwan* (The Brotherhood). The *Ikhwan* was a religious militia dedicated to the purification and unification of Islam that followed the teaching of Muhammad ibn Abd al-Wahhab, so its members were identified by others as "Wahhabis." This organization undertook to replace the tribal loyalties of its followers with loyalty to Islam alone and to settle Bedouin tribesmen at oases and wells. Abd al-Aziz also cultivated close ties at this time to Wahhabi religious scholars.

In 1915, just as they were also building an allegiance with the Hashemite Sharif Hussein, the British signed a treaty with Abd al-Aziz in which he pledged to keep fighting the Al Rashid, who had been allied with the Ottomans. Abd al-Aziz did not initiate hostilities against them for five years, claiming that payments he was receiving from the British were inadequate to go after them. In any event, once he commenced fighting, he defeated the Al Rashid and annexed all their territories within two years. He then negotiated a new treaty with the British in which, in exchange for more payments, he agreed not try to expand his territories into areas strategically important to them, specifically Iraq and the Persian Gulf coast.

Building the New Kingdom

Instead, he continued westward, driving Sharif Hussein out of Mecca and Medina in 1926. Over the next six years, his armies annexed much of the Arabian Peninsula, so that he adopted the name Saudi Arabia for his domains and had himself proclaimed its king in 1932. Halfway

through this expansion process, he attacked and defeated at the Battle of al-Sabla a group of the *Ikhwan* forces that he had created, because they disobeyed his orders and had attacked Iraq. Controlling and channeling the religious zeal of the Ikhwan forces would become an important issue for him after the establishment of the Saudi kingdom. One way to do this was to create a **Saudi National Guard** in which the *Ikhwan* were incorporated into a force designed to protect the Saudi royal family from internal threats, should the need arise.

Abd al-Aziz was a very talented manager of fractious nomadic tribesmen because he was so skilled at incorporating them into his ranks. He had the reputation of being magnanimous in victory to his opponents, offering them inclusion into his forces instead of ill treatment. Another technique that he employed to create ties was to marry wives from tribes whom he had conquered. Such alliances produced children that tied groups in distinct geographical areas much more closely to the Saudi royal clan, creating a ruling family that knit the country together through a network of kin relationships.

The early 1930s also witnessed the beginnings of modern life in the Arabian Peninsula, traditionally a peripheral zone relative to the coastal cities of the region. Abd al-Aziz quickly understood the potential benefits of using new Western technologies to link the dispersed settlements of his homeland. He chose to bring in automobiles and later airplanes to reach distant parts of his territory in a fraction of the time previously required. He built an information network with wireless telegraphs to extend his eyes and ears across the country. In this very conservative country, many were opposed to such technological novelties, but Abd al-Aziz took time to demonstrate the value of these tools.

In one demonstration, Abd al-Aziz finally overcame the opposition of clerics to the telephone by inviting them to listen to recitations from the Quran being read over it. When he saw that they had heard this, he said, "Read your Quran. Does it not say that the devil and his [followers] cannot pronounce even one word of our Holy Book? This miracle therefore is not of the devil but of nature."[5] It was this very practical approach that reconciled many Saudis to the rapid expansion of technology and modern devices that followed upon the discovery of oil and its transformation into the mainstay of the Saudi economy.

Oil Discovered

The first discovery of oil in the Middle East in Iran by the British in 1908 raised interests in future petroleum prospects in the surrounding area. This precipitated the creation of the Turkish Petroleum Company (TPC) in 1912, a joint venture company launched by Armenian Ottoman petroleum entrepreneur Calouste Gulbenkian (1869–1955). The TPC's major shareholders originally were Royal Dutch/Shell Oil Company, the Ottoman Bank, and the Deutsche Bank. By March 1914, the British government, an original majority owner of the Ottoman Bank, succeeded in having the Ottoman Bank's shares in the TPC transferred to the Anglo-Persian Oil Company (in which the British government had just acquired a majority interest).

With the advent of hostilities, the commercial activities of the TPC became frozen until after World War I. By the 1920s, the TPC shares that had belonged to the Deutsche Bank had been reallocated to the French Petroleum Company (now known as "Total") as reparations and an American element had also been brought in: the Near East Development Corporation consisting of a consortium of five U.S. oil companies. When the TPC (known as the **Iraq Petroleum Company** [IPC] after 1929) finally discovered oil in Iraq in the late 1920s, its exploitation there was carefully controlled by the British.

The British created the Red Line Agreement in 1928. It specified that participants in the IPC would not undertake any oil exploration projects within former Ottoman domains that did not fully include other partners in this company. Since Saudi Arabia and most of the Persian Gulf region were not really regarded as former Ottoman domains, companies that did not belong to the IPC would presumably be able to act as independent agents in seeking oil concessions there.

Standard Oil Company of California (SOCAL, later called Chevron)—a company not bound by the Red Line Agreement—asked Harold St. John Philby to broker a deal between it and the Saudis in May 1932. Philby was a British convert to Islam who had earlier played an important role in the first years of the Transjordan mandate. By the 1930s, he was living in Jedda, Saudi Arabia and had become an important member of Abd al-Aziz's inner circle. He was willing to help SOCAL negotiate this, but decided that some competition might get a better deal for the Saudis.

He contacted the IPC to see if it might be interested in joining discussions. The IPC sent Stephen Longrigg, a veteran negotiator, to represent it, but he soon bowed out because the Saudis wanted payment in gold, instead of the Indian rupees that the IPC was offering. In May 1933, SOCAL signed a concession agreement with Abd al-Aziz for long-term exploration and extraction of oil in the al-Hasa region along the Persian Gulf.

In the end, SOCAL built a good relationship with Abd al-Aziz because he felt that the company focused solely on business, and lacked the imperialist baggage of British and other European firms. Saudi income from the SOCAL concession helped bridge a revenue gap created by the huge decrease in the number of Hajj pilgrims after the beginning of the Great Depression in 1929. A new subsidiary company of SOCAL, **California Arabian Standard Oil Company (CASOC)**, was created in 1933 to move ahead with prospecting.

---

[5] Abd al-Aziz ibn Saud, quoted in William A. Eddy, "King Ibn Sa'ud: 'Our Faith and Your Iron,'" *Middle East Journal* 17, no. 3 (Summer, 1963): 257–263.

Because of global economic weakness during the early 1930s, it was difficult to raise enough cash to keep the project going. In addition, the IPC, as a hostile competitor to CASOC and SOCAL, did not allow CASOC to use its extensive petroleum marketing and distribution networks in Asia. To get around this obstacle, SOCAL finally sold 50 percent of CASOC to Texaco, a Texas oil company that controlled extensive Asian supply markets beyond IPC's reach.

The style of the first oil prospectors who came to the Dammam area in the mid-1930s also helped move things along. They quickly created good working relationships with the local population. Some historians attribute this success to their status as prospectors who did not bring with them the official military and diplomatic personnel who usually were part of Western powers' projects in the region. Within a fairly short time (at a desert camp just southwest of Dammam that would be named Dhahran in February 1939), a fenced, prefabricated American community was built, complete with a recreation hall and a movie theater that was quite different from previous Western commercial towns and settlements in the region.

The atmosphere created by this project sustained the search for oil from unpromising beginnings in the depths of the Great Depression until commercial quantities of oil began to flow from Dammam Well #7 in March, 1938. The output of this well alone (more than 1,500 barrels per day) far exceeded the yield of most American wells at that time. King Abd al-Aziz made an extraordinary three-day car trip from Riyadh to attend the opening ceremony on May 1, 1939. At that time, he turned the tap to fill the first tanker of Saudi crude oil sent to Bahrain from the Ras Tannura dock.

Questions to Think About

1. What were the six principles of Kemalism, and how do they help explain Ataturk's revolution?
2. What were Ataturk's most important specific reforms, and why were they important?
3. What was the nature of opposition to Ataturk's changes, and how did he handle this?
4. Why did Reza Shah admire Ataturk, and why did he conduct his modernization program so differently?
5. Why was Reza Shah removed from the throne in Iran?
6. What led to the success of Abd al-Aziz as a ruler?
7. Why did Abd al-Aziz award the oil exploration concession to SOCAL, an American company, instead of IPC, a British-dominated company?

For Further Reading

Ansari, Ali M. *Modern Iran Since 1921: The Pahlavis and After*. London: Pearson Education, 2003.

Anscombe, Frederick F. *The Ottoman Gulf: The Creation of Kuwait, Saudi Arabia, and Qatar*. New York: Columbia University Press, 1997.

Atabaki, Touraj, and Erik Jan Zürcher. *Men of Order: Authoritarian Modernization under Ataturk and Reza Shah*. London: I.B. Tauris, 2004.

Azak, Umut. *Islam and Secularism in Turkey: Kemalism, Religion and the Nation State*. London: I.B. Tauris, 2010.

Kostiner, Joseph. *The Making of Saudi Arabia, 1916–1936: From Chieftaincy to Monarchical State*. New York: Oxford University Press, 1993.

Lewis, Bernard. *Turkey to-Day*. London: Hutchinson, 1940.

Mango, Andrew. *Atatürk*. Woodstock, NY: Overlook Press, 2000.

Parla, Taha, and Andrew Davison. *Corporatist Ideology in Kemalist Turkey*. Syracuse, NY: Syracuse University Press, 2004.

Renda, Günsel, and C. Max Kortepeter. *The Transformation of Turkish Culture: The Atatürk Legacy*. Princeton, NJ: Kingston Press, 1986.

Stegner, Wallace. *Discovery; The Search for Arabian Oil*. Beirut, Lebanon: Middle East Export Press, 1971.

Troeller, Gary. *The Birth of Saudi Arabia: Britain and the Rise of the House of Sa'ud*. London: F. Cass, 1976.

Vitalis, Robert. *America's Kingdom: Mythmaking on the Saudi Oil Frontier*. Stanford, CA: Stanford University Press, 2007.

Yalman, Ahmet Emin. *Turkey in My Time*. Norman: University of Oklahoma Press, 1956.

12

Making New Nations from Imperial Regions

EGYPT AS AN INDEPENDENT COUNTRY

Egypt's formal status as an independent nation began in 1922. At that time, the British government unilaterally declared that its protectorate there, in force since the beginning of World War I in 1914, was finished. Sultan Fuad I immediately became King Fuad I, but the British retained control over four "reserved points." A British army detachment was to be kept in place to protect the Suez Canal, the British were to retain control of the Sudan, the British would protect Egypt against foreign aggression, and Britain retained the right to protect foreign interests and citizens in Egypt. This declaration came after two years of diplomatic turmoil, during which the British and Egyptians could never agree on conditions for the British to grant Egypt total independence. The Wafd party leadership never accepted the "reserved points," which it saw as unacceptable restrictions of Egyptian sovereignty.

Government Stalemate

The situation became more complex when the Wafd party won the first real parliamentary elections held in independent Egypt with an overwhelming majority in January 1924. They came into power promising to make Egypt into an independent parliamentary democracy and constitutional monarchy. There were three main obstacles to this in the 1920s. The hereditary rulers of the nation, descendants of Muhammad Ali first called khedives and then sultans, had now become kings. They enjoyed less formal power than before, but remained reluctant to cede any power at all to the elected parliament. In the parliament, the Wafd party wielded its electoral majority in a fairly authoritarian fashion. Saad Zaghloul, first elected prime minister of the kingdom of Egypt, always led the party to promote its own interests, instead of seeking compromise with others. Finally, the British continued to interfere in Egyptian internal affairs much as they had before. Egyptian politics thus devolved into a permanent contest between the king, the Wafd, and the British through the 1930s.

For better or for worse, the Wafd, which had come to power with the promise of enacting a broad range of social reforms, gradually became a voice for the nation's commercial and professional elites. It slowly distanced itself from the Egyptian peasants and masses. It began to promote the Europeanization of all aspects of life, which estranged it from those at all levels of society who respected traditional Muslim values.

Some intellectuals began to emphasize the country's "Mediterranean" and "pharaonic" heritage as more authentic than its Islamic past, in order to align Egypt more closely with Europe, but also to assert that it was older and somehow more "authentic" than Europe. This **"Pharaonism"** had its roots in the discoveries made by Egyptologists in the early nineteenth century and rose to prominence after World War I. Its most notable literary proponent was the writer Taha Hussein (1889–1973) and it became a popular philosophy in Egyptian nationalist discourse between World War I and World War II.

However, the Wafd party's actual support for Taha Hussein during the acrimonious controversy that erupted after he published *On Jahiliya* [*Pre-Islamic*] *Poetry* in 1926 revealed the limits of its public commitment to intellectual ideals. This work was Hussein's scholarly attempt to apply modern analytical techniques to a canon with strong religious overtones: the pre-Islamic [*jahiliya*] Arabic poetry that provided the literary context of the Quran. In it, Hussein stated that he wanted to examine this genre of writing with a modern critical eye. When his study also tried to analyze the Quran as a work of literature, it ventured into sensitive territory. Hussein asserted that the story of Ibrahim and Ismail (Abraham and Ishmael) at the Kaaba in the Quran was included to demonstrate Mecca's glorious past—to show it as comparable to ancient Rome.[1] Such discussions unleashed a predictable barrage of criticism from Egyptian Islamic scholars.

A group of professors from the Muslim university of al-Azhar issued a statement accusing Hussein of straying from Islamic principles, choosing to insult Islam, and spreading heresy in his capacity as a university teacher. Because the leaders of the Wafd party, then the majority group in parliament, remained silent, the government was pressured to start legal action against Hussein. Many petitions were presented asking for him to be formally charged with defaming the Islamic faith: a crime under Egyptian law. In the end, the government prosecutor concluded that Hussein's accusers had taken his words entirely out of context and that there was no evidence that Taha Hussein had deliberately maligned Islam, thus closing the case. The passive attitude of Wafd leaders to the case revealed how the party handled this according to political expediency.

Mustafa Nahhas Pasha, leader of the Wafd after Zaghloul's death in 1927, served several times as prime minister over the next two decades and personified this style. His ability to stay in office, beyond winning elections, depended upon whether he was in or out of favor with the king and the British. He happened to be prime minister in 1936, when a renegotiated treaty between Egypt and Britain was signed. Although it was somewhat of an improvement on the 1922 Declaration of Egyptian Independence, the 1936 agreement preserved for the British many of the privileges covered in the four reserved points. This caused former Wafd supporters to demonstrate against the party's current leadership for showing such duplicity. The new treaty did contain language that appeared to leave room for renegotiation, but all was put on hold when a new monarch, the sixteen-year-old Farouk, suddenly took the throne upon his father's death in 1936.

Muslim Brotherhood

Most politics in Egypt during this era, despite the way the Wafd party continued to present itself as the representative of the Egyptian people, was conducted, as before, at a fairly elite level.

---

[1] http://weekly.ahram.org.eg/2001/535/chrncls.htm (accessed August 27, 2010).

Parliamentary and royal maneuvering took place in constant interplay with the British and had little real impact on ordinary people. The great promises that the Wafd had made in its rise to power remained unfulfilled.

Some people, particular those uprooted by economic upheavals and displacement in the 1920s and 1930s, turned to a new organization: the Muslim Brotherhood. A schoolteacher named Hasan al-Banna started it in the Suez Canal town of Ismailiya in 1928. Al-Banna had been inspired by the reformist, modernist messages of Jamal al-Din al-Afghani and Muhammad Abduh. As a teenager, he had been struck by the intensity of the 1919 revolt against the British. Now, with the same level of passion, he resolved to launch a campaign to defend Islam and Muslim values against Western domination and encroachment.

Al-Banna tried to revive the practice of Islam as a working faith for ordinary people and to promote its teaching—no longer part of the curriculum of modern secularized schools. He tried to do this by creating networks of families and Islamic discussion groups who pledged to honor a list of Muslim principles, which included not drinking alcohol, not lending or borrowing money at interest, and promoting modest dress for women. Unlike the Islamic modernists who had inspired him in his youth, al-Banna came to see the proper goal of contemporary Muslim believers as returning as much as possible to the pure, unadulterated Islam of Muhammad's time when he led the umma in Medina.

When the **Muslim Brotherhood** combined this message of purification with building hospitals, cottage industries, and mosques, it attracted a multitude of followers very quickly, boasting more than 500,000 members and many more sympathizers by the time Hasan al-Banna was killed in 1949. The attraction of this group is not hard to fathom. When most other organizations came to be perceived as established for and run by members of the social elite, the Brotherhood was perceived as sincerely reaching out to the masses.

As the 1930s progressed, the organization grew incredibly quickly, particularly after its headquarters moved to Cairo in 1932. The way that the organization was funded, by its individual members buying shares, shielded it from the pressures of both the government and wealthy individual donors. Although its focus remained on education and social welfare throughout this period, it began to take some political stands, particularly by sending financial support to the Palestinians during their 1936–1939 revolt. The society gradually developed an intensely hierarchical structure, but with members' position in the hierarchy determined by their performance of Islamic duties and participation in the society's study groups. Such a meritocratic system stood in stark contrast to the conventional system of patronage that defined most Egyptian organizations and was very appealing to the middle class. Despite this level of organization, al-Banna kept the organization at a distance from party politics, believing this to be too much in the hands of the elites, who in turn were too closely associated with the British.

Hasan al-Banna (1906–1949)

AFP/Getty Images/Newscom

Throughout this period, there was continuous pressure from some of its more ardent members for it to take a more activist stance in combating the British. Al-Banna tried to manage this pressure by creating "Battalions" of dedicated members who would receive more spiritual and physical training, but would pledge not to engage in any militant activity unless all peaceful means of resistance had been exhausted. This fragile equilibrium was to be challenged by the onset of the Second World War.

PALESTINE IN THE 1920S AND 1930S

Although Egypt confronted numerous issues in gaining its partial independence under Britain's aegis after 1922, it saw nothing as complex as the challenges the British faced in setting up the Palestine mandate. The 1920s and 1930s witnessed a British attempt to administer it according to the terms of the League of Nations charter that established it in 1922, but the provisions of this document were ambiguous and contradictory at best. One of its most problematic clauses was its call for the British (as the territory's administrators) to "facilitate Jewish immigration…[and] encourage close settlement by Jews on the land, including State lands and waste lands not required for public purposes."[2] They were called to do this "while ensuring that the rights and position of other sections of the population are not prejudiced": not an easy task under the best of circumstances.

The Palestinian Arab leadership continually asked the British to grant their people national and political rights, such as representative government, in the part of the Palestine mandate that had been designated to include a Jewish homeland. The British appealed to the terms of the mandate though, to reject the principle of simple majority rule or other measures that would give the Arabs majority control over the government. The Palestinians also faced a gradually but constantly changing demographic situation. Because of steady immigration, even in the face of various restrictions, the Yishuv (Hebrew word for the Jewish Zionist community in Palestine) increased during the mandate from one-sixth to almost one-third of the total population.

Another great challenge was that during the mandate period, the Jewish part of the Palestinian economy grew at around 13 percent per year, while the Arab sector of the economy lagged behind with growth at only half that rate (6.5 percent annually). The economic strength of the Jewish part of the economy had completely overtaken the Arab sector by 1936, with Jews in Palestine now earning between twice and three times on average as much as Palestinian Arabs. Due in part to better funding, the educational infrastructure of the Jewish community in Palestine outpaced the Arabs in development as well. For example, two first-class institutions of higher learning for the Yishuv were founded in the mid-1920s, the Technion in Haifa and the Hebrew University of Jerusalem, that both remain important educational institutions in the modern state of Israel. For Palestinian Arabs in the mandate, the main educational opportunity remained traditional religious schooling, with those seeking modern university education being required to travel to other countries such as Lebanon and Egypt.

Arab and Jewish Leadership in the Mandate

The British adopted a top-down management style for the Palestinian Arabs, dealing only with the elite instead of the middle or lower classes. This did not encourage Palestinian leaders to seek mass support for their policies and actions. The British approach resulted in a continuation of the political situation that had prevailed for the Arabs during the Ottoman period, when they had been dominated by a ruling elite accustomed to having its commands obeyed.

---

[2]http://www.mideastweb.org/mandate.htm (accessed on August 27, 2010).

In contrast to the Arabs, the Jewish community was run by a network of representative institutions. One of its principal organizations was the Jewish Agency, created in 1929 as an offshoot of the World Zionist Organization. The Jewish Agency was managed by a general council, half of whose members were chosen by the World Zionist Organization and the other half by other Jewish communities around the world. The British gave the Agency authority to issue immigration permits to Palestine (with the number of permits fixed by the British) and to distribute funds donated by Jews abroad.

Adult Jewish residents of Palestine (including women) first elected a General Assembly in 1927 with new elections held every four years after that. This assembly in turn selected a forty-member National Committee. The British treated this National Committee as a provisional governmental authority and allowed it to collect its own taxes. Because of the economic trends through the Mandate period, in which the balance of prosperity shifted in favor of the Jews, more and more of the revenue raised by the Mandate government came from the Jewish community. Most of the Mandate government's expenses, though, were allocated to funding administration and services for the Arab majority. The British thus allowed the National Committee to administer most services for the Jewish population independently, permitting it to function as a government within a government. This was particularly true for education and health care among the Jewish population, which were administered by the major Zionist organizations and funded by municipal taxes, donations, and fees.

There were definite divisions within the Jewish community in Palestine, most obviously between ultraorthodox Jewish religious communities and Zionists. The ultraorthodox always viewed Zionists as anathema. They felt that Zionism promoted gathering Jews in a renewed Israel *before* the coming of the messiah: an unpardonable heresy.

A more serious rift developed within Zionism itself upon the emergence of Revisionist Zionism in the 1920s. Led by Ze'ev Jabotinsky (1880–1940), who had served in World War I in the British Army with distinction, the **Revisionist Zionists** formally broke with mainstream Zionists in 1935 over the issue of partition of the Palestine mandate into Arab and Jewish sections, which they totally opposed. Their alternative concept was to promote an expansive Israeli state that existed on both sides of the Jordan River, whose inhabitants would live a middle-class European lifestyle instead of the socialist orientation of the Labor Zionists, who promoted farming and the kibbutz movement. Although the Revisionists made peace with the mainstream Zionists in 1947 on the eve of the Israeli War of Independence, the two main political blocs during the first fifty years of Israeli history, Labor and Likud, had their origins in these differing visions of what Israel ought to be.

Arab Revolt (1936–1939)

Disagreements within the Zionism movement paled in comparison with mounting popular discontent among Palestinian Arabs over rising Jewish immigration to Palestine in the 1930s. The Jewish population there increased from around 11 percent in 1922 to around 30 percent in 1940, with considerably more of the increase occurring after 1930. Discontent at the popular level promoted grassroots demonstrations by independent activists, but such initiatives were thwarted and weakened by Palestinian notables, who saw more advantages in collaborating with the British than in forcefully opposing them. This quiescent state of affairs prevailed until 1936, when a violent Palestinian uprising broke out, whose origins lay in the activism of charismatic, populist Islamic figures such as **Izz al-Din al-Qassam** (1882–1935).

Born near Latakia in Syria, al-Qassam attended al-Azhar University in Cairo where he apparently attended lectures on Islam and modernity by Muhammad Abduh and Rashid Rida. Upon his return, he became a teacher and imam at his local mosque. In 1911, he intended to go to Libya to help Ottoman forces there, but never made it. He served as an Ottoman military chaplain during World War I at a base near Damascus, received some military training, and organized a guerrilla unit to fight the French in Syria after the war.

After the defeat of Faisal by the French, al-Qassam was among those sentenced to death for opposing them. He was able to flee to Haifa, now under British control. In some ways reminiscent of Hasan al-Banna in Egypt, al-Qassam reached out to the lower classes there, setting up an Islamic night school for workers and proselytizing on the streets among ordinary people. Many of his followers were landless tenant farmers who had come to Haifa from the Upper Galilee region, where they had been forced to leave agricultural lands recently purchased by the Jewish National Fund.

Unlike al-Banna, al-Qassam's incendiary political and religious speeches called on peasants to create guerrilla units and stage attacks on British and Jews. After a set of clashes between Arab Palestinians and Jews in 1929, he sharpened his calls to action and began to organize military training courses. By 1935, he had organized hundreds of followers into small covert cells, and provided them with bombs and firearms to kill and terrorize Jewish immigrants, as well as commit acts of vandalism against Jewish communal farms and British installations.

In November 1935, al-Qassam and twelve of his men fled to the hills between Jenin and Nablus. The British police launched a manhunt, found him hiding in a cave, and killed him in a gun battle there. His heroic last stand as a religious martyr caught the imagination of young Palestinians, and his funeral was one of the largest gatherings that ever took place in Palestine during the mandate period. By April 1936, anti-Zionist sentiments boiled over into an Arab general strike across Palestine that continued for the next six months. Thousands of Jewish farms were destroyed, and Jewish civilians were attacked and killed by small militant groups who took inspiration from al-Qassam and his followers.

In 1937, a British investigative commission led by Lord Peel offered the first partition plan for Palestine. The Zionists would be given a small Jewish state whose Arab population would have to be moved out, while a larger Arab state would be created that would be attached to Jordan. Arab leaders immediately rejected the proposal, but the World Zionist Congress, although not happy with its specifics, accepted the general concept of this plan as the starting point for negotiations.

After a lull in violence, during which the **Peel Commission** conducted its inquiry, unrest resumed in the fall of 1937. The uprising now began to get out of control in two important towns, Nablus and Hebron, where civil order broke down. Confronted with much more serious and organized threats of violence, British troops applied massive force to quell the unrest, aided by 6,000 armed Jewish auxiliary police. Orde Wingate, a British army intelligence officer who happened to be a Christian evangelical Zionist, had organized by June 1938 Special Night Squads (SNS) composed of British soldiers and a small contingent of Jewish volunteers such as Yigal Allon (later an Israeli commander in the 1948 war and a politician).

From the official British perspective, the primary mission of the Special Night Squads was to defend the Iraqi Petroleum Company (IPC) pipeline that ran from Iraq through Transjordan and Palestine to the port of Haifa, as well as to protect the electric power grid of Palestine from guerrilla attacks. In their raids on Arab villages and guerrilla camps, the SNS units pioneered brutal counterinsurgency tactics later adopted by the Special Air Service (SAS) units of the British army. These SNS units continued in service until September 1939, when they were disbanded following the general shift in British policy that occurred upon the issuance of the 1939 **White Paper**, which called for Jewish immigration to be severely reduced and favored Arab Palestinian interests.

The SNS units were not the only Jewish armed groups that had gotten involved in confronting the **Arab Revolt** militarily. Another was the Revisionist Zionist militia known as the **Irgun** (also called by its initials: IZL, pronounced "Etzel"), founded in the early 1930s. Beginning in 1936, the Irgun started to use violence against Arab civilians, attacking marketplaces and buses, in retaliation for Arab attacks on Jews.

The 1936–1939 Arab Revolt resulted in the deaths of 400 Jews and 200 British soldiers, with approximately 5,000 deaths and 10,000 wounded among the Palestinians. The Arab Revolt had several long-term impacts. It prompted the rapid expansion of Jewish underground militias, primarily the main military force known as the Haganah. Jewish commanders gained valuable experience battling Palestinians in the Arab Revolt, which proved decisive in Israel's battlefield successes in the 1948 War of Independence. For both sides, this conflict showed that the two communities could not be easily reconciled, marking the real beginning of serious diplomatic efforts in favor of partition and a two-state solution.

As the unrest diminished in intensity, the British government issued a White Paper in May 1939, offering the main official policy response to Arab grievances. It severely restricted Jewish land acquisitions and immigration just on the eve of the Second World War. After war began, it was not even possible to fill this smaller immigration quota. The policy of exclusion created by this White Paper represented for many an abandonment of the Balfour Declaration's support for Palestine as a Jewish refuge. This now radicalized segments of the Jewish population, particularly among the Revisionist Zionists, who began to see in this new document a real justification for fighting the British.

The 1936–1939 Arab Revolt had a deleterious effect on the Palestinian Arabs, because the harsh response by the British to the challenges that it posed had fragmented Palestinian leadership. Many leaders had been killed off and others, such as Hajj Amin al-Husayni, sent into exile. Palestinian Arab social cohesion had been badly damaged, setting the stage for the Palestinian problems in the 1948 War: a more epochal challenge than any confrontation of the 1930s.

IRAQ AS AN INDEPENDENT NATION

Like Palestine, Iraq was beset by problems immediately after its creation as a British mandate in 1920. The coronation of Faisal, son of Sharif Hussein and recently ousted from Syria by the French, as first **ruler of the Hashemite Kingdom** of Iraq in August 1921 did not improve matters, because he lacked any local constituency. Unrest continued among Sunni and Shii Arabs as well as Kurds in various regions of the country through the 1920s. The British restored order by using two military forces that they directly controlled, the Iraq Levies and **Royal Air Force** (RAF) Iraq Command, as well as creating an Iraqi national army as part of Faisal's new government.

The Iraq Levies grew out of an irregular force of Arabs, Kurds, Turcoman, and Assyrian troops that had assisted the British after their initial campaign in Mesopotamia at the end of World War I. By 1923, half of the soldiers in the Levies were **Assyrians**, and the other half Kurds, along with a few Marsh Arabs and Turcomans. Five years later, the Levies were almost entirely Assyrians, and the force had now primarily been assigned to guard RAF bases in Iraq. The Assyrians were members of an Aramaic-speaking Christian minority group, many of whom now in Iraq had fled during the war from areas in Ottoman Anatolia. Because of their minority, newcomer status in Iraq, they remained steadfastly loyal to the British through the 1920s.

When the RAF established an Iraq Command in 1922, it became one of the first major British military units ever to be commanded by an air force officer, and it employed several new military techniques. Royal Air Force planes, for example, dropped delayed-action bombs outside Sulaymaniya in 1923 to prepare the area for British occupation and to compel its Kurdish leader, Sheikh Mahmud Barzanji, to flee to Iran. A short time after that, the RAF flew 280 Sikh troops into Kirkuk in the first British military airlift operation.

The Iraqi national army reflected Ottoman social divisions, with Sunni Arabs (and some Kurds) serving as its officers, and its enlisted personnel being drawn from Iraq's Shii population, particularly the tribal element of this religious group. As the status and influence of the army grew, this tended to reinforce the existing higher status of Sunnis serving in it, despite their lesser numbers in the country's overall population.

The most important factor in stabilizing Iraq during the first few years of the mandate became King Faisal himself. Despite his foreign origins, he effectively balanced the competing interests of vastly divergent groups for a considerable length of time. Faisal was assisted by several able lieutenants, most notably Nuri al-Said and Sati al-Husri. Nuri al-Said was an Ottoman officer from Iraq who rose from fairly humble circumstances to eventually become Faisal's deputy during World War I. He was well-poised to be Faisal's liaison with the native Iraqi Arab elite, but without himself having an independent power base, given his middle-class origins. Sati al-Husri had built a career in the Ottoman educational system. He emerged as an associate of Faisal after the war, first in Syria, and then in Iraq, where he became national director of higher education through the 1920s. In reshaping school curricula, he emphasized secularism and Arab nationalism in ways that shaped the thinking of those who later assumed important leadership roles in the country.

Problems of Iraqi Unification in the 1930s

Despite the relative success of the beginning of Hashemite rule in Iraq, several issues continued to weigh on the country for decades after the 1920s. One was the Anglo-Iraqi Treaty of 1922, by which the British were seen to have inappropriate influence over Iraq's government (even though the agreement was rewritten more favorably for Iraq in 1930). Another problem was Iraq's paltry oil income. It did not receive substantial revenues until the 1950s because of agreements and concessions secured by the IPC at the outset of the mandate. The IPC, really a consortium of several foreign companies, managed to broker an agreement extending many years into the future, which gave it excellent terms. Finally, the sheer poverty of the country severely curtailed its operating budget, exacerbated by the fact that Iraq still had to pay a part of the remaining Ottoman public debt until finally retiring its share in 1934. Anger over Iraq's dependence on and indebtedness to foreigners in all these issues caused the growth of a robust nationalist movement across ethnic, religious, and economic lines.

Nationalist agendas began to shape Iraqi politics even more after 1932, when the British mandate in Iraq formally ended and the nation received nominal independence. When Faisal died after a sudden heart attack in 1933, he was succeeded on the throne by his son Ghazi: a monarch much less interested than his father in ruling and whose focus on fast cars ended in his own swift demise in an auto wreck in 1939. Ghazi in turn was replaced by his three-year old son Faisal II, whose government was administered by a regent until 1953. The sudden loss of Faisal I meant that the crucial role he played as a mediator and broker between the many Iraqi political factions remained unfilled until the fall of the monarchy in 1958. The fragile national unity secured in the 1920s quickly broke down under the pressures of a series of large internal rebellions in the mid-1930s, among the most important of which was the Assyrian uprising.

Upon Iraq's 1932 declaration of independence, Assyrians, under the leadership of their young patriarch Mar Shamun, tried to reassert the autonomous status they once enjoyed in the Ottoman *millet* system when they lived in eastern Anatolia. Under British protection, they had become the backbone group of the Iraq

Levies. Shamun presented a case to the League of Nations for an autonomous Assyrian enclave in northern Iraq, which would have included a large area inhabited by Kurds, who did not wish to be part of an Assyrian region.

The tensions that this created led to a spate of intercommunal violence, including a notorious set of massacres in Assyrian villages by troops from the Iraqi national army in the summer of 1933. The commander blamed or credited for this was Bakr Sidqi. He was an officer who used this affair to bolster his own standing as an Arab nationalist and to introduce universal conscription in order to create a large Iraqi national army, which remained dominated by a Sunni Arab officer cadre that had carried over from Ottoman times.

TRANSJORDAN UNDER ABDULLAH

Since the British had drawn the borders of Transjordan in a somewhat quirky fashion, partly to facilitate the transport of oil from Iraq to Haifa, Abdullah faced considerable challenges in establishing his right to rule there. He was an Arab, but not from this part of the Arabian Peninsula. His task was to fit into existing networks of loyalties here in which he was an outsider, while keeping his British patrons happy at the same time.

Politics in this new kingdom revolved around balancing interests of three distinct groups. First were local tribal notables zealously guarding their independence and autonomy. Next, Abdullah's government was mostly made up of urban Arab bureaucrats still dreaming of establishing an independent Arab state in Damascus. Finally he had to answer to the British. The British, themselves focused on maintaining regional stability while not angering the French, sent Abdullah a £5,000 monthly stipend, so he owed it to them to listen to their requests.

Abdullah appealed in different ways to each group. For the local tribal chiefs, his task was to establish how his Hashemite status justified rule over them. To the bureaucrats, he had to convey that he shared their dream of a larger Arab Syrian state centered in Damascus without provoking reactions from the French, jealous guardians who had driven out Faisal to control Syria. Finally, he had to keep the British convinced that he was the best choice to rule this area and that he could work productively with their administrators in Palestine.

In the rapidly evolving situation in the Middle East, the British sent T.E. Lawrence and Harold St. John Philby, two experts with long experience in the Middle East, to consult with Abdullah. Philby ended up becoming his resident advisor, helping him govern in ways that reassured the British and French. Philby also succeeded in getting rid of many fervent Arab nationalists who had joined Abdullah's government. After Abdullah's visit to London in 1922, the British government formally announced that it had put Transjordan on a path to independence under his rule.

The difficulty was that this announcement foresaw the creation of a constitutional government with an elected parliament: a system that Abdullah completely opposed but Philby strongly supported. This disagreement created hard feelings between the two men, which exploded in June 1923 when Abdullah ordered the destruction of an ancient Byzantine basilica in order to build a mosque in Amman. This made Philby so angry that it ended his previously cordial relationship with Abdullah.

Abdullah had managed to keep his relationship with the British relatively stable by reducing the power and number of extreme Arab nationalists working in his government. He ran into trouble with some local leaders when the Adwan tribe mounted a revolt against him. They became angry when they heard that taxes collected from them were going to be given to the Bani Sakhr, a rival group. The Bani Sakhr had the reputation of being specially favored by Abdullah, because their lands had long been principal targets of regular raids by Wahhabis striking from farther south in the Arabian Peninsula.

When the Adwan attacked, they were defeat by the **Arab Legion**: an elite force commanded by British officers totally loyal to Abdullah. Local urban elites interpreted this as a sign of how much the British stood behind Abdullah and protected him. Britain used its increased standing after this affair to remove remaining Arab nationalists from important positions in Abdullah's government and army. This incident also meant that British administrators lost some confidence in Abdullah's ability to manage his kingdom and began to consider other options for governing Transjordan.

Just as this tension loomed between Abdullah and the British, Abdullah's father Sharif Hussein arrived from the Hejaz for a visit in January 1924. Hussein's presence overshadowed Abdullah during the two months of his stay, culminating in his precipitous assumption of the title of caliph, upon its being taken away from the last Ottoman ruler in March. To a certain extent, this had been the Hashemite dream since the beginning of World War I, when this possibility was discussed in the Hussein-McMahon correspondence.

Now, the results were mixed. Arab populations of the Syria and Palestine mandates, to show their collective opposition to British and French overlords, expressed enthusiastic support for Hussein as caliph. The Saudi ruler Abd al-Aziz immediately attacked his declaration as illegitimate. He used this against Hussein to build momentum for the military campaign against Hashemite rule in the Hejaz that he launched a short time later.

Back in Transjordan, after the distraction and excitement of Hussein's visit had subsided, the British decided to exert more direct control over Abdullah. Without warning, Britain suddenly cut its subsidy to him. Upon his return from a hajj pilgrimage in August 1924, the British handed him an ultimatum. It declared that he could not stay on the throne if he did not agree to a list of demands that dramatically increased Britain's control over Jordan's internal and foreign affairs. His acceptance

made him far more dependent on the British than before: the way his reign became defined for many years to come. British control was further enhanced after Abd al-Aziz ibn Saud swiftly took control of the Hejaz, leaving Iraq and Jordan as the only places still ruled by Hashemites.

Abdullah's reputation as an Arab leader was also tarnished by his failure to assist anti-French rebels in Syria. He failed to help Sultan al-Atrash, Druze leader of the **Great Syrian Revolt** of 1925–1927 (see p. 186), primarily due to British pressure.

This was interpreted by many Syrians as his bid to appease the French, because in an earlier Druze rebellion, Abdullah had given sanctuary to al-Atrash. In any event, the series of upheavals in both Syria and the Hejaz in the 1920s brought many refugees to Transjordan. Some found work there in the government, while others joined the emerging commercial infrastructures of cities like Maan and Amman.

By the late 1920s, despite the vagaries of creating a new nation, Transjordan had been stabilized. Central authority under King Abdullah I had been secured, but at a price, which was Britain's implicit oversight of all government policies and actions, however trivial. Nevertheless, Transjordan gradually became one of the more stable nations carved out of Ottoman Syria after World War I: a **state of affairs that continued beyond World War II**.

DEVELOPMENTS IN LEBANON AND SYRIA

Syria, the mandate carved out of the old Ottoman province of Syria for France, had a very different history from neighboring territories assigned to the British. Iraq, Palestine, and Jordan had all been created either by slicing off parts of an existing Ottoman province (Palestine and Transjordan) or by combining several provinces together (Iraq). French Syria, in contrast, encompassed territories that historically had functioned as the political center of the Levant region. Most recently, its capital Damascus had been the center of the attempt to create a united Arab kingdom under Faisal, which had been crushed by the French in 1920.

The heart of that part of the Syrian mandate in which the Republic of Lebanon was declared on September 1, 1926, was the autonomous Ottoman region of Mount Lebanon. It had been dominated by the French since 1861, when the central Ottoman government had issued a *Reglement Organique* (Organic Statute) for this area in order to end the ongoing Druze-Maronite War. This document had given European nations, particularly France, greatly increased power and influence over this coastal region, as well as the Syrian hinterlands inland from it.

By the 1920s, France's goal, in carving Lebanon out of Syria, was to empower the Maronites to secure a stable foothold for France from which to rule Syria. Beyond Mount Lebanon, "Great Lebanon" under the French now included the former Ottoman districts of Tripoli and Sidon as well as the Bekaa Valley. At first, almost all of the Muslim population in this area (as well as many non-Maronite Christians) had resisted its creation, but their protests were suppressed by a series of fairly brutal French campaigns, particularly in south Lebanon.

During the entire time that the French held Lebanon, tension continued due to their presence there, although armed resistance diminished in the 1930s. There was always a paradox in Lebanon for its dominant group: the Maronites. Either they could choose a separate Christian state, or they could create an economically viable state, but having both would prove very difficult.

The first few years after the establishment of "Great Lebanon" in 1920 witnessed continuous political struggles over the proper representation of various religious and ethnic groups in its government. The outbreak of a broad armed uprising against the French across Syria and Lebanon in 1925 prompted the French government to establish a clearer set of rules on the rights and privileges of each ethnic and religious community. This was reflected most clearly in the first Lebanese constitution promulgated on May 23, 1926. Based loosely on the governmental structure of the French Third Republic, it had a Chamber of Deputies, a president, and a Council of Ministers. The Chamber of Deputies elected the president for a single six-year term, with its deputies popularly elected in proportion to the voting populations of each ethnic/religious group.

The practice arose that major public officials were to be chosen according to the proportional strength enjoyed by their respective ethnic/religious communities as well. This eventually coalesced into the tradition that the president should be a Maronite Christian, a Sunni Muslim should be chosen as prime minister, and a Shii Muslim selected as speaker of the Chamber of Deputies—a pattern that only solidified many years later. In theory, the Chamber of Deputies performed a legislative function, but in reality, the president and his cabinet prepared bills submitted to the Chamber of Deputies, which passed with little discussion. In this system, a French high commissioner exercised supreme power: an arrangement that allowed the French to intervene on a regular basis to select officials and impose policies to protect their interests.

When elections were held, Charles Debbas, not a Maronite but a Greek Orthodox politician, was elected as Lebanon's first president. When he finished his first term in 1932, there was a bitter competition to succeed him between two Maronite presidential candidates. Since they had equal support in the Chamber of Deputies, Muhammad al-Jisr, a Muslim leader from Tripoli, was proposed as a compromise candidate.

However, because al-Jisr was Muslim and the French authorities did not want a Muslim president, the French High Commissioner suspended the constitution and extended the term of Debbas for one year. The next French high commissioner appointed one Maronite, Habib Pasha al-Saad, as president for two years until another Maronite, Émile Eddé, could be elected. The French had always tried to skew Lebanese politics in their favor, but their own domestic situation soon changed.

The election of a leftist government in France in the spring of 1936 caused French policy toward Lebanon and Syria to alter considerably. The new French government now seemed willing to negotiate terms for the eventual independence of these two places as separate nations. It signed a treaty in September 1936 with Syria that specified how this would take place. As a logical corollary to this agreement, Lebanon, represented through a delegation led by Eddé, signed its own Treaty of Friendship and Alliance with France in November. However, although the French *signed* both treaties, they did not *ratify* either one, leaving the relationship between France and its two most important central Middle Eastern territories ambiguous in the years just before World War II.

This first French–Lebanese agreement emphasized the need for the rights of each ethnic and religious community to be respected, in ways that foreshadowed the **Lebanese National Pact** soon to follow. Nevertheless, the French government soon retreated into defensive mode in Lebanon, epitomized by the high commissioner's suspension of the Lebanese constitution in September 1939 just at the beginning of World War II. Events of the war drastically changed the situation there, as in many other parts of the region.

The Great Syrian Revolt

Even more than Lebanon, Syria had been the center of much political activity in the Middle East after World War I, and intrigues there continued after the French took control. One of the main problems was that the French were not content merely to divide-and-rule. They also tried to micromanage politics in ways that traditional leaders viewed as continual threats

to their status, in contrast to the general British approach in the Middle East of empowering local elites and allowing them degrees of autonomy. One of the first groups to feel such a threat from the French in the 1920s was the Druze political elite led by the al-Atrash clan, rulers of the Jabal Druze area. This group felt that it had come under direct attack from the French authorities when the French tried to impose modernization programs such as secularizing the Druze judicial system and appointing local officials more compliant with the wishes of the central authorities in Damascus.

In particular, there was great anger at the appointment of Captain Gabriel Carbillet as governor of Jabal Druze. Carbillet quickly became infamous for drafting locals to perform forced labor on road-building projects and other public works schemes. In addition, he responded to popular protests against his actions with forceful repression. Tensions built until the summer of 1925, when the Jabal Druze leader Sultan Pasha al-Atrash officially declared war on France.

Al-Atrash managed to enlist the participation of several different communities of Syrians in a revolt that now spread across the country. Rebel forces initially achieved a number of victories against the French, but this was countered when France sent in large Moroccan and Senegalese contingents armed with modern weaponry, in addition to augmenting its air force in Syria. These reinforcements allowed the French to regain control of the situation, although fierce resistance lasted for nearly two more years. Sultan al-Atrash and other rebel leaders were sentenced to death, but he and his followers eventually escaped to Transjordan and were ultimately pardoned.

This rebellion had several important results. It forced the French to start moving away from their divide-and-rule strategy, and they agreed to hold the first Syrian national elections in 1928 (although the formal reunification of four of the ministates of French Syria: Damascus, Aleppo, the Alawite state, and Jabal Druze did not occur until 1936). These were won by an opposition group, the **National Bloc** led by notables such as Ibrahim Hanano and Hashim al-Atassi, many of whom had been prominent in the effort to create an Arab kingdom under Faisal after World War I.

"National Bloc"

A group of notables had met in October 1927 to create this National Bloc: a coalition group that would organize the Syrian nationalist movement over the next two decades. The Bloc promoted Syrian independence through diplomatic rather than violent means, with Hashim al-Atassi elected as its permanent president. In 1928, he was also elected president of the Constituent Assembly and charged with drawing up Syria's first constitution. This assembly immediately ran into trouble since it continued to support the 1920 proclamation of an independent Syrian state—totally out of bounds for the French—and was dissolved by the French high commissioner in May 1930.

The French authorities then imprisoned al-Atassi for several months on Arwad Island, located in the Mediterranean just off the Syrian coast. Upon being freed, he was elected as a parliamentary deputy. Al-Atassi opposed the 1934 treaty with France because it kept certain parts of Syria under French control. The National Bloc mobilized massive street demonstrations and riots to protest this. In the end, the French government was compelled to acknowledge the Bloc as truly representing the Syrian people and to invite al-Atassi to Paris for new talks. Six months later, the 1936 Franco-Syrian Treaty of Independence became the first agreement between France and this Syrian group that supported Arab nationalism.

This accord finally charted a clear path toward Syrian independence over a twenty-five year period, with the eventual re-incorporation of previously autonomous territories into Syria (except for Lebanon). In return, Syria pledged to support France in any wars, allow French planes to use its airspace, and permit France to keep military bases there. Based on the signing of this treaty, al-Atassi became the first head of state of Syria as a recognized independent nation in November 1936.

Part of the success of this diplomacy and the creation of a new relationship between France and Syria was due to the new French government led by the leftist Popular Front between 1936 and 1938. However, as with the agreement between France and Lebanon, the Franco-Syrian treaty was *signed* but not *ratified* by France. Various influential sectors of the French government began to develop reservations about relinquishing any French holdings or influence in the Middle East in the face of the emerging threat posed by Nazi Germany. One deathblow to the Franco-Syrian treaty and to al-Atassi's leadership was the resolution of the issue of the status of Alexandretta in favor of it becoming part of Turkey. This area, a former Ottoman district occupied by the French since World War I and now administered as a part of the Syrian mandate, had been claimed by the Turks since the founding of the Turkish Republic in 1923.

After the signing of the Franco-Syrian treaty and the Syrian parliamentary elections in 1936, two deputies were elected from Alexandretta who strongly supported Syria's total independence from France. This prompted the Turkish government to renew its campaign to claim this region. Growing uncertainty over France's future in the Middle East, which had led the French not to ratify the Franco-Syrian treaty, now also persuaded them to accede to Turkish pressure first to give autonomy to Alexandretta, and finally to allow it to become a Turkish province in 1939 after a referendum (which Syrians never accepted as fair). Due to the failure of the treaty actually to be implemented and the final loss of Alexandretta, al-Atassi resigned as prime minister in July 1939 and would not hold public office again until 1949. The outbreak of World War II only two months later threw the whole situation into turmoil, with all discussion of Syrian independence deferred indefinitely.

"Special Troops of the Levant"

Another lasting effect of the 1925–1927 Revolt had been the creation of a force called the **Special Troops of the Levant** (*Troupes Spéciales du Levant*). It was augmented by North African infantry (*tirailleurs*) and cavalry (*spahis*), Foreign Legion (*Légion étrangère*), and Colonial Infantry units (of metropolitan French and Senegalese origin). This entire force was called the Army of the Levant and had responsibility for keeping order in both Syria and Lebanon between the two world wars.

The French organized the *Troupes Spéciales du Levant* in order to favor religious and ethnic minorities: a military extension of their general divide-and-rule philosophy in running Syria. Sunni Muslim Arabs, who constituted 65 percent of Syria's population, were discouraged from serving in the *Troupes Spéciales*, whose personnel was mainly composed of members of the Druze, Christian, Circassian, and Alawite communities. In addition to the main military forces, there were several companies of Lebanese light infantry and squadrons of Druze, Circassian, and Kurdish mounted infantry designated as auxiliary troops. They provided a form of military police (*gendarmerie*) for internal security purposes and were primarily deployed in the areas of their recruitment. A military academy (*École Militaire*) was established at Homs to train Syrian and Lebanese officers and specialist noncommissioned officers (NCOs), creating a cadre of trained professional military officers largely from the minority groups of Syria. This would have political implications in the future, due to the lack of participation (proportionally) of members of the majority Sunni Arab group in this type of training.

Questions to Think About

1. What defined Egyptian politics after Egypt was given its independence in 1922?
2. What was Pharaonism, and why was it popular?
3. What was the Wafd party's approach to governing?
4. What were the agendas of the Muslim Brotherhood?
5. How was the Muslim Brotherhood organized as a group?
6. What were the particular challenges faced by the Palestine mandate in the 1920s?
7. How did Arab and Jewish leadership in the Palestine mandate compare and contrast with each other?
8. Who were the Revisionist Zionists and what was their impact?
9. How did the 1936–1939 Arab Revolt affect the situation in Palestine?
10. What was the 1939 White Paper?
11. What were the issues confronted by Iraq as it first became a British mandate and then an independent nation?
12. What roles did the Iraq Levies and the RAF play in the Iraq mandate?
13. What were the big challenges to Iraqi stability in the 1930s?
14. How did Abdullah secure power in Transjordan?
15. How did the French try to rule Lebanon and Syria after they became mandates?
16. How did the Great Syrian Revolt of 1925–1927 affect French policy toward Syria?
17. What was the "National Bloc" and how did it shape Syrian politics?
18. Who were the Special Troops of the Levant, and what was their function in Syria and Lebanon?

For Further Reading

Beinin, Joel, and Zachary Lockman. *Workers on the Nile: Nationalism, Communism, Islam, and the Egyptian Working Class, 1882–1954*. Princeton, NJ: Princeton University Press, 1987.

Botman, Selma. *Egypt from Independence to Revolution, 1919–1952*. Syracuse, NY: Syracuse University Press, 1991.

Gelvin, James L. *Divided Loyalties: Nationalism and Mass Politics in Syria at the Close of Empire*. Berkeley: University of California Press, 1998.

Goldschmidt, Arthur, Amy J. Johnson, and Barak A. Salmoni. *Re-Envisioning Egypt 1919–1952*. Cairo: American University in Cairo Press, 2005.

Jabotinsky, Vladimir. *The Jewish War Front*. Westport, CT: Greenwood Press, 1975.

Mitchell, Richard P. *The Society of the Muslim Brothers*. London: Oxford University Press, 1969.

Provence, Michael. *The Great Syrian Revolt and the Rise of Arab Nationalism*. Austin: University of Texas Press, 2005.

Salibi, Kamal S. *A House of Many Mansions: The History of Lebanon Reconsidered*. Berkeley: University of California Press, 1988.

Segev, Tom. *One Palestine, Complete: Jews and Arabs under the Mandate*. New York: Metropolitan Books, 2000.

Shelef, Nadav G. *Evolving Nationalism: Homeland, Identity, and Religion in Israel, 1925–2005*. Ithaca: Cornell University Press, 2010.

Shepherd, Naomi. *Ploughing Sand: British Rule in Palestine, 1917–1948*. New Brunswick, NJ: Rutgers University Press, 2000.

Wien, Peter. *Iraqi Arab Nationalism: Authoritarian, Totalitarian, and Pro-Fascist Inclinations, 1932–1941*. London: Routledge, 2006.

Wilson, Mary C. *King Abdullah, Britain, and the Making of Jordan*. Cambridge: Cambridge University Press, 1990.

13

World War II and Its Aftermath

W orld War II had a different impact on the Middle East from World War I. It was not as devastating for this region in terms of lives lost, battles fought, and empires/nations dismantled or rearranged. However, its impact was still enormous, particularly given the far-reaching effects of the war in other parts of the world. The conflict's effect on European nations was felt quite strongly (if indirectly) across the Middle East, particularly where European powers still had direct control. Although the experience of this was different in each country, events revealed that the imperialist approach long used there by France and the UK was swiftly being overshadowed by the activist diplomacy of the USSR and the United States: rising champions of communism and capitalism. The rapid diminishing of Western European presence in various parts of the region during the war and just after it had a large impact on what was to follow.

IRAN

Changing Rulers

One good example of this shift can be seen in Iran. Although Iran had declared its official neutrality upon the outbreak of war in 1939, Britain became extremely worried that Germany might try to invade Iran to meet rapidly growing fuel needs. Such fears remained vague and ambiguous until June 22, 1941, when Germany successfully and precipitously invaded the Soviet Union in Operation Barbarossa.

Suddenly, Iran became a very strategic potential convoy area to the Soviets for military supplies, particularly with the new Trans-Iranian Railway after 1939. Britain and the Soviet Union put pressure on Reza Shah to allow Iran to be used for transporting military cargo, which caused a series of pro-German riots in Tehran. When he refused to declare Iran's clear allegiance to the Allies and would not expel Germans from the country, Britain and the USSR invaded the country, arrested Reza, and deported him to the island of Mauritius on September 16, 1941. They established direct control over Iran's communications and railway system.

Before he left, Reza abdicated his throne in favor of his eighteen-year-old son, Mohammad Reza Pahlavi. Iran then became a major avenue for transporting supplies in the Lend-Lease program: a way the United States used to provide war materiel to various nations fighting against Germany and its allies. In 1942, the United States, now formally an ally of Britain and the USSR, sent a military force to Iran to help maintain the highway and railroad networks there. In that same year, Britain and the USSR signed an agreement with Iran that after using the nation as a supply conduit, they would still respect Iran's independence and agree to withdraw their troops within six months of the war's end, a commitment joined by the United States in 1943.

Iran even played host to a major Allied summit meeting, the **Tehran Conference**, in November and December 1943. This gathering, one of only two occasions at which Churchill, Stalin, and Roosevelt met face-to-face, became one of the key gatherings for the Allies to plan the end of the war, and in which serious negotiations on a myriad of international issues were conducted. The newly-crowned Mohammad Reza Pahlavi and his Iranian subjects were virtually excluded from any participation in it, epitomized by the fact that the three world leaders who attended each held only brief, perfunctory meetings with the Iranian monarch. As the war dragged on, the presence of significant numbers of foreign troops in Iran became a large burden on the country, creating hyperinflation in prices and severe food shortages, which, coupled with bad harvests in 1942, led to large-scale famine.

At the same time, **Mohammad Reza Shah's** relative weakness at first and his initially mild approach as a ruler meant that Iran's political system became increasingly open during the war. Political parties reemerged, and genuine parliamentary elections were held in 1944 for the first time in many, many years. The new shah's goal was to continue the reform

policies of his father, but a contest for control of the government soon developed between him and **Mohammad Mosaddeq** (1882–1967).

Mosaddeq, an experienced politician whose mother was a Qajar princess, had been elected to the first Iranian parliament created after the 1906 Constitutional Revolution and served in various official positions after that. When he was elected to the reestablished parliament in 1944, he became the head of Iran's National Front (*Jebhe-ye Melli*). This group was created by a group of prominent nationalists who shared the goals of broadening democratic institutions and improving governance in Iran, as well as ending foreign domination of the country's economy, most notably by nationalizing the Anglo-Iranian Oil Company (AIOC).

In the end, Mohammad Reza Pahlavi was unwilling to be transformed into a mere constitutional monarch and simply defer to the power of elected legislators. With a management style relying more on indirect manipulation than on decisive action, Mohammad Reza turned to building up the army as his main power base, while he continued to have strained relations with the parliament. In 1949, an assassination attempt on him blamed on the pro-Soviet **Tudeh** Party resulted in the banning of that party and the gradual expansion of the shah's executive powers. This set the stage for a showdown with Mosaddeq and his followers over the control of Iran's oil resources that developed into open conflict just a few years later.

The oil industry was critically important, since it featured foreign control over the key component of the nation's economy. Its nationalization was perceived by Iranian nationalists as the most direct way to reduce foreign domination over the country. With the end of hostilities against Japan by September 1945, Iranians became hopeful that foreign troops would honor their commitments and leave soon. However, the USSR decided that it did not have immediate plans to leave Iranian Azerbaijan, where it had been cultivating pro-Soviet autonomy movements during the war.

The Azerbaijan Crisis

Iran became one of the first places of conflict in the emerging Cold War: an indication of its strategic importance in the postwar rivalry between the United States and the USSR. Instead of withdrawing from the country entirely after the end of hostilities as promised, Stalin declared the establishment of two People's Democratic Republics in northwest Iran: the Azerbaijan People's Republic and the **Kurdish Republic of Mahabad**. Under strong American pressure, the Soviet Union finally withdrew its army from Iran and ended these political experiments there. Although the leaders of its Azerbaijani enclave escaped to Soviet Azerbaijan, the leaders of its Kurdish Republic were tried and executed in Mahabad by Iranian authorities in 1947. Despite removing its troops from Iran in the end, the Soviet Union did receive a new oil concession from Iran in exchange for this withdrawal.

The British presence in Iran, as reflected by the oil industry, remained apparently unchanged after the war, but anti-British feelings under the surface were rapidly increasing. The Anglo-Iranian Oil Company (AIOC), whose majority shareholder remained the British government, continued to produce and market most Iranian oil. Many of its workers belonged to Iranian trade unions that established closer ties with the Soviet Union during the war.

The Russians used these links to create problems for the British at refineries in Khuzestan. By making such connections, the Soviet Union also tapped into the steadily growing sentiment in Iran that favored nationalization of the country's oil industry. After the end of World War II, this blossomed into a major popular movement that boosted support for the National Front.

Such sentiments were magnified by the public realization of how poorly Iran was being compensated by the Anglo-Iranian Oil Company for its oil in comparison with the equal profit-sharing arrangement that **ARAMCO** had with Saudi Arabia. The AIOC gave Iran just £7 million in 1947—a year in which the company reported total after-tax profits of £40 million ($160 million). This sense of inequity contributed to the surge in nationalist feeling that resulted in Mohammad Mosaddeq becoming prime minister in 1951.

TURKEY IN WORLD WAR II

The situation in Turkey, which managed to retain its neutrality in the Second World War despite severe pressures from both sides, was substantially different from what happened in its neighbor Iran. Ataturk died in November 10, 1938, at the relatively young age of fifty-seven. The day after his death, the Turkish Grand National Assembly elected Ismet Inonu, a key associate of Ataturk since the Turkish War of Independence, to succeed him as president.

With the disastrous experiences of the Ottomans in the First World War always in mind, Inonu decided to keep Turkey neutral in any new conflict. He took diplomatic steps to maintain balanced relations with all powerful European nations. Just after Germany signed a nonaggression pact with the Soviet Union in August 1939 (the major proximate cause of the outbreak of World War II), Turkey signed a treaty of mutual nonmilitary assistance with Britain and France two months later. To hedge bets on the other side, the Turks also concluded a nonaggression treaty with Germany in June 1941, just days before the German invasion of Russia.

Despite continuous pressure, Turkey never permitted the passage of troops, ships, or aircraft in its land area or its waters, and continued to enforce the terms of the 1936 Montreux Convention diligently in the Bosphorus and Dardanelles. Turkey finally broke diplomatic relations with Germany in August 1944 and declared war against it in February 1945: a necessary condition for attending the conference in San Francisco in April 1945 at which the UN was created. This allowed Turkey to sign the United Nations Charter as one of the fifty original UN members on October 24, 1945.

Enjoying a neutral stance not far from areas of conflict in the Balkans and the Middle East, Istanbul also became a center of international intrigue and espionage during the war. Spies from Axis and Allied powers continuously pursued their respective war aims covertly there. The United States established an important branch there of the **Office of Strategic Services**: a clandestine organization created in June 1942 to coordinate American intelligence activities around the world. The activities of its Istanbul agents focused on guiding covert operations targeted at the Balkans. The German intelligence service used its Istanbul operatives principally to supervise and conduct activities in the Arab Middle East and Iran, particularly during the attempt by General von Rommel to seize the Suez Canal and thwart the British in Egypt during the early phases of the war.

Although Turkey escaped the physical damage inflicted on most of Europe during the war, it experienced terrible inflation and food shortages during the conflict. To meet its debts, the Turkish government in November 1942 imposed a **capital levy**: an extraordinary tax on personal wealth that everyone would be required to pay within thirty days. It soon emerged that non-Muslim minorities were being assessed at much higher rates than Muslim Turks. Around two thousand who could not pay the tax within the time alloted were sent to labor camps in eastern Anatolia. After this caused a few deaths, the levy was finally ended in the winter of 1944 after relentless public criticism.

Having weathered the war with fighting not far away from it in the Balkans, the Aegean and the Mediterranean, while maintaining careful neutrality, Turkey positioned itself to join the victorious Allies after the war as part of a front line against the emerging Communist bloc led by the Soviet Union on Turkey's northern frontiers. As a part of this new identity, Ismet Inonu introduced multiparty democracy in 1946 and witnessed the Republican People's Party (created by Ataturk in 1923 and later the sole political party) sweep from power in

1950 by the Democrat Party. Turkey, although still in close relationship with other parts of the Middle East, began to establish for itself a gradually more and more European identity—a component of Ataturk's modernization programs.

ARAMCO AND SAUDI ARABIA

Modernization also swept across other parts of the region as a direct result of economic demands imposed by the war, in particular, the enormous increased need for fuel. Already by 1940, Saudi Arabia was producing several thousand barrels of oil per day, enabling the completion of a full refinery at Ras Tannura by 1945 and a complete oil processing facility there by 1950 under the California-Arabian Standard Oil Company (CASOC)'s new name: the "Arabian-American Oil Company" (ARAMCO).

ARAMCO initiated many changes in Saudi life when it began digging its wells. It mapped the oil industry's future in modern maps and charts, produced detailed geological reports, built modern harbors, brought in asphalt roads and a radio system, as well as dug modern water wells at Dammam, Qatif, Riyadh, and Jidda. It had been instrumental in the building of an eleven-mile canal, pumps, and irrigation channels at al-Kharj just south of Riyadh, a town that has now grown into a major food-producing oasis. As oil revenues increased, Riyadh itself experienced a construction boom, almost doubling in population by the end of the 1940s.

In May 1943, General Patrick Hurley, President Roosevelt's personal representative in the Middle East, visited Dhahran and Riyadh. Hurley went there because the United States was beginning to look upon Saudi oil production with great interest, but also to extend American Lend-Lease aid to Saudi Arabia, suffering from war shortages that hampered the completion of various projects. By this point in the war, the focus of American military planning had shifted to operations against the Japanese in Asia, and the logical source of fuel for any new military offensives there would be the Persian Gulf. The U.S. government now proposed to buy into CASOC, finance a big refinery at Ras Tanura, and construct a pipeline from there to the Mediterranean, now under secure Allied control for some time.

If the American government had succeeded in purchasing even a minority share in CASOC, the company might have been transformed into an entity resembling the Anglo-Persian Oil Company at the beginning of World War I, which evolved into a quasi-official arm of British policy in Iran. The petroleum engineers who ran CASOC's field operations, however, highly valued their status as private citizens. They felt that the favor shown them by King Abd al-Aziz resulted from their lack of official political ties. They worked hard to prevent any greater degree of official American involvement by conducting extensive lobbying in Washington. In the end, they secured official U.S. support for completing a 50,000-barrel-per-day refinery at Ras Tanura, but kept the U.S. government from directly investing in this project.

This project became the stimulus for a huge expansion of ARAMCO activities, given the massive increase in scale of oil exports that it allowed. It also brought in a horde of western construction workers who lacked sensitivity about Arab sensibilities, pride, and culture. This created problems that only the anticipated royalties from daily exports of 350,000 barrels might justify to the Saudi Government. Around one thousand American and foreign workers, all on limited contracts with the Bechtel Corporation, began to arrive and depart in swift succession on the Ras Tanura job. They did not find in Saudi Arabia what the pioneer American oil prospectors had seen ten years earlier, but focused on more mundane complaints about housing conditions, food, lack of air conditioning, and bad laundry service. Gradually the situation improved. Indian workers who had been striking because of the food situation settled down; the Iraqis proved to be good craftsmen.

Soon, the total workforce there included more than 900 Americans. Dhahran no longer felt like the ends of the earth. This American commercial presence was swiftly followed by a military presence. After he had consulted with the British and met with Franklin Roosevelt on board a U.S. warship near the Suez Canal, Abd al-Aziz agreed in August 1945 to allow the United States to construct a military airfield at Dhahran and to permit American navy ships to call at Saudi ports. When the airbase was finished, it inaugurated an official U.S. military presence in and around Saudi Arabia that has continued ever since.

ARAMCO became one of the main vehicles of modernization and change in the country during the reigns of Abd al-Aziz and his sons who followed him on the throne. Because of steadily increasing petroleum revenues, Saudi Arabia was able to put off many hard social choices as it modernized, keeping its traditional social structure, political system, and religious practices remarkably intact. Nevertheless, its rapid pace of technical and industrial modernization greatly affected all parts of the Middle East, as its oil boom attracted skilled workers from many neighboring countries. Upon his death in 1953, Abd al-Aziz ibn Saud presided over a country that had already been quite radically transformed, but in fact had only just begun its process of real change.

EGYPT IN WORLD WAR II

As Saudi Arabia's strategic importance began to emerge during World War II, Egypt's central role for the security of the British Empire never seemed more obvious than when Axis forces threatened to capture the Suez Canal. Britain believed that it had to secure Egypt's stability as a strategic conduit for the duration of the war. This severely constrained British toleration for Egyptian attempts to assert more independence and autonomy.

Most Egyptians perceived World War II as a European affair and would have preferred to avoid any entanglement in it. Germany's early successes captured Egyptian attention and reawakened longstanding Middle Eastern admiration for Germany as Britain's enemy, and therefore, Egypt's friend. It became a key British priority to forestall any warming of relations between Egypt and Germany.

Paradoxically, this agenda gave the Wafd party, which had risen to power because of its staunch opposition to British domination, a chance to return to government. Among the Egyptian people, the Wafd became discredited by its failure to oppose the 1936 Anglo-Egyptian treaty forcefully enough. In spite of this, it retained enough clout in elite political circles to be of immediate use to the British as they tried to secure their position in Egypt following a spate of German victories early in the war.

Farouk and the British

When war broke out in Europe, Ali Maher had just become Egypt's prime minister, leading a coalition of generally anti-British independent politicians. The British grew more and more nervous about any actions he might take against them, so they tried to get King Farouk to appoint someone to lead the government whom they could trust. Farouk resisted, until the British forced him to allow the Wafd to take power in February 1942.

By that time, German forces in North Africa led by General Erwin Rommel were advancing rapidly toward the British army holding the Libyan town of Tobruk. When the Germans secured it, their plan was to drive into Egypt toward the Nile. In a dramatic gesture, Sir Miles Lampson, Britain's ambassador to Egypt since 1936, drove to King Farouk's palace accompanied by a squadron of British tanks, and compelled Farouk to appoint a more overtly pro-British government headed by Mustafa Nahhas, perennial leader of the Wafd Party. Although humiliated, Farouk capitulated to this demand and allowed Nahhas to stay in power through 1944.

The appeasement of the British by Nahhas and the Wafd dramatically tarnished their reputation in Egypt, which was further sullied by the publication in 1943 of an exposé of Wafd corruption by a disgruntled insider, Makram Ubayd. After the government of Nahhas was dissolved in 1944, political momentum shifted toward groups that took a more militant approach, such as the secular nationalist Young Egypt movement and the Muslim Brotherhood.

Egypt after the War

When Great Britain elected an anti-imperialist Labour government in July 1945 in the first general elections held there since 1935, there was hope in Egypt that this might mark a change in British policy. By December 1945, Mahmud Nuqrashi, first a member of the Wafd but split from it since 1938, was now serving as Egypt's prime minister. When he officially requested the British to revise the 1936 treaty and remove their troops from Egypt, the British Foreign Office responded that the turbulent circumstances of World War II proved "the essential soundness of [the treaty's] fundamental principles," adding that Britain saw no reason to renegotiate it now. In angry response, students and workers across the country organized huge protests and carried out attacks against British institutions and personnel.

The deteriorating situation forced Farouk to install a new prime minister, Ismail Sidqi. Sidqi, a political independent who had been powerful in the early 1930s, was now in poor health. When he took over negotiations with the British, he was opposed at every step by Nahhas and the Wafd, now in the opposition.

British prime minister Atlee agreed to remove British troops from Egyptian cities by September 1949. All British forces soon left, except for detachments stationed at the Suez Canal. The question of Sudan's future status was what finally stalled discussions. Britain wanted the Sudan to be granted immediate independence, while Egyptian nationalists remained adamant that it was an integral part of Egypt. In the end, the Egyptians referred the Sudan issue to the new United Nations. The Muslim Brotherhood capitalized on continued popular anger against the British to organize strikes and protests, calling for a jihad against them. Negotiations with the British remained unfinished up to the outbreak of the first full-scale Arab-Israeli War in May 1948: an event that transformed the whole situation in the region.

PALESTINE IN WORLD WAR II

The British White Paper of May 1939 backed away from the commitment Britain made to the Zionist movement in the Balfour Declaration by severely curtailing the number of Jewish immigrants to be allowed into Palestine. In addition, the document established as a British goal the establishment of an Arab Palestinian state within a decade. Both Palestinian Arab and Zionist leaders felt that its terms were unfavorable to them and opposed it. Ben-Gurion, serving as head of the Jewish Agency in Palestine, was reported to have declared in September 1939: "We shall fight the war against Hitler as if there were no White Paper, and we shall fight the White Paper as if there were no war."[1]

Although this statement set the agenda for Zionist activities during World War II, its implicit paradox was borne out by the complexity of Jewish military involvement in the war. One example of this can be found in the story of the elite strike group of the Zionist defense forces known as the Palmach. It was first established in May 1941 as a joint project of the British military and the Haganah, the main Zionist military force in Palestine, to help the British protect their Middle Eastern territories from the German threat taking shape

over in North Africa and to participate in the Allied invasion of Syria and Lebanon. By this time in the war, both of these French mandates had fallen under the control of **Vichy France**: the pro-Fascist French government now allied with Germany whose capital was located in the resort town of Vichy. British experts trained **Palmach** troops in sophisticated military techniques and equipped them with small arms and explosives.

However, after securing Allied control over Syria and Lebanon, as well as achieving a crucial victory over Rommel's army at **El Alamein** in November 1942, the British ordered this elite group to be disbanded. Instead, the organization merely went underground. It started to organize illegal Jewish immigration to Palestine. More than 100,000 Jews were taken to Palestine through operations in which Palmach forces played important roles, while the Haganah began to take on the task of covertly organizing demonstrations against British immigration quotas.

In this new clandestine mode, Palmach soldiers would now be supported by working and living on the kibbutz communal farms. Each farm would host a platoon of Palmach troops and supply them with food and housing. In return, these units would safeguard the kibbutzim and help with their agricultural work. This system became the basis for closer integration of kibbutz farms with the military defense structures of the Zionist movement. An easily-mobilized military force could be maintained and groups of settlers with military training and experience could be easily formed to create future settlements. Through training and indoctrination, the Palmach produced field commanders encouraged to take initiative and serve as examples for their soldiers. This force maintained several naval, air, and commando groups for a variety of special missions.

At about this same time, the perception grew among many Zionist leaders that Britain was turning irreversibly away from them,

---

[1]http://www.jewishagency.org/JewishAgency/English/ Jewish+Education/Compelling+Content/Eye+on+Israel/ Activities+and+Programming/Israel-Ben+Gurion/Chapter+ 1++The+White+Paper+of+1939.htm (accessed August 27, 2010).

leading them to build new connections with the United States. As part of such a strategy, Zionist leaders held an important conference at New York's Biltmore Hotel in May 1942 later known as the "Biltmore Conference." **David Ben-Gurion** called it to secure support from American Jewish organizations, in the face of British opposition to any plans of establishing a Jewish state after the 1939 White Paper. The Biltmore Program adopted at this gathering called for removing any limits on Jewish immigration to Palestine and calling on it to be established as a Jewish "commonwealth."

In keeping with the paradoxical goals earlier articulated by Ben-Gurion both to support the British against the Nazis while fighting Britain to defeat the 1939 White Paper, Jewish units continued to fight alongside Allied forces against the Germans even after Rommel's defeat, at exactly the same time that a Zionist insurgency against the British began to form in Palestine. In 1943, after a long series of requests and negotiations, the British Army announced the creation of the **Jewish Brigade Group**. While Palestinian Jews had been permitted to enlist in the British army since 1940, this was the first time an exclusively Jewish military unit served in the war under a Jewish flag. The Jewish Brigade Group consisted of 5,000 soldiers and was deployed in Italy in September 1944. By the time the unit was disbanded in 1946, more than 30,000 Palestinian Jews had served in the British army during the war.

In addition to Palmach efforts against the British to maintain a steady flow of refugees from Europe, a more militant Zionist insurgency campaign began in early 1944. It was waged by members of the Irgun and an offshoot from it called Lehi: two groups that saw themselves locked in a struggle against the British for survival that required immediate armed action. The Irgun had reemerged under the leadership of Menachem Begin.

Begin had been a Revisionist Zionist leader in Poland before the war, but was arrested by the Soviets when they invaded there. They first interned him in a labor camp, but he was subsequently freed and sent to the Middle East with the Polish army of General Anders after the Soviet Union joined the Allies following the surprise German invasion of 1941. When Begin arrived in Palestine, where this Polish force eventually ended up in 1943, Irgun leaders prevailed on his commanders to let him join their organization.

He quickly rose to become the commander of the Irgun, which issued a Declaration of Revolt on February 1, 1944, calling for armed insurrection against the British. This document argued that by issuing the 1939 White Paper, the British abandoned the promises of the Balfour Declaration just before thousands of Jewish soldiers fought for the Allies in the war and European Jews suffered annihilation under the Nazi onslaught. The declaration unleashed a wave of anti-British violence, the most spectacular incident of which was the November 1944 assassination of Lord Moyne (then British minister of state for the Middle East) by members of the offshoot **Lehi** group (led by Abraham Stern and also known as the Stern gang).

Less militant Zionist leaders saw this radical approach as a great potential threat to the entire Zionist project. To avoid cutting all ties with the British, the Haganah then chose to work with British forces to identify and even help deport some Irgun members to British detention camps in Africa. This activity, which took place in late 1944 and early 1945, came to be called the *saison* ("hunting season" in Hebrew). It greatly upset some Haganah members to be working against their own people, but Begin remained cautious, ordering his Irgun followers not to go after Haganah units in any hostile actions at this time.

At the end of the war, the Haganah, Irgun, and the Lehi tried to unite into a coalition to be called the Hebrew Resistance Movement. This quickly broke down because of Operation Agatha: a coordinated and devastating British attack on all these different groups in June 1946. This was followed a month later by the Irgun's retaliatory bombing of the King David Hotel. Both incidents were opening rounds in the larger postwar struggle over the future of Palestine and the beginning of Israel.

TRANSJORDAN IN WORLD WAR II

King Abdullah, as one of Britain's staunchest allies in the Middle East, was quick to send a message of support to the British and to offer the support of the Arab Legion upon the outbreak of hostilities in 1939. It would play a role in the British **Operation Exporter** invasion of Lebanon and Syria in 1941 (described below), but Abdullah was somewhat upset not to have been consulted in the planning and preparation of this operation. The Arab Legion was commanded after 1939 by John Bagot Glubb **(Glubb Pasha)**, who had already served for a number of years as a commander in Abdullah's military. It was under Glubb that the Legion's numbers grew, and it gained combat experience through operations in Syria and Lebanon. At the end of the day, Glubb Pasha was perceived to have remained loyal throughout his service in the Middle East to British interests: a perception that also reflected the continued close ties of Abdullah to Britain and would come under close scrutiny when the Arab Legion became involved in the 1948–1949 **Arab–Israeli War**.

COMPLEXITIES IN LEBANON, SYRIA, AND IRAQ

Operation "Exporter"

The coming of World War II had a notably different impact on the French mandates of Syria and Lebanon, compared with territories administered or dominated by the British in the Middle East. By the outbreak of hostilities, Britain had already granted two of its mandated Middle Eastern territories, the Hashemite Kingdoms of Jordan and Iraq, degrees of nominal independence that the French were not really interested in considering at that time. The chaotic and rapid flow of events during the first three years of war (1939–1942) meant that the French were forced to reconsider all assumptions about their colonial empire when the nation became divided into two warring governments in July 1940 following its invasion and occupation by Germany.

At that time, one part of the French government accepted defeat at the hands of Germany and formed a French State with its administrative center at Vichy (know as Vichy France) that became a German ally. The other part fled to exile in England and became known as the Free French, fighting alongside the British for the liberation of their country. French officials in many French colonies and overseas possessions, including Syria and Lebanon, sided with the Vichy regime. This created an enormous problem for the British, who suddenly saw a German ally controlling territories dangerously close to important oil-producing regions upon which they depended more than ever during wartime.

The most important of these was Iraq, already in a precarious political situation at the beginning of World War II. By that time, its king was the four-year Faysal II, whose regent, his uncle Abd al-Ilah, was unable to keep the prime minister, a staunch nationalist named Rashid Ali al-Gaylani, from drifting closer to Germany and Italy and away from Britain. Abd al-Ilah finally compelled al-Gaylani to resign his position, but al-Gaylani created a secret plan to take back power in a coup that he carried out in April, 1941. Iraqi forces under his control laid siege to the RAF Habbaniya airbase, one of the key outposts of British military power in Iraq west of Baghdad just a few days later, forcing Abd al-Ilah to seek refuge with his Hashemite relatives in Jordan.

The British were not going to permit this, and with reinforcements from India and additional RAF forces, launched the Anglo-Iraqi War of 1941. Although it lasted only a few weeks until the end of May, this marked the Allied defeat of a significant German foray into Iraq that had had a reasonable chance of success.

On May 11, a German diplomatic mission, including a personal representative of Adolf Hitler, reached Baghdad. It met there with al-Gaylani, where the decision was taken to prevent the RAF from relieving Habbaniya, while Iraqi ground forces were simultaneously sent in to capture it with German air support. In the end, the Luftwaffe detachment did not have the planned impact, and British forces at the besieged base drove away attacking Iraqi ground troops even before any relief force had reached them. A few days later, soon after the British relief force had finally gotten there, British and Indian ground troops advanced to seize Faluja, from where they moved on toward Baghdad.

On May 28, the Germans sent a panicked message from Baghdad that British forces were closing on the city with over one hundred tanks, and that there were only two German aircraft still functioning: two bombers with only four bombs between them left to drop. The next day, al-Gaylani and his key supporters fled, followed one day later by the German military mission. On May 31, the British and Iraqis signed an armistice, soon after which Abd al-Ilah brought King Faysal II back with him to Baghdad and restored his government.

The British did not stop after securing Iraq. They pressed on with Operation Exporter: code name for the invasion of Syria and Lebanon carried out in June and July 1941 to remove the Vichy French from power there. In the wake of the just-thwarted German foray into Iraq, the British wanted to prevent these territories from ever being used again in a similar fashion.

During the operations in Iraq that took place in May, there had already been a number of clashes between British, German, Vichy French, and Italian aircraft. At first, there was reasonable parity between the Vichy French

and Allied forces opposing each other in Syria and Lebanon. After the Germans abandoned their adventure in Iraq, they were not asked by the Vichy French commander in Syria to send any forces there. Their only real contribution to Vichy French efforts was to allow French aircraft to refuel at a German-controlled airbase in Greece. The British relied on forces assembled from detachments stationed in Palestine and Iraq, augmented by two Free French brigades, two Indian units, the Arab Legion from Transjordan, and a detachment of the Zionist irregular force mentioned earlier known as the Palmach, which also supplied interpreters and guides to other Allied units. In a series of fairly hard-fought battles that began on June 8 and continued for about five weeks, the Allies secured control of these French territories by July 12.

Independence for Syria and Lebanon

After fighting ended, General Charles de Gaulle, head of the Free French government, visited the area. Under political pressure from the Lebanese and the British, the Free French announced in November 1941 that Lebanon could become independent, with the provision that France would retain some authority there. After new elections took place in 1943, the newly-elected government unilaterally abolished the French mandate. The French reaction was to throw that entire government into prison. In the face of international pressure, France released these officials on November 22, 1943, and finally agreed to Lebanese independence. Nevertheless, the last French troops did not leave Lebanon until 1946.

Lebanon's unwritten National Pact was established in 1943 as the basis for proportional power sharing between the country's different religious and ethnic groups. It required that the Lebanese president be a Maronite Christian, its speaker of parliament a Shii Muslim, its prime minister a Sunni Muslim, and the deputy speaker of its parliament a member of the Greek Orthodox faith. National policy came to be set largely by a relatively small cohort of traditional regional and sectarian leaders. The Pact allocated political power in ratios based on the 1932 census, whose data was not updated because no new census was ever taken. Proportional parliamentary representation ensured that there would be six Christians for every five Muslim delegates, with a similar ratio for government employees. In subsequent negotiations, groups that benefited the most from the 1943 formula fought to preserve it, while those at a disadvantage pushed to update it or abolish it entirely. The interplay for position and power among the religious, political, and party leaders and groups produced an extraordinarily complex political system.

Syria was granted independence on January 1, 1944. From then until 1946, it was occupied by both British and French forces. As in Lebanon, the Free French had proclaimed Syria independent just after Operation Exporter in 1941. This position was strongly supported by the British, who were only willing to acknowledge French predominance in Syria as long as France fulfilled its promise to grant the country full independence. The election as Syria's president in August 1943 of Shukri al-Quwatli, a strong leader in the National Bloc before the war, represented a major victory for Syrian nationalism.

As in Lebanon, the French were also reluctant to leave Syria. The situation came to a head in 1945. At that time, France's refusal to relinquish control over key parts of Syria's economy as well as over parts of its armed forces led to a military confrontation. This culminated in a French bombardment of Damascus that caused over two thousand civilian casualties. When the British intervened, an agreement was finally reached for simultaneous British and French withdrawal from Syria and Lebanon by April 1946.

Questions to Think About

1. Why did the British and the Russians choose to remove Reza Shah from the throne of Iran at the beginning of World War II?
2. How did the accession of Mohammad Reza Shah Pahlavi to the throne affect politics in Iran?
3. Who was Mohammad Mosaddeq?
4. What was the significance of the Azerbaijan Crisis?
5. How was World War II in Turkey very different from World War I, and what happened in Turkish politics after the war?
6. How did the creation of ARAMCO affect Saudi Arabia in the 1940s?
7. What happened to Egypt in World War II, and how did changes in Britain after the war affect Egypt's relationship with it?
8. What was the impact of World War II on the Palestine mandate?
9. How did different parts of the Zionist movement come to conflict with each other during World War II?
10. What was Operation Exporter, and how did it affect the fate of the mandate system in the Middle East?
11. How did World War II expedite the independence of Syria and Lebanon?
12. What was the Lebanese National Pact, and why was it established when it was?

For Further Reading

Beckman, Morris. *The Jewish Brigade: An Army with Two Masters, 1944–1945.* Rockville Centre, NY: Sarpedon, 1998.

Deringil, Selim. *Turkish Foreign Policy during the Second World War: An "Active" Neutrality.* Cambridge: Cambridge University Press, 1989.

Katouzian, Homa. *Musaddiq and the Struggle for Power in Iran.* London: I.B. Tauris, 1999.

Kolinsky, Martin. *Britain's War in the Middle East: Strategy and Diplomacy, 1936–42.* New York: St. Martin's Press, 1999.

Roshwald, Aviel. *Estranged Bedfellows: Britain and France in the Middle East during the Second World War.* New York: Oxford University Press, 1990.

Seale, Patrick. *The Struggle for Arab Independence: Riad El-Solh and the Makers of the Modern Middle East.* Cambridge: Cambridge University Press, 2010.

Stark, Freya. *Dust in the Lion's Paw; Autobiography, 1939–1946.* London: J. Murray, 1961.

Tamkin, Nicholas. *Britain, Turkey, and the Soviet Union, 1940–45: Strategy, Diplomacy, and Intelligence in the Eastern Mediterranean.* Houndmills, Basingstoke, Hampshire: Palgrave Macmillan, 2009.

14

War Over Israel/Palestine

Among the watershed developments of Middle Eastern history, the creation of the state of Israel and the ensuing Arab-Israeli conflict of 1948 had an impact on the region and its relations with the rest of the world that has continued ever since. After this, the United States and the USSR took increasingly active roles there, as the global battle for influence that defined the Cold War took shape. What happened in 1948 affected everything that would take place over the next few decades in the Middle East. The focus here will be to examine the sequence of events following World War II that led up to the establishment of Israel as a nation: the time when the modern contours of the continuing conflict over the Holy Land emerged.

The British elections of 1945 unexpectedly brought the Labour Party led by Clement Atlee to power. Among its policy priorities were decolonization and refashioning the British Empire into a "commonwealth of nations." As part of this shift, Atlee's government turned immediately to the question of Palestine. It formed an Anglo-American Committee to find solutions for the growing refugee and military crises that had arisen there by the end of the war. The refugee problem had multiplied, because the 1939 White Paper curtailed Jewish immigration to Palestine just as various clandestine organizations were trying to get as many Jews out of Europe as fast as they could. By 1945, thousands of Jewish refugees had been removed from ships transporting them illegally to the beaches of Palestine and detained in camps in Cyprus set up by the British.

The Committee's April 1946 report, unanimously approved by all of its American and British members, recommended an immediate increase in the number of Jews allowed into Palestine to 100,000. It stated that Palestine ought to be "a country in which the legitimate national aspirations of both Jews and Arabs can be reconciled without either side fearing the ascendancy of the other."[1] Immediately upon publication, the report was challenged by the British government, which refused to admit more Jewish refugees unless it received American military and financial help to carry this out.

Such a demand made the report into a dead letter. Since the American Joint Chiefs of Staff had advised President Truman that use of American forces

---

[1]*N.Y. Times*, May 1, 1946, p. 15.

in Palestine might so embitter Arab opinion against the United States that the Soviet Union could attain predominant power and influence in the region, he was not prepared to assist the British in this way. In the end, the British just adopted a tougher military policy, also due to the fact that British troops were being targeted and attacked more and more frequently by various Zionist insurgency groups.

With the end of World War II, the major Zionist military organizations—the Haganah and the Irgun—at first agreed to cooperate against the British. Ironically, the Zionist commando force that the British had helped create and train, the Palmach, now began to function as one of the key insurgent forces against its former allies. Its units carried out attacks on strategic bridges, railways, radar posts, and police stations. The Palmach's leaders had become reintegrated into the Haganah and later played essential roles in the establishment of the Israeli army.

As noted, the fragile sense of a united Zionist military effort in this postwar era was totally shattered by the quick succession of Operation Agatha and the King David Hotel bombing. When the British carried out Operation Agatha in June 1946 against all the Zionist military groups and arrested approximately 2,700 people, the leaders of these groups agreed at first on the need to retaliate. A high-ranking Haganah commander sent a letter in early July to Irgun leader Menachem Begin signaling (in coded language) the Haganah's general approval of an Irgun plan to blow up the King David Hotel as a strike against one of the main symbols of official British presence in Palestine.

AFTER KING DAVID: BEGINNING OF THE MANDATE'S END

The actual operation killed so many British officials and soldiers that it caused a huge international uproar, creating enormous bad publicity for the Zionists in the British press. Worried that the British would now impose even more severe measures, Labor Zionist swiftly broke with the Irgun and denounced the event very emphatically. David Ben-Gurion declared in an interview that the Irgun was "the enemy of the Jewish people." A meeting of Zionist leaders in Paris on August 5, 1946, decided to end armed struggle against the British in Palestine.

This decision created resentment even among many members of the Haganah, some of whose members continued to sabotage British naval vessels that were hunting down illegal immigrants. Part of the anger expressed by other Zionist leaders arose from the way that the King David incident diverted world attention from the plight of hundreds of thousands of Holocaust survivors now housed in DP (displaced persons) camps across Europe who hoped to go to Palestine—a key factor in garnering broader public support around the world for the creation of a Jewish state.

At this point, the Irgun and Lehi groups began to conduct armed resistance totally on their own. Although Labor Zionist leaders tried to play this down, the harsh tactics of the Irgun and Lehi met with some success. The British position in Palestine became increasingly untenable, with British dependents forced to leave, British officials and soldiers confined to secure areas while subject to attacks, and martial law eventually being declared for lengthy periods of time. By the beginning of 1947, there even more British troops were in Palestine than were stationed in India. Diplomatic channels also had failed to produce any solution beyond the plan proposed by the Anglo-American committee, which both the Arabs and Jews had rejected.

In the end, the British never settled on how to manage the growing problem of refugees and displaced persons who would not return to their homelands in Europe: a situation that continued to stoke international public opinion against British policy. The Truman administration put increasing pressure on the UK to change its course in Palestine and admit more refugees: a request that postwar Britain was not in a good position to ignore, given its reliance on American economic aid to reconstruct its war-torn economy.

Moreover, since it was now led by a Labour government, Britain's official attachment to its empire had begun to wane rapidly. This new leadership would bring British rule in India to an abrupt end by August 1947, soon after Britain had informed the United States that it could no longer bear the financial burdens of bolstering Greece and Turkey against potential communist encroachment. The variety of international and domestic pressures being felt by the British government also put pressure on it to do something rapidly with respect to Palestine. Thus on February 18, 1947, Britain suddenly announced that it would turn the problem over to the United Nations to find a solution.

UNSCOP PARTITION PLAN

The question of Palestine became one of the first major issues brought before the UN. Although this new international organization was already shaping up to be the main diplomatic battleground between a Western bloc now led by the United States and a Soviet bloc led by the USSR, the question of the future of Palestine and its partition into separate Zionist and Palestinian states paradoxically was a subject about which the United States and the Soviet Union had arrived at general agreement by the spring of 1947. For the Soviet Union, this was a matter of *realpolitik*. Stalin and his advisers perceived support for Zionism as a way to further diminish British influence in the Middle East. For the United States, such support offered a practical way to champion the cause of Jewish refugees displaced by the war. The case for this approach was presented more and more convincingly by representatives of American Zionist organizations, who focused on rising American domestic political support for helping displaced persons as they met with Truman and his advisers.

The British request led to the establishment of the **United Nations Special Committee on Palestine (UNSCOP)** on May 15, 1947, with representatives from eleven countries. None of these nations were among the permanent members of the UN Security Council, but with the exceptions of Iran, India, and Yugoslavia, neither did any of them have any close connections with the Middle East. This made their representatives prime targets to be persuaded and influenced by public relations campaigns.

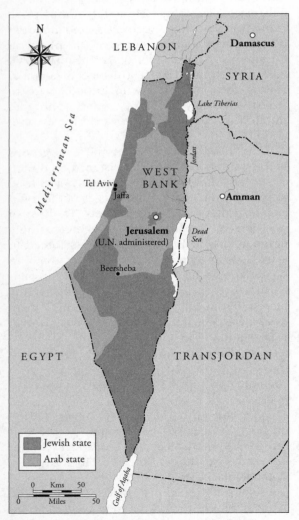

MAP 14.1 UN Partition Plan for Palestine (1947)

As the UNSCOP delegates conducted hearings and investigations, as well as sending observers to assess the situation on the ground in Palestine, Zionist leaders immediately saw an opportunity to influence them. They set about presenting a strong case for partition, making powerful cases to representatives of the committee about the specifics of how it should draw the partition lines on its final report in ways that would subtly support the Zionists' position and undermine that of Arab Palestinians. In addition, one group of UN observers happened to witness the forcible removal and deportation in July 1947 by British authorities in Haifa harbor of about 4,500 Jewish refugees attempting to land illegally in Palestine. They were taken off of an old American steamship purchased by the Haganah and renamed *Exodus 1947*: an incident that became the basis for the popular 1960 American film *Exodus* starring Paul Newman.

In contrast to the public relations successes achieved by Zionist spokesmen with UNSCOP, the Arabs did not reach out to this committee at all. Arab Palestinians refused to meet officially with the UN group, given their total rejection of any partition plan at this time. Rejection of any partition plans was not merely the position held by different Palestinian Arab groups; it was one of the founding agendas of the Arab League. This organization of newly-independent Arab countries, formed under the aegis of Egypt in 1945, had as one of its prime objectives the creation of a single, unified Palestinian state.

The situation on the Arab side was made even more complex by the activities of Abdullah I, ruler of the newly established **Hashemite Kingdom of Jordan**. Upon the full independence of his country in March 1946, Abdullah had begun to negotiate separately and secretly with Zionist leaders about dividing the territory of the Palestine mandate between him and them, in exchange for limiting Jordan's involvement in any possible combined future Arab attack on Zionist forces. In the end, different Arab groups came to the debate about the future of Palestine divided among themselves and with differing agendas. This meant that they were not able to have the impact on UNSCOP that the Zionists enjoyed.

When UNSCOP issued its final report on August 31, 1947, a majority of its members voted to recommend that an independent Arab and an independent Jewish state be created, with Jerusalem to be placed under international administration. Since they saw this plan as creating the conditions for a viable Jewish state, Zionist leaders embraced it wholeheartedly. In contrast, given the established Arab consensus for a unitary Palestinian state, Arab leaders in Palestine and around the Arab world denounced the plan. These two responses set the stage for military confrontation between the Yishuv of Zionist Jews in Palestine and the larger Arab world around it.

CIVIL WAR

The true catalyst for the civil war that erupted at the end of the Palestine mandate period was the vote on November 29, 1947, by the United Nations General Assembly (33-13) to accept the UNSCOP report. This meant that its partition plan would now be carried out. UN resolution 181, which specified the terms of the partition, also set August 1, 1948, as the latest date for the end of the British mandate. In reaction to this new UN resolution, a huge wave of violence swept through the cities of Palestine the very next day.

The British government, for its part, used the resolution to establish two policies at a December 4 cabinet meeting that would define how it would govern as the mandate came to an end. First, it was made clear that "British troops and the British administration should in no circumstances become involved in enforcing that decision or in maintaining law and order while the United Nations Commission enforced it." This effectively set the stage for British forces to step aside as waves of violence between Jews and Arabs began and escalated.

Second, May 15, 1948, was set as the formal end of the mandate government: a date that began to shape the activities of all the interested parties in the conflict.

Through the months of December 1947 and January 1948, a series of bombings and reprisals by Palestinian and Zionist militants killed around 1,000 people and injured more than 2,000. David Ben-Gurion, leader of the Labor Zionist movement, called on his followers to stay on their lands and to resist their occupation by others. Abd al-Qadir al-Husayni, a nephew of the mufti Hajj Amin al-Husayni, returned covertly to Palestine after being in exile since the 1936–1939 Arab Revolt. He began to develop a plan to surround and cut off the Jewish community of Jerusalem, staging numerous attacks to cut off Jewish supply convoys from the west and south. Within a few weeks, Arab ambushes drastically curtailed the food supply to Jewish communities in Jerusalem and in the Galilee.

The British also began in January (whether by design or lack of oversight) to allow foreign Arab forces to enter Palestinian territory. This reflected disagreements among British officials serving in different capacities in the Middle East. The loyalties of officers and diplomats to different sides of the emerging struggle between Arabs and Zionists complicated the situation as the official British focus shifted to exploring how the United Kingdom could leave most expeditiously. When Palestine Mandate High Commissioner Sir Alan Cunningham complained to London that no serious effort was being made to stop outside incursions in this emerging struggle, the first British ambassador to newly-independent Jordan, Sir Alec Kirkbride, criticized Cunningham's hostile tone and threats in a message to Foreign Secretary Ernest Bevin. After a secret meeting between Bevin, Sir John Glubb, commander of the Arab Legion, and the new Jordanian prime minister Tawfiq Abu al-Huda in early February 1948, the British began to support the incorporation of the Arab sector of Palestine into Jordan, while even U.S. support for the partition plan was beginning to waver under the pressures of Arab opposition to it.[2]

Arab Disunity

Although the Arabs by this time were becoming more confident that they could forestall a partition of Palestine, their leaders did not all share the same precise goals for what should happen instead. One insurgent group, led by Abd al-Qadir al-Husayni and known as the "Army of the Holy War," conducted its activities separately and sometimes at odds with other militant organizations such as the "Arab Liberation Army." The Arab Liberation Army (ALA) was a force of irregular recruits in Palestine commanded by Fawzi al-Qawuqji and supported by member nations of the Arab League. As long as the British still directly ruled Palestine, other Arab nations remained wary of intervening directly in the emerging conflict there with their own forces, choosing instead to provide indirect support for internally led Palestinian militia groups.

In addition, indirect Arab involvement kept the focus off of deep tensions between Arab nations over their own questions of political legitimacy. For example, the president of Syria at that time, Shukri al-Quwatli, greatly feared that embroiling the Syrian army too deeply in Palestine would leave his country exposed to incursions from Jordan's King Abdullah. Abdullah had never totally renounced Hashemite claims to Syria, continuing to dream of a Greater Syria that might include parts of Syria, Lebanon, Jordan, and Palestine in a revival of the united kingdom his brother Faisal had briefly formed after World War I.

Abdullah, for his part, remained interested in exploring possible ways to divide Palestine between himself and the Zionist movement. He continued to engage in secret negotiations with Zionist leaders in the months after the partition plan was announced.

[2]Yoav Gelber, *Palestine, 1948* (Eastbourne, UK: Sussex Academic Press, 2006), 71.

With regard to partition, it also soon became clear that the British saw great merit in assisting Abdullah to assert control over portions of the mandate allocated to the Arabs in the new partition plan. They favored this as the best way to sideline elements of the Palestinian elite, particularly the al-Husayni family, whose leader Hajj Amin had drifted too close to Germany during the war for the British to trust again.

Plan Dalet (D)

By early April 1948, the growing severity of the political crisis unleashed by the announcement of the UN partition plan prompted the Haganah to implement a new operational strategy with the code name *Tokhnit Dalet* (Plan D). This plan shifted the focus of Zionist armed units from defensive to offensive action, envisioning the transformation of the Haganah from an insurgent group into a regular army, with all able-bodied Jewish adults immediately mobilized into military training units. It called for the Haganah to secure control of all areas of the planned Jewish state as well as areas of Jewish settlement outside its borders. The plan presented a program for Zionist territorial control to be strengthened through the fortification of strongholds in areas and on roads that connected parts of Zionist-controlled territory, as well as by taking over Arab villages close to Jewish settlements and occupying British bases and police stations (after the British had abandoned them). It also provided for the acquisition of weapons and war materiel from Europe through a clandestine supply system.

The military operations carried out under this plan that focused on reopening the supply routes to Jerusalem were quite successful. Over the six weeks between the beginning of April and May 15, 1948, when Israel declared its existence as an independent nation, the Haganah occupied about 100 Arab villages to create territorial continuity between almost all Jewish settlements in Palestine, excluding Jerusalem.

Nakba and Deir Yassin

This happened simultaneously with several disasters on the Palestinian Arab side. Many of its leaders fled the country while others, such as Abd al-Qadir al-Husayni, were killed in battle. By the end of March, more than 100,000 Palestinian Arabs had fled the country: the beginning of waves of Arab emigration away from Palestine that would continue over many years.

One of the bitterest collective memories of Palestinians about that period concerns the attack on April 9, 1948, by members of the Irgun and Lehi groups on the village of **Deir Yassin**, located on the western outskirts of Jerusalem. This assault resulted in the deaths of around 120 villagers there and caused a huge impact because of how widely it became reported. The Deir Yassin attack took place in the context of Operation Nachshon. This was code name for the attempt by Zionist military forces to secure control of the overland route between Tel Aviv and Jerusalem, which involved capturing Arab settlements and villages in the area and forcing their populations to leave.

Although all the expulsions of Palestinians from this era have been remembered by the Arabs as key episodes in the removal of people from their homes now known as the Nakba ("Catastrophe") of 1948, the Deir Yassin incident has stood out for its gratuitous brutality. Ironically, Deir Yassin was not one of the Arab villages in this area that had sided with Palestinian insurgents at the time. Instead, it had carefully nurtured a policy of neutrality and built good relations with the orthodox Jewish community of Givat Shaul next door. As evidence of this, leaders of Deir Yassin had intervened with the ALA forces in the area and persuaded them to leave Givat Shaul alone.

Deir Yassin was not even a target of the main Haganah contingent there—the principal Zionist armed force in the area. The Haganah had focused its regional efforts on securing the main strategic point in the vicinity—the fortress/village of al-Kastel, against which it began an offensive on April 6. Despite their rivalry with the Irgun and Lehi groups, Haganah commanders invited them to help in this operation. The Irgun and Lehi fighters in the area chose instead to move against Deir Yassin. They decided that conducting an independent operation against a high-visibility target could raise their profile in what was shaping up to be the main battle for Zionist independence. A more implicit aim of their plan, particularly from their right-wing Zionist perspective, was that if it were conducted in a decisive, "take-no-prisoners" way, this might help scare more Palestinians to flee the country.

Deir Yassin became famous for the atrocities committed against civilians there, with accounts circulated about entire families being filled with bullets and grenade fragments and buried under their houses that were blown up on top of them. Such rumors helped persuade Palestinian Arabs to begin taking flight in large numbers. Reports of the incident also became an important catalyst for other Arab countries to commit their armies to the battle against Zionist forces. Menachem Begin, the Irgun leader, later wrote that he was "convinced ... that our officers and men wished to avoid a single unnecessary casualty in the Dir Yassin battle," while Azzam Pasha, then head of the Arab League, commented that "the massacre of Deir Yassin was to a great extent the cause of the wrath of the Arab nations and the most important factor for sending [in] the Arab armies."[3] It is not possible to reconcile the differing historical memories of this occasion, since different sides have directly discordant views of what happened that depend directly on vastly divergent general perspectives on the Arab-Israeli conflict as a whole. At a minimum, Deir Yassin can be viewed as a complex tragedy in which a planned raid by irregular fighters degenerated into an episode of brutality and slaughter of civilians.

---

[3]Menachem Begin, *The Revolt: Story of the Irgun* (New York: Schuman, 1951), 164, and Azzam Pasha quoted in Tom Segev, *1949: The First Israelis* (New York: Henry Holt, 1998), 89.

The effects of Deir Yassin were immediate. This incident took the Jewish Agency in Tel Aviv by surprise, but it quickly issued a public condemnation as well as delivering a formal apology to King Abdullah for what had happened—an overture that he rebuffed. A large Arab retaliatory massacre was staged on April 13, 1948, when Palestinian forces killed about seventy Jewish medical personnel in an ambush of a convoy heading to Mt. Scopus near Jerusalem. Ultimately, these military encounters in and around Jerusalem set the stage for the beginning of the first Arab-Israeli War, which really started after Israel's Declaration of Independence at midnight on May 14, 1948.

Eve of Israeli Independence

The prelude to the actual declaration of independence, which took place on the day before the formal end of the British mandate, was marked by complex behind-the-scenes maneuvers in preparation for the anticipated conflict. By the beginning of May, the military situation on the ground had shifted in favor of the Zionist forces, because of the success of Plan Dalet and several major Arab military defeats. Haganah, Palmach, and Irgun units had established control over such important places along the coast as Tiberias, Haifa, Jaffa, and Acre.

The British had essentially withdrawn their troops. The negative publicity created by the Deir Yassin incident and other Arab setbacks in April was now putting a great deal of pressure on leaders of neighboring Arab states to become involved, but their armies were not yet ready to deploy. There was one important exception: the Arab Legion of Jordan commanded by Glubb Pasha. The monarch who controlled this force, King Abdullah I, had already made separate arrangements with the British in February to occupy areas allotted to the Arabs under the UNSCOP partition plan and incorporate them into his territories, thus thwarting any alternate Palestinian-run state.

At the very same time, Abdullah conducted one final round of discussions with the

Zionist side in a secret encounter on the night of May 10 with Golda Meir (later Israel's first female prime minister), whom he first met in November 1947. Abdullah had already been engaged in convert discussions with Jewish leaders for about two years, continually trying to convince them to accept a plan for Palestine that would give him political authority over the whole of the existing mandate, with the Jewish community and its territories becoming an autonomous enclave under his sovereignty in a federal system. By the time of the final UNSCOP partition plan, however, Zionist leaders would accept nothing less than full independence and control over the portions of territory allotted to the Jewish state in the plan: a demand that Abdullah apparently accepted at his November 1947 meeting with Meir.

In May 1948, when Meir and Abdullah finally met again to discuss the situation, Abdullah rescinded his acceptance of an independent Jewish state and tried to reintroduce the concept of an autonomous Jewish enclave within his larger Hashemite kingdom. He explained that he was now bound to negotiate as only one member of a larger group of Arab nations. He noted that his diplomatic options had become quite constrained, given the intense negative feelings created by Deir Yassin and other recent disastrous setbacks, as well as the fact that the Haganah had recently been conducting military operations to secure territory beyond the 1947 partition borders. The meeting with Meir also included Abdullah's plea that the Zionist movement not declare an independent Jewish state too soon after the end of the British mandate.

Nevertheless, Abdullah saw Hajj Amin al-Husayni and his associates on the Palestinian Arab Higher Committee as his real political adversaries, in particular since they were now being championed by other members of the Arab League (as a counterweight to Abdullah). Consolidation of his own political authority over the West Bank and other parts of Palestine allotted to the Arabs in the UN partition plan remained one of Abdullah's main political goals during the First Arab-Israeli War. In the end,

the Arab League assigned Abdullah command over all the Arab forces, but the reality was that each Arab military unit operated on its own. Events on the ground increased the momentum toward conflict. On May 13, a large force of Arab irregulars, including some units of the Arab Legion, struck and occupied the Zionist settlement of **Kfar Etzion** on the **West Bank**, where all but four of the Jewish defenders were killed.

WAR OF 1948

David Ben-Gurion and a group of Zionist leaders who had constituted themselves the provisional government of the nascent Jewish state voted 6-4 to declare Israel's independence on the afternoon of May 14, the day before Britain's Palestine Mandate was set to expire. Israel was first recognized as a nation informally by U.S. President Truman, in a statement he had read eleven minutes after the declaration was issued, and was first formally recognized by the Soviet Union three days later. The informal recognition extended to Israel by Truman caught U.S. State Department officials by surprise, since they had just been at work on a new UN trusteeship plan to avert an open military conflict.

David Ben Gurion (1886–1973)

Later that evening and continuing over the next few days, several thousand troops from neighboring Arab countries invaded Palestine. The Arab League issued a statement on May 15 explaining that Arab armies had come into this country to protect the rights and properties of its Arab inhabitants and would oppose the implementation of the UN Partition Plan because it had been rejected by the Arabs. Four thousand Jordanian troops from the Arab Legion immediately invaded the separate zone created by the partition plan that defined greater metropolitan Jerusalem, as well as areas designated to form part of the Arab state in the UN partition plan. Larger Arab armies were supplemented by small detachments of volunteers from Saudi Arabia, Libya, and North Yemen. In their declaration, the Arab states announced that their goal was to form a United State of Palestine in lieu of the UN Partition Plan.

This Arab action was condemned by both the United States and the Soviet Union as an illegal act of aggression, but the British focused on withdrawing the last of their troops and officials as fast as they could. The Arabs and Israelis started the war with fairly unequal forces that grew more unequal as time progressed. At the beginning of the conflict, the Israelis had about 35,000 troops and the Arabs approximately 25,000. Over the next few months, the differential increased significantly, such that by the spring of 1949, the Israeli forces had grown to 115,000 while the Arab could only claim around 60,000 soldiers. The Israeli advantage was the direct result of the progressive mobilization of Israeli society and a huge influx of an average of 10,000 immigrants each month after the declaration of Israeli independence. By May 26, the new **Israel Defence Forces** (IDF) had incorporated the soldiers of the Haganah and Palmach, and their erstwhile right-wing rival military force: the Irgun.

After the Israeli Declaration of Independence, several major arms purchases that had been negotiated earlier began to arrive. One good example were twenty-five Avia S-199 planes from Czechoslovakia that began to arrive in Israel on May 20, causing the balance of air power to shift in favor of the Israeli Air Force. These aircraft ironically were postwar versions of the workhorse Messerschmitt Bf-109 fighter planes used so extensively by the German Luftwaffe during World War II.

The IDF's first mission was to keep the Arab armies away from major Jewish settlements until reinforcements and weapons came. The Arab Legion and the IDF had the most severe clashes at various places in Jerusalem and on the Jerusalem–Tel Aviv road. On May 17, Abdullah gave Glubb Pasha the command to enter the city of Jerusalem. After ten days of intense house-to-house combat, the Arab Legion had dislodged Israeli soldiers from the Arab sections of Jerusalem and had secured control of the Jewish Quarter of the Old City. The IDF had stopped the Syrian army at Kibbutz Degania in the north on May 21.

In the south, Egyptian troops did penetrate the defenses of several Israeli kibbutzim, but suffered heavy casualties. The most notable battle occurred at Kibbutz Yad Mordechai, in which the Israeli force, consisting of 130 fighters from the surrounding area and 20 Palmach fighters, held off an assault by a much larger Egyptian force for several days. Soon after that, the Haganah halted the Egyptian offensive a short distance to the north on the Mediterranean Coast near Ashdod.

First UN Truce

The UN arranged a twenty-eight–day truce that came into effect on June 11. Israeli and Arab forces both used this interval to improve their tactical positions, but the Israelis were able to resupply units more effectively than the Arabs. The IDF managed to acquire weapons from Czechoslovakia (which had just become part of the Soviet bloc) as well as improve its military training and organization. In addition, the Israel army nearly doubled its manpower during the truce.

After the truce was in place, the UN tried to address the issue of how to achieve a political settlement but with no success, so fighting resumed on July 8. It continued again for ten days until the UN Security Council arranged a second truce starting on July 18. On September 16, chief UN negotiator Folke Bernadotte proposed a new partition plan, once again rejected by both sides. On the next day, Bernadotte was assassinated by the militant Zionist group Lehi, which feared that the Israeli government would ultimately accept the plan, but the government had already decided to reject it and resume combat in a month.

After October 15, when fighting again commenced, the Israelis used the next few months of combat to secure defensible borders for their territory. The IDF launched operations in order to take control of the Negev and push back Egyptian forces. It then occupied the entire Upper Galilee, driving ALA and **Lebanese forces** back across the Lebanese border. By January, the IDF had forced the Egyptian army, now trapped in the Gaza Strip, to withdraw and accept a cease-fire. One final key operation took place in March 1949, when IDF forces took control of the site on the Red Sea where the port town of Eilat would later be built.

UN Resolution 194

In December 1948, the UN passed Resolution 194. It stated that in the context of a general peace agreement "refugees wishing to return to their homes and live in peace with their neighbors should be permitted to do so" and that "compensation should be paid for the property of those choosing not to return." These parts of the resolution were never implemented, since there were no real attempts at this time to seek a solution for the Palestinian refugee crisis.

Aftermath

In 1949, Israel signed separate armistice agreements with Egypt, Lebanon, Jordan, and Syria. The new borders of Israel, as defined by these agreements, included about 78 percent of the territory of the Palestine mandate as it had stood after the independence of Jordan in 1946. This in turn was about 18 percent more than the 1947 UN partition plan had allotted to it. The **Gaza Strip** and the West Bank were occupied by Egypt and Jordan, respectively.

During the conflicts in Palestine and Israel in 1947–1948, around 750,000 Palestinians fled or were expelled from their homes. The problem of Palestinian refugees and the debate around their right of return have remained major issues ever since this first conflict. Arab Palestinians around the world hold annual demonstrations and protests every year on May 15.

During the 1948 War, around 10,000 Jews were forced to evacuate their homes in Palestine or Israel, but in the three years following the war, around 700,000 Jews settled in Israel, mainly along the new nation's borders and in lands formerly occupied by Arabs who had fled. Many of these new immigrants were part of the continued flow of displaced persons from Europe, while others were Middle Eastern Jews who had left the Arab world after the conflict of 1948 created a hostile environment for them in their home countries.

Questions to Think About

1. What was the refugee problem created by World War II that was important for Palestine?
2. Why didn't the British government accept the Anglo-American Committee's report?
3. What was Operation Agatha?
4. What was the impact of the King David Hotel bombing?
5. Why did the British decide to leave Palestine?
6. What factors shaped the UN peace plan and why wasn't it more successful?

7. How did Jordan's King Abdullah I try to shape any peace settlement with the Zionists to his advantage?

8. What was Plan Dalet?

9. What was Deir Yassin, and why was it important?

10. What were the most important consequences of the 1948 War?

For Further Reading

Anglo-American Committee of Inquiry on Jewish Problems in Palestine and Europe. *Report to the United States Government and His Majesty's Government in the United Kingdom, Lausanne, Switzerland, April 20, 1946*. Washington: U.S. Govt. Print. Off., 1946.

Begin, Menachem. *The Revolt: Story of the Irgun*. New York: Schuman, 1951.

Benson, Michael T. *Harry S. Truman and the Founding of Israel*. Westport, CT: Praeger, 1997.

Cohen, Michael Joseph. *Truman and Israel*. Berkeley: University of California Press, 1990.

Gelber, Yoav. *Palestine, 1948: War, Escape and the Emergence of the Palestinian Refugee Problem*. Brighton: Sussex Academic Press, 2001.

Morris, Benny. *The Birth of the Palestinian Refugee Problem, 1947–1949*. Cambridge: Cambridge University Press, 1987.

Morris, Benny. *1948: A History of the First Arab-Israeli War*. New Haven: Yale University Press, 2008.

Morris, Benny. *The Road to Jerusalem: Glubb Pasha, Palestine and the Jews*. London: I.B. Tauris, 2003.

Rogan, Eugene L., and Avi Shlaim. *The War for Palestine: Rewriting the History of 1948*. Cambridge: Cambridge University Press, 2007.

Shlaim, Avi. *Collusion Across the Jordan: King Abdullah, the Zionist Movement, and the Partition of Palestine*. New York: Columbia University Press, 1988.

Tal, David. *War in Palestine, 1948: Strategy and Diplomacy*. London: Routledge, 2004.

15

Impact of the 1948 War

The effects of the first Arab-Israeli conflict were far-reaching and quite long-lasting across the entire Middle East. The Arab world now confronted a new enemy, Israel, which it identified as the latest incarnation of an old one: European colonialism and imperialism. Israel saw itself, in contrast, as the modern incarnation of a centuries-old dream to establish a Jewish homeland. The impact of defeat was felt quite differently in various Arab nations, but nowhere was it felt more bitterly than among the Palestinians.

PALESTINIANS IN EXILE

Palestinians accurately saw the Israeli victory as an enormous challenge to plans for a unitary Arab state in Palestine. In addition, they perceived the debacle of the conventional Arab military response in 1948 to this challenge as a tactical lesson. Many chose the path of indirect resistance to the Zionist vision of a unitary Jewish state. After neighboring countries had all signed cease-fires with Israel, small Palestinian armed bands began to launch continuous incursions and raids into Israeli territory. These were organized by groups formed in new Palestinian refugee camps in Jordan and Egypt. These camps were created by the new **United Nations Relief and Works Agency (UNRWA)** after the war to accommodate hundreds of thousands of people who fled their homes during the conflict.

The war also left the Palestinians and other Arabs deeply divided among themselves. Many prominent Palestinian leaders, including the leading members of the al-Husayni family, left Jerusalem due to tense relations with the ruler of Jordan, who had assumed formal control there upon the end of the Palestine mandate and the conclusion of hostilities with Israel. Over the next few years, tensions among different groups of Arabs escalated greatly. Palestinians feared that Jordan and Lebanon were both on the verge of making separate peace treaties with Israel, while many Syrians felt that Lebanon was really a part of their country that had been illegitimately taken away by the French.

On July 17, 1951, Riyad al-Sulh, first prime minister of Lebanon after it had become fully independent from the French and one of the architects of the 1943 Lebanese National Pact, was shot as he was visiting Amman, the Jordanian capital. His assassin was a sympathizer of the **Syrian Social Nationalist Party**: an extremist group that promoted the unification of all the former British and French mandates into a greater Syria. Then, just before he was scheduled to give a eulogy at al-Sulh's funeral, King Abdullah I of Jordan himself was assassinated by a Palestinian dissident as he attended Friday prayers at the al-Aqsa mosque in Jerusalem. He was accompanied there by his grandson Hussein (later king of Jordan), who, although only slightly wounded in the attack, was left with an indelible sense of the constant potential threats to him.

For some time before, during, and after the war, Abdullah had been in secret negotiations with Zionist leaders in order to broker a lasting peace. This channel of discussion continued after he established formal Jordanian political control over the West Bank following the April 1949 cease-fire. When all Palestinians resident in the West Bank were given automatic Jordanian citizenship in April 1950, some became terrified that Abdullah was on the verge of signing a permanent treaty with Israel that would end their hopes for their own nation: a fear that ultimately led to his murder.

Another key group of Palestinian refugees in the Gaza Strip now fell under Egyptian control after the Egyptian-Israeli cease-fire signed in February 1949. At that time, Egypt recognized the "All-Palestine Government," created by the Arab League in September 1948 during the war, as the official government of Palestine, to administer Gaza until the eventual recovery of all mandate lands from Israel. Since this All-Palestine Government had been dominated by the al-Husayni family and its activities staunchly opposed by Jordan, the Jordanians convened several Palestinian congresses of their own in December 1948, calling for the unification of Jordan and the West Bank: a step that the Jordanians took eighteen months later. As it was promoted by different groups in different ways, the Palestinian cause thus became both a component of the international political struggle between different Arab nations and the rallying cause for them to unite against a common enemy. It has continued to play these contradictory roles up to the present in the Arab world.

EGYPT AFTER 1948

Egypt fielded one of the largest military contingents in the 1948 Arab-Israeli War and suffered the greatest losses among the Arab armies, but another real impact of the war was the damage it did to King Farouk's legitimacy. He had already been challenged by numerous political factions before 1948, but popular discontent with him really welled up in the wake of the Egyptian defeat in Palestine. This anger was also directed at the British, long perceived by the Egyptian people as the main imperialist power that had created so many of the region's problems. Such resentments were skillfully exploited by activists of the Muslim Brotherhood, which had sent volunteers to fight in the 1948 war. To quell rising unrest and mitigate the Brotherhood's growing impact, the Egyptian government formally banned the organization in December 1948.

By that time, the Muslim Brotherhood had created a network of hospitals, factories, and schools, as well as a secret military wing. With all of these ways to exercise influence in the society, the Egyptian government began to worry that it could form a parallel political authority seen by ordinary Egyptians as more legitimate than the nation's actual government. Seeing this threat, the police arrested many of its members and kept Hasan al-Banna, its overall leader, under strict surveillance. As a response to this crackdown, an activist affiliated with the organization assassinated Prime Minister al-Nuqrashi, recently reappointed to lead the government.

Al-Banna quickly repudiated this act and called on Brotherhood members to cease any violent actions. He produced a pamphlet condemning all violence committed by Brotherhood members, although he pointed out that this had occurred due to a loss of public confidence in the Egyptian government and the disastrous outcome of the war in

Palestine. The upshot was that al-Banna himself was killed only a few weeks later by agents of the police, probably following official orders. A wave of Brotherhood arrests and trials then ensued, but the underlying problems that had created the unrest did not go away.

When the Wafd Party returned to power in 1950, it restored the rights of the Muslim Brotherhood to exist legally. This did not stem the rising tide of popular resentment against the British and their continued presence in the country. By October 1951, the political climate reached such a state that the new Wafd leader Mustafa Nahhas Pasha, prime minister in 1936 when the Anglo-Egyptian Treaty was first signed and put in again with British assistance in the "soft coup" of 1942, unilaterally declared the 1936 treaty to be ended. Massive street demonstrations were organized in support of this act.

The Egyptian army, together with large numbers of activists, including many members of the Brotherhood, began preparing for a showdown with the British in the Canal Zone. Popular fervor boiled over into antigovernment riots when nationalists became impatient with Nahhas Pasha's lack of action. Tensions rose steadily over the next several weeks as different groups sorted out what their next moves would be.

Egypt's 1952 Revolution

On October 16, 1951, local police failed to suppress a particularly violent riot that had broken out in Ismailia near the Suez Canal, so British troops were brought in to restore order. Some Egyptian police then did more than just stand aside—they joined the rioters to attack British troops. By early January 1952, after thirty-three British soldiers had been killed and sixty-nine wounded, the British commander ordered all Egyptian troops in Ismailia to be disarmed. When a British army unit tried to carry out this order, it was met with a volley of fire. British forces ended up forcing their way into the walled compound of the Egyptian auxiliary police barracks. After a few hours under siege, the majority of the Egyptian police holed up there surrendered peacefully, but not without having forty-one troops killed and seventy-three wounded.

This clash became the spark for a vast mass uprising. Large riots broke out the next day in Cairo during which mobs tore down and torched places particularly associated with the British: Shepheard's Hotel, the offices of BOAC airlines, and the Turf Club. Mustafa Nahhas's government immediately was dissolved, replaced by a succession of short-lived cabinets, each lasting only a few weeks.

At this same time, a shift in power within the leadership of the Egyptian military was taking shape that would soon have great effects. After the debacle of the 1948 Arab-Israeli War, a group of junior military officers had formed a clandestine **Free Officers' Movement**. Its members were mostly of middle-class origin, young officers who had risen on their own merits. They saw their mission as ending the corrupt elitism and nepotism that crippled Egypt and rendered it helpless against the plots of imperialist powers such as Britain and France. Its charismatic leader was an army officer from a small village in southern Egypt who distinguished himself during the 1948 war: **Gamal Abdel Nasser** (1918–1970). Just thirty-two years old when he became the movement's head in 1950, Nasser embodied the hopes and dreams of the hardworking Egyptian middle class.

The Free Officers tapped a more senior military leader, General Muhammad Naguib, to be their public figurehead as they prepared to stage a coup, which rapidly-changing circumstances prompted them to carry out on July 23. That morning, a group of the Free Officers led by Naguib seized power. They proclaimed their goal to be freeing Egypt from "bribery, mischief, and the absence of governmental stability." Within three days, King Farouk fled into exile, abdicating in favor of his infant son, now installed as the figurehead King Fuad II.

Egypt was now ruled by a Revolutionary Command Council (RCC) composed mainly of leaders of the Free Officers' Movement. At first, veteran politician Ali Maher was asked to form a new civilian government to continue under the RCC's aegis, but he resigned within a few weeks because he thought the Free Officers' plans for land reform were too radical. Naguib became prime minister. He secured passage of an agrarian reform law that initiated a major land redistribution for peasant farmers and placed a limit of 200 acres on individual land ownership. The new law also put limits on land rents and established a minimum wage.

The land reform enjoyed a reasonable degree of success because its aims were relatively modest. The 95 percent of owners who had owned only 35 percent of the land before the reform now received control of more than 50 percent of the land. This change substantially lessened inequalities in Egyptian agriculture and promoted Egypt's social stability for many years after its implementation.

However, it was not just in the area of land reform that substantial adjustments were made. The Free Officers put forward a revolutionary agenda. They got rid of the Egypt's constitution—its founding document as an independent nation issued in 1923—"in the name of the people." All existing political parties were dissolved in January 1953 with only the RCC left.

Several new mass political organizations were created to mobilize popular support. On June 18, 1953, Egypt was declared a popular republic. The monarchy was finally abolished, and Naguib appointed as the first president and prime minister. Nasser, now thirty-five, was appointed deputy premier and minister of the interior. A Revolutionary Tribunal composed of key members of the RCC, Abdel Latif Boghdadi, **Anwar Sadat**, and Hassan Ibrahim, was established to put politicians of the old regime on trial for their corruption and misdeeds.

The Muslim Brotherhood, which had joined with the Free Officers in opposition to King Farouk and had fought alongside them in Palestine against the Israelis, now came under attack. It did not agree with the secular nationalist agendas that the Free Officers began to promote now that they had consolidated power. After clashes in January 1954 between Muslim Brothers and activists of the new Liberation Rally popular movement, the RCC again outlawed the Muslim Brotherhood, and it remained an officially illegal political organization in Egypt until June 2011.

Divisions within the RCC ultimately resulted in the ouster of General Naguib by the fall of 1954. Nasser gradually assumed more and more power, first as chairman of the RCC and prime minister, and finally became president. Accounts of one incident during this period later evolved into an enduring legend about him. A member of the Muslim Brotherhood fired eight shots at Nasser as he was delivering a speech in October, 1954.

Although Nasser was not hit, his audience panicked. He was reported to have calmly said to them: "If Abdel Nasser dies, then everyone of you is Abdel Nasser. Gamal Abdel Nasser is of you and from you and he is willing to sacrifice his life for the nation."[1] Nasser, with great natural stage presence, transformed this situation into a confirmation of why he deserved to be the nation's **supreme leader**.

It also gave him a pretext to conduct one of the most severe political crackdowns in the country's history. Thousands of Muslim Brothers, Communists, and Wafd Party members were arrested, tortured, and put to death. To consolidate his hold on power and bring the masses over to his side, Nasser went around the country giving speeches. Also at this time, he secured control over the Egyptian state radio network and newspaper production system in order to circulate his messages more easily at home and abroad. **Umm Kulthum**, considered one of the greatest Egyptian and Arab singers of recent times, recorded numerous songs lauding Nasser that began to be broadcast across the Middle East on Radio Cairo.

---

[1]Gamal Abdel Nasser quoted in Said Aburish, *Nasser: The Last Arab* (New York: Thomas Dunne Books, 2004), 54.

Through this period, his speeches, now presented every week on the radio, were explicitly framed in the context of Arab nationalism. Nasser stressed particular nationalist words such as *watan* (homeland) and *khalq* (people) in his descriptions of the Arabs as a single unit, instead of referring in more general terms to the Arab peoples or Arab region. He was first installed by the RCC in January 1955 as Egypt's interim president, but then given permanent tenure in that office a few months later, after the revolutionary movement had secured its hold on power.

Nasser on the World Stage

Over the next few months, Nasser began casting his activities in an increasingly international context and returning to the question of Israel. He took an important step in this direction in February 1955 after a major Israeli attack on the Gaza Strip, the part of Palestine administered by Egypt after 1949, had killed a number of Egyptians. A low level of conflict between Israel and Palestinian refugees in Gaza had continued since 1948, but such activities were not really supported by Egypt, and it in fact tried to restrict them.

After this attack, which generated a lot of publicity, Nasser changed strategies. He now decided to take more direct control of Palestinian groups and coordinate their operations with what Egypt was doing. Nasser built new momentum for another direct confrontation with Israel, as well as with Britain and France. He began harping on Israel's role as the latest vehicle of imperialist and colonialist encroachment in the region. He also became a leading member of the NAM **(Non-Aligned Movement)**: a group of nations that declared themselves independent of the two emerging global capitalist and communist power blocs.

When Nasser attended the Bandung Conference in Indonesia in April 1955, he was recognized as the leading representative of the Arab countries. In collaboration with Tito and Nehru, the renowned postwar leaders of Yugoslavia and India, Nasser began proclaiming a foreign policy of "positive neutralism." This approach sought to build connections with the East bloc led by the Soviet Union, while at the same time developing similar ties with the West and its leading champion, the United States.

The most immediate impact of Nasser's attempt to befriend both sides in the rapidly emerging and expanding Cold War was to alienate Western countries, particularly Britain, France, and the United States. Tensions first surfaced in connection with his desires to get modern weaponry. As a military officer, Nasser was particularly sensitive to the need to acquire state-of-the-art weapons. Western countries, although friendly to him up to a point, became increasingly wary of his revolutionary rhetoric.

In the end, he could not persuade them to supply him with weapons under terms as good as those offered by the Soviets and their allies. When Nasser accordingly signed a major arms agreement with Czechoslovakia in September 1955, this was regarded as traitorous by Western Europe and the United States. In fact, the Egyptians had first tried to make a deal with the Americans, but this fell through because the United States insisted on cash payments, instead of accepting goods as the Soviets were prepared to do.

At home, news of the Czech arms deal was then presented as a sign of Nasser's credibility as an independent Arab leader who could defy the West, bolstering his image at home at an important time. In January 1956, a new constitution for the country was issued that had a decidedly authoritarian tone. Henceforth, Egypt would only have one political party: the National Union. When the party chose someone to stand for the presidential election, this choice would simply be ratified by a popular referendum.

An overwhelming majority voted in favor of Nasser filling this post in June 1956, so the RCC was abolished, and its members resigned from their military positions. Egypt's sudden shift to one-man rule alarmed foreign observers, but was met with broad domestic support as Nasser built a reputation for standing up to foreign pressure more than Egypt's leaders had done for many years.

Nasser's shift to a more activist and revolutionary style both at home and abroad was also part of his attempt to reach out to the masses in neighboring Arab countries. In his speeches, he began to criticize Britain's close relationships with Iraq and Jordan, the two Hashemite Arab kingdoms that it had helped create, as threatening to Egypt's rising power and prestige throughout the Arab world. For Nasser, these threats were made concrete in 1955 with the creation of the Baghdad Pact (also known as the Central Treaty Organization, or CENTO). From a Western perspective, this alliance marked a tentative postwar attempt by the British to assemble Iran, Iraq, Pakistan, Turkey, and the United Kingdom into a NATO-like military group that could resist Soviet designs on the Middle East. Nasser had a totally different perspective. He portrayed this initiative as proof that Britain was remaking the eastern Middle East into a bloc centered in Iraq that was sympathetic to Britain, but cut out Egypt entirely.

Nasser took numerous steps to thwart what he perceived as British plans to isolate him. He reached out in particular to strength his ties with Saudi Arabia—longstanding enemy of both the Hashemite kingdoms of Jordan and Iraq—to counter any British plans to draw Syria, Jordan, or Lebanon into CENTO. Nasser used sympathizers in Jordan, who were Arab nationalist activists, to promote domestic unrest there. They helped create a situation in which King Hussein had to fire Glubb Pasha, British commander of his Arab Legion, to counter charges that he was a British lackey. Finally, through Egypt's weapons purchases from the Soviet Bloc, Nasser heightened Western concerns about whether he was drifting too close to the Communist bloc.

Global alignments were in state of upheaval and adjustment at this time, which created some diplomatic paradoxes. Although the United Kingdom looked to the United States for support in keeping Nasser under control, President Eisenhower was also influenced in these circumstances by the attitudes of Saudi Arabia: one of the closest U.S. allies in the region at that time. The Saudis were just as opposed to the Baghdad Pact, dominated by their rival Iraq, as was Egypt. For its part, the United States saw the Baghdad Pact as focusing too much on the partnership between parts of the Middle East and the United Kingdom, whose role in the region the United States was keen to reduce in favor of bolstering its own influence.

SUEZ

All these developments came to a head during the **Suez Crisis** of 1956. The immediate origins of the crisis can be found in the American cancellation of financial support for the **Aswan Dam** project on July 19. The announced reason for this action was that the United States had lost confidence in Egypt's ability to carry out this project. This decision was also designed as a signal sent by the American secretary of state, John Foster Dulles, that the U.S. government would not tolerate Egypt's attempts to befriend both capitalists and communists in a neutral way. One recent action alone, Nasser's formal diplomatic recognition of the People's Republic of China in May, had immensely angered Dulles, who viewed the world in fairly bipolar terms. In the end, the Soviet Union financed and built the Aswan Dam between 1960 and 1970.

Building on the growing momentum of nationalist fervor at that moment, Nasser's next act was to nationalize the Suez Canal. Nasser intentionally made reference to Ferdinand de Lesseps, architect of the canal, in a speech he gave in Alexandria on July 26, 1956: a prearranged signal for Egyptian troops to occupy it. When his forces had secured it, he declared it nationalized.

The explanation for this was that Egypt now needed money to finance the Aswan Dam project, and the only source for this would be Canal revenues. This act was immediately

Gamal Abdel Nasser (August 1956)

Rue des Archives/The Granger Collection, NYC

In addition, as time went by, it became obvious that Egypt would allow all ships (except for Israeli vessels) to travel through it, thus removing the only real pretext for outside intervention under the existing agreement that governed its use.

Military Actions in Suez

For reasons of its own, as well as the trauma of being displaced from an important remnant of its imperial presence in the Middle East, the British government decided that it would move militarily against Egypt. Because it had no overt grounds to do this, it made a secret agreement with France and Israel to retake the canal. The French and Israelis had their own motives for moving against Nasser. The French had verified that he was clandestinely supplying nationalist guerillas then fighting against them in Algeria, while the Israelis feared Nasser's ability to unite the Arabs against them. On the surface, the aggrieved British and French worked through diplomatic channels, starting in early August with a meeting between them and the Americans.

This was followed by numerous conferences over the next few months, none of which produced any concrete results. Meanwhile, the British, French, and Israelis concluded a secret agreement at Sèvres in October, calling for the Israelis to attack the Sinai, with the British and French forces being invited to "separate" them from the Egyptians and meanwhile retake the canal. The British left the Americans totally in the dark about this plan, hoping that Nasser's drift toward the Soviet bloc would persuade them to accept these British and French actions without too much protest.

The Israeli army began operations by invading the Sinai Peninsula. It also placed units on the Israeli-Jordanian border on high alert, fearing Jordanian participation in any developing conflict. As a security measure, the Israeli army ordered all Arab villages in Israel near the frontier with Jordan to be put under a

perceived by the British as a direct blow to their vital national interests. The British prime minister at the time, Anthony Eden, had resigned in 1938 as British foreign minister to protest what he saw as appeasement by then–prime minister Neville Chamberlain of Adolf Hitler at the Munich Conference. Eden now characterized Nasser's moves as resembling those of Hitler, issuing a charge that set the stage for military engagement.

This crisis placed the United States in a dilemma. Despite having canceled the Aswan Dam project, the Americans did not support any British or French moves to retake the Canal by force. Egypt, in the end, had eminent domain over it, and it had been scheduled to be returned to Egypt anyway a few years later.

strict curfew between 5 P.M. and 6 A.M each day. There was confusion about the start times and rules of the curfew in different areas, causing the deaths of forty-eight unarmed Palestinian men, women, and teenagers in one area. When this incident was finally made public, it caused a scandal that helped change Israel's policy toward its own Arab citizens, whom it had often treated before this time as enemy combatants.

Crisis Unfolds

Soon after the beginning of the Israeli attack in Sinai, Israel's armed forces quickly secured numerous strategic points across the peninsula. After British and French planes had flown in, ostensibly to "separate" the Israelis and Egyptians, Nasser sent his own air force as a defensive strategy to bases in southern Egypt. This pullback allowed Israeli planes to strike Egyptian troops at will while their ground troops advanced across the Sinai. On the morning of October 30, Britain and France sent Nasser an ultimatum that he must remove his forces at once from the Canal Zone, to which he responded by scuttling all ships then parked in the Canal. On November 5 and 6, British and French ground forces were brought in and quickly secured control of the canal region, which ended the military phase of the crisis.

The British-French military operation to retake the Suez Canal was a great military success but a political disaster. Nasser requested help from the United States on November 1, this time without requesting any Russian assistance. The United States demanded that the invasion stop and helped create a UN cease-fire resolution that Britain and France, as permanent members of the Security Council, vetoed. Ultimately, the UN General Assembly held an emergency special session that established the first **United Nations Emergency Force (UNEF)** and called for an immediate cease-fire. After this, Britain and France quickly withdrew from Egypt.

The resolution of the crisis was also expedited by the possibility of sanctions. The United States threatened to put financial pressure on Great Britain by selling off some of its holdings of British bonds. In parallel with such actions, Saudi Arabia embargoed oil shipments to Britain and France until they agreed to leave Egypt, with the United States (as well as other NATO members) refusing to make up the shortfall.

Global Impact

This outcome greatly accelerated the pace at which Britain was letting go of its empire. British foreign policy now began to focus on cooperative action with other European powers, in place of grand gestures reminiscent of the imperial era. The UN-imposed end to the crisis clearly revealed how much less important the United Kingdom and France had become as global powers. While the conflict bolstered Israel's confidence in its own military capabilities, Nasser's standing in the Arab world specifically and the Third World in general was also greatly enhanced, with his reputation and stature now more and more closely tied to his embrace of Pan-Arabism.

UNITED ARAB REPUBLIC

Nasser's success electrified the Arab world, which turned to him as the panacea for what ailed it. By 1957, after a military takeover several years earlier and a series of generally weak governments, numerous communists had gained positions of power in Syria. Nasser once told a visiting Syrian delegation that they needed to get rid of the communists in their government. They responded that the only way to forestall the encroaching power of communists in Syria would be for it to unite with Egypt completely—to make good on the Pan-Arab dream of political union.

When this was proposed as a real possibility, Nasser at first resisted actual union with Syria, but finally gave in. The United Arab

Republic (UAR) was created by the joining of Syria and Egypt on February 1, 1958: the first step toward a state that would bring all Arabs together. Since Pan-Arab sentiment was widespread in Syria and Nasser was now the major hero of Pan-Arabism after the Suez Crisis, Syria and Egypt were the two most logical countries to pursue such a venture.

The realities of Arab unity were much less attractive. When Nasser became the UAR's president, he took the same approach that he used in Egypt when he took power there. He cracked down swiftly on Syrian Communists and on opponents of the UAR concept, removing several prominent Syrian politicians from power. Nasser's conditions for taking over Syria were reminiscent of the rules established in Egypt upon the takeover of the Free Officers' movement.

In Syria, he called for holding a popular plebiscite on the UAR, dissolving political parties, and removing the army from political activity. While the concept of a popular referendum seemed reasonable to most Syrian leaders, they thought that getting rid of political parties and taking the military totally out of political affairs might harm their interests. Despite such worries, they realized that they would be wiser not to resist Nasser, since popular sentiment in Syria overwhelmingly supported him.

Life in the UAR

As Syria's leaders chafed under Nasser's new rules, they retained hope that he would use the existing Baath Party apparatus as his primary method of controling Syria. In reality, Nasser never intended to give the Syrian Baath any power at all. His new provisional constitution created a 600-member National Assembly (400 from Egypt and 200 from Syria) and dissolved all other political parties, including the Baath. Nasser assigned each area two vice-presidents, with one former Baath Party member appointed in Syria. While Nasser did permit some former Baath officials to serve,

they never reached positions as high as those enjoyed by Egyptian officials.

In 1959 and 1960, Nasser slowly moved prominent Syrians out of influential positions, replacing them with his close Egyptian associates and cronies. Nasser formed a committee of two Syrian **Baath party** leaders together with one of his Egyptian loyalists to oversee developments in Syria, but they all lived in Cairo. Situating this group in Egypt was another way to neutralize the impact of important Syrian politicians.

The Syrian reaction against these changes was fairly swift. Army officers suddenly resented being put under the authority of Egyptians. Syrian bedouin tribesmen began receiving considerable amounts of money from Saudi Arabia to prevent them from becoming loyal to Nasser. Syrians also began to resent the Egyptian-style land reform program now being imposed on them, and Baath intellectuals who had supported the concept of Arab union totally rejected Nasser's concept of a single political party. Nasser's response to problems in Syria was to appoint Egyptians from his inner circle to serve as viceroys there.

Regional Impact

All experiments in Arab unity that included Egypt and/or Syria were interpreted as major threats by the Jordanians. Their perceptions of Syria as a perennial instigator of conspiracies against King Hussein and Egypt as an enduring foe of the Hashemites only added to their fears. Hussein's response to Nasser's Pan-Arab initiative was to propose to his cousin King Faisal II of Iraq that an Arab Federation of Jordan and Iraq be formed to counter the UAR. This new confederation, created on February 14, 1958, was to allow each member state its own domestic policies, but with common military and foreign policies. The agreement foresaw the creation of a unified military command between the two states, 80 percent of whose budget was to be supplied by Iraq and 20 percent by Jordan.

Camille Chamoun, Lebanon's president and an opponent of Nasser, also viewed the creation of the UAR with worry, since he saw it destabilizing the complex mosaic of political forces that governed his own country. Pro-Nasser factions there, mostly comprised of Muslims and Druze groups, began clashing with Chamoun's loyalists among the Christian Maronite population. These tensions culminated in the first **Lebanese civil war** that took place in July 1958. Nasser had no plans to incorporate Lebanon into the UAR, seeing it as a special case among Arab nations. Despite this, Nasser remained a revolutionary instigator who backed his loyalists there, sending them funding, weapons, and providing training for their leaders.

In this situation of rising tensions across the Arab world, a group of Iraqi army officers launched a military coup on July 14 that overthrew the Hashemite monarchy there—ending the Arab Federation experiment. Nasser immediately recognized this new government, declaring any military action taken against it to be the same as "an attack on the UAR." As a preventative measure and in the wake of the upheaval in Lebanon, the United States sent its Marines there and the United Kingdom sent its special forces to Jordan to forestall any similar actions by Nasserists in these countries. This marked the first significant deployment of U.S. troops in the central Middle East since World War II. The operation was viewed as a great success, since only four American soldiers died, three in an accident and one killed by a sniper.

From the Egyptian perspective, the Iraqi revolution marked another step on the road toward eventual Arab unity. For several years after the 1958 coup, Iraq became the most supportive among the other Arab states for expanding the **United Arab Republic**. It tried actively to join the UAR over the next few years, and even after the original federation collapsed, Iraq proposed to rebuild another one in 1963 with Egypt and Syria as its partners. Iraq then adopted a new three-star flag to symbolize the three members of this proposed

union—a banner that continued as Iraq's national flag (with some Islamic exhortations later added) until 2008.

However, such experiments in Pan-Arab union were not destined to last. The Iraqi military leaders who unseated the Hashemite monarchy in 1958 called themselves a Revolutionary Command Council in imitation of their Egyptian counterparts, and most saw uniting Iraq with the UAR as their eventual goal. However, their leader Abdel Karim Qasim did not agree with them. It has been suggested that Qasim saw Nasser as a dangerous potential challenge to his standing in Iraq.

When the 1958 Lebanon crisis subsided after U.S. intervention there, the United States used quiet diplomacy to persuade President Chamoun to allow Fuad Chehab to be chosen as Lebanon's new president. When Nasser and Chehab, both career military officers, held a meeting at the Lebanese-Syrian border, Nasser told Chehab that he never envisioned Lebanon joining the UAR. His only concern was that it not be used as a base against Pan-Arabism. This encounter marked the end of the crisis in Lebanon, since Nasser agreed to stop giving material support to his activist Lebanese followers, and the United States set a deadline for its military withdrawal from the area.

Meanwhile, within the UAR, Nasser tried to introduce economic reforms in June 1960 to increase the government's role in the Syrian economy and to make Syria's government resemble the strong Egyptian public sector. His agents carried out an extraordinary campaign of nationalizations in both Syria and Egypt, but in Syria, these took place largely without input from top Syrian economic officials. The entire Syrian cotton trade was taken over by the government, as well as all import-export firms.

Collapse

Although Nasser failed to implement massive economic reforms in Syria that were designed to parallel changes in the Egyptian economy, the failure of the UAR experiment in Syria was directly tied to his refusal to include Syrian leaders in his team. Syrian Baath leaders shared most of Nasser's political, social, and economic views and would have been his natural allies. Abdel Hakim Amer, Nasser's viceroy in Syria and his old Egyptian army colleague, shut out the Baath thoroughly in elections, assisted by Colonel Abdul Hamid Sarraj (one of Nasser's most loyal Syrian followers): a policy that permanently alienated Syrian Baath leaders. In the end, the UAR administered Syria with a harsh security system focused on crushing opposition and centralizing authority.

Nasser consolidated regional Syrian governments into one central authority, but this left him without any trustworthy loyalists in different parts of Syria to keep tabs on the political situation. Thus, Nasser was taken by surprise when a group of Syrian officers staged a coup on September 28, 1961, to take Syria out of the UAR.

These officers first offered to negotiate with Egypt over the creation of a new agreement for an Arab union in which Syria would have more equal status with its partner. Nasser rejected all such overtures, but continued to declare for many years after this break that he would never give up his dream for a complete Pan-Arab political union some day. The UAR experiment with Syria would remain the closest he ever came to that goal.

NORTH YEMEN CIVIL WAR

Another place where Nasser's revolutionary fervor had begun to catch fire by the late 1950s was North Yemen. In 1958, its hereditary monarch, Imam Ahmad ibn Yahya, had announced that his kingdom would enter into a loose federation with the UAR. When a Nasserite faction took power in a 1962 coup, overthrowing Ahmad's successor Imam Badr and proclaiming the Yemen Arab Republic, its action marked the beginning of the **North Yemen Civil War**. This struggle set troops loyal to the new republic (assisted by Nasser's Egyptian army) against the forces of the

recently deposed traditional ruler, Imam Badr, who was strongly supported by Saudi Arabia and Jordan. This conflict continued sporadically until 1967 when Egyptian troops were withdrawn just after the Six-Day War. After the collapse of the original UAR experiment in 1961, this became Nasser's second attempt to promote his vision of Pan-Arabism. It remained a steady drain on Egyptian resources over the five years just before the 1967 Six-Day War: the next transformative Middle Eastern conflict.

Nasser's failure in the North Yemen War sheds light on the obstacles confronted by secular Arab nationalists in trying to build Arab political unity while fostering collectivist schemes of modernization across the region. With its backwardness and the poor reputation of its rulers, Yemen might have seemed an ideal place for Nasser's modernization dreams to take hold, but it was so poor and so divided geographically that its politics often devolved into struggles to stay in power. Imam Ahmad bin Yahya inherited the Yemeni throne in 1948, and was almost overthrown in 1955 in a military coup led by an officer trained in Iraq, but survived through his sheer brutality. After this incident, there was constant tension between the Yemeni army and the country's ruler, who struggled to maintain control of a country extremely difficult to manage even in the best of times.

Outbreak of War

When Ahmad, who had been in poor health for several years, died a natural death in mid-September 1962, he was immediately succeeded as Imam by Badr. Badr at first had sympathized with Nasser's Pan-Arab movement, so one of his first official acts was to select one of Nasser's main supporters in the Yemeni army, Colonel Abdullah Sallal, to lead the palace guard. Colonel Sallal, in consultation with the Egyptians and with promises of military support from them, decided that it was the right time to transform Yemen into a republic. Thus on September 26, Sallal led a coup to overthrow Badr and proclaim the Yemen Arab Republic.

In Nasser's view, the decisive and rapid victory of republican forces over royalists in Yemen might have helped restore confidence in him across the Arab world, since his public image had suffered after the UAR's collapse. In addition, the successful overthrow of the monarchy in North Yemen could serve as a prelude to the liberation of South Yemen and its strategic port capital of Aden from British control: setting the stage for another campaign to further his anticolonialist and anti-imperialist agendas.

With substantial Egyptian assistance, the Yemeni army managed to seize control of Sanaa, North Yemen's capital, and on September 28, announced Badr's death. Soon after that, Colonel Sallal, who had taken power as the revolution's leader, gathered tribal leaders in Sanaa and admonished them that "anyone who tries to restore … [the monarchy] is an enemy of God and man!" By then, he had learned that Badr had not been killed but taken refuge with royalist tribesmen in the north, eventually escaping to Saudi Arabia a few days later.[2]

Nasser sent a detachment of Egyptian Special Forces to help Sallal consolidate control. This intervention, together with Badr's arrival in Saudi Arabia, prompted the Saudis to move troops to the Yemeni border. The situation turned somewhat chaotic when a Saudi cargo plane filled with military equipment being sent to the Yemeni royalists along the Yemeni-Saudi border failed to land in Najran on October 3. It was flown instead by its crew to Egypt, who then immediately defected there *en masse* to Nasser's cause.

The fact that *all* these pilots had all been trained by the U.S. military assistance mission to Saudi Arabia, together with the subsequent defection of three more crews with their planes over the next few days, was deeply shocking

to the Saudi king. He grounded all native air crewmen, relying now on American TWA pilots to deliver cargo to the front lines in Yemen. One of the Saudi princes, Talal, who had taken refuge in Cairo in 1961 as a prominent Saudi dissident and supporter of Nasser, announced that he was forming an Arab Liberation Front to overthrow the Saudi monarchy.

None of this amounted to much in terms of real action, but it prompted the Saudis to intensify their efforts on behalf of the Yemeni royalists. The bigger problem was that all this took place at the height of the Cold War: in precisely the same month as the main showdown of the Cuban Missile Crisis. Because of these circumstances, the conflict immediately acquired international importance. For example, when the Soviet Union became the first nation (even before Egypt) to recognize the new Yemen Arab Republic Soviet leader Nikita Khrushchev cabled to Colonel Sallal that any aggressive act against Yemen would be viewed as an act of aggression against the Soviet Union itself. The United States tried to avert a larger conflict by using a diplomatic campaign to pressure Nasser's troops to withdraw from Yemen in exchange for Saudi Arabia and Jordan halting assistance to the royalist forces, but negotiations broke down because the Saudis and Jordanians did not trust Nasser.

In the end, the United States was placed in the difficult position of supporting the Saudis as their close allies, but was also forced to recognize that Nasser's allies had secured control in Yemen. On December 19, 1962, the United States formally recognized the Yemen Arab Republic—a gesture that only emboldened the Yemenis and their Egyptian helpers. One month later, Egyptian planes bombed Najran, a Saudi city with an important airbase near the Yemeni border. In March 1963, veteran U.S. Middle East negotiator Ralph Bunche met with Nasser in Cairo, where Nasser was reported to have told him that Egypt would remove its forces from Yemen if the Saudis would end their support for the royalists.

---

[2]"Yemen: Arabia Felix," *Time*, October 26, 1962.

Operation "Hard Surface"

Soon thereafter, the American government decided to send U.S. planes to protect Saudi airspace from Egyptian incursions. The main point of this intervention, called **Operation "Hard Surface,"** was to induce the Saudis to cease their aid to Yemeni royalist forces. Under pressure from the United States, Saudi King Faisal agreed to curtail his country's involvement in Yemen, and Nasser met with the Americans in Beirut to confirm that he would still honor the withdrawal agreement that he had made with Bunche. In order to keep peace, a UN Yemen Observation Mission was to be established under the command of a Swedish general in order to create a demilitarized zone on the Yemen-Saudi border. This planned mission was finally abandoned in late 1964. This turn of events froze the civil war into a much longer standoff, since Operation Hard Surface had already been terminated by King Faisal several months earlier.

War Continues

Over the next three years, the Saudis spent millions to equip royalist soldiers and hire hundreds of mercenaries, and kept the royalists fighting a steady series of small skirmishes and conflicts with republican forces. They were joined at various times in providing aid by Pakistan, Iran, the British, and the United States. In 1965, the U.S. Army Corps of Engineers was deployed in Saudi Arabia to supervise the construction of military facilities and provide the Saudi military with combat vehicles, all of which constituted an indirect form of U.S. aid in the Yemen war.

Imam Badr commanded two royalist units that controled much of northern and eastern Yemen, with numerous locations where the royalists controlled the mountains while the Yemeni republicans and their Egyptian allies retained the towns and fortresses. Royalist tactics became confined to guerrilla warfare, including surprise assaults on conventional Egyptian and Yemeni republican forces in addition to attacking their supply lines. By late 1965,

55,000 Egyptian troops were in Yemen, but they were beset by continuous logistical difficulties. Egypt was spending millions of dollars to keep its troops and their Yemeni allies equipped.

In 1966, after numerous peace conferences and attempts to solve the conflict had failed, Yemeni republican and Egyptian forces began to resort to fairly drastic measures, including the use of poison gas. One of the biggest gas attacks took place in January 1967, when 140 people were killed in an attack that targeted a member of Yemen's royal family. In February 1967, Nasser asserted that Egypt was ready to "stay in Yemen twenty years if necessary," to which a royalist spokesman countered, "We are prepared to fight for fifty years to keep Nasser out, just as we did the Ottoman Turks." In a bitter mood, Nasser complained that "as the situation now stands, Arab summits are finished forever."[3]

Six-Day War: End of the North Yemen Civil War

The human and material costs of the June 1967 Six-Day War, effectively forced Egypt to end its involvement in Yemen. After the Suez Canal had been shut down in June, Egypt began to lose at least $5 million per week in toll revenue, while Israel now controlled Sinai wells that had provided half of Egypt's oil supply. In August 1967, Nasser recalled 15,000 troops from Yemen to make up for losses in the Six-Day War. On the domestic front, Egypt imposed higher taxes, reduced overtime pay, cut the sugar ration, curtailed many major industrial programs, and raised staple prices drastically. Nasser and Saudi King Faisal then signed a treaty in which Nasser agreed to remove all remaining Egyptian troops from Yemen, in exchange for Faisal curtailing Saudi arms shipments to Imam Badr. To ease Egypt's financial woes, Saudi Arabia, Libya, and Kuwait agreed to pay it $266 million per year, of which Saudi Arabia would provide $154 million.

---

[3]"The Middle East: Revolt within a War," *Time*, February 17, 1967.

Questions to Think About

1. What was the impact of the 1948 war on the Palestinians?
2. How did different Arab countries try to influence the Palestinians?
3. How did the loss of the war in 1948 affect Egypt, and what caused the Egyptian revolution of 1952?
4. How did the Free Officers' Movement and Gamal Abdel Nasser try to change Egypt?
5. What happened to the Muslim Brotherhood under Nasser?
6. How did Nasser use the media to promote his agendas?
7. What was positive neutralism, and why wasn't it successful?
8. What led to the Suez Crisis of 1956, and what were its effects?
9. Why was the United Arab Republic formed, and why did it dissolve within three years?
10. What caused Nasser's intervention in the North Yemen Civil War?
11. Why was Pan-Arabism such an important ideology during the 1950s and 1960s in the Middle East?

For Further Reading

Aburish, Said K. *Nasser: The Last Arab*. New York: St. Martin's Press/Thomas Dunne Books, 2004.

Badeeb, Saeed M., and John Peterson. *The Saudi-Egyptian Conflict over North Yemen, 1962–1970*. Boulder, CO: Westview Press, 1986.

Berger, Earl. *The Covenant and the Sword: Arab–Israeli Relations, 1948-56*. London: Routledge & K. Paul, 1965.

Gordon, Joel. *Nasser: Hero of the Arab Nation*. Oxford: Oneworld, 2006.

Haykal, Muḥammad Ḥasanayn. *The Cairo Documents: The Inside Story of Nasser and His Relationship with World Leaders, Rebels, and Statesmen*. Garden City, NY: Doubleday, 1973.

Jankowski, James P. *Nasser's Egypt, Arab Nationalism, and the United Arab Republic*. Boulder, CO: Lynne Rienner Publishers, 2001.

Kyle, Keith. *Suez: Britain's End of Empire in the Middle East*. London: I.B. Tauris, 2003.

McNamara, Robert. *Britain, Nasser and the Balance of Power in the Middle East, 1952–1967: From the Egyptian Revolution to the Six-Day War*. London: Frank Cass, 2003.

Morris, Benny. *Israel's Border Wars, 1949–1956: Arab Infiltration, Israeli Retaliation, and the Countdown to the Suez War*. Oxford: Clarendon Press, 1993.

Podeh, Elie. *The Decline of Arab Unity: The Rise and Fall of the United Arabic Republic*. Brighton: Sussex Academic Press, 1999.

Shalom, Zaki. *David Ben-Gurion, the State of Israel and the Arab World, 1949–1956*. Brighton: Sussex Academic Press, 2002.

Smith, Simon C. *Reassessing Suez 1956: New Perspectives on the Crisis and Its Aftermath*. Aldershot, England: Ashgate, 2008.

Vatikiotis, P. J. *Nasser and His Generation*. New York: St. Martin's Press, 1978.

16

Six-Day War

The 1956 Suez Crisis and its termination did not deal with any of the larger regional problems of the Middle East. They were also not addressed by the Pan-Arab projects and plans of the late 1950s. The events of 1956 had excluded any real possibility that an Arab country would now be able to recognize Israel: a situation that formed the backdrop of events leading to another war one decade later.

With this sense of stymied political initiative across the region, some individual regimes became more radicalized, such as the rulers of Syria and Iraq. After Syria's political divorce from Egypt upon the collapse of the UAR in 1961, Syrian politics became quite turbulent over the next eighteen months. This period culminated in a March 1963 coup by a stridently radical Baath group: the National Council of the Revolutionary Command (NCRC).

Because a Baathist group had also just taken power in Iraq just one month earlier, negotiations soon commenced about making another attempt at a united Arab government now to include Egypt, Iraq, and Syria. Such discussions ended when the new Iraqi Baathist regime was overthrown in November 1963. Iraq was then ruled by the two Arif brothers in succession through 1968: both non-Baathist career military officers who supported Nasser's policies but were not ready to create a political union with him.

After this final Pan-Arab experiment in 1963 failed to work, Syria's rulers became successively more militant with each new government. Amin al-Hafiz, the Baathist Syrian army officer who took power in the March 1963 coup, steered the country toward a more socialist approach and aligned it more and more closely with the Soviet bloc. The turbulence of politics in this area had other unpredictable consequences. Between 1961 and 1963, al-Hafiz had been in semi-exile from Syria, serving as the Syrian military attaché in Buenos Aires, Argentina. While there, he became friends with a man who presented himself as a Lebanese merchant, Kamal Amin Thaabet, but was in fact an Israeli spy named Eli Cohen. Cohen succeeded in making himself a trusted adviser of al-Hafiz and even moved to Syria in 1962, from where he relayed valuable information to Israel. When Cohen was finally unmasked in 1965, al-Hafiz had him executed and arrested many of his friends in a purge, but Syria was not entirely able to mitigate the impact of the valuable military intelligence he provided to Israel on the eve of the Six-Day War.

BAATH RULE IN SYRIA AND IRAQ

Even the Pan-Arab Baathism of al-Hafiz and his supporters (often labeled the *qawmi* or "nationalist" bloc) was ultimately not radical enough for another Syrian Baath faction: the *qutri* ("regionalist") bloc. It called for the restoration of a Greater Syria (in echo of the Syrian Social Nationalist Party). In the end, this more radical faction overthrew al-Hafiz in the wake of the Cohen affair in February 1966. Most portentous for Syria's political future, it was strongly supported by military officers from religious minorities, such as the Alawites and the Druze, in contrast to al-Hafiz, from a Sunni family in Aleppo.

By the late 1960s, different branches of the Arab Baath Socialist Party had become established as the ruling groups in both Syria and Iraq, holding power there over the next several decades. The Baath party is secularist, modernist, and staunchly Arab nationalist, seeing itself as a vanguard against "Western imperialism" while calling for the "renaissance" or "resurrection" (*baath*) of the Arab World in one unified state. The words of its motto, "Unity, Freedom, Socialism" (*wahda, hurriya, ishtirakiya*), expressed its basic principles: (1) an unyielding dedication to Arab unity, (2) its call for the freedom of the Arab world from non-Arab control and foreign interference (typified by the long recent Ottoman domination of the region), and (3) Arab socialism (contrasted with European socialism and communism).

The party had been founded in the 1940s in Damascus by Syrian intellectuals Michel Aflaq (of Orthodox Christian background), and Salah al-Bitar, with an ideology that offered a rough synthesis of nationalist and socialist concepts. It attracted a significant number of Christian Arabs as its founding members, because it did not have an overtly Islamic orientation. In 1955, an internal coup against Aflaq and Bitar split the Syrian and Iraqi branches of the party into rival organizations. Like other revolutionary movements, when it did not hold power, the Baath was organized into cells, which helped inhibit outside repression and infiltration.

After securing power in Syria and Iraq by the mid-1960s, the branches of the Baath Party in both countries gradually evolved into patronage networks that eventually became closely interwoven with the official government bureaucracy. Party structures soon became virtually indistinguishable from the state, and membership rolls were increased to transform previous vanguard groups into regime-supporting mass organizations.

Salah Jadid, a member of the Alawi minority and the Baath ruler of Syria who came to power in 1966, aligned Syria ever more closely with the Soviet bloc, and increased promotion and sponsorship of Palestinian guerrilla raids against Israel. As a result of the radicalization of the new regime's ideology, these raids were now being framed less in Arab or Palestinian nationalist terms and more in strictly Marxist terms as the operations of a "people's war of liberation." These activities were promoted in part as a way to deflect domestic opposition to Baathism, but also paradoxically meant that radical Arab states came to depend more on more for legitimacy on how stridently they opposed Israel.

NASSER AND EGYPT IN THE 1960S

Nasser, for his part, tried not to lose the Pan-Arabist and revolutionary initiative for which he had become famous in the late 1950s. As noted, he put a lot of effort into creating a Yemen Arab Republic to replace that country's hereditary monarchy beginning in 1962, but his radical programs had a domestic component as well. Despite Syria's exit from the UAR, Nasser retained this Pan-Arabist title as Egypt's official name and in December 1962, created an Arab Socialist Union as the UAR's sole political party and the main instrument of his new National Charter announced in 1964.

Much like programs introduced during the previous decade, the Charter offered an program of nationalization, as well as agrarian and constitutional reform, but on a more radical and thorough basis than before. The ultimate result of Nasser's programs was to transfer seven billion Egyptian pounds of private assets to the public sector. Banks, insurance companies, large shipping companies, and major industries were placed under public control. The new laws reduced the maximum amount of private land ownership from 200 to 100 acres, and a maximum 90 percent tax rate was imposed on yearly incomes over ten thousand Egyptian pounds. Company boards of directors now had to include a minimum number of ordinary workers, with workers and peasants guaranteed at least half of the seats in the People's Assembly.

It is noteworthy that in Egypt, even the most radical and far-reaching of these reforms were described as "socialist" and not "communist": Private enterprise was never totally abolished. While there were attempts to reduce social class distinctions, there were not real attempts to eliminate them by law. In the realm of social and religious life, Nasser did press for real changes. His National Charter called for women's legal equality with men and for providing support for programs to encourage family planning.

In 1961, Nasser began implementing reforms designed to modernize the received wisdom of the leaders of the al-Azhar Mosque, long regarded as the *de facto* Sunni Islamic religious legal authority. His goal was for al-Azhar to be a vehicle of his programs and modernizing agendas, for its scholars to function as religious authorities with more legitimacy than the populist clerics associated with the Muslim Brotherhood. In the larger Muslim world, the wisdom of al-Azhar could also compete with the rigid Islamic doctrines being more and more aggressively promoted by Saudi Arabia and its conservative Wahhabi clerics.

One of Nasser's most notable direct interventions in religious practice occurred when he put pressure on the main religious authority of al-Azhar, Mahmud Shaltut, to issue a *fatwa* affirming the status of Shii Muslims as adherents of a legitimate rite (*madhhab*) in Islam, in contrast to centuries of Sunni *fatwas* denouncing members of this group as heretics and apostates. Also during this time, Nasser had the administrators of al-Azhar make changes in their course curricula: a shift that had an impact on lower levels of the Egyptian educational system as well. His government permitted mixed-gender schools, allowed the theory of evolution to be taught, changed divorce laws, and merged Islamic religious courts into civil ones.

SAYYID QUTB: ARCHITECT OF MODERN ISLAMISM

This, of course, was all taking place at a time when the Muslim Brotherhood organization was still formally outlawed and many of its leaders were serving long prison sentences. Among its most important philosophers was Sayyid Qutb (1906–1966), one of the main theorists of modern Sunni Muslim fundamentalism or "Islamism." Qutb, of fairly humble peasant origin, had risen through the Egyptian bureaucracy to become an official in the Ministry of Education, which sent him for two years in the late 1940s to the United States to study. He spent this time in Greeley, Colorado (1948–1950), where he became horrified by the Western materialism and decadence that he saw rampant there. Sometime after his return to Egypt, he joined the Muslim Brotherhood, and for awhile, became allied with the Free Officers' Movement that overthrew the Egyptian monarchy.

Qutb quickly became disillusioned with Egypt's new rulers as it became clear that Islamic principles and doctrines would not guide their régime. When the government cracked down on Muslim activists, particularly the leadership of the Brotherhood, they detained Qutb, who stayed in prison between 1955 and 1964. Just after his release, Qutb published his most famous work: *Maalim fi al-Tariq*

(*Milestones on the Path*). In this book, he accuses contemporary Muslim societies of being not Islamic but *jahili*: a word previously used to refer to the ignorance of pre-Islamic times. In this work, Qutb reinterprets this word to refer to *all* non-Islamic ideas and regimes, past and present, as "pagan" and "barbaric." Qutb's use of the term *jahili* here also implied apostasy by many contemporary Muslims from Islam itself: an unpardonable offense.

As Qutb perceived the situation, his Muslim contemporaries made a great mistake to view the Quran as a source of culture and information. They were not able to see how its teachings and guidance could *really* be employed to reshape societies and liberate men from enslavement to other men, allowing them to serve God alone. In his view, the real Islamic community "had been extinct for a few centuries" as Muslim societies reverted to *jahiliya* ("the state of being ignorant of God's guidance"), since those who now called themselves "Muslims" no longer actually followed Islamic law (Sharia).[1]

Qutb believed that only the authentic reestablishment of Sharia would redeem the world and restore harmony to it. Attempts to confuse people by introducing elements of socialism or nationalism into Islam could be regarded as reversions to the *jahiliya* (the pre-Islamic "time of ignorance") and thus constituted acts against God. A vanguard (*talia*) modeled on the original group of Prophet Muhammad's "companions" (*sahaba*) would be assembled.

It would watch over the reestablishment of a righteous political order based on Islamic law. Through its total fidelity to true Islamic precepts and practices, this vanguard would overcome the evil forces of the pagan *jahiliya* now reestablished with the rise of materialism and modern decadence. The spiritual awareness of this group would guard it from seduction by non-Muslim cultures and let its members turn away from non-Muslim friends and family.[2] The vanguard considered the Quran as a set of orders to obey, not merely a text to be interpreted for "knowledge and information" or to find solutions to personal problems.

Qutb explained that use of force would be necessary to pursue this struggle, since it was naive to assume that any rulers who had usurped God's authority would give up power without a fight. His theories were the origins of modern radical Sunni fundamentalism. His extension of the traditional Muslim legal concept *takfir* (the act of identifying someone as a *kafir* [unbeliever] or even as an apostate [for those born Muslims] who deserved the death penalty) to include contemporary Muslim leaders and rulers was an unprecedented innovation. Qutb's stridency perhaps reflects great despair about the monumental difficulty of challenging the powerful currents of modernization sweeping over the Middle East in the 1950s and 1960s.

Despite Qutb's intense antipathy toward "Western" culture, many of his ideas strongly resembled certain doctrines of European fascism. These included the concept of the "decline" of contemporary Western civilization and the "infertility" of its democracy, as well as a desire to restore an earlier golden age under a totalitarian social, political, and economic system, his concept of victimization by malicious foreign conspiracies, and his advocacy of violent revolution to force change. Less than a year after his initial release, Qutb was arrested again, now accused of treason, helping to plan a coup, and aiding in a plot to assassinate Nasser. His trial was conducted in a military court, by whose judgment he was executed in 1966. By the end of his life, Qutb had become a legend among certain followers of the Muslim Brotherhood, and many found

---

[1] Sayyid Qutb, *Milestones* (Damascus: Dar al-Ilm, 1993), 9, 93.

[2] Ibid., 15.

his philosophies appealing after the massive Arab defeat of the Six-Day War in 1967.

Just as governments in the region were attempting to suppress Islamic activism, a trend toward secular radicalization of politics at this time was also having an impact in many parts of the Middle East as well. One notable example among on the Palestinians can be seen in the career of George Habash. Habash was an Orthodox Christian Palestinian from Lydda who, at the time of the 1948 war, had been a medical student at the American University of Beirut. He could not go back to his hometown, so after graduating first in his medical school class, he joined his family in Jordan, where they had moved after the war.

Habash did volunteer service in refugee camps as a young doctor: an experience that transformed him into an avid supporter of armed Palestinian guerrilla action against Israel. He founded the "Arab Nationalist Movement" (ANM) in 1951: a group at first closely aligned with Nasser's vision of Arab unity. Habash became implicated in plots to overthrow Jordan's King Hussein and fled to Syria, but headed back to Beirut after the collapse of the UAR in 1961. The ANM, founded as a group closely aligned with Nasser, now split into various factions in different Arab countries. Some factions were more nationalist and others more Marxist in focus. Habash and his followers created one of the more radical Marxist branches of the group in 1964—the Palestinian Regional Command of the ANM—a precursor to even more militant revolutionary groups that emerged after the Six-Day War.

CREATING THE PLO

The increasing radicalism in various parts of the Arab world created concern among more conservative states about the potential for uncontroled militancy to destabilize the whole region in dangerous ways. By this time, Israel had been functioning as nation for almost two decades. The increased polarization felt against it among more radical Arab leaders can

be seen in the extremely negative reaction to Habib Bourguiba's March 1965 Jericho speech. Bourguiba, first president of independent Tunisia and a well-respected fighter against French imperialism and colonialism, delicately called on his Arab brethren in these remarks to negotiate a lasting peace with Israel, but found himself denounced across the region as a traitor who had abandoned the Palestinian cause.

For his part, Nasser was reasonably satisfied with the results of revolutionary initiatives he had sponsored and supported, but mistrusted the radical plans and programs of others. In particular, he began to get very worried about how Syrian support for more and more radical Palestinian raids into Israel by the mid-1960s could further destabilize the situation. This fear about events getting out of control became one of the main reasons for Nasser's creation, under the auspices of the Arab League, of the "**Palestine Liberation Organization**" (**PLO**) in June 1964. The PLO was designed to serve as an umbrella organization that could be managed by other Arab countries, particularly Egypt, and could ride herd on more radical Palestinian factions. Its first chairman, Ahmad al-Shuqairy, was a prominent Palestinian lawyer and politician who had served as a diplomat and civil servant in numerous Arab regimes, but was somewhat disconnected from younger Palestinians now growing up in the refugee camps.

Looming ever larger as a factor in the rise of militancy across the Middle East by 1960s was the continuing unresolved question of what to do about these refugees. Many thousands were still living in camps, from which Arab governments were not anxious to resettle them, because of the perception that this might imply recognition of the status quo in Israel. In this vein, the 1964 Palestinian National Charter explicitly called for a single Arab state of Palestine to replace Israel.

While Egypt and Jordan promoted the creation of this Palestinian state on land regarded as occupied by Israel, they made sure that the text of the 1964 Palestinian National

Charter specified that the PLO would not have authority over the Gaza Strip, the West Bank, or the Himma area: territories then controlled by Egypt, Jordan, and Syria, respectively.[3] This clause was rendered moot after Israel's occupation of these places in 1967, but reflected continued uncertainty among Arab nations regarding what *specific* Arab lands belonged precisely to *which* Arab nation, leaving aside the whole question of what belonged to the Israelis or to the Palestinians.

One of the rising Palestinian groups of this era was the **Fatah** movement, whose name (meaning "retaking" or "conquest") was the reverse acronym of the Arabic initials for Palestine Liberation Movement (*Harakat al-Tahrir al-Filastini*). Fatah was in essence a nationalist group founded in 1954 by Palestinian doctors, lawyers, and other professionals working in the Persian Gulf States after they fled their homeland following the 1948 war. One of the prominent members of this group was Yasser Arafat, Egyptian-born member of a Palestinian family from Gaza who had been the president of the General Union of Palestinian Students at Cairo University in the early 1950s.

Fatah presented itself as an organization made up of the "youth of the catastrophe" (*shibab al-nakba*; with "catastrophe" referring to the 1948 war), who committed themselves to armed struggle against Zionism. Its first major guerrilla attack came on January 3, 1965. On that day, a Fatah group (styling its members as "*fidayin*": "those who sacrifice their lives") tried unsuccessfully to sabotage the Israeli National Water Carrier by planting a bomb in one of its pumping stations that failed to detonate. The Water Carrier was a distribution system Israel had recently put into operation. It diverted large quantities of water from the Jordan River (which forms the border between Jordan and Israel) to meet Israel's

growing water needs. Although Israel repelled this attack fairly easily, it was a harbinger of what was to follow over the next few years as Palestinian raids increased.

ISRAEL AS A NEW NATION: THE STRUGGLE OVER WATER

Despite a constant low level and intermittent high level of conflict with its Arab neighbors through the 1950s, Israel faced many other challenges at this time, due to substantial waves of new Jewish immigration and the new nation's programs of rapid modernization. As part of fulfilling the modern Zionist dream of creating a national home for Jews, Israeli leaders also sought to create a just society that offered equality of opportunity for all Jewish immigrants with a guarantee of certain standards of living. Until the era of Israel as an independent nation, this goal had mainly been pursued by "pioneer" Zionists, relatively well-educated Jews who had emigrated primarily from Europe and North America to build a new society based on such principles.

After World War II, Jews coming to Israel were primarily part of a "rescue immigration" program that included Holocaust survivors and Middle Eastern Jews expelled from Arab countries during and just after the 1948 war. This group had not had any real chance to prepare for their immigration. Lacking any training or education designed to equip them to function in this modern society, the socialization of these newcomers became one of the main social challenges for Israel in the 1950s.

A variety of public works projects were instituted in this era to reduce unemployment among this new, unskilled immigrant population. One of the most important was the building of the **Israeli National Water Carrier**. This was a system of pipes, canals, and tunnels started in 1953 to bring water from the Sea of Galilee to the Negev and central Israel, a project that was finally completed in 1964. The Water Carrier project, though, did not merely

---

[3]http://www.un.int/palestine/PLO/PNA2.html (accessed August 28, 2010).

have domestic ramifications. Because its ultimate sources lay in the territory of hostile countries on its borders, this created a constant flashpoint for armed conflict between Israel and its Arab neighbors as each nation in the region tried to meet its increasing water demands.

In 1953, as a way to reduce tensions after the 1948 Arab-Israeli War, the United States had presented the Jordan Valley Unified Water Plan (named the Johnston Plan for American representative Eric Johnston): the latest attempt to end the longstanding battle over this vital resource. In the late 1930s and mid 1940s, both the government of Transjordan and the World Zionist Organization (in its capacity before Israel's founding as the de facto government of the Jewish community in Palestine) had already produced scientific studies with conflicting visions of water use in the Jordan Valley. The study commissioned by Jordan asserted that the water supplies of the Jordan valley were not sufficient to sustain a Jewish state, while the Zionist study concluded that by diverting water from the Jordan basin to the Negev region, approximately four million new immigrants to a Jewish state could be supported—research that became the origins and rationale for the National Water Carrier project. Meanwhile, Jordan concluded an agreement with Syria to dam the Yarmouk River and use its water to irrigate Jordanian territory before it flowed to the Sea of Galilee: an act that could spark another armed confrontation with Israel very rapidly.

To defuse this increasingly tense situation, U.S. President Eisenhower dispatched Ambassador Johnston to the region to work out a plan that would regulate water usage. His scheme followed principles used in the 1930s in the United States to set up the Tennessee Valley Authority (TVA) as a model to optimize usage of the water of an entire river basin as a single unit. It called for various dams to be built on rivers flowing into the Sea of Galilee and the Jordan River, as well as canals

and waterworks created to utilize the water flow from wadis more efficiently and provide irrigation for parts of the West Bank. The plan proposed that as a fair allocation, Israel should receive 394 million cubic meters, Jordan 774 million cubic meters, and Syria 45 million cubic meters of this water annually. Intense diplomatic negotiations ensued over this plan, and by 1955 technical representatives from Israel and the Arab League had agreed to this division. Although the technical experts from both sides had accepted details of the plan, the Israeli parliament and the Arab League council never formally ratified it, although both sides made an implicit commitment to abide by the Johnston plan rules.

The 1956 Suez Crisis changed the diplomatic situation entirely. Now none of the Arab states (except Jordan) wanted to do anything at all that implied cooperation with Israel. They strongly opposed the Johnston plan and began to make arrangements to choke off Israel's water supplies upstream. Nevertheless, Israel continued building its National Water Carrier project, and Jordan proceeded with its own East Ghor Main Canal project, both of which were funded in part by the United States. In the new climate after Suez, the United States demanded assurances from both Israel and Jordan that they would still abide by the original parameters of the Johnston plan, despite the Arab opposition that had arisen.

The situation remained in an unresolved stalemate until July 1964, when Israel began taking water from the Jordan River to supply its just-completed National Water Carrier. At an Arab League summit in Cairo in January 1964 convened to discuss this issue, a Headwater Diversion Plan was announced in which Syria would create a canal to divert the flow of the Banias River away from Israel and down the slopes of the Golan Heights toward the Yarmouk River. Lebanon would then link the Hasbani River to the Litani River and on to the Banias River to complete the flow channel.

The goal was to divert between 20 and 30 million cubic meters of water from tributaries of the Jordan River to be used by Syria and Jordan instead of Israel.

When Israel found out about this, it attacked the worksites, all very near its frontier, first with tanks in March 1965 and then as work shifted eastward, with airstrikes in May and August of that same year. These planned diversion works would have reduced the installed capacity of Israel's carrier by about 35 percent, and Israel's overall water supply by about 11 percent. Such attacks by the Israel Defence Forces (IDF) helped escalate the level of border violence that led directly to outbreak of the 1967 war, but they did not mark the first use of hostile force in the struggle over control of water resources.

ISRAEL, JORDAN, AND PALESTINIANS IN THE WEST BANK

Among the first such confrontations was the January 1965 attack on the pumping station already mentioned (which the Fatah organization still regards as its first real guerilla operation): an incident that marked the beginning of a wave of small attacks by Fatah teams over the next two years. These were carried out by Palestinian volunteers trained in camps in Syria and Algeria. Such operations were led primarily by Fatah activists living in Syria, but funded by wealthy Palestinians living in other countries. This was also when Yasser Arafat, who had moved to Syria from Kuwait in 1962, became one of Fatah's leaders.

Even more strategic than the Syrian frontier, the long border between Jordan (then still controlling the West Bank and east Jerusalem) and Israel became the most important area of confrontation during this part of the conflict. While Syria, with its increasing radicalism, became the main supporter of these cross-border attacks, Israel held Jordan responsible for raids launched from its territory. This put Jordan's King Hussein in an extremely difficult position.

INCIDENT AT SAMU

With the majority of his country's population being of Palestinian origin, Hussein could not afford to suppress such Palestinian activities too harshly, lest he be accused of favoring Israel. More than sixty Fatah raids were carried out (mostly unsuccessfully in a military sense) through 1966, but Fatah was good at creating publicity and making a name for itself among Palestinians. As a close ally of Syria, it was regarded with great suspicion by Egypt, since Egypt had been promoting the PLO (at that time quite separate from Fatah), which Nasser had recently helped establish as the most legitimate Palestinian movement.

This round of Fatah incursions culminated on November 11, 1966. On this date, an Israeli border patrol vehicle ran over a land mine, which killed three soldiers and injured six. The Israelis immediately suspected that the mine had been planted by Fatah sympathizers staging their attack from the village of Samu, just across the border in the southern West Bank. This led the Israeli government to approve a significant military retaliation against Samu called Operation "Shredder." Although King Hussein of Jordan quickly wrote a personal letter of condolence to Israel that he had transmitted via the U.S. ambassador to Israel, it was not delivered in time to stop the Israeli operation.

The next morning, Israeli troops crossed into the West Bank and entered Samu, where they destroyed several houses after their inhabitants had been removed. In an unexpected turn of events, Jordanian troops arrived there and soon engaged the Israelis in combat, the results of which were inconclusive, since there were relatively few casualties and actual fighting continued for only about four hours. The diplomatic consequences of the event were far more substantial. Hussein had been conducting secret negotiations with the Israelis over the previous three years. He felt that they had let him down with an excessive military response: a sentiment shared by the

United States and the UN. To manage domestic anger over this event, Hussein mobilized his armed forces but also tried to crack down on any more guerrilla operations being launched from Jordan.

The real wild card in this increasingly tense confrontation was Syria. As it played a more activist role, the Syrian government both helped Palestinian militants stage attacks on Israel through Jordanian territory, as well as continually shelling Israeli civilian communities from its own artillery emplacements on the Golan Heights. The Syrian government, itself taken over by the more militant Baathist faction of Salah al-Jadid in 1966, refused to accept responsibility for activities carried out by Fatah activists or other Palestinians.

The constant low level of military conflict and confrontation that had continued in the Demilitarized Zone (DMZ) between Syria and Israel on the Golan Heights since the armistice agreements of 1949 suddenly was placed in a new context in 1966. In that year, tensions increased markedly with the increase in the number of Palestinian raids and the conclusion of a new mutual defense pact brokered by the Soviet Union between Egypt and Syria, calling for joint action in case of an Israeli attack against either of them.

Over the next few months, tensions gradually went up, so that by April 1967, a minor incident on the Syrian-Israeli DMZ resulted in a major aerial battle over the Golan Heights. Six Syrian MiG-21s were shot down by Israeli planes, which then flew over Damascus. This was accompanied by various skirmishes between land artillery forces, but still did not erupt into full-scale military conflict, although a fierce diplomatic war of words escalated through May.

UNEF TROOPS LEAVE SINAI

On May 18, Egypt asked the United Nations Emergency Force (UNEF) stationed in Sinai since 1956 to leave: the logical precursor to a new Arab attack on Israel. Four days later, the Egyptian government closed the Straits of Tiran. Since they connected the main Israeli port of Eilat to the Red Sea, this presumably was another clear sign of impending Arab war plans. Israel asked the United States and the United Kingdom to reopen the Straits of Tiran as they had pledged to do after the Suez Crisis, but only the United Kingdom and the Netherlands were willing to supply ships to do this in 1967. In any event, the closure of the Straits was something Israel had faced before between 1951 and 1956, and thus was not perceived by the Israeli government as an immediate threat.

Of greater concern was whether Jordan would join other Arab states in a conflict against Israel. The pivotal surprise gesture occurred on May 30, when King Hussein signed a mutual defense treaty with Egypt, perhaps indicating the pressure he felt from his Palestinian subjects to go along with Nasser's Pan-Arabist agenda to join the fight against Israel. Nasser stated in a radio address broadcast on that day that any differences between him and King Hussein (whom he had called an "imperialist lackey" only two days earlier) had been erased "in one moment." When Nasser announced that the "basic objective will be the destruction of Israel. The Arab people want to fight," Jordanian forces were placed under the command of an Egyptian general and two battalions of Egyptian commandos were flown to Jordan just three days before the war actually started.

FIGHTING FOR SIX DAYS

The sense of impending conflict brought the United States and the USSR into the diplomatic discussion, but neither side was able to influence what was happening in military terms. On June 3, U.S. President Johnson, having consulted with both Israeli and Egyptian senior officials, issued a statement committing the United States to no specific action but calling for diplomacy and patience. This apparently convinced the Israeli government that it could wait no longer, but must move immediately on its own accord. The Egyptians were also furiously preparing for something to happen soon. In a report from Cairo dated June 4, 1967, an American reporter observed that "Cairo does not want war and it is certainly not ready for war. But it has already accepted the possibility, even the likelihood, of war, as if it had lost control of the situation."

Israel's air attack on Egypt early on the morning of June 5 commenced what would later be called the "Six-Day War." The main imperative for Israeli commanders was to act quickly and decisively, because so many of Israel's troops were reservists who could not be mobilized indefinitely without severely constraining the nation's economy.

In very approximate terms, the manpower of the Israeli armed forces was roughly equal to that of the combined Arab forces, but the Israelis were far better disciplined and trained, with superior equipment and more competent leadership. With its citizen army, Israel benefited from the morale boost of fielding a force that had a clear understanding of what its mission was and how it should be carried out. The Arab armies, in contrast, were composed of soldiers with more complex systems of loyalties, shaped by the twists and turns that had created new Middle Eastern countries within recent memory.

The initial Israeli air attack by Israel that began at 7:45 A.M. on June 5 remains a model of achieving surprise and good execution. The Israelis used all but twelve of their two hundred combat aircraft in raids destroying Egypt's airfields and most of its planes on the ground, including more than ninety MiG-21s, then the best Soviet fighter plane available. Paradoxically, the Egyptian government had shut down its air defense system out of fear that rebel forces in the Egyptian ranks might shoot down a plane carrying Egyptian commanders to the Sinai. Only nineteen Israeli planes were lost, mostly due to logistical failures. By sunset on the second day of the war, June 6, Israel had also wiped out most of the air forces of Jordan, Syria, and Iraq. The success of these

attacks was a very crucial factor in the swift overall Israeli victory in this war.

Beginning on the morning of the war's first day, Israeli general **Ariel Sharon** began a carefully planned ground assault on the Sinai Peninsula, resulting in the swift seizure of Abu Ageila, a key point on the main central highway through Sinai, by noon on the second day. When Field Marshal Amer, Nasser's defense minister and close associate, heard about this, he ordered the retreat of all Egyptian units from the Sinai. This prompted the Israelis to go around these retreating forces to head them off and annihilate them in mountain passes in the western part of Sinai. By the end of the day on June 8, the Egyptian army had been defeated, and Israel controlled the Sinai Peninsula all the way to the Suez Canal.

In the West Bank

Although Jordan's King Hussein had been reluctant to enter the war, when it started, he cast his lot with Nasser. This battlefront of the war was much more challenging than the conflict against Egypt. The initial Israeli plan had been to stay in a defensive posture against Jordan, to allow Israel's army to concentrate on Egypt. However, on the morning of June 5, just as Israeli planes were attacking Egypt, the Jordanian air force and artillery hit targets in central Israel.

None of these assaults caused much damage, and Israel sent an immediate message in which it promised not to begin any military action against Jordan if King Hussein did not enter the war. His swift reply was that it was too late and that the die had already been cast for Jordan to join in the conflict on the Arab side. For a very brief period of time, the Israelis hesitated about what to do next, but when Jordanian troops advanced across the 1949 armistice lines in Jerusalem and occupied UN headquarters in the Demilitarized Zone by noon on the first day, Israeli units were dispatched within minutes to move against Jordanian forces into the West Bank.

During the afternoon of that same first day, Israeli Air Force (IAF) strikes destroyed the Royal Jordanian Air Force. By nightfall, Israeli forces had completed the encirclement of Jerusalem after several bouts of fierce house-to-house fighting. The Israeli commander on this front, General Moshe Dayan, forbade his troops to enter the old city itself, fearing damage to holy places. Over the next two days, Israeli forces secured control of key strategic points across the West Bank after heavy fighting in many areas.

On the morning of June 7, acting on information suggesting that the UN was about to arrange a cease-fire but without consulting the Israeli government, General Dayan authorized his troops to occupy Jerusalem's Old City where intense street fighting, conducted mostly by paratroopers, led to Israeli troops finally securing and holding it within a matter of hours. It is important to note that at this point, no strategic decisions had been made by the Israeli government about whether or not to secure and hold *any* territories in the West Bank at all. When intelligence reports revealed that Hussein had withdrawn his troops across the Jordan River, Dayan commanded his forces to capture and hold the West Bank.

On the Syrian Front

The leadership of Syria, as in many circumstances, adopted a very cautious approach at the beginning of the war, and began by shelling and conducting air raids on northern Israel. It soon fell victim to the second wave of Israeli air assaults, in which Israeli planes destroyed two thirds of Syria's air force on the night of June 5 and immobilized the remaining third for the rest of the conflict. A minor Syrian ground force tried to capture one of the Israeli water stations near the Golan Heights but failed, while a broader Syrian ground offensive also collapsed due to numerous logistical problems. Syria's military commanders gave up all hopes of staging a ground attack and shifted to pursuing a campaign of intensively shelling Israeli settlements in the Hula Valley that continued over the next few days.

Syria announced that it would accept a cease-fire at 3 A.M. on June 9. Four hours later at 7 A.M., Dayan issued an order for Israeli troops to begin a land invasion of Syria by attacking the Golan Heights. Israel had made claims on the area around Mount Hermon for a long time, and Syria had created a lot of trouble for Israel over the previous few years by sponsoring raids and shelling Israeli targets from the Golan, so there was some sentiment among Israeli leaders in favor of entering Syrian territory there. Arguments against doing this from a military perspective included the argument that such an attack would literally be an uphill battle against a fortified opponent that could be very costly, as well as the fear that an attack on Syria itself was likely to involve the Soviet Union much more directly in the situation, since the current Syrian regime was among its closest Middle Eastern allies.

All of these factors taken together had at first convinced Dayan to oppose an invasion, but the situation was changing. At this point in the war, Dayan authorized the invasion since battlefronts in Egypt and the West Bank had quieted down, intelligence reports suggested that there was less likelihood of Soviet intervention on Syria's behalf, and an intercepted cable revealed that Nasser was asking Syrian President al-Jadid to accept a cease-fire without delay.

The mountainous terrain of the Golan and its lack of good roads severely taxed combat logistics there. In addition, Syria had built a substantial network of fortifications resembling the Maginot Line in its intricacy, which was hard for Israeli planes to attack. Israel did have very good intelligence about these emplacements and Syria's plans for them collected by their spy, Eli Cohen, unmasked and put to death in Syria only two years earlier.

The key to Israeli success in the Golan Heights in 1967 was that Syrian forces did not have good military discipline or rapport between officers and enlisted. Syrian officers and their men soon fled. By nightfall on June 9, Israeli forces had crossed through the Golan Heights to the plateau beyond it. There, they completed their offensive by occupying strategically good positions. These positions eventually formed a cease-fire perimeter known as the Purple Line.

Superpowers and the Conflict

The Six-Day War occurred at a very tense time in international relations, which had an impact on its course and outcome. By the summer of 1967, the United States was already heavily involved in Vietnam and so was not as able to get as directly involved in the unfolding Middle East situation as it might otherwise have been. The Soviet Union sensed an opportunity to extend its influence in the Middle East at U.S. expense by prodding its Arab allies, particularly Syria, to take a tough stance against Israel. Finally, after hostilities had actually commenced, Arab leaders, particularly Nasser, began to use radio addresses to accuse Western powers, particularly the United States, of helping Israeli achieve its remarkably devastating initial wave of airstrikes. They tried to capitalize on the skepticism of the average Arab that Israel could have accomplished such military achievements on its own.

On June 8, the USS *Liberty*, a U.S. electronic intelligence monitoring ship traveling in the Mediterranean north of al-Arish just outside of Egypt's territorial waters, was attacked by Israeli air and naval units. These forces nearly sank it and caused heavy casualties among its crew. The Israeli government said that its units had attacked because of mistaken identity. It apologized for the error, paying compensation to the victims and their families. After an investigation, the United States officially accepted Israel's explanation, although claims are still made today that the attacks were deliberate, designed to constrain American intelligence gathering about Israeli operations at the end of the war.

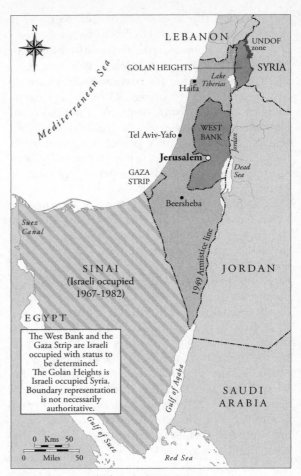

MAP 16.1   Israel after the 1967 War

End of the War: Impact on Israel

In any event, Israel finished its attack in the Golan Heights by June 10, and a lasting cease-fire was arranged on the next day. Israel now occupied the Golan Heights, the entire West Bank of the Jordan River (including East Jerusalem), as well as the Gaza Strip and the Sinai Peninsula. This gave it control of three times more territory and offered far greater strategic depth than it ever had before (which proved useful for the 1973 **October War**). Approximately one million Palestinian Arabs lived in the areas that Israel had taken so suddenly.

The implications of Israel's stunningly quick victory in the Six-Day War were large for both sides. Israel had proven to its citizens and to its supporters around the world that it could win a huge victory against a formidable adversary, with results far more conclusive than any of the conflicts fought before. In addition, taking control of the Old City of Jerusalem, with its Temple Mount as the holiest site in Judaism, had an enormous psychological impact on Israelis, who could now pray again at the Western Wall after being kept from visiting since 1948.

This immediately presented numerous issues. Just a few days after the end of the war, Moshe Dayan visited the mosque of al-Aqsa on the Temple Mount and met with Muslim religious leaders in charge of it. He requested that they hold the usual religious services there on the next Friday, and guaranteed that Israeli troops would be removed from the site and stationed outside the compound. They were ordered not interfere in the private affairs of Muslims, who were formally recognized to have authority over their own sanctuaries. Dayan had already given orders on the day of the capture of the Old City of Jerusalem that an Israeli flag someone had hoisted over the Dome of the Rock must be taken down.

This did not resolve any issues. In 1967, August 16 corresponded to the ninth of Av, 5727, in the Hebrew calendar. To celebrate this holiday, the day designated to remember the destruction of the ancient Jewish Temple, Shlomo Goren, chief rabbi of the Israel Defence Forces (IDF) held a prayer service on the Temple Mount accompanied by several followers. When complaints were lodged about this, no Israeli official wanted to go on record formally stating that Jews were *forbidden* to pray on the Temple Mount. Instead, the decision was made to impose an indefinite, de facto ban on Jews praying there. While this postponed any definitive resolution of the issue, like so many other "solutions" in the Arab-Israeli confrontation, it functioned merely to put off discussion of any real remedy for the problem.

An even more complex situation presented itself in the West Bank town of Hebron (called in Arabic "al-Khalil"). Hebron is the site of the Cave of the Patriarchs containing the tombs of Abraham, Sarah, and their family, thus extremely holy to both Muslims and Jews. The Israeli government's goal there was not to arrange for a division of authority and rights over different parts of the site, as in the case of the Temple Mount, but to broker harmonious coexistence—a very complex process in the decades since 1967.

In addition to having religious feelings that surfaced when Israel took control of the most sacred sites in Judaism, Israelis were enthralled by how their use of technology as well as military prowess shaped this victory, as explained in a speech given by the main army commander, Yitzhak Rabin, soon after the event:

> Our airmen who struck the enemies' planes with such accuracy that no one understands how it was done and the world seeks to explain it technologically by reference to secret weapons; our armoured troops who stood their ground and overcame the enemy even when their equipment was inferior to his; our soldiers in all the several branches of the army who withstood our enemies everywhere despite the superiority of their numbers and fortifications: what they all showed was not only coolness and courage in battle but a passionate faith in the justice of their cause, the certain knowledge that only their personal, individual resistance against the greatest of dangers could save their country and their families, and that the alternative to victory was annihilation.[4]

By June 27, Israel had formally incorporated East Jerusalem together with adjacent

---

[4]http://www.mfa.gov.il/MFA/Facts+About+Israel/State/ Address+by+IDF+Chief-of-Staff+Lieut-Gen+Yitzhak+Ra. htm (accessed September 15, 2011).

areas of the West Bank to the north and south into Jerusalem's new municipal boundaries. Among the Arab inhabitants of the West Bank, only those in East Jerusalem and the Golan Heights became entitled to receive full Israeli citizenship, since Israel formally incorporated these territories, but the vast majority refused to do this. Within a few years after the Israeli conquest of all these territories, a large effort was begun to create Jewish settlements in them, with major consequences for the future.

ARABS AND THE WAR

In predictable contrast to the Israeli reaction, the 1967 war was regarded in the Arab world as a disaster on par with the conflict of 1948. It produced another wave of refugees with thousands more Palestinians fleeing to neighboring countries during the fighting and over the following months. Perhaps as much as a quarter of the existing West Bank population (between two hundred and two hundred and fifty thousand people) fled to the East Bank into Jordan, and few ever returned. Around seventy thousand left Gaza and went to Egypt or elsewhere in the Arab world, and more than eighty thousand Syrians departed from the Golan Heights region, with 20,000 alone leaving the city of Quneitra.

Among Arab heads of state, the national leader most grievously affected by the 1967 Arab disaster was Nasser, who announced in a televised speech on the fifth day (June 10) of the Six-Day War that he was resigning as Egypt's leader. In his speech, Nasser transferred all his powers to his longtime deputy Zakaria Mohieddin. When he heard this news, Mohieddin was completely taken by surprise and refused to step into Nasser's role, but instead resigned himself.

Just after Nasser made this speech, tens of thousands demonstrators rushed into streets in mass demonstrations across the Arab world rejecting Nasser's resignation and chanting slogans of support for him. Upon hearing of such reactions, he announced the next day that he had decided to stay in office. Riding this wave of popular support, he chose instead to arrest a large number of senior army commanders to provide a scapegoat for the military failures.

The Arab League convened a summit in Khartoum, Sudan, on August 29. The most important symbolic shift there was that Saudi King Faisal was now perceived as the leader of the Arab world, having displaced Nasser, although the two rode hand in hand in an open limousine through the streets of Khartoum to show solidarity. The conference was also made famous by the "Three No's" resolution: No peace with Israel, no recognition of Israel, no negotiations with Israel. It also marked the formal beginning of regular financial assistance from wealthy Arab oil states, which included Kuwait, Libya, and Saudi Arabia, to the front-line states (Egypt, Jordan, and Syria) that had lost the war in order to help them rebuild their militaries. The meeting emphasized the right of the Palestinians to control all of Palestine—reaffirming the Arab League's commitment to the total elimination of the state of Israel. Finally, Nasser and Faisal agreed to a cease-fire in the North Yemen Civil War that had gone on since 1962.

When he returned to Egypt, Nasser acted quickly to reassert power. Several senior officials under house arrest were allowed to commit suicide, most notably his close associate Abd al-Hakim Amer. Despite consenting to Amer's demise, Nasser said that he lost "the person closest to me" and would carry the burden of his former comrade's death. Soon thereafter, Nasser took additional titles as Egypt's prime minister and commander-in-chief of the armed forces as he tightened his personal grip on power.

THE SIX-DAY WAR AND THE WORLD

Through the 1950s and early 1960s, there had been some ambiguity in the relationships of various Arab countries with the United States and the USSR. After 1967, though, the situation became more clearly defined, with the USSR now resupplying Egypt with about half of its former arsenal of weapons and breaking diplomatic relations with Israel. Immediately following the war, six Arab countries broke off diplomatic relations with the United States, and Lebanon withdrew its ambassador from Washington. The United States drew considerably closer to Israel after this, although it tried to maintain relations with the Arab world as much as it could.

In broad terms, the disastrous outcome of the Six-Day War for the Arabs was also an important factor in the increasingly radicalization and anti-Americanism of the Middle East: a process that paralleled the growth of radical leftist and religious fundamentalist movements, and the increasing use of terrorism as a weapon. The leftist reaction, strongly encouraged by the Soviet Union, was based on disbelief that the Israelis could have beaten the combined force of the Arab armies together so swiftly without any outside assistance. The religious reaction went beyond the Arab world and spread to other Islamic countries such as Iran and Pakistan. It was fueled by anger at the Israeli takeover of Jerusalem and the Dome of the Rock, whose sanctity as an Islamic holy site was now considered compromised.

UN RESOLUTION 242

Although the Khartoum Resolution had been strident in delivering its three "no's" to Israel, it also in effect marked a shift in Arab views of the conflict from centering on the very question of Israel's legitimacy toward a debate about what the specific territories and boundaries in a final peace arrangement might be. Despite all the discussions at Khartoum, Egypt and Jordan formally accepted **United Nations Security Council Resolution 242** as ratified on November 22, 1967. This resolution introduced the concept of "land for peace," calling for Israeli withdrawal "from territories occupied" in 1967 in exchange for "the termination of all claims or states of belligerency." The writers of this document took into account that there were likely to be some territorial adjustments in the final settlement, so avoided putting the words "*all*" or "*the*" before the phrase "*territories occupied*" in the official English-language version of the text. Resolution 242 became the basis for all subsequent peace negotiations in the conflict up to the present day.

Questions to Think About

1. What made Arab politics turbulent in the mid-1960s?
2. What were the origins of the Baath Party, and why did it become more popular in the 1960s in Syria and Iraq?
3. What further revolutionary measures did Nasser introduce in Egypt in the 1960s?
4. Who was Sayyid Qutb, and how can he be considered the founder of modern radical Islamism?
5. What were Sayyid Qutb's views on Egypt's rulers?
6. Why was the PLO created?
7. What was Fatah?
8. What was the Israeli National Water Carrier, and what problems did it solve and create?
9. How did the Samu incident affect relations between Jordan and Israel?
10. What gave Israel the strategic advantage in the Six-Day War?
11. What happened on the Syrian front in the Six-Day War?
12. What was the Six-Day War's impact in the Middle East and internationally?
13. What did UN Resolution 242 specify and not specify about ending the Arab-Israeli conflict?

For Further Reading

Abu Jaber, Kamel. *The Arab Ba`th Socialist Party: History, Ideology, and Organization.* Syracuse, NY: Syracuse University Press, 1966.

Badeeb, Saeed M., and John Peterson. *The Saudi-Egyptian Conflict over North Yemen, 1962–1970.* Boulder, CO: Westview Press, 1986.

Berger, Earl. *The Covenant and the Sword: Arab-Israeli Relations, 1948–56.* London: Routledge & K. Paul, 1965.

Calvert, John. *Sayyid Qutb and the Origins of Radical Islamism.* New York: Columbia University Press, 2010.

Cobban, Helena. *The Palestinian Liberation Organisation: People, Power, and Politics.* Cambridge: Cambridge University Press, 1984.

Dunstan, Simon, and Peter Dennis. *The Six-Day War, 1967: Jordan and Syria.* Oxford: Osprey, 2009.

Gordon, Joel. *Nasser: Hero of the Arab Nation.* Oxford: Oneworld, 2006.

Hudson, Michael C. *Arab Politics: The Search for Legitimacy.* New Haven: Yale University Press, 1977.

Hussein, Vick Vance, and Pierre Lauer. *My War with Israel.* New York: Morrow, 1969.

Kerr, Malcolm H. *The Arab Cold War: Gamal `Abd Al-Nasir and His Rivals, 1958–1970.* London: Published for the Royal Institute of International Affairs by Oxford University Press, 1971.

Khadduri, Majid. *Arab Contemporaries: The Role of Personalities in Politics.* Baltimore: Johns Hopkins University Press, 1973.

Khatab, Sayed. *The Political Thought of Sayyid Qutb: The Theory of Jahiliyyah.* London: Routledge, 2006.

Oren, Michael B. *Six Days of War: June 1967 and the Making of the Modern Middle East.* Oxford: Oxford University Press, 2002.

Qutb, Sayyid. *Milestones.* Cedar Rapids, IA: Mother Mosque Foundation, 1981.

Rubin, Barry M. *Revolution Until Victory? The Politics and History of the PLO.* Cambridge: Harvard University Press, 1994.

Segev, Tom. *1967: Israel, the War, and the Year That Transformed the Middle East.* New York: Metropolitan Books, 2007.

Shemesh, Moshe. *Arab Politics, Palestinian Nationalism and the Six-Day War: The Crystallization of Arab Strategy and Nasir's Descent to War, 1957–1967.* Brighton: Sussex Academic Press, 2008.

17

Turkey and Iran after World War II

TURKEY AFTER WORLD WAR II

Emergence of Multiparty Politics

Turkey had remained neutral during World War II, taking great care to avoid becoming caught up in conflict the way that the Ottoman Empire had been during World War I. Although it had indeed survived through the war without major catastrophe, the postwar era saw major changes and upheaval in nations around Turkey. In 1946 alone, Greece was thrust into a full-scale, bloody civil war; Bulgaria was transformed into a loyal people's republic of the Soviet bloc; and the short-lived Kurdish Republic of Mahabad was declared in Iranian Azerbaijan near Turkey's eastern border. Syria and Iraq, both emerging from their time under French and British control, experienced considerable political turmoil after the war as well.

Turkish politics, although considerably more peaceful than what was going on in surrounding countries, entered its own era of change. In June 1945, several prominent political leaders including **Adnan Menderes** (an important banker and landlord), Fuat Koprulu (a well-known historian from an old Ottoman family), and Jelal Bayar (former Turkish prime minister) introduced a proposal to cancel extraordinary laws controling the economy and press freedom imposed during the war as well as to permit multiple political parties. Ismet Inonu, Ataturk's handpicked successor, was still serving as president. The only political party allowed at this time, Ataturk's Republican People's Party (RPP), totally rejected this proposal, and its supporters were expelled from the party, except for Bayar, who resigned.

This group formed a new political organization in January 1946: the Democrat Party (DP). Creation of this party was a new beginning for politics in Turkey, because despite the rejection of the earlier proposal, the government gradually began to relax many wartime controls and liberalize the political process. The DP, headed by Bayar and Menderes, quickly evolved into the RPP's main opposition.

By the general elections of July 1946, the DP won 62 seats out of 465 in the assembly. It represented the interests of private businesses and industry, but received strong support as well in rural areas, particularly among more religiously conservative voters. By May 1950, the DP won 408 seats in the assembly compared to only 69 for the RPP, whose unbroken hold on power since the beginning of the Turkish Republic was suddenly ended. The new assembly elected Bayar to replace Inonu as president and selected Menderes as prime minister. His new administration moved away from promoting state control over large parts of the economy to encouraging private enterprise and foreign investment in industry.

Member of the World Community of Nations

These domestic changes coincided with Turkey's international realignment as it developed closer alliances with Western nations in general and the United States in particular. This trend was seen as a natural extension of Turkey's membership in the United Nations, which it had joined in 1945 as one of the original signatories of the UN Charter. Ties with the United States were expanded in a 1947 agreement that specified American intentions to secure Turkey and Greece against Soviet aggression: an important early phase of implementing the Truman Doctrine at the outset of the Cold War. Over the next few years, the United States sent considerable aid to Turkey and dispatched civilian and military personnel there to help in its economic development and provide military training.

Turkey became a member of the Council of Europe in 1949 and was brought into the North Atlantic Treaty Organization (NATO) in 1952. Upon the outbreak of hostilities in Korea in 1950, the Turkish army sent an infantry brigade there to serve under the UN command. Over the next three years, over seven hundred Turkish soldiers were lost in combat. Despite these casualties, Turkey's participation in this international mission was perceived very favorably by the Turkish public as a sign of the nation's emergence as a full-fledged member of the larger community of nations. Izmir became NATO'S headquarters for southeastern Europe, and the Turks permitted other NATO installations to be located in Turkey and allowed the United States to station troops there.

The Turkish electorate responded favorably to these changes in Turkey's international and domestic situations, so in the elections of 1954, the DP enlarged its parliamentary majority even more. The government of Menderes took this as a license to push through various pieces of legislation that angered the RPP, now in the opposition. The two main political parties became unable to cooperate in the assembly, paralyzing the legislative process for a considerable period of time.

Cyprus and the 1955 Istanbul Riots

The next few years saw a considerable escalation of tensions with Greece over the status of Cyprus and were also marked by greater international tensions. Both Turkey and Greece had become members of the NATO alliance in 1952, but their cooperation in NATO operations was compromised by their longstanding dispute over the Cyprus issue. In the 1950s, Cyprus was still a British crown colony (as it had been since 1878). Greek Cypriots campaigned hard for the end of British rule and the political union (*enosis*) of Cyprus with Greece. Turkish Cypriots, numerically fewer than Greeks on the island, sought a division of its territory between the two communities.

Proponents of various visions of the island's future sought international support for their causes. In 1954, Greece proposed to the UN Security Council that Cyprus be granted independence, but British and Turkish pressure defeated this initiative. To keep up this pressure, Turkish nationalist organizations organized violent demonstrations against the Greek minority in Istanbul as well as the

Ecumenical Patriarchate, head of all Orthodox Christianity, still located in the old city there. This anti-Greek campaign was facilitated by the government (still led by the DP) and various national newspapers. One major Turkish newspaper, *Hurriyet*, wrote on August 28, 1955, that "If the Greeks dare touch our brethren, then there are plenty of Greeks in Istanbul against whom to retaliate."[1]

At a 1955 London conference between Turkey, Greece, and the UK, Prime Minister Menderes denounced Istanbul's Greek minority population, using them as a convenient scapegoat during an economic crisis in which the Turkish economy contracted. The DP's emphasis on private investment caused inflation to skyrocket, and when it could not control this problem through policy, the DP leadership, particularly Menderes, adopted a more rabble-rousing approach to governing.

DP policies had allowed huge movement from rural areas to cities, particularly Istanbul, Ankara, and Izmir. New city residents, clustered in poor shantytowns, were prime targets to be roused for political activity. News that the Turkish consulate in Thessaloniki (which also housed Ataturk's birthplace) had been bombed brought the peace conference to an end, and unleashed riots against the Greek residents of Istanbul. It was later revealed that DP leaders had planned these events and that the fuse for the bomb detonated in Thessaloniki had been sent a few days earlier from Istanbul. Just after the London conference ended, a large riot broke out in Istanbul's Taksim Square that was followed by huge amounts of looting of Greek properties in the Beyoglu (Pera) district and along Istanbul's main shopping street, Istiklal Avenue. Many Greek Orthodox churches around the city were also damaged.

Turkey's vital importance as a Cold War ally led Britain and the United States to shield Menderes and the DP from any direct blame for these disturbances. The Cyprus problem did not go away, but after much negotiation over the next five years, the island did become a non-aligned republic in 1960 with a complex power-sharing arrangement between the Greek and Turkish communities. Although this allowed Britain to declare Cyprus an independent nation and transfer authority to local control, its new constitution ultimately became the framework for another era of conflict there.

Back on the Turkish mainland, the DP had failed to solve Turkey's economic problems, which continued to mount through the late 1950s when inflation was not stopped. Violence flared as RPP leader Inonu toured through central Anatolia in early 1960, prompting the Menderes government to suspend political activity and impose martial law. On April 28, 1960, police fired on students in Istanbul protesting against the government and defying martial law, killing several. The following week, military cadets marched in solidarity with the students, involving the military in a confrontation with the government.

COUP OF 1960

Ataturk had maintained a firm belief that the Turkish armed forces should never get involved in politics. While military commanders generally agreed with this philosophy, it was with the caveat that the Turkish military had a duty to stand on guard to protect the constitution and Kemalism. In 1960, senior commanders of the military decided that the civilian government had strayed too far from Kemalist principles, particularly in not being vigilant enough in enforcing secularism as a state policy, and was too corrupt. They saw this as justifying their intervention in politics at that time.

On May 27, 1960, army units occupied important government buildings, detaining President Bayar, Prime Minister Menderes, and most of the DP members of the Grand National Assembly, along with many other public officials. This coup was not very violent and was received calmly throughout the country.

---

[1] Alexis Alexandris, *The Greek Minority of Istanbul and Greek-Turkish Relations 1918–1974*, 2nd ed. (Athens: Centre for Asia Minor Studies, 1992), 256.

A committee of senior military officers took over the government and selected a civilian cabinet to carry out its day-to-day functions. The Menderes government left behind high inflation and heavy debt, forcing the imposition of emergency austerity measures. In 1961, a new constitution was ratified by a fairly slim popular referendum (60 percent). It made substantial changes in the 1924 constitution while continuing to embody the principles of Kemalism, thus marking the beginning of Turkey's so-called "Second Republic." Hundreds of former government officials were put on trial, and all but about 100 were found guilty of various crimes, with three death sentences, including one for Menderes, pronounced and carried out.

In the first elections held under the new constitution, no party gained a majority, so a coalition was necessary. The new legislature, now bicameral, chose retired General Gursel, not involved in the recent coup, as president. Inonu then served as prime minister, but cobbled together a series of weak coalitions. Eventually, all but a very few politicians convicted of crimes after the coup were released. The DP's successor party, called the Justice Party (JP), won elections in 1965 and 1969, cultivating a more conservative populist constituency. The JP was careful never directly to challenge the principle of secularism as a key part of Kemalism, but its encouragement of the open expression of traditional Islamic belief appealed to many conservatives. Like the DP, the JP also encouraged the private sector more vigorously than before and was open to foreign investment in Turkey.

This was an era in which European economies, particular West Germany's, played an important role in improving Turkey's economic health with the *Gastarbeiter* program. This program, beginning in 1961, allowed Turks to get temporary work visas in Germany as a way to ease work shortages created by the enormous losses of manpower during World War II. While this plan was intended originally only as a temporary measure, it led to a growing long-term presence of Turks in West Germany who never returned to Turkey. There were approximately seven thousand Turkish guestworkers living in Germany when the program started in 1961, but only a decade later in 1971, this number had ballooned to nearly seven hundred thousand Turkish citizens, all of whom were sending remittances back to the impoverished rural areas of their native country.

In foreign policy, the Cyprus question continued to be a main concern. Shortly after the implementation of the 1960 constitution, disputes again arose between the Turkish and Greek communities there. Open fighting broke out on December 21, 1963, in Nicosia, which soon spread across the island and caused the fragile power-sharing government to collapse. One week later, an interim peacekeeping force of British, Turkish, and Greek troops moved in to restore order, soon replaced by a UN peace keeping detachment. Conflict between the two communities led to major crises in 1964 and again in 1967, during which Turkey and Greece—both NATO members—came to the brink of war. After a flurry of activity in 1967 when a group of colonels staged a coup and seized power in Greece, the situation once again fell into a stalemate for a few more years.

TURKISH DEMOCRACY IN CRISIS: THE 1970S

Turkey soon entered its own period of renewed political crisis. The JP government's majority in the Turkish Grand National Assembly eroded after the 1969 general election as Prime Minister Demirel's supporters abandoned him. In 1970, three small conservative parties previously in coalition with the JP now united among themselves as the National Salvation Party: an explicitly Islamic-oriented group that now made much more stringent demands on Demirel as the price of continued support. Some JP members deserted in 1971 to form a right-wing secular party while the JP's more liberal members just left it to become independents.

All these realignments resulted in the JP losing its parliamentary majority. This happened just as acts of violence and terrorism began to increase around the country. Unrest, as in the past, was fueled by longstanding grievances of economic distress, social inequities, and slowness of reform. Leftist activists now increasingly targeted their protests at Turkey's military and economic ties to the West. As a consequence of this instability, the armed forces chiefs told the president in March 1971 that if he did not assemble a "strong and credible government," or if economic and social reforms called for in the 1961 constitution were not implemented, the military would step in again. This led to Demirel's immediate resignation, followed by a series of weak caretaker governments that ruled until elections were held in October 1973.

These elections again resulted in no party achieving a majority. This prompted an unlikely coalition between Ejevit, leader of the RPP (which had now moved much farther to the left than in previous times) and Nejmettin Erbakan, leader of an Islamically oriented party. This lasted for only a few months in 1974. Coalitions became the norm over the next few years, which meant that government was not really able to address the nation's mounting long-term problems very effectively.

Cyprus and the 1974 War

The Cyprus issue had some new twists. In July 1974, the longstanding president of Cyprus, Archbishop Makarios III, was deposed by a coup arranged in Greece. The goal of the coup plotters was to install a government that would unify Cyprus and Greece without a vote. Turkish prime minister Ejevit immediately announced that unilateral imposition of such a union would be in direct violation of the 1960 Cyprus independence agreement, and authorized military action to protect Turkish Cypriots. On July 20, 1974, 30,000 Turkish troops, including naval and air units, landed in Kyrenia (in northern Cyprus) and

began to march on Nicosia, the capital. The UN arranged a cease-fire two days later, by which time Turkish troops controled the road between Nicosia and Kyrenia as well as large amounts of territory on both sides of it: the area of Cyprus with the most substantial Turkish population.

The Greek military government collapsed a few days later as a result of its involvement in this plot. Peace talks began but soon collapsed. After some more fighting, the Greek forces accepted a Turkish cease-fire offer that left the Turks in control of all territory on the island north of a particular line. In February 1975, the Turkish Federated State of Cyprus was established in the northern region with Rauf Denktash as its president. This was later renamed the Turkish Republic of Northern Cyprus, but remains a country today recognized only by Turkey.

The partition of Cyprus made about one third of the island's population into refugees. About 10,000 Turkish Cypriot refugees from the southern part of the island fled to northern Cyprus through airlifts from British bases via Turkey. At the same time, Greek Cypriot leaders alleged that the Turkish military was bringing settlers from Anatolia to occupy lands in the northern part of the island from which Greek Cypriots had fled. This constant tension flared up in a series of naval confrontations in the Aegean Sea during the late 1970s between Greece and Turkey.

Domestic Political Tensions

Despite increasing electoral success, the RPP failed to win enough seats in the Turkish parliament in the next general elections in 1977 either to claim a majority or even form a governing coalition. Demirel again assembled another right-of-center coalition that depended on a mere four-seat majority. Continuing public disillusionment over the government's failure to address economic problems and restore public order led to Demirel's ouster at the end of 1977.

Ejevit was now asked to lead a new government, also backed by a slim four-seat parliamentary majority. By December 1978, the government imposed martial law in various regions to quell huge outbreaks of sectarian violence. This only produced a transitory calm, and Ejevit resigned in October 1979, now replaced again by Demirel. He brought in a nonpartisan group of technocrats to impose drastic economic restructuring plans.

When their measures were challenged by a series of trade union strikes, Demirel extended martial law to restrict union activity and public gatherings. Apart from pressures from the left, popular religious activism was influencing politics at this time in a way that deeply concerned military leaders, who perceived this as another clear assault on secularism.

Economic Woes

One of the greatest challenges faced by Turkey's economy was the rapid increase in the price of oil after 1973. Within four years, the country's economic situation had plunged into a deep crisis, with a rate of inflation rising to over 50 percent by 1977 and an unemployment rate unofficially calculated that year to be nearly a third of the total workforce. Under pressure from the International Monetary Fund, Demirel's government devalued the currency by 10 percent and raised some government-subsidized prices.

Despite such measures, another major devaluation of the Turkish lira, and a rescheduling of the foreign debt, there was still no clear economic recovery by 1978. The economic restrictions imposed actually had the effect of contracting the economy, so industrial production fell and unemployment kept growing. Demirel's focus, when he came back into office in the fall of 1979, was much more on private sector–driven initiatives. Turgut Ozal, an economist, was tasked to direct this program.

Although this new approach made some headway in economic development, it seemingly had no impact on the increasing

tempo of political violence that began to appear unstoppable. All through the 1970s, many political organizations created adjunct street-fighting units. Many were directly connected with the extreme right, but there were a substantial number on the radical left who identified themselves either as revolutionary Marxists or as partisans of the Kurdish nationalist movement. The military's collective frustration over this breakdown of civil authority came to a head in September 1980.

THE COUP OF SEPTEMBER 12, 1980

The last straw was a massive demonstration in Konya on September 6. It was supported by pro-Islamist political parties, who called for Islamic law to be reimposed in Turkey. There were reports that protestors there showed disrespect to the Turkish flag and its national anthem—gestures seen by the military as an open attack on Kemalism and a direct challenge to it.

The armed forces moved quickly to seize control of the country. In contrast to the 1960 and 1971 military coups, which had taken place to force institutional change and reform, the goal of this action was to stabilize and rejuvenate the system created after those earlier episodes of military involvement in politics. Although the military eventually formed a Consultative Assembly to write a new constitution for what would become Turkey's "Third Republic," its first priority was pacifying the country.

The nation was put under martial law, and many people were arrested, particularly prominent political leaders. The cornerstone of national sovereignty of the Turkish Republic, the Grand National Assembly, was dissolved and its members excluded from political activity for several years. Whole political parties were abolished, trade unions purged, and strikes banned. Approximately 30,000 people were said to have been arrested just after the coup. One year later, 25,000 were still in custody, and there were still 10,000 being detained two years later, some held without charges. As a reaction to the severity of this crackdown, the European Community suspended all financial assistance to Turkey, and the Council of Europe refused to seat Turkish delegates in its assembly.

The Turkish economy performed significantly better in the first two years after the coup than it had for many years. The new rulers kept Turgut Ozal in their government, and he made sure that Demirel's economic stabilization program would continue. Because of strict budget-tightening measures, Turkey's inflation rate dropped to only 30 percent by 1982. Ozal's strict monetarist policies put the Turkish economy on a free-market, free-trade path, radically different from anything it had experienced since the founding of the Turkish Republic. This new vision has continued to guide the Turkish economy to the present, through an era of significant political and social change.

IRAN AFTER WORLD WAR II

Mosaddeq Nationalizes Iran's Oil

In Iran, during and after World War II there were increasing demands for the nation to be freed from foreign influence and domination. The immediate postwar years marked the time when Mohammad Reza Pahlavi, the young ruler installed by the British during the war, came into his own as a real leader. He introduced Iran's First Development Plan (1948–1955): one of the clearest descriptions of what the nation needed to do to use its oil wealth most effectively.

The British government still received far more direct income from the Anglo-Iranian Oil Company (AIOC) than Iran: a situation that Iranian nationalists found hard to reconcile. Through the 1940s, more supporters of renegotiating the oil agreement were elected to parliament. Recent deals signed by Saudi Arabia with its oil concessionary company, ARAMCO, and Venezuela with its concessionary company,

Mohammad Mosaddeq (around 1951)

Standard Oil, gave Saudis and Venezuelans a 50-percent share of oil profits. Because the British were used to getting their way in Iran, they continually rejected a more equitable distribution of oil revenues there.

Subsequent negotiations between the AIOC and the Iranian parliament did not achieve success. General Ali Razmara, who had been made prime minister in June 1950 at the behest of the British, had not proven a good intermediary between the parliament and the AIOC. When the company final presented a fifty-fifty profit-sharing deal in February 1951, nationalist feeling in the country and in the parliament had risen to such a pitch that popular sentiment in favor of nationalizing the oil industry had become nearly unstoppable. Soon thereafter, Razmara advised against nationalization, arguing that Iran did not then possess the requisite technical skill to administer the oil concession effectively by itself. He was assassinated in March 1951 by an Islamic activist from a militant group called Fadayan-e Islam (those who sacrifice themselves for Islam). In that same month, the Iranian parliament passed legislation to nationalize Iran's oil industry. Mohammad Reza Shah, giving into political pressure and street demonstrations, appointed the staunch nationalist Mohammad Mosaddeq as prime minister in April.

The British lost no time in responding to this challenge. They brought Iranian output to a virtual standstill, withdrawing their technicians and imposing a worldwide embargo on the purchase of Iranian oil. In September 1951, Britain froze Iran's assets in the UK and banned all exports of goods to Iran. When Britain disputed the legality of Iran's oil nationalization before the International Court of Justice at The Hague, that court ruled in favor of Iran.

This prompted the AIOC to present another profit-sharing offer to Iran on better terms than ever before. The strong nationalist feelings stirred up by the confrontation, combined with Iran's general anti-British feeling at that time, agitation by activists, and a shared belief among Mosaddeq's inner circle that the British would ultimately accept Iran's maximum demands, led the Iranian government to reject any new British offers. This caused substantial economic stress when Iran's economy began to decline after the loss of foreign exchange and oil revenues.

Mosaddeq's open defiance of Britain resulted in a huge and sudden surge of popularity for him, but also created great friction between him and the shah. In the summer of 1952, Mosaddeq resigned when Mohammad Reza Pahlavi refused his demand that the Iranian prime minister be allowed to appoint the minister of war himself (and thus control the armed forces). This caused three days of pro-Mosaddeq rioting. The unrest compelled the shah to beg Mosaddeq to return, but the confrontation lessened Mohammad Reza's personal prestige among his subjects.

Upon reinstatement, Mosaddeq adopted a more dictatorial approach to governing as revenues continued to drop and the economy suffered more. In August 1952, the parliament granted him full governing powers for a six-month period, which it later extended. As support for him in parliament diminished rapidly with the worsening economic situation, Mosaddeq pushed through a referendum on August 3, 1953, on the question of whether the parliament ought to be dissolved entirely. He did close it down after claiming a resounding vote in favor of this proposal.

Although President Truman had at first been supportive of Iran's nationalist aspirations, the Eisenhower administration (which took office in January 1953) agreed more with the view of events being promoted by the British. This held that there could be no possible reasonable compromise with Mosaddeq due to his close alliance with Tudeh (the Iranian Communist Party) and that his personal consolidation of power was making a communist takeover in Iran more and more likely.

In June 1953, the United States agreed to collaborate with the British in an operation to overthrow Mosaddeq code-named "Ajax." Kermit Roosevelt, an agent of the new U.S. Central Intelligence Agency (and Theodore Roosevelt's grandson), carried out a clandestine mission in Iran to permit the shah and the Iranian military, led by General Fazlollah Zahedi, to remove Mosaddeq from power. When the shah appointed Zahedi to replace Mosaddeq as prime minister on August 13 (following the secret plan), Mosaddeq refused to step down. Instead, he arrested the shah's messenger. This reaction set in motion the second plan of Operation Ajax: a military takeover. At first, when this scheme did not seem to be working, the shah lost his nerve, fled to Rome, and General Zahedi went undercover.

After four days of rioting (which had been strongly supported and encouraged by Roosevelt and his team), the tide turned. On August 19, pro-shah army units and street crowds prevailed over Mosaddeq's forces, permitting the shah to come back to Iran and Zahedi to emerge from hiding. Mosaddeq at that point was arrested, tried, and sentenced to three years in prison for attempting to overthrow the monarchy, but was kept under house arrest in his native village near Tehran until he died in 1967. Hundreds of his close political associates as well as National Front and Tudeh political activists were imprisoned and some put to death.

AFTER MOSADDEQ: IRAN AS FRIEND OF THE UNITED STATES

In the wake of this upheaval and in order to counter Iran's economic difficulties, the U.S. government sent Iran $45 million in immediate economic assistance. Although the Iranian government restored diplomatic relations with Britain in December 1953, an entirely new oil agreement was created in 1954 that replaced the Anglo-Iranian Oil Company (now renamed "British Petroleum" [BP]) as sole concessionary agent with a consortium of several companies: an arrangement in which BP now only had a 40 percent share. The shah, fearing internal opposition, sought to bolster his regime by becoming a major strategic partner of the United States in the Cold War on Russia's southern frontier, and joined the Baghdad Pact (to form part of the organization known as CENTO) in 1955 along with Iraq, Turkey, and Pakistan. Iran and the United States signed a multifaceted, long-term defense agreement in 1959, expanding further a major U.S. presence in the country that began to take root in the late 1940s.

In this Cold War setting, relations with the Soviet Union were correct but not friendly—Iran always remaining wary of the potential for the Russians to intervene militarily in its affairs as they had done so many times before. To secure his own hold on power, the shah suppressed the Tudeh, Mosaddeq's National Front, and many other political parties. He curbed press freedoms, exercised close control over parliamentary elections in 1954 and 1956,

and began to appoint a series of prime ministers who would follow his orders. Perhaps most importantly he strengthened his secret police. In 1956, it was renamed the Organization for National Intelligence and Security with the Persian acronym: **SAVAK**. SAVAK was trained at first by a team of career U.S. CIA agents, later replaced by trainers from the Israeli intelligence service Mossad.

Economic recovery from the upheaval of the oil nationalization happened slowly. The sudden infusion of oil money upon the resumption of production created huge inflation, while severe restrictions on free speech and political activity closed off outlets for expressing discontent. Parliamentary politics became a sort of game after 1957, when, upon ending the state of martial law in force since 1953, the shah had two of his senior officials form a majority party and a loyal opposition party as the basis for a two-party system. These groups were called the *Melliyun* (Nationalist) and *Mardom* (Peoples') parties. Such officially created artificial organizations proved completely unsatisfactory for actual political representation, and this new system could not suppress a growing suspicion among the people that fraud and corruption were on the rise across Iran.

Ali Amini and the White Revolution

Faced with increasing domestic discontent and under pressure from the new U.S. administration led by John F. Kennedy, the shah chose Ali Amini, a wealthy landlord and senior government official considered a proponent of reform, to become his prime minister in May 1961. In order to facilitate his ability to govern effectively, the shah allowed him to dissolve the parliament entirely and rule by decree for six months.

Amini immediately instituted a number of important reforms by creating a freer press, as well as allowing suppressed parties such as the National Front to rejoin the political arena and arresting several former senior officials on

Hope, Bob/Mirrorpix/Newscom

Mohammad Reza Shah Pahlavi (December 1960)

corruption charges. Under his aegis, the Iranian government pursued a plan to reorganize the civil service, and in January 1962, approved a sweeping land redistribution law: the single most important measure of Amini's tenure in office.

Amini's government soon encountered many problems directly caused by the sweeping reforms that he tried to introduce. His economic reforms might have been deemed necessary for long-term prosperity, but they created more unemployment and economic hardship in the short term for the merchant and business communities. His attacks on corruption were resented by senior officials, and the independence of his government came to be seen as too great a challenge to royal authority. Finally, instead of being satisfied with the somewhat expanded freedoms and greater political liberalism brought in by Amini for the first time in many years, the National Front and

other opposition groups lobbied for even more reforms. Faced with a large budget deficit, the shah's refusal to cut the military budget, and a decline in support from the United States, Amini resigned in July 1962.

The three men who served as Iran's prime ministers for almost the entire remainder of the shah's reign—Asadullah Alam, Hasan Ali Mansur, and Abbas Hoveyda—were all close associates of Muhammad Reza Pahlavi, indicating how the shah, in the end, drew the reins of power close to himself and kept them there.

At first, he capitalized on the successful reception of Amini's land distribution program by holding a national referendum on six initiatives in January 1963. In addition to formalizing the land reform process, these included provisions for industrial workers to have profit-sharing in private companies, the legal recognition of traditional common lands through the nationalization of forests and pastureland, the sale of government-run factories to pay for land reform, changes in the electoral law to give more representation on governing councils to ordinary workers and farmers, and the creation of a Literacy Corps to allow young men to fulfill their military service requirement by teaching literacy in villages: a program inspired by the new U.S. Peace Corps. The shah labeled this collection of projects the **White Revolution**, and reported a 99 percent vote in favor of their implementation. In addition, the shah announced in February 1963 that women would henceforth be given the right to vote.

Although the 99 percent affirmative vote was clearly for show, these programs did generate a fair amount of support among certain social groups. They failed, however, to address Iran's biggest problems with sufficient speed. The rural poor still eked out a living under very difficult circumstances. There was also substantial opposition from provincial landholders to any land reforms, and Iran's Shii clerical establishment was concerned about changes in the status of women and non-Muslims that these reforms included.

In general, there was concern about the degree to which the White Revolution would increase the shah's power and authority.

Opposition to these changes found its voice in **Ayatollah Sayyid Ruhollah Musavi** Khomeini. Khomeini was a well-respected teacher at the Faiziye seminary in Qom who led clerical opposition to these reforms. He was arrested a few days after he gave an inflammatory speech against the White Revolution on the day of Ashura (June 3, 1963). In it, he compared Mohammad Reza Shah to the Umayyad Caliph Yazid (the ruler responsible for the death of the third Shii Imam Husayn, Ali's younger son, on that day). When Khomeini's arrest caused some of the most violent riots in Iran since the overthrow of Mosaddeq, the shah put them down with a huge show of force. Khomeini was kept in prison for several weeks, remaining under house arrest for several months more after that. Although it seemed at that time that the shah had decisively silenced his main opponent, this was only to be a brief respite.

Mohammad Reza Tries to Transcend Politics: 1964–1974

Iranian parliamentary elections in September 1963 signaled the creation of yet another new political group: the *Iran Novin* (New Iran) Party. This was an exclusive organization of senior civil servants, presented as committed only to a program of economic and administrative reform, renewal, and modernization. The National Front and other groups were not represented in these elections at all, since they were limited only to a very small group of officially approved parties and candidates such as *Iran Novin*. In March 1964, Mansur replaced Alam as prime minister, leading a government also staffed by members of *Iran Novin*.

The shah presented this as the way to rise above petty politics, to create a government both loyal to him and attractive to the growing number of Iranians being educated in technical and scientific professions both at home and abroad. *Iran Novin*'s participants were almost all from a select cohort of the younger generation of civil servants, Western-educated technocrats, and business leaders. According to the shah's vision, their leadership would replace the rough-and-tumble of traditional Iranian politics with harmonious economic planning. As long as rising oil prices kept the economy steadily improving and opportunities expanding, this approach was generally successful.

Among the few laws during this era to attract any real parliamentary opposition was the 1964 Status of Forces Bill. It offered diplomatic immunity for U.S. military personnel serving in Iran and their families. The measure allowed these Americans to be tried under U.S. rather than Iranian law for crimes committed in Iranian territory. This provided a humiliating reminder of the nineteenth-century capitulations imposed on Iran by European powers. There was sufficient opposition to the bill that sixty-five deputies abstained, and sixty-one opposed the bill when it came up for a vote: an unprecedented turn of events in such a closed political system.

The legislation stirred up strong emotions across the society. Khomeini, recently released from house arrest, gave a public sermon to a large audience in Qom in November 1964 in which he stridently attacked this measure. When tapes of this sermon and leaflets summarizing it went into wide circulation, Khomeini was again taken into custody, but was now exiled to Turkey. In October 1965, he was allowed to move to the Shii shrine city of Najaf, Iraq. He lived there for the next thirteen years, but stayed closely connected with his religious followers back home via the clandestine circulation throughout Iran of cassette tapes of his sermons as well as a constant flow of Iranian pilgrims to the Shii holy cities of Iraq.

The new prime minister, Mansur, attempted to address lingering budget problems created by the White Revolution through heavy new taxes on gasoline and kerosene and on exit permits for Iranians leaving the country. The lower classes opposed these new taxes since they used kerosene as their main heating fuel. When there were large-scale strikes, Mansur canceled the new taxes only six weeks after they had been imposed. Just at this time, a large new amount of cash flowed in from various petroleum projects, easing budgetary stresses considerably.

Such a new financial cushion helped Mohammad Reza Shah Pahlavi to preserve relative stability in the country despite Mansur's assassination in January 1965 by members of a radical Islamic group closely tied to Khomeini and an attempt on his own life made by a non-religious group a few months later. As Mansur's replacement, the shah chose another techno-crat, Amir Abbas Hoveyda, who had run the National Iranian Oil Company (NIOC) and helped create the *Iran Novin* party.

Hoveyda's appointment inaugurated a period of nearly ten years of impressive economic growth and political stability. In this period, Iran's rapidly growing economic and military strength gave the country more and more influence over its neighbors in the Persian Gulf region, and Hoveyda promoted good rela-tions between Iran and all of the nations around it. His twelve years as prime minister became the longest term of any of Iran's modern prime ministers. As a fulfillment of the shah's earlier plan, *Iran Novin* remained the dominant group in the government and the parliament, receiv-ing large electoral majorities in the elections of 1967 and 1971. Both elections were carefully managed by the authorities, who only per-mitted a few parties to run in them alongside *Iran Novin*. Among Hoveyda's lasting accom-plishments was his substantial increase in the number of institutions of higher education, bringing many students from rural and lower middle-class backgrounds into the new com-munity college system, and creating several new institutions of fairly high academic standing.

The late 1960s also witnessed substantive gains in women's status. This trend was encour-aged by the Iranian Women's Organization led by the shah's sister, Princess Ashraf. In 1967, a Family Protection Law was enacted to

reform marriage, divorce, and family law, but in accordance with a Shii rule that provisions can be added to the marriage contract that is part of any legitimate Islamic marriage. The new Family Protection Law now required that modernizing provisions, such as the rule that a husband could not take more than one wife without the first wife's consent, be included now in *all* marriage contracts. Similar modern-izing clauses with regard to divorce and child guardianship rules were to be included as a matter of secular law, but in a form that was religiously acceptable to Shii scholars. It is a testament to the success of this law in reinter-preting and modernizing norms of traditional Shii family law that it became one of the very first regulations formally abolished by the new Islamic Iranian government in 1979.

Despite promoting modernization initia-tives in numerous areas of Iranian life, the shah still had to deal with the ancient monarchical question of who his heir would be. He had remarried in 1959 (after two marriages that did not produce a son), and his new queen, Farah Diba Pahlavi, gave birth to a male heir, Reza, in 1960. In 1967, the shah standardized the process of royal succession, and finally cele-brated the achievements of his reign by staging a coronation ceremony for him and his queen, which had not been done at the time that he assumed the throne in 1941. Just as his father Reza Shah had done, he now placed the crown on his own head.

In 1971, the shah convened celebrations to mark 2,500 years of uninterrupted monarchy in Iran since the founding of the Persian Empire by Cyrus the Great: an occasion designed pri-marily to affirm the monarch's status as Iran's absolute and unchallenged ruler. The lavish Hollywood-style ceremonies held in the ruins of the ancient capital at Persepolis excluded most Iranians from attendance, while invited foreign heads of state and dignitaries were the main honored guests. A sermon by Khomeini condemning these celebrations and the regime received wide distribution. Later, there was also widespread feeling in Iran that the shah had insulted traditional sensibilities in 1975, when the parliament, at his behest, voted to alter the Iranian calendar so that years would be aligned henceforth with the first year of the reign of the ancient emperor Cyrus, instead of the beginning of the Islamic era.

None of this royal pomp and circumstance was as important ultimately as the fact that Iran experienced a long period of unprecedented and sustained economic growth in the late sixties and early seventies. The land distribution program launched in 1962, along with steadily expanding employment possibilities, a dramatic improvement in living standards, and the relatively low level of inflation between 1964 and 1973 all contributed to relative domestic political calm. There was dissent from opposition groups on the left and religious activists on the right, but this was effectively controlled by a growing and increasingly efficient secret police and security apparatus.

Mohammad Reza Pahlavi continued to expand Iran's role in Persian Gulf affairs. Along with the Saudis, he supported the royalists in the North Yemen Civil War and helped the sultan of Oman suppress a rebellion in the southwestern Omani province of Dhofar starting in 1971. The shah gave up any Iranian claims to Bahrain just prior to that nation's independence from Britain in December 1971. Upon Britain's withdrawal from the area, Iran occupied three islands, Abu Musa as well as the Greater and Lesser Tunbs, also still claimed by the **United Arab Emirates (UAE)**. Iran-Iraq relations remained unsettled up to 1975, when the two nations signed the **Algiers Agreement**. In it, Iraq consented to equal navigation rights for Iran in the Shatt al-Arab waterway, in exchange for which the shah agreed to stop supporting Kurdish rebels in northern Iraq.

To enhance Iran's role in the Gulf, the shah also used oil revenues to expand and equip his armed forces. His concept that Iran would become the main guarantor of Gulf security in the aftermath of Britain's withdrawal from the region paralleled President Nixon's visions for the area's future. The goal of the 1969 Nixon Doctrine was to encourage United States allies to shoulder greater responsibility for regional security. In this vein, Nixon took the unprecedented step while on a 1972 visit to Iran to announce that he would permit the shah to purchase *any* conventional weapon in the U.S. arsenal in whatever quantities the shah believed necessary for Iran's defense. U.S.-Iranian military cooperation broadened further when the United States was permitted to establish two listening stations in Iran in the early 1970s to monitor Soviet ballistic missile launches and other Russian military operations.

Political Opposition in the Late 1960s and Early 1970s

In the wake of the severe government crackdown on any political opposition after the June 1963 riots, little overt political dissent was possible in Iran. It became harder as well to sustain underground political opposition, given the success of the economy. In spite of this, opposition groups gradually reemerged as more violent new groups appeared, some of which were created by adherents of more radical Islamic ideologies.

The leadership of Tudeh, the Iranian communist party, remained in exile, forgoing a major role in Iranian politics until the Islamic Revolution of 1979. The National Front was sidelined because of various internal splits that sapped its strength. Its most prominent subgroup was the **Iran Freedom Movement (IFM)**. This small faction was led by Mehdi Bazargan, who sought to build ties to the moderate clerical opposition. Bazargan acknowledged the political relevance of Islam to the younger generation of his followers. One of the most important intellectuals connected with the IFM was **Ali Shariati**, a sociologist who promoted his vision of Islamic activism. His vision of Islam focused on it as a vehicle to promote political struggle, social justice, and the cause of the deprived classes in ways that resembled revolutionary calls to activism articulated in classic Marxist-Leninist thought.

Khomeini, although still in exile in Iraq, continued to issue denunciations of the Iranian government, to make personal attacks on the shah, and to rally his supporters. In a series of lectures delivered to students in Najaf between 1969 and 1970, later published in a book entitled *Velayat-e Faqih* (*The Guardianship of the Islamic Jurisprudent*), Khomeini argued that monarchy was anathema to Islam as a form of government, that sincere Muslims must strive for the establishment of an Islamic state, and that the leadership of the state rightfully belonged to the *faqih,* or Islamic legal scholar (jurisprudent), because of his ability to discern the true interpretation of holy scripture and law with greatest accuracy. A network of Shii clerics arose to promote Khomeini's ideas in Iran, spreading his message in particular via the medium of clandestine cassette tapes. Increasing difficulties in rural Iran during the early 1970s, combined with rising corruption and an increasingly skewed distribution of wealth, gradually won Khomeini a substantial number of sympathizers across the country.

Another very influential work of this period (although published a few years earlier and clandestinely in 1962) was Jalal Al-e Ahmad's *Gharbzadegi* (*Weststruckness/Occid entosis*). In this work, Al-e Ahmad described twentieth-century Iranians as "Weststruck" (*gharbzade*) with the dual meaning of being "stricken" (as if by a debilitating disease) by Western culture and materialism, but also "infatuated or intoxicated" by it (as if by a drug or alcohol). He compared *gharbzadegi* with cholera and frostbite, but also paralleled it to flies that infest wheat from within, leaving its surface looking healthy.[2] In his view, the only element of Iranian life not polluted by *gharbzadegi* was Shii Islam. Ayatollah Khomeini agreed with him in a 1971 attack on "the poisonous culture of imperialism [that was] penetrating to the depths of towns and villages throughout the Muslim world, displacing the culture of the Quran, recruiting our youth en masse to the service of foreigners and imperialists...."[3]

Some Iranian youth, disillusioned with the suppression of all legal opposition to the regime and attracted by the success of guerrilla movements in Cuba, Vietnam, and China, formed their own radical clandestine groups to pursue armed struggle. Almost all of these organizations were eventually infiltrated and destroyed by the shah's security forces, but two kept going longer than others: the *Fadayan* (*Cherikha-ye Fadayan-e Khalq* or "Detachments of those who sacrifice for the People"), and the *Mojahedin* (*Mojahedin-e Khalq,* or "Holy Warriors of the People"). These two movements differed ideologically but were quite similar in their methods. The *Fadayan* were politically Marxist-Leninist, while the *Mojahedin* used an Islamic basis for their political and economic struggles. Both groups attacked police stations; bombed foreign diplomatic offices; as well as assassinating government officials and U.S. military personnel, but neither was able to become more than a marginal extremist group until the Islamic Revolution of 1979.

Fundamentally, Iran's prosperity through the 1960s and 1970s was based almost entirely on its continuously and gradually increasing oil revenues. Iran's political stability at this time depended on having an effective security service to stifle dissent, combined with the ability to harness the efforts of a technocratic elite educated abroad. The cataclysmic challenges that this system would suddenly experience in the late 1970s remained unanticipated during the early years of that decade—perceived neither by ordinary Iranians, for whom things were proceeding well enough to remain hopeful about the country's gradual improvement, nor by foreigners, most of whom were involved in aspects of the country's rapid modernization programs.

---

[2]Roy Mottahedeh, *Mantle of the Prophet* (Oxford: Oneworld Publications, 2008), 296.

[3]Ayatollah Ruhollah Khomeini, *Islam and Revolution: Writings and Declarations of Imam Khomeini*, trans. Hamid Algar (Berkeley: Mizan, 1980), 195.

Questions to Think About

1. How did Turkish politics change just after World War II?
2. How did Turkey become more aligned with the United States, the UN, and NATO in the 1950s?
3. What impact did the Cyprus issue have on Turkish foreign and domestic politics in the 1950s?
4. Why did the Turkish military mount a coup in 1960?
5. What was the *Gastarbeiter* program, and how did it affect Turkey?
6. Why did Turkish democracy experience a crisis in the 1970s?
7. What were the causes and consequences of the Turkish military invasion of Cyprus in 1974?
8. Why did Turkey experience large economic problems in the 1970s?
9. How did the issue of nationalizing the oil industry become an important political question for Iran after World War II?
10. What role did the United States play in dealing with Mosaddeq and the nationalization of oil in Iran?
11. How did the shah reestablish his control of Iran after the oil nationalization issue?
12. What was the White Revolution, and how was it received in Iran?
13. Who was Ayatollah Khomeini and why did he attack the shah?
14. What would be the best form of government, in Khomeini's view?
15. How did women's legal status in Iran change under the shah?
16. Who was Ali Shariati?
17. Why did Jalal Al-e Ahmad perceive modern Iranians as "Weststruck"?
18. Who were the *Mojahedin-e Khalq*?

For Further Reading

Ahmad, Feroz. *The Turkish Experiment in Democracy, 1950–1975*. Boulder, CO: Westview Press, for the Royal Institute of International Affairs, London, 1977.

Al Aḥmad, Jalal, R. Campbell, and Hamid Algar. *Occidentosis: A Plague from the West*. Berkeley: Mizan Press, 1983.

Ansari, Ali M., and Ali M. Ansari. *Modern Iran: The Pahlavis and After*. Harlow: Longman, 2007.

Dodd, C.H. *The History and Politics of the Cyprus Conflict*. Houndmills, Basingstoke, Hampshire: Palgrave Macmillan, 2010.

Gül, Murat. *The Emergence of Modern Istanbul: Transformation and Modernisation of a City*. London: Tauris Academic Studies, 2009.

Katouzian, Homa. *Mosaddeq and the Struggle for Power in Iran*. London: I.B. Tauris, 1999.

Kinzer, Stephen. *All the Shah's Men: An American Coup and the Roots of Middle East Terror*. Hoboken, NJ: J. Wiley & Sons, 2003.

Landau, Jacob M. *Radical Politics in Modern Turkey*. Leiden: Brill, 1974.

Rahnama, Ali. *An Islamic Utopian: A Political Biography of Ali Shari'ati*. London: I.B. Tauris, 1998.

Stern, Laurence M. *The Wrong Horse: The Politics of Intervention and the Failure of American Diplomacy*. New York: Times Books, 1977.

Tamkoç, Metin. *The Warrior Diplomats: Guardians of the National Security and Modernization of Turkey*. Salt Lake City: University of Utah Press, 1976.

VanderLippe, John M. *The Politics of Turkish Democracy: Ismet Inönü and the Formation of the Multi-Party System, 1938–1950*. Albany: State University of New York Press, 2005.

Vasileiou, Giorgos. *From the President's Office: A Journey towards Reconciliation in a Divided Cyprus*. London: I.B. Tauris, 2010.

18

From Six-Day War to October War

Israel's swift and decisive victory in the Six-Day War gave it control of an enormous amount of new territory, but left all of the underlying issues of the conflict completely unresolved and created many new problems. The Arab summit held in Khartoum had agreed on an agenda of "no recognition, no peace and no negotiations with the State of Israel," but this common statement of purpose masked major political realignments taking place across the Arab world immediately after the war.

Among the Palestinians alone, there were considerable readjustments. Just after the end of the war, Nasser proclaimed Arafat "leader of the Palestinians." In December, there was a new chairman chosen for the PLO, Yahya Hammuda, who brought Arafat and his guerrilla group Fatah into the PLO's Executive Committee, in which Fatah was now given one-third of the seats.

KARAMEH AND THE RISE OF ARAFAT

After its victory, Israel launched military operations against Palestinian militants to stop the series of attacks that Palestinian groups had been launching before, during, and after the war. The focus of the Israeli counterstrike was the village of Karameh in Jordan, site of a Palestinian refugee camp as well as Fatah headquarters. Coincidentally, *karameh* in Arabic also means "dignity," offering to the site a certain symbolic meaning after the recent military disaster.

When other militant groups, such as the new "**Popular Front for the Liberation of Palestine**" (PFLP) recently set up by George Habash, heard rumors that the Israelis were going to move against the town, they left. When Arafat's aides advised him to flee too, he was reported to have declared, "We want to convince the world that there are those in the Arab world who will not withdraw or flee" and ordered his men to stay (with the assurance that Jordanian forces would come to their aid if necessary). On March 21, the IDF mounted a substantial assault on Karameh using armored tanks, heavy artillery, and fighter aircraft. Fatah soldiers stood their ground, forcing the Israelis to strengthen their efforts. When this prompted the intervention of Jordanian regular units, the Israelis chose to retreat.

When the shooting stopped, almost two hundred Palestinian and Jordanian soldiers and twenty-eight Israeli soldiers had been killed. In spite of its greater losses, Fatah claimed this battle as a victory because it had forced Israeli forces to retreat. Although Arafat's exact role in leading this battle was unclear, he received credit from his followers for his presence there. The Battle of Karameh became a significant indication of his growing reputation among the Palestinians and bolstered his status across the Arab world.

In practical terms, this meant much greater financial support for Fatah as well as larger donations of weapons and equipment from Arab countries. Significant numbers of young Arabs, even those not of Palestinian origin, joined Fatah. In February 1969, Arafat became chairman of the PLO: a post in which he then remained until his death in 2004, assuming numerous other leadership responsibilities within the organization over the next few years to secure control of it.

BLACK SEPTEMBER

Israel's inability to deliver a decisive blow against Palestinian militant forces in the months following the Six-Day War gave militant leaders, particularly Arafat, the feeling that irregular tactics might be the road to success. This increasing militancy put a big strain on Jordanian–Palestinian relations, because Palestinian groups in Jordan now started to create their own autonomous zones there as a state within a state. After the success of Karameh, Fatah guerillas began to set up roadblocks, challenge Jordanian police forces, and levy their own taxes.

Although King Hussein saw such behavior as a direct threat to his kingdom's sovereignty and attempted to disarm the militias, he was very anxious to avoid open confrontation with them. He offered an extraordinary olive branch when he even invited Arafat to become Jordan's prime minister at one point. By this time, Arafat was totally focused on building stature among the Palestinians and turned him down.

Palestinian Refugee Camp in Jordan (April 1969)

Terry Fincher/Photo Int/Alamy

Such gestures were not able to stem the tide of quickly rising militancy in Jordan, particularly among groups such as the PFLP, which adopted a considerably more radical approach than Fatah. The PFLP, in fact, was now moving beyond the basic agendas of Palestinian nationalism as championed by Fatah and most member organizations of the PLO. The PFLP soon evolved into one of the militant organizations promoted by the Soviet Union in the late 1960s, whose main goal was to incite Communist revolutions around the world. It thus broadened its potential range of targets, most spectacularly with an infamous series of plane hijackings.

Its first big action occurred on September 15, 1970, when it hijacked five European and American commercial jetliners, landing three of them at an airfield thirty miles east of Amman. PFLP militants took all the passengers off and then blew up three of the planes. The impact of this action was largely negative for Arafat, since he was now held accountable for the deeds of more radical Palestinian factions such as the PFLP, which were loosely under the PLO's aegis. For his part, King Hussein took the opportunity to reestablish authority over Jordan and declared martial law. Arafat was then appointed supreme commander of the PLA (the PLO's military wing) and armed conflict between the Jordanians and Palestinians ensued.

Various Arab leaders intervened to restore peace. As his last act of diplomacy, Gamal Abdel Nasser convened an emergency Arab League summit in Cairo on September 21, but this failed to resolve the problems between the Palestinians and King Hussein. Nasser himself suffered a fatal heart attack a short time after the summit ended.

The next few days saw substantial fighting between the Jordanian army and Palestinian forces. The Jordanians reestablished control by September 25, and within two days Arafat and Hussein signed a cease-fire agreement. In this short period of fighting, thousands of Palestinians died, creating a level of tension that soon eroded the effects of this cease-fire. In June 1971, Hussein ordered the Jordanian army to remove all remaining Palestinian forces from northern Jordan. Arafat and about two thousand of his followers initially fled to Syria, but because of tensions between him and Syrian leader **Hafez al-Assad**, the Palestinian group eventually was allowed into Lebanon, where they joined PLO forces already in place and set up a new headquarters in Beirut.

INTERNATIONAL TERRORISM

Arafat secured control of the situation by relocating his whole organization to a new country. As the more militant sections of the PLO continued their global scope of terrorist activities, he was obliged to portray himself more and more stridently as a revolutionary leader to retain legitimacy as the PLO's chairman. Several incidents in 1972 became hallmarks of the PLO's new international militancy: the hijacking of Sabena flight 571, the Lod Airport massacre, and the Munich massacre.

In early May 1972, a new subgroup of Fatah calling itself "**Black September**" (in memory of the Jordanian-Palestinian clash of September 1970) hijacked a Belgian airliner on its way to Vienna, forcing it to land at Ben Gurion Airport in Lod, Israel. There was relatively little loss of life because Israeli commandos intervened quickly. The PFLP and the Japanese Red Army next conducted a shooting spree now known as the Lod Airport Massacre at the same airport on May 30, killing twenty-four civilians. A few months later at the 1972 Olympic Summer Games, members of Black September abducted and put to death eleven Israeli athletes. Uncertainty has lingered regarding how closely Arafat was involved in these operations, but it has been fairly well substantiated that he authorized the Munich operation and at least knew its general plan.

This event had an enormous media impact. Because of the popularity of the Olympic Games, substantial viewing audiences around the world followed the drama as hostages were taken and transported with their captors to a NATO airport in military helicopters, where an attempt to free them was made and failed, with all hostages being killed. The Munich crisis can also be seen as the beginning of modern counterterrorism techniques that grew out of investigations of this incident. The negative publicity was so great, in fact, that Arafat eventually suppressed the Black September group and commanded the PLO not to carry out any terrorist acts of violence against targets outside of Israel, the West Bank or the Gaza Strip.

He was not able to suppress all such operations. In March 1973, a group of Black September operatives killed five diplomats and five other people at the Saudi Embassy in Khartoum, Sudan—an operation Arafat was accused of having approved. However indirectly, he still supported these organizations and therefore could not be said to have abandoned terrorism totally. The effectiveness of terrorism as a way to advance the Palestinian cause has continued to be a subject of intense debate. It is undeniable that these activities garnered such media attention that to prevent them in future, law enforcement agencies around the world began to study how to develop effective counterterrorism strategies.

WAR OF ATTRITION

Alongside the emergence of terrorism as an unconventional military strategy used by Palestinians after the Six-Day War, the conventional military confrontation still continued (although at lower intensity) even after Arab states had accepted a cease-fire with Israel.

Despite this, there were diplomatic indications of a shift in the agendas of different Arab nations. Nasser had accepted UN Resolution 242 in November 1967. Resolution 242 called for Israel's withdrawal from "territories" that it had occupied in war, without precisely specifying which territories this meant. Notwithstanding the uncertainties

of its diplomatic language, Nasser's mere acceptance of this resolution signaled that he was now ready to negotiate the Palestinian issue, instead of using it merely as a rallying cry for Arab unity.

Nasser was also committed to building better relations with moderate Arab countries, including Jordan, Saudi Arabia, and Arab states of the Persian Gulf following the **Khartoum summit**, since he had now begun to accept financial support from many of them. On the other hand, his traditional allies in the Pan-Arab cause, including Syria, Iraq, Algeria, and the PLO, stood firm against any peace negotiations with Israel. This group now included Libya, where a junior Air Force officer, Muammar al-Qaddafi, led a 1969 coup modeled on Nasser's Free Officers' Movement to overthrow that nation's hereditary monarch King Idris I.

Faced with somewhat contradictory choices in dealing with Israel, Nasser decided in January 1968 to maintain, through a war of attrition, a constant level of military pressure on it but without reigniting overt hostilities. First, he ordered units to harass Israeli military positions east of the now-blockaded Suez Canal and allowed the Soviets to begin building several improved naval bases in Egypt. Two months later, after the Palestinian success at Karameh, Nasser invited Arafat to Cairo, where he offered Fatah financial and military support. He recognized Arafat formally as the leader of the Palestinian struggle against Israel, but expressed his desire for Arafat to think of an eventual peace with Israel that would include a Palestinian state in the West Bank and Gaza. To promote this idea internationally, Nasser traveled with Arafat in July to Moscow, where they met with the leaders of the Soviet Union. For Arafat, the most pressing issue at that time was his need to maintain credibility with the most militant subgroups of the PLO.

Israel responded swiftly to Egyptian assaults on its Sinai fortifications. It launched several bombing strikes along the Canal, forcing Egyptians to flee. To keep the situation from getting out of control, Nasser immediately halted all military operations, but rebuilt his defenses. He resumed another round of open hostilities in March 1969, just as he began receiving financial aid from the Gulf Arab states. By November, Nasser had arranged for the Palestinians to use Lebanese territory as a staging ground for attacks on Israel. He appointed Anwar Sadat as one of his vice presidents in December 1969, since his relationships with other members of Egypt's ruling elite had become strained.

To keep credibility in his dual roles as both warrior and peacemaker, Nasser, supported by King Hussein, accepted a new peace plan presented in June 1970 by the U.S. secretary of state, William Rogers. Because it called for Israel to withdraw from areas it had taken in the Six-Day War, without any guarantees of lasting peace from Arab states, the Israelis refused even to begin discussions about it. Later in 1970, any potential diplomatic breakthroughs became totally overshadowed by the Black September confrontation between the Jordanians and the Palestinians.

SADAT ASSUMES POWER

Following Nasser's fatal heart attack, which happened just hours after the end of a conference he had convened to restore peace between Jordan and the Palestinians, Vice President Anwar Sadat succeeded him as Egypt's leader on October 5. Sadat shifted his focus away from promoting Pan-Arab unity to restoring Egypt's own identity and regaining territory it had lost in 1967. Through careful but deliberate steps, Sadat began to move away from Nasserism as an ideology and a plan for action, which alienated many Egyptians from him.

Sadat did not end the war of attrition, since it preserved the option of an immediate escalation to full-scale hostilities if necessary. Its continuous low level of military operations kept a constant low level of military tension in the area around the Canal, but this also maintained a state of readiness within the Egyptian armed forces. The level of military friction there was

also inadvertently increased by complacency on the Israeli side, created by the completion in late 1969 of the **Bar Lev Line**: a system of fortifications built by Israel on the eastern side of the Canal designed to thwart any Egyptian land attack.

The Line (constructed at a cost of $300 million) began with a huge continuous sand wall twenty to twenty-five meters high, backed up by a concrete barrier that ran along almost the entire Canal. Its goal was to prevent penetration by any armored or amphibious units without a substantial engineering breach, which Israeli intelligence experts predicted Egypt was incapable of doing quickly enough. The next barrier was a line of small fortifications, each manned by infantry platoons and a few tanks. Between these were placed barbed wire and fields of mines sunk deep into the ground. Finally, this was backed up by strongholds built along sandy hills five to eight kilometers behind the canal that each could hold a company of infantry. As a culmination, the Israelis put in a system that could pump crude oil directly into the Suez Canal, which would then be lit and made into a sheet of flame on the Canal's waters.

Defensive plans were created in which the Bar Lev Line could be held at all costs for the first forty-eight hours of any conflict. The Egyptian General Staff devoted large amounts of time and resources to figure out how to penetrate this system. Since Israeli commanders believed it to be an insurmountable obstacle for the Egyptians, the Bar Lev Line encouraged a sense of security. In fact, the steady pressure on Israel caused by the war of attrition was largely mitigated by the creation of the Bar Lev Line. With the Line in place, Sadat perceived that the strategic situation now worked against him. It became more and more obvious that Israel could not be forced, through diplomatic negotiations, to withdraw to its pre-1967 borders, but would have to be compelled to do so militarily.

Sadat reckoned that Egypt's situation in any final settlement with Israel could be improved by even partial military success against it. He perceived that achievement of some sort of victory against Israel was the best way for Egypt to restore its national honor, perceived to have been lost in 1967. Finally, because Sadat was poised to dismantle many aspects of Nasser's Pan-Arabist, socialist program, he sensed that a military victory would give him a positive standing among the people that could allow him to carry out otherwise unpopular reforms.

Syria's new ruler, Hafez al-Assad, also favored a military option but for different reasons. He saw the retaking of the Golan Heights as a fundamental Syrian national strategic goal, and had been carrying out a massive rearmament program with Soviet assistance to prepare for that eventuality. Assad believed that if Egypt and Syria could mount a coordinated attack on Israel in which Syria could swiftly retake the Golan Heights, this would push Israel to negotiations and force it to give up the West Bank and Gaza as well as offer other concessions.

For its part, Jordan had no desire for any further military encounters with Israel, fearing further losses of territory and more instability, but Sadat managed to win the support of many other Arab nations for a renewed military approach. He also began a massive rearmament program in 1972, receiving large shipments of new planes, missiles, and other equipment from the Soviet Union. Sadat strove to overhaul his military planning by introducing Soviet battlefield tactics into his preparations. He also fired generals whom he saw as too political and whom he held responsible for the 1967 defeat, replacing them with commanders he considered more competent.

The perspective of Nasser's Soviet patrons now diverged significantly from the views of their Egyptian allies. The Soviets were increasingly wary of a new Arab-Israel war, lest this spark a nuclear confrontation with the United States. Serious negotiations over nuclear arms reduction in the process later labeled détente were getting underway in earnest, and

neither the Soviets nor the Americans wanted the Arabs or the Israelis to get in the way of this larger diplomatic process.

This Egyptian-Soviet divergence in strategic goals rapidly became too great to ignore. When Egyptian intelligence found out that the Soviets were getting too much information about Egyptian preparations for a surprise move against the Canal, Sadat expelled most of the Soviet Union's 20,000 military advisers in Egypt. He redirected his country's foreign policy to move somewhat closer to the United States, although the Syrians remained closely aligned with the Soviet Union.

MOVES TOWARD WAR

In October 1972, Sadat told his generals that he planned to go to war with Israel even if the Soviets did not fully support him. He gambled that even limited military success against Israel offered the best way to gain future negotiating room in a final settlement of the conflict. He started covert planning for this in 1971, but informed his major commanders of the war plan just shortly before the attack.

He gave his plan to attack Israel jointly with Syria the code name "**Operation Badr.**" This name commemorated the Battle of Badr, first major victory of the Muslims in 624 over the Quraysh rulers of Mecca. In the first few months of 1973, Sadat made occasional verbal threats of war with Israel and had Arab armies conduct exercises. This brought the Israelis to high levels of alert a few times, but these were feints meant to convince Israel that all such Egyptian threats were mere rhetoric. This technique seemed to have worked, because the Israelis dismissed Sadat's threats as typical Arab brinkmanship.

Israel's leaders remained supremely confident that Israel's air force and defensive systems on its borders such as the Bar Lev line were more than adequate for its defense. Israeli intelligence analysts had begun to track the growing rift between the Soviet Union and Egypt, which they believed would greatly reduce the likelihood of an Arab attack and led them to dismiss other evidence of impending conflict. The Egyptians helped to reinforce such misinterpretations, producing a steady stream of incorrect information implying that they had big maintenance problems as well as personnel and equipment shortages.

Sadat selected the major Jewish holiday of Yom Kippur as an obvious time to initiate hostilities. This is virtually the only holiday when activities across Israel come to a complete halt. It is a day when both secular and religious Jews fast, stop driving, and do not use electricity or communications devices at all. This is also a day on which many soldiers are on leave, rendering Israel more open to attack. By coincidence, Yom Kippur in 1973 was also the ninth day of Ramadan, the Muslim month of fast and penitence. Paradoxically, beginning the attack on Yom Kippur helped Israel mobilize reservists, since they were at home, where they could quickly be contacted. In addition, the roads were relatively free of traffic, allowing them to get to the fronts more quickly.

King Hussein made clear at a summit meeting in September 1973 with Sadat and Assad that he could not take part in any renewed hostilities against Israel, because of the enormous risks this posed to Jordan's stability and even survival as a nation. On September 25, Hussein made a secret trip to Tel Aviv, where he personally warned Israeli Prime Minister Meir about an impending Syrian assault. Israeli intelligence analysts, though, discounted this warning as simply more evidence of a complex disinformation campaign being organized by Egypt and Syria.

Although the principal element in all Israeli strategic plans at that time for conflict with the Arab world was for Israel to launch a preemptive strike (reminiscent of 1967), this option was rejected by the Israeli leadership in a meeting on the morning of Yom Kippur (October 6, 1973), out of fear of adverse international reaction and because intelligence reports did not point to an imminent Arab attack. At that meeting, Meir was reported to

have declared, "If we strike first, we won't get help from anybody."[1]

There was also the sense that a boycott by Arab oil-producing members of the OPEC oil cartel would have an enormously negative secondary impact on Israel, since many European countries had already curtailed military exports being sent there under threat of an oil embargo. The Israeli leadership understood its own total dependence on the United States for military supplies and saw anything that threatened this source as a major problem. The United States supported Israel's decision to avoid launching a pre-emptive strike, reaching out at this time to the Soviet Union to keep hostilities from breaking out, but diplomatic efforts were too late.

OCTOBER WAR OF 1973

On October 6, 1973, Syria and Egypt commenced a surprise campaign against Israel that began on the Jewish holy day of Yom Kippur. The first great tactical surprise for the Israeli commanders that day was the speed with which the Egyptians broke through the Bar Lev Line. Their technique was to use water cannons that drew from the canal through hoses attached to dredging pumps. This technique reduced breaching times for the sand walls to less than two hours. Once many substantial breaches had been made, the Egyptians attacked the Bar Lev Line with two large ground forces. These ground troops received cover from 250 Egyptian planes and approximately 2,000 artillery pieces, and so were able to advance quite rapidly into the Sinai.

Shielded by this air support and artillery barrage, the Egyptian assault force of 32,000 Egyptian ground troops crossed over the Canal in various places through the afternoon in what became known in Arabic as *al-Abur* (the Crossing). They held their ground and

---

[1]Abraham Rabinovich, *The Yom Kippur War* (New York: Schocken, 2005), 89.

captured most of the Bar Lev forts within a few days. Despite suffering substantial casualties, Egyptian elite units fought extremely hard and caused considerable panic among Israeli units, which hindered their ability to focus on stopping the assault across the canal. Two relatively large units of Egyptian forces advanced a considerable distance into the Sinai desert, so that by the following morning, several hundred Egyptian tanks had crossed over the canal.

Israeli forces defending the Bar Lev Line were also relatively unprotected by Israeli aircraft, most of which had suddenly been called to defend against the Syrian invasion of the Golan Heights. Israel, which had been so effective in the air in 1967, saw the power of its air force in Sinai effectively curtailed in the initial phases of the 1973 conflict by Egyptian SAM missile units.

Egyptian preparations for this operation were unusually meticulous. Small groups of frogmen went out late in the evening on October 5 to block underwater openings to the Canal through which Israelis were planning to pump crude oil and start fires on the Canal's surface. The Egyptians not only succeeded in their initial breakthrough of the Bar Lev Line but were ready for the Israeli counterattack, deploying units carrying large numbers of portable antitank weapons. The coordinated Egyptian use of these weapons, in combination with the lack of Israeli planes, kept Israeli armored units from advancing very far at first.

After the initial breakthrough, Egyptian forces consolidated their hold on the town of Qantara. Their commando units thwarted several counterattacks of Israeli reservists over the next few days, but at the high cost of more than half of these highly-trained soldiers. Stable front lines had developed in the Sinai by October 9: the third day of fighting.

Three days later, Israeli intelligence received information suggesting that Egypt was planning a major new assault. Sadat, supported by some (but not all) of his commanders, now decided to try to seize the strategic Mitla and Gidi Passes along with the Israeli command center at Refidim. The goal was to reduce pressure on Syria (now on the defensive), since Israel would have had to transfer important units from the Golan to Sinai to take these sites back if they had been captured. Egyptian forces launched this attack on October 14, but an Egyptian commando unit brought in by helicopter to disrupt Israeli forces just as the main Egyptian units were advancing was quickly overcome by an Israeli reconaissance unit: a small but critical defeat that shifted battlefield momentum away from the Egyptians. Soon their whole plan fell apart. This encounter, later called the Battle of the Sinai, became a turning point in the Sinai campaign, since it allowed Israeli forces to break through a gap that had arisen between the Egyptian Second and Third Armies and move rapidly toward the Canal.

On the night of October 15, hundreds of Israeli paratroopers crossed the Canal on rubber boats and knocked out several Egyptian SAM batteries. By October 18, the Israelis had landed at least one division of troops on the west bank of the Canal—very troubling news for Sadat and his commanders. By the end of the war, which occurred just a few days later, Israelis had come within seventy miles of Cairo and secured control of 1,600 square kilometers on the Canal's western shore. Even this late in the hostilities, the Egyptians still held onto much territory on the east bank of the Canal, occupying around 1,200 square kilometers in Sinai itself.

Syria in the War

On the first day of fighting, the Syrian Army attacked Israeli forces in the Golan Heights with an overwhelming superiority of forces. This forced Israel to put every tank it had in the Golan Heights into combat at once. The Syrians also dropped a commando force behind Israeli lines to seize an Israeli installation on Mount Hermon, so the situation began with difficulties for Israel. However, mobilized reservists arrived at the Golan many hours before they were anticipated by the Syrians and went into action immediately.

The first day of battle was relatively successful for the Syrians with their overwhelming numerical advantage. Six hours after the attack began, Israel's first defensive lines were breached. One Syrian tank brigade reached a road running directly across the Golan straight to Nafah: a key crossroads that was also the Israeli headquarters in the area. That evening, a lone Israeli tank operator held this unit back for twenty hours in a running battle.

Over the next four days, a small Israeli tank unit defended the northern Golan and the Nafah headquarters against repeated Syrian attacks. At one point, a Syrian force from the southern Golan came right up to Nafah, but stopped advancing before going into the camp there. By October 8, Israeli reservists began to arrive at that front in sufficient numbers to halt the Syrian offensive. On October 11, Israeli units finally turned the tide and moved into Syria, advancing far enough to secure gun positions from which they would be able to shell the outskirts of Damascus if necessary.

This Israeli advance into Syria put enormous pressure on King Hussein, who desperately wanted to stay out of this war. In the end, he agreed to send an expeditionary force to Syria to help defend it. However, he still would not allow Israel to be attacked from Jordan itself, hoping that this would forestall any Israeli air attack on him. Although the Israelis did not attack Jordan in the end, this was mainly because their forces and resources were stretched so thin on the Egyptian and Syrian fronts. Then the Iraqis sent a detachment to Syria, and these combined Arab forces prevented any further Israeli advances. The remaining Syrian forces behind Israeli lines, a group of elite troops on Mount Hermon that had secured positions there on October 6, were finally dislodged by two Israeli commando units in an arduous battle that ended on October 22.

Global Context

Much more than the Six-Day War, the October War was a conflict in which the United States remained actively engaged in resupplying Israel, while the Soviet Union provided support for Egypt and Syria on a continuous basis throughout the war. At first, the United States expected the Israelis to establish control of the battlefield very soon, but by October 8, when Israel was having a variety of military and logistical problems, a feeling of crisis began to creep in. On that day, it was reported that Prime Minister Meir ordered tactical nuclear weapons to be made ready for use if necessary.

This was done in an easily detectable way, in order to send a clear signal of the gravity of the situation. When Henry Kissinger, the U.S. secretary of state, got word of this, President Nixon ordered an immediate American airlift to resupply all military equipment and weapons that Israel had lost so far, perhaps in an attempt to keep the Israelis from even contemplating any nuclear options. The first U.S. resupply airlift arrived on October 14, and U.S. assistance quickly mushroomed into a massive effort, whose total cost was then about US$800 million (US$3.91 billion in 2010 dollars).

UN Resolution 338

On October 22, the UN passed Resolution 338, which called for an immediate cease-fire. At this point, General Ariel Sharon's Israeli forces were still in the middle of their attempt to capture the city of Ismailia and to cut off the Egyptian Second Army. Other Israeli forces were just a few hundred meters away from cutting off the last road controled by the Egyptians that linked Cairo with Suez. In the southern area of operations, there was a patchwork of Israeli and Egyptian units across the battlefield, with no clear front lines. As units on both sides were trying to reassemble in preparation for a cease-fire, fighting did not stop.

Fighting was not ending despite the announcement of a cease-fire, and nine Israeli tanks were destroyed on the night that it was declared. Israeli ground commanders used continued skirmishes to keep moving southwards and seize a road to cut off the Egyptian Third army, still deployed east of the Canal. Israeli troops also tried to take the town of Suez, but were repulsed by the Egyptian garrison and some local militia forces there.

By October 23, when it became clear that the cease-fire was not taking hold, there was a round of very tense diplomacy in which the Soviet Union accused the Israelis of not complying with what they had agreed to do. At this time, Kissinger saw a diplomatic opportunity for the United States to claim credit for saving the Egyptian Third Army if all fighting could be halted immediately, and so he pressured Israeli commanders not to pursue this unit.

Threat of Nuclear Showdown

The diplomatic scramble to create a stable cease-fire continued for the next two days, resulting in the dispatch of a "very urgent" letter from Soviet leader Leonid Brezhnev to President Nixon in which he announced, "I will say it straight that if you find it impossible to act jointly with us in this matter, we should be faced with the necessity urgently to consider taking appropriate steps unilaterally. We cannot allow arbitrariness on the part of Israel."[2]

This constituted one of the clearest threats of direct Soviet intervention in an international conflict since the Cuban Missile Crisis of 1962. Nixon's response was reportedly to allow Kissinger (as secretary of state) to take whatever action was necessary. This showdown coincided exactly with the period of maximum stress on Nixon during the Watergate political crisis (which ultimately forced his resignation in August 1974). By this time, Nixon had plunged into such a psychological crisis that Kissinger was apparently forced to handle this predicament mostly on his own without involving the president directly.

Kissinger convened a group of senior officials including the director of the CIA, the secretary of defense, and the White House chief of staff to plan what to do next. This group produced a friendly, nonconfrontational response to Brezhnev dispatched in Nixon's name, but with a decision being made simultaneously to raise the nuclear alert status of U.S. forces up one level from DEFCON four to DEFCON three. Another message (with Nixon's signature) was then sent to Sadat, calling on him to cancel requests for more substantial Soviet help and threatening direct U.S. intervention if the Soviets got directly involved.

As a response to the changed U.S. defense posture, the Soviets put seven airborne divisions on alert with airlift capability, if it became necessary to send them to the Middle East. In addition, seven Soviet amphibious warfare ships were sent into the Mediterranean. When the Soviets found out about the American change in nuclear alert status, they were overwhelmed and ceased any further escalations and preparations. The Egyptians also agreed to the American request, dropping their request for possible greater Soviet assistance, so the immediate superpower crisis was defused.

End of the War

As in Egypt, the war showed no signs of slowing down in the north on the Syrian front, and a large air battle took place in the skies near Damascus on October 23. Word came of the UN cease-fire call just as Syrian forces, now augmented by detachments from Jordan and Iraq, were preparing for a massive ground strike on Israeli positions near Damascus. By this time, the Soviet Union had replaced most of Syria's tanks lost at the beginning of the war. Many of Assad's commanders argued that this attack should still go forward, while others countered that this would give the Israelis cover to continue their destruction of the Egyptian Third Army and allow them then to attack Syria with greater intensity. In the end, Assad announced that he would accept the cease-fire as well.

---

[2]Walter Boyne, *The Two O'Clock War* (New York: Thomas Dunne Books, 2002), 245.

The UN was compelled to pass another resolution (339) on October 24: a renewed call for the cease-fire already presented in Resolution 338. Even with this, fighting still did not totally cease, and military tensions remained very high. Facing continued Israeli advances, the Egyptian government sent Kissinger an unprecedented message that it would begin direct negotiations with the Israelis if Israel would allow nonmilitary supplies to reach its besieged Third Army and agree to a complete termination of hostilities.

At a press conference on October 25, Kissinger set the stage for subsequent Middle East diplomacy to resolve the Arab-Israeli conflict by announcing the formula known as "land for peace": "The problem will be to relate the Arab concern for sovereignty over the territories to the Israeli concern for secure boundaries. We believe that the process of negotiations between the parties is an essential component of this."[3] A short while later, the UN adopted its final statement on ending the October War, Resolution 340, after which a total cease-fire commenced in Egypt, but not in Syria, where a war of attrition continued at a low level until May 1974.

The first round of disengagement talks took place on October 28, at Kilometer 101 on the road between Cairo and the Suez Canal, and all Israeli troops had withdrawn from the western side of the Canal by March 1974. In the Golan Heights, Israel and Syria reached a disengagement agreement through Henry Kissinger's shuttle diplomacy by May 1974. It included an exchange of POWs, Israel's withdrawal to the 1967 lines, and the creation of a UN buffer zone. The negotiations to create these agreements marked the first direct public meetings between Arab and Israeli officials since armistices signed after the 1948 war.

---

[3]William Quandt, *Peace Process: American Diplomacy and the Arab-Israeli Conflict since 1967*, rev. ed. (Berkeley: University of California Press, 2001), 124.

REGIONAL IMPACT OF THE WAR

Overcoming the grave challenges posed by the initial coordinated Egyptian-Syrian surprise attack, Israel emerged at the end of the October War as the victor on all fronts in military terms. The striking Israeli victory, achieved even in the face of Arab armies successfully carrying out their best strategic plans, greatly increased Egypt's and Syria's inclination to avoid another conflict. Israeli achievements at the end of the war exposed important vulnerabilities in these regimes' hold on power in their respective countries. The outcome of the war created the basis for the peace process soon to take place between Egypt and Israel.

From a different perspective, the fact that Egypt and Syria enjoyed any success at all in their surprise attack on Israel became very important across the Arab world in healing the trauma of the sudden, shocking defeat in 1967. Arabs were able to feel somehow that their honor had been redeemed, even if Egypt and Syria experienced setbacks at the conclusion of hostilities. It was also easy enough for Arabs to credit Israel's striking recovery by the end of the war to the emergency help it had gotten from the United States.

Sadat created a new image for himself as the "**Hero of the Crossing**" [of the Suez Canal], with his bargaining position in any eventual peace negotiations with Israel now greatly improved. This increased popularity also gave him firmer control of Egypt, affording him the chance to enact difficult but necessary reforms. The impact of the conflict was not all positive. Despite capitalizing on the war to bolster his standing, Sadat also took action against commanders who disagreed with him. Assad, for his part, executed at least one subordinate for military failure, and another deputy who had been defeated in action against Israeli troops died under suspicious circumstances.

The public face of the war's memory in Arab countries was presented positively. October 6 became an Egyptian national holiday known as Armed Forces Day and was also made a holiday in Syria. Hosni Mubarak, who succeeded Sadat as Egypt's president, observed in 2006 that the war "breathed new life" into Egypt, characterizing initial Arab success in it as a way to reduce bitterness over the 1967 defeat.[4]

In contrast to generally positive feelings about the outcome of the war among many Arabs, Israelis often remembered it as a situation in which they barely escaped complete disaster. There was a strong feeling that Israeli leaders became too complacent after 1967. An official commission, which studied events before the war and the disasters of its first few days, recommended that several senior intelligence analysts and military commanders be dismissed for failing to identify military threats correctly. Although the commission exonerated Prime Minister Meir and Defense Minister Dayan for such failures, its critical report soon led to their resignations.

OIL EMBARGO

The most enduring effect of the October War worldwide was the 1973 oil embargo, which had a major impact on public awareness of energy sources and conservation. On October 16, 1973, OPEC announced its decision to raise the posted price of oil by 70 percent, to $5.11 a barrel. The next day, oil ministers announced a cut in production by 5 percent from September's output, with continued production cuts to follow over time in increments of 5 percent until their economic and political objectives were met, which included ending the October War in a just manner.

When President Nixon requested on October 19 that Congress appropriate $2.2 billion in emergency aid to Israel, including $1.5 billion in grants, Libya declared an embargo on all oil shipments to the United States. Saudi Arabia and the other OPEC states immediately

signed on to this initiative, with the result that the market price for oil shot up overnight to $12 per barrel. The world economy, already reeling at this time from the recent dismantling of the Bretton Woods international monetary system, plunged into a series of downturns and experienced high inflation over the next decade. The oil embargo, which lasted until March 1974, set off a search for new energy sources, encouraged energy conservation, and fostered a more restrictive monetary policy to fight inflation.

Substantial rapid increases in the price of oil also dramatically enhanced the wealth of oil-exporting nations. Oil-producing countries, long dominated by foreign oil companies, suddenly began to receive far greater profits from their most valuable exports. The traditional flow of capital in the world reversed as oil-exporting nations accumulated vast new wealth. Some of this income was given out as charity to underdeveloped nations, whose economies had been weakened by the combined effects of higher oil prices and lower prices for their own exports and raw materials. Much of this new abundance also became channeled into large arms purchase programs, raising tensions across the Middle East.

PLO AND THE WAR

Although the PLO had only a small contingent of troops fighting in the 1973 war alongside the Egyptians, the effects of the war on it were important, because it had to adjust its message to a new situation in which the Egyptians, in particular, had offered to begin direct negotiations with Israel. In 1974, the PLO leadership issued a Ten Point Program. This initiative offered an official Palestinian formula for compromise with the Israelis. It foresaw the establishment of a Palestinian national authority over every part of "liberated Palestinian territory," referring specifically to areas captured by Arab forces in the 1948 Arab-Israeli War (the present-day West Bank, East Jerusalem, and the Gaza Strip). This sign

---

[4]http://www.upi.com/Top_News/2008/10/06/Mubarak-reflects-on-1973-Yom-Kippur-War/UPI-59221223312625/ (accessed on August 28, 2010).

of the PLO's willingness to compromise at all with Israel caused such major discontent among several of the PLO's constituent factions that many of them, including the radical PFLP and **DFLP**, formed a "**Rejectionist Front**": a rival coalition designed to supplant the PLO and continue to promote the uncompromising agendas of the Khartoum Declaration of 1967s.

In the same year, the PLO became recognized by the Arab League as the "sole legitimate representative of the Palestinian people" and was admitted to full membership at the Rabat Summit. Arafat became the first representative of a nongovernmental organization to address a plenary session of the UN General Assembly. He also became the first speaker at the UN to wear a holster (although it contained no weapon). In a very theatrical manner, Arafat declared: "I come bearing an olive branch and a freedom fighter's gun. Do not let the olive branch fall from my hand."[5] His appearance there dramatically enhanced the visibility of the Palestinian cause internationally and built sympathy for it.

CONCLUSIONS

Overall, the war created a more realistic impression among Arab and Israeli leaders about the real way to negotiate peace. Both sides were left with much more accurate views of the strengths and weaknesses of their opponents. Myths that Sadat and Assad might have harbored about their abilities to engage in small, contained wars to achieve limited diplomatic objectives, as well as feelings that the Israeli leadership might have had about Israel's ability to detect and withstand any Arab moves against it were all totally dispelled as a result of what happened militarily in the various phases of the 1973 encounter. This was bolstered by a new Israeli public awareness of vulnerabilities, which, coupled with a popular Arab feeling that military honor with Israel had now been restored to counter the 1967 disaster, created a momentum toward discussing peace.

At the same time, this renewed feeling of confidence was conditional because victory had not been total. Forces in the Middle East that did not support peace with Israel under any circumstances began to regroup. In particular, Islamist forces, brutally suppressed by Arab nationalist regimes, found in the uncertain sense of achievement after 1973 an opening for ill will to coalesce against Sadat, Assad and their secular supporters. For the time being, their militancy was suppressed and managed by secular nationalists, but they gradually gained more followers.

Questions to Think About

1. What were the effects of the Six-Day War on Palestinian organizations?
2. What was Black September, and how did it affect Jordan and the Palestinians?
3. What was the PFLP, and what were its tactics?
4. Who was Yasser Arafat, and how did he rise to power?
5. What was the impact of the Munich massacre?
6. What was the War of Attrition?
7. How did Anwar Sadat change policies in Egypt when he took power there?
8. What was the Bar Lev Line, and why was it popular in Israel?
9. Why and how was Sadat successful at the beginning of the October War?

---

[5]Barry and Judith Rubin, *Yasir Arafat: A Political Biography* (Oxford: Oxford University Press, 2005), 72.

10. Why was it so difficult to reach a cease-fire at the end of the October War?
11. How did the superpowers get involved in ending the October War?
12. What was the local impact of the October War in the Middle East?
13. How was the October War connected to the 1973 Oil Embargo?

For Further Reading

Alexander, Yonah. *Palestinian Secular Terrorism.* Ardsley, NY: Transnational Publishers, 2003.

Amuzegar, Jahangir. *Managing the Oil Wealth: OPEC's Windfalls and Pitfalls.* London: I.B. Tauris, 2001.

Badri, Hasan, Taha Majdub, and Diya al-Din Zuhdi. *The Ramadan War, 1973.* Dunn Loring, VA: T.N. Dupuy Associates, 1977.

Cubert, Harold M. *The PFLP's Changing Role in the Middle East.* London: F. Cass, 1997.

Haykal, Moḥammad Hasanayan. *The Road to Ramadan.* London: Collins, 1975.

Herzog, Chaim. *The War of Atonement.* London: Greenhill Books, 2003.

Klein, Aaron J. *Striking Back: The 1972 Munich Olympics Massacre and Israel's Deadly Response.* New York: Random House, 2005.

Korn, David A. *Stalemate: The War of Attrition and Great Power Diplomacy in the Middle East, 1967–1970.* Boulder, CO: Westview Press, 1992.

Kurz, Anat. *Fatah and the Politics of Violence: The Institutionalization of a Popular Struggle.* Brighton: Sussex Academic Press, 2005.

Lippman, Thomas W. *Egypt after Nasser: Sadat, Peace, and the Mirage of Prosperity.* New York: Paragon House, 1989.

Rabinovich, Abraham. *The Yom Kippur War: The Epic Encounter That Transformed the Middle East.* New York: Schocken Books, 2004.

Rubin, Barry M., and Judith Colp Rubin. *Yasir Arafat: A Political Biography.* New York: Oxford University Press, 2003.

Sadat, Anwar. *In Search of Identity: An Autobiography.* New York: Harper & Row, 1978.

Sayigh, Yazid. *Armed Struggle and the Search for State: The Palestinian National Movement, 1949–1993.* Oxford: Clarendon Press, 1997.

Van Creveld, Martin. *Military Lessons of the Yom Kippur War: Historical Perspectives.* Beverly Hills: Sage Publications, 1975.

19

Arab Middle East in the 1970s

BREAKDOWN OF THE LEBANESE POLITICAL SYSTEM

Lebanon had experienced the same waves of political tension that swept over the rest of the Middle East in the 1950s and 1960s, but because of its relative stability, Beirut had been called the "Paris of the Middle East." It was seen as the capital of a tolerant, open, and substantially westernized society in which Europeans and Americans felt more at home than in other parts of the region. It was only after 1967 and the arrival of Palestinian leaders from Jordan in the early 1970s that Lebanon became a central area of conflict in larger regional upheavals. This façade of stability masked great underlying sectarian tensions, kept in check by the savvy political maneuvering of the nation's political leaders. The arrival of the Palestinian leadership in Lebanon following Black September was what really began to unravel this fragile peace.

Before this, Palestinian groups had used Lebanon as a secondary operations center for years, claiming many active members among the hundreds of thousands of Palestinian refugees living in camps there. Their activities in the 1950s and 1960s had always been carefully monitored and intermittently controlled by the Lebanese "Deuxième Bureau": a military security agency modeled on its French namesake. This organization was answerable directly to the Lebanese military commander-in-chief, a post always given to a Maronite Christian.

In 1969, as the result of an agreement brokered in Cairo by Nasser between Yasser Arafat and Emile Boustany, Maronite commander-in-chief of the Lebanese army at that time, a Palestinian group affiliated with the PLO was given jurisdiction over security in the UN camps of Palestinian refugees. In addition, Palestinians were formally acknowledged to have the right to pursue armed struggle against Israel. Now this agreement became the basis for the Palestinian leadership to begin to create in Lebanon the "state within a state" that it had tried (and failed) to establish in Jordan. Over time, this put enough additional pressure on Lebanon's delicate sectarian balance to destabilize the country's power-sharing system.

Some Lebanese groups began to see Palestinians as useful allies in the country's own internal political struggles. Many in the Muslim community, for example, saw joining with the Palestinians as a way to put pressure on Christians to abandon the 1943 Lebanese National Pact: the unwritten framework for the division of power between sectarian communities in Lebanon. Other activists envisioned making the Palestinians their allies in a push toward a more Pan-Arabist, socialist, and Nasserist vision of Lebanon.

All these ideas about how to use the Palestinians had their roots in tensions over the division of political power between Lebanon's numerous religious and ethnic communities. Many people, particularly Muslims, lobbied for a new census to be taken (since the last one had been conducted in 1932), which would alter the structure of power sharing, given the substantial rise in Muslim and decrease in Christian populations over the past few decades. The Christians (particularly the Maronites) saw such proposals as a direct attack on them.

In any case, tensions in Lebanon rose rapidly upon the arrival of armed Palestinian groups from Jordan. Through the 1970s, numerous Palestinian factions carried out a steadily increasing number of small raids across the border against Israeli civilian and military targets. With these Palestinian groups as their models, different Lebanese factions began to take power into their own hands, creating armed militias to carry the political battle into military struggles.

Within a few years, these groups became more powerful than the regular army, itself already very small and divided according to a fixed ratio between members of different religious communities. Members of the army, especially Muslims, began to leave and join the militias of their respective groups.

Given the sectarian character of armed groups, noncombatant civilians soon became prime targets. As violence became the norm, militias mutated into mafia-style gangs who turned to blackmail, extortion, and smuggling to raise money. Many began to receive subsidies from outside powers and frequently changed loyalties. With the collapse of central government and law enforcement, Lebanon finally evolved into a major center of illegal drug production and paper money counterfeiting, turning the Bekaa Valley into a major world hashish-growing zone.

Arrival of the PLO in Lebanon

Although the arrival of the Palestinian leadership in the early 1970s was a brutal shock to the fragile Lebanese political system, the actual seeds of the problem were planted just after the Six-Day War. As noted, Lebanon in 1969 had been forced to sign the Cairo Agreement, which permitted the PLO to launch attacks on Israel from Lebanese soil. Because this agreement also gave the PLO authority over Palestinian refugee camps in Lebanon, much of the southern part of the country fell totally under Palestinian control after its leadership's arrival: a completely unanticipated development.

As Palestinian guerrillas set up more bases in south Lebanon, their presence came to weigh heavily on the local villagers. Various Palestinian factions also took the law into their own hands, which became a source of deep resentment among the conservative Shii locals. The quick erosion of support for the PLO and its constituent groups was reminiscent of how the Palestinians had recently become unwelcome in Jordan.

When they first arrived, the PLO leadership and Arafat initially tried to avoid getting too closely involved in Lebanese sectarian struggles, but the militant agendas of affiliate groups such as the PFLP and DFLP again put pressure on the PLO to take sides, lest its revolutionary authenticity and credentials be questioned. Arafat began to link the PLO with a group called the **Lebanese National Movement** (LNM): an organization with Communist and Nasserist tendencies. The LNM was led by

Kamal Jumblatt, a Lebanese leader of Druze origin, and favored a nonsectarian, nonethnic approach to Arab unification. Its close ties with the PLO were based to a great degree on personal affinity between Jumblatt and Arafat.

Beginning of the Lebanese Civil War

A gradual increase in PLO activities launched from Lebanon against Israel, coupled with ever-growing PLO involvement in domestic Lebanese politics, brought the situation to a turning point in February 1975. At that time, some Palestinians became involved in a dispute between Muslim and Christian fishermen in the coastal city of Sidon. Local Muslim fishermen were afraid that a new Christian-owned fishing company would push them out, with the national government's support. The company's main patron was former president Camille Chamoun, a powerful Maronite Christian politician. When Sidon's mayor, a staunch Nasserist and Palestinian sympathizer, was shot in suspicious circumstances during a demonstration, armed clashes broke out between units of the Lebanese National Army, commanded by Christians, and armed groups of Pan-Arab activists seeking vengeance for the mayor. This later group was then joined by radical Palestinian militants loosely affiliated with the PLO who, as staunch Marxists, opposed the Lebanese government's actions on ideological grounds.

The situation rapidly descended into violence over the next few weeks, culminating in a shooting on April 13 that killed four people at a church service in Christian East Beirut. That service was being attended by another major Maronite leader, Pierre Gemayel, whose two bodyguards were killed (although Gemayel himself survived). Later that same day, Maronite gunmen ambushed a bus carrying Palestinians from Sabra and Shatila to the Tel Zaatar refugee camp and killed twenty-seven people. The attackers were members of the right-wing **Phalange Party**, whose name was reminiscent of extreme right-wing movements in Italy and Spain in the 1930s. The two attacks set off a series of armed strikes across Beirut that evening continued through the next few days: a set of confrontations later remembered as round one of the civil war.

At first, fighting took place between right-wing Maronite groups (principally the Phalange) and a loose confederation of leftists and activists supported by radical elements of the PLO. After the outbreak of actual hostilities, it became less and less clear that Lebanon's standing army, now commanded by a rightist Maronite general, could remain an honest broker in any efforts to restore the status quo. The Lebanese army was rapidly devolving into just another armed faction.

On December 6, 1975, later infamous as Black Saturday, four murdered Christian militiamen were found in an abandoned car in East Beirut. This prompted Phalangists to construct roadblocks across Beirut to check ID cards, killing those identified as Palestinians or Muslims. Other Phalangists took hostages and staged attacks on Muslims in East Beirut. Retaliations by Palestinian and Lebanese Muslim militias then caused several hundred more people to be killed, and the situation degenerated into continuous fighting.

Christian East Beirut, an area surrounded by a number of heavily armed Palestinian camps, fell under siege and experienced severe fuel and food shortages. Phalangist units and their Christian allies then retaliated by putting Palestinian camps under siege one by one and attacking them. In January 1976, Christians sacked the well-defended Karantina camp near Beirut harbor in an operation that killed about one thousand Palestinians. In retaliation, the PLO assaulted Damour on the coast, killing many Christians there and looting cemeteries, for which Maronites retaliated by laying siege to the Palestinian camp at Tel Zaatar. This upheaval led large numbers of civilians to seek refuge in areas controlled by their respective groups, gradually transforming East and West Beirut effectively into separate Christian and Muslim enclaves. The war grew from a

Palestinian-Maronite confrontation into a bigger sectarian conflict.

By June 1976, Maronite militias were on the verge of being defeated militarily by Palestinians and their Lebanese allies. This led the sitting Lebanese president, the Maronite Suleiman Frangieh, to request Syrian intervention, pointing out how Syria's economic prosperity depended upon Lebanon being stable. Syria complied with this request, but in supporting the Lebanese government, it was actually helping a regime now functioning more as a Maronite factional force than a national administrative body.

Syria paradoxically now was assisting the same faction in the emerging Lebanese conflict as Israel, which had also recently started giving military equipment and advisers to Maronite forces. Syria's political interests in intervening were totally distinct from Israel's, however. The paramount Syrian interest was to go after any Islamist sympathizers and allies of the Muslim Brotherhood in Lebanon. Their Muslim allies in Syria were perceived by the Baathist government there as one of the main internal threats to its control.

At first, the Syrian army secured the northern Lebanese city of Tripoli and the Bekaa Valley, imposing a cease-fire there. This intervention allowed Maronite forces to overcome the defenses of the Tel Zaatar camp, causing another mass killing in August, this time of several hundred Palestinian refugees.

By October 1976, the Arab League had secured a cease-fire. After this, Syria was allowed to keep 40,000 "peacekeeping" troops in Lebanon as an "Arab Deterrent Force," ostensibly to restore calm. Syria came to regard this as a blank check to keep troops stationed there for the next twenty-nine years, until 2005. The 1976 cease-fire was declared to be the end of the Lebanese Civil War, but produced at best only a temporary lull in the conflict.

None of the underlying issues driving participants were discussed, much less resolved. What did result was further consolidation of two broad coalitions dominant on different sides of Beirut. West Beirut became the stronghold for the PLO and its Lebanese militia allies, at that time drawn from Druze, leftist, and Sunni Muslim groups. East Beirut, combined with the Christian sector of Mount Lebanon, was given over to the Christians. The dividing line, running right through central Beirut, became known as the **Green Line**.

Through 1977, these coalitions evolved in very different ways. Christians became more and more consolidated under the Phalangists and their commander Bachir Gemayel in an umbrella group called the Lebanese Front. It was modeled on and designed to counter the leftist, Pan-Arab Lebanese National Movement created by Druze leader Kamal Jumblatt. In March 1977, Jumblatt was assassinated in an attack linked to the Syrians. This loss caused the Lebanese National Movement to lose momentum and devolve back into its disparate leftist, Shii, Druze, Sunni, and Palestinian components. Through these years, Syrian president Hafez al-Assad played a complex *realpolitik* game of targeted killings and shifting alliances to keep Lebanon slightly unstable in ways that benefited Syria.

PLO-Israel Struggle Resumes

The October 1976 cease-fire did nothing to address the continuing state of hostility between the PLO and Israel. Small operations against Israel had continued while the PLO consolidated its position in Lebanon. By 1978, large-scale attacks had resumed. One of the most infamous was the Coastal Road massacre of March 1978, in which about ten Fatah commandos landed on boats near the Coastal Road between Haifa and Tel Aviv in Israel. They commandeered a bus, killing thirty-seven Israeli civilians. As retaliation, the Israeli Army conducted **Operation Litani**: the temporary Israeli occupation of southern Lebanon up to the Litani River. This Israeli incursion prompted Arafat to move PLO forces north into the Palestinian stronghold of West Beirut.

As soon as Israeli forces withdrew, Palestinians resumed attacks on Israel, putting pressure on it to respond again militarily. A continuous string of incidents over the next few years kept tensions high in Lebanon, with PLO militants kidnapping Lebanese policemen and killing innocent civilians. Israel often responded to PLO strikes against it with massive and deadly reprisals, which ended up killing many non-Palestinian Lebanese civilians who just happened to be in the way.

As a buffer, Israel retained control over a 12-mile "security zone" on the Lebanese border. To police this, Israel used as its proxy the South Lebanon Army (SLA): a militia composed mostly of Christian soldiers. When PLO forces attacked the SLA, this gave Israel an excuse to carry out air raids on PLO bases and strengthen the SLA as its buffer force.

HAFEZ AL-ASSAD: NEW CHALLENGES IN SYRIA

A key participant in the Lebanese drama of the 1970s was Syrian president Hafez al-Assad. He had used Syria's recovery from the Six-Day War to consolidate his power. The loss of the Golan Heights had set off a power struggle between the more pragmatist wing of the Syrian Baath Party dominated by military officers and the more militant, ideological group led by civilians.

Al-Assad was an air force officer and a member of the Alawite religious minority group who had served as minister of defense during the Six-Day War. After the war, he emerged as leader of a Baathist group of military officers. When the group felt strongly that Syria's current ruler Salah al-Jadid had acted irresponsibly when he tried to intervene in the Black September conflict between Jordan and the Palestinians, they successfully mounted a nonviolent coup called "The Corrective Revolution" to replace him in November 1970.

Upon taking power, al-Assad created a political structure reminiscent in some ways of what Nasser had made in Egypt. The Syrian

Baath party held a "regional" congress in March 1971 to create a twenty-one–member Regional Command to govern the country. The Command was led by al-Assad, who was also confirmed as president at that time in a national referendum. To broaden its support, the Command created a popular legislature known as the People's Council, with about half of its seats going to Baath Party members. One year later, al-Assad created the National Progressive Front, a coalition of groups led by the Baath Party to strengthen national solidarity. Through these institutions, the Baath Party functioned more and more like a patronage system closely linked to the state bureaucracy, with the political organization transformed from its previous role as a vanguard group into a mass organization.

The most visible public-works project created during this period, reminiscent of Nasser's Aswan Dam, was the Tabqa (or Thawra) Dam: an earthwork barrier built on the Euphrates in northern Syria between 1968 and 1973 with Soviet help. It created Lake Assad, Syria's largest water reservoir. Although this dam was originally built to generate hydroelectric power and facilitate irrigation, it fell short in both areas, although it still provides most drinking water today for northern Syria. The dam project was almost totally supported by Soviet in the end, since Syria had so firmly aligned itself with the Soviet camp by the late 1960s. An attempt was made to resettle the several thousand Arab families displaced by Lake Assad along the borders with Iraq and Turkey. This was done in order to create an "Arab belt" to separate Syria's Kurdish population from Kurdish communities in Turkey and Iraq, but this was only partially implemented.

Going considerably beyond what Nasser did in Egypt, al-Assad attempted to remake Syria as an authoritarian state. He became the focus of an official personality cult, depicted in endless portraits and posters put up across the country as a remarkably wise, just, and strong leader. In practical terms, his regime did bring stability, in contrast to continuous government upheavals over the previous two decades. The regime brought public schooling to large segments of the population and achieved a notable rise in living standards at all social levels. Al-Assad's staunchly secular approach (as a Baathist and member of the Alawi religious minority) persuaded members of Syria's many religious minorities to support him, out of fear that their status could be diminished under any more conservative Sunni regime that might replace him.

As a career military officer, al-Assad was well-disposed to increase Syria's military strength substantially with Soviet help. To legitimize his rule, al-Assad relied on a Soviet-style propaganda campaign depicting his regime as the only true champion of the Arab nation against the imperialism and aggression of Western powers: a strategy to unite diverse groups through feelings of national pride.

Always pragmatic, al-Assad took a sophisticated approach to defending his absolute rule. Instead of treating dissenters with brutality, the Syrian government often bribed or threatened them first, only resorting to more severe methods of persuasion after these had failed. In such situations, the government acted very decisively to quell any opposition.

Serious challenges to his rule came from outside and within the country, but his regime withstood all the blows dealt it. The October War of 1973 became a major setback for him when the Syrian army not only failed to retake the Golan Heights, but lost additional territory. By 1976, the Syrians also become deeply embroiled in Lebanon, where their troops would remain for the next three decades.

Sunni Muslim Activists Rise Up: 1976–1982

The most serious challenge of this period occurred in the late 1970s, when Sunni Muslim fundamentalists sustained an armed insurgency against al-Assad's government between 1976 and 1982. There had been a branch of the Muslim Brotherhood in Syria since the

late 1940s, although it had been outlawed and suppressed by successive Baathist rulers since the early 1960s.

By the 1970s, more radical Brotherhood supporters were angered by the staunch secularism of the Baath party and objected in particular to rule by al-Assad, as a member of a religious minority linked with Shii Islam. Similar to al-Assad, many Baath party members had risen to prominence from poor, rural backgrounds. This group tended to favor radical economic policies for redistributing wealth and wanted the government to manage economic affairs to promote equality. Syrian Sunni Muslim elites in contrast, who had historically dominated Syria's traditional market and agrarian economies, saw government involvement in the economy as very negative. Although few moderate Sunni leaders supported the religious stridency of the Muslim Brotherhood activists, they perceived that militants aligned with the Brotherhood might be useful as a political tool to pressure the Baath ruling group.

Whatever their origins, radicals carried out a series of violent actions after Syrian troops went into Lebanon in 1976. These began with an assassination campaign against high-ranking Syrian military officers and bureaucrats in addition to professionals, teachers, and doctors, many of whom were Alawis. This first wave of violence culminated in June 1979 with a massacre of cadets at an Aleppo military academy, carried out by Islamist militants in collaboration with turncoat sympathizers among the officers there. This attack was followed by an intensified campaign of violence whose targets were prominent Alawis, Baath Party officials, and a wide variety of police and military targets. Over the next two years, militants claimed the lives of hundreds of victims in Aleppo and other Syrian cities in attacks that included assaults using hand grenades and car bombs.

Al-Assad's regime was calculating but brutal in its retaliation. In June 1980, government paramilitary forces commanded by Hafez al-Assad's brother Rifaat massacred around five hundred Islamist inmates at Tadmur prison (near Palmyra), and membership in the Muslim Brotherhood was made a capital offense. Over the next two years, targeted killings at home and abroad eliminated hundreds of people deemed to be enemies of the state or Islamic militants. One notable opponent of al-Assad to be murdered was **Salah al-Din Bitar**, cofounder of the Baath Party, who was killed in Paris in July 1980. The Syrian government never took responsibility for these killings, but they were clearly seen as retaliation for what Muslim activists had done, as well as settling scores within the Baath Party.

The final major act of official retaliation by the Assad regime against this insurgency was the Hama massacre of February 1982. The city of Hama, long a center of conservative Sunni Muslim landholders and their allies in the Muslim Brotherhood, became an important symbolic target. In the early morning of February 3, Islamic militants there suddenly declared Hama to be a "liberated" city, and mosque loudspeakers broadcast calls for jihad against the government. In response, Islamic activists attacked the homes of Baath Party leaders and government officials, killing many.

Assad retaliated by sending Special Forces troops (commanded by his brother Rifaat) to occupy the city warning that anyone staying there would be treated as a rebel. It took the government three weeks to reestablish authority over the whole city. During this operation, Syrian army units carried out a series of artillery barrages, leveling large parts of the town and causing the deaths of thousands of civilians. The Hama massacre and the earlier killings effectively ended this large-scale Sunni Islamist insurgency and crushed Islamic activist networks across the country. There were no other serious internal challenges to the Assad regime after this event until the Syrian part of the Arab Spring uprising that began in January 2011, with many seeking to oust his son, Bashar al-Assad, from power. Rifaat al-Assad mounted a failed coup attempt against Hafez al-Assad in 1984, for which he was permanently exiled to France.

Hafez al-Assad succeeded in defending his regime against a serious challenge by Muslim activists through severe repression. While this suppressed Syria's internal problems, the complex changes in its relationships with all of its immediate neighbors, particularly Israel and Lebanon, would continue to occupy much of his government's attention through the rest of his years in power.

CAMP DAVID

Egypt, too, faced a new situation with Israel following the October War. Sadat, like al-Assad, had gone to war in 1973 with the goal of retaking territory lost in 1967. He, however, had been much more committed than al-Assad to engaging in a real peace process after the war. By 1977, only very slight, incremental progress had been made toward this goal.

The new U.S. president, Jimmy Carter, decided to abandon Henry Kissinger's concept of shuttle diplomacy. Kissinger's approach had relied on using his status as a high-level American intermediary to travel back and forth between heads of state numerous times to fine-tune agreements. His method had achieved a partial Israeli withdrawal from Sinai, now codified in the Sinai II agreement signed in Geneva in September, 1975, but had little else to show for considerable diplomatic efforts.

Carter now sought to arrange a more comprehensive negotiating session, possibly in Geneva, where all the parties could meet face-to-face and all outstanding issues could be put on the bargaining table. Carter made a point of visiting all relevant heads of state several times in 1977 and wrote up a plan of action to begin such talks soon. His strategy had to be adjusted when in June of that year, a right-wing coalition led by Menachem Begin took power in Israel. For the first time in its history, the country would not be governed by a coalition led by the Labor Party, but by a considerably more conservative group.

On one hand, it was anathema for Begin, who had been one of the leaders of the Irgun militant Zionist organization during and after World War II, even to think of including the PLO in any diplomatic discussions, given that PLO's charter presented the destruction of Israel as one of its basic goals. On the other, he was quite happy with the prospect of concluding a lasting peace agreement with Egypt. Secret Egyptian-Israeli talks (brokered by Rumania and Morocco) soon got underway, completely separate from any ongoing American diplomatic initiatives. Begin was ready to begin serious negotiations about returning the Sinai to Egypt, but was adamantly opposed to any discussion of Israel's withdrawal from the West Bank. He was actually pushing for the establishment of even more Jewish settlements there, perceiving this territory as integral to Israel's identity as a Jewish state. Begin's readiness to begin direct talks became a key to the success of Carter's peace plan, but other unanticipated events soon dramatically affected the situation.

By the fall of 1977, Sadat, too, had decided that the peace process was not moving forward as quickly as he desired. There were disagreements among various Arab nations about the format of upcoming talks, and he felt that President Carter was not applying sufficient pressure to force Israel to make necessary concessions. Sadat decided to allay his frustration with the lack of progress by making a dramatic gesture.

After secret preparations, Sadat paid a surprise visit to Israel for three days in November 1977. There, he presented a peace plan directly to the Israeli parliament. Sadat's speech broadly discussed the parameters of peace, the question of the West Bank, and the plight of Palestinian refugees, but went totally beyond the parameters of the international diplomatic planning then underway, which was focused merely on reviving face-to-face negotiations between Israel and its Arab neighbors.

Although he was certainly committed to Egypt playing a principal role in the larger Arab-Israeli peace process, Sadat's strong push to reach a settlement with Israel was also part of his plan to repair Egypt's ties with the West in order to revive its stymied economy. Sadat was striking out on a different path from Nasser, motivated by his conviction that it was time for Egypt to pay more attention to its own national interests and concerns than serve as the spokesman for the entire Arab world. Parallel to this new concept of Egypt's place in the world, he envisioned a firm accord between Israel and Egypt as the catalyst for similar agreements between Israel and its other Arab neighbors: treaties that might ultimately form the basis for a final, peaceful resolution of the Palestinian problem.

Begin saw many advantages for Israel to conduct bilateral talks with Egypt, but for reasons that did not correspond to Sadat's ideas at all. For Begin, such negotiations could effectively thwart the desire of any larger Arab delegation to present unwelcome or unacceptable demands. The U.S. administration had no inkling that the Israelis and Egyptians had already been conducting extensive secret talks in Morocco led by Moshe Dayan and Sadat's representative, Hassan Tuhami. Despite having been taken completely by surprise with the news of this diplomatic channel, American diplomats scrambled to build on the positive momentum that it appeared to have created.

Sadat's historic visit created a large amount of immediate positive energy, enhanced even more by Begin's reciprocal trip to Egypt that soon followed. However, not enough real negotiating had yet taken place between the two countries to create a basis for sustained diplomatic progress. The situation soon regressed back to the impasse that Sadat's dramatic trip had tried to get beyond. An Israeli-Egyptian summit on Christmas Day 1977 in Ismailiya, near the Suez Canal, resulted in nothing more than a cordial photo opportunity. Although talks continued through the winter and spring of 1978, there was a sense that real progress had stalled.

At a cabinet meeting in July, President Carter threw out the idea that a small summit be held at the secluded presidential retreat at Camp David, Maryland. His concept was that only he, Prime Minister Begin, and President Sadat with their close aides would be present, and the group would agree to shut itself off from the outside world until the terms of a realistic agreement could be produced. Carter's advisers were at first quite skeptical.

When U.S. secretary of state Cyrus Vance presented the idea to Begin and Sadat, both readily agreed to it. Thus, the two leaders, each accompanied only by a small team of associates, came to Camp David for two weeks of intensive negotiations in early September 1978. Carter maintained such unremitting determination not to allow anyone to leave before an agreement was produced that this achieved a successful result.

Even in this closed situation, it was not easy to make progress. Because Begin and Sadat had such personal antipathy toward each other, Carter was required to perform his own version of shuttle diplomacy between their different cabins to convey the substance of discussions.

Carter also managed to thwart many attempts made by both Egyptians and Israelis to stop the negotiations. When discussions reached the question of whether to remove Israeli settlements from the Sinai as well as the airing of disagreements over the status of the West Bank, an impasse emerged. Carter was only able to get around this by allowing Begin to table discussion of the West Bank until some later time, while standing firm in support of Sadat's call for all Israeli settlements to be cleared from the Sinai. For a break, Carter brought the two leaders to the Gettysburg battlefield to allow them to muse together about parallels between the American Civil War and their own struggles.

Two agreements (later called the "Camp David Accords") were produced by these negotiations: *A Framework for Peace in the Middle East* and *A Framework for the Conclusion of a Peace Treaty between Egypt and Israel*. The latter document became the basis for the comprehensive Israel-Egypt Peace Treaty concluded in March 1979.

The first agreement, far more ambiguous and open-ended than the second, presented a framework for negotiations on how to create an autonomous self-governing authority in the West Bank and the Gaza Strip and as well as calling for the full implementation of UN Resolution 242. This document's deliberate imprecision produced vastly different interpretations of it by Israel, Egypt, and the United States. Treatment of some of the most divisive issues, such as any discussion of the final status of Jerusalem, was deliberately excluded from it.

The second agreement presented in a fairly detailed way the terms of the peace treaty soon to be signed, in particular with regard to the situation in Sinai. Israel agreed to a complete withdrawal of all troops and civilians from the Sinai with sovereignty over the peninsula fully restored to Egypt, in exchange for the normalization of diplomatic relations and guarantees of free passage through the Suez Canal and nearby waterways (most important of which were the Straits of Tiran). As an incentive for the agreement to be honored, the United States agreed to provide several billion dollars worth of aid annually to both Israel and Egypt, which continues to be given at the present time.

Larger Impact

Within the Middle East, perhaps the most important change created by the Camp David was that Egypt came to be viewed by other Arabs not as the leader of the Arab world, but as a pariah that had left behind Arab interests, particularly those of the Palestinians. As a reflection of this sentiment in the region, Egypt's membership in the Arab League was suspended between 1979 and 1989. Egypt's realignment created a power vacuum in the Arab world that has yet to be filled again by it or any other nation, although it has in recent years regained much of its former stature as a cultural and intellectual capital of the Arab world. From a different perspective, though, the improbable achievements of Begin, Sadat, and Carter at Camp David suggested that Arab-Israeli negotiations could in fact achieve real progress through intensive direct efforts at communication and cooperation: a realization that influenced the course of numerous subsequent peace talks.

Assassination of Sadat

Just as importantly, the **Camp David Accords** did not bring any solutions to Egypt's internal economic and social problems. Sadat had created an "open door" economic liberalization policy in the mid-1970s designed to modernize Egypt's stagnant economy and connect it more with world economic trends, but there were large popular protests against the lifting of price controls on bread and other staples, presented as necessary changes to promote economic prosperity.

Militant Islamist activists, particular those associated with radical groups that had broken away from the Muslim Brotherhood, were enraged by Sadat's peace process with Israel. Several militant organizations began recruiting military officers and started procuring weapons in order to launch an Islamic revolution in Egypt. One of these organizations had recruited a high-ranking insider, an army intelligence specialist with the rank of colonel named Abbud al-Zumar who drew up comprehensive plans to seize state institutions and set off an Islamic uprising.

Sadat responded harshly to such perceived threats and had thousands of people across the political spectrum arrested in 1981 on charges of sedition and political intrigue. His dragnet failed to uncover one particular militant cell in the army led by Lieutenant Khalid Islambouli. This group succeeded in assassinating Anwar Sadat on October 6, 1981, during the annual victory parade held in Cairo to commemorate Egypt's successful crossing of the Suez Canal during the 1973 October War. A fatwa

approving this assassination had been issued by Omar Abd al-Rahman, a Muslim cleric later convicted in the United States for his role in the 1993 World Trade Center bombing.

Although Sadat was being guarded by multiple layers of security, a troop truck suddenly halted right in front of his presidential reviewing stand. Lt. Islambouli, riding on the truck as the main assassin, got out and appeared to be about to salute. As Sadat stood up to receive his greeting, Islambouli threw three grenades at him, only one of which exploded. More assassins then jumped out of the truck and fired assault rifles into the stands in Sadat's general direction. The attack lasted only two minutes, but twelve people were killed. A mass insurrection had been organized to start in the town of Asyut in Upper Egypt simultaneously with the assassination. Rebels took control of the city for a few days and killed sixty-eight policemen and soldiers. The Egyptian government was only able to reestablish control there after paratroopers arrived from Cairo.

Sadat was succeeded by his vice president Hosni Mubarak, whose hand was slightly injured during the attack. Mubarak became the longest-serving president in Egypt's history, being forced to leave office only after a sudden, large popular political upheaval in February 2011. In the trials that followed Sadat's killing, over three hundred Islamic radicals were indicted along with Khalid Islambouli, including **Ayman al-Zawahiri**, Omar Abd al-Rahman, and Abd al-Hamid Kishk, all of whom would later be linked to radical Islamist groups.

When the trials were covered by the international press, al-Zawahiri's knowledge of English made him the de facto spokesman for the defendants. Al-Zawahiri was released from prison in 1984 and eventually made his way to Afghanistan. There he eventually became a close associate of **Osama bin Laden**, as well as one of the founders and now the leader of the **al-Qaeda** militant Islamist group. Abd al-Rahman and Kishk, both blind clerics, served as spiritual guides for militant extremists and were eventually released from detention. Abd al-Rahman also first traveled to Afghanistan, but came to the United States in 1990, where he is now serving a life sentence for involvement in the 1993 World Trade Center bombings. Kishk, who passed away in 1996, was released from an Egyptian prison in 1982 by Mubarak, with the provision that he would no longer be a public activist. Despite this, his messages continued to be circulated through widely distributed tape recordings of his sermons and he retained a large informal following.

OIL POWER

In parallel with all these major political developments in the Middle East during the 1970s, the global economy first began to take real notice of the importance of Middle Eastern oil production as a result of what happened to oil prices in the October War. Petroleum exports from the Middle East had been steadily increasing since the 1940s. Production and distribution were largely controlled by major Western oil companies known as the "**Seven Sisters**" (including Chevron, ExxonMobil, and BP), who kept price rises fairly modest for many years. Although twelve major non-Western oil-producing countries, including Iran and seven Arab nations, had created the **Organization of Petroleum Exporting Countries (OPEC)** in 1960 as a bargaining unit to increase their share of revenues, this cartel did not really began to assert itself until the early 1970s.

The first event that brought it to take action was when the United States took the dollar off the gold standard in August 1971 in an effort to secure its domestic economic health. This change suddenly created tremendous uncertainty about oil producers' future incomes, since all oil was priced in dollars and there was uncertainty about what would happen to foreign exchange rates. OPEC at first announced that its members would tie the price of oil to gold as a more stable index, but this proved hard to implement. The result

was a period of intense oil price fluctuations, compared to the previous two decades when the price of crude had been kept somewhat artificially stable and risen by less than 2 percent per year.

The halcyon period of cheap oil, during which many Western economies were able to raise their energy consumption by 5 per cent per year without paying any real economic price, was about to end. The crisis point happened when the Arab members of OPEC started using oil as a political weapon during the October War of 1973. In August of that year, Anwar Sadat and Saudi King Faisal agreed that oil embargoes would be part of any future Arab-Israeli conflict. When OPEC learned midway through the war that the United States had resupplied Israel with critical military supplies, the organization immediately raised its posted price of oil by 70 percent to over five dollars per barrel. Arab oil ministers then imposed an embargo on the United States, and announced a general 5 percent production cut, with more cuts to be imposed over time until economic and political objectives were attained.

On this news, open-market world oil prices shot up from $3 to $12 per barrel. This had an immediate global economic impact, since demand for oil drops little even if its price is raised substantially. By January 1974, after various production cuts and price rises had been imposed, Arab oil-producing nations agreed to freeze prices for three months. Although the oil embargo against the United States was lifted in March, the situation would never return to what it had been before the war. Over the long term, the oil embargo created a much greater consciousness in the West of the finite nature of oil as an energy resource, and initiated a general trend toward energy conservation. Large oil price increases also brought sudden vast new amounts of wealth to particular Middle Eastern countries, which tremendously exacerbated economic imbalances between producers and nonproducers in the region.

Middle East in the World Economy

A handful of Middle Eastern countries, so long dominated by Western companies that controlled and managed the price and distribution of their petroleum exports, could finally amass real wealth through their control of this vital world commodity. The particular impact of the Arab use of the "oil weapon" in 1973 has remained a point of debate ever since then. Some argue in fact that U.S. fears of Soviet involvement in the conflict probably drove U.S. policies more than concerns about oil and that the groundwork for the Arab-Israeli peace process that evolved after the October War had already been in place long before the war itself. The 1973 oil embargo did initiate a long-term effort to find alternative sources of energy, whether through new exploration for sources of petroleum or the creation of new technologies.

These sudden price increases immediately shocked Western consumers. Their concerns caused the implementation of various rationing plans in Western countries, with a national maximum highway speed limit of 55 miles per hour being declared in the United States in 1974 to conserve fuel. Most importantly, this event put the Middle East on the mental map of many westerners as never before.

Even when the embargo was ended and prices were frozen for a few months, the general rise in oil prices continued unabated through the 1970s. This crisis also marked the beginning of a divergence in approach to the Arab-Israeli conflict among different industrialized nations. Western Europe and Japan, importing between 80 and 90 percent of their oil from the Middle East, began to adopt more pro-Arab policies instead of favoring Israel, in contrast to the United States, which imported only 10–12 percent of its oil from Middle East countries at that time and for many years thereafter.

The oil crisis also substantially increased the visibility of the Middle East in world politics. Before the oil crisis and the October War, the Middle East had been only one arena of the global competition between the United States and the USSR as superpowers, in which Israel, Saudi Arabia, and Iran on the U.S. side, versus Egypt, Syria, and Iraq on the Soviet side, were part of the vast global geopolitical competition for world influence. When oil prices increased so dramatically and rapidly after 1973, the Soviet Union started to boost its own oil production and export so much by the late 1970s that it began to perceive OPEC countries as its economic competitors.

This, in turn, heightened fears among the leaders of Middle Eastern OPEC nations, still largely conservative monarchies, that this growing economic competition might prompt the Soviet Union to engage in military action against them—perhaps as an offshoot of its 1979 intervention in Afghanistan. This potential Soviet threat prompted the oil producers of the Gulf to lean on the United States for new security guarantees against any Soviet military action in the region, boosting the U.S. role substantially as a security guarantor in the Persian Gulf during the 1970s.

Economic Rise of Saudi Arabia

With regard to their domestic economies, these OPEC-member states assumed greater control over their own natural resources in the 1970s, augmenting their financial power even more. Saudi Arabia, for example, acquired full operational control of ARAMCO, its national oil company, completely nationalizing it in 1980 under the leadership of longtime Saudi oil executive Ahmad Zaki Yamani. Other OPEC nations adopted similar courses of action, and their incomes soared. With enormous new cash reserves, Saudi Arabia pursued a series of wide-ranging development plans valued in the hundreds of billions of dollars.

Increased sale of American weapons and technology to countries that suddenly could afford much more of them also had an impact. Both Saudi Arabia and Iran became increasingly dependent on U.S. weapons to help them cope with emerging external and internal threats. By 1979, the amount of

American weapons purchased annually by the Saudis was more than five times larger than what Israel purchased from the United States. Oil-producing countries' enormous new wealth paradoxically led them into a more dependent relationship with the West, because their economies became even more closely integrated with economies there.

After the immediate crisis of 1973 in oil prices had settled down, Saudi Arabia adopted a fairly consistent policy to moderate the price and production of oil, both to stabilize its own growing investments in the Western economic system effort, as well as to forestall development of alternative methods of energy production. Much of its immediate success was due to the skilled leadership of King Faisal (ruled 1964–1975), who established a good connection with Sadat in the years leading up to the October War and became the main coordinator of the oil embargo during that conflict.

This action became Faisal's defining act as king, and secured his lasting global prestige. Saudi Arabia's new oil income now allowed him to greatly expand subsidies to Egypt, Syria, and the PLO, and to deepen ties with Pakistan, which assisted in particular with the development of Saudi Arabia's military and internal security forces and renamed its third-largest city Lyallpur as Faisalabad in his honor in 1977.

His reign was cut short when he was assassinated at a weekly royal audience in a revenge killing carried out by one of his nephews in March 1975. Prince Khalid, another son of Abdul Aziz ibn Saud (but by a different wife from Faisal's mother), took the throne, but ceded the day-to-day running of the country to another brother, Crown Prince Fahd, who succeeded him as king upon his death in 1982. Both Khalid and Fahd continued to pursue policies similar to those of Faisal, their courses of action facilitated by the enormous continued influx of wealth into the kingdom.

One mission that this wealth facilitated was religious and charitable outreach to the Muslim world. This had long been one of Saudi Arabia's important foreign policies, in its capacity as the country in which the Muslim holy sites of Mecca and Medina are located. This was accomplished through a nongovernmental organization: the Muslim World League, whose mission was to promote and support Islamic institutions around the world. Founded in Saudi Arabia in 1962, the Muslim World League had received a substantial boost in its funding from the Saudi government after the increase in oil wealth, which it used to expand its outreach considerably. In 1979, it created a subsidiary called the International Islamic Relief Organization, specifically to provide charity and support for Muslims in need worldwide.

Because of Saudi Arabia's official support for Wahhabi teachings and doctrine, both organizations have focused their support on mosques, schools, and charitable organizations that agree with this approach to Islam, which has produced criticism from Muslims and non-Muslims who do not wish to see Wahhabism promoted in this way.

GRAND MOSQUE SEIZURE

The tension between the fervent traditionalism of Wahhabi loyalists in Saudi Arabia and the rapid modernization of all aspects of life there by the late 1970s created currents of dissent under the surface of the nation's prosperity. The Saudi monarchy derived its strength from the complex interwoven networks of loyalty between different branches of the royal family and prominent provincial notable and religious families. In addition, it was supported by a security system that relied on the internal cohesion of the Wahhabi movement as well as the latest security technologies and expertise from abroad. The Saudi system had proved extremely resilient in the face of numerous threats over the years. The most serious challenge ever posed to it though, came from a group of several hundred dissidents who successfully invaded and seized Mecca's Grand Mosque on November 20, 1979: corresponding to the first day of 1400 A.H.: the first year of the Islamic fifteenth century.

It was taken over by a group of dissidents led by Juhaiman al-Utaibi. Al-Utaibi was a member of one of the main families of Nejd the central part of Saudi Arabia where the Saudi royal family also had its origins. He had been a career soldier in the Saudi National Guard, a tribal military force separate from the regular Saudi army with a strongly conservative religious character. In the early morning of that day, he entered the mosque with several hundred well-armed followers and fairly quickly secured the central mosque sanctuary.

Because it was so well-armed and had a good knowledge of the mosque precincts, this group managed for two weeks to repel all outside forces that tried to attack it and was able to broadcast its message through the mosque loudspeakers set up around the complex. Al-Utaibi declared his brother-in-law Muhammad Abdullah al-Qahtani (who was there with him) to be the Mahdi, or Islamic messiah whose arrival signaled the advent of the end times as predicted in Islamic scriptures. In his declarations, he also called for the export of oil from Saudi Arabia to the West to be halted, for the Saudi dynasty to be overthrown, for Western culture to be eradicated from Saudi Arabia, and for all non-Muslims to be expelled from the country. Many in this group had been theology students at the Islamic University in Medina, an institution closely associated with radical exiled Egyptian members of the Muslim Brotherhood. Saudi religious authorities in fact had previously investigated al-Utaibi and al-Qahtani on charges of heresy, but they were exonerated when it was determined that they were only fervent traditionalists whose views were reminiscent of the original Ikhwan, like al-Utaibi's grandfather, and not a threat.

After the occupation went on for two more weeks, Saudi troops, assisted by French and Pakistani special forces, were finally able to dislodge this group, but with many deaths and casualties. Curiously, it was widely believed across the Muslim world that the United States had somehow been responsible for this action—a belief that led to the seizure of the U.S. embassy in Islamabad, Pakistan, which killed a U.S. Marine security guard there. This was followed by numerous anti-American demonstrations in Muslim countries from Libya to Bangladesh, indicating a rapidly rising anti-American sentiment across the Muslim world. Nowhere was this more dramatic than in Iran, where the departure of the shah and the arrival of Imam Khomeini earlier in 1979 signaled the culmination of the beginning phase of a revolution that had started a few months earlier and would soon create a totally new regime in Iran.

Questions to Think About

1. How did the arrival of the Palestinian leadership in Lebanon after Black September destabilize its political system?
2. Who was Kamal Jumblatt, and what role did he play in Lebanese politics?
3. What actually triggered the start of the Lebanese Civil War?
4. How did Hafez al-Assad consolidate his power in Syria?
5. What were the effects of the Camp David peace process on the Middle East, and what was achieved and not achieved in terms of final agreements?
6. Why was Anwar Sadat assassinated, and who was responsible for his death?
7. How did the sharp rise in oil prices in the 1970s affect the Middle East and how did it change international attitudes about the region?
8. How was Saudi Arabia affected by the oil price rise?

For Further Reading

Abir, Mordechai. *Saudi Arabia in the Oil Era: Regime and Elites: Conflict and Collaboration*. Boulder, CO: Westview Press, 1988.

Alexander, Yonah. *Palestinian Secular Terrorism*. Ardsley, NY: Transnational Publishers, 2003.

Bulloch, John. *Death of a Country: The Civil War in Lebanon*. London: Weidenfeld & Nicolson, 1977.

Deeb, Marius. *The Lebanese Civil War*. New York: Praeger, 1980.

El-Khazen, Farid. *The Breakdown of the State in Lebanon, 1967–1976*. Cambridge: Harvard University Press, 2000.

Fisk, Robert. *Pity the Nation: Lebanon at War*. London: A. Deutsch, 1990.

Haugbolle, Sune. *War and Memory in Lebanon*. New York: Cambridge University Press, 2010.

Haykal, Muhammad Hasanayn. *Autumn of Fury: The Assassination of Sadat*. New York: Random House, 1983.

Hinnebusch, Raymond A. *Syria: Revolution from Above*. London: Routledge, 2001.

Quandt, William B. *Camp David: Peacemaking and Politics*. Washington, DC: Brookings Institution, 1986.

Seale, Patrick, and Maureen McConville. *Asad of Syria: The Struggle for the Middle East*. Berkeley: University of California Press, 1989.

Stein, Kenneth W. *Heroic Diplomacy: Sadat, Kissinger, Carter, Begin and the Quest for Arab-Israeli Peace*. New York: Routledge, 1999.

Telhami, Shibley. *Power and Leadership in International Bargaining: The Path to the Camp David Accords*. New York: Columbia University Press, 1990.

Van Creveld, Martin. *Military Lessons of the Yom Kippur War: Historical Perspectives*. Beverly Hills: Sage Publications, 1975.

Weinberger, Naomi Joy. *Syrian Intervention in Lebanon: The 1975–76 Civil War*. New York: Oxford University Press, 1986.

Weizman, Ezer. *The Battle for Peace*. Toronto: Bantam Books, 1981.

20

Revolution in Iran, Saddam, and the Iran-Iraq War

It was not just Arab members of OPEC who were transformed by the enormous sudden increase in oil prices. Iran too was profoundly affected by the oil boom. There was a quick rise in inflation because there was so much more money to spend. Because of the extremely uneven distribution of this new wealth, the gap between rich and poor as well as between the rural and urban populations increased dramatically. Thousands of foreign skilled workers had come into the country, an influx now seen as a threat to traditional Iranian cultural values.

Shah Mohammad Reza Pahlavi's own family reaped the greatest benefit from this windfall. By 1976, he had personally amassed around 1 billion dollars; while his family and foundations controlled billions more. At this time, his government imposed economic austerity measures to combat rampant inflation. The impact of these new regulations was felt most directly by thousands of poor and unskilled young men flocking from rural areas to cities to find employment on construction projects. This group was quite conservative culturally and religiously, and made up the core of demonstrators and martyrs in the revolution that soon took place.

RASTAKHIZ AND THE REVIVAL OF OPPOSITION

Through the White Revolution and other initiatives of the 1960s, the shah had already tried to marginalize political forces that opposed him, using all kinds of techniques and strategies. In 1975, he took his political experiments one step further by creating the *Rastakhiz* (Resurgence) Party, to be led by his technocratic prime minister Amir Abbas Hoveyda.

This was designed to be a single body to replace all existing political organizations, in which enrollment and payment of dues became obligatory. It

Wally McNamee/Historical/CORBIS

Mohammad Reza Shah Pahlavi and Empress Farah (December 1977)

immediately became very unpopular among large segments of the society, particularly the merchants of bazaars in the main towns, because it was seen as an unwarranted intrusion into hitherto private political, economic, and religious spheres of people's lives. A youth branch of *Rastakhiz* was also created, presented by Hoveyda as a vanguard of modernization and development.

Soon, the organization launched a campaign against what it identified as excessive profit-taking by merchants, particularly those in the main city bazaars. These *bazaari* shopkeepers were charged with harming the economic future of the nation by raising prices too high, and were made scapegoats for the recent rapid inflation. Attempts to combat inflation by assessing large fines on merchants and even imprisoning them for price gouging actively turned the bazaar against the regime. This was dangerous, since this group had the wealth and connections to make its political positions heard, even if only through disturbances and demonstrations.

The other new factor, beginning in 1977, was that when Jimmy Carter became president, he inaugurated a campaign to force important U.S. allies to uphold human rights and allow freedom of speech. The shah did not welcome this initiative, but as the United States was his main ally, he felt obligated at least to appear to be going along with this American program and released some prisoners. This new American position emboldened his opponents to be more vocal and express political opposition more openly.

The sudden deaths of Ali Shariati, a well-regarded Islamic modernist and **Mustafa Khomeini**, Ayatollah Khomeini's son, raised tensions. Both were blamed on SAVAK, the shah's secret police, and caused large demonstrations through early 1978. At this exact time too, the shah was also dealing with the fact that he had been diagnosed with cancer three years earlier, although he was able to keep this a complete secret from everyone beyond his close family circle until after he had left Iran in 1979.

PRELUDE TO REVOLUTION: CYCLES OF MARTYRDOM

What is often regarded as the real turning point in this prerevolutionary situation and the beginning of the path toward an outright revolution in Iran was a demonstration held in the city of Qom on January 8, 1978. This took place on the day after a slanderous article accusing Ayatollah Khomeini of being a foreign spy was published in a government-produced newspaper. The Iranian army was sent in to disperse demonstrators and several students were killed.

A single political demonstration in Qom against the shah would not, in and of itself, have been considered a major event. Forty days later, groups in several cities staged memorial services (known as *arba'in*) to commemorate those killed at this gathering—now considered religious martyrs (*shahidan*). When yet more people were killed at these new events, this set in motion a cycle of memorial services every forty days to recognize demonstrators who had been martyred in the previous memorial services. With each new memorial, there was more violence and severe repression by the shah's security forces.

On May 10, government troops broke into the home of a politically moderate but greatly respected and influential cleric, Ayatollah Kazem Shariatmadari. They killed two of his disciples right in front of him, supposedly for not pledging loyalty to the shah. This shocked Shariatmadari into giving up his aloof stance toward any worldly political involvement. He now aligned himself and his followers with the growing opposition movement to the monarchy.

There was great uncertainty in the U.S. government about how to respond to this rapidly evolving situation. The CIA produced a study in August 1978 concluding that Iran was "not in a revolutionary or even a prerevolutionary situation."[1] While U.S.

officials assured the shah of U.S. support, some American officials began to doubt the regime's ability to stay in power.

The pace of events slowed down briefly in the early summer. On June 17, Shariatmadari was able to stop the cycle of protests being held every forty days by issuing a call for calm on the streets that was finally heeded. When the shah fired his secret police commander and made a commitment to hold elections soon, affairs seemed to be settling down.

However, protests resumed with new intensity two months later. Unrest now became fueled by young unskilled men, recently laid off in budget cuts made to cut inflation. The shah tried to quell this fresh outbreak by installing a new prime minister and legalizing opposition political parties, but his gestures were too late. The government imposed martial law, but thousands of protestors assembled in central Tehran on Friday, September 8, despite this crackdown.

This became known as "Black Friday" in memory of the dozens of demonstrators killed by police that day. This soon was followed by a general strike in October that shut down Iran's economy, and the revolutionary movement now began to attract large popular support. As a last-ditch attempt to weaken the clerics' position, the shah prevailed upon the Iraqi government to deport Khomeini, who had been living in Najaf since 1965. When Khomeini ended up in a suburb of Paris, his new situation there paradoxically gave him far better access to communications with Iran and much more visibility in the international press than he had enjoyed in Iraq. On December 10 and 11, millions of demonstrators, perhaps as much as 10 percent of the nation's entire population, assembled across Iran to demand that the shah leave and Khomeini come home.

In desperation, the shah appointed Dr. Shahpour Bakhtiar as prime minister on January 3, 1979. Bakhtiar had been a close associate of Mosaddeq in the 1950s and led the **Iranian National Front** political group in the 1960s and 1970s when it was a

---

[1] Jimmy Carter, *Keeping Faith: Memoirs of a President* (Fayetteville: University of Arkansas Press, 1995), 446.

banned organization. Although he had spent considerable amounts of time in prison and was no friend of the shah, he accepted his call to take this job.

Bakhtiyar was a staunch Iranian nationalist who had been a faithful disciple of Mosaddeq. He feared a revolution in which either communists or Islamic clerics took over the country: outcomes he felt had the potential to destroy Iran. The shah's choice of Bakhtiyar to lead his government, as a concession to his most strident opponents, had no impact at all on Khomeini and other religious militants. They all denounced Bakhtiyar as a traitor and labeled his government illegal.

A constitutional democrat at heart, Bakhtiyar soon prevailed on the shah to leave the country. On January 16, 1979, Mohammad Reza Pahlavi and Empress Farah took refuge in Egypt, where they were welcomed by President Sadat. This set off huge celebrations in Iran and within a short time, most statues and memorials of the Pahlavi dynasty were taken down and destroyed.

Despite the fact that Bakhtiyar immediately liberalized the Iranian government, freed political prisoners, instituted freedom of the press, and disbanded the SAVAK secret police, he was quickly swept away by revolutionary turmoil when he allowed Khomeini to return. Bakhtiyar calculated that he could permit Khomeini to return and restrict him to a Vatican-like enclave in Qom, while leading Iran to his own long-sought goal of liberal constitutional democracy.

KHOMEINI ARRIVES: THE REVOLUTION REALLY BEGINS

Events did not follow this plan. Khomeini flew back to Iran from France on February 1, 1979, and was greeted at the airport by a frenzied crowd of several million Iranian devotees. His reception now marked him as the main leader of the revolution, with hordes of people greeting him as the Imam. This title, of course, could simply refer to his status as an Islamic prayer leader, but it also alluded in Shii Islam to the Hidden Twelfth Imam, coloring Khomeini's arrival in a mystical, religious hue.

Three days after his arrival, Khomeini appointed Mehdi Bazargan, who like Bakhtiyar, had been a close ally and supporter of Mosaddeq but had developed much closer ties than Bakhtiyar to Shii clerical leaders, as his new interim prime minister. He ordered Iranians to accept, as a religious obligation, Bazargan instead of Bakhtiyar as their leader, forcing Bakhtiyar out of Iran within a few months. Khomeini appointed Bazargan by invoking the concept that spiritual guardianship (*velayat*) to rule the country was granted to him (Khomeini) in his capacity as a religious scholar (*faqih*).

This marked the first public pronouncement upon his return to Iran of the doctrine of *Velayat-e Faqih* (Guardianship of the Islamic Jurist) that he had developed in the late 1960s and early 1970s while in exile in Iraq. This was based on the idea that the only legitimate government in Islamic countries was not monarchy, but rule by a Muslim scholar with the ability to interpret Islamic law. Khomeini declared, "This is not an ordinary government. It is a government based on *sharia* [Islamic holy law]. Opposing this government means opposing Islamic *sharia*.... Revolt against God's government is a revolt against God. Revolt against God is blasphemous."[2]

There were a few scattered clashes between military forces loyal to different sides in this upheaval, but when the main military command declared its neutrality between the governments of Bazargan and Bakhtiyar on February 11, this marked the effective end of Bakhtiyar's authority as prime minister. Revolutionaries and rebel soldiers immediately began occupying police stations and military installations, giving out weapons to the public.

The next few months were crucial for the consolidation of revolutionary power by

---

[2]Baqer Moin, *Khomeini* (New York: Macmillan, 2000), 204.

Ayatollah Khomeini (November 1978)

Bettmann/Corbis

Khomeini and his supporters, because not all the activists who had participated in the shah's overthrow supported the idea of creating an Islamic state. There was a fairly widespread idea that Khomeini would function as more of a spiritual guide than an actual political ruler, since he was already in his mid-seventies, had never held public office, and had been in exile from the country for many years.

It is noteworthy that from the very moment of his return to Iran, Khomeini and his disciples began to work toward the implementation of a government based on his concept of the Guardianship of the Islamic Jurist by using temporary allegiances (such as with Bazargan) to further their cause, while systematically removing from power everyone opposed to their ideas.

At first, Bazargan and his associates kept up a façade of government as usual, but real power in this radical phase of the Iranian Revolution rapidly flowed to several different organizations: a central Revolutionary Council, various parajudicial revolutionary tribunals, paramilitary Revolutionary Guards, and a network of neighborhood revolutionary committees (*komitehs*).

The Revolutionary Council was formed from a group of Khomeini's inner circle of advisers in January 1979 just before he left France to return to Iran. At first its authority overlapped with that of Bazargan's government, but this ambiguity was resolved after Bazargan and his entire cabinet resigned when the American Embassy was seized and its diplomats taken hostage on November 4, 1979. The Revolutionary Council then functioned as Iran's government until the election of a new parliament in August 1980.

The first revolutionary tribunal was convened secretly in Tehran in the school where Khomeini had set up his headquarters, and issued death sentences carried out on February 16, 1979. The judges were clerics personally chosen by Khomeini, and their decisions were not subject to any judicial appeal. Trials were limited to a few hours or even minutes. Those on trial could be found guilty on the basis of their reputations and there were no defense attorneys. The charge of "sowing corruption on earth" became widely applied in these tribunals to cover a variety of offenses. Although they were strongly criticized, complaints were waved off in this time of revolutionary fervor. By early November 1979, these revolutionary tribunals had condemned more than five hundred people to death.

The Revolutionary Guards were set up in May 1979 to counter leftist militias as well as watch over the regular Iranian armed forces. They have evolved over time since then into a military organization parallel to the regular army and navy, now commonly called the "Iranian Revolutionary Guards Corps" (IRGC). Affiliated with this military force was a mass group, the *Baseej-e Mostazafin* (Mobilization of the Oppressed), which Khomeini established in November 1979. Since that time, this has been an auxiliary volunteer force mobilized to do the Islamic government's bidding in many capacities.

Many neighborhood revolutionary committees (*komitehs*) were also formed, often centered in local mosques, to enforce revolutionary ideology among the people. Soon after Khomeini's return, the Islamic Republican Party was formed as an organization for mass mobilization to promote the concept of theocratic government found in Guardianship of the Islamic Jurist (*velayat-e faqih*). The muscle of the revolution was provided by Hizbullahi (Party of God) groups of tough guys—thugs available to attack demonstrators and offices of newspapers critical of Khomeini.

Among their first targets were supporters of three groups that had been integral parts of the revolutionary anti-shah movement. Two of them, the Muslim People's Republican Party and the National Democratic Front, were both groups formed after the shah's ouster that represented major factions of the revolutionary movement, but neither supported Khomeini's concept of Guardianship of the Islamic Jurist. The National Democratic Front, a coalition of secular leftist groups led by Mosaddeq's grandson Hedayatollah Matin-Daftari, opposed any religious government at all, while the moderate religious Muslim People's Republican Party, associated with Grand Ayatollah Shariatmadari, wanted a more collective religious leadership than Khomenini's vision of having a single Islamic jurist as leader implied. The third group, the People's Mojahedin of Iran, had forged an eclectic combination of Islamic, Marxist, and nationalist values strikingly similar to the revolutionary Islam espoused in the 1960s by Ali Shariati. Its adherents began to be attacked by Khomeini's followers immediately after the revolution, and it still continues today to oppose the Islamic Republic of Iran.

Very soon, the revolutionaries set in motion the process of actually creating an "Islamic republic." There had been a referendum held at the end of March 1979 on the simple question of whether the monarchy should be replaced with an "Islamic Republic," with the phrase "Islamic Republic" not being defined anywhere on the ballot. The only political groups who opposed this ballot openly were the National Democratic Front, a small group of Iranian socialists, and a few Kurdish parties. In the end, such dissent was meaningless, since the results were soon announced, with 98.2 percent reporting as being in favor of creating an "Islamic republic," whatever this might mean.

AN "ISLAMIC" CONSTITUTION

In June 1979, the Bazargan government issued a draft constitution for an Islamic Republic that had been in development for several years. It was modeled on the 1958 constitution of the French Fifth Republic, and was strikingly similar to the 1906 Iranian Constitution, except that it substituted a French-style president for the monarch. It included a **Guardian Council** to veto legislation deemed to be against Islamic values, but did not feature Khomeini's guardianship of the Islamic Jurist and did not empower the clergy at all in running day-to-day governmental affairs. Although Khomeini pronounced the document "correct" as a first draft to thwart leftist objections to it, a seventy-three-member **Assembly of Experts** for the Constitution (made up largely of Khomeini's clerical supporters) was created that summer to produce a final version of the constitution.

The result was a document altered almost beyond recognition. It included a powerful post of "guardian jurist," intended specifically for Khomeini. This official was to be given control over the military and security services, and would be permitted to select key administrative and judicial officials. In addition, this constitution increased the number of clerics who made up the Council of Guardians and their power, granting that body authority over elections as well as the ability to veto laws passed by the ordinary legislature.

THE IRAN HOSTAGE CRISIS

Now revealed to have been suffering from terminal cancer (undetected by major Western intelligence agencies for several years), the shah was finally allowed to come to the United States for treatment in October 1979, which caused an outcry in Iran. On November 4, youthful militant university students, calling themselves Muslim Student Followers of the Imam's Line, stormed the U.S. embassy compound and took its staff hostage.

There was considerable fear that the United States might organize a coup against the new Islamic government of Iran in order to bring the shah back—a development these militants were determined to forestall. They also wanted to work against Bazargan's government. They suspected it was planning to normalize relations with the United States: a serious threat, in these militants' view, to the current Islamic fervor in Iran that might undermine the revolution totally.

They immediately demanded that the shah be returned to Iran for trial and execution, that the United States apologize for the overthrow of Mosaddeq and for continually interfering in Iranian politics, and that Iran's assets frozen by the United States be released. Although the students had first planned to take the embassy over and hold it only for a short time, they reevaluated their situation after they began to grasp the popularity of what they had done and realized that they had Khomeini's full support.

The taking of hostages became immediately popular among the Iranian public, partly because it drew attention away from the unfolding chaos of the revolution and directed it toward the United States: a nation against which many Iranians could unite to harbor anger due to its long support for the shah. Khomeini immediately understood how useful the situation could now be, explaining "This action has many benefits.... It has united our people. Our opponents do not dare act against us. We can put the constitution to the people's vote without difficulty...."[3] This became a platform for rhetorical assaults on the United States as the shah's main ally, with it now labeled the "Great Satan" and endless accusations being made about "evidence of American plotting."

The hostage-taking was enormously helpful to revolutionary hardliners in Iranian domestic politics just as they were trying to consolidate power. This situation caused the immediate collapse of Bazargan's government, clearing the way for the Revolutionary Council to take full control of Iran. This dramatic event, as it unfolded, also deflected attention from the controversial new constitution that codified the theocratic system and was due for a referendum on approval a few weeks later.

After this referendum passed, revolutionaries used allegations of pro-American sentiments to attack any opponents who disagreed with them. In addition, the careful release of selected diplomatic dispatches and reports seized at the embassy over the next few months helped discredit and remove from power many moderate politicians, including Bazargan himself. Fifty-two American hostages were held captive in various and changing locations for 444 days until January 1981. This ordeal dragged on so long, partly because there was great political danger for any Iranian leader perceived as doing anything to accommodate the United States, as numerous failed negotiations and one aborted rescue attempt delayed any possible release even further.

The hostage-taking also created a new feeling of patriotism in the United States that had been so divided over the recent Vietnam conflict. It was a huge story for television news, and in fact was the origin of the ABC program later called *Nightline*, launched

---

[3]Ibid., 228.

with the title *The Iran Crisis—America Held Hostage*. There was also harassment of individual Iranians living in the United States.

The hostage crisis damaged Carter's presidency and probably ruined his chances for re-election, because he was seen as unable to solve the problem. Talks brokered by Algeria finally resolved the situation. An agreement signed there just before the end of Carter's term in office called for the immediate release by Iran of the hostages, release by the United States of $7.9 billion of Iranian assets, as well as an American guarantee of immunity from lawsuits Iranians might face in the United States and a formal pledge by the United States "not to intervene, directly or indirectly, politically or militarily, in Iran's internal affairs."[4] In the end, the hostages were released on Ronald Reagan's first day as president, and relations have still not been normalized between the two nations several decades later.

CREATING AN ISLAMIC REPUBLIC

One of the most important lasting impacts of this turbulent period was the creation of the structure of the Islamic Republic of Iran (IRI), whose constitution was ratified partly as a result of popular approval of the new regime at the time of the hostage crisis. Although it has been amended, the constitution is still the governing document of the IRI today, so its provisions are worth examining.

The Islamic Republic is led by a guardian jurist known as the Supreme Leader. He is chosen by the Assembly of Experts, a deliberative body of eighty-six Islamic scholars also empowered to oversee the Supreme Leader as well as dismiss him if they so choose. The Supreme Leader serves as the absolute head of the Iranian government, ranking above all other officials including the president. He has final say in all internal and foreign policies,

controls all armed forces, runs state media, and appoints the head of the Judiciary.

According to Khomeini, political allegiance, during the occultation and absence of the Twelfth Imam, had to be given to the current Islamic guardian jurist, based on the idea of emulating him (*taqlid*). In this new system, the jurist now oversees all governmental affairs. Many prominent Shii clerics criticized Khomeini's concept of the Guardianship of the Islamic Jurist as presented in this constitution. They see the Supreme Leader becoming too involved in daily political affairs, noting that to exercise such powers justly while participating in all aspects of life as a scholar would only really be possible for the Twelfth Imam: still believed to be in occultation (mystical hiding) pending the end of the world.

The president is Iran's chief executive, elected for a four-year term through universal adult suffrage. The Supreme Leader can dismiss the president at will and prevent the implementation of laws through institutions under his control, which include the Guardian Council and the Expediency Council. Presidential candidates must be approved by the Guardian Council. Since half of its twelve members are appointed by the Supreme Leader, and its mission is to preserve the values of the Islamic Republic, its approval process is quite restrictive. Only a small number of potential candidates are allowed to stand for election. In the election of 1997 for example, the Guardian Council approved only four of 238 candidates to run for president.

There is only one parliament, the Islamic Consultative Assembly, but all of its legislation must be reviewed and approved by the Guardian Council. While all Guardian Council members vote on whether laws presented by the Assembly are compatible with the constitution, only the six clerics on the council are permitted to decide on whether they harmonize with Islamic law. If the Guardian Council rejects a law, it returns it to the Assembly for correction. If the Assembly and the Council of Guardians cannot agree, the issue is sent to the Expediency

---

[4]http://www.iusct.org/general-declaration.pdf (accessed on March 21, 2011).

Council for a decision. The Guardian Council also serves as a constitutional court, with the authority to interpret the constitution based on a three-quarters majority vote. All candidates for national elections, as well as prospective members of the Assembly of Experts, must be vetted by the Guardian Council, which is also charged with supervising elections.

The constitution of the Islamic Republic of Iran defines it as the only government in the region in which formal religious authority will be recognized as the basis for governmental decision making and policy, in a way that is supposed to be combined with democratically elected institutions. All other governments of the Middle East, whether or not they regard Islam as their "established" religion, function as secular authorities, even if their regimes are of radically different types.

Iran's unique attempt to create a theocratic democracy in the late twentieth century that began in 1979 continues to evolve today. It is also important to remember that much of what makes Iran the way it is today is not merely based on what was put in place at the time of the 1979 revolution, but is shaped by how that system was affected by the apocalyptic devastation of the 1980–1988 **Iran-Iraq War**.

SADDAM'S IRAQ

A radically different type of regime from the Islamic Republic of Iran can be found in Baathist Iraq, the nation against which Iran became embroiled in a brutal conflict between 1980 and 1988. Iraq had a turbulent history of Baathist rule beginning in the early 1960s similar to Syria's. **Saddam Hussein**, like Hafez al-Assad, was from a poor family and belonged to an ethnic minority as a Sunni Arab in Iraq. Despite these commonalities, the two rulers had radically different styles. Al-Assad had risen through the ranks as a career military officer, while Saddam learned his skills as a political organizer and enforcer of Baath party discipline.

In 1968, Saddam helped organize a fairly nonviolent coup in which Ahmad Hassan al-Bakr unseated Abd al-Rahman Arif as Iraq's president. Although Saddam acted as al-Bakr's faithful deputy on the surface, he was involved in a lot of behind-the-scenes internal Baath party politics and political maneuvering. In the early 1970s, Saddam devoted considerable energy as vice chairman of Iraq's Revolutionary Command Council (Baathist governing body of the country) to creating cohesion in a nation defined by its profound social, ethnic, religious, and economic divisions. His approach was to combine massive political repression with promoting a vast improvement of living standards and infrastructure, facilitated after 1973 by the rapid rise in oil income. Although al-Assad engaged in his share of repression, he always did it in a much more calculating and deliberate way than Saddam, and Iraq's far greater wealth gave Saddam many more resources to carry out his plans that al-Assad could ever count on.

Iraq's government under Saddam grew into something of a modern Leviathan: formidable and menacing enough to counter internal and external threats to its hegemony, while actively promoting the rapid modernization of all sectors of its economy. He remained attentive to the requirements of building mass support among the different communities he led, carefully monitoring how government welfare and development programs were being administered and applied. The real key to his success was taking total control of Iraq's oil wealth when he nationalized the petroleum industry in June 1972, just in time for vastly increased revenues in the fall of 1973. Using this windfall, Saddam's Iraq was soon providing social services and launching infrastructure improvement projects unprecedented in the region.

Saddam established a national campaign to eliminate illiteracy and supported free education for Iraqis through the university level. The Iraqi government generously supported families of soldiers, offered its people free hospitalization, and provided substantial subsidies for farmers. Iraq's new public health systems even won a UNESCO award as Saddam launched a campaign to build roads, promote mining, and bring electricity to almost every city in the country.

His approach to governing was thoroughly secular and modernizing. To the consternation of Islamic conservatives, women in his regime were given added freedoms and offered high-level jobs in government and industry. Saddam also created a Western-style legal system, greatly reducing the role of Sharia law in the Iraqi legal system.

His strategy for retaining loyalty to his regime in the rural areas consisted of mechanizing agriculture on a large scale, and giving out land and other benefits to peasant farmers. Soon, in the eyes of many Iraqis, Saddam was being credited with the success of welfare and economic development programs. After he formally took supreme power in July 1979, he tried to consolidate his own power even more over the government and the Baath Party. He carefully cultivated his personal relationships with important party members and Saddam soon built a powerful inner circle of supporters.

This had become very important for him early in 1979 when his nominal boss al-Bakr made an agreement with Syria to unify the two countries. Since Syrian president Hafez al-Assad would have become the deputy leader of such a union, Saddam would probably have had considerably less power. To prevent this, he forced al-Bakr to quit in July 1979 and became Iraq's president himself.

Saddam's next step was to conduct a brutal purge of Baath Party leaders. A video-tape of a meeting held that year of high party officials shows him accusing people of trea-son on camera and having them led away one by one, revealing a penchant to document his own brutality as ruler that continued through-out his regime. By August 1, 1979, hundreds of high-ranking party members had been executed by firing squads composed of other high-ranking members of the party to secure Saddam's position at the top.

The fragmentary nature of Iraqi society continually hampered his plans to increase national unity. His core constituency always remained the 20 percent minority of working-class, peasant, and middle-class Sunni Arabs living primarily in central and western Iraq. Iraq's Arab Shii population, who always remained in the numerical majority and were concentrated in the south, generally opposed the secularizing policies of the Baath regime. This caused the government to wonder about this group's loyalties. With the constant flow of Shii pilgrims and religious scholars between Iran and Iraq, this uncertainty was compounded by fears of how the revolutionary upheaval overtaking Iran in 1978 might spread to other countries.

In the north, *peshmerga* units of Kurdish guerilla fighters had been at war with Iraq's rulers on and off for many decades. Overt hostilities came to a temporary halt when Iran agreed to stop supporting this insurgency in 1975 when it signed the Algiers Accord, but this became more of a pause in Kurdish resistance than its real termination. By the end of the 1970s, most Iraqi Kurds had become affiliated with two political organizations: the **Kurdish Democratic Party** (KDP), a new name for the traditional group long dominated by the Barzani tribal clan, and the **Patriotic Union of Kurdistan (PUK)**, a newer, more urban, and more leftist group formed in 1975 by Jalal Talabani. Saddam would alternately try to co-opt these rebel groups, which sometimes worked, or terrorize them, if co-opting failed. He also relocated Arabs to northern Iraqi cities from other parts of the country to change the demographic mix there.

Saddam's ideology resembled the Pan-Arab nationalism of his Syrian Baathist rivals, but was promoted with even greater intensity. He presented Iraq as the true heartland of the Arab world and the crossroads of all human civilizations, with himself as its uniquely versatile leader. He was depicted in thousands of paintings, posters, statues, and murals across the country. In these, Saddam wore a wide variety of costumes and showed up in numerous different guises to create a personality cult appealing to diverse elements of the society. He appeared in Bedouin garb, the traditional garments of the Sunni Arab Iraqi peasant, and even Kurdish clothing, while also being depicted in elegant Western suits, as well as assuming the guise of a devout Muslim, with full headdress and robe, praying toward Mecca.

At a more practical level, Saddam also created a Machiavellian network of competing security police bureaucracies and armed forces that kept each other in check. Iraq's good financial situation meant that all these organizations were kept well-equipped and became important clients of arms manufacturers worldwide. Saddam was also able to purchase a test nuclear reactor **(Osirak/Tammuz I)** from France to begin the process of eventually producing nuclear weapons, but it was destroyed in a surgical strike by the Israeli Air Force in June 1981.

IRAN-IRAQ WAR

By September 1980, Saddam had built a formidable state prosperous enough to support his visions of personal and national aggrandizement, as manifested in the dozens of palaces that he had constructed for himself and his family around the country. Bolstered by his successes so far, he now chose to revisit the old Iran-Iraq border dispute as a way to pursue these goals beyond the borders of Iraq proper, as well as keeping his society united in its focus on an outside threat.

In that month, he launched a war with Iran, using the tired and specious pretext that the Ottoman Turks, when they ruled Iraq as foreigners, had surrendered Arab territories to Iran that he was now acting to "restore" to the Arab homeland. Iraq had long claimed parts of southern Iran (in the province along the Persian Gulf known as Khuzestan) as its territory. The majority of the people in this area were indeed Arabic-speaking, but they had been under Iranian rule for centuries and considered themselves Iranians.

KPA/ZUMA Press/Newscom

Saddam Hussein (December 1995)

The new rulers of the Islamic Republic of Iran, now steeped in the messianic fervor of their young regime, were ready to do battle with Saddam. They had a strong sense that this conflict might offer the chance to expand their revolution beyond Iran's borders. Perhaps Muslims around the world, particularly Shii populations of Iraq, Saudi Arabia, and the other Arab countries of the Persian Gulf, would follow the Iranian example by revolting against their own governments to form a united Islamic republic. Khomeini and his followers also had a special spiritual hostility toward the secular, Arab nationalist ideology of Baathist Iraq under Saddam, whom Iranian propaganda had recently labeled "a puppet of Satan."[5]

The Iran-Iraq War that followed between September 1980 and August 1988 was known as the "Imposed War" or the "Holy Defense" in Iran, but called "Qadisiyat Saddam" in Iraq, in memory of the Arab victory over Sassanian forces at the Battle of Qadisiya in 636 during the early Muslim conquests. Both titles were rhetorical devices that failed to convey the true costs of this clash, but each revealed the ideological agendas of the two sides very clearly. After the initial attacks, the war bogged down into a steady slog back and forth across a limited front line in which hundreds of thousands of Iranians and Iraqis lost their lives. The impact of this struggle is often compared to the effects of World War I in terms of human loss and because both wars saw extensive use of trench warfare, human wave attacks by soldiers lacking adequate equipment and training, as well as the extensive use of chemical weapons like mustard gas.

Both sides entered the conflict with misconceptions about the situations of their forces and those of their opponents. By this time, Iran's professional armed forces had been severely weakened by extensive purges of the officer corps during the revolution and were

also now beset by severe shortages of spare parts for their American-made equipment. The Iranian military was now forced to rely on badly-armed, although ideologically fervent militias. Iran possessed few defenses in the Shatt al-Arab waterway. Iraqi commanders mistakenly believed that Arabic speakers and Sunnis in Iran would welcome and join them, not grasping the hold of Iranian nationalism there.

First Phase

At first, advancing Iraqi forces met with success, since Iranian regular military units and the Revolutionary Guards were not able to coordinate their activities properly and suffered in battle as a result. Within two days, the Iranian navy had counterattacked by destroying two Iraqi terminals near the port of Fao, severely curtailing Iraq's ability to export oil for a considerable time. Iran's air force also soon commenced a campaign to hit strategic Iraqi industrial and economic targets. At the same time, Iraqi ground forces were able to gain ground fairly rapidly against a disorganized Iranian resistance, creating a wide front that drove deep into Iranian territory.

By March 1981, this Iraqi advance had stalled. Gradually, the Iranians had gained control of the air war, using their nation's larger geographical scale to their advantage. By this time too, Iran's people had mobilized to defend the country, with hundreds of thousands of additional volunteer troops going to the front over the next few months. When Iraqi forces were pushed back into their own territory by June 1982, Iran vowed to press on until Saddam was removed from power and replaced by an "Islamic republic" in Iraq.

Iran mounted its own offensive now, with volunteer troops reciting slogans such as "War, War until Victory" and "The Road to Jerusalem Goes through Karbala." This offensive featured extensive use of human wave attacks by volunteers in which the troops had been fired up before going into battle by professional storytellers, who dramatically

---

[5]Kenneth M. Pollack, *The Persian Puzzle: The Conflict between Iran and America* (New York: Random House, 2005), 183.

recited the story of Ashura, recalling the Battle of Karbala and praising the glory of the martyrs who had fallen there. Sometimes an actor would play the part of Imam Husayn by riding a white horse down the lines: a vision of battlefield heroism to inspire them as they went forth.

When they now attacked into Iraq, Iranian forces came up against substantial defenses and a larger Iraqi army. These Iraqi preparations paid off. When Iran had been fighting on its own soil, it used human-wave attacks, supported by artillery, tanks, and aircraft, with considerable success. In contrast, launching such attacks on Iraqi soil put these volunteers against well-built Iraqi artillery emplacements, with the result that tens of thousands of Iranian soldiers died in each successive attempt to invade Iraq after 1982, with no significant impact on Iraqi defenses. The consequences of this became particularly grisly when Iranian boy volunteers were sent to run across minefields to clear the way for older soldiers behind them. Such tactics produced a multitude of legless veterans who languish today as middle-aged patients in Iranian hospitals. Iranian forces were also brutalized by Iraqi's use of chemical weapons such as mustard gas, which left yet many more as permanent invalids.

Over the next three years, Iranian commanders continued to believe that their numerical superiority would enable them to break through Iraqi defenses if only a coordinated joint attack could be launched. Logistical disorganization prevented such an assault from taking place. Weapons merchants across the globe were happy to deal with both sides, so the stalemate dragged on. To break this, Saddam launched air and missile attacks against selected Iranian cities in February 1984: a move met by swift Iranian retaliation. This "war of the cities" would continue intermittently through the rest of the conflict, but did not affect the ground situation very much. In the end, these attacks on cities did not affect Iran's will to fight very much.

After several more indecisive Iranian offensives, which saw some minor territorial advances but vast more waves of casualties, Saddam had begun to receive enough financial support from other Arab nations to launch his own offensive against Iran for the first time in several years. In return, Iranian commanders began to shift their own tactics, given the failure of their unsupported human wave attacks. Their new approach included developing more coordination between the Revolutionary Guards and the regular Iranian army. Although this did help the Iranians take a part of the Baghdad–Basra highway that they could not capture in previous attempts, Saddam responded to this new challenge with another series of chemical attacks on Iranian positions in Iraq and by starting another "war of the cities."

In contrast to some leaders during difficult times in war, who rhetorically invoke more nationalist imagery, Khomeini's approach to the Iran-Iraq war as it dragged on became more and more deeply religious. He declared in 1985, "It is our belief that Saddam wishes to return Islam to blasphemy and polytheism.... If America becomes victorious ... and grants victory to Saddam, Islam will receive such a blow that it will not be able to raise its head for a long time.... The issue is one of Islam versus blasphemy, and not of Iran versus Iraq."[6] It is noteworthy how clearly Khomeini linked Saddam with the United States, in depicting the war as part of a cosmic religious struggle between good and evil.

Iran-Contra Affair

During the early years of the war, the United States remained very uncertain about how to deal Iran: its recently staunch ally that had suddenly become its worst enemy in the region. This uncertainty produced the huge

---

[6]Daniel Brumberg, *Reinventing Khomeini: The Struggle for Reform in Iran* (Chicago: University of Chicago Press, 2001), 133.

political scandal of the **Iran-Contra affair**. This occurred when senior members of the Reagan administration agreed on a secret plan to facilitate arms sales to Iran, then under a U.S. arms embargo. The idea was to promote better relations with moderate elements within the new Islamic regime as well as secure the release of American hostages being held in Lebanon by **Hezbollah** forces, who were Iran's allies there. As a side benefit, several senior officials decided to divert proceeds from these sales secretly to fund anti-Communist Nicaraguan rebels known as the "contras."

The problem with all these schemes was that they violated the official arms embargo against Iran as well as the Boland Amendment: a law that made direct funding of Nicaraguan rebel groups, including the "contras," illegal. In the end, there were several shipments of arms to Iran, and six American hostages were released in Lebanon, with funds from these arms shipments being sent to the contras via the Central Intelligence Agency.

Although it was never proven that the president himself had approved the transfer of funds to the contras, numerous high-level investigations were conducted and criminal indictments made in this case, none of which resulted in any sustained convictions. The net impact of the affair was to reduce any official American interest in making contact with any elements of Iran's Islamic government. At this time, American focus on this conflict was shifting to its increasing impact on the Persian Gulf, which was creating a direct challenge for the U.S. in guarding maritime commerce there.

During various phases of the war, over thirty countries offered support to Iraq, Iran, or both. This ambiguity of international support grew out of the uncertain alignments of both these nations during this final phase of the Cold War. Both developed extraordinarily complex clandestine procurement networks to obtain needed materiel, munitions, and critical parts, involving agents and countries across the globe.

Tanker War: Conflict in the Gulf

There was less ambiguity about the strategic importance of maintaining stability of commerce in the Persian Gulf: one of the main conduits, by the 1980s, of the world's energy needs. Early in the Iran-Iraq War, ship battles had broken out in the Gulf, but they proved so costly to both sides that there were no serious naval encounters over the next two years. This pause ended abruptly when in March 1984, Iraq began to use French aircraft armed with Exocet missiles to attack tankers carrying oil from Iran, even those flying neutral flags. In retaliation, Iran launched attacks on tankers carrying Iraqi oil from Kuwait and then began to target tankers belonging to any Persian Gulf states that were providing financial support to Iraq.

This began what was later called the "tanker war." Iraq was looking for a way out of the stalemate of the land war by now trying to cut off Iran's oil exports, which might force Tehran to seek peace. However, repeated Iraqi attacks on Kharg Island failed to put the facility there out of operation.

These attacks were able to substantially reduce Iranian oil exports and cut the amount of shipping in the Gulf as a whole by 25 percent. This prompted insurance rates on tankers there to increase, which further increased the price of Gulf oil. When the Saudis shot down an Iranian jet that had strayed into Saudi waters and the situation grew dangerously tense, both Iraq and Iran accepted a UN-sponsored moratorium on shelling any civilian targets. Iraq very quickly reneged on compliance with this agreement and resumed airstrikes on any tankers transporting oil from Iranian terminals, even those registered with its Arab allies in the Gulf, which continued through 1986 and 1987.

When Iran responded by resuming its own attacks on tankers traveling from Arab ports in the Gulf, Kuwait sought the assistance of the United States and the Soviet Union in the fall of 1986, asking them to help protect its shipping. When the Soviet Union agreed to allow Kuwait to use several Soviet tankers in early 1987, the United States agreed to allow the Kuwaitis to "reflag" their tankers as U.S. ships in Operation "Earnest Will." This direct U.S. involvement was also made more urgent by the Iraqi missile attack on the USS *Stark* in May 17, 1987, in which several dozen American sailors were killed. Although this was written off as a mistake, it did become the impetus for much greater U.S. involvement in protecting shipping in the Gulf.

Although Iran stopped short of direct attacks on U.S. ships, it harassed them in various ways, by laying mines, for example, and sending out hit-and-run missions by small patrol boats (manned by the naval branch of the militant Revolutionary Guards). When Iranian forces hit and badly damaged the reflagged tanker *Sea Isle City* in October 1987, U.S. retaliation consisted of destroying two Iranian oil platforms in Operation "Nimble Archer." While there was always some pressure to avoid escalating the conflict any further and keep oil supplies flowing, at the same time there was also continuing pressure to prolong the war.

By early 1988, the Gulf had become quite crowded, with ships from several foreign and regional navies patrolling it. By this time there were almost weekly incidents that crippled or severely damaged merchant ships, which kept shipyards in Bahrain and Dubai fully occupied doing repair work. The USS *Samuel B. Roberts* was badly damaged in April 1988 when it struck an Iranian mine, which left ten sailors wounded but none dead. The U.S. response, Operation "Praying Mantis," featured the U.S. Navy's largest engagement of surface warships since the Second World War. Two Iranian oil platforms, two Iranian ships, and six Iranian gunboats were destroyed, and one American helicopter crashed during this operation.

Throughout this period, U.S. Navy forces in the Gulf remained on very high alert. Soon after Praying Mantis, the USS *Vincennes*, an American guided-missile cruiser, mistakenly shot down an Iranian civilian airliner on a routine flight to Dubai on July 3, 1988, killing 290 passengers and crew.

Operation "Anfal": War on the Kurds

During the first few years of the Iran-Iraq War, Saddam's government tried to reconcile with Kurdish groups in order to persuade them not to assist Iran. Although the PUK agreed to end its conflict with Iraq, the KDP continued in rebellion against the Iraqi government. By 1987, the Iraqi government decided on a strategy to end its Kurdish problem for once and for all. In a military context, Iraq decided to create an empty buffer zone in its border region with Iran. This took place under the extreme pressure of the stalemate that had developed by the end of the war. To achieve this, Iraq forced Kurds living in villages along the Iran–Iraq border to leave their homes between 1987 and 1989 in the Anfal campaign, in which thousands were killed and their villages destroyed. The word *anfal* means "the spoils of war," referring to the section of the Quran describing the triumph of Muslims over pagans at the Battle of Badr in 624 AD. In this case, it was used to describe a campaign of mass killing and looting led by Saddam Hussein's cousin Ali Hassan al-Majid.

Although horrifying enough as an episode of mass killing, with thousands transported to detention camps and murdered, what stood apart in this episode was the widespread use of chemical weapons, including mustard gas and the nerve gas Sarin against the town of Halabja as well as in dozens of other Kurdish villages. The attack on Halabja marked one of the largest scale chemical weapons attacks ever launched against a civilian population.

End of the War

On July 20, 1987, the UN Security Council passed U.S.-sponsored Resolution 598, calling for an end to fighting between Iran and Iraq and a return to prewar boundaries. Iraq, which had lost important pieces of land over the course of the war, accepted the resolution quite promptly. The leaders of Iran, in contrast, still felt that total victory was so close for them that they kept fighting for nearly one more year, finally "quaffing the chalice of poison" (in Khomeini's words) and accepting a cease-fire in early July 1988.[7]

The final chapter of this conflict occurred after that, though, when the group known as the People's Mojahedin of Iran, originally part of the coalition of revolutionaries in Iran in 1979, commenced a ten-day attack from Iraq against western Iran and Kermanshah, with Iraq providing air support that continued for ten days starting in late July 1988. Under great international pressure, Saddam pulled back his planes. The operation ended in a decisive defeat for the People's Mojahedin, which suffered thousands of casualties as well as seeing many of its supporters imprisoned in Iranian jails executed.

Physical Impact of the Iran-Iraq War

The Iran-Iraq War exacted an enormous human cost, with well over 1 million people killed or wounded on both sides. It was estimated in 1991 that Iran suffered more than 50,000 casualties from Iraq's repeated use of chemical weapons against it, with thousands of Iraqis perishing by this method as well. The real number of gas victims will eventually be far larger, since long-term effects of gas have continued to produce deaths since then.

Because of the extensive use of airstrikes and missiles, cities on both sides had also been considerably damaged. The two countries' oil industries were also severely affected by the war. As a consequence of the upheaval created by Islamic Revolution and the Iran-Iraq War, Iran's crude oil production capacity dropped from over 6 million barrels per day in 1978 to just over 2 million by 1988, with Iraq's output falling from 3.7 to 2.5 million barrels per day during the same interval. The millions of shells that landed across one of Iraq's main oil fields near Basra have remained a serious

obstacle for the restoration of previous levels of production as well.

Although both sides suffered grievous human and material losses, the financial toll was more burdensome for Iraq than Iran, since the latter used tactics that cost more lives but were less expensive. This placed Saddam in a difficult position, since the largest portion of the $130 billion that he owed at the end of the war was the $67 billion debt to Kuwait, Saudi Arabia, Qatar, the UAE, and Jordan: a circumstance that directly contributed to Saddam's 1990 decision to invade Kuwait and threaten Saudi Arabia.

Saddam's government commemorated the war by erecting several large sculptures in Baghdad, such as the Hands of Victory statue and the Al-Shaheed Monument, but his original territorial goals for the war were not achieved. The fighting left the borders between Iran and Iraq unmodified. In 1990, Saddam formally acknowledged Iranian rights over the eastern half of the Shatt al-Arab, returning to the terms he had accepted in the Algiers Accord of 1975 with the shah.

In Iran, there was a concerted effort to use the war's impact to bolster the nation's new Islamic government. Stringent wartime conditions of life there were used to strengthen the regime's hold on power and radicalize the youth population. A continuous stream of propaganda articles appeared in government newspapers throughout the conflict, depicting how ordinary Iranians were joining the war effort in droves to seek martyrdom on the battlefield.[8]

THE IRAN-IRAQ WAR AND THE IRANIAN CULTURAL REVOLUTION

Over the course of the war, the new regime also consciously pursued a Cultural Revolution (*enqelab-e farhangi*): a prolonged attempt

---

[7]Ayatollah Ruhollah Khomeini, quoted in Ramin Jahanbegloo, *Iran: Between Tradition and Modernity* (Lanham, MD: Lexington Books, 2004), 119.

[8]For an example, see an April 1983 account in *Etelaat* newspaper cited in Geoffrey Wawro, *Quicksand: America's Pursuit of Power in the Middle East* (New York: Penguin Press, 2010), 399.

to leanse Iranian universities and institutions of higher learning of Western and un-Islamic influences. The initial impetus for this program was to purge universities of secular leftists and Marxists whom the regime had now declared its enemies, but others were targeted as well.

A few months before the war broke out, Khomeini gave a speech harshly attacking the universities in which he declared, "We are not afraid of economic sanctions or military intervention. What we are afraid of is Western universities and the training of our youth in the interests of West or East [not Islamic values]."[9] A "Committee for the Islamization of Universities" was created to examine curricula in every subject from engineering to the humanities and abolished many courses. Students had to appear before revolutionary committees and those found to disagree with Khomeini's doctrine of Guardianship of the Islamic Jurist were expelled. Non-Muslim students were excluded from all programs of study except accounting and foreign languages.

This program closed many universities for three years between 1980 and 1983. When they finally reopened, many books had been taken out of their libraries and banned, while thousands of students and professors had been dismissed from their faculties. This dealt a heavy blow to the lives and careers of many academics, causing the emigration of numerous scholars and scientific experts. One of the most active sponsors of this academic inquisition was the current Supreme Leader, Ali Khamenei, who for much of the 1980s served as president of the Islamic Republic.

Aided by tighter and tighter social controls established over the course of the Iran-Iraq War, the Iranian revolutionary regime succeeded through this Cultural Revolution in establishing control over university campuses and suppressing the teaching of subjects considered harmful to its agendas. Due to this change, Iran became greatly weakened in the scientific and technical fields required for it to develop its society and infrastructure. Although this Cultural Revolution was not directly linked to the war, its implementation was really made possible by the war situation, making this among the most important indirect, but lasting impacts of the Iran-Iraq War on Iranian society as a whole.

Questions to Think About

1. What was the impact of oil price increases on Iran, and how did it affect politics there?
2. How did events in Iran begin to lead to greater and greater popular discontent there in 1978?
3. Why did Shah Mohammad Reza Pahlavi leave and Ayatollah Khomeini return to Iran in early 1979?
4. How did Islamic groups take control of the revolution, and what were their goals?
5. Why did the hostage crisis happen, and what was its impact?
6. How does the Islamic Republic of Iran function as a government, and how does it combine theocratic and democratic elements?
7. How did Saddam's rule of Iraq compare with Syria under Hafez al-Assad as a Baathist government?
8. Why did Saddam Hussein begin a war with Iran?
9. Why is the Iran-Iraq War often compared with World War I?
10. How did the United States become involved in the Iran-Iraq War?
11. What was the Anfal campaign, and why was it launched?
12. What was the impact of the Iran-Iraq War on life in the Islamic Republic of Iran?

---

[9]Shaul Bakhash, *The Reign of the Ayatollahs* (New York: Basic Books, 1986), 122.

For Further Reading

Afkhami, Gholam R. *The Life and Times of the Shah*. Berkeley: University of California Press, 2009.

Ahmadzadeh, Habib, and Paul Sprachman. *A City under Siege: Tales of the Iran-Iraq War*. Costa Mesa, CA: Mazda Publishers, 2010.

Amuzegar, Jahangir. *The Dynamics of the Iranian Revolution: The Pahlavis' Triumph and Tragedy*. Albany: State University of New York Press, 1991.

Bowden, Mark. *Guests of the Ayatollah: The First Battle in America's War with Militant Islam*. New York: Atlantic Monthly Press, 2006.

Buchta, Wilfried. *Who Rules Iran? The Structure of Power in the Islamic Republic*. Washington, DC: Washington Institute for Near East Policy, 2000.

Cordesman, Anthony H. *The Iran-Iraq War and Western Security, 1984–87: Strategic Implications and Policy Options*. London: Jane's, 1987.

Farber, David R. *Taken Hostage: The Iran Hostage Crisis and America's First Encounter with Radical Islam*. Princeton, NJ: Princeton University Press, 2005.

Houghton, David Patrick. *US Foreign Policy and the Iran Hostage Crisis*. Cambridge: Cambridge University Press, 2001.

Makiya, Kanan. *Republic of Fear: The Politics of Modern Iraq*. Berkeley: University of California Press, 1998.

Marr, Phebe. *The Modern History of Iraq*. Boulder, CO: Westview Press, 2004.

Milani, Abbas. *The Shah*. New York: Palgrave Macmillan, 2011.

Milani, Mohsen M. *The Making of Iran's Islamic Revolution: From Monarchy to Islamic Republic*. Boulder, CO: Westview Press, 1988.

Pelletiere, Stephen C. *The Iran-Iraq War: Chaos in a Vacuum*. New York: Praeger, 1992.

Rajaee, Farhang. *Iranian Perspectives on the Iran-Iraq War*. Gainesville: University Press of Florida, 1997.

Takeyh, Ray. *Hidden Iran: Paradox and Power in the Islamic Republic*. New York: Times Books, 2006.

Wise, Harold Lee. *Inside the Danger Zone: The U.S. Military in the Persian Gulf, 1987–1988*. Annapolis, MD: Naval Institute Press, 2007.

21

Middle East at the End of the Cold War, 1979–1993

I ran and Iraq were not the only places in the Middle East to endure great turbulence in the 1980s: the last years of the Cold War. The Soviet Union conducted a very costly war in Afghanistan, and the Lebanese Civil War worsened, while there was a revolt of Palestinians living in the West Bank and the rise of an insurgency among the Kurdish population in eastern Turkey. All these wars were deeply affected by the dynamics of current global contests for power and influence between East and West, but they originated in longstanding local conflicts that continued in new guises.

SOVIET WAR IN AFGHANISTAN

The Soviet war in Afghanistan, which went on for ten years, is a good example of this. It had its origins in an attempt by the Soviet Union to preserve a Communist government it had installed in the late 1970s: the latest "Communist" version of Russia's drive to expand influence and control southward begun over a century earlier in its Great Game struggle with Britain. The Afghan Communist government's main foes were guerrilla warriors called *mujahidin*. The *mujahidin* formed small groups of fighters whose allegiances coalesced around regional tribal leaders from Afghanistan's diverse collection of ethnic and religious groups.

Many outside powers supported these groups, but their most important backers were Pakistan, Saudi Arabia, and the United States, all of whom had different motives for their aid. Pakistan was always most concerned about keeping control of its own complex ethnic mixture, with members of the same ethnic groups straddling the border between Pakistan and Afghanistan. Saudi Arabians perceived Afghanistan as the ideal place to promote a return to Islam by all the Muslim peoples of the Soviet Union, particularly in Central Asia, whose religious life had been suppressed by the Communists for decades. For the United States, Afghanistan was a strategic theater of the Cold War in which to confront Communist expansionism face to face.

The first Soviet troops entered Afghanistan on Christmas Eve (December 24) 1979 and the last left in February 1989. This war was so prolonged, so costly, and caused so many casualties that it is often referred to as the Soviet Union's Vietnam War, to draw a parallel with the costs that the Vietnam conflict had exacted on the United States.

Mohammed Daoud Khan and Afghanistan's First Republic

Russian military activities in Afghanistan had not begun recently, but commenced in the competition between the Russian and British Empires known as the "Great Game" for predominance in Central Asia. Although this changed dramatically after the British left India following World War II, the Soviet Union that had risen up after the collapse of the Russian Empire remained engaged in Afghanistan, primarily by sending it generous military and economic help in the 1960s and 1970s. Over this same period, the United States countered this Soviet assistance program through its own economic aid missions. The U.S. Agency for International Development, for example, built a hydroelectric project between 1949 and 1979 to improve water utilization in Afghanistan's **Helmand Valley**, among the most fertile regions of the country.

Until 1973, Afghanistan had been a monarchy dominated for two centuries by the **Durranis**, one of the main Pashtun tribal confederations. In that year, Mohammed Daoud Khan, a cousin of King Mohammed Zahir Shah who had been on the throne for the previous four decades, staged a coup and declared himself president of the first "republic" in the history of Afghanistan. His seizure of power occurred after several years of bad harvests, a decline in foreign aid, and rising concern among the country's ruling elite that the governing style of the ruling monarch was too laissez-faire and hands-off.

Daoud had served as Afghanistan's prime minister in the 1950s and always saw the active modernization of his country as his primary goal. When he regained power in 1973, he tried to continue a policy of modernization and staying nonaligned: playing the United States and USSR off against each other while preserving stable relations with neighbors India, Pakistan, and Iran. It soon proved quite difficult to balance all the competing interest groups that Daoud had to satisfy to stay in power.

During his years out of office, Daoud had built ties with members of Afghan's new urban intelligentsia, as well as with leaders of the Afghan officer corps largely trained by the Soviets. In 1974, he signed an agreement with the Soviet Union to bolster Afghanistan's military capabilities, and for an extended period of time, the Afghans received a generous flow of advanced Soviet military equipment. The Soviet Union was pleased to have an ally on its strategic southern border, which, although still ruled by a member of the traditional royal family, had recently been proclaimed a republic and seen its monarchy abolished. For his part, Daoud remained wary of depending too much on his pro-Soviet colleagues in the Afghan military and gradually removed many of them from important positions. This slowly soured relations with the Soviet Union, which ultimately proved dangerous for him.

At this same time, he had to confront another group that had initially supported his rise to power: Islamist members of the Muslim Youth Organization. This group had been founded at Kabul University in 1969, at a time when that campus was wracked by an intense ideological struggle between Marxist revolutionaries and Islamists. Muslim activists there were inspired by the philosophy of the radical Egyptian thinker Sayyid Qutb. Qutb's main text, *Milestones,* had just been translated into Dari, one of Afghanistan's main languages (and very similar to Persian/Farsi), by a member of the university's Islamic law faculty, Burhanuddin Rabbani.

When Daoud banned the Muslim Youth Organization in 1974, all its leaders fled to Pakistan. There, they organized an Afghani Muslim resistance supported by the Pakistani government. Pakistan's aid to these activists was partly motivated by its continued long-running dispute with Afghanistan over the border between the two nations. Known as the **Durand Line** and created by the British in 1898, this border ran right through the middle of the homelands of the Pashtun people, the largest single ethnic group (though not a majority) in Afghanistan's population. As a result, this frontier has remained a constant source of friction between the rulers of Afghanistan and Pakistan.

Fairly soon, Daoud was able to ease tensions with Pakistan through a new agreement brokered by the United States and Iran. Any improvements in relations between Afghanistan and Pakistan were in turn opposed by Afghan Communists and their Soviet supporters. The Soviets were also put off by how Daoud was building closer relationships with major Middle Eastern nations such as Iran and Egypt. When Afghanistan concluded a military cooperation treaty with Egypt to bring in Egyptian officers to train the Afghan military and police forces, this provided an unpleasant reminder for the Soviet leadership of how Egypt had recently distanced itself from its Soviet patrons before and after the 1973 October War.

Adopting a tactic used by other modernizing Middle Eastern rulers in the twentieth century, Daoud issued a new national constitution and established a single political party, the National Revolutionary Party, in 1976, and declared all other parties abolished. With a nod to Afghan tradition, he also convened a *loya jirga* (traditional Pashtun assembly of tribal elders) in early 1977 to confirm his new constitution and party.

"Democratic Republic" of Afghanistan

All of these developments were unsettling for the Russians. At a meeting with Daoud in 1977, Soviet leader Brezhnev broke away from planned scripted expressions of friendship, bluntly admonishing him not to stray too far away from Soviet influence. This startled Daoud, who quickly responded that Afghanistan would never let the Russians dictate to its leaders how to run their country. At a practical level, Daoud was able to answer such Soviet threats in this way because the Afghani Communist Party remained weak. For many years, it had been divided into two opposing groups: the *Parcham* (flag) and *Khalq* (people) factions.

As Daoud became increasingly alienated from both factions, this brought them together. At the April 1978 funeral of Mir Akbar Khyber, a member of the *Parcham* group who had died under suspicious circumstances, thousands of Communists from both factions staged a joint demonstration in Kabul. This prompted Daoud to suppress them all, so Communist cells in the Afghan army staged a coup and killed Daoud a few days later.

Nur Muhammad Taraki, secretary general of Afghan Communist Party and leader of the *Khalq* faction, became the first prime minister of a new "Democratic Republic of Afghanistan." During their first few months in power, the Communists remade Afghanistan into a Soviet-style totalitarian state, collectivizing land holdings and abolishing Islamic law entirely. The new government tolerated no opposition to these changes. To enforce them, it imprisoned and executed thousands of prisoners, including many village religious leaders and headmen, at the infamous Pul-e-Charkhi prison east of Kabul. This caused an immediate and violent reaction among the rural population, and by late 1978, there were already signs of a civil war in various parts of the country.

By the middle of 1979, the Communist government had lost control over large parts of the country and began requesting substantial Soviet assistance. The Soviets were reluctant at first to become too embroiled in the situation, because it was clear that factional divisions which had long separated the Afghan Communist party were only deepening after its seizure of power and that the USSR would stand to lose more than it would gain through direct intervention. Meanwhile, anticommunist rebels were pleased to receive covert aid from the United States. The CIA offered financial support to Afghan rebel factions and was permitted to conduct propaganda operations against the communist government, according to an executive order signed by President Carter at this time.

Within the Communist ruling elite, factional divisions continued to cause big problems. In September 1979, Deputy Prime Minister Hafizullah Amin (longtime leader of the *Parcham* [flag] faction) took power after a gun battle in which President Taraki (of the *Khalq* faction) was murdered. Amin had a hard time securing his control over the situation. He was forced to move against his Communist opponents while simultaneously quelling a growing popular rebellion. When the KGB station in Kabul sent a warning to Moscow that Amin's continued rule would lead to "harsh repressions, and as a result, the activation and consolidation of the opposition," this caused great alarm among the Soviet leadership.[1] In the end, it chose to intervene with Russian troops in December.

A KGB team came to Kabul, had Amin tried and executed by a tribunal of the Afghan Revolutionary Central Committee, and finally replaced him with Babrak Karmal. Karmal was another leader of the *Parcham* faction who subsequently ruled Afghanistan until 1986. Although he adopted a notably milder approach than either of his predecessors, it came too late. By late 1980, more than half of the 80,000-man Afghan army had deserted or joined the rebels. Within a few days after Karmal took power, more than 100,000 Soviet troops had arrived in Afghanistan. Although

this was met with an immediate international outcry, it had no effect on the situation in the country itself.

Pursuing the War: 1980–1987

Soviet troops found themselves immediately thrust into putting down uprisings in the major cities, battling tribal armies, and going after mutinous Afghan army units. Once Soviet forces had secured the cities, the war fell into a pattern over the next few years. The Soviet army controlled the cities and main roads, while the *mujahidin* (as the rebels were now calling themselves), broke into small groups to wage continuous guerrilla war. Nearly 80 percent of the entire country was never controlled by the central government during this period. Every so often, Soviet forces would stage huge offensives in rebel-controlled areas, but they still could never establish government control over them.

When Mikhail Gorbachev became the new Soviet leader in March 1985, he set a one-year deadline for a solution to be found to the Afghan problem. The Soviet military arranged for a troop surge to produce this result, which increased fighting across the country and made 1985 the bloodiest year of the war. Gorbachev's plan did not meet with success, and the *mujahidin* continued their successful resistance against Soviet power.

By this time, the U.S. government had come to view the Afghan conflict as a major part of the Cold War, authorizing the CIA to aid the *mujahidin* by way of allies in the Pakistani intelligence services. Muslim countries, in particular Saudi Arabia, also provided them help and contingents of volunteers who became known as the "**Afghan Arabs**." These were young Muslims from other countries who wished to assist in a jihad against atheistic communists. One of them was Osama bin Laden, who became one of the founders of al-Qaeda after he had lived in Pakistan and been aiding the "Afghans for" several years.

The Afghan resistance movement functioned and ruled in chaos, with all combat

---

[1]Martin Walker, *The Cold War: A History* (New York: Macmillan, 1995), 254.

being waged locally by regional warlords. After years of war, there were hundreds of bases from which the *mujahidin* operated. Most were affiliated with several major groups headquartered in western Pakistan, with its border cities of Quetta and Peshawar serving as important conduits for supplies and communication.

The channeling of large amounts of aid promoted growth in some sectors of Pakistan's economy, but in general the war was vastly more harmful than beneficial. The siphoning off of military materiel sent through the port of Karachi produced disorder and violence there, and there was a huge increase in the amount of heroin being imported into Pakistan from Afghanistan to pay for weapons. During the conflict, Pakistan also brought in millions of Afghan refugees (mostly Pashtun) who mostly stayed in the border regions, where many of them still live today. A smaller amount, but still numbering in the millions, took refuge in the eastern provinces of Iran.

The impact of the war on Afghanistan itself was far greater than on Pakistan, with the entire infrastructure of the country being essentially destroyed by the end of the 1980s. The population of Afghanistan's second largest city, Kandahar, for example, was reduced from 200,000 before the war to about 25,000 inhabitants after a prolonged campaign of carpet bombing and bulldozing conducted by the Soviets and their Afghan allies in 1987. Land mines took the lives of 25,000 Afghans during the war and 10–15 million mines remain scattered across the country today, with an estimated 3–4% of the Afghan population (in 2005) crippled or disabled by mines.

Ending the War: 1987–1992

After trying and failing to transfer the burden of fighting to its Afghan allies, the Soviet Union announced that whatever else happened, by mid-1987 it would start withdrawing its own forces. In 1988, the governments of Pakistan and Afghanistan, backed officially by the United States and Soviet Union, signed the Geneva Accords: an agreement to resolve their major disputes. This included a timetable for the full withdrawal of Soviet troops, finally completed in February 1989.

After the Soviet pullout, the Communist Afghan government withstood the attacks of the *mujahidin* for three more years. It continued to get Soviet funding and arms until the collapse of the Soviet Union itself in 1991. During this interim period, the government army's performance surpassed anything it had ever achieved while the Soviet military was still there. This effort suffered a major blow in 1992, when Abdul Rashid Dostum, one of the government army's leading generals, joined the *mujahidin* and helped them occupy Kabul. Although the 1988 Geneva Accords offered a diplomatic framework to allow the Soviets to leave, they totally failed to address the problem of what would follow after that. The Soviet withdrawal also ended official U.S. interest in Afghanistan, whose problems were then left for others to sort out.

When major disagreements arose between *mujahidin* factions, regional powers played the situation to their own advantage. The swift rise to power of the **Taliban** in 1994 was, in large part, one of the main consequences of the nearly complete breakdown of civil society across Afghanistan that gradually took place after the 1989 departure of the Soviets and the final collapse of their puppet regime three years later in 1992.

1982 WAR IN LEBANON

The Soviet-Afghan War of the 1980s had a pivotal impact on the Soviet Union's sense of itself, with one of its lasting impacts being a loss of confidence among its leadership that became a critical factor in the demise of the Soviet Union, which occurred only a few years after the end of the debacle in Afghanistan. For Israel, the 1982 Lebanon War had a decisive impact as well, since this was the first war Israel fought in which there was significant domestic dissent about how the war was conducted and for what ends it was pursued. Originally labeled Operation "Peace for Galilee" to reflect its limited goal of ending Palestinian incursions into Israel from Lebanon, the conflict dragged Israel into an occupation of southern Lebanon lasting many years and helped create the Shii Hezbollah terrorist organization, now one of Israel's main enemies.

It began on June 6, 1982, with the Israeli army's invasion of southern Lebanon. The invasion took place under a somewhat curious pretext: the attempted assassination of Israel's ambassador to the United Kingdom. This operation had no connection with any of the main Palestinian groups in Lebanon at all. Instead, it had been carried out by a freelance Palestinian terror group based in Syria known as the Abu Nidal Organization—opposed to the PLO since the 1970s.

The bigger issue was that by this time, the Lebanese frontier had become Israel's most challenging border. Israel tried to secure it through Operation Litani in 1978: a limited military intervention in Lebanon in response to increased Palestinian activities there in the previous few years. Following the 1978 incursion, a UN monitoring force (UNIFIL) was put in place, and Israel began to use Lebanese Christian militia forces to provide a buffer between it and the PLO. Its main partner became the predominantly Christian South Lebanon Army (SLA), many of whose members then began to train at Israeli military schools.

A steady exchange of limited hostile encounters continued between the Israelis and the PLO over the next four years, keeping this area in a constant state of tension. The military problem with these attacks was that because PLO weapons stockpiles were widely dispersed, this made them very hard for the Israelis to attack and destroy. When Israel did attack them, this often resulted in many civilian Lebanese deaths. There was finally a cease-fire arranged in July 1981, but it was broken by a new round of attacks in the spring of 1982.

Right-wing Israelis then serving in the government of Menachem Begin, particularly the new minister of defense, Ariel Sharon, began to conceive of a more substantial political-strategic alliance between Israel and the Lebanese Christians as a potential long-term solution to the problem of what to do about the Palestinians in Lebanon. The concept was that a strongly pro-Israeli Christian government in Lebanon might eventually be persuaded to expel the PLO and many of the Palestinian refugees living there. When Israel completed its withdrawal from the Sinai in 1982 according to the terms of its recent peace treaty with Egypt, the conservative Israeli government decided to devote its attention to resolving the problem of the PLO in Lebanon for once and for all.

The 1982 war began when Israel started a conventional advance into Lebanon to force PLO forces to move 25 miles to the north. With peace on its other borders, Israel's ability to field a much larger force in Lebanon than before permitted it now to take control of the battleground and maintain the element of surprise. Israel wanted to avoid a full-scale war and took some pains to avoid engaging Syrian ground forces in the fighting. Instead, it focused on neutralizing Syrian air power, which it did by destroying a total of 86 Syrian planes.

As Israeli ground forces quickly progressed toward Beirut, the Israeli Navy landed tanks, armored vehicles, and paratroopers north of Sidon to seal off PLO escape routes. Tyre and Sidon (two major cities in southern Lebanon located less than 25 miles north of Israel) suffered serious damage, and Israeli also forces bombed and shelled Beirut, killing many PLO members and civilians. Israeli troops finally took the Beirut airport and occupied several of the city's southern suburbs after intensive shelling, during which the city remained under siege for long periods at a time.

When American negotiator Philip Habib arranged a cease-fire on August 18, 1982, American, French, and Italian peacekeepers were sent to Beirut as peacekeepers in the "Multinational Force in Lebanon." In August and September, more than 14,000 PLO warriors left the country. Tunis, Tunisia, eventually became the new PLO headquarters when the organization's leaders finally arrived there from northern Lebanon in December 1983. In return for the PLO's acceptance of this agreement, Ambassador Habib gave assurances that Palestinian civilians in refugee camps would not be harmed.

Gemayel's Assassination and the Sabra and Shatila Massacres

On September 1, 1982, Bachir Gemayel, senior leader of the Maronite Phalange Party, commander of the Lebanese Forces militia, and president-elect of Lebanon, held a meeting with Israeli prime minister Begin in northern Israel. Begin demanded that Gemayel sign a peace treaty with Israel as soon as he became president, since Israel was providing so much support for his Lebanese Forces militia. Gemayel replied that he could not do this immediately but needed more time to achieve consensus among supporters on this issue.

Gemayel was assassinated two weeks later on September 14 by a fellow Maronite. His killer happened to be a member of the Syrian Social Nationalist Party and had links to Syrian intelligence. When questioned about what he had done, he said that he had taken action out of fear that Gemayel would sell out Lebanon to Israel.

The next day, Israeli forces reoccupied West Beirut. In violation of the cease-fire agreement arranged by the United States, Israel allowed about 150 members of the Lebanese Forces militia to enter the Sabra and Shatila refugee camps, claiming that "two thousand PLO terrorists" were taking refuge there. The result was that at least eight hundred civilians were murdered by these forces as Israeli units circled the camps with tanks and set up checkpoints, monitoring who came out and went in.

A later official Israeli investigation found that Ariel Sharon bore "personal responsibility" for not stopping the massacre once he learned it was underway. It recommended that he

resign as defense minister and never hold any future position in the Israeli government. At first, Sharon ignored the call to leave his post, but after the death of an Israeli protester demonstrating against the war, he did quit his job as defense minister, although he remained in the cabinet as a minister without portfolio.

Results of the 1982 War

Thousands of Lebanese lost their lives as a result of this war, which also did hundreds of millions of dollars' worth of material damage. Although the conflict did result in the relocation of the PLO's headquarters from Beirut to Tunis, where it remained until the 1990s, Israel never secured a final peace agreement with Lebanon and was unable to destroy organized Palestinian resistance to it.

By May 1983, Israel and Lebanon made an arrangement brokered by the United States. According to it, Israel would withdraw from Lebanon, providing that it could patrol a "security zone" in the south in conjunction with the regular Lebanese Army. This agreement was not formally ratified by either side, although Israel more or less followed its provisions. Instead of having the regular Lebanese army as its partner, the Israelis used the South Lebanon Army as its client in a "security zone" along the border, where they now stationed troops that would only leave Lebanon permanently in 2000, seventeen years later.

The events of the war wrecked any possibility of an alliance developing between Israel and Lebanon's Maronite community, thwarting Sharon's dream of installing a pro-Israeli Christian Lebanese government. The conflict, in fact, prompted 850,000 Christians to leave the country, most on a permanent basis. Domestically, Israel experienced significant challenges to the longstanding rule there about not publicly criticizing the military. Ordinary Israelis became disillusioned with military leaders after this war: a significant problem for a society that relied on its citizen-soldiers.

Militancy and the Rise of Hezbollah

Perhaps the most unintended and unforeseen consequence of the war in Lebanon itself was how it caused many Shiis, who had not been supporters or allies of the PLO before this conflict, to turn against Israel after it had invaded and then occupied their lands for a long time. Opposition to this Israeli occupation became one of the main causes for the most militant Lebanese Shiis to take inspiration from the millenarian revolutionary zeal then sweeping over Iran and to form Hezbollah. Twenty years later (by the early twenty-first century), Hezbollah has evolved into a versatile militant Islamist fighting force against Israel and the United States that has replaced the Palestinians as Israel's primary opponent in southern Lebanon (although the Palestinians are still threats elsewhere).

Hezbollah began as an association of Lebanese Shii militants inspired by the recent Iranian revolution and Ayatollah Khomeini. Ending Israel's occupation of southern Lebanon was the primary focus of its early activities. As Hezbollah became more formally organized over the 1980s, it also evolved into a major provider of social services for thousands of poor Lebanese Shiis: operating schools, hospitals, and agricultural services as well as playing a more and more influential role in Lebanese politics.

Even before Hezbollah had coalesced as an organization, the failure of Israeli troops to withdraw from Lebanon after the 1982 cease-fire, as well as the presence of American and European troops, coincided with the first major use of a new tactic: suicide bombing. Between 1982 and 1986, militants carried out several dozen suicide attacks against American, French, and Israeli targets in Lebanon resulting in hundreds of deaths. Among the most infamous occurred in 1983 with the bombing of the U.S. Embassy in Beirut in April, followed by the October 23 simultaneous truck bombings against U.S. and French contingents of the Multinational Force, in which 241 American and 58 French soldiers died.

A shadowy organization calling itself "Islamic Jihad" claimed responsibility for these deeds in a statement released to a French news agency, declaring, "We are the soldiers of God....We are neither Iranians, Syrians, nor Palestinians, but Muslims who follow the precepts of the Koran....We said after that [embassy bombing] that we would strike more violently still. Now they understand with what they are dealing. Violence will remain our only way."[2] Just a few weeks later, this Islamic Jihad also took responsibility for the murder of Malcolm Kerr, president of the American University in Beirut (whose predecessor, David Dodge, had been kidnapped and released by militants). The actual identity of Islamic Jihad has remained unclear since then. Some have argued that this label was an alias used by another organization, possibly Hezbollah, others have concluded it to have been a cover for intelligence operatives from Iran, while still others have described it as a network or phony company: a front behind which to conceal its true identity.

In any event, Hezbollah formally proclaimed its own existence and issued a formal mission statement in February 1985 as "an open letter to all the Oppressed in Lebanon and the World." It announced that its goals were to expel the Americans, French, and their allies from Lebanon, putting an end to any colonialist presence in the country. It also called for bringing Christian Phalangist militiamen to justice for their crimes, while asking for the Lebanese people to be given the right to choose freely whatever form of government they might desire. Finally, the letter advised the Lebanese to choose an "Islamic government," since only this would really be able to secure liberty and justice for all. The document referred to Ayatollah Khomeini as the leader whose "orders we obey" and called on Christians to embrace Islam. It noted that "God had made

---

[2]Robin Wright, *Sacred Rage: The Wrath of Militant Islam* (New York: Simon & Schuster, 2001), 73.

it intolerable for Muslims to participate in a government not based on Islamic holy law" and called Israel "the vanguard of the United States in the Islamic world."[3]

As Israel's occupation of southern Lebanon continued during the next few years, Hezbollah developed into its own state within a state in the parts of Lebanon that it controlled, as its own armed forces engaged in continuous small skirmishes with Israeli units serving in the occupation army. Hezbollah leaders had originally envisioned transforming Lebanon into a formal Islamic republic along Iranian lines. Eventually, this goal was abandoned in favor of building the organization into a military action/social welfare agency with a leadership structure similar to that of Iran's clerical ruling group, in which final authority and power rested with the senior cleric. In keeping with Khomeini's concept of Guardianship of the Islamic Jurist (*velayat-e faqih*) they deemed this to be Khomeini himself. As long as Khomeini was alive, the leadership of Hezbollah turned to him as their authority when it could not agree on how to proceed in a given circumstance. Many ordinary Shiis began to perceive Hezbollah as an important source of medical, economic, and educational assistance in addition to its military activities. By the late 1980s, it was playing as crucial a role in the reconstruction of damaged parts of the country as the actual official government of Lebanon.

Final Unraveling of Lebanese Politics

As Hezbollah evolved into a formidably independent institution, sectarian conflict worsened as efforts at national reconciliation broke down. The departure of the Multinational Force in February 1984 set off a showdown between the **Amal movement** (manned by

---

[3]See an English translation of the document's text in Joseph Alagha, *The Shifts in Hezbollah's Ideology: Religious Ideology, Political Ideology, and Political Program* (Amsterdam: Amsterdam University Press, 2006), 223–238.

Lebanese Shii troops who had not joined Hezbollah but were now being helped by Syria) and PLO forces remaining in Lebanon after the PLO leadership had left. This grew into a "War of the Camps" that extended through 1985 and 1986, causing many more Palestinian deaths, with several remaining Palestinian camps being virtually obliterated.

By 1987, this new round of clashes began to center on Beirut, where a coalition of Palestinian soldiers, Lebanese leftists, and Druze militiamen rose up against Amal. A violent confrontation also took place there between Amal and Hezbollah, in which Hezbollah forces easily captured several parts of the city held by Amal. Even in the midst of the turmoil, as militias battled for control and civil order broke down, the national government had continued to abide by the National Pact all this time, appointing requisite members of different religious minorities to their respective official posts.

The real crisis of the system finally occurred when the term of the president, Maronite politician Amin Gemayel (brother of the assassinated Bachir Gemayel), ended in September 1988. Because of the security breakdown and boycotts by several Christian politicians, it was not possible to assemble a quorum of the Lebanese parliament to select his successor. In a purely political maneuver, Gemayel appointed General **Michel Aoun**, a Maronite leader, to be Lebanon's temporary prime minister just minutes before his own term as president expired.

Gemayel's action was intended to preserve the Maronite power that went along with the presidency, but it violated the National Pact rule that the prime minister had to be a Sunni Muslim. When challenged, Gemayel invoked the precedent of 1952, when Maronite general Chehab became temporary prime minister in a transition government. Muslim politicians and warlords now refused to recognize Aoun as prime minister, so two rival national governments were formed. One, under Sunni politician Selim al-Hoss, was supported by Syria.

Its headquarters were in West Beirut, and it was run mostly by civilians and Muslims. The other, led by Aoun and a group of Christian military officers, controlled East Beirut and surrounding areas.

At first, Aoun was supported by about 60 percent of the regular Lebanese army, including nearly all of its tank and artillery units. He was also backed by Samir Geagea, commander of the Lebanese Forces militia since January 1986. Geagea was a charismatic Christian military leader who had greatly expanded the Lebanese Forces' military capabilities and level of training.

At the same time, he had also built a social services network (reminiscent of Hezbollah) to help Christians in places where official government services were no longer provided. Geagea's group collected unofficial taxes from Christians, but also offered them extensive medical coverage (including free open-heart surgical operations). He began a sister cities program, pairing Christian towns with their counterparts in Europe and North America. There was even an attempt to open a new airport in Halat (north of Beirut), since the Beirut International Airport, long under the control of Syrian forces, had become virtually inaccessible to Lebanese Christians.

By the spring of 1989, Aoun's alliance with the Lebanese Forces fell apart when Geagea turned against him. In order to collect more customs revenues, Michel Aoun began to use troops under his control to wrest control of seaports held by Geagea's forces. Syria was drawn more and more directly into this dispute, until Aoun declared a "war of liberation" against Syria after it attacked the Lebanese presidential palace and ministry of defense on March 14, 1989.

Paradoxically, the U.S. government now was backing the Syrians against Aoun in this confrontation, in exchange for Syrian support against Saddam Hussein. Aoun had developed a close friendship with Iraqi president Hussein, who had begun to see Aoun as a useful ally in Iraq's rivalries with Syria and Iran. Through the spring and summer of 1989, fierce artillery battles between Aoun and the Syrians over control of Beirut drove most inhabitants out of the city, leaving only about 100,000 people there when it was over.

Aoun drew closer and closer to Iraq, accepting arms and military supplies from Saddam Hussein. Lebanon had become by this time a proxy battlefield for the conflict between Iran and Iraq—a situation that continued even after the actual Iran-Iraq War had ended. To counter Iran's strong links with Amal and Hezbollah, Iraq backed Christian military leaders such as Aoun.

Taif Accord

The rapid further deterioration of civil order in Lebanon caused concern in the Arab League. This led to a peace initiative brokered by Kuwait, Saudi Arabia, Algeria, and Morocco. Members of the last elected group of the Lebanese National Assembly (chosen in 1972 before the civil war began) met in the Saudi city of Taif in October 1989. This meeting produced a National Reconciliation Accord (later usually called the **Taif Accord**), marking the beginning of the final end of the Lebanese civil war that had started in 1975.

The agreement restructured the power-sharing system of the National Pact. It took away some power that the National Pact had given the Maronites. Under the National Pact, the Maronite president had appointed the Sunni Muslim prime minister, so that the prime minister was always directly responsible and answerable to him. Under the Taif Accord, the prime minister was now made responsible to the legislature as well.[4]

Although the accord called for an end to political sectarianism, it specified no definite way to carry this out. It enlarged the parliament to 128 members, now equally divided between Christians and Muslims, to replace the ratio of

---

[4]See the Taif Accord text in David Sorenson, *Global Security Watch—Lebanon: A Reference Handbook* (Santa Barbara, CA: Praeger, 2009), 174.

six Christian to five Muslim deputies specified in the National Pact. Similar to the parliament, the cabinet was to have equal numbers of Christians and Muslims.

The accord also required all militia groups to disarm. Hezbollah alone was permitted to keep its arms, because it was now redefined as a "resistance force" against Israel instead of a militia per se. Finally, the agreement acknowledged a large role for Syria in Lebanese affairs in a way that angered many Lebanese.

General Aoun refused to attend the meeting that produced it, calling those who signed the accord traitors, and formally dissolved the Lebanese National Assembly that had agreed on it. After signing the Taif agreement, this group returned to Lebanon in November 1989 and elected René Moawad as the new Lebanese president. His term of office lasted only seventeen days until he was killed by a car bomb. His successor, Elias Hrawi (who remained as president until 1998), appointed General Lahoud to command the regular Lebanese army and ordered Aoun to leave the presidential palace.

Aoun ignored this order, but his position became weaker and weaker as his former allies, Geagea's Lebanese Forces militia, waged war on him between January and October 1990. When Aoun's supporter Saddam Hussein invaded Kuwait in August, 1990, Syria's decision to back the United States against Saddam was reciprocated by official U.S. support for Syrian action against Aoun. On October 13, 1990, Syrian forces captured the presidential palace, where Aoun had made his last stand and forced him to flee to France.

On December 24, the new president Elias Hrawi created a half-Christian, half-Muslim unity government with a cabinet that included seven former militia commanders. Within three months, the Lebanese parliament passed a law granting amnesty for most political crimes committed before the law was approved, except for offenses committed against foreign diplomats and certain other crimes specified by the Lebanese judicial authorities.

By May 1991, all militias (except Hezbollah) were dissolved, and the official Lebanese Armed Forces had been restored as a nonsectarian institution. Although Lebanon experienced numerous crises and periods of instability since then, it has remained far more peaceful in the two decades following the Taif Accord than in the fifteen years before it.

FIRST INTIFADA (1987–1993)

Although the challenges posed to Israel by Lebanon's continuing upheaval did not end after Israeli troops withdrew to a southern defensive perimeter in June 1985, they were greatly reduced. Israel confronted a much more serious problem when the Palestinian uprising now referred to as the First Intifada erupted in Gaza, the West Bank, and East Jerusalem in 1987.

After removing the PLO leadership from Lebanon and driving it to Tunisia by 1983, Israelis began to feel that their security could no longer be threatened by forces coming from just over the border, either from Egypt, Jordan, or Lebanon. What this calculation did not take into account was the growing restiveness of Palestinians under Israeli military occupation since 1967. Unlike Palestinians under Israeli rule since 1948 (with recognized rights as citizens of Israel), or Palestinians who had fled to other countries (where they dreamed of returning someday but had no direct contact with Israelis), Palestinians living in the occupied territories had to deal on a daily basis with Israeli soldiers, who regarded them as potential security threats and whose main job was to keep them pacified, without worrying about disrespecting them or violating their rights.

Encounters between Israelis and Palestinians in this setting created a rising level of stress and tension that could always erupt into something bigger, given the right circumstances. This finally happened when an Israeli military transport truck ran into a group of Palestinians from a refugee camp at a border crossing in early December 1987, killing several of them. The incident caused substantial riots across Gaza, the West Bank, and East Jerusalem. Unrest was fueled by widespread Palestinian anger over house demolitions and deportations, carried out by the Israeli military as the governing authority in these areas.

Ordinary Palestinians were also frustrated by the political stalemate that had arisen in diplomatic attempts to resolve the Arab-Israeli conflict. Many felt that Arab nations, in general, and the PLO, in particular, were doing very little to alleviate daily Palestinian suffering in areas under Israeli occupation. The PLO was perceived as out of touch after it had relocated to Tunis.

It angered many Palestinians that a general Arab summit convened in Amman in the fall of 1987 glossed over their concerns almost totally, focusing instead on finding a solution to the Iran-Iraq War. For Palestinians in the West Bank and the Gaza Strip, there was much more concern about the high levels of unemployment and poverty there.

Israel responded aggressively to quell disturbances when they broke out, as indicated by then-Defense Minister Yitzhak Rabin who stated in January 1988 that "might, power, and beatings" would be used to confront any demonstrators making trouble. After another round of riots broke out in April of that year, sparked by the killing of a PLO official in Tunis, the Arab League committed financial support to this *intifada* (Arabic for "shaking off" or "uprising") at its next summit in 1988 in Algiers. The PLO also made house demolitions into a stimulus for Palestinian resistance when it began making payments to families whose dwellings had been destroyed.

Although the First Intifada came to be marked by significant violence, it also featured many acts of civil disobedience. One example occurred in the fall of 1989 when local committees in Beit Sahour, a small, predominantly Christian town just east of Bethlehem, began to withhold taxes from the Israel to protest its conduct as an occupier. The Israeli response was to imprison activists and levy huge fines, as well as removing and destroying equipment, furnishings, and goods from Palestinian stores, factories, and homes. When such measures were reported as overreactions by the international media, this generated substantial negative publicity for Israel.

Lacking central coordination, the First Intifada was a mass movement, which although not totally spontaneous, was organized at a grassroots level. This approach succeeded in changing international perceptions of the Palestinians. In foreign press accounts, Israel's harsh responses to these protests made the Palestinians into "Davids" against an Israeli "Goliath." This turned upside down the way Israelis had been seen themselves as Davids against the Goliath of the combined Arab armies in 1967. Media reports about the First Intifada depicted in harsh clarity the extraordinary stresses experienced by the Israeli army, manned as it was by citizen-soldiers, in maintaining a prolonged occupation force where it was not welcome. Major American newspapers and television networks began to criticize Israeli actions in ways not seen before, which had quite a negative impact on tourism to Israel and its general image abroad.

The First Intifada had more tangible results as well. It prompted the PLO to try to win back the spotlight it was perceived to have lost after its recent debacle in Lebanon. One way to do this was to issue a Palestinian Declaration of Independence in November 1988. This document was presented at the same time as a call for peace negotiations based on UN Resolution 242. This implied official Palestinian acceptance of the existence of Israel and a two-state solution, which Yasser Arafat made explicit in a speech delivered to the UN General Assembly in December 1988. Upon the PLO's acceptance of the terms of UN Resolution 242, the United States officially accepted it as a negotiating partner, which in turn began the process toward the next round of the peace process culminating in the 1993 **Oslo Accords**.

RISE OF HAMAS

Another equally important result of the First Intifada was the creation and evolution of Hamas as an important Palestinian organization, which was founded during the first set of uprisings in December 1987. It was formed by Palestinian sympathizers of the Egyptian Muslim Brotherhood who had organized a Palestinian branch of the Brotherhood in Gaza in the 1970s.

Its main founder, Sheikh Ahmad Yassin, had himself grown up in Gaza, and had worked during the 1970s to revive a branch of the Brotherhood there in the wake of 1967. This organization was renamed Hamas in December 1987: an acronym for the Arabic initials of "Islamic Resistance Movement" as well as an Arabic word meaning "zeal." One of its main goals, as stated in its covenant issued in 1988, is the elimination of Israel and its replacement with an Islamic state in Palestine.

In terms of methods, it has been prepared to move toward that goal gradually, using different techniques and methods appropriate to different phases of its pursuit. In pursuit of this long-term goal, it engaged in a multifaceted set of activities, some very peaceful and some very militant. Its public face became associated with social welfare activities comparable to those of the Muslim Brotherhood in Egypt or Hezbollah in Lebanon, with a particular focus on ministering to the neediest segment of the Palestinian population living in Gaza. The second part of its strategy was to engage in political and religious consciousness raising, in a bid to replace the PLO as the "true" voice of the Palestinians. Finally, its August 1988 founding covenant declaration that "Jihad is ... [the organization's] path and death for the sake of God is the loftiest of its wishes," conveyed that it had a more confrontational and belligerent dimension.[5]

The more militant side of **Hamas** began to emerge toward the end of the First Intifada in the "war of the knives" after 1990, as the more violent encounters between Israelis and Palestinians came to be known. Hamas, which developed a fairly intricate and interwoven organizational structure during the first two years of the First Intifada, had been severely weakened in May 1989 by the mass arrest of many hundreds of its members and sympathizers, including Ahmad Yassin. It was reorganized soon thereafter by Musa Abu Marzuq, a Palestinian then living in United States, who, while on a brief visit back to Gaza, helped transfer leadership responsibilities away from its members in Israel, Gaza, and the West Bank to those in other countries. His task was facilitated by the fact that several senior Hamas leaders had just been deported by Israel to Lebanon, where they went into hiding.

This had the effect of making it much harder for the Israelis to "decapitate" this organization through campaigns of mass arrests. The organization became broken up into small cells that went underground, so despite Israeli attempts to suppress it, Hamas ended the First Intifada by carrying out its first series of suicide bombing attacks, with the very first at the Mehola Junction, a rest stop on a highway in the West Bank, on April 16, 1993. The focus in Middle Eastern affairs by that time had shifted to the revived Israeli-Palestinian peace process, which resulted in the signing of the Oslo Accords on September 1993 by Israeli Prime Minister Rabin, PLO Chairman Arafat, and U.S. President Bill Clinton.

TURKEY'S STRUGGLE WITH THE PKK: 1978–1999

Problems faced by Middle Eastern governments in dealing with conflicting national identities were not confined to disputes between Israelis and Palestinians, but took many different forms elsewhere in the region. This was particularly true in Turkey in its relations with its Kurdish population. By the 1980s, Turkey had

---

[5]See the text of the 1988 Hamas covenant at http://avalon. law.yale.edu/20th_century/hamas.asp (accessed August 29, 2010).

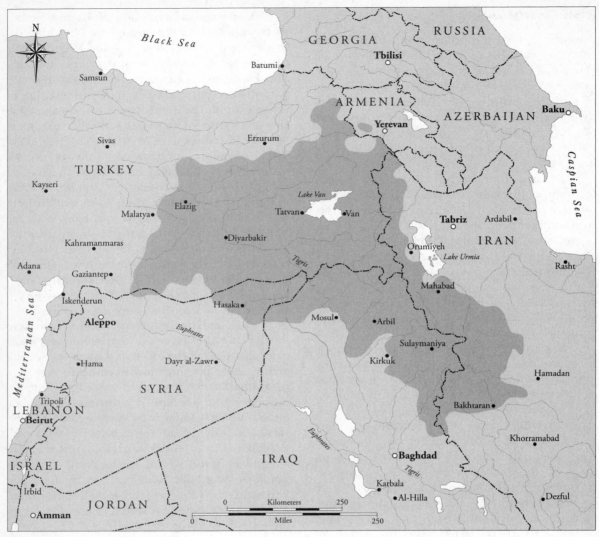

MAP 21.1 Kurds in the Middle East

weathered upheavals in its foreign relations with Greece and in its domestic affairs with the rise of leftist insurgencies countered by military coups, the most recent of which had taken place in September 1980. It had brought in a liberalizing, free-market government led by Prime Minister Turgut Ozal to address the nation's economic weaknesses. One of Turkey's great unsolved problems remained the under-development of eastern Anatolia, home of the Kurds, who had been a source of instability for so long in the nation's history.

After the suppression of the 1937–1938 Dersim rebellion, the last serious Kurdish rebellion in Anatolia during the early years of the Turkish Republic, the Turkish government had explored solving the Kurdish problem by promoting ethnic mixing through migration to and from eastern Anatolia, but with uncertain results. It also tried various economic development programs, culminating later in the "Southeast Anatolia Project" (Turkish initials, "GAP"), but the eastern half of the country continued to lag behind its western part.

The situation changed with the founding of the Kurdistan Workers' Party (known by its Kurdish initials "PKK") in November 1978. This new group injected the energies of revolutionary leftist agitation into the long Kurdish nationalist struggle centered in eastern Turkey, and the result was lethal. Beginning in August 1984 and continuing through September 1999, a **long war** between the Turkish military and the PKK resulted in the destruction of many villages and the deaths of thousands of people in eastern Anatolia.

The PKK had its origins in the early 1970s with a group of radical university students in Ankara led by Abdullah Ojalan (often referred to by his nickname "Apo"), and its early activities reflect its radical Marxist/Maoist origins. On November 27, 1978, the group adopted the name Kurdistan Workers' Party ("PKK" in Kurdish). Unlike earlier Kurdish political parties organized in Turkey that took a conservative approach to politics as groups affiliated with tribes or religious orders, the PKK adopted a political agenda promoting Kurdish identity and nationalism but also espousing a Marxist, revolutionary, modernizing program of change. Its longevity can be attributed to its early establishment of a disciplined but decentralized organizational structure that would enable it to survive many different attacks and pressures.

When the organization moved its focus from Ankara to border towns on Turkey's southeastern frontier, this gave it an effective platform to reach out to Kurdish groups there, long a source of problems for the central government. Since its founding, the Turkish Republic had judged people or groups asserting their Kurdish identity or differences from Turks as threats to Turkey's national identity, and acted to suppress them with force if necessary.

The PKK launched its first violent activities against Kurds who were perceived as government collaborators and Kurdish tribes

that had coexisted peacefully with the government. In August 1979, it tried unsuccessfully to assassinate Mehmed Jelal Buchak, a wealthy Kurdish landlord and important member of the national Turkish Justice Party (successor to the Democrat Party of Suleyman Demirel). Although the attack was unsuccessful, it set off a long conflict between the Buchak tribe and the **PKK** that continued over many years.

To avoid capture, Ojalan fled to Lebanon. There, he made connections with leftist militants from around the Middle East living in Palestinian camps. Ultimately, Syria provided a safe haven for the PKK in the Bekaa Valley of Lebanon and in Syria itself until 1999. After the 1980 Turkish coup, the PKK had been violently suppressed in Turkey, but its leadership set up an elaborate organization to continue activities even while its members were in prison or abroad.

By 1984, the PKK began to conduct military actions in eastern Turkey, targeting government officials and civilians associated with the GAP project. GAP had been launched in the late 1970s and was well underway by the mid-1980s with dam projects along the upper Euphrates River. It had evolved into a multisector project, which included irrigation and hydroelectric power generation, as well as providing improvements in urban and rural infrastructures, forestry management, education, and health care.

PKK attacks were able to impede the implementation of GAP quite severely in some areas. At this time, too, the uncertain situation in northern Iraq produced by the Iran-Iraq War allowed the PKK to stage continual cross-border attacks into Turkey. By the late 1980s, the PKK was launching most attacks on Turkey from two places: Syria and northern Iraq. Turkish troops pursued PKK forces across the border into northern Iraq in numerous incursions that Saddam Hussein permitted, but in 1988, the Iranian government also gave permission for the PKK to open camps close to its border with Turkey.

PKK guerrilla operations reached their highest intensity during the Gulf War between

August 1990 and February 1991. This war had removed vestiges of the Iraqi central government's control over the Kurds of northern Iraq, enabling the PKK to establish yet more bases and training camps there. After the Gulf War, the situation in Iraq settled into a stalemate defined by the no-fly zones in the north and south enforced by the United States. The PKK opened branches in numerous other countries to make it a more difficult target for Turkey to attack.

The Turkish authorities accepted that they could not eliminate the PKK as a military force as long as it had safe havens in Syria, Iraq, and Iran. Although various countries made regular financial contributions to the PKK, it also became more involved in drug trafficking after the Gulf War, which was quite lucrative. Fighting the PKK was very expensive for the Turkish government, which eventually came to spend as much as 10 percent of its annual income on this problem.

Between 1994 and 1997, there was an intermittent and very bloody civil war between the two main Kurdish groups in northern Iraq, the KDP led by Massoud Barzani and the PUK (Patriotic Union of Kurdistan) led by Jalal Talabani. During this period, the Turkish army mounted several operations into Iraq to go after the PKK. The first, Operation "Steel," brought 35,000 Turkish troops into northern Iraq between March and May 1995 to clear out PKK strongholds there, but was not totally successful. This was followed by Operation "Hammer" in May and Operation "Dawn" in September 1997: two more attempts to root out the PKK from northern Iraq that also failed. After the KDP and PUK finally signed a lasting cease-fire in November 1997 (followed by a formal treaty in 1998), this put pressure on the PKK to curtail its activities, but it managed to keep them up through a series of suicide bombings conducted by women from conservative rural areas in eastern Anatolia in 1998 and 1999.

Turkey also increased pressure on the other Kurdish safe haven, Syria, when the head of the Turkish armed forces announced in October 1998 that because of the Kurds, there was an undeclared war between Syria and Turkey. As a result of this, Syria finally ceased its support for the PKK, and in 1999, Turkish authorities were able to track down Ojalan and capture him in Kenya. He was prosecuted and sentenced to death, but his punishment was later commuted to life imprisonment, since it had become a condition for Turkey's admission to the European Union that it abolish the death penalty.

The capture of Ojalan marked a real turning point in this long conflict, because after his arrest, he ordered PKK members to refrain from violence. In fact, he called for dialogue with the government of Turkey on all outstanding issues. Although some violence did eventually resume, the end of Ojalan's active leadership role in the PKK created considerable momentum toward peaceful resolution of the Kurdish problem. This was marked in various small ways, such as with the advent of Turkish radio and television stations permitted to broadcast in the Kurdish language after 2004 (as the next step after the 1991 lifting of a ban on the use of Kurdish in Turkish publications).

More importantly, various openly Kurdish political parties have been allowed to participate in elections since 1994, although each party whose members were elected to the parliament was eventually banned. Nevertheless, nineteen members of the latest such party to be shut down (the Democratic Society Party, declared illegal by the Turkish constitutional court in December 2009) have continued to sit in the parliament. They all have joined a new "Peace and Democracy" Party (Turkish acronym: "BDP"). The chairman of the last banned Kurdish group described this new association as a continuation of all the earlier disbanded parties in its campaign to defend Kurdish rights.[6] It has received support

---

[6]http://www.todayszaman.com/news-195998-dtp-deputies-retreat-from-resignation.html (accessed November 9, 2011).

from Ojalan, who expressed approval from prison of how it had been careful to act within the formal legal constraints of the Turkish political system.

With all these fits and starts, the Turkish government has continued a gradual process of dismantling legal restrictions on the Kurds—a normalization process supported by the current Turkish government now led by the moderate Islamist Justice and Development Party. Despite all these changes, the PKK's operational bases in northern Iraq have not been dismantled, and hard-line PKK militants have turned against some former colleagues who entered mainstream Turkish politics and assassinated them.

Questions to Think About

1. What kind of government did Mohammed Daoud Khan try to create for Afghanistan, and why did his rule make his Soviet allies uncomfortable?
2. Why did the Pakistani government make allegiances with Muslim students from Afghanistan?'
3. Why did the Soviets invade Afghanistan in December 1979?
4. Why were the Soviets unable to defend the communist government of Afghanistan in the 1980s?
5. Who were the *mujahidin* in Afghanistan, and why did the United States, Pakistan, and Saudi Arabia support them?
6. What ended the Soviet war in Afghanistan, and what were its consequences for the country?
7. What caused the 1982 Lebanon War?
8. What were the effects of the 1982 Lebanon War on the Palestinians?
9. What were the effects of the war on the United States?
10. What happened at Sabra and Shatila, and what was its impact?
11. Why was Hezbollah organized, and what were its goals?
12. How did the Lebanese political system unravel in the late 1980s?
13. How did the Taif Accord change the rules for Lebanon specified by the Lebanese National Pact?
14. What caused the First Palestinian Intifada?
15. How did the First Intifada change international perceptions of Israelis and Palestinians?
16. What was Hamas, and how did it compare to the Muslim Brotherhood of Egypt and Hezbollah of Lebanon?
17. What was the PKK, and how did it change the political situation for Kurds in eastern Turkey?
18. How was the PKK able to continue its struggle against Turkey for so long?
19. What was the GAP project and why did the PKK attack its sites?
20. How has the PKK changed since 1999?

For Further Reading

Arnold, Anthony. *Afghanistan's Two-Party Communism: Parcham and Khalq.* Stanford, CA: Hoover Institution Press, 1983.

Avnery, Uri. *My Friend, the Enemy.* Westport, CT: L. Hill, 1986.

Azani, Eitan. *Hezbollah: The Story of the Party of God: From Revolution to Institutionalization.* New York: Palgrave Macmillan, 2009.

Bradsher, Henry S. *Afghan Communism and Soviet Intervention.* Oxford: Oxford University Press, 1999.

Friedman, Thomas L. *From Beirut to Jerusalem.* New York: Farrar, Straus, Giroux, 1990.

Harub, Khalid. *Hamas: A Beginner's Guide.* Ann Arbor, MI: Pluto Press, 2010.

Hirst, David. *Beware of Small States: Lebanon, Battleground of the Middle East.* New York: Nation Books, 2010.

Hunter, F. Robert. *The Palestinian Uprising: A War by Other Means.* Berkeley: University of California Press, 1991.

Hyman, Anthony, and Anthony Hyman. *Afghanistan under Soviet Domination, 1964–83*. New York: St. Martin's Press, 1984.

Maley, William. *The Afghanistan Wars*. Basingstoke, UK: Palgrave Macmillan, 2009.

Marcus, Aliza. *Blood and Belief: The PKK and the Kurdish Fight for Independence*. New York: New York University Press, 2007.

O'Ballance, Edgar, and Edgar O'Ballance. *Afghan Wars*. London: Brassey's, 2002.

Rasanayagam, Angelo. *Afghanistan: A Modern History: Monarchy, Despotism or Democracy? The Problems of Governance in the Muslim Tradition*. London: I.B. Tauris, 2003.

Roy, Olivier. *Islam and Resistance in Afghanistan*. Cambridge: Cambridge University Press, 1990.

Rubin, Barnett R. *The Fragmentation of Afghanistan: State Formation and Collapse in the International System*. New Haven: Yale University Press, 2002.

Schiff, Zeev, Ehud Yaari, and Ina Friedman. *Intifada: The Palestinian Uprising—Israel's Third Front*. New York: Simon and Schuster, 1990.

Schiff, Zeev, Ehud Yaari, and Ina Friedman. *Israel's Lebanon War*. New York: Simon and Schuster, 1984.

White, Paul J. *Primitive Rebels or Revolutionary Modernizers? The Kurdish National Movement in Turkey*. London: Zed Books, 2000.

22

The Middle East after the Cold War

With the end of the Cold War, the fall of the Soviet Union, and the collapse of the Warsaw Pact in July 1991, a whole new international situation began to take shape. Old regional conflicts in which the Soviet bloc and the Western alliance had taken different sides continued, but old systems of alliances were being replaced by entirely new ones. Nevertheless, long-standing allies of the United States in the Middle East such as Saudi Arabia and Israel continued to influence American actions in the region, although there was no longer the same need to assess how the Soviet bloc might respond to what the United States did in any given situation.

FIRST GULF WAR: 1990–1991

One of the first conflicts of the post–Cold War world (although it technically happened at the very end of the Cold War) was the **Persian Gulf War** of August 1990–February 1991. This involved a coalition of many countries (including NATO members as well as Warsaw Pact nations) who came together to force Iraq to leave Kuwait, which it had invaded and annexed in August 1990.

One of Iraq's main motives for this invasion was the severe economic crisis it experienced at the end of the Iran–Iraq War. By the end of the war in the summer of 1988, Iraq was virtually bankrupt, and owed large sums to Saudi Arabia and Kuwait. Saddam Hussein put pressure on both countries to forgive this debt, but they turned him down. He accused Kuwait of exceeding its OPEC quotas and driving down the price of oil, thus further hurting the Iraqi economy. Saddam was both weighed down by the costs of the war and puffed up by the sense that he had triumphed over Iran. Steeped in Baathist paranoia, he may also have suspected Kuwait of creating a conspiracy to destroy his economy, to which responding with force would be justified.

Iraqis often viewed Kuwait with a certain jaundiced eye. Iraqi leaders had been making claims since their nation became independent in 1932 that Kuwait actually was part of Iraq. They had long asserted that Kuwait was a creation of British imperialism in the late nineteenth century on territory that had belonged to the Ottoman (later Iraqi) province of Basra for centuries before that. Kuwait's historical rulers, the Al Sabah, signed a treaty in 1899 making Great Britain their protector. The British then had drawn the border between Iraq and Kuwait in order to limit Iraq's coastline, to keep any future rulers of Iraq from challenging British predominance in the Persian Gulf. Iraq accepted this border but only because of British pressure, and it took the deployment of British troops to Kuwait after it declared independence in 1961 to persuade the Iraqi government to recognize the Kuwaiti government formally in 1963.

In early July 1990, Iraq issued its first threats to take military action against Kuwait and moved troops to the border. On July 25, Saddam Hussein met with his new U.S. ambassador, April Glaspie. At that meeting, Glaspie was reported to have said, "We [i.e., officials of the U.S. government] have no opinion on your Arab-Arab conflicts, such as your dispute with Kuwait."[1] Her comments were later criticized as giving Saddam the impression that the United States would not act to defend Kuwait if he invaded. Other evidence suggests that the idea that Iraq might *invade* Kuwait seemed so preposterous at that time that neither Kuwait nor the United States regarded this as a real possibility.

In retrospect, it appears that Saddam had already decided on this course of action several days before this meeting. When negotiations arranged by Saudi Arabia between Iraq and Kuwait in Jedda on July 31 failed disastrously, the situation moved swiftly toward conflict. On August 2, Iraq launched its invasion with an air raid on Kuwait City. Commandos flew in on helicopters and rode in on boats to attack from the coast, while Iraqi army divisions occupied Kuwait's airports and airbases.

Because there was no anticipation of an actual invasion, Kuwaiti forces had not been placed on any alert status at all. Thus, it only took two days of fighting for the Iraqi Republican Guard to end all Kuwaiti resistance. After this quick victory, Saddam Hussein installed his cousin, Ali Hassan al-Majid (Chemical Ali), brutal commander of **Operation Anfal** against the Kurds in the late 1980s, as governor of "Kadhima": the name Saddam bestowed on Kuwait in its new status as Iraq's nineteenth province.

Within a short time, UN resolutions were issued to condemn Iraq's invasion, call for its withdrawal, and put it under economic sanctions to be enforced by a naval blockade. The Arab League soon passed its own resolution offering a solution to the conflict to be handled totally within its organization, warning against the intervention of outsiders. U.S. President George H.W. Bush immediately dispatched American forces to Saudi Arabia, invoking the 1951 Saudi-U.S. defense agreement last used in 1963 during Operation Hard Surface in the early part of the North Yemen Civil War.

An international military coalition to forestall any further Iraqi moves was assembled quite rapidly, with approximately two-thirds of its $60 billion cost covered by Saudi Arabia. Syria, among Arab states, joined this force while Jordan stayed out of it, reflecting these nations' differing historical relationships with Iraq. On November 29, the UN Security Council authorized the use of force against Iraq if it did not leave Kuwait by January 15, 1991, which it failed to do.

The military campaign to remove Iraqi troops from Kuwait commenced with an aerial bombardment of Iraq and Kuwait on January 17, 1991. A few hours after these attacks, Saddam Hussein declared on Iraqi radio in his theatrical style that "the great duel, the mother of all battles has begun. The dawn of victory nears as this great showdown begins."[2] Just

---

[1]Christopher Cerf and Micah Sifry, eds., *Iraq War Reader: History, Documents, Opinions* (New York: Simon & Schuster, 2007), 68.

[2]Saddam Hussein on Baghdad State Radio, January 17, 1991.

after this, Iraq launched its first Scud missile strikes against Tel Aviv and Haifa, Israel—a ploy to drag Israel into the war that didn't work. Another Scud fired at U.S. forces in Saudi Arabia was shot down by a Patriot missile—the first of many mid-air interceptions by this new weapon. Over the course of the war, Iraqi fired over thirty Scud missiles into Israel, which caused some damage but few casualties. The Israelis were most afraid of poison gas being launched this way, so they distributed gas masks. There was a lot of pressure put on Israeli leaders to retaliate, but they showed restraint, going against their usual preference to strike back.

The use of Scuds set off an urgent U.S. mission to find and destroy all mobile missile launchers in Iraq. Batteries of U.S. Patriot missiles were also hastily moved to Israel. The most devastating Scud attack happened on February 25, when a missile hit a building at Dhahran airbase in Saudi Arabia, killing twenty-eight U.S. soldiers, all of whom were Army reservists from Pennsylvania.

The initial aerial bombing campaign lasted a few days. It resulted in the dropping of over 80,000 tons of bombs, which devastated Iraq's military and civilian infrastructure. On January 23, Iraq dumped between two and three hundred million gallons of crude oil into the Persian Gulf, causing the largest offshore spill to that date in history. This action has been explained as a tactic to keep U.S. Marines from coming ashore, since American warships had shelled Failaka Island off Kuwait's coast during the war as a deception.

On January 29, Iraqi forces advanced over the Kuwaiti border and captured the Saudi city of Khafji. Although it had not been well defended, the battle to retake it was over within two days, as the Iraqi invasion force was driven back by U.S. Marine Corps units assisted by Saudi and Qatari forces. There were significant casualties on both sides, although the Iraqis forces suffered more dead and had more men captured than the coalition forces.

The conflict at Khafji became a strategically important turning point for the Iraqis.

Saddam had ordered this attack to try to secure a small victory over the coalition, figuring that at best, his battle-hardened troops would easily outdo their American opponents and at worst, they could take many Americans prisoner. Instead, the encounter revealed many weaknesses in the performance of Iraq's elite troops, persuading U.S. commanders that a ground invasion of Kuwait might be far easier than previously imagined.

This was helpful in planning the main advance into Kuwait, which began on February 23. Coalition forces quickly liberated Kuwait, advanced into Iraq, and declared a cease-fire only one hundred hours after the start of their initial advance. During this operation, Iraq continued to fire missiles against targets in Saudi Arabia. Although the weaponry of Iraqi and coalition forces was fairly evenly matched, coalition forces were able to use new GPS navigational and other electronic systems. This allowed them to navigate without reference to roads or other fixed landmarks, so they could go after specific Iraqi sites instead of wasting time searching for possible targets.

This whole operation happened far more rapidly than anticipated. Iraqi troops started a mass retreat from Kuwait on February 26 after setting Kuwaiti oil fields on fire. They formed a long, motley convoy inching along the main highway between Kuwait and Iraq: a perfect target for coalition bombers. Hundreds of Iraqis were killed there, and their convoy was hit by so many bombs that the road came to be known as the "Highway of Death." American, British, and French forces soon pushed into Iraq, eventually advancing to positions one hundred miles south of Baghdad before pulling back. President Bush announced a cease-fire on February 28 and declared Kuwait liberated.

Western media reports initially described the Iraqi army as numbering between 550 and 600,000 soldiers, but this number proved greatly exaggerated. Moreover, many Iraqi troops were young conscripts lacking adequate equipment and proper training. By contrast, there were 540,000 well-equipped and trained troops in the coalition force. With 100,000 Turkish soldiers along the Turkish-Iraqi border, the Iraqis were forced to thin their units to cover their borders.

Iraq had acquired a lot of military hardware during the Iran–Iraq War from international arms dealers. However, it now owned many different types of equipment that were difficult to maintain and keep running. Iraqi troops also could not defend themselves against high-tech thermal sights and special antitank rounds used by coalition tanks. Iraqi units failed to do battle in any urban areas: the one place where they could have negated the other side's technological advantages. They tried to use Soviet command and control techniques, but were hampered by constant airstrikes that destroyed their communications centers and command bunkers.

End of the War

After a cease-fire was arranged, a peace conference was convened in the portion of Iraqi territory now occupied by coalition forces to negotiate and sign an armistice agreement. Iraq received permission to fly armed helicopters on its side of the temporary border for transport purposes, on the pretext that this would compensate for damage done to its transportation system. A short time later, these helicopters were deployed to crush a Shii revolt in southern Iraq. This rebellion had been encouraged by coalition radio broadcasts in Arabic proclaiming a massive uprising and promising liberation from Saddam. In the north, Kurdish leaders took American statements to heart that the United States would support their revolt against the Baghdad government and began fighting.

However, when no U.S. support was forthcoming for any rebellions, Iraq's main military commanders decided to remain loyal to Saddam and harshly suppressed uprisings against him in the north and south. Millions of Kurdish refugees fled across the mountains seeking refuge in Turkey and Iran. These tragic events finally resulted in the U.S. imposition of no-fly zones in northern and southern Iraq in 1992, but only after significant damage had been done and lives lost. Kuwait's ruler was restored to power, and many suspected Iraqi collaborators were put on trial there. Thousands of people were expelled from the country, including a large number of Palestinians who had shown their support for Saddam.

The United States and its coalition partners were criticized for allowing him to remain in power. The rejoinder to this at that time was that trying to remove him would have incurred too much political and human cost. Dick Cheney, who served as U.S. defense secretary during the war, observed that "if we had gone in there, I would still have forces in Baghdad today": a curious premonition of what would actually happen during the first decade of the twenty-first century.[3]

With the end of the war, the United States hoped that Saddam Hussein would be overthrown through an internal coup, instead of requiring its own further military involvement. The CIA tried to use its collaborators inside Iraq to mobilize such a revolt, but was easily thwarted by the multiple layers of Iraq's internal security system.

In March 1991, over five hundred thousand American troops began to move out of the Persian Gulf. From the perspective of the American people, the war was over with only 148 Americans killed in combat. However, approximately a quarter of the U.S. troops who served in the war still suffer from a range of serious medical symptoms (known as Gulf War Syndrome) whose causes are not fully understood but may be the result of exposure to toxic chemicals. For the Iraqis, who sustained thousands of casualties during the war and lived under harsh economic sanctions over the next twelve years, the impact of the conflict also lingered.

---

[3]Stephen F. Hayes, *Cheney: The Untold Story of America's Most Powerful and Controversial Vice President* (New York: HarperCollins, 2007), 251.

Operation "Southern Watch"

Following the Gulf War, the United States maintained around 5,000 troops in remote desert bases in Saudi Arabia, a deployment that ended in 2003 when many of these forces were moved to Qatar. Operations "Provide Comfort" and "Southern Watch" enforced no-fly zones over northern and southern Iraq established in 1992 as oil tankers in the Persian Gulf continued to be protected by the U.S. Fifth Fleet with its headquarters in Bahrain.

After the Gulf War revealed how many U.S. forces were stationed and deployed on Saudi territory, Muslim activists around the world became upset by this permanent non-Muslim military presence so near Mecca and Medina. In the view of an activist with a growing reputation at that time, Osama bin Laden, Prophet Muhammad had forbidden the continuous presence of infidels in the Arabian Peninsula.[4] The fact that U.S. troops remained there after the Gulf War thus became cited as one cause of the attacks of September 11, 2001, as well as other terrorist actions.

Media and the War

The Gulf War was a remarkably well-televised war. Viewers around the world could see live pictures of missiles hitting their targets and fighters taking off from aircraft carriers. In the United States, the major networks (ABC, NBC, and CBS) all had correspondents in Baghdad who reported live during the war's first airstrikes, but it was the coverage of the Cable News Network (CNN) that became regarded as a landmark event in this network's history. When all the other American TV correspondents' telephones went dead while the bombing took place, CNN became the only service able to provide live coverage because it had secured a stable phone line. Its main correspondent, Peter Arnett, became for a period of time the only American TV correspondent reporting live from Iraq.

MAP 22.1   West Bank and Gaza (1967–2011)

The United States established a much stricter policy regarding what the media was allowed to report than during the Vietnam War. Only a few selected reporters were allowed to visit the front lines or conduct interviews with soldiers, and their reports were subject to military prior approval as well as censorship. A new feature of this war's coverage was how instantaneously reports could now be presented. As soon as the Iraqi government chose to allow live satellite transmissions from the country by Western news organizations, U.S. journalists hurried back there.

MORE ATTEMPTS AT PEACE: THE OSLO ACCORDS

World media certainly covered the Gulf War, as well as the First Intifada of the late 1980s in considerable depth, but the process leading up

---

[4]Peter Bergen, *Holy War, Inc.: Inside the Secret World of Osama Bin Laden* (New York: Simon and Schuster, 2001), 3.

to the Oslo Accords was kept out of the press spotlight until it was fairly well underway. The 1993 Oslo Accords, officially known as the "Declaration of Principles on Interim Self-Government Arrangements," became the first agreement concluded directly between Israel's government and the PLO. The plan was for this to become the framework for all future negotiations between Israel and the Palestinians, leading to the resolution of all outstanding issues.

Negotiations to produce this declaration grew out of the 1991 Madrid Conference. In a speech just after the end of the Gulf War, President Bush presented his vision for a new Middle Eastern order. He renewed the U.S. commitment to keep a permanent naval presence in the Persian Gulf and provide funds for Middle Eastern economic development, but more importantly, promised to work on creating an Arab-Israeli peace agreement based on the principle of "**land for peace**" that also recognized the rights of the Palestinians. Bush announced that he would convene a peace conference in Madrid to discuss how to pursue this last goal.

Bush and his secretary of state James Baker felt that their diplomatic initiative could succeed because it would emphasize process rather than specific points of discussion and that it was happening soon after the successful conclusion of the Gulf War. Middle Eastern participants in this discussion had different concerns from their American counterparts. Israeli prime minister Yitzhak Shamir, who had succeeded Menachem Begin as head of the right-wing Likud Party but was even more conservative, was concerned about getting $10 billion in loan guarantees from the United States. He explained that these funds would be allocated to help absorb Israeli's recent immigrants from the Soviet Union. The problem was that the United States could not verify whether or not its previous loan guarantees to Israel (made in October 1990) had been used for expanding Jewish settlements on the West Bank, which the Americans were trying to stop.

Following the pattern of earlier American envoys, Baker made numerous shuttle trips around the Middle East over the next few months trying to find a formula for convening a peace conference that all parties could accept. He did not have an easy time, particularly on the issue of Palestinian representation. Because Shamir was such a staunch supporter of settlements in Gaza and the West Bank, many Arabs saw his request for loan guarantees as a test of America's objectivity as a mediator.

The loan guarantee issue remained a point of contention. In September 1991, the Bush Administration asked Congress to delay discussion of loan guarantees for a few months as a way to keep the focus on a peace conference and buy some time, as well as tone down the domestic discussion of this charged issue. Shamir and Israel's supporters in Washington decided to push for the loan guarantees against Bush's request. Since Bush then had a very favorable approval rating, he was not going to acquiesce to this.

Shamir at first thought that he would be able to get around Bush and Baker on the loan guarantees issue, but their unwillingness to back down, as well as the president's high approval ratings, led him to give up. The opening conference session took place in Madrid at the beginning of November. Its purpose was to create a forum for bilateral and multilateral discussions that also involved the larger international community. This resulted in the first-ever public bilateral talks between Israel and its neighbors (beyond Egypt). The opening session was followed by many more meetings held in Washington between December 1991 and January 1994.

Simultaneous talks were launched in Moscow in January 1992. They continued through 1993 at five forums held in various locations around Europe and in the Middle East, each focusing on a specific diplomatic issue (such as water, the environment, and arms control). Not all parties participated in all (and in some cases, any) of the multilateral discussions. The most concrete result of these bilateral talks came in the Israeli-Jordanian track, which led to a peace treaty between Israel and Jordan in 1994. The Israeli-Syrian sessions did produce a series of follow-on meetings without ultimately resulting in a peace treaty.

Beginning the Oslo Process

With Shamir's archconservative government representing Israel, the bilateral Israeli-Palestinian track was not really destined to lead very far. In this case, the Madrid talks rapidly became overshadowed by the Oslo Process: an initially clandestine discussion track started just after the 1992 Israeli elections. These elections brought in a Labor government headed by Yitzhak Rabin, who pledged to end Shamir's support for settlements and generally sought to realign Israeli positions on various issues.

The impact of the Gulf War was felt not only by President Bush and the American government. The war helped convince many Israelis that with Scud missiles, the defensive value of territory was more illusory than they had realized, and that technology and a good air force were at least as important in winning wars as control of territory.

The PLO came away from the war with the sense that it had lost some important sources of patronage and support. There was no longer a Soviet Union upon which it could rely, and Arab Gulf states had cut off their assistance to the PLO because of anger over its friendship with Iraq during the war. Due to Israeli discomfort, the PLO had not even been invited to the Madrid Conference, although it stayed in very close contact with the Palestinian delegation there.

As the official Madrid track of negotiations was continuing at a meeting in London in December 1992. Israel's deputy foreign affairs minister Yossi Beilin, and a Norwegian researcher, Terje Rød-Larsen, arranged for a secret meeting between a PLO representative, Ahmad Qurei, and an Israeli history professor, Yair Hirschfeld. These two men established a

good personal connection and agreed to get together again in Oslo for what became a series of fourteen meetings.

They agreed about the general parameters of an eventual accord after only a few sessions. This attracted the attention of Israel's foreign affairs minister Shimon Peres, who sent a high-ranking deputy and a military lawyer to participate in these talks. Meetings had mostly been limited to short, formal encounters in the Madrid track. In Oslo by contrast, Israeli and Palestinian delegations lived and ate together, which increased their mutual respect and built connections. Working behind the scenes, the Norwegian government facilitated this process in a very helpful way by keeping it totally out of the media spotlight.

By August 1993, the delegations had finalized a complete agreement. Peres came to Oslo and signed this "Declaration of Principles" secretly. He then brought it to the United States, where he showed it to Dennis Ross, the chief American negotiator, who was very surprised to learn what had happened. Final terms were then hammered out in a hotel in Paris. There, the document's text was approved by Yasser Arafat and Yitzhak Rabin just in time for an official signing in Washington in the presence of the new U.S. president, Bill Clinton.

Sixty percent of Israelis supported the Oslo Accords when they were first presented, because they represented such an attractive alternative to the violence and unrest that had swept over the country since the outbreak of the First Intifada. In essence, this document called for Israel to withdraw from parts of the Gaza Strip and the West Bank, affirming the Palestinians' right to self-government in areas under a "Palestinian Interim Self-Government Authority."

Provisions of the Declaration of Principles would be implemented one month after its signing, beginning a five-year interim period. "Permanent status negotiations" to produce a final agreement were to be started during this interval, but by no later than May 1996. The major issues to be discussed in this phase were to include all the thorniest diplomatic questions: the status of Jerusalem, the fate and rights of Palestinian refugees, the future and status of Israeli settlers in the West Bank and Gaza, and final guarantees for security and fixing borders. Israel also agreed to grant the Palestinians increasing levels of interim self-government in stages.

At the same time that it signed the Declaration of Principles, the Israeli government formally recognized the PLO as the legitimate representative of the Palestinian people. The PLO reciprocated by officially accepting Israel's right as a state to exist and renouncing terrorism as well as other forms of violence. It formally abandoned its desire for the destruction of the Israeli state. Both sides agreed that the eventual permanent settlement had to be based on the provisions of UN Security Council Resolutions 242 and 338.

Free, general elections were to be held to select a Palestinian Council to run the Interim Authority. This Council's jurisdiction was to extend generally over the West Bank and Gaza Strip, except for issues to be resolved in the permanent status negotiations. A redeployment of Israeli military forces in the West Bank and the Gaza Strip would take place. Both sides recognized the West Bank and Gaza as a single territorial unit.

The IDF would hand over authority for the administration of education and culture, health, social welfare, direct taxation, and tourism in certain areas to authorized Palestinians. The Palestinian Council was also tasked with creating an effective police force, with Israel retaining control over external defense. A committee for Israeli-Palestinian economic cooperation was also to be established in order to develop and implement cooperative economic plans in the spirit of the accords.

Reactions to Oslo

In Israel, left-wing politicians generally supported this agreement, while those on the right generally were against it. After several days of discussion in the Israeli parliament, sixty-one

King Hussein, Yitzhak Rabin, Bill Clinton, Yasser Arafat, and Hosni Mubarak (September 1995)

members voted to support it, with fifty against it, and eight abstentions. Palestinian politicians also had mixed reactions to what had transpired in Oslo. While members of Fatah, the core PLO group whose members had represented the Palestinian side in the negotiations, generally accepted the Oslo agreement, Islamist groups such as Hamas and Palestinian Islamic Jihad, as well as "rejectionist" groups such as the PFLP, rejected it, given that denial of Israel's right to exist remained one of their core values.

In the end, Rabin, Arafat, and Peres were all awarded the 1994 Nobel Peace Prize for their efforts. On behalf of his fellow Israelis, Rabin declared, "We who have fought against you, the Palestinians, we say to you today, in a loud and a clear voice, enough of blood and tears ... enough!"[5] The success of the Oslo Accords produced positive momentum in another part of the Arab-Israeli peace process: negotiations with Jordan. Rabin and Peres continued the Israeli-Jordanian talks that had begun in the Madrid process with King Hussein, aided by strong support from U.S. president Clinton, who promised that the United States would forgive Jordan's debts if a peace could be concluded.

After a final round of negotiations, Jordan and Israel signed a full peace treaty in October, 1994. In contrast to its uncertain reactions to the Oslo Accords, the Israeli public was in complete support of this treaty. Predictably, the Egyptian government praised the agreement, while Syria's leadership ignored it. Hezbollah protested it by shelling Israeli settlements in the northern Galilee just a few minutes before the signing ceremony. However, Israeli settlers under attack brought radios and mobile TVs into their shelters in order not to miss the historic signing of a second peace treaty between Israel and an Arab state. Following the normalization of relations, Israel and Jordan began allowing tourists, business people, and workers to travel freely between the two states.

Israeli tourists started to visit Jordan, many of them coming especially to see Petra—a famous ancient city that Israelis had been visiting secretly for many years.

RABIN'S ASSASSINATION

Despite the joy felt in Israel by this new peace treaty, growing resistance to what the Oslo Accords had produced eventually turned violent. Rabin, despite his long career as an Israeli soldier, came under personal attack from ultraorthodox religious conservatives and leaders of the right-wing Likud Party. They began to charge that the Oslo peace process was a mask to conceal the surrender of the occupied territories, which for very religious settlers would include giving away land promised by God to the Jews: a heinous religious crime.

Contrary to such accusations, Rabin's plan was to consolidate Jewish settlements in the West Bank in order to create a situation in which the settlers could remain there, but finally in peace with their Arab neighbors. In accordance with the framework laid out in the Declaration of Principles, he foresaw eventually turning over control of 90 percent of the Arab population of the West Bank to the PLO, while keeping Israeli control over 70 percent of the land there. In one speech to the Israeli parliament, Rabin affirmed that in this situation, Israel would still maintain "total freedom of action in order to fulfill the security aims that touch upon the permanent solution."[6]

This did not diminish the rising anger at Rabin. Likud and other right-wing political groups organized rallies where the tone became increasingly hateful and threatening. In October 1995, Likud leader (and later prime minister) Benjamin Netanyahu charged that Rabin's government was "removed from Jewish tradition ... and Jewish values."[7] He was addressing

---

[5]Yitzhak Rabin, quoted in William Safire, *Lend Me Your Ears: Great Speeches in History* (New York: Norton, 2004), 172.

[6]http://www.mfa.gov.il/MFA/MFAArchive/1990_1999/1995/10/PM+Rabin+in+Knesset-+Ratification+of+Interim+Agree.htm (accessed August 29, 2010).

protesters at a demonstration where posters were displayed that depicted Rabin in a Nazi SS uniform and as a target in the cross hairs of a gun. When Rabin accused Netanyahu of provoking violence, Netanyahu strongly rebuffed his criticism.

Left-wing supporters of the Oslo Accords began to organize their own rallies as well to counter this atmosphere. After one of these pro-Oslo gatherings had just concluded in downtown Tel Aviv on November 4, 1995, Rabin was walking down the city hall steps toward his car when a far right-wing ultraorthodox Jewish law student, Yigal Amir, fired three shots and killed him. Amir was a militant opponent of the Oslo Accords, and had come to view Rabin as a *rodef* (Hebrew for "pursuer" or "attacker") who put Jewish lives in danger because of his support for these agreements and their implications for the West Bank settlers. In Amir's view (shaped by his ultraorthodox education), this justified Rabin's murder. Ironically, Rabin was carrying in his shirt pocket the words to a peace song he had just sung at the rally. It expressed the need for peace since the dead cannot be brought back to life.

As a nation, Israel was aghast at Rabin's assassination, and this had a negative effect on implementation of the Oslo Accords. Palestinians living in the West Bank and Gaza did not see their living conditions improve, and the number of Israeli settlers there almost doubled. A campaign of suicide bombings that Hamas had begun in 1993 continued, and subsequent retaliatory actions carried by the Israeli military further diminished prospects for progress.

Even among the accords' initial supporters there had been some skepticism, which increased as time passed. Many Israelis began to worry that Oslo had only been a tactical ploy by the Palestinians, who they suspected

were not sincere about wanting lasting peace and coexistence with Israel. Israeli faith in the accords was more seriously compromised by the fact that attacks against Israel continually increased after the signing. Finally, the new Palestinian Authority that was supposed to be functioning as a government did not really stop these attacks.

When violence flared up in a 1996 incident for example, Palestinian police turned their guns on Israelis in clashes which left sixty-one Palestinians and fifteen Israeli soldiers dead. Palestinians, for their part, grew more and more skeptical that Israel would ever dismantle any settlements in the West Bank, especially in the area around Jerusalem. They feared that paradoxically, this agreement might even accelerate the settlement program in the long run, and facts on the ground had begun to bear out this worry.

In part as a reaction to this fear, Netanyahu was elected prime minister in 1996. Upon taking office, he initiated a policy he called "reciprocity." Israel would no longer engage in the peace process if Arafat continued to incite or support terrorism, directly or indirectly. Even on a more limited basis, the peace process still continued, with two more agreements being concluded: the January 1997 Hebron Agreement and the October 1998 Wye River Memorandum. Both dealt with the redeployment of Israeli forces in the West Bank and other issues connected with the implementation of the Oslo Accords. They were significant in that they indicated that even Likud, led by Netanyahu, had finally agreed to use the Oslo framework for negotiations.

However, when left-wing Israelis became dissatisfied that Netanyahu was not really moving the peace process along and the right-wing felt that he was giving away too much, this brought a Labor government back into power led by Ehud Barak: a retired career military officer (like Rabin) who was elected prime minister in May 1999.

---

[7]Charles Smith, *Palestine and the Arab-Israeli Conflict* (Boston: Bedford/St. Martin, 2001), 474.

JULY 2000: CAMP DAVID SUMMIT

Upon taking office, Barak fulfilled a campaign promise to end decades of Israeli military presence in southern Lebanon, which he did in May 2000. He also tried to revive the Oslo process with new negotiations, leading to the Camp David Summit of July 2000. At this meeting, Barak was reported to have offered Arafat immediate total control over approximately 73 percent of the West Bank (to later increase to around 90 percent) and 100 percent of the Gaza Strip, as well as Palestinian sovereignty over *parts*, but not *all* of East Jerusalem. In exchange, sixty-nine Jewish settlements (housing 85 percent of the West Bank's Jewish settlers) would be transferred to Israel.

The Palestinian delegation countered that Israeli annexations would block road connections between major Palestinian population centers, with for example, the Israelis retaining control over a road between Jerusalem and the Dead Sea. The major disagreements were disputes over the right of Palestinians to return to lands from which they had been displaced since 1948, as well as the question of the final status of Muslim holy sites in Jerusalem.

Although there was some discussion of how a right of return might be implemented, the Palestinians were not willing ultimately to give up demands for a full right of return for all Palestinians, which the Israelis could not accept. Even more serious was the disagreement over holy sites, particularly the Temple Mount. The Israelis were willing to concede "custodianship" of the Temple Mount to the Palestinians but not "sovereignty" over it. This divergence, in the end, became the key deal-breaker. Any Palestinian government that would sign this away would be seen as traitorous by the Palestinian public, but would also have to worry about incurring the wrath of the whole worldwide Muslim *umma*, in the case of any concessions made concerning the Temple Mount.

Given such pressures, Arafat rejected Barak's offer without proposing an alternative, and no formulas were found by negotiators to work around this, even after intense U.S. diplomatic pressure. Following this failed attempt at closure, there were various attempts to restart discussions, but none had a lasting impact. The whole peace process was very soon overshadowed by a new wave of unrest: the al-Aqsa (or "Second") Intifada, which broke out in September 2000 to protest Ariel Sharon's visit to the Temple Mount.

THE AL-AQSA INTIFADA

This unrest was named for the al-Aqsa Mosque located on the Temple Mount, because of rioting that erupted there on Friday September 29, 2000, the day after Ariel Sharon had visited. Tensions between Palestinians and Israelis were already rising sharply after the failure of the Camp David Summit, and Sharon's visit caused them to explode.

As noted, the Dome of the Rock, located near the al-Aqsa Mosque on the Temple Mount, is regarded by Muslims as the site of Muhammad's "night journey" to heaven, and is thus considered to be the third-holiest site in Islam (after Mecca and Medina). As the location of the ancient Jewish temple, it is also seen as the holiest site in Judaism. Sharon did not actually enter the al-Aqsa Mosque or the Dome of the Rock. He paid his visit to the site during normal tourist hours to assert the right of all Israelis to go to the Temple Mount if they chose to do so. A Likud spokesman stated that his other purpose in making this trip was to demonstrate that "under a Likud government, [the Temple Mount] will remain under Israeli sovereignty," one of the main sticking points at the Camp David Summit. The country was then in the throes of an election campaign, which gave this visit an important political dimension. Several senior Palestinians contacted Sharon and begged him to call it off, but to no avail. Sharon's name was still infamous among Palestinians for his role in allowing the Sabra and Shatila massacres to take place during the 1982 Lebanon War (see p. 311).

The day after Sharon's visit, huge riots erupted around the Old City of Jerusalem following Friday noon prayers. Palestinians began throwing rocks from the Temple Mount over the Western Wall down onto tourists and Jewish worshipers there. This prompted Israeli riot police to storm the Temple Mount compound. There, they began firing rubber-coated steel bullets that killed four and injured as many as two hundred protesters.

Over the next several days, demonstrations broke out across the West Bank and Gaza in which dozens of Palestinians were killed and hundreds wounded. In one West Bank city, a Palestinian police officer conducting a joint patrol with an Israeli policeman suddenly pulled out his gun and shot the Israeli dead. Clashes continued through October that now involved Arab citizens of Israel as well as Palestinians from Gaza and the West Bank.

On October 12, police serving in the Palestinian Authority force arrested two Israeli army reservists who had accidentally come to Ramallah. When rumor spread that they were members of an elite undercover Israeli unit sent there, an agitated Palestinian mob stormed the police station, beat them to death, and threw their mutilated bodies into the street from a second floor window. In retaliation, Israel conducted air strikes against Palestinian Authority targets, which destroyed the police station where this had taken place.

SHARON'S ELECTION

In the wake of this breakdown and partly as a result of it, Ariel Sharon, at the time leader of the Likud Party, triumphed over Barak in a special election to become prime minister in February 2001. He refused to meet in person with Yasser Arafat, and this put further progress on the peace process in a state of limbo for some time. The new U.S. administration of President George W. Bush also did not take a very active role initially in trying to get peace talks restarted.

Over the next two years, Palestinian Islamic militants from Hamas and Islamic Jihad (another Islamist Palestinian militant group) continued to mount a steady stream of terror attacks against which Israeli forces retaliated. Two of the most spectacular were the suicide bombings against the Tel Aviv Dolphinarium dance club in June 2001 and the Sbarro pizza restaurant in Jerusalem in August 2001. New tactics began to be seen as well, in which boats carrying weapons and supplies for Palestinian militants were brought covertly to the Gaza coast, where some were intercepted by Israeli naval commandos.

OPERATION "DEFENSIVE SHIELD"

Operation "**Defensive Shield**," conducted by Israel between March and May 2002, became the most significant military operation in the West Bank since the Six-Day War in 1967. It was prompted by the increasing number of Israeli deaths from terrorist attacks. Its first part consisted of a strike on Ramallah, carried out on March 29, 2002, that laid siege to Yasser Arafat's compound there. Attacks on the West Bank's six largest cities soon followed. It was estimated that during the three weeks of Operation Defensive Shield, at least 200 Palestinians were killed and 500 wounded with 30 Israeli soldiers dead and 127 wounded. Substantial sectors of the Palestinian population were made homeless by the operation, and long after it ended, it was difficult to repair damaged infrastructure.

During the first two weeks of April, there was a showdown in the Palestinian refugee camp of Jenin that became a flash point. Various accusations of war crimes committed there by Israeli forces were made, but none ever proven. Starting at about the same time and continuing into May, there was an armed standoff at the Church of the Nativity in Bethlehem. Israeli soldiers surrounded the church as Palestinian militants held civilians and priests inside as hostages. During the confrontation, IDF snipers killed seven and wounded more than forty people inside the church. The standoff ended with the deportation to Europe of the thirteen most hard-core Palestinian hostage takers there, which ended the IDF's thirty-nine–day siege.

BEIRUT SUMMIT AND THE ROAD MAP FOR PEACE

Just as all these new clashes were taking place, Arab nations held the Beirut Summit in March 2002 to present an "Arab Peace Initiative," but it offered no really new ideas. Its main points were that Israel should make a full withdrawal to its 1967 borders and ensure the right of return for the Palestinian refugees.[8] Although Israeli foreign minister Shimon Peres welcomed this plan as a point of departure, he reminded its authors that "the details of every peace plan must be discussed directly between Israel and the Palestinians, and to make this possible, the Palestinian Authority must put an end to terror, the horrifying expression of which we witnessed just last night in Netanya."[9] Peres was referring to yet another spectacular suicide bombing that had just taken place at a large Passover seder at a hotel in Israel the night before, as well as the fact that the Beirut Summit totally avoided any discussion of terrorism.

In June 2002, President Bush presented the next diplomatic initiative: a "road map" for peace developed by the "quartet," meaning the United States, the European Union, the United Nations, and Russia. This called for the creation of an independent Palestinian state as well as for Israel and the Palestinians to take independent actions separately, leaving contentious issues until rapport could be reestablished after the current round of violence.

As its first step, the Palestinian Authority was asked to "undertake visible efforts on the ground to arrest, disrupt, and restrain individuals and groups conducting and planning violent attacks on Israelis" and to rebuild its security apparatus to confront "all those engaged in terror." For its part, Israel was called to dismantle all settlements created after March 2001, freeze all settlement activity, withdraw its troops from Palestinian areas occupied after September 28, 2000, end curfews, and ease restrictions on movement of persons and goods.[10]

Although it was formulated by the summer of 2002, the "road map" was not officially presented until April 2003. This was because neither the United States nor Israel was willing to negotiate directly with Arafat, distancing themselves from him because he had not acted vigorously enough in their view to oppose terrorism among his Palestinian followers. This problem of not being willing to meet with Arafat directly was solved when Arafat appointed Mahmud Abbas (also called "Abu Mazen") to be the first prime minister of the Palestinian Authority in April 2003. Despite this new "road map," the main development since 2003 in the Israeli-Palestinian situation has been the rapidly increasing importance of Hamas, particularly since Arafat's death in 2004.

AFGHANISTAN: REFUGE FOR ISLAMIC MILITANCY

Afghanistan had been thrown into chaos by warring factions in the wake of the abrupt Soviet withdrawal in 1989. The Pakistani intelligence services took this opportunity to promote a previously unknown group of religious students calling themselves the Taliban, and continued to support this group through the 1990s.

At first, the Taliban were welcomed by ordinary Afghans. They had become sick of

---

[8]http://www.al-bab.com/arab/docs/league/peace02.htm (accessed August 29, 2010).

[9]http://www.mfa.gov.il/MFA/About+the+Ministry/MFA+Spokesman/2002/Response+of+FM+Peres+to+the+decisions+of+the+Arab.htm (accessed August 29, 2010).

[10]http://www.bitterlemons.org/docs/roadmap3.html (accessed August 29, 2010).

warlords, now perceived as primarily focused on getting rich and fighting among themselves. The Afghan people were ready to accept the vow of Taliban leader Mullah Omar to rid the country of such criminals. By the 1990s, a group of truck owners based in Pakistan who specialized in transporting goods to and from Afghanistan began to support the Taliban. They saw this new group as the only force capable of ending bandit control of Afghanistan's southern transport routes, which could relieve them of the large sums of protection money these truckers were constantly forced to pay.

Many Afghan Taliban leaders, including Mullah Omar, had been students at a conservative Muslim religious school in Pakistan's Northwest Frontier Province known as the Darul Uloom Haqqania. Dominated by ethnic Pashtuns, the Taliban movement experienced its first major military success in the fall of 1994, when it took control of Kandahar, one of the main cities in the Pashtun heartland. It rapidly gained momentum, and by September 1996 the Taliban controlled Kabul. There, they captured, tortured, castrated, and executed Muhammad Najibullah: last president of Soviet Afghanistan and hated symbol of the old regime.

Taliban Rule

The Taliban imposed a regime that interpreted Sharia law as forbidding a wide variety of activities. The Afghan people were prohibited from watching movies or television, listening to music, engaging in any forms of dancing, displaying portraits or pictures in their homes, applauding during sports events or other public gatherings, and such frivolous amusements as flying kites. This set of moral regulations was decreed by a "Ministry for the Promotion of Virtue and Suppression of Vice" and enforced by a "religious police" reminiscent in some ways of the guardians of public morality in Saudi Arabia, but much more severe even that their Saudi counterparts. In towns just conquered by the Taliban, religious police would beat men and women whom they deemed transgressors of their moral code with long sticks.

They punished theft by amputating right hands, executed those convicted of rape, and stoned to death married people convicted of adultery. In Kabul, punishments typically were carried out in public at the city's old soccer stadium. Men were now obliged to cover their heads and grow long beards, but it was the behavior of women that became the particular focus of Taliban restrictions. Women were forbidden in general from working, from wearing any articles of clothing considered to be too attractive, from taking taxis without being escorted by their male relatives, or even from washing clothes in streams. They were obliged to wear burqas: traditional robes cloaking the whole body except for a small screen through which to peer out.[11]

After the Taliban secured control of Kabul, they placed even heavier restrictions on women. In February 1998, religious police forced all women to stay off of Kabul's streets. They even issued regulations that ordered all house windows to be blackened, so women would not be visible from outside. Home schooling for girls was now prohibited, and in June 1998 the Taliban began to allow women to use only one hospital in Kabul. During this period, many reports circulated of women being beaten for violating provisions of the Taliban version of Islamic law.

Movie theaters were closed and music banned. Hundreds of cultural artifacts considered idolatrous were destroyed, including collections of museums and private art galleries. In February 2001, the Taliban used sledgehammers to destroy priceless representational works of art kept at the National Museum of Afghanistan. They even banned the traditional Afghan New Year *Nowruz* celebration and for a while prohibited Shii commemoration of the day of Ashura. The most infamous episode of Taliban cultural suppression occurred in March 2001.

---

[11]Ahmad Rashid, *Taliban* (2000), 218–219.

At that time, the Taliban ordered the demolition of two ancient Buddha statues both over 100 feet tall and about 1,500 years old carved into cliffs at Bamiyan.

In the summer of 1998, Taliban sought out and massacred members of the Hazara, a mostly Shii group that lived in the Mazar-i-Sharif area. Mullah Nizai, Taliban commander of the attack on the Hazaras, called them infidels and threatened to kill them if they did not convert to Sunni Islam. In later years, there were still more Hazara massacres.

Northern Alliance Fights Back

After the Taliban took over Kabul in September 1996, an Uzbek warlord who was a former Soviet commander, General Abdul Rashid Dostum, joined forces with a Tajik warlord and hero of the anticommunist *mujahidin*, Ahmad Shah Massoud, to form a Northern Alliance against the Taliban. Although both commanders considered themselves devout Muslims and wanted to promote the use of Islamic law in Afghanistan, they did not agree with the severity of Taliban interpretations of it. They were supported by Russia and Iran, while the Taliban were given financial aid by the UAE, Saudi Arabia, and Pakistan.

Through 1997 and 1998 the Northern Alliance and the Taliban fought constantly for control of the country—a turbulent period that only ended when the Taliban took definitive control of Mazar-i Sharif in August 1998. By 1999, the Taliban had pushed the Northern Alliance back to the Panjshir Valley. Over the next couple of years, Ahmad Shah Massoud was successful in defending this stronghold against further Taliban advances and brought the war to a standstill.

On September 9, 2001, a suicide bomber, posing as a journalist, blew himself up after gaining access to Ahmad Shah Massoud's office. Massoud was hit in the chest with shrapnel from the bomb and died shortly after being taken to Tajikistan for emergency care. It has been reported that the militant Islamist group

al-Qaeda helped carry out this attack, with the killing itself probably arranged by al-Qaeda leader Osama bin Laden's main deputy Ayman al-Zawahiri.

This may have been a way for al-Qaeda to do the Taliban a favor. As the **Northern Alliance's** most effective commander, Massoud was also being discussed as an obvious replacement for the Taliban to rule Afghanistan. If al-Qaeda at that time had begun to focus on coordinating the attacks of September 11, 2001, on the United States, they knew that they would have to depend on strong Taliban protection from a predictably severe U.S. reaction, which may have given them a very concrete reason to help out their Taliban sponsors in this way.

AL-QAEDA

Afghanistan under Taliban rule had been a fairly congenial place for al-Qaeda, since it was there in the late 1980s that this organization itself began to take shape. It seems to have been created in August 1988 at a meeting between leaders from Egyptian Islamic Jihad (one of the militant offshoots of the Muslim Brotherhood in the 1970s), Abdullah Azzam (a Palestinian Islamic activist and longtime member of the Muslim Brotherhood), and Osama bin Laden (a wealthy Saudi who had come to Afghanistan in the early 1980s to help the war effort there). This group agreed that it would combine bin Laden's funds with the organizational and logistical expertise of Egyptian Islamic Jihad to fight in support of militant Islam elsewhere in the world after the Soviets had left Afghanistan.

There was already quite a track record for international Islamic financial support in the struggle against the Soviets. Much funding had been provided through international Muslim organizations such as the *Maktab al-Khidamat* (Services Bureau), a group whose funds came in part from the millions of dollars donated annually to the war effort by the Saudi government and individual wealthy Saudis linked to representatives such as Osama bin Laden. Bin Laden and Azzam had set up the *Maktab al-Khidamat* in Peshawar, Pakistan, in 1984. Beginning around 1986, it began to establish a fund-raising and support network for the war in Afghanistan in the United States and other countries, one hub of which was apparently a refugee center in Brooklyn, New York.

This organization ran guest houses in Peshawar near the Afghan border and collected supplies for building paramilitary training camps to prepare foreign recruits (who became *mujahidin*) for the war front in Afghanistan. Bin Laden became a major financial supporter of Afghan and foreign *mujahidin*, spending his own money and using connections with Saudi royals and wealthy Gulf Arabs to raise more funds. After 1987, Azzam and bin Laden began creating camps inside Afghanistan. The role played by this organization and other foreign volunteers, called "Afghan Arabs" by some, was not large in Afghanistan, since there were not more than two thousand volunteers in the field at a time. They had a much greater impact when they went back to their home countries to help launch wars that cost, in some cases, thousands of lives, such as what happened in Algeria in the 1990s.

Militant Islam Goes Global

Toward the end of the Soviet war in Afghanistan, some activists wanted to expand operations to include militant Islamist struggles taking place elsewhere, such as in Israel and Kashmir. Bin Laden sought to expand activities into nonmilitary operations in other parts of the world; Azzam, by contrast, wanted to remain focused on fighting. After Azzam was assassinated by a mysterious car bomb in 1989, bin Laden took over the *Maktab* and merged it with al-Qaeda.

Osama bin Laden by then had gone back to Saudi Arabia. When Iraq invaded Kuwait in August 1990, Osama met with Prince Sultan, the Saudi defense minister, and offered him the services of experienced soldiers from Afghanistan to remove Iraq from Kuwait. Bin Laden told him that Saudi Arabia could easily avoid the indignity of allowing an army of American unbelievers to defend it. The prince thanked him but was skeptical. "There are no caves in Kuwait," he observed. "You cannot fight them from the mountains and caves. What will you do when he [Saddam] lobs the missiles at you with chemical and biological weapons?" Bin Laden was reported to have replied, "We fight him with faith."[12] The subsequent U.S. deployment in his homeland angered bin Laden, who thought that this sullied sacred Islamic soil so near to the holy sites of Mecca and Medina. After speaking out in public against the Saudi government for allowing foreigners to come in and defend the country, he was banished to Sudan.

In Khartoum, Osama and his followers were the guests of the Islamist theologian Hasan al-Turabi between 1992 to 1996. There had recently been an Islamist coup d'état in Sudan led by Colonel Omar al-Bashir, whose government bin Laden offered financial assistance (using his inherited wealth) to set up various business ventures and create training camps for militants. Osama and al-Zawahiri continued to conduct various terrorist operations against the Saudi and Egyptian governments from Sudan, but this created such pressure on the Sudanese to control this that they were finally led to expel al-Qaeda and bin Laden in 1996.

Shelter with the Taliban

When the Sudanese made it clear that bin Laden was no longer welcome in their country, Taliban-controlled Afghanistan provided a perfect safe haven where Osama and al-Qaeda could escape. As noted, many of the main

---

[12]"A Nation Challenged: Saudi Arabia; Holy War Lured Saudis As Rulers Looked Away," *N.Y. Times,* December 27, 2001.

leaders of the Taliban movement had been graduates of the Darul Uloom Haqqania school of Muslim theology, which by the 1980s was largely funded through private donations from wealthy Arabs.

Many of bin Laden's contacts from those days were still engaged in funneling charitable donations through friendly Islamic banks, in order to distribute money to a network of charities functioning partly as fronts for militant groups. Al-Qaeda came under Taliban protection and acquired a measure of legitimacy as a designated part of the Taliban Ministry of Defense. Many of the *mujahidin* who later joined the Taliban had fought years earlier alongside Afghan Arab fighters connected to bin Laden, which further cemented the ties between them.

Upon his arrival in Afghanistan, al-Qaeda sought to open an "offensive phase" of his global jihad campaign around the world. In 1998 bin Laden issued a fatwa, in essence a public declaration of war against the United States and its allies. He channeled al-Qaeda's resources toward generating large-scale, spectacular strikes: "The ruling to kill the Americans and their allies—civilians and military—is an individual duty for every Muslim who can do it in any country in which it is possible to do it, in order to liberate the al-Aqsa Mosque [in Jerusalem] and the Holy Mosque [in Mecca] from their grip, and in order for their armies to move out of all the lands of Islam, defeated and unable to threaten any Muslim."[13] Although bin Laden possessed no traditional Islamic scholarly qualifications to be able to issue such a fatwa, he rejected, following the approach of Sayyid Qutb, the religious authority of most so-called contemporary Muslim scholars, since he viewed them as paid servants of *jahiliya* rulers and thus without legitimate standing as "Muslims," much less "Islamic scholars."

In December 1998, the CIA reported to the U.S. president that "Bin Ladin [*sic*] and his allies are preparing for attacks in the US, including an aircraft hijacking."[14] Before that point, al-Qaeda operatives had carried out several major terrorist attacks, and in each case its leadership planned the operations well in advance. It was also very difficult for the United States to strike back in a meaningful way against these assaults.

One example of this problem was the attempted retaliation for the 1998 bombings of U.S. embassies in Kenya and Tanzania that had resulted in the deaths of over three hundred people, mostly East Africans. The U.S. military did obliterate an al-Qaeda base in Afghanistan by firing a barrage of cruise missiles, but such a loss did not really harm the organization's operational capacity. While al-Qaeda militants in the Middle East continued to achieve success with such attacks as the strike against the USS *Cole* in an October 2000 suicide attack in Yemen that killed seventeen U.S. servicemen and seriously damaged the vessel, al-Qaeda's organizers began to envision and prepare for an attack that would take place in the United States itself.

September 11, 2001

The attacks of September 11, 2001, became the most damaging terrorist acts in the history of the United States, resulting in the deaths of approximately 3,000 people. Two commercial airliners were deliberately flown into the World Trade Center towers, which both collapsed soon after the impact, a third crashed into the Pentagon, and a fourth, originally intended to hit the United States Capitol, crashed in a field in rural Pennsylvania.

Al-Qaeda suicide teams carried out these attacks, acting in accord with bin Laden's

---

[13]John Calvert, *Islamism: A Documentary and Reference Guide* (Santa Barbara: Greenwood Press, 2008), 227.

[14]*Nine/Eleven Commission Report, Final Report of the National Commission on Terrorist Attacks upon the United States* (New York: Norton, 2004), 128.

Osama bin Laden on al-Jazeera (October 2001)

1998 fatwa under the direction of bin Laden, al-Zawahiri, and others. The team leader for the operation was an Egyptian named Muhammad Atta, with bin Laden, al-Zawahiri, and Khalid Shaikh Mohammed serving as its key overall planners. Bin Laden praised the attacks in messages issued shortly after September 11, 2001, but denied direct involvement. U.S. investigators were fairly quickly able to identify the perpetrators and their connections to al-Qaeda because the luggage that Muhammad Atta had checked did not actually get loaded onto the plane that he crashed and contained much revealing information.

GWOT: THE GLOBAL WAR ON TERROR

Immediately after the attacks, the U.S. government quickly identified bin Laden as the main person whom it would hold responsible, and

began to prepare to overthrow the Taliban regime that it assessed was furnishing al-Qaeda a safe haven. The U.S. offered Taliban leader Mullah Omar a chance to surrender bin Laden and his top associates. The Taliban leadership offered to turn him over to a neutral country for trial if the U.S. could provide evidence of his responsibility for the attacks. U.S. President Bush responded, "We know he's guilty. Turn him over."[15]

On October 7, 2001, the United States and its allies invaded Afghanistan, and supported by the Afghan Northern Alliance, removed the Taliban government from power in the country by December 2001. It quickly destroyed Taliban and al-Qaeda training camps, and disrupted

---

[15]*Public Papers of the Presidents of the United States: George W. Bush, 2001* (Book 2: July 1 to December 31, 2001) (Washington: National Archives and Records Administration, Office of the Federal Register, 2003), 1238.

al-Qaeda's operating structure. After being driven out of the organization's strongholds in the Tora Bora area near the Pakistani border, some al-Qaeda fighters tried to regroup in Gardez.

Under the cover of intense aerial bombardment, U.S. infantry and Afghan forces attacked there, shattering al-Qaeda positions and killing or capturing many militants. By early 2002, al-Qaeda's operational capacity had been severely curtailed. In late 2004, the U.S. government announced that two-thirds of the most senior al-Qaeda figures active in 2001 had been captured and interrogated by the CIA. After years of investigation and preparation, the United States was finally able to hunt down and kill bin Laden in May 2011 after he had been hiding for many years in a modest compound in Abbottabad, Pakistan: a city in the hills just a few miles north of the capital Islamabad that is also home to the main Pakistani military academy. While al-Zawahiri has since taken over as the head of al-Qaeda, the future of the organization remains in question, since al-Zawahiri is not thought to have the same personal charisma or leadership style that bin Laden used to attract followers.

Questions to Think About

1. How was the international situation changing at the time of the First Gulf War, and how did this affect its outcome?
2. Why did Saddam Hussein start the First Gulf War, and what were his claims about Kuwait's status?
3. What was the impact of the war in military terms, and how did it affect Iraqis?
4. How did the Oslo Accords represent a new phase in the Arab-Israeli peace process?
5. What was the impact of the Oslo Accords?
6. How did the Arab-Israeli peace process change after 2000 and the al-Aqsa Intifada?
7. Who are the Taliban, and how did they take power in Afghanistan in the 1990s?
8. What is al-Qaeda, and how did it take refuge in Afghanistan?
9. How did Osama bin Laden and al-Qaeda justify the September 11, 2001, attacks on the United States?

For Further Reading

Atkinson, Rick. *Crusade: The Untold Story of the Persian Gulf War*. Boston: Houghton Mifflin, 1993.

Beilin, Yossi. *Touching Peace: From the Oslo Accord to a Final Agreement*. London: Weidenfeld & Nicolson, 1999.

Bergen, Peter L. *The Longest War: The Enduring Conflict between America and Al-Qaeda*. New York: Free Press, 2011.

Brown, Nathan J. *Palestinian Politics after the Oslo Accords: Resuming Arab Palestine*. Berkeley: University of California Press, 2003.

Chayes, Sarah. *The Punishment of Virtue: Inside Afghanistan after the Taliban*. New York: Penguin Press, 2006.

Cordesman, Anthony H. *Kuwait: Recovery and Security after the Gulf War*. Boulder, CO: Westview Press, 1997.

Freedman, Lawrence, and Efraim Karsh. *The Gulf Conflict, 1990–1991: Diplomacy and War in the New World Order*. Princeton: Princeton University Press, 1993.

Freedman, Robert Owen. *The Middle East and the Peace Process: The Impact of the Oslo Accords*. Gainesville: University Press of Florida, 1998.

Gerges, Fawaz A. *The Rise and Fall of Al-Qaeda*. Oxford: Oxford University Press, 2011.

Gohari, M. J. *The Taliban: Ascent to Power*. Karachi: Oxford University Press, 2000.

Golan, Galia. *Israel and Palestine: Peace Plans and Proposals from Oslo to Disengagement*. Princeton: Markus Wiener Publishers, 2007.

Goodson, Larry P. *Afghanistan's Endless War: State Failure, Regional Politics, and the Rise of the Taliban*. Seattle: University of Washington Press, 2001.

Ibrahim, Raymond, Ayman Zawahiri, and Osama Bin Laden. *The Al Qaeda Reader*. New York: Doubleday, 2007.

Kepel, Gilles, Jean-Pierre Milelli, and Pascale Ghazaleh. *Al Qaeda in Its Own Words*. Cambridge: Belknap Press of Harvard University Press, 2008.

Maley, William. *The Afghanistan Wars*. Basingstoke, UK: Palgrave Macmillan, 2009.

Parsons, Nigel Craig. *The Politics of the Palestinian Authority: From Oslo to Al-Aqsa*. New York: Routledge, 2005.

Quray, Ahmad. *From Oslo to Jerusalem: The Palestinian Story of the Secret Negotiations*. London: I.B. Tauris, 2006.

Rashid, Ahmed. *Taliban: Militant Islam, Oil and Fundamentalism in Central Asia*. New Haven: Yale University Press, 2001.

Sifry, Micah L., and Christopher Cerf. *The Gulf War Reader: History, Documents, Opinions*. New York: Times Books, 1991.

23

The Middle East in World History after September 11

OPERATION "ENDURING FREEDOM" AND THE WAR IN AFGHANISTAN

Within three months after the United States and the UK invaded Afghanistan in Operation "Enduring Freedom" on October 7, 2001, Taliban control had been removed from the country. The goals of "Enduring Freedom" were to bring al-Qaeda's leaders to justice, destroy al-Qaeda as an organization, and remove the Taliban regime. By June 2011, the United States had been engaged in this operation for 116 months, 13 months longer than it had pursued the Vietnam War. It had accomplished much of what it originally set out to do, but its exit strategy from Afghanistan remained unclear. It had killed Osama bin Laden, but not destroyed the Taliban, although it rather quickly displaced them from power. As for previous occupiers of Afghanistan, stabilizing the situation there became a great challenge for the International Security Assistance Force (ISAF): the U.S.-led international force assigned to bring peace to the country.

From another perspective, the American invasion brought sudden relief from the severe restrictions of Taliban rule. Radio Mazar-i-Sharif, the former Taliban Voice of Sharia radio station, now went on the air with music introduced by a female announcer—unimaginable during the Taliban era. A transitional government took power in the summer of 2002, after a traditional Afghan *loya jirga* assembly of different tribes and ethnic groups was held in Kabul to choose a new leader. It selected Hamid Karzai, commander of an important Pashtun militia force who played a critical role in the success of the final big offensive against the Taliban: the battle to take Kandahar in early December 2001.

Karzai, although later accused of corruption, was elected to the office of president in 2004 and 2009. This indicated that he maintained a meaningful level of support in a country known for its political fragmentation. After this

343

government was put in place, activities of the ISAF force shifted to a counterinsurgency campaign.

The largest tactical challenge was that Taliban warriors easily established sanctuaries just across border in Pakistan, because the people in that region of Pakistan were their ethnic kin. Pakistan's central government was extremely sensitive to the potential of these areas to destabilize the whole country, so ISAF could not easily pursue guerrilla teams who jumped over the border to attack them and then hurried back to Pakistan. Within Afghanistan, the extraordinary remoteness of southern provinces such as Kandahar and Helmand made it easy for small Taliban contingents there to melt away into the hills as Afghan warriors had done for centuries.

By early 2003, the Taliban had created small, movable training camps to educate a growing cadre of new recruits. They were mainly Afghan refugees attending the same religious schools in Pakistan that had trained the founders of the Taliban movement. Soon, new Taliban bases arose in Pakistan that the Pakistani government was unable (or unwilling) to suppress. Over the next summer, the Taliban conducted many ambushes of isolated American and Afghan government units. These continual small clashes sapped the morale of ISAF troops.

By January 2006, ISAF's strategic focus turned to expanding "Provincial Reconstruction Teams" (PRTs). These teams were composed of civilian and military experts sent all over Afghanistan to enhance security arrangements, support the government's authority, and enable rebuilding of the infrastructure. The Taliban immediately perceived the threat of such stabilization operations and vowed to resist them.

The struggle against the Taliban was weighed down by the classic problem of counterinsurgency: how to avoid collateral casualties among civilians. On March 4, 2007, U.S. Marines, reacting to an ambush, killed at least twelve civilians and injured thirty-three in one district near the Pakistani border. After large protests around the country, the unit that had carried out this attack was asked to leave Afghanistan, since it was decided that this had damaged its relations with the local population beyond repair.

As the conflict passed into 2008, both the United States and the UK increased troop strengths in Afghanistan, since Taliban resistance continued strong. The Taliban freed hundreds of inmates from the main Kandahar prison, in an operation against a facility where the Canadian government had just spent about $1 million making improvements.

Following this setback, British troops in ISAF had success in Operation Eagle's Summit. Their mission was to move a 220-ton turbine to the Kajaki dam in Helmand province through Taliban-controlled areas. In 1953, the U.S. Agency for International Development (USAID) had built the Kajaki dam to bring electricity and modern irrigation to Helmand and Kandahar provinces for the first time. The dam had fallen into disrepair after the 1979 Soviet invasion.

Although the Taliban restored it in early 2001, the dam was then bombed just a few months later during the U.S. invasion. By 2005, USAID had restored one turbine, but needed to bring in another new one. The transport of this new piece of machinery in a convoy of 100 vehicles spread out over two miles was reported have been one of the largest logistical operations carried out by the British Army since World War II. It took five days to travel 110 miles, but only one soldier was killed during the operation, in a traffic accident.

In early September 2008, American forces again entered Pakistani territory by helicopter and attacked three houses in a village, killing several people. When an unnamed American official announced that President Bush had authorized such raids, the Pakistani military said that it would "open fire" on any American soldiers who crossed the border. On October 1, a drone (undoubtedly of U.S. origin) fired a missile against a militant base in Pakistan that appears to have killed six people.

The Pakistanis became so furious that they announced that they would cut supply lines through their country to ISAF forces for an indefinite amount of time, but goods continued to be delivered.

In the next two months, there was a wave of arson attacks, hijackings, and robberies carried out in Pakistan against convoys supplying ISAF troops. In December 2008 alone, raids destroyed around three hundred cargo trucks and Humvees at a NATO depot near Peshawar. Despite continued American frustration with Pakistan's lack of action against militants taking refuge there, Pakistan remained unwilling to turn its back on old allies: the Afghan Taliban whom it had help put in power many years earlier. From the Pakistani perspective, the Afghan Taliban might prove useful allies in future confrontations with India over Afghanistan after the Americans had left. Pakistanis have always perceived India as their main strategic threat, and they see Afghanistan as a key place where the conflict between them and India is continuously played out by proxy. As an alternative to this supply route through Pakistan, U.S. commanders began to work in 2009 on boosting the shipping capacity of the Northern Distribution Network to Afghanistan through Russia, Uzbekistan, and Kyrgyzstan.

By the fall of 2009, the American ambassador to Afghanistan, retired three-star general Karl Eikenberry, began expressing concern about how merely sending more U.S. troops there had become a kind of panacea to "solve" the Afghanistan problem, conveying frustration with the lack of funds being allocated for development and reconstruction. President Karzai, now newly re-elected, implored the United States to begin direct talks with Taliban leaders, but it only began to explore the possibilities of starting this process beginning in 2011.

In 2009, President Obama sent thirty thousand more U.S. troops to the country, continuing the strategy of keeping continuous pressure on the Taliban that had defined U.S. counterinsurgency operations in Afghanistan over its years there, but a timetable for their withdrawal was announced in June 2011.

In early January 2010, there were preliminary talks between the United Nations and representatives of the Taliban—the first time that such discussions had ever happened. Later that year, the United States installed a new commander in Afghanistan, General David Petraeus, with extensive knowledge of counterinsurgency techniques. Petraeus presented an initiative to President Karzai in July 2010 to create "Local Police Forces" to bolster security in remote areas. Karzai had fought this, fearing return to the days of the country being split into local militias. Similar schemes had been tried in the past, but Petraeus, as a commander with a lot of experience in how to manage counterinsurgency in Iraq, was able to point to some success in Afghanistan by the time he left there in July 2011.

One of the main issues in Afghanistan for the United States by the summer of 2011 was the great pressure on President Obama to scale down U.S. involvement more rapidly than his military commanders wanted him to do. In June, he announced that he would withdraw troops in Afghanistan sent in the earlier "surge" on a somewhat expedited schedule. The question of how to sort out future negotiations with the Taliban and the current Afghan government concerning the country's future remained the paramount issue confronting the United States and its ISAF partners at that time.

Afghanistan's Economy and Opium

No matter who controls it ultimately, Afghanistan's biggest challenges will continue to be poverty and its lack of infrastructure. It has the highest infant mortality rate in the world and 70 percent of its population does not have access to clean water. The country has also been rated one of the two most corrupt countries in the world.

The key economic question that faces the country concerns the fate of its most lucrative cash crop: opium. By 2008, Afghanistan had become the largest producer of illegal opium producer in the world. In 2007, 93 percent of the opiates on the world market had their origins there. Afghanistan produces the most hashish of any nation in the world as well.

Opium production rose during the Soviet war when warlords were searching for easy ways to make money to buy weapons and continued after they left for the same reasons. In a remarkable turnaround, in July 2000, Taliban leader Mullah Mohammed Omar, whose regime had previously allowed poppy cultivation, suddenly declared that growing poppies was against Islamic values and banned this crop. Opium poppy cultivation dropped by 91 percent. By late 2001, facing an economic collapse, many farmers went back to growing opium for export. Recent growing seasons have seen record levels of poppy cultivation as corrupt officials and continued unrest in the rural areas have undermined efforts to control this.

It has been alleged that Karzai's government as well as the Taliban, and in fact all political forces in Afghanistan as well as criminals are benefiting from this production. Serious proposals have been made to use Afghanistan's opium production to produce legal medical products, but there is still a lot of debate over how and whether this would work to solve the problem. Although opium cultivation on the current scale was not historically a major part of Afghanistan's economy, it has now evolved to where the country is highly dependent on this product. It has been estimated that nearly 10 percent of the population is involved in some way in opium cultivation.

Afghanistan on the New Silk Road

If its circumstances improve, Afghanistan could use its location at the historical nexus of Eurasian financial and trade networks greatly to its advantage. Central Asia and the Silk Road flourished as a conduit for trade goods in times past, and other countries in the region are developing a similar role in the modern global economy.

One way for Afghanistan to join this trend would be to create a trans-Afghanistan natural gas pipeline to link Turkmenistan and Pakistan—a project that the Taliban had almost signed an agreement with UNOCAL oil company to build in 1997. In December 2002, the new Afghan government, Turkmenistan, and Pakistan concluded a new agreement to build this pipeline. Although the project stalled for a while after that due to instability in the region of Afghanistan through which the line would flow, it appeared by 2011 to be back on track for completion within a few years, which would be quite a boon for Afghanistan, since it is scheduled to receive 8 percent of its proceeds.

Afghanistan also has mineral riches that have attracted the attention of its neighbors. In 2007, China became the country's largest foreign investor when it won a $3.5 billion contract to develop copper mines at Aynak, southeast of Kabul and one of the world's largest copper deposits. In June 2010, a team of American geologists prepared a confidential report suggesting that Afghanistan may possess as much as $1 trillion in untapped mineral resources, far beyond any previously known reserves. The report asserted that Afghanistan could become the "Saudi Arabia of lithium," possessing vast quantities of a key raw material in the manufacture of batteries for laptops and cell phones. Nevertheless, all of these possibilities remain only potentials until the country achieves greater social and political stability.

2003 IRAQ WAR

The other major war during the new millennium in which the United States became involved, the Iraq War, has also continued to the present. **Operation "Iraqi Freedom"** began on March 20, 2003, when a multinational force led by soldiers from the United States and the UK invaded Iraq. The American and British governments had alleged that Iraq possessed weapons of mass destruction (WMDs), posing an urgent threat to their security and that of their allies. Due to American and British pressure, the UN Security Council passed a resolution calling on Iraq to cooperate fully with UN inspectors to prove that Iraq had no WMDs.

In the end, the United Nations found no evidence that Iraq possessed any WMDs. Research after the invasion of Iraq confirmed that it had ended nuclear, chemical, and biological weapons programs in 1991 and had no active programs in 2003 (although it had plans to resume production if sanctions imposed in the 1990s were lifted). A few U.S. officials also accused Saddam Hussein of supporting al-Qaeda, but no evidence for this was found.

Based on tenuous claims about Iraq's possession of WMDs and its support for terrorism, U.S. President Bush (joined by British Prime Minister Blair) pushed to move into Iraq preemptively. Joined by small detachments from about forty other nations that became labeled the "Coalition of the Willing," U.S. and British troops commenced the invasion of Iraq in March 2003.

The invasion's stated goals were to end the Saddam Hussein regime, destroy any WMDs that were found, destroy any Islamist militant organizations in Iraq, distribute humanitarian aid, secure Iraq's petroleum infrastructure, and help create a representative but cooperative Iraqi government to serve as a model for other nations in the region. As in the case with Afghanistan, some of these goals had been partially (or completely) achieved by 2010, but also as in Afghanistan, the America military presence in the country had not ended by then.

After some fairly intense combat, Baghdad was taken on April 9, 2003. Its abrupt fall created massive civil disorder there, with much looting of government buildings. Hundreds of thousands of tons of ordnance was stolen that was later believed to have been used by insurgents. By April 15, after Saddam's hometown of Tikrit had surrendered, the invasion was declared over.

A "Coalition Provisional Authority" (CPA) was created that ran the country from late April 2003 until June 2004. It set up its command post in the "Green Zone" a heavily fortified area in central Baghdad that had functioned as the headquarters of earlier Iraqi regimes. For most of its lifespan, the CPA was run by a former U.S. diplomat who had developed a second career as counterterrorism expert: L. Paul Bremer.

The CPA's first act was to order the dismantling of the Baath Party apparatus and structure that had played a role in oppressing Iraqis, and it also formally disbanded the Iraqi army. Both measures created large groups of unemployed and impoverished former bureaucrats and soldiers who now had the time, connections, knowledge, and motivation to cause a lot of trouble. In July 2003, the CPA formed the "Iraqi Governing Council" and appointed its members. The Council consisted largely of Iraqi expatriates who had previously fled the country during the rule of Saddam Hussein or dissidents who had been persecuted by him. Various political factions felt left out of this council, an omission that in the case of urban Shii communities in the Sadr City section of Baghdad and in Basra led to demonstrations.

On May 1, 2003, President George Bush had given a speech on an aircraft carrier under an enormous banner reading "MISSION ACCOMPLISHED" in which he declared victory in Iraq. Soon after this speech, there was a huge wave of attacks, particularly in the region northwest of Baghdad known as the "**Sunni Triangle**" for its large Sunni Muslim population. At first, resistance was led by loyalists to Saddam who relied on weapons hidden away prior to the invasion.

Soon, religious radicals and unaffiliated Iraqis joined in the battles, causing many American deaths. These fighters used guerrilla techniques of all sorts, employing many IED (improvised explosive devices) and RPGs (rocket-propelled grenades). By the end of 2003, these attacks had increased in intensity. To counter this, coalition forces began to use artillery and airplanes.

The cumulative effects of years of sanctions, war, bombings, and decay had already left many Iraqi cities barely functioning before the invasion, but the failure of the CPA to provide basic services created much anger and discontent. When Saddam was captured in December 2003, it was hoped that this would help end the insurgency, and the United States then promised $20 billion in aid for reconstruction in the form of credits against Iraq's future oil income.

At this point, a Sunni insurgency, inspired by both nationalist and Islamist agendas, started gaining power across the country. Simultaneously, a militant Shii "Mahdi Army" led by Muqtada al-Sadr, charismatic son of a revered Shii cleric murdered by Saddam, also began attacking coalition targets in an attempt to seize control from Iraqi security forces. The cities of south and central Iraq erupted in urban guerrilla battles as multinational forces attempted to maintain order. Violence also increased during this period because foreign fighters from around the Middle East, as well as "al-Qaeda in Iraq" (an offshoot of the main al-Qaeda organization) led by Abu Musab al-Zarqawi, a Jordanian trained in Afghanistan, expanded the number of insurgents.

Abu Ghraib and the First and Second Battles of Fallujah

On March 31, 2004, a group of insurgents in Fallujah ambushed a convoy providing security for a food service delivery to U.S. troops. They killed the convoy's guards, who were not soldiers, but private security personnel working for Blackwater USA (a private American security contractor), set them on fire, and displayed their burnt corpses on a bridge over the Euphrates River. When photos and videos of this event circulated worldwide, they prompted an attempt to "pacify" the city in April later called the First Battle of Fallujah.

When this did not succeed, another offensive took place in November known as the Second Battle of Fallujah. This was remembered as one of the bloodiest battles of the Iraq War, featuring the most intense urban combat for U.S. troops since Vietnam. The American use of white phosphorus as an incendiary weapon against insurgents in this battle became somewhat controversial. The battle, lasting about six weeks, was perceived as a victory for the coalition, with 95 U.S. soldiers killed versus approximately 1,350 insurgents. The city of Fallujah was severely damaged during the fighting, although most civilians had fled before it took place.

The Abu Ghraib scandal also became publicized in 2004. Reports of prisoner abuse at the detention facility of Abu Ghraib, as well as graphic pictures showing U.S. military personnel taunting and abusing Iraqi prisoners there, were publicized in a television news report and discussed in a magazine article. These revelations were damaging to the moral authority of the occupation, especially in Iraqi eyes, and called the continued U.S. presence in Iraq into question.

Iraqi Transitional Government

Despite the violence still taking place, elections were held in January 2005 to create an "Iraqi Transitional Government," tasked with drawing up a permanent constitution. Although many Sunnis stayed away, most Kurdish and Shii voters who were eligible to vote did participate, and the level of violence subsided somewhat. Any hopes for greater calm diminished in May 2005, due to a wave of suicide bombings carried out by disaffected Iraqi Sunni Arabs. These attacks damaged important Shii sites and killed many Shiis.

Despite this, a new Iraqi constitution was ratified in October 2005. Elections were held for the new National Assembly in December, in which Sunni Iraqis now participated along with their Kurdish and Shii fellow citizens. The first government of Iraq under the new constitution took office on May 20, 2006.

Sectarian violence also expanded to new levels of intensity in 2006. The most spectacular attack in terms of destruction was the al-Askari Mosque bombing in Samarra in February, believed to have been caused by a bomb planted by al-Qaeda militants. The *Iraq Study Group Report*, issued in December by a high-level study led by former Congressman Lee Hamilton and former secretary of state James Baker, concluded that "the situation in Iraq is grave and deteriorating."[1] In that month, Saddam Hussein was hanged, having been found guilty of crimes against humanity by an Iraqi court after a trial lasting for a year.

Iraq's New Constitution

Over its history as a modern nation, Iraq had a series of constitutions, but the 2005 Constitution is remarkably explicit in its description of Iraq as a nonsectarian, voluntary federation. Its preamble, for example, describes the Iraqi nation as a "union" (*ittihad*) established through "freedom and choice." This implies, at least from a Kurdish perspective, the presumption of a right to secede. There is no reference to Iraq as an "Islamic" state, although some politicians had wanted this. The document recognizes Islam as "the official religion of the state" and "a foundation source of legislation," but follows this with a guarantee of full "rights to freedom of religious belief and practice of all individuals."[2]

The details of wording are subtle but significant, because they reflect a compromise between legislators who insisted on describing Islam as "*the* foundation source" and those who preferred it to be "*a* foundation source" among several. It is also interesting that this section of the constitution does not refer explicitly to "Islamic law," just "Islam." In a later provision, the constitution calls for experts in "Islamic jurisprudence" to be part of the judicial system, although not as its only source of legal authority.

On the other hand, the document forbids the creation of any law that contradicts "the established provisions of Islam." This provides a way to acknowledge the importance of Islamic jurisprudence and honor its "established provisions" (*thawabit*), meaning in this case general and fairly broad principles. However, it also avoids the more controversial discussion of specific "legal rulings" (*ahkam*) about which Muslims might have significant differences. Just after this discussion, there is a clause that forbids enactment of any law violating the principles of democracy or limiting stipulated rights and freedoms. The constitution presents religious rights in communal rather than individual terms, although also offers explicit discussion of individual freedom of thought, conscience, and creed. It specifically prohibits the practice of *takfir* (accusation of apostasy or religious unbelief), often associated with radical Sunni militants declaring Shiis to be apostates.

Its provisions for a federal state with different powers reserved for different levels of regional and national governance are innovative by the standards of the Middle East, most of whose regimes remain highly centralized in law and practice. Nevertheless, the complexities of apportioning powers can be seen in its wording. Article 13 states, "Any text in any regional constitutions … that contradicts this Constitution shall be considered void," while Article 115 indicates, "With regard to … powers shared between the federal government and the regional government, priority shall be given to the law of the regions … in case of dispute."[3] How federalism might work in practice will eventually be an issue for Iraq to sort out as it determines how the constitution will apply. This will always remain a major challenge for Iraq, given its diversity. The bigger challenges that Iraq faced in 2006 and 2007 remained the restoration of civic order and the suppression of violence that threatened to unravel this whole system.

[1] James Baker III and Lee Hamilton, *The Iraq Study Group Report* (New York: Vintage Books, 2006), 11.

[2] http://www.uniraq.org/documents/iraqi_constitution.pdf (accessed on August 29, 2010).

[3] http://www.uniraq.org/documents/iraqi_constitution.pdf (accessed on August 29, 2010).

More Violence and the 2007 Surge

In January 2007 President Bush proposed sending several thousand more troops to Iraq, and providing additional funding for its reconstruction. The United States had decided to try a new "surge" strategy whose main goal was to support the new Iraqi government with additional U.S. forces in specific areas.

Although the results were somewhat mixed at first, with no real abatement in violence, casualties did significantly drop by the end of 2007. Some studies attributed this directly to the troop surge, while others suggested that the decrease in violence might be due to the rise of ethnic uniformity in different neighborhoods in Baghdad, which reduced the possibility of incidents between members of distinct groups. By July 2008, U.S. forces sustained the lowest number of casualties for one month since the initial invasion of Iraq in 2003.

Withdrawal of American Forces: 2008–2010

The new Iraqi government approved a U.S.-Iraq Status of Forces Agreement in December 2008. It determined that U.S. combat forces would withdraw from Iraqi cities by June 30, 2009, and that all U.S. forces would be completely gone from Iraq by the end of 2011. Although there have been protests against some of its provisions that were considered to give the United States too much leeway, it set a timetable for U.S. withdrawal has so far proceeded as planned.

By November 2009, Iraqi civilian casualties dropped to their lowest level since 2003 as well. The question of how well the new Iraqi government can confront the fragmentary pressures of sectarianism and regionalism remains to be seen, because there were additional waves of violence in 2011. Despite its announced timetable for withdrawal, the United States is creating four "super bases" for permanent deployment. One will be adjacent to Baghdad, two close to the southern and northern oil field regions, with a fourth in the western part of the country near the Syrian border.

New Oil Contracts

One measure of sustainability for Iraq's new government will be to see how fast it can get the nation back on its feet economically. In 2009, the Iraqi oil ministry of oil finally awarded contracts to international oil companies to tap some of Iraq's many oil fields, production in which had been under capacity for years. If oil does begin to flow again in greater quantities, this will be enormously important for restoring infrastructure and promoting further economic development. As in all sectors of the economy, much will depend on the ability of the government to establish and increase security across the nation.

ARAB-ISRAELI CONFLICT AFTER 9/11

Even before the events of September 11, 2001 transformed the situation in the Middle East, the failure of the Israeli-Palestinian peace process and a new wave of Palestinian and occasional Hezbollah terrorist attacks led Israel's political leadership to lose confidence in the prospects of a final, negotiated peace with the Palestinian Authority in any near future. Israelis began to suspect that Palestinians viewed their peace agreements with Israel so far as temporary expedients and lost faith in the process. Many Israelis thus became more anxious simply to disengage from the Palestinians.

In response to a wave of suicide bomb attacks, the most serious of which had been the Passover Massacre of March 2002, Israeli prime minister Ariel Sharon had launched Operation "Defensive Shield." He also began construction of a barrier around the West Bank (although not totally in favor of this plan himself) to seal Israel off from the Palestinians. His forceful approach helped his Likud coalition gain the most seats in the January 2003 parliamentary elections, but revealed a deeply-divided Israeli electorate, since even Likud received only a 29 percent plurality of the vote.

Sharon's Disengagement Plan

In June 2004, Sharon's government approved a plan to take all Israelis out of the Gaza Strip and from four settlements in the northern West Bank. Although Likud had rejected a proposal to do this at a party conference in May, he reformulated it and proceeded to act on it. Following the approval of the plan, it was decided to close the Erez industrial zone, a major commercial center in the Gaza Strip, and move its factories to development towns in Israel proper.

Sharon's aggressive presentation of this plan alienated many of his conservative supporters but gained unexpected approval from the Israeli left. Conservatives accused him not only of abandoning the platform upon which he had been elected, but of stealing ideas from his Labor opponent, Amram Mitzna, who had recently presented a smaller disengagement plan that had Sharon had campaigned *against* during the elections. Sharon had support for his plan in the government but not from within his own party, so he had to create a unity government in coalition with the Labor Party in January 2005 to proceed. The plan's opponents, including Benjamin Netanyahu, advised Sharon to hold a national referendum on the issue, but he refused.

On August 7, Netanyahu resigned just before the Israeli cabinet approved the first phase of the plan by a large majority. He sharply criticized Sharon for moving "blindly along" with the plan as he downplayed an increase in terrorist activity that had been predicted. Sharon responded that the disengagement plan was an important diplomatic initiative for Israel that was badly needed at that time in the peace process. The evacuation continued through late August, more or less peacefully, and the Israel army completed its final pullout by the middle of September. Partly because of his loss of support in Likud,

Sharon formed a new centrist party, Kadima ("Forward"), in November 2005. It brought together leading politicians from Likud and Labor who were ready to accept that the peace process would finally result in the creation of a Palestinian state.

Hamas Wins the Vote

Any hope that Sharon's bold withdrawal from Gaza might create new momentum in the peace process ended when Hamas won a large plurality in the Palestinian Legislative Council elections in January 2006: the first elections for this body held since 1996. In reaction to these results, Israel, the United States, the European Union, and others, including various Arab states, imposed sanctions that stopped aid to the Palestinians upon which they were depending.

This group of donors promised to resume aid shipments if Hamas officially recognized Israel, accepted agreements made by the Palestinian Authority under its previous administration led by Fatah, and renounced violence. Despite sanctions and successful border interdictions, Hamas leaders were able to smuggle enough money and materials into the Palestinian territories, particularly Gaza, to maintain basic health and educational services (even as the defeated Fatah group kept control of much of the Palestinian security service). It was also not, at this time, prepared to rethink any basic principles.

Several factors were pushing toward a new Palestinian-Israeli clash. Since the Israeli withdrawal from Gaza in September 2005, militants had fired hundreds of missiles from there into Israel. Israel responded with airstrikes and barrages of thousands of artillery shells of its own. The political landscape had also changed somewhat, because just three weeks before the Palestinian elections, Ariel Sharon became permanently incapacitated by a severe stroke on January 4, 2006, with Ehud Olmert thereafter serving as acting prime minister: a post to which he was elected in March as head of the new Kadima Party. He had little time to settle into this new job, because on June 25, 2006, Hamas activists captured an Israeli soldier, Gilad Shalit, in a raid on a border post just north of Gaza.

2006 Israel-Gaza Conflict

The suppression of rocket attacks as well as securing Shalit's release became the basis for Operation "Summer Rains" an Israeli incursion into Gaza that commenced on June 28 and continued through mid-July, 2006. During this operation, Israel arrested numerous Hamas officials (both in Gaza and on the West Bank). Among them were Palestinian Authority cabinet ministers as well as people who had just been elected to the Palestinian Legislative Council such as its speaker, Aziz Dweik. Although some were freed within a few days, others subsequently spent periods of up to four years in Israeli prisons, being tried and convicted by Israel on charges of helping and supporting terrorist operations. Many other Hamas officials went into hiding when this happened. Israel announced that these officials had not been arrested to be used as bargaining chips to secure the release of Corporal Shalit.

At the start of Operation Summer Rains, Israel stated that the operation could stop if Corporal Shalit were let go. On August 15, a senior Hamas official responded that his group would only release Shalit if Israel released thousands of Palestinians it was holding. When another Israeli incursion, Operation "Autumn Clouds," ended in late November with Israeli forces finally withdrawing from Gaza and a cease-fire being declared between Israel and Hamas, there was still no agreement about setting Shalit free. (He was finally released on October 18, 2011 in exchange for 1,027 Palestinian prisoners.)

The cease-fire never really went into effect completely, with thirty to forty rockets continuing to strike Israel each month from Gaza before the next major flare-up of violence in May 2007. This partial reduction in hostilities was soon totally overshadowed by a bitter internecine struggle that erupted between Hamas and Fatah.

Lebanon War

Just as problems were heating up with the Palestinians in Gaza, the Israelis faced another set of challenges on their northern border with Lebanon, resulting in a war there with Hezbollah in July and August, 2006. After Israel had totally withdrawn from Lebanon in 2000, this led to the immediate collapse of its proxy Lebanese militia, the South Lebanon Army (SLA). Hezbollah soon establish control over the border area. On the pretext of trying to oust the Israelis from the disputed **Shebaa farms region** and freeing Lebanese prisoners in Israel, Hezbollah intensified attacks across the Israeli border and began trying to seize Israeli soldiers to exchange.

In July 2006, Hezbollah militants fired missiles at two Israeli Humvees patrolling on the Israeli side of the border fence. The ambush killed three soldiers, and two others were captured (either dying or dead) and taken back to Lebanon. Five more died in a failed rescue attempt.

Israel decided to respond with massive airstrikes and artillery fire against Lebanese targets. This severely damaged parts of the Lebanese civilian infrastructure, including Beirut Airport, which Israel asserted had been used as a weapons and supply site for Hezbollah. It also mounted an air and naval blockade, and undertook a short ground invasion of southern Lebanon.

In response, Hezbollah fired around four thousand rockets into Israel and engaged Israeli troops in guerrilla fighting. More than 1,500 people were killed, mostly Lebanese civilians. Around one million Lebanese were forced to leave their homes, with 300,000 to 500,000 Israelis also temporarily displaced, and billions of dollars in damage was done to the Lebanese infrastructure.

On August 11, 2006, UN Resolution 1701 was issued in an attempt to end the hostilities. It called for the disarmament of Hezbollah, Israel's withdrawal from Lebanon, and the deployment of regular Lebanese army soldiers as well as an enlarged **United Nations Interim Force in Lebanon (UNIFIL)** detachment in the south. UNIFIL's mission was expanded and now included the ability to use force to keep hostile activities for occurring in its area. By October 2006, most Israeli troops had left Lebanon, although a small contingent of troops stayed behind in Ghajar, a village straddling the border between the Golan Heights and Lebanon. Despite this UN resolution, neither the Lebanese government nor UN forces in Lebanon have taken any actions to end Hezbollah's continued military activities.

Reactions to the 2006 Lebanon War

After the war, the Lebanese army sent 15,000 soldiers, backed by a UNIFIL force of 12,000, south of the Litani River to replace Hezbollah there, although the Lebanese government explicitly stated that it would never disarm Hezbollah by force. The war sharpened disagreements within the Lebanese public over Hezbollah's status as the only armed militia not disarmed after the Lebanese Civil War. Some admired it as the last group left willing to fight Israel, while others dismissed it as a dangerous proxy force dedicated primarily to carrying out Iranian and Syrian policies in Lebanon. In Israel, there was a widely-held view that Prime Minister Olmert had mishandled the conflict, with 63 percent of Israelis polled in late August 2006 wanting him to resign.

2006–2007 Fatah-Hamas Conflict

Very soon, attention turned to another emerging problem: conflict between Hamas and Fatah over leadership of the Palestinian Authority. After the 2006 election, Hamas began to fear that the Palestinian Authority's Presidential Guard force was being prepared to occupy Gaza. This force, loyal to Palestinian Authority president and Fatah leader Mahmoud Abbas, had been enlarged by August 2006 to 3,500 men with U.S. assistance and training. Between March and December 2006, Fatah commanders began to refuse to take orders from officials of the newly-elected Palestinian government (who were mostly members of Hamas), and there was an escalating campaign of violence between the two sides in which many were killed.

Tensions kept rising until December 2006, when Abbas called for another Palestinian general election. Hamas challenged the need to hold an early election, maintaining that its members had the right to continue in office for their full elected terms. Fighting between the groups broke out soon after Palestinian security forces began firing on a Hamas rally in Ramallah.

Hamas then accused Fatah of attempting to assassinate Ismail Haniya, the Palestinian prime minister. This set off intense fighting in Gaza in December 2006 and January 2007. Finally, a cease-fire was arranged in February 2007 between Hamas and Fatah representatives meeting in Mecca, Saudi Arabia, but intermittent clashes continued.

In May and June, a final showdown between the two groups took place in Gaza, in which more than one hundred people were killed. On June 14, Abbas dissolved the current Palestinian government and declared a state of emergency. Prime Minister Haniya was dismissed (although he did not accept this as a valid action), and Abbas began to rule Gaza and the West Bank by decree. According to the 2003 Palestinian Constitution, Abbas was allowed to declare a state of emergency and dismiss the prime minister, but after 30 days the Palestinian Legislative Council was required to renew it. Abbas never convened a meeting of the council, since its Hamas members would have blocked any continuation of the emergency situation.

After this crisis, the two sides have remained locked in conflict ever since. On June 15, 2007, Abbas appointed Salam Fayyad, a non-Fatah, non-Hamas financial expert, to serve as interim prime minister. Fayyad was then reappointed to this office by Abbas in May 2009, but both before and after this, a continuous low-level civil war has continued between Hamas, headquartered in Gaza, and Fatah, headquartered on the West Bank. In March 2008, Hamas and Fatah leaders met in Sanaa, Yemen, to sign an agreement that called for a return to the situation in Gaza as it existed before June 2007, but this did not take hold. The conflict between the two groups has continued to grind on until the present. As a Hamas spokesman once explained to a radio interviewer, "We are fighting for our faith and Fatah are fighting for their salaries. That is why we will win."[4]

The government of Abbas has received widespread international support. In late June 2008, Egypt, Jordan, and Saudi Arabia said that the West Bank–based cabinet formed by Abbas was the sole legitimate Palestinian government. Hamas, after June 2008, began removing officials connected to Fatah from positions of power and influence in Gaza. The organization has tried to collect guns from all militias, clans, and other groups not tied to them, and took control of supply tunnels to Egypt. It has shut down newspapers and made trouble for journalists. Pro-Fatah gatherings have been forbidden or suppressed, and Hamas gangs have attacked Christian bookstores and libraries.

2008–2009 Gaza War

Over the past three years, members of Hamas and other Gaza militants have continued to shoot Qassam rockets into Israel, and Israel has responded with shelling and airstrikes. The Egyptian border with Gaza was closed and then reopened in the spring of 2011 after the fall of the Mubarak regime, but with still only a relatively small number of people allowed to cross it each day.

Since 2008, Israel has continued to take a fairly hard line with Gaza. In November of that year, Israel placed a blockade there in response to rocket and mortar attacks. Food, power, and water could still come in from Egypt if the

Egyptian authorities allowed them to pass, or if brought in clandestinely through secret tunnels. After one twenty-four–hour period during which no rockets or mortars were fired into Israel, the Israelis allowed the transfer of more than thirty truckloads of food, basic supplies, and medicine into Gaza, and sent fuel to its main power plant. Because two rockets were launched the next day, Israel again quickly stopped any cargo shipments there.

On December 27, 2008, Israeli jets conducted air strikes on targets in Gaza. These struck police stations, schools, hospitals, UN warehouses, mosques, and various Hamas government buildings. Israel described the strikes as another response to continued Hamas rocket attacks on southern Israel. The Israeli army began a ground invasion of the Gaza Strip on January 3, 2009. Over one thousand Palestinians and thirteen Israelis were killed and hundreds of millions of dollars of damage done in twenty-two days of war. Israel then made a unilateral decision to stop fighting and pulled out within three weeks. The Israeli blockade of the Gaza Strip has continued since the end of this war to the present, although Israel does allow some quantities of aid to arrive there on a regular basis.

February 2009 Israeli Elections

In 2008, Prime Minister Olmert came under investigation for corruption, leading him to announce that he would step down when Tzipi Livni took over as new leader of the Kadima Party in September of that year. Although she won the election, she was not able to form a coalition, so Olmert stayed in office until the general election of February, 2009.

In that election, although Likud won twenty-seven seats and Kadima twenty-eight, right-wing parties won a majority of seats, so Benjamin Netanyahu became prime minister for the second time.

Netanyahu, who does not support a two-state solution to the Palestinian-Israeli problem, came under immediate pressure from

---

[4]"http://www.time.com/time/world/article/0,8599,1632614,00.html" (accessed August 29, 2010).

new U.S. president Barack Obama to freeze the growth of Israeli settlements in the West Bank: a recurring demand of American presidents since President George H.W. Bush posed it in the early 1990s. Obama and his secretary of state Hillary Clinton continued to press for a two-state solution, reflecting a long-standing American policy position.

In June 2009, Netanyahu stated for the first time that he could accept a Palestinian state if Jerusalem remained the united capital of Israel, the Palestinians had no army, and the Palestinians would give up their demand for the right of return to pre-1948 lands. He also asserted that existing Jewish settlements in the West Bank had the right to "natural growth" while their permanent status is up for further negotiation. In general, this speech was far more conciliatory than Netanyahu's previously more hawkish stance against the peace process. Nevertheless, in March 2010, Israel's government approved construction of over one thousand new apartments in a Jewish housing development in Jerusalem, despite the opposition of the current U.S. administration to such actions.

Gaza Flotilla Raid

In May 2010, Israel boarded and seized six ships of the Gaza Freedom Flotilla. These ships were assembled by an international coalition of human rights activist groups, with the mission of breaking through the ongoing blockade of the Gaza Strip and bringing humanitarian aid, medical supplies, and construction materials there. As the flotilla approached the Israeli coast carrying 663 people from 37 countries, Israel requested to have the ships' cargos inspected at its port of Ashdod. When the flotilla refused this request, Israeli commandos boarded and seized these ships in the Mediterranean Sea in international waters.

Activists on the largest vessel, the Turkish ship *Mavi Marmara*, clashed with Israeli Special Forces troops as they landed on the vessels' decks. Nine activists were killed by Israeli troops, dozens were injured, and hundreds detained, with seven Israeli troops injured. Both sides issued accusations and counteraccusations about the misuse of weapons and violent attacks, but much uncertainty has remained about what actually transpired. Although the Gaza Freedom Flotilla marked the ninth attempt since 2008 to break the blockade by sea, it was the first that resulted in any deaths. After seizing its cargo, Israel transferred seventy truckloads of it to the United Nations to arrange for its delivery to Gaza. Although Hamas authorities at first would not take this aid, they later accepted it.

The raid prompted major international condemnation and demonstrations around the world. The United Nations condemned its "acts resulting in civilian deaths," demanded an inquiry, and called for Israel to release immediately any civilians it had arrested. Israel soon freed most detainees and deported them to their countries of origin. The incident further degraded already worsening relations between the moderate Islamist government of Turkey, from where the flotilla had originally departed, and Israel. This incident has also put pressure on the rulers of Egypt, particularly the new government that overthrew Mubarak in early 2011, to ease restrictions on traffic passing through the Rafah border between Egypt and Gaza.

LEBANON AND THE 2005 "CEDAR REVOLUTION"

The 2006 Lebanon War, although it caused enormous damage and human suffering in Lebanon, was in political terms part of the long struggle between Israel and the Hezbollah movement that had begun in the early 1980s with the foundation of the organization itself. The 2005 **Cedar Revolution**, although less costly in human terms, had an important impact on the country as well. It began with a series of demonstrations across Lebanon set off by the murder of the prominent Sunni politician, former Lebanese prime minister Rafik Hariri, on February 14, 2005.

In general, activists who arranged these demonstrations wanted to restore a degree of independence and autonomy to Lebanon that it had not enjoyed for many years. The most important step to achieve this, in their view, was to secure the withdrawal of the Syrian army units that had occupied Lebanon since 1976 and to oust a government heavily under Syrian influence. Only a few months earlier, the United Nations passed Resolution 1559 calling on Syria to remove its troops from Lebanon and for Hezbollah's armed wing to finally disarm, but neither Syria nor Hezbollah wanted to comply. Many Lebanese also wanted former prime minister Michel Aoun to be able to return from fourteen years in exile, and for Lebanese Forces commander Samir Geagea, imprisoned since 1994, to be released. The organizers of the Cedar Revolution were also pushing for an impartial international commission to investigate Hariri's assassination, and demanded the resignation of certain Lebanese security officials to ensure that their other demands would be carried out. They were also calling for new and free parliamentary elections, the final key step in ending the Syrian influence that had weighed for so long on the Lebanese political system. By the time that their demonstrations started, approximately 14,000 Syrian soldiers and intelligence agents were still deployed in Lebanon. In the end, Syrian troops completely withdrew from Lebanon by April 2005, and its pro-Syrian government was also removed from office.

The name "Cedar Revolution" was a term used by American officials to draw parallels with the Rose Revolution of Georgia, and the Ukraine's Orange Revolution, but in the Arab world, this was better known as Lebanon's *Intifadat al-Istiqlal* (Independence Uprising) or Cedar Spring, to recall respectively the **First Palestinian Intifada** and the 1968 Prague Spring in Czechoslovakia.

No serious evidence has ever surfaced to identify Hariri's actual killers, but Lebanese immediately placed the blame on the Syrian government for his murder. Hariri had a severe falling-out with Syria just before he resigned as prime minister in October 2004, and was replaced by a Syrian ally. Bashar al-Assad, who had succeeded his father Hafez al-Assad as Syria's leader in 2000, was reported to have told Hariri, "If you and [French President] Chirac want me out of Lebanon, I will break Lebanon."[5] One week after Hariri died, tens of thousands of protesters held an anti-Syrian demonstration at the location where he was killed. After that, substantial protests were organized in central Beirut every week, with huge supporting rallies held in Lebanese immigrant communities around the world.

By the end of February, Hariri's pro-Syrian replacement as prime minister, Omar Karami, had quit. This did not appease opposition leaders, and the fires of popular discontent were fanned when a UN investigative team reported that the Syrian presence in Lebanon had greatly heightened the instability immediately preceding the assassination.

To counter all this, Hezbollah leader Hassan Nasrallah arranged his own large rallies to outdo the earlier anti-Syrian events. They were designed to show the extent of popular support for Syria in Lebanon and to emphasize that Hezbollah continued to reject UN Resolution 1559, since it called into question the continued existence of its military wing. Exactly one month after Hariri's death, a larger anti-Syrian protest was held in central Beirut.

This turned into one of the largest gatherings in modern Lebanese history with over one million people in attendance. Holding this demonstration in downtown Beirut in Martyrs' Square was also a way to commemorate Hariri. This was the site of his grave but had also been a focal point of reconstruction efforts he led to bring Beirut back to how it had been before the war.

---

[5]Bashar al-Assad, quoted in Neil MacFarquhar, "Behind Lebanon Upheaval, 2 Men's Fateful Clash," *N.Y. Times*, March 20, 2005.

Not all reactions to this event were protests. There were also a series of killings that targeted anti-Syrian Lebanese politicians, and bombs were detonated in Christian neighborhoods. In retaliation, many Syrians working in Lebanon had their houses set on fire, or were beaten, shot, and robbed after Hariri's death. In the wake of all these developments, the last remaining Syrian troops began to leave Lebanon on the weekend of April 9 and 10, ending their presence in Lebanon almost exactly thirty years after they had come in.

After the Cedar Revolution

When new elections took place in early June, Saad al-Hariri's anti-Syrian bloc won 72 of the 128 available seats in the Lebanese parliament. This became the first Lebanese government to include members of Hezbollah as well as members of a new political group formed by Michel Aoun, just back from fifteen years in exile.

One of this new government's first great challenges was to bring the 2006 Lebanon War to an end. On July 27, 2006, the new prime minister, Fouad Siniora, announced a plan to end the conflict that became the basis for UN Resolution 1701 (as discussed on p. 352). Although the provisions of the Siniora Plan were generally accepted by all factions in Lebanon, including Hezbollah, the unity of his government was fleeting. On November 13, 2006, Shii politicians serving in his cabinet resigned just before the question of establishing an international tribunal to try Hariri's killers was to be discussed.

At this point, Amal and Hezbollah asserted that these resignations ended the legitimacy of Siniora's government, because his group no longer included all religious groups in the country. This paralyzed political activity for the time being, which also meant that a new president could not be chosen after pro-Syrian Emile Lahoud's term expired in November 2007.

Political violence in Lebanon, already significantly reduced since the end of the Lebanese Civil War in 1990 and the withdrawal of Israeli forces in 2000, remained at a fairly low level after the Cedar Revolution. Nevertheless, new clashes could still provide clear reminders of the enormous tensions lurking just below the surface. In February 2007, members of an Islamist group called "Fatah al-Islam" living in the Nahr al-Bared Palestinian refugee camp were blamed for two bombings in Ain Alak, a predominantly Christian village in the Beirut suburbs. This Fatah al-Islam group was accused of having ties to al-Qaeda as well as Syrian intelligence, itself seen to be using these militants as tools to prolong Lebanon's internal destabilization.

On May 20, 2007, Lebanese police raided a house in Tripoli being used by these so-called Fatah al-Islam militants—triggering armed clashes in the Nahr al-Bared camp itself. Several men reportedly resisted arrest there, and militants went after a Lebanese military post at the camp gate, murdering twenty-seven soldiers in their sleep, seizing several vehicles, and killing a number of civilians who had come to the army post's defense.

Through the next day, militants in the camp continued battling against units of the Lebanese army as Lebanese army tanks and artillery kept up a steady volley of shellfire. The camp soon became totally surrounded by Lebanese army forces, who were now apparently being resupplied from the United States, among other sources. By June 1, Lebanese army tanks had massed outside the camp and began to enter it. After two days of intense fighting, militant forces had pushed the Lebanese army contingent back out of the camp.

A few days later, a different group of Islamist militants, "Jund al-Sham," at yet another Palestinian refugee camp, Ain al-Hilweh in south Lebanon, fired a grenade at an army checkpoint that caused another clash with the army. When the Lebanese army attacked Nahr al-Bared again, they ran into booby-trapped buildings and took many casualties before they were stopped. On June 11, militants killed two Lebanese Red Cross workers outside Nahr al-Bared as they were evacuating civilians.

The Lebanese army kept up a heavy bombardment of the camp. By then, the army had given up any plans of entering the camp itself. On June 21, the Lebanese government declared an end to its operations against the camp, since it had determined that all Fatah al-Islam positions in the outlying areas of the camp had been taken or destroyed.

Heavy fighting then erupted in the city of Tripoli. On June 25, forces of the mainstream secular Palestinian Fatah organization went into the Nahr al-Bared camp to fight Islamic militants there and killed three of them. Three days later, the Lebanese military attacked another group of Fatah al-Islam militants who had holed up in a cave near Tripoli.

The conflict then subsided for about two weeks until July 12. On that date, the Lebanese army marched into the center of Nahr al-Bared camp and engaged the remaining Islamist militants there in heavy combat. Within a week, only three hundred square yards remained under Islamist militant control in the camp, but the army's assault on them was blocked by the large numbers of booby traps in many surrounding buildings. The military was hoping to declare victory there on August 1—Lebanese Army Day—but fighting in the camp dragged on through September 7, by which time many of the Fatah al-Islam fighters and most of their leaders had been able to escape into the mountains.

The Doha Agreement

Many Lebanese believe that the Syrians were behind the activities of this Fatah al-Islam—a charge repeatedly denied—but a more serious confrontation soon loomed between Lebanese opposition parties and the government. Opposition party demonstrations against the government had been continuing since December 2006, and opposition party parliamentary deputies had stopped attending sessions in protest. By 2008, tensions between the government and the opposition had escalated to such an extent that on May 7, a group of opposition parties and movements carried out a joint military strike on targets around Beirut, in one of the most violent attacks since the end of the Lebanese civil war.

After several hundred people died in a few days of intense fighting, Lebanese leaders met in Doha, Qatar, and concluded the **Doha Agreement** on May 21, 2008. This finally gave minority opposition political parties veto power, resulted in the election of President Michel Suleiman, and forced all political groups to pledge that weapons would no longer be used for internal political battles. This did not completely end all fighting, since episodes of intense combat continued to occur around the country, particularly in the north.

Nevertheless, it has helped facilitate the conclusion of many long-standing feuds that had persisted around Lebanon. For example, on September 8, 2008, Alawi and Sunni leaders signed a reconciliation agreement, ending thirty years of fighting and tension between them that had plagued Tripoli since the end of the civil war.

After this latest round of problems, things started to look up somewhat for Lebanon. Despite global economic problems in 2009, Lebanon enjoyed 9 percent economic growth and welcomed the largest number of tourists who had ever visited in its history. Despite this, the results of the 2009 Lebanese elections were similar to those of 2005, suggesting that the same political divides that defined the situation then still persist.

IRAN: 1997–2011

Iran also, despite having seen some temporary changes during the two terms of President Mohammad Khatami from 1997 to 2005, continued on a similar trajectory as before Khatami with the current president, Mahmoud Ahmedinejad, who has ruled since 2005.

Muhammad Khatami

Khatami's presidency witnessed attempts at reforms to promote democracy, reinforce the rule of law, and improve the enforcement of

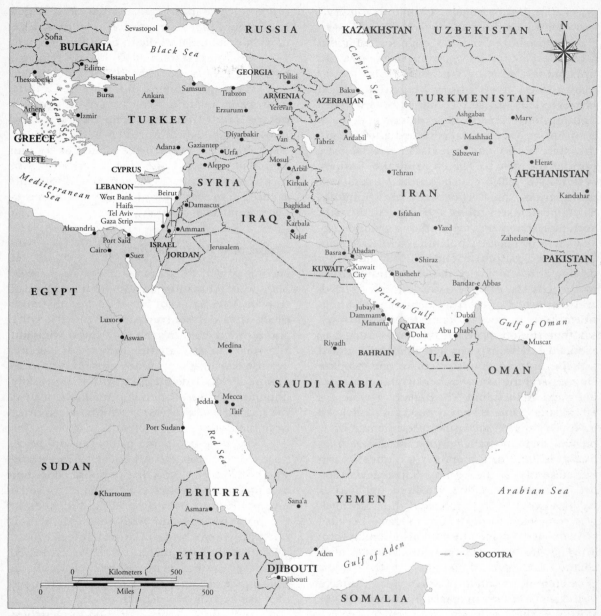

MAP 23.1   Middle East in 2011

rights. This included supervising city council elections more carefully, promoting stricter adherence to Iran's constitution, permitting criticism of high-ranking political authorities, allowing a wide range of political views, reopening foreign embassies, reorganizing the Ministry of Intelligence, and initiating an international forum known as the "Dialogue among Civilizations." Iran's large number of young people (with around half of the nation's population born after the Islamic Revolution) provided Khatami great support.

In pushing for such changes, Khatami faced fierce opposition from very powerful opponents serving in Iran's unelected institutions (over whom he had no legal power). This caused constant tension and fighting between his government and these institutions (such as the Guardian Council, the state radio and television service, the police, the armed forces, and the judicial system). In 1999, courts banned over sixty newspapers that supported him. Some of Khatami's closest allies were arrested, tried, and imprisoned on very dubious grounds.

Tehran mayor Gholamhossein Karbaschi had been a faithful friend of Khatami and a driving force in many modernization efforts in the city. In 1998, he was arrested, tried, and convicted on corruption charges, which prompted huge student demonstrations. Another big supporter, Abdullah Nouri, had founded a newspaper called *Khordad,* named for the Iranian month (equivalent to late May–early June) in which Khatami had won his great victory in 1997. Based on what his newspaper printed, he was tried and convicted in November 1999 for insulting Islamic values by pushing for democratic reforms and dishonoring Imam Khomeini's memory by questioning the authority of the current Supreme Leader, Ali Khamenei. In 2002, Hashem Aghajari, a well-known history professor and reformist, was sentenced to death for apostasy because he called for "Islamic Protestantism" and reform in Islam. He was released two years later after paying a large sum of money.

Supporters of reform won about 65 percent of the seats in parliamentary elections in 2000. However, their attempts to repeal restrictive press laws were struck down by Supreme Leader Khamenei. Despite this standoff, President Khatami easily won reelection in 2001.

Khatami worked to improve relations with other countries. He announced Iran would accept a two-state solution for Palestine if Palestinians agreed to one, eased official pressure on Bahais, and assured the UK that Iran would not carry out Khomeini's 1988 fatwa for Salman Rushdie to be put to death. In 1998, Britain reestablished diplomatic relations with Iran broken since the 1979 revolution.

The United States did not substantially improve its relations with Iran, which further deteriorated after President Bush labelled Iran, Iraq, and North Korea an "Axis of Evil" in 2002. Tensions between the United States and Iran also increased after the American-British invasion of Iraq in 2003, and as U.S. officials accused Iran ever more forcefully of trying to develop nuclear weapons.

Mahmoud Ahmadinejad

Having served as Tehran's mayor since 2003, Mahmoud Ahmadinejad ran for president of Iran in 2005 as a conservative populist who pledged to fight corruption, defend the poor, and strengthen Iran's security internationally. He won by a wide margin in a runoff election against Rafsanjani, a former president running again. Ahmadinejad benefited from the popularity of his economic program as well as the fact that supporters of reform stayed away from the polls.

From the beginning of his time in office, he used a lot of anti-American rhetoric and was criticized for how his populist economic measures of offering cheap loans to small businesses and providing large subsidies to the poor for gas and food resulted in high unemployment and inflation. International human rights organizations have criticized the deteriorating state of human rights in Iran under his rule. There has been a notable increase in arbitrary detentions and arrests. In 2007, the Tehran police launched the harshest enforcement campaign for many years to enforce women's Islamic dress codes.

In the June 2009 election, his victory was hotly disputed by enormous protests. These were among the largest public displays of opposition to the Islamic Republic's unelected leadership in its history. Despite great popular enthusiasm for his reformist challenger Mir-Hossein Mousavi, Ahmadinejad was officially declared to have won by a wide margin over his opponents. There were a torrent of charges concerning voting irregularities that spawned violent protests, and by July 1, 2009, more than one thousand people had been arrested for demonstrating.

Ahmadinejad has renewed Iran's already close relationships with Syria and Hezbollah. He has tried to develop closer connections with Iraq as it establishes more and more autonomy from the United States, and has reached out internationally to opponents of American foreign policy such as Hugo Chávez of Venezuela. He has made a number of anomalous public statements, including a letter that he sent to President Bush exhorting him to uphold "monotheism and justice," as well as telling an Iranian audience, "We are proud to declare that we are to implement a dynamic and progressive economy to put an end to [sic] liberal economy."[6] In September 2009, he made a series of controversial statements about Israel and the Holocaust, asserting that the Holocaust had largely been fabricated by Western powers in order to justify Zionism and the establishment of a Jewish state in Palestine.[7]

Iran's Nuclear Program

Since the era of Shah Mohammad Reza Pahlavi, Iran has been involved in researching the use of nuclear power, primarily for electricity generation, and continued such programs after the revolution. The Islamic Republic began to collaborate with Russian scientists on nuclear issues in the 1990s and made considerable inroads in building facilities by the early 2000s. At that point, UN and European inspectors began seeking to verify that Iran was not working toward any weapons development.

While inspectors found nothing to suggest that Iran was trying to develop weapons, they also verified that Iran had *not* reported its nuclear activities as it was required to do under international agreements it had signed.

Based on this breach, the United Nations' International Atomic Energy Agency (IAEA) voted to refer Iran to be evaluated by the UN Security Council for sanctions in February 2006. A battle then ensued, in which the United States began to demand that Iran cease all uranium enrichment, which it refused to do (and was in fact not required to do according to UN rules). The result was the issuance of UN Resolution 1696, calling on Iran to suspend all enrichment activities because it had been "unable to provide assurances about Iran's undeclared nuclear material and activities."[8] This was followed by six more resolutions, 1737 (2006), 1747 (2007), 1803 (2008), 1835 (2008), 1887 (2009), and 1929 (2010), all repeating calls for sanctions on Iran for not complying with resolution 1696. The situation has continued to escalate as Iran turned away two UN nuclear inspectors in June 2010 and U.S. President Obama enacted new unilateral U.S. sanctions on Iran that went beyond the UN sanctions in July 2010.

ARAB COUNTRIES OF THE PERSIAN GULF AFTER 9/11

After their independence from Britain in 1971, the sheikhdoms of the Persian Gulf have all done well economically because of either their own oil resources or those of neighboring countries. Due in part, perhaps, to the smaller scales of their societies, all of which have experienced rapid increases in national wealth with the oil price rises of the past three decades, they have been able to build societies with much less turmoil than the larger states around them. Another important factor in their success has been their continued restriction on the number of people allowed to be full citizens of their

---

[6]IRNA, "Ahmadinejad: Iran to Implement Dynamic, Progressive Economy to Put End to Liberal Economy," October 30, 2008.

[7]"Ahmadinejad's Holocaust 'myth' comments slammed," Agence France Presse, September 18, 2009.

[8]http://www.un.org/News/Press/docs/2006/sc8792.doc.htm (accessed on April 1, 2011).

nations. This has allowed these countries to benefit from a foreign workforce that has remained fairly cheap. Because these workers' status has always remained transitory and dependent on the goodwill of the citizens, this has concentrated political power in each of these countries in a fairly small cohort of people. This has had different effects on each one, though.

Since September 11, Qatar has strengthened its ties to the United States, by hosting several major American military facilities that previously had been located in Saudi Arabia. It possesses the third-largest proven natural gas reserves in the world. Like other small Persian Gulf states, its exclusive citizenship rules have kept its population numbers limited, such that its citizenry has the highest per capita income of any Middle Eastern country.

The current ruler of Qatar, Sheikh Hamad al-Thani overthrew his father, Khalifa al-Thani, in a peaceful coup in 1995. Since then, he has pursued the political liberalization of his country, but very slowly and deliberately. Sheikh Hamad has tried to diversify the economy and improve the nation's educational system, allowing several major U.S. universities to create satellite campuses and affiliates there. In its most important liberalization experiment, the Qatari monarchy founded "**Al-Jazeera**," the world's first all-news satellite television network broadcasting in Arabic, in 1995. In April 2003, Qatari voters approved a new constitution that officially granted women the right to vote and run for national office. Despite its status as the host to several large American military facilities, Qatar has experienced relatively less social turbulence than some of its neighbors. When an Egyptian carried out a suicide car bomb assault in 2005 on a theater on the outskirts of Doha, Qatar's capital, this marked the very first terrorist attack in Qatar directed at civilians.

Just as economically vibrant as Qatar, the relatively open societies and economies of the member emirates of the United Arab Emirates society have flourished so far in the twenty-first century. They have also endured financial excesses, fought social ills such as prostitution and human trafficking, and had to deal with restive populations of foreign workers. There is a sense that despite social tolerance and economic freedom, members of the elite in different emirates usually benefit from favoritism in court cases, business opportunities, and in influencing national decisions. Keeping an eye on its neighbors, the UAE held its first democratic elections in 2006, although it kept them very limited in scope.

The most prosperous economically of the seven emirate members of the UAE is Dubai. In recent years, its GDP per capita has been slightly higher than that of the United States (taking into account, though, that this only includes UAE citizens, who make up just under 20 percent of the 8.19 million people living in

Burj Khalifa, Dubai, UAE (January 2010)

Gavin Hellier/Robert Harding Picture Library Ltd/Alamy

the country). Revenues from oil and natural gas currently account for less than 6 percent of the emirate's revenues, in contrast, for example, with Qatar, whose oil and gas revenues make up more than 60 percent of its GDP. Dubai's top trade partner is now India, but it also has important trade relationships with Iran, Iraq, China, and the United States (US $7.57 billion). Its port at Jebel Ali has the largest man-made harbor in the world and ranked seventh globally for the volume of container traffic it supports.

Bahrain, another one of these countries that cannot depend directly on oil revenues, experienced real instability due to major unrest among its Shiii majority in the 1990s. In the twenty-first century, it has still not made enough changes in its political system to include this group as fully as it wants in the political process, which created fresh unrest there in the spring of 2011.

This has been especially troublesome to Saudi Arabia, just a few miles away across the Persian Gulf, and the United States, with its major naval base in Manama, Bahrain's capital. For the Iranians, this unrest has been seen as somewhat of an opportunity to exert more influence regionally, given the fact that a majority of Bahrainis are Shii Muslims. Since the United States has designated Bahrain as a "Major Non-NATO Ally," and given it some special security assistance, it has been very concerned about stabilizing the internal situation there before it gets out of control.

Kuwait, a key U.S. partner during the last two decades of American involvement in Iraq, has been recently stuck in a struggle between its elected parliament and the ruling Al Sabah family primarily over the family's political role and power in the government. Kuwait's 2009 elections, though, did result in the first four women ever being chosen to sit in its parliament.

Saudi Arabia, following its very different history from its Arab oil-producing neighbors in the Gulf region, has taken a much more active role than them in brokering solutions to regional conflicts in the Middle East, such as the Arab-Israeli conflict and the ongoing turmoil in Lebanon. It has also continued a deliberate and careful program of domestic political reforms under King Abdullah, which have codified royal succession rules, begun restructuring the justice system, and changed some educational curricula and practices that were blamed for inculcating extremism in its population. Saudi Arabia's long-lasting defense ties with the United States have continued strong, while there have been more substantial issues over the past decade on which the two countries have been in some disagreement, such as how to solve the Arab-Israeli conflict and how to deal with the threat of terrorism.

PROBLEMS OF YEMENI UNIFICATION: 1990–2011

Not all the smaller Arab states in the region have been as stable as the oil-rich nations of the Persian Gulf. Yemen, for example, like Lebanon, experienced several major episodes of conflict after its unification in 1990, with a civil war in the 1990s and an insurgency in the mid-2000s. Following the end of the final clashes in the North Yemen Civil War by 1970, Yemen had emerged as two different nations, the Yemen Arab Republic (YAR) in the north and the People's Democratic Republic of Yemen (PDRY) in the south.

In the 1970s, the Soviet bloc had strongly supported the PDRY, while YAR had remained loosely aligned with Saudi Arabia and the United States. Strong Soviet support for the PDRY provided the Soviet Union access to important naval facilities in South Yemen. There was continuous discussion for many years of general plans for the unification of the two Yemens, but with no concrete actions being taken. In May 1988 though, the YAR and PDRY governments set off on a path toward unification, which finally took place in May 1990.

When the united Republic of Yemen was then declared, this began a complex process of bringing together two very different political and economic systems. Within three years, conflicts within the ruling coalition that had taken power after the new nation's first elections resulted in the self-imposed exile of Ali Salim Al-Bidh, former leader of the PDRY, as well as a rise in civil unrest. The situation finally broke down into a civil war in 1994, which led to the secession of the south between May and July of that year. Despite this breakdown, the unified Republic of Yemen was restored and held its second multiparty parliamentary elections in April 1997.

This was not the end of problems. In 2004, a fresh insurgency arose in north Yemen led by the Houthis, a militant Shii group there, who claimed that Yemeni Shiis were not being properly treated by the government. Over the next five years, there was a continuous series of armed clashes between the Houthis and government forces. Finally in August 2009, the Yemeni army launched a fresh offensive against these rebels, which spilled over into Saudi Arabia and displaced hundreds of thousands of people. A tentative truce was arranged in January 2010, but the country still remained unsettled by this uprising, as well as after the recent turmoil of 2011, in which Yemeni President Saleh was injured in a grenade attack in June and forced to flee to Saudi Arabia for a period of time, after which he agreed to step down as Yemen's president in the near future.

EGYPT AFTER SEPTEMBER 11

Egypt was affected indirectly by all of the regional problems that arose after September 11, but its leadership cautioned against haste by outside forces in dealing with them. Mubarak opposed the 2003 invasion of Iraq by Britain and the United States. He made a strong case that the Israeli-Palestinian conflict should remain the first priority in the region, and stated that foreign occupation of Iraq would produce "100 Bin Ladens."[9]

Egypt's economic situation improved slightly in the first decade of the twenty-first century, but its political system was stagnant. By 2005, there was substantially greater pressure for reforming Egypt's autocratic one-party, one-ruler system.

Mubarak actually allowed multiple candidates to run in the 2005 election. All electoral institutions and the nation's security apparatus remained under his direct supervision, though, so the change was more cosmetic than substantive. There was some expansion of press freedom, with new independent news outlets being allowed to present occasional criticisms of the ruler and his family.

When Mubarak was chosen in September in an election in which vote rigging was confirmed to have taken place, the main opposition candidate, Ayman Nour, contested the results and demanded that the election be redone. When Nour was then tried and convicted of forgery, being sentenced to five years of hard labor in prison, this confirmed that nothing had really changed in Egypt's political system. The true question facing the country concerned Mubarak's succession, since he was not a young man and had been experiencing some health problems.

TURKEY SINCE 2001

Because of Turkey's earlier successes in creating real democratic institutions, it experienced more upheaval than Egypt in the first decade of the twenty-first century, particular in conflicts over the proper roles of secularism and religion in government. As discussed, political parties have emerged in Turkey starting in the 1980s and continuing until the present that are perceived as challenging the secular status of the Turkish government. They are suspected of having the long-term goal of restoring religion to the central place in government it enjoyed in Ottoman times. Each time such Islamist political parties achieved electoral success, they eventually were banned, until the "Justice and Development" Party.

[9]"Mubarak Says Iraq War Will Produce '100 Bin Ladens,'" Reuters News Agency, March 31, 2003.

The Justice and Development Party (AKP), created in 2001 with Islamist roots, won the 2002, 2007, and 2011 national elections by wide margins. Its electoral victories, though, have not ended the rising tension between supporters of complete secularism in government and those who favor a more religious approach to politics. The AKP narrowly survived an attempt to close it through a 2008 lawsuit that accused it of undermining secularism. While the Constitutional Court did find that the AKP had been a "focal point of anti-secular activities" in violation of the Turkish Constitution, the Court only made it pay a fine instead of banning it altogether.

AKP efforts to elect one of its members as Turkey's president provoked another crisis. The nominee, Foreign Minister Abdullah Gul, had roots in Turkey's Islamist movement and, with a wife who wore a headscarf, was considered by secularists to be a threat to the Turkish republic. In May 2007, they were able to have the Constitutional Court block his election. After the AKP won a huge plurality (46.6%) in parliamentary elections in July 2007, Gul became president after a new election was held in August.

In 2008, police unearthed an alleged conspiracy led by a secret group of ultranationalists and secularists called "Ergenekon." They were accused of carrying out a plot designed to sow chaos and provoke the military to overthrow the government. Several high-ranking retired officers have been arrested in this inquiry, including two four-star generals. Hearings in the case began in October 2008 and have caused a lot of controversy. Some view this affair as showing that Turkey has matured as a democracy. As they see it, the nation's legal system is finally confronting an elite that has covertly manipulated and controlled the political system for five decades. Others charge that the AKP is using the affair to intimidate its opponents and that the authorities' treatment of the accused has fallen short of international judicial standards. The Turkish military has tried to avoid becoming too closely involved

in the Ergenekon case, although appears to be cooperating with its ongoing investigation. In February 2010, more than forty high-ranking officers were arrested and then formally charged with attempting to overthrow the government in another conspiracy: the so-called "Sledgehammer" plot that may be related to the Ergenekon matter.

Through this domestic political turmoil, the **AKP** government has continued to conduct a very active foreign policy in the Middle East. It has engaged Iraq in order to fight the PKK and to prevent the emergence of an independent Kurdish state in northern Iraq. In its first years in power, it facilitated indirect Israeli-Syrian peace talks and improved its political and economic relationship with Syria. More recently, it had a major diplomatic conflict with Israel after its boarding and seizure of the ships of the Gaza flotilla that had set out from Turkey in May 2010. In 2011, Turkey had a very serious diplomatic rupture with Syria due to civil unrest there, which has caused many refugees to flee across the Syrian-Turkish border. The Turkish government has also been playing an important role in efforts to avert conflict over Iran's nuclear program. At the same time, the AKP has continued to press for Turkey's admission to the European Union, but this may be stymied by the situation in Cyprus, which has reached another stalemate, as well as lack of improvement in Turkey's relations with Armenia over various issues.

EPILOGUE: THE MIDDLE EAST IN THE WORLD TODAY AND THE ARAB UPRISING

By the 1990s, many Western commentators (and some Middle Eastern ones, such as the authors of the 2002 *Arab Human Development Report*) had begun to view the Middle East not merely as a zone of conflict, but also a zone of backwardness.[10] Many nations across

[10]See the text of the UNDP's *2002 Arab Human Development Report* at http://www.arab-hdr.org/publications/other/ahdr/ahdr2002e.pdf (accessed August 30, 2010).

Eastern Europe, Latin America, East Asia, and parts of Africa were perceived to be surpassing their Middle Eastern counterparts as they were rapidly evolving into more robust political democracies while all these regions became increasingly integrated into the globalizing world economy.

In the Middle East, it was difficult to see that real democratic institutions had spread beyond only a small number of countries and sectors of various societies. Although many countries in the region had legislative assemblies, most had little real power, or were chosen by electorates whose right to vote was constrained by religious and/or ethnic identity as well as citizenship, making real political participation a rarity in some of the region's countries. Outside observers have examined how the negative impacts of political repression, economic corruption and social cronyism, overspending on arms and projects to aggrandize rulers, combined with depending too much on oil revenues, have all inhibited the creation and growth of strong nations with healthy economies in the Middle East.

Many commentators from within the region have also focused on the broad, negative effects of outside, Western intervention and interference in the region. They ascribe true blame for many, if not most, of the region's problems to outsiders. Foreign commentators, following the approach of Edward Said, have echoed this. They point to the West's creation, starting in the late eighteenth century, of an imaginary "Orient" that the West used to control and exploit the Middle East on its own terms.

The debate about what has caused the Middle East's lack of advancement and progress in recent history can continue endlessly. The only certain thing, though, is that it will remain, even if only by virtue of its geographical situation, at the middle of global affairs. It has been, is, and will continue to be a world crossroads, with all that is good and bad about that.

This has suddenly been demonstrated again by the precipitous events unfolding in the region in the first months of 2011 in what is being labeled the "Arab Spring" or "Arab Uprising." This began in December 2010, when Mohamed Bouazizi, a twenty-six–year old fruit vendor in a small town in Tunisia, set himself on fire to protest government corruption, of which he had been a victim. This started a wave of popular protests there against the government, which grew so massive and so quickly that they led to the overthrow of President Zine El Abidine Ben Ali, who had ruled Tunisia for twenty-three years, on January 14, 2011.

This in turn, sparked a series of mass protests in Egypt that began in late January, culminating in the ouster of President Hosni Mubarak on February 11. Power was transferred to a council of high-ranking military officers, who allowed the first round of free parliamentary elections to be held beginning on November 28, 2011. Mubarak had ruled for almost thirty years, and his fall from power has created a situation in which the well-accepted rules of the existing social order in Egypt are being contested and challenged.

The next country to be affected by this wave of popular sentiment was Libya, where a civil war began in mid-February 2011. After a wave of popular protests, an interim opposition government (the National Transitional Council [NTC]) was established in the city of Benghazi to depose Libya's ruler of forty-two years, Colonel Muammar Qaddafi. Although Qaddafi retained power in much of the western part of the country with his headquarters in the capital city of Tripoli for several more months, he was eventually defeated and killed by forces under the NTC, supported by NATO airstrikes, in his hometown of Sirt on October 20. The NTC issued a "Constitutional Declaration" in August 2011 to guide Libya's transition to a new democratic government, and the country is now moving toward that goal.

Numerous other Middle Eastern countries have experienced greater and lesser degrees of civil unrest and upheaval, with Bahrain, Syria, and Yemen as the countries that are most seriously affected, although many regimes have been challenged. These revolutions and upheavals have captured the imagination of the region, particularly through the far greater access of ordinary Middle Easterners to television channels covering these changes such as Qatar's "al-Jazeera" and "al-Arabiya" from Dubai. They have inspired great hopes for the future as well as great fears—but only in the course of time will the impact of these upheavals be clear. Whatever happens, it will bring substantial changes across the region, and it can only be hoped that the net effect of such changes will be positive and helpful.

As this unfolds, it remains important to keep an eye on where the region has been: to place all that is happening and will happen in historical context. With this in mind, the basic goal of this work has been to explore the region's recent history, to enable readers to put this region in a more accurate context when their paths cross it in some way.

Questions to Think About

1. What were the goals of Operation "Enduring Freedom," and how well were they achieved?
2. What have been the greatest challenges faced by the United States since it came into Afghanistan, and how has it tried to manage them?
3. What has been Pakistan's role in Afghanistan since 2001, and what role does Afghanistan play in Pakistan's regional foreign policy?
4. What are Afghanistan's future economic prospects, and what are its greatest economic challenges at present?
5. What were the reasons that the United States began Operation "Iraqi Freedom" in March 2003, and have its goals for Iraq been achieved?
6. What have been the greatest challenges faced by the United States since it entered Iraq, and how has it tried to manage them?
7. What are the most important provisions of the new Iraqi constitution, and what do they reveal about Iraq?
8. What developments have occurred in the Arab-Israeli peace process since 2000?
9. Why has the Gaza Strip recently been so important?
10. How have Lebanese politics in the 2000s changed, and how have they stayed the same?
11. What have been the results of the recent conflict between Fatah and Hamas among the Palestinians?
12. What did Mohammad Khatami represent in Iranian politics?
13. How has Ahmadinejad affected Iranian politics?
14. What have been the most significant political, social, and economic dynamics in the Arab states of the Persian Gulf since September 11, 2001?
15. What has happened in Egypt and Turkey in the 2000s?
16. What are the implications so far of the "Arab Spring" or "Arab Uprising" of 2011?

For Further Reading

Abdullah, Thabit. *Dictatorship, Imperialism and Chaos: Iraq since 1989*. London and New York: Zed Books, 2006.

Ali, Tariq. *The Duel: Pakistan on the Flight Path of American Power*. New York: Scribner, 2008.

Arjomand, Said Amir. *After Khomeini: Iran under His Successors*. Oxford: Oxford University Press, 2009.

Boyne, Walter J. *Operation Iraqi Freedom: What Went Right, What Went Wrong, and Why*. New York: Forge, 2003.

Chandrasekaran, Rajiv. *Imperial Life in the Emerald City: Inside Iraq's Green Zone*. New York: Alfred A. Knopf, 2006.

Dyer, Gwynne. *After Iraq: Anarchy and Renewal in the Middle East*. New York: Thomas Dunne Books/St. Martin's Press, 2008.

Elsheshtawy, Yasser. *Dubai: Behind an Urban Spectacle*. New York: Routledge, 2010.

Freedman, Lawrence. *A Choice of Enemies: America Confronts the Middle East*. New York: Public Affairs, 2008.

Hale, William M., and Ergun Özbudun. *Islamism, Democracy and Liberalism in Turkey: The Case of the AKP.* New York: Routledge, 2010.

Jones, Seth G. *In the Graveyard of Empires: America's War in Afghanistan.* New York: W.W. Norton, 2010.

Kilcullen, David. *The Accidental Guerrilla: Fighting Small Wars in the Midst of a Big One.* Oxford: Oxford University Press, 2009.

Maloney, Sean M. *Enduring the Freedom: A Rogue Historian in Afghanistan.* Washington, DC: Potomac Books, 2005.

Naji, Kasra. *Ahmadinejad: The Secret History of Iran's Radical Leader.* Berkeley: University of California Press, 2008.

Packer, George. *The Assassins' Gate: America in Iraq.* New York: Farrar, Straus and Giroux, 2005.

Ricks, Thomas E. *Fiasco: The American Military Adventure in Iraq.* New York: Penguin Press, 2006.

United Nations Development Programme, and Arab Fund for Economic and Social Development. *The Arab Human Development Report 2005: Towards the Rise of Women in the Arab World.* New York: United Nations Development Programme, Regional Bureau for Arab States, 2006.

Wawro, Geoffrey. *Quicksand: America's Pursuit of Power in the Middle East.* New York: Penguin Press, 2010.

GLOSSARY

Note: All dates are Common Era except BCE = Before the Common Era and AH = Year of the Hegira; l. = lived; d. = died; r. = ruled. In Arabic, "ibn" means "son of."

Abbas I (l. 1571–1629; r. 1587–1629) Regarded as one of the greatest Safavid shahs.

Abbasid caliphs Rulers of the Muslim world between 750 and 1258 CE, whose capital was Baghdad, Iraq.

Abd al-Aziz ibn Saud (l. 1876–1953; r. 1902–1953) Ruler credited with creating the modern kingdom of Saudi Arabia.

Abdulhamid II (l. 1842–1918; r. 1876–1909) Ottoman sultan brought in to support the first Ottoman Constitution, who ruled as an absolute monarch between 1878 and 1908.

Abdullah (l. 1882–1951; r. 1921–1951) First Hashemite ruler of Transjordan ("Jordan" after 1946).

Abduh, Muhammad (l. 1849–1905) Egyptian scholar, champion of Muslim educational reform in the early modern era.

Abraham (Arabic: "Ibrahim") Regarded by Jews as father of the Jews and by Christians as a man of great faith. Believed by Muslims to have built the Kaaba helped by his eldest son Ishmael (Arabic: "Ismail").

Abu Bakr (d. 634; r. 632–634) First "Rightly-Guided" caliph.

Abu Hanifa (l. 699–767) Founder of Hanafi school of Muslim jurisprudence.

Abu Sufyan (d. 650) Tribal leader in Mecca.

Abu Talib (d. 619) Muhammad's uncle, leader of the Banu Hashim, and Ali's father.

Achaemenid Empire (c. 550–330 BCE) Ancient Empire centered in Mesopotamia and Persia controlling much of the modern Middle East.

"Afghan Arabs" Muslim volunteers, in particular from Saudi Arabia, who helped fight against the Soviets in Afghanistan in the 1980s.

al-Afghani, Jamal al-Din (l. 1838–1897) One of the earliest Islamic modernists, al-Afghani sought ways to harmonize modernization and traditional Islamic values. He also called for Muslims worldwide to become more united.

AKP (Turkish: "Adalet ve Kalkinma Partisi" ["Justice and Development Party"]) Turkish political party with an openly Islamic orientation, ruling Turkey since the 2002 elections.

Al Rashid Nejd Arab tribal clan, rival of the Saudi clan.

Algiers Agreement Accord in 1975 that gave Iraq and Iran equal navigation rights in the Shatt al-Arab waterway, for which Iran withdrew its support for Kurdish rebels in northern Iraq.

Ali (d. 661; r. 656–661) Muhammad's cousin and son-in-law; fourth "Rightly-Guided" caliph and first Shii Imam.

Aliyah (Hebrew: "aliyah" = "ascent"/"going up") Wave of modern Zionist immigration to Palestine.

Amal Lebanese Shii militia group founded in 1975.

al-Andalus (Spanish: "Andalucía") Southern parts of the Iberian Peninsula ruled by Muslims between the eighth and the fifteenth centuries.

Anfal, Operation Saddam Hussein's war on the Kurds between 1986 and 1989 in which he used poison gas.

Anglo-Persian Oil Company (APOC; "Anglo-Iranian Oil Company" after 1935) British company founded in 1908 to manage oil production in Iran.

Anglo-Turkish (Balta Limani) Convention of 1838 Agreement substantially lowering tax rates on British imports into the Ottoman Empire.

ansar (**English: "helpers"**) Converts to Islam from among Medina's natives.

Aoun, Michel (l. 1933–) Military officer who served as prime minister of Lebanon between 1988 and 1990 (variant spelling: "Michel Awn").

Arab Awakening (Arabic: "al-Nahda") Nineteenth-century movement promoting Arab culture and the union of Arabic speakers into one nation.

Arab Legion Jordanian military force commanded by British officer John Bagot Glubb ("Glubb Pasha") after 1939.

Arab Revolt of 1916 Uprising of Arabs in the Hejaz against the Ottomans that began in June 1916, led by Sharif Hussein with British assistance.

Arab Revolt of 1936 Violent mass Palestinian Arab uprising arising from popular discontent over the mandate.

Arab-Israeli War of 1948 War fought between May 1948 and January 1949 by Palestinian militia groups, assisted by a coalition of Arab armed forces, against Israel.

ARAMCO ("Arabian-American Oil Company") New name of CASOC after 1944, fully nationalized by Saudi Arabia in 1980.

Armenian Revolutionary Federation Armenian nationalist group founded in Tsarist Georgia in 1890, commonly called the Dashnak Party.

Ashura In general, Muharram 10 of the Muslim calendar, but specifically referring to Muharram 10, 61 AH [= October 2, 680], remembered by Shii Muslims for the martyrdom of Imam Husayn at the Battle of Karbala.

askeri (**Turkish, from Arabic "askari"**) Ottoman ruling class, defined as "those who receive tax revenues." Word also generally means "military."

Assassins (ca. 1092–1265) Militant extremist group of Ismaili Shiis in northern Iran, whose name originated in the belief that they used hashish, and has passed into general use as a term to describe political killers (variant: "*Hashshashiyun*").

Assembly of Experts Deliberative body of Shii Muslim religious scholars in the Islamic Republic of Iran empowered to oversee the Supreme Leader as well as dismiss him.

Assyrians Aramaic-speaking Christian group from Mesopotamia and eastern Anatolia, mostly concentrated in Iraq after World War I.

Aswan Dam Dam built on the Nile by Gamal Abdel Nasser between 1960 and 1970 with Soviet assistance.

Ataturk, Mustafa Kemal (l. 1881–1938; r. 1921–1938) Founder and first president of the modern Republic of Turkey.

Ayman al-Zawahiri (l. 1951–) Egyptian doctor and Muslim activist who ended up in Afghanistan by the mid-1980s. There, he became an associate of Osama bin Laden, as well as a founder and now leader of al-Qaeda.

Ayn Jalut, Battle of (1260) Important strategic defeat by Mamluks of the Mongols in 1260. The Mamluks were among the only Muslim military forces ever to defeat the Mongols.

Ayyubids Dynasty founded by Salah al-Din (Saladin) that ruled Egypt and the central Middle East between 1171 and 1250.

al-Azhar Center of Islamic learning founded in Cairo in the tenth century, still an important Muslim educational institution.

Baath Party Political group founded in Damascus in the 1940s by Michel Aflaq and Salah al-Bitar. Its ideology synthesized Arab nationalist and socialist concepts, but lacked an overtly Islamic orientation (variant spelling: "Ba`th").

Badr, Battle of First major victory of the Muslims in 624 over the Quraysh rulers of Mecca.

Badr, Operation Anwar Sadat's plan to attack Israel jointly with Syria in 1973. Its name commemorated the Battle of Badr.

Baghdad New Abbasid capital city, built in 762 about twenty miles northwest of Ctesiphon, the Sassanian capital.

Bahaullah (I. 1817–1892) Iranian prophet of a new religion, the Bahai faith.

Balfour Declaration Declaration issued in November 1917 by the British government supporting a Jewish "national home" in Palestine.

Banu Hashim Important subgroup of the Quraysh tribe in Mecca.

Bar Lev Line System of fortifications completed by Israel in late 1969 on the eastern side of the Suez Canal. It was designed to thwart Egyptian land attack, but failed.

Baseej-e Mostazafin (Persian: "Mobilization of the Oppressed") Mass militant group in Iran affiliated with the Revolutionary Guards, established in November 1979 as an auxiliary volunteer force. (variant spelling: *Basij-e Mostaz`afin*).

Bedouin Desert dwellers in the Middle East and North Africa (variant spelling: *Badawiyyun*).

Ben-Gurion, David (l. 1886–1973; r. 1948–1954, 1955–1963) First prime minister of Israel.

Berat The *Berat* (Turkish: "certificate") system allowed foreign nations to bestow citizenship and other privileges on certain non-Muslim Ottoman subjects in exchange for payment.

Biltmore Conference May 1942 conference of Zionist leaders in New York to build support among American Jewish organizations for a Jewish state in Palestine.

Bin Laden, Osama (l. 1957–2011) Militant Saudi Islamist leader who helped form al-Qaeda in 1988.

Black September Military confrontation in September 1970 between Jordan and the Palestinians that resulted in Palestinian leaders moving to Lebanon.

Buyids Military family from northern Iran. Although loyal Shiis, they held secular and military power under the authority of the Sunni Abbasid caliphs in the tenth and eleventh centuries.

Byzantine Empire Eastern Roman Empire, governed from Constantinople and ended in 1453 by the Ottomans.

California Arabian Standard Oil Company (CASOC) Company created in 1933 as a subsidiary of Standard Oil of California (SOCAL) to explore for oil in Saudi Arabia.

caliph (Arabic: "khalifa") Successor of Muhammad as leader of the *umma* (Muslim community).

Camp David Accords September 1978 framework agreements signed after peace negotiations between Israeli leader Menachem Begin, Egyptian leader Anwar Sadat, and U.S. president Jimmy Carter. Led to the March 1979 Israel-Egypt Peace Treaty.

capital levy Tax on personal wealth imposed in 1942 by Turkey, assessed at much higher rates for non-Muslim minorities than Muslim Turks. Ended in late 1944.

capitulations Provisions of diplomatic agreements that gave European powers and their subjects various special financial, legal, social, and diplomatic privileges in the Ottoman Empire, Iran, and various Asian countries.

Cedar Revolution Political activity in Lebanon forcing Syrian troops to leave Lebanon entirely by April 2005 and removing Lebanon's pro-Syrian government from office.

Chaldiran, Battle of Major Ottoman defeat in August 1514 of the Safavids in eastern Anatolia.

Circassians Muslims from the northern Caucasus, resettled during the late nineteenth century in marginal areas of the Ottoman Empire after homeland was conquered by Russia.

Committee of Union and Progress (CUP) Secret society whose precursor was formed in 1889 at the Ottoman Imperial Military Medical School. It became the most important part of the Young Turk movement in the 1908 Ottoman Constitutional Revolution.

Constantinople Capital of the Eastern Roman (later Byzantine Empire) founded in 330 by

Emperor Constantine. It was captured in 1453 by the Ottoman Sultan Mehmed II, "the Conqueror," and eventually renamed Istanbul.

Constitution of Medina Document issued in Medina soon after the hegira specifying rights and duties for all of Medina's inhabitants, as well as relationships between different groups there, including those between Muslims, Jews, Christians, and other People of the Book.

Crusades In Middle East context, Christian attempts to retake the Holy Land from the Muslims. Christian rulers conquered Jerusalem and the central Middle East in the First Crusade (1096–1099). Muslims led by Saladin reconquered Jerusalem in 1187, and various Crusades continued over the next several centuries.

D'Arcy Agreement In May 1901, an English/Australian prospector named William D'Arcy received a sixty-year concession to export much of Iran's oil. The agreement stipulated that Iran would receive only 16 percent of annual profits.

Defensive Shield, Operation Most significant Israeli military operation in the West Bank since 1967, conducted between March and May 2002.

Deir Yassin Palestinian village west of Jerusalem attacked on April 9, 1948 by members of the Irgun and Lehi groups. Assault resulted in around one hundred and twenty Palestinian deaths and was widely reported.

Democrat Party (DP) First major opposition party in Turkey formed in the new multiparty system in 1946. When it won parliamentary elections in 1950, its leader, Adnan Menderes, become prime minister.

derebeys (Turkish: "mountain valley chiefs") Rulers who began to emerge as hereditary minor princes all over the Ottoman Empire with the decline of the *timar* system in the eighteenth century.

devshirme Conscription of non-Muslim boys to become slaves of the Ottoman sultan and serve as officials, bureaucrats, and soldiers in the Ottoman ruling class.

DFLP (Democratic Front for the Liberation of Palestine) Militant Marxist-Leninist Palestinian group organized in 1969 that broke off from the PFLP (Popular Front for the Liberation of Palestine).

dhimmi (Arabic: "protected") Status of Jews, Christians, and Zoroastrians known as People of the Book under Islamic law. Dhimmi groups were allowed to maintain their religious practices and retained significant legal, political, and social autonomy.

divan Ottoman cabinet of royal advisers.

Doha Agreement May 2008 agreement signed in Doha, Qatar that gave minority opposition political parties in Lebanon some veto power and forced political groups to renounce the use of force in internal political battles.

Dome of the Rock Shrine on the Temple Mount in Jerusalem built in the seventh century CE over the very stone where Muslims believe Muhammad commenced his miraculous Night Journey to heaven. The location coincides with the site considered by many scholars to be the center of the Jewish Second Temple.

Druze Religious sect with roots in Shiism and many followers in Lebanon.

Durand Line Border between Pakistan (then British India) and Afghanistan created by the British in 1898 that ran right through Pashtun homelands.

Durrani One of the main Pashtun tribal confederations in Afghanistan from which most of the country's rulers have been chosen since the mid-eighteenth century.

Eastern Question Set of issues connected with Russia's rise and the Ottoman Empire's decline in Europe and Asia in the nineteenth century.

Ecumenical Patriarchate Head of all Orthodox Christianity, located in the old city of Istanbul.

El Alamein Site of pivotal battles in central Egypt in 1942, where German forces led by

Erwin Rommel were pushed back by Allied forces commanded by Bernard Montgomery.

Enduring Freedom, Operation Invasion of Afghanistan led by the U.S. and the UK to remove the Taliban that began on October 7, 2001.

enosis In the post-World War II context, usually referring to the plan for political union (Greek: *enosis*) of Cyprus with Greece.

Enver Pasha Ismail (l. 1881–1922) Member of the CUP governing triumvirate in the Ottoman Empire during World War I.

Esmail (l. 1487–1524; r. 1501–1524) Charismatic Safavid leader, later considered founder of the Safavid dnasty. He took the title "shah" in 1501 when Safavid armies captured the city of Tabriz (variant spelling: "Isma'il").

Exporter, Operation British invasion of Lebanon and Syria in 1941 launched from Iraq, which used many British Indian troops.

Farouk (l. 1920–1965; r. 1936–1952) Last descendant of Muhammad Ali to rule Egypt (variant spelling: "Faruq").

Fatah Palestinian nationalist group founded in 1954 by Palestinian professionals working abroad. A prominent early member and leader was Yasser Arafat.

Fatima Muhammad's only daughter recognized by all Muslims to have survived him.

Fatimids Dynasty of Ismaili Shii rulers that ruled over a caliphate rivaling the Abbasids, first in Tunisia and later in Egypt, from the tenth to the twelfth centuries.

fiday **(Arabic: "one who sacrifices himself")** Term commonly used in the Middle East to refer to irregular forces in battle. (variant spellings/plurals: *fedai/faday/fedayeen/fidayin/fadayan*).

First Fitna Period of struggle during Ali's caliphate.

Five Pillars of Islam Five most basic required acts of Islamic worship: (1) reciting and believing the Muslim Testament of Faith, (2) performing ritual prayer at intervals throughout the day, (3) fasting during daylight in the month of Ramadan, (4) giving alms, (5) performing pilgrimage to Mecca once in a lifetime (if able).

Free Officers' Movement Group of young Egyptian military officers formed after the 1948 Arab-Israeli War that launched Egypt's 1952 revolution.

Fourteen Points Woodrow Wilson's speech to the U.S. Congress in January 1918 presenting U.S. goals in World War I. The twelfth point discussed future of the Ottoman Empire.

gastarbeiter **(German: "guest worker")** Turkish (or other foreign) worker allowed to receive temporary work visas in Germany beginning in 1961.

Gaza Strip Strip of land along the Mediterranean controlled by the Egyptian army at time of the Arab-Israeli cease-fire of February 1949, which became an important Palestinian refugee site.

Gharbzadegi **(Persian: "Weststruckness/ Occidentosis")** Influential Iranian work of the 1960s by Jalal Al-e Ahmad. In it, Al-e Ahmad described modern Iranians as "weststruck" (Persian: "*gharbzade*") with the dual meaning of being "stricken" by Western culture and materialism, but also "intoxicated" by it.

al-Ghazali, Muhammad (l. 1058–1111) Islamic philosopher whose master work, *Revival of the Religious Sciences* (*Ihya Ulum al-Din*), blends an orthodox approach to studying religious texts with a mystical exploration of their more esoteric dimensions.

ghazi Arabic term meaning "warrior for Islam" (variant spelling: "*gazi*").

ghulam General term in Arabic for slave soldier in medieval Muslim empires, but specific referring in Iranian history to a soldier in Safavid units established under Shah Abbas I in the early seventeenth century (variant spelling: "*gholam*").

Glubb Pasha (l. 1897–1986) Lieutenant-General Sir John Bagot Glubb, British commander of the Arab Legion.

Gokalp, Ziya (l. 1876–1924) One of the founders of modern Turkish nationalism.

Great Game Nineteenth-century competition between Britain and Russia for predominance in Asia.

Great Lebanon Mandate of Lebanon established under the French in the early 1920s.

Great Syrian Rebellion Mass uprising against French rule in Syria between 1925 and 1927.

Green Line Dividing line during the Lebanese Civil War between West and East Beirut.

Guardian Council Group of six Muslim scholars and six lawyers in the Islamic Republic of Iran charged with ensuring that laws passed by parliament are valid according to Islamic rules and norms. This group also vets candidates for president and the parliament.

hadith Report of what Muhammad said and did during his life.

Hafez al-Assad (l. 1930–2000, r. 1971–2000) Air force officer and member of the Alawite religious minority group who served as Syria's president (and absolute ruler) between 1971 and 2000. (variant spelling: Hafiz al-Asad.)

Haganah (Hebrew: "Defense") Clandestine Zionist self-defense militia units first organized in the 1920s, evolving into the main Zionist defense forces in the 1930s and 1940s.

hajj Pilgrimage to Mecca to commemorate events in the lives of Abrahim (Ibrahim), Hagar (Hajar), and Ishmael (Ismail). Muslims are enjoined to make a hajj pilgrimage once in a lifetime if they can afford it and are physical able.

hakimiyet-i milliye **(Arabic/Turkish)** Term adopted for the concept of national sovereignty during the Second Ottoman Constitutional Period.

Hamas (Acronym for Arabic *"Harakat al-Muqawama al-Islamiya"* ["Islamic Resistance Movement"]) Islamic political organization founded at the beginning of the First Palestinian Intifada in December 1987 by Palestinian sympathizers in Gaza of the Egyptian Muslim Brotherhood.

Hamidiye units Ottoman cavalry regiments of Kurdish horsemen formed in the late nineteenth century and modeled on the Russian Cossacks.

Hard Surface, Operation Sending of U.S. planes in the summer of 1963 to protect Saudi airspace from Egyptian incursions.

harem In general, the guarded sanctuary of a traditional Muslim family dwelling. Specifically, the Ottoman sultan's palace where his wives, concubines, and their children lived. The harem was usually ruled by the mother of the reigning sultan (known in Turkish as the *valide sultan*).

Harun al-Rashid (l. ca. 763–809; r. 786–809) Abbasid caliph whose reign is often perceived as the height of Abbasid power.

Hasan (l. 625–669) Ali's eldest son (Muhammad's grandson), recognized as the Second Imam of Shii Islam.

Haseki Hurrem Sultan (l. 1506–1558) Ottoman Sultan Suleyman I's wife (also known as Roxelana), famous as Suleyman's adviser, as well as in her capacity as founder of charitable institutions.

Hashemite Kingdom of Iraq (1921–1958) Kingdom founded at the beginning of the British mandate under Faisal (son of Sharif Hussein, ruler of the Hejaz), ultimately overthrown by a coup of military officers.

Hashemite Kingdom of Jordan [originally Transjordan] (1921–) Kingdom founded at the beginning of the British mandate under Abdullah (brother of Faisal and son of Sharif Hussein, ruler of the Hejaz) that continues today.

Hashemites Lineal descendants of Muhammad who ruled the Hejaz (western Arabia) for many centuries until the 1920s, when they were removed by the Saudis.

Haskalah Eighteenth- and nineteenth-century European Jewish enlightenment movement.

Helmand Valley Among the most fertile regions of Afghanistan, located in the southwest of the country.

Herzl, Theodor (l. 1860–1904) Austrian Jewish journalist whose *Jewish State* (1896) presented a plan for a modern Jewish state that became the foundational text of the Zionist movement, which he helped start in 1897.

Hezbollah (Arabic: "Party of God") Militant Lebanese Shii political group that emerged after 1982. Other Islamic militant organizations that use the same name (but are distinct from the Lebanese Hezbollah) exist in Iran, Iraq, and Turkey (variant spellings: "Hizbollah," "Hizbullah").

hijra **(hegira)** Flight of Muhammad and his Muslim followers from Mecca to Medina in 622. This event marks the beginning of the Muslim calendar.

Histadrut Labor federation founded in 1920 offering social services, job protection, and health benefits for Zionist emigrants to Palestine.

House of Wisdom Abbasid caliph Harun al-Rashid established the *Bayt al-Hikma* (Arabic: "House of Wisdom") in Baghdad in the late eighth/early ninth centuries to promote interchange among scholars from a variety of academic backgrounds.

Husayn ibn Ali (l. 626–680) Ali's son and Muhammad's grandson; Third Shii Imam.

Hussein, Saddam (l. 1937–2006; r. 1976–2003) Iraqi Baathist dictator, who held absolute power in Iraq between 1979 and 2003 (variant spelling: "Saddam Husayn").

Hussein ibn Ali, Sharif (l. 1854–1931, r. 1908–1924) Ottoman governor of the Hejaz and leader of the Hashemites (variant spelling: "Sherif Husayn ibn Ali").

Ibn Khaldun (l. 1332–1406) North African scholar who made one of the first attempts to analyze social dynamics of nomadic conquests.

Ibn Rushd, Abu al-Walid Muhammad (l. 1126–1198) Famous Islamic philosopher known in the West as Averroes, who argued that religion and philosophy were not in conflict with each other, since they provided different ways to reach the same ultimate truth.

Ibn Sina, Husayn (l. 980–1037) Known in the West as Avicenna, he served as a doctor to numerous rulers and wrote many treatises. The most voluminous of these, the multivolume *Qanun fi al-Tibb* (*Canon of Medicine*), remained a medical reference book in the Middle East and Europe until the eighteenth century.

Ibn Taymiya (l. 1263–1328) Muslim religious scholar who charged that Mongol converts to Islam were not true Muslims since they continued to follow tribal laws, proving that they were living in *jahiliya* (a traditional Islamic term describing the pre-Islamic state of ignorance before Muhammad and the revelation of the Quran). His innovative use of the concept of *jahiliya* was later adopted by twentieth-century Islamic militants like Sayyid Qutb.

ijtihad Muslim legal term for "independent legal reasoning."

Ikhwan **(Arabic: "Brotherhood")** Religious militia in Saudi Arabia who followed the teachings of Muhammad ibn Abd al-Wahhab, proponent of a strict interpretation of Islamic law.

ilm al-fiqh **(Arabic: "science of jurisprudence")** Muslim legal discipline focused on how to apply religious legal rules in practice.

iltizam **system** Tax-farming system that expanded in the Ottoman Empire in the mid-seventeenth century.

Imam (Arabic word with basic meaning of "prayer leader") In general, leader who guides those assembled in a mosque in prayer. For Shii Muslims, Imams are the lineal descendants of Ali and Fatima authorized to lead the community of Muslim believers.

Imperial Rescript February 1856 Ottoman decree promising all Ottoman subjects equal treatment in taxation, education, military service, justice, and an equal opportunity to serve as government officials.

Institut d'Égypte Research institute established in 1798 by Napoleon on his arrival in Egypt that collected an immense amount of information and important artifacts, including the Rosetta Stone.

Intifada, al-Aqsa (or "Second Palestinian") Palestinian uprising in September 2000 to protest Ariel Sharon's visit to the Temple Mount (site of the al-Aqsa Mosque).

Intifada, First Palestinian (1987–1993) Popular Palestinian uprising that erupted in Gaza, the West Bank, and East Jerusalem in 1987.

Iran-Contra Affair Secret plan made in the early 1980s by senior members of the Reagan administration to facilitate arms sales to Iran, then under a U.S. arms embargo. Senior U.S. officials diverted funds from these sales secretly to fund anticommunist Nicaraguan rebels known as the contras. Several were prosecuted, but none convicted of legal violations in this affair.

Iran Freedom Movement (IFM) Faction of the Iranian National Front led by Mehdi Bazargan. The IFM was founded in 1961 and emphasized the political relevance of Islam.

Iranian Constitutional Revolution (1905–1907) Upheaval that caused the establishment of a parliament and a constitution in Iran, which became a constitutional monarchy.

Iran-Iraq War and the Iranian Cultural Revolution (Persian: "*enqelab-e farhangi*") Systematic attempt in the early 1980s to cleanse universities and institutions of higher learning of Western and un-Islamic influences.

Iran Hostage Crisis Fifty-two American hostages held captive in Iran in various and changing locations for 444 days between November 1979 and January 1981.

Iran-Iraq War Conflict between Iran and Iraq that lasted from September 1980 to August 1988, which bogged down into a steady slog back and forth across a limited front line that cost hundreds of thousands of lives.

Iraq Levies Irregular force of Arabs, Kurds, Turcomans, and Assyrians assisting the British in Mesopotamia after World War I. By 1923, almost half the Levies were Assyrians and the other half Kurds. Five years later, the Levies were almost entirely Assyrians, now assigned to guard RAF bases in Iraq.

Iraq Petroleum Company (IPC; "Turkish Petroleum Company" before 1929) Company established in 1912 by Armenian Ottoman petroleum entrepreneur Calouste Gulbenkian (1869–1955). It became the major oil producer in Iraq when oil was discovered there in 1927. The Iraqi government did not receive its promised share of revenues from the company for many years.

Iraqi Freedom, Operation Invasion of Iraq on March 20, 2003, led by soldiers from the United States and the UK.

Irgun Revisionist Zionist militia (also called by its initials: IZL, pronounced "Etzel") founded in the early 1930s. It used violence after 1936 against Arab civilians in retaliation for Arab attacks against Jews.

Islam Submitting to the will of God and God's message as communicated to Muhammad.

Isra Muhammad's mystical one-night voyage on a winged horse (Buraq) from Mecca to "the farthest mosque" (Arabic: "*al-masjid al-aqsa*"), later identified by Muslims with the al-Aqsa Mosque in Jerusalem.

Israel Defence Forces (IDF) Israel's military, created upon the founding of Israel in May 1948. It incorporated soldiers of the Haganah and Palmach, and their erstwhile right-wing military rival force: the Irgun.

Israeli National Water Carrier Water distribution system diverting large quantities of water from the Jordan River (the border between Jordan and Israel) to meet Israel's growing water needs.

Jafar al-Sadiq (l. 702–765) Sixth Shii Imam (great-grandson of Third Shii Imam Husayn) and renowned Islamic legal scholar (variant spelling: "Ja'far").

janissary (Turkish: "*yenicheri*" ["new soldier"]) Infantry troop, part of an elite Ottoman military force. This force was first created in the late fourteenth century and ultimately abolished by Sultan Mahmud II in 1826.

al-Jazeera World's first all-news satellite television network broadcasting in Arabic, founded in 1995 and based in Doha, Qatar.

Jemal Pasha, Ahmed (l. 1872–1922) Member of the CUP governing triumvirate of the Ottoman Empire during World War I (modern Turkish spelling: Ahmet Cemal Paşa).

Jevdet Pasha, Ahmed (l. 1822–1895) Government official involved in a wide range of Ottoman Tanzimat-era modernization projects (modern Turkish spelling: Ahmet Cevdet Paşa).

Jewish Brigade Group First exclusively Jewish military unit permitted to serve in World War II.

Jewish National Fund Charity established in 1901 to buy land for Jewish settlement in Palestine.

jihad **(Arabic)** Striving to fulfill God's wishes, considered by some Muslim thinkers as a "sixth pillar" of Islam. One definition, described as the "lesser" jihad, is associated with waging war to defend (or in some cases expand) territories ruled by Muslims. Another, labeled the "greater" jihad, describes an individual's struggle to improve him or herself religiously and morally.

Kaaba Meteorite encased in a stone cube in Mecca that at one time formed the focal point of Mecca's polytheistic worship, now at the heart of the hajj pilgrimage (variant spellings: "Ka'bah," "Kaba").

kadi **(Turkish from Arabic "*qadi*")** Ottoman judge.

kafes **(Turkish: "cage") system** Confinement of princes to the harem section of the Ottoman royal palace until they reached maturity, creating many princes with few real-world leadership skills.

Karbala, Battle of On the tenth of Muharram, 61 AH (October 10, 680 CE), Husayn was heading to Kufa to assemble an army to fight Yazid. On Yazid's orders, an Umayyad force intercepted and killed him on his way there, along with family members and companions. The event is remembered as Ashura: one of the primary commemorations of martyrdom among Shii Muslims. Shiis consider Husayn to be the Third Imam (variant spelling: "Kerbala").

Karlowitz, Treaty of 1699 agreement between Austria and the Ottoman Empire marking first substantial and permanent loss of territory for the Ottomans in Europe.

Kemal, Namik (l. 1840–1888) One of the founders of the Young Ottoman group and an early and influential proponent of Turkish nationalism.

Kemalism Ideology of Mustafa Kemal Ataturk in founding the Turkish Republic, which combined republicanism, populism, secularism, revolutionism, nationalism, and statism.

Kfar Etzion Jewish settlement on the West Bank, where all but four of the Jewish defenders were killed in May 1948.

Khadija Widow fifteen years older than Muhammad: his first and only wife for twenty-five years.

khan Turkish and Mongol title for ruler.

Khartoum Summit Arab League meeting in Khartoum, Sudan, on August 29, 1967, that produced the "Three No's" resolution: No peace with Israel, no recognition of Israel, no negotiations with Israel.

khedive Honorific title adopted by Muhammad Ali's grandson Ismail (r. 1863–1879) to exalt the status of the rulers of Egypt beyond mere Ottoman provincial governors.

Khomeini, Ayatollah Sayyid Ruhollah Musavi (l. 1902–1989; r. 1979–1989) Khomeini was a well-respected religious teacher in Iran who led opposition to Shah Mohammad Reza Pahlavi's White Revolution. He became the Islamic Republic's first Supreme Leader in 1979.

khums For Shii Muslims, 20 percent of yearly profits, of which the first half must be given to the current Imam (or during his current absence, to a respected Shii scholar) (variant spelling: "*khoms*").

Khuzestan Area in southern Iran along the Persian Gulf with an Arabic-speaking majority, but under Iranian rule for centuries.

al-Khwarizmi, Muhammad ibn Musa (l. 780–850) Muslim scientist born in Central Asia and one of the main scholars to work at the House of Wisdom in Baghdad.

klepht **(Greek: "brigand")** Armed Greek highwayman of the late nineteenth century.

komiteh **(Persian: "committee")** Neighborhood revolutionary committee set up in Iran in 1979 to reinforce the impact of the Islamic revolution.

Koprulu Era (1656–1703) Time of leadership in the Ottoman Empire by the able grand viziers of the Koprulu family.

Kuchuk Kaynarja, Treaty of Agreement ending the Russo-Turkish War of 1768–1774. It recognized the Ottoman sultan as the *spiritual* head of Crimean Muslims there, with the Russian emperor acknowledged as *political* sovereign over the Crimea. In turn, the Russian emperor was made protector of all Orthodox Christian subjects of the Ottoman sultan (modern Turkish spelling: Küçük Kaynarca).

Kurdish Democratic Party (KDP) Iraqi Kurdish political group long dominated by the Barzani tribal clan.

Kurdish Republic of Mahabad First independent Kurdish state, established in northwest Iran between January and December 1946.

Land for Peace Formula that guided the 1979 Camp David negotiations between Israel and Egypt. This emphasized Israel's need to withdraw from lands occupied in 1967 in exchange for permanent peace with its Arab neighbors.

Land Laws of 1858 and 1867 Ottoman Tanzimat law codes designed to distinguish more clearly between state and private lands.

Lausanne, Treaty of Treaty in 1923 ending the Turkish War of Independence that recognized the Republic of Turkey.

Lebanese Civil War War between 1975 and 1990 involving all ethnic and religious groups in Lebanon.

Lebanese Forces Maronite Christian militia group during the Lebanese Civil War that became a political party after the war ended in 1990.

Lebanese National Movement (LNM) Lebanese political organization with Communist and Nasserist tendencies led by Kamal Jumblatt, a Druze leader.

Lebanese National Pact Unwritten 1943 agreement providing for proportional power sharing between Lebanon's different groups.

Lehi Radical Zionist group that broke away from the Irgun in 1940, conducting many attacks on the British in Palestine during the mandate period.

Lepanto, Battle of Important 1571 Ottoman naval defeat off the coast of modern Greece.

Litani, Operation 1978 Israeli occupation of southern Lebanon up to the Litani River.

Long War Extended Ottoman-Habsburg conflict between 1593 and 1606.

madhhab One of the four Sunni schools of legal interpretation: the Hanafi, Shafii, Maliki, and Hanbali schools of jurisprudence.

madrassa Traditional Islamic school.

Mahdi Arabic term for "redeemer of mankind who will come to earth just before the Day of Judgment and end injustice and tyranny." Comparable to Christian and Jewish concepts of a messiah or deliverer.

Mahmudiye Ottoman warship built in 1829 in Istanbul. It remained in service for forty-five years and was the largest warship in the world for a long time.

Mamluks Military slaves originally from Central Asia, who established a realm that governed an Islamic empire based in Egypt between 1250 and 1517.

Mandate Territory described in the 1919 Treaty of Versailles as an independent nation subject to administrative help from an outside power.

Maronites Important Catholic Christian group in Lebanon.

mawali **(Arabic: "clients")** New non-Arab converts to Islam in the early period of Muslim expansion.

Maysalun, Battle of French defeat of the Hashemite ruler Faisal in July 1920 near Damascus.

mazalim **courts** Beginning in the early Abbasid period, Muslim rulers supplemented religious courts with this parallel system of administrative law over which they had sole control.

Mecca Major trade and pilgrimage city in the western part of the Arabian Peninsula. Regarded by Muslims as the first place on earth established to worship God, as well as site of key events in the life of Abraham (Arabic: "Ibrahim"), his son Ishmael (Arabic: "Ismail"), and his wife Hagar (Arabic: "Hajar").

Medina City two hundred miles north of Mecca where Muhammad and his Muslim followers fled during the hegira in 622.

Megali Idea **(Greek: "Great Idea")** Nineteenth- and early twentieth-century concept of recreating a "Greater Greece" including Thrace, possibly Istanbul (to be rechristened "Constantinople"), as well as large parts of Anatolia.

Mehmed II (the Conqueror; l. 1432–1481, r. 1444–1446, 1451–1481) Ottoman sultan who conquered Constantinople.

Menderes, Adnan (l. 1899–1961, r. 1950–1960) First prime minister of the Republic of Turkey not from Ataturk's Republican People's Party.

Mesopotamia Located in modern southern Iraq, center of a series of the earliest civilizations in human history.

Middle East Region of the world between the Nile River in Africa and the Oxus (Amu Darya) River in Central Asia (from west to east), and between the Balkans (in southeastern Europe) and the Indian Ocean (from north to south).

millet (Arabic/Turkish: "nation") Self-governing community of non-Muslim Ottoman subjects, organized according to religion.

Miraj Muhammad's mystical night tour of heaven and hell, during which he spoke with earlier prophets such as Abraham, Moses, and Jesus.

Mojahedin-e Khalq **(Persian: "Holy Warriors of the People")** Radical clandestine Iranian extremist group founded in 1965. It has pursued armed struggle using an ideology combining Marxist and Islamic concepts strikingly similar to the revolutionary Islam espoused in the 1960s by Ali Shariati.

Mosaddeq, Mohammad (l. 1882–1967, r. 1951–1953) Prime minister of Iran who nationalized Iran's oil and was deposed by Mohammad Reza Shah Pahlavi.

Mosque (Arabic: "masjid") Place to conduct Muslim ritual daily prayers.

Mount Lebanon Maronite heartland in Lebanon.

muhajirun **(Arabic: "emigrants")** Muslims who made the hegira to Medina from Mecca.

Muhammad al-Mahdi Twelfth Shii Imam, believed to have gone into hiding in the 870s and expected to return just before the Day of Resurrection.

Muhammad Ali (l. 1769–1849, r. 1805–1849) Ottoman governor of Egypt whose descendants would rule there for the next 150 years.

Muhammad (l. 570–632) Prophet of Islam.

mujahidin General Arabic word for Muslim soldiers engaged in jihad, but specifically Muslim guerrilla fighters who were the main foes of the

Afghan communist government beginning in the late 1970s (variant spellings: "*mujahideen*," "*mojahedin*").

mujtahid Muslim legal scholar who emphasizes the use of *ijtihad* (independent legal judgment) in formulating opinions. Such scholars became particularly prominent during the eighteenth and early nineteenth centuries in Iran (variant spelling: "*mojtahed*").

Mulla Sadra (l. c. 1571–1641) Important philosopher and Islamic scholar during the Safavid era in Iran.

Muslim Brotherhood Mass organization founded by Hasan al-Banna in the Egyptian Suez Canal town of Ismailiya in 1928 to defend Islam and Muslim values against Western domination and encroachment.

Muslim Believer in the Islamic faith; Arabic active participle of the same verb for which "Islam" is the verbal noun (variant spelling: "Moslem").

Naqshbandis Adherents of a worldwide Muslim Sufi order founded in the thirteenth century in Bukhara (in modern Uzbekistan).

Naser al-Din Shah (l. 1831–1896, r. 1848–1896) Qajar ruler of Iran (variant spelling: "Nasir al-Din").

Nasser, Gamal Abdel (l. 1918–1970, r. 1956–1970) Charismatic leader of the Free Officers' Movement in Egypt, Nasser served as Egypt's president from 1956 until his death in 1970 (variant spelling: "Jamal Abd al-Nasir").

National Bloc Political coalition created in the late 1920s to represent the Syrian nationalist movement over the next two decades and promote Syrian independence through diplomacy instead of violence.

National Front, Iranian (Persian: "Jebhe-ye Melli") Iranian nationalist political coalition founded in 1949 by Mohammad Mosaddeq.

Nawruz Persian New Year's Day coinciding with the March spring equinox.

Nightingale, Florence (l. 1820–1910) British nurse who established one of the world's first modern military hospitals in Ottoman army barracks across the Bosphorus from Istanbul during the Crimean War.

nizam-i jedid (Ottoman Turkish: "new order") Reform program instituted by Ottoman Sultan Selim III in the late eighteenth century to integrate European military techniques and doctrines into Ottoman practice.

Nizamiya Muhammad Ali's new military force created in the 1820s, closely patterned on British and French models.

Noble Rescript of the Rose Chamber (Turkish: "*Gulhane Firmani*") Document issued in 1839 that reinterpreted the basis of the Ottoman sultan's sovereignty and legitimacy while redefining his subjects as "citizens" of the empire with specific rights.

Non-Aligned Movement (NAM) Group of nations declaring themselves independent of the two emerging global capitalist and communist power blocs in the early 1950s.

North Yemen Civil War Conflict between supporters of the king of North Yemen and defenders of the Yemen Arab Republic between 1962 and 1970.

Northern Alliance Afghani force formed in 1996 by an Uzbek warlord, General Abdul Rashid Dostum, and a Tajik warlord, Ahmad Shah Massoud, to fight the Taliban.

October War War in 1973 between Israel, Syria, and Egypt that began with a surprise Arab attack on the Jewish holy day of Yom Kippur. Also known as the Ramadan War and the Yom Kippur War.

Office of Strategic Services Clandestine U.S. organization created in June 1942 to coordinate American intelligence activities around the world, forerunner of the CIA.

Organization of the Petroleum Exporting Countries (OPEC) Association created in 1960 to establish common oil prices among exporting countries. More powerful after Arab OPEC members started using oil embargoes as a political weapon during the October War of 1973.

Orientalism Term used by Edward Said to explain how Westerners intimately involved in the Middle East constructed an Oriental "other" based on romantic concepts of the Middle East. This "other" could be then classified as inferior, dominated, and controlled.

orthodoxy Importance for a religion of having correct beliefs about God and his message.

orthopraxy Importance for a religion of following correct ritual practices.

Osirak/Tammuz I Test nuclear reactor purchased from France by Iraq, and destroyed in a surgical strike by Israel in June 1981.

Oslo Accords Peace agreement signed in September 1993 by Israeli Prime Minister Yitzhak Rabin, PLO Chairman Yasser Arafat, and U.S. President Bill Clinton.

Osman I (l. 1258–1324, r. 1299–1324) Turkish prince in western Anatolia later regarded as the founder of the Ottoman dynasty.

Ottoman Red Crescent Society Ottoman branch of the International Red Cross Movement established in the late 1860s.

Ottomans (r. 1352–1923) Staunch defenders of Sunni Islam, Ottomans formed a Turkish dynasty that became one of longest-lasting Islamic empires. It ruled at various times most of the Middle East (except Iran), North Africa, and parts of southeastern Europe.

Pahlavi, Reza Shah (l. 1878–1944; r. 1925–1941) First rose to power as commander of the Persian Cossack Brigade; then took the Iranian throne as Reza Shah in 1925.

Pahlavi, Mohammad Reza Shah (l. 1919–1980; r. 1941–1979) Son of Reza Shah Pahlavi and shah of Iran between 1941 and 1979.

Pahlavi (1) Written form of the Persian language used by the Sassanian rulers. (2) Name of the Iranian ruling dynasty established by Muhammad Reza Shah in 1925.

Palestine Liberation Organization (PLO) Palestinian nationalist organization founded in Cairo in June 1964.

Palmach Elite strike group of Zionist defense forces organized at the beginning of World War II.

Pan-Slavism Ideology promoting the union of Slavic peoples and their liberation from Ottoman rule.

Pan-Turkism Ideology promoting the union of Turkish and Turkic peoples.

Patriotic Union of Kurdistan (PUK) Urban, leftist Iraqi Kurdish political group formed in 1975 by Jalal Talabani.

Pax Britannica Late nineteenth-century period when Britain controlled the world's maritime trade routes and enjoyed unchallenged naval supremacy.

Peel Commission British commission formed in 1937 that offered the first partition plan for Palestine.

People of the Book Monotheists such as Jews and Christians whom Muslims accept as fellow believers in God.

Persian Gulf Residency British post created in 1822 with its headquarters in Bushehr, Iran, operating under the control of the British East India Company in Mumbai (Bombay).

Persian Gulf War (1990–1991) War to force Iraq to leave Kuwait, which it invaded and annexed in August 1990. Also known as the "First Gulf War."

Persian Gulf Body of shallow water south of Iraq, west of Iran, and east of the Arabian Peninsula, also called the Arabian Gulf.

peshmerga Kurdish guerrilla fighter in northern Iraq.

Phalange Party Right-wing political movement formed in the 1930s that played a major role in the Lebanese Civil War during the 1970s.

pharaonism Philosophy made popular by Egyptian writer Taha Hussein (l. 1889–1973) that celebrated Egypt's ancient traditions more than its Islamic and Arab heritage.

PFLP (Popular Front for the Liberation of Palestine) Militant Marxist-Leninist Palestinian national liberation group organized in 1967.

PKK (English: "Kurdish Workers' Party") Kurdish militant group founded in eastern Turkey in November 1978 that blended revolutionary leftist agitation with Kurdish nationalism.

al-Qaeda Militant Islamist group created in 1988 by leaders from Egyptian Islamic Jihad who joined forces with Abdullah Azzam and Osama bin Laden.

Qarmati Shiis Revolutionary militant Shii movement that arose in Bahrain, Syria, and the southern Arabian Peninsula in the late ninth and early tenth centuries.

al-Qassam, Izz al-Din (l. 1882–1935) Charismatic, populist, Islamic Palestinian activist.

Qezelbash Shii sympathizers among the Turcoman tribes in eastern Anatolia. Their name derives from the Turkish phrase for "red head," referring to their distinctive red headgear. Prominent between the fifteenth and seventeenth centuries (variant spellings: "Qizilbash, Kizilbash").

Quran For Muslims, final book revealed by God to his last prophet, Muhammad. Divided into 114 chapters (*suras*) arranged in descending order of length (except for the first sura; (variant spelling: Koran)).

Quraysh Main ruling tribe of Mecca and guardians of the Kaaba.

Qutb, Sayyid (l. 1906–1966) Egyptian Islamic thinker who became one of the main theorists of modern Sunni Muslim fundamentalism or Islamism.

Ramadan During the month of Ramadan, Muslims must not eat or drink between dawn and dusk in ritual fasting (Arabic: "*sawm*"). At this time, it is customary to read the Quran at night and have an *iftar* (Arabic: "breaking of the fast") meal just after dusk.

***reaya* (Arabic: "*raaya*")** Ottoman subject class of those who grew food and produced goods ("those who pay taxes").

Red Sea Strategic waterway between the Arabian Peninsula and the coasts of Egypt and Sudan.

***Reglement Organique* (French: "Organic Statute")** 1861 Ottoman Law that gave European nations, particularly France, increased influence over the coastal region of Lebanon as well as its Syrian hinterlands.

Rejectionist Front Coalition of radical Palestinian groups and their Arab allies formed in 1974 to oppose the PLO, accused of being insufficiently anti-Israeli in its positions.

Revisionist Zionism Founded by Ze'ev Jabotinsky (1880–1940), Revisionist Zionists formally broke with mainstream Zionists in 1935 over the issue of partition of the Palestine mandate into Arab and Jewish sections, which they totally opposed. They wanted a Jewish state on both sides of the Jordan River, whose inhabitants would live a middle-class European lifestyle instead of the socialist vision of the Labor Zionists.

Revolutionary Guard Corps, Iranian (IRGC) Set up in May 1979 to counter leftist militias as well as watch over the regular Iranian armed forces. It has evolved since then into a military organization parallel to the regular army and navy.

Rightly-Guided Caliphs (Arabic: *Rashidun*) First four Muslim caliphs who ruled 632–661.

Robert College (now Bosphorus University) Educational institution founded in Istanbul by American missionaries in 1863, taken over by the Turkish government in 1971.

Rumi, Jalal al-Din (l. 1207–1273) Major Sufi poet who remains a major literary figure across the world today. Born in Balkh (in modern Afghanistan), Rumi spent many years in Konya (in modern Turkey) and traveled widely through the medieval Islamic world. His most famous poem, the *Masnavi-ye Manavi (Spiritual Couplets)*, is sometimes described as the Quran of Sufism.

Rum Seljuks Branch of the Seljuks that ruled over a fairly substantial empire in Anatolia and the Middle East between the late eleventh and early fourteenth centuries. "Rum" was another name for Anatolia (variant spelling: "Saljuqs").

Rushdiye ("adolescence") schools Intermediate educational institutions created during the Ottoman Tanzimat to give several generations of students broad exposure to modern arts and sciences.

Sabbatai Zevi (l. 1626–1676) Messianic figure who led a group of Jews through the Ottoman Empire in the 1640s. There, they ended up converting en masse to Islam and establishing a special community centered in Salonika (later Thessaloniki, Greece), where they became known as *donmes* (Turkish for "converts").

Sadat, Anwar (l. 1918–1981; r. 1970–1981) President of Egypt and signer of the Egyptian-Israeli Peace Treaty; assassinated by renegade Egyptian army officers.

Safavids Rulers of Iran between 1501 and 1722. They spoke Turkish and began as a Sufi order in the thirteenth century. By the early sixteenth century, they had emerged as a messianic Shii movement that established modern Iran as a Shii political entity.

al-Saffah, Abu al-Abbas Abdullah (l. 721–754; r. 750–754) First Abbasid caliph.

Safi al-Din (l. 1252–1334) Founder of the Safavid Sufi order.

Sakarya, Battle of Major Turkish victory (August–September 1921) during the Turkish War of Independence that stopped the final Greek offensive in Anatolia.

Salah al-Din (Saladin) al-Ayyubi (l. c. 1138–1193; r. 1171–1193) Muslim commander of Kurdish origin who took Jerusalem back from the Crusaders in 1187 after the Battle of Hattin, prompting the Third Crusade of 1189–1192.

salat Ritual prayer, one of the Five Pillars of Islam. A short ritual prayer must be performed five times daily in the direction of the Kaaba in Mecca.

Samarkand Central Asian city in modern Uzbekistan where some of the first paper mills outside of the Far East were built in the early Abbasid era.

Sassanian Empire Persian empire that arose in the third century CE, ruling over much of the eastern Middle East until defeated by Muslim conquerors in the seventh century CE.

Saudi Arabia Modern country covering much of the Arabian Peninsula formed in 1932 by the Saudi family. It united the regions of Nejd and the Hejaz.

Saudi National Guard Saudi military force incorporating the *Ikhwan,* designed to protect the Saudi royal family from potential internal threats.

Saudis Tribal nomadic group based in the central Nejd region of Arabia. Became followers of Muhammad ibn Abd al-Wahhab (l. 1703–1792), a cleric who launched a conservative Islamic revival movement in the mid-eighteenth century.

Savak Iranian intelligence service under Mohammad Reza Shah Pahlavi.

sayyid (Arabic: "lord") Honorific title used for descendants of Muhammad through his daughter Fatima.

Second Ottoman Constitutional Period Period of Ottoman history after 1908 following the reinstatement of the original 1876 constitution, in which politics came to be dominated by the "Committee of Union and Progress" (CUP).

Selim I (l. 1470–1520, r. 1512–1520) Ottoman sultan who defeated the Safavids and the Mamluks, bringing all of Anatolia, Syria, and Egypt under Ottoman control. He became the first Ottoman ruler to claim the title "custodian/servitor of the two holy places" in recognition of his conquest of Mecca and Medina.

Selim III (l. 1761–1808, r. 1789–1807) Ottoman sultan credited with introducing the first comprehensive program of modernizing military reform.

Seljuks Turkish dynasty that gradually took power in Iraq and the central Middle East under the Great Sultanate in the eleventh and twelfth centuries. Seljuk rulers actively promoted Sunni Islam to defend against the efforts of Shii missionaries (variant spelling: "Saljuqs").

Seven Sisters Major Western companies that largely controlled the production and distribution of world oil supplies and kept price rises fairly modest through the early 1970s.

Sèvres, Treaty of Punitive peace treaty comparable to the Treaty of Versailles signed by the Ottoman government in 1920, superseded by the Treaty of Lausanne in July 1923.

Shadow Caliphs Abbasid rulers maintained as figureheads in Cairo by the Mamluk rulers of Egypt between the thirteenth and the early sixteenth centuries.

shahada **(Arabic: "testament of faith")** "There is no god but God, Muhammad is the Prophet of God."

Sharia Islamic Holy Law, based on the Quran and hadith reports (compiled during the Umayyad and Abbasid eras into collections), offers guidance on all aspects of life and culture.

Shariati, Ali (l. 1933–1975) Iranian sociologist with a vision of Islamic activism as a vehicle to promote social justice.

sharif **(Arabic: "noble")** Honorific title for descendant of Muhammad through his daughter Fatima.

Sharon, Ariel (l. 1928–, r. 2001–2006) Controversial Israeli general and political leader.

Shaykh al-Islam Chief religious official of the Ottoman Empire (variant spelling: "Şeyhülislam").

Shebaa farms region Disputed border region between Syria, Lebanon, and Israel.

Shia Muslim group (originally "faction") supporting the right of Ali and his family to rule the Muslim umma (variant spellings: "Shi'a," "Shi'ah").

Shii Member of the group supporting the right of Ali and his family to rule the Muslim *umma* (variant spelling: "Shi'i").

Shiis (Ismaili) Shiis who accepted Jafar's son Ismail as his successor and the authentic Seventh Imam.

Shiis (Twelver) Shiis who believe in Twelve Imams. Their Seventh Imam was not Ja'far's son Ismail, but Ismail's brother Musa al-Kazim.

Social Democrat "Hinchak" ("Bell") society Armenian nationalist group founded in Geneva, Switzerland in 1887.

Socialist Zionists Prominent in the Zionist community in Palestine after 1905, focused on creating rural collective farms called *kibbutzim* and embracing Hebrew as a common language.

Special Troops of the Levant (*Troupes Spéciales du Levant***)** Military force organized in Syria during the French mandate, which favored religious and ethnic minorities.

Suez Crisis Nasser's nationalization of the Suez Canal in 1956, which provoked an international crisis involving Britain, France, and Israel.

Sufism Following a mystical path to God to transcend the experience of religion in the material world.

Suleyman I (the Magnificent; the Lawgiver; l. 1496–1566, r. 1520–1566) Sultan long considered one of the greatest Ottoman rulers.

Sultan Mehmed VI (l. 1861–1926, r. 1918–1922) Last Ottoman sultan.

sultan Arabic word for "ruler with temporal, secular power."

Sun Language theory Theory promoted by Turkish nationalists in the early twentieth century that the Turkish language was the origin of all human languages.

sunna Muhammad's sayings and practices.

Sunni Someone who follows Muhammad's sayings and practices.

Sunni Triangle Region northwest of Baghdad in Iraq known for its large Sunni Muslim population.

Supreme Leader Guardian jurist who leads the Islamic Republic of Iran and serves as the absolute head of the Iranian government, ranking above all other officials including the president.

Sykes-Picot Agreement Secret May 1916 agreement in which Britain consented to French predominance in the coastal regions of Ottoman Syria. It called for direct British and French control over certain areas and indirect influence over others.

Syrian Protestant College (SPC) American Protestant missionary school founded in 1866 and renamed the American University of Beirut (AUB) in 1920.

Syrian Social Nationalist Party Extremist Arab political group that promoted the unification of all the former British and French mandates into a greater Syria.

tafsir Discipline of interpreting the Quran and uncovering its meanings.

Taif Accord Agreement concluded in 1989 at the end of the Lebanese Civil War. It slightly restructured the power-sharing system of the 1943 Lebanese National Pact.

takfir Traditional Muslim legal concept defined as the act of identifying someone as a *kafir* (unbeliever) or even as an apostate (for those born Muslims).

Talas, Battle of Clash between Muslim and Chinese forces at a site located in modern Kyrgyzstan in 751.

Talat Pasha, Mehmed (l. 1874–1921) Originally a postal clerk from Edirne who later became one of the three main leaders of the Ottoman "Committee of Union and Progress" (CUP).

Taliban Extremely conservative religious students who ruled Afghanistan from 1994 to 2003 using a very strict interpretation of Islamic law (variant spelling: "Taleban").

Tanzimat (Turkish/Arabic: "Reordering" or "Reorganization") Ottoman period of modernization between 1839 and 1876.

tariqa Sufi order, organized group of Islamic mystics. Sufi disciples (*murids*) followed the teachings of a particular master (sheikh or *murshid*).

tawhid **(Arabic "God's unity and oneness")** Belief in divine unity, which forms the basis for all Islamic belief.

Tehran Conference Important World War II Allied summit meeting held in Tehran in November and December, 1943.

Tel Aviv City in Israel just north of Jaffa on the Mediterranean coast, founded in 1909 and named using the Hebrew title of Theodor Herzl's utopian novel *Old-New Land*.

Temujin (d.1227, r. 1206–1227) Mongol tribal leader of the early thirteenth century, later given the title Genghis Khan (meaning "oceanic" or "universal" ruler) and regarded as founder of the Mongol Empire.

terjuman **(dragoman)** Official Ottoman court translator. Dragomans were often Greek natives of Istanbul (modern Turkish spelling: *tercüman*).

timar **system** Ottoman land-tenure system to distribute revenue to cavalrymen and other members of the *askeri* ruling class. They were given land revenues as payment for military service.

Timur (Tamerlane) (l. 1336 –1405, r. 1370–1405) Turco-Mongol conqueror who secured control of much of Central Asia, the eastern part of the Middle East, Anatolia, and the northern part of the Indian subcontinent.

Topkapi Palace Main imperial palace in Istanbul of the Ottoman sultans between the late fifteenth and early nineteenth centuries.

Trans-Iranian Railway Railway constructed by Reza Shah Pahlavi between the Caspian Sea and the Persian Gulf in the 1930s.

Translation Bureau (Turkish: "*Terjumeodasi*") Ottoman office created in 1821 by Mahmud II to educate Muslims on how to translate important foreign books and documents into Ottoman Turkish.

Tudeh Iranian communist party closely aligned with the Soviet Union.

Turcomans Name given to various Turkish tribal groups across Anatolia, Iran, and northern Iraq, who had migrated there around the time of the rise of the Seljuks (variant spellings: *Turkmens/Turkmans*).

Turkish Grand National Assembly Parliament of the Turkish Republic.

Turkish Hearth Association (Turkish: "Turk Ojagi") Turkish nationalist group organized just before World War I that spread the modernizing and nationalist ideas of the CUP.

Turkish Petroleum Company See **Iraq Petroleum Company**.

Turkish Red Crescent Society New name of the Ottoman Red Crescent Society after the founding of the Turkish Republic.

Turkmenchay, Treaty of 1828 Russian-Iranian agreement that recognized northern Iran as a Russian zone of influence where Russia would henceforth be free to play a major part in Iran's internal affairs.

Twelfth Imam Last descendant of Ali and Fatima, now believed to be in hiding by Twelver Shiis.

Tzympe (Turkish: "Jinbi") First Ottoman base in Europe at the Dardanelles near Gallipoli, established in 1354.

Umar (r. 634–644 CE) Second Rightly-Guided caliph who led Muslim forces into Iran and Egypt.

Umar ibn Abd al-Aziz Umayyad caliph between 717 and 720, during whose reign the first collections of hadith accounts were assembled.

Umayyad caliphs Ruled the Islamic *umma* between 661 and 750 with their capital at Damascus.

Umm Kulthum (l. 1898–1975) One of the greatest Egyptian and Arab singers of the twentieth century.

umma Community of all Muslims in the world.

United Arab Emirates (UAE) Confederation of small Arab states on the Persian Gulf formed in 1971.

United Arab Republic (UAR) Political union of Syria and Egypt on February 1, 1958, seen as the first step in uniting all Arabs in a single state. Syria left the UAR on September 28, 1961 after a military coup.

United Nations Emergency Force (UNEF) UN force deployed in the Sinai and Gaza in 1956 to bring the Suez Crisis to an end.

United Nations Interim Force in Lebanon (UNIFIL) UN monitoring force brought in after Israel's 1978 incursion into Lebanon.

United Nations Relief and Works Agency (UNRWA) Agency charged with helping Palestinian refugees during and after the Arab-Israeli conflict of 1948.

United Nations Resolution 242 Resolution ending the Six-Day War, ratified on November 22, 1967. It introduced the concept of "land for peace," calling for Israeli withdrawal "from territories occupied" in 1967 in exchange for "the termination of all claims or states of belligerency."

United Nations Special Committee on Palestine (UNSCOP) UN Commission formed in 1947 that presented a partition plan accepted by the Zionists but rejected by the Palestinian Arabs.

Urabi, Ahmad (l. 1841–1911) Colonel in the Egyptian army who led a revolt in 1882 to prevent European powers from taking more control of the Egyptian government.

Usulis Faction of Shii legal scholars that became prominent in the eighteenth and nineteenth centuries who argued that pure reason was the best basis for legal opinions. This faction still dominates Shii legal thinking.

Uthman (r. 644–656) Third Rightly-Guided caliph who oversaw production of a formally compiled text of the Quran.

Uzbeks Turkic rulers of Central Asia between the sixteenth and nineteenth centuries.

Veiled Protectorate System put in place after 1882 in which Britain managed Egypt, but only behind the scenes, with Egyptian officials remaining formally in charge.

velayat-e faqih (Persian: "Guardianship of the Islamic Jurisprudent") Ayatollah Khomeini's concept that leadership of the state rightfully belonged to the Islamic legal scholar (jurisprudent), because he could find the most accurate interpretation of Muslim scripture and law.

Vichy France Pro-Fascist French government allied with Germany (1940–1944) with its capital in the southern French resort town of Vichy.

vizier High-ranking and skilled political adviser to caliphs and sultans in Islamic domains.

Wafd (English "delegation") Nationalist Egyptian political party founded after World War I by members of a delegation sent to the Paris Peace Conference. It became a major force in Egyptian politics over the next several decades.

waqf (Arabic: "charitable foundation") Income from any property formally set aside, under Islamic law, for charitable purposes. *Waqfs* helped support numerous public institutions, such as hospitals, schools, and mosques.

War of Turkish Independence Conflict between Turkey and Greece that started in 1919 and ended in 1923, culminating in the establishment of the Republic of Turkey in October 1923.

Well-Protected Domains Ottoman name for the Ottoman Empire. It was intended to describe a place with a political system regarded, in its ideal form, as a model of Islamic governance.

West Bank Land controlled on the west bank of the Jordan River by the Jordanian army at the cease-fire of 1949, which became an important Palestinian refugee site and was incorporated into Jordan between 1949 and 1967. After 1967, it was occupied by Israel.

White Paper British document issued in May 1939 that severely restricted Jewish land acquisitions in Palestine and immigration there just on the eve of the Second World War.

White Revolution Iranian political reform program introduced in 1963 that included creating a freer press, arresting former senior officials on corruption charges, redistributing land, and allowing women the right to vote.

Yasa Law code proclaimed by Genghis Khan in the early thirteenth century for the Mongol empire.

Yathrib Old name for the town of Medina in the Arabian Peninsula.

Yazid I (l. 645–683, r. 680–683) Muawiya's son and second Umayyad caliph.

Yishuv Hebrew word for the Jewish Zionist community in Palestine.

Young Ottomans Secret society formed in 1865 by Ottoman exiles in Europe. Young Ottomans called for a real constitutional government to promote reform, based on a creative understanding of Islamic law in light of Enlightenment political theories.

Young Turks Ottoman dissident movement that united a variety of political groups through a shared vision of popular sovereignty. They were the main force behind the Young Turk Revolution of 1908.

zakat (Arabic: "alms") One of the Five Pillars of Islam, requiring Muslims to give alms to the poor.

Zamzam Sacred well at Mecca.

Zanj Black slaves in the salt marshes around Basra who conducted a revolt in the late 860s, which was crushed by 883.

Zionism Modern movement whose goal was to establish a home for the Jewish people in Palestine.

Zoroastrianism Dualistic monotheism with origins in the teachings of the prophet Zoroaster, who lived in Iran probably before the sixth century BCE.

INDEX